Standard Arabic

An advanced course

This course is designed for students who have completed a first-level course in Arabic and wish to pursue the subject to degree level. It aims to develop thoroughly the four basic language skills of reading, writing, speaking and listening, making extensive use of authentic Arabic materials. Each of the twenty chapters is based around a particular topic relating to the culture, history, politics, geography or society of the Arab Middle East, to give students an insight into important aspects of the region. This topic-based approach allows students to tackle vocabulary and structures in a coherent and concentrated manner.

Each chapter contains materials for translation into and from Arabic, aural texts, précis passages, suggested oral discussion topics, and a variety of exercises including comprehension in English and Arabic.

Accompanying cassettes and a teacher's handbook containing sample answers to many of the exercises are also available.

James Dickins has held lectureships in Arabic at Heriot-Watt University in Edinburgh and the University of Durham, and has also taught Arabic at the universities of Cambridge and St Andrews. His research work has concentrated on functional linguistics, and Sudanese Arabic grammar and lexicography, and his book *Extended Axiomatic Linguistics* appeared in 1998.

Janet Watson has held lectureships in Arabic at the universities of Edinburgh, Durham and Salford, and has also taught at Manchester University. She travels regularly to the Middle East and has spent extended periods in Yemen and Egypt. A specialist in Yemeni Arabic, her book publications include *A Syntax of San'ani Arabic and Ṣbaḥtū! A Course in San'ani Arabic*.

Standard Arabic
An advanced course

JAMES DICKINS
University of Durham

JANET C. E. WATSON
University of Durham

CAMBRIDGE
UNIVERSITY PRESS

PUBLISHED BY THE PRESS SYNDICATE OF THE UNIVERSITY OF CAMBRIDGE
The Pitt Building, Trumpington Street, Cambridge, United Kingdom

CAMBRIDGE UNIVERSITY PRESS
The Edinburgh Building, Cambridge CB2 2RU, UK
40 West 20th Street, New York, NY 10011–4211, USA
477 Williamstown Road, Port Melbourne, VIC 3207, Australia
Ruiz de Alarcón 13, 28014 Madrid, Spain
Dock House, The Waterfront, Cape Town 8001, South Africa

http://www.cambridge.org

First published 1999
Reprinted 2001, 2003, 2005

Printed in the United Kingdom at the University Press, Cambridge

Typeset in Times 10/12.5

A catalogue record for this book is available from the British Library

ISBN 0 521 632110 hardback
ISBN 0 521 635586 paperback

This book is dedicated to I.K.A. Howard.

Contents

Acknowledgements

A book of this size and scope could not have been produced without the help and support of a great number of people. In particular we wish to thank the following:

Fahd al-Liheibi for checking a number of the Arabic texts and Arabic translations of English texts.

Othman al-Misned for checking a number of the Arabic texts and Arabic translations of English texts.

Ralph Austin for reading and commenting on the course at an early stage, for suggesting some material (particularly classical material), and for checking our translations of classical texts.

Geoffrey Bowder for reading an early version of the course and for making a number of useful suggestions.

Kathleen Burrill for reading an early version of the coursebook and for discussing the course and its acceptability in the United States with various colleagues.

Mike Carter for encouragement and for suggesting some (particularly classical) material.

Fadia Faqir for checking English–to–Arabic translations and for teaching working versions of the coursebook.

Margaret Greenhalgh, Avril Shields and Ruth Carey for help in finding relevant material in the Middle Eastern Documentation Unit, University of Durham.

Clive Holes for encouragement.

Ronak Husni for much time spent offering expert advice on English–to–Arabic and Arabic–to–English translations and for teaching working versions of the coursebook.

Emma Murphy for providing details about the Arab–Israeli dispute, the Gulf War, Islamic fundamentalism, and Max Weber.

Tim Niblock and Anoush Ehteshami for checking some of the political and historical background material.

Riyadh Nourallah for suggesting some material.

Saadiya Salloum for pointing out a number of mistakes in the Arabic texts.

Abdellatif Sellami for proof–reading the Arabic texts and Arabic translations.

Paul Starkey for providing some material; also for providing the chronology of Arabic literature in chapter 17.

Gill Thomas, Marigold Acland, Kate Brett, Alison Gilderdale and others at Cambridge University Press.

Jack Wesson for teaching some of the coursebook, and making many useful comments over the past five years.

Anonymous reviewers for Cambridge University Press for making a number of useful suggestions.

All errors in the book are of course our responsibility alone.

We would also like to thank the following publishers and firms for permission to reproduce materials for which they hold copyright:

University of Chicago Press for a passage from Marshall G.S. Hodgson, *The Venture of Islam*, vol. 1, 1974.

The BBC, and particularly Suzannah Kirkland, for various BBC Arabic Service news broadcasts and 'Harvest of the Month' recordings. In addition we thank the following for giving us permission to reproduce their recordings for the BBC: Tony Allan, Nicola Ziyada, John Wright, John King, Jareer Abu-Haidar, and particularly Walid Arafat for checking his original recording and the typescript.

Oxford University Press for three passages from Bernard Lewis, *The Arabs in History*, new edition, 1993.

John Murray (Publishers) Ltd. for a passage from Charles Issawi, *An Arab Philosophy of History*, 1955.

Cambridge University Press for a passage from R.A. Hudson, *Sociolinguistics*, 1980.

MIT Press for a passage from Sami K. Hamarneh 'The life sciences' in John R. Hayes (ed.), *The Genius of Arab Civilisation: Source of Renaissance*, 1975.

Librairie du Liban Publishers for a passage from M. Hinds and El-S. Badawi, *A Dictionary of Egyptian Arabic*, 1986.

Blackwell Publishers for a passage from David Crystal, *A Dictionary of Linguistics and Phonetics*, 1985.

Pantheon/Schocken Books for two passages from Inea Bushnaq (translator), *Arab Folktales*, 1986.

HarperCollinsPublishers and David Higham Associates for a passage from Dilip Hiro, *Islamic Fundamentalism*, 1988.

Curtis Brown Ltd, London on behalf of Sir Wilfred Thesiger for a passage from Wilfred Thesiger, *The Marsh Arabs*, 1964 (1983).

Peters, Fraser & Dunlop Group Ltd. for a passage from Peter Mansfield, *The Arabs*, 1980.

B T Batsford Ltd. for a passage from H. Bleaney and R. Lawless, *The Arab–Israeli Conflict* 1947–67, 1990.

Editions du Seuil and Penguin Books UK for a passage from Maxime

Rodinson, *Mohammed*, 1976.

Europa Publications Ltd. for a passage from *The Middle East and North Africa 1996*, 1996.

Guardian News Service Ltd. for three passages from *The Guardian* and one passage from *The Guardian Special Gulf Report*.

Organization of Arab Petroleum Exporting Countries (OAPEC) for a passage from OAPEC *Monthly Bulletin*, February 1990.

An-Nahar for various passages from *An-Nahar*.

Middle East International for two articles from *Middle East International*.

Brintons Carpets Limited for a passage on Brintons.

The Arab Research Centre for a passage by احمد كمال ابو مجد from الباحث العربي.

The authors and publishers have made every effort to obtain permission from copyright owners of works still in copyright. If, however, any have been overlooked, they apologise for the omission and will make suitable acknowledgement in future reprints.

Introduction

Standard Arabic: an advanced course is designed for students who have mastered a general introduction to the modern standard language (such as *Elementary Modern Standard Arabic*), and is intended typically to be taught over two academic years. The course can therefore be used with students who have completed one year of intensive Arabic, for example in a three–year undergraduate degree course which does not include a year abroad in the Arab world. In terms of the British university system, where undergraduates spend three years studying Arabic at their home university (possibly with one year at a university or another institution in an Arab country), the twenty chapters of the course would cover the two final years of an undergraduate degree. Chapters 1 to 10 of the course would be typically covered during the penultimate year, while chapters 11 to 20 would be covered during the final year of the degree.

The course is principally topic–based, but within this overall framework it includes material of various genres (academic writing, journalistic writing, highbrow fiction, anecdotal materials), periods (classical and modern), rhetorical text–types (argumentative, narrative, descriptive, instructive), and channels (written and spoken). The course comprises twenty topics laid out in chapters. Each of the chapters is divided into thirteen sections. The sections are described below.

The aim of the course is to develop the four basic language skills of reading, writing, speaking and listening to an advanced level, and to give students general competence in both Arabic>English and English>Arabic translation. The course is also designed to provide students with an insight into important aspects of the Middle East, and to this end the materials chosen are designed to be genuinely interesting and informative (and in some cases controversial). From the point of view of the mechanics of language learning, the topic–based approach allows students to tackle vocabulary and structures in a coherent and concentrated manner.

As far as possible we have attempted to choose topics which will not date too quickly, and which will appeal to differing student interests. The materials in the course are designed in such a way as to give teacher and student a choice. We do not imagine that anyone would wish to use all the material in every chapter. In some cases, whole chapters could be skipped, if the teacher wished. A lot of the work could be done by students at home – in particular where the answer is provided later in the book (as in the transcription of early aural texts). For some topics – such as the Arab–Israeli conflict, Democracy and Islamic Fundamentalism – teachers may wish to supplement more current material.

The chapter titles are as follows. Working on the three broad categories of social, cultural and political, chapters followed by an **S** are mainly social in orientation, those followed by a **C** are mainly cultural, and those followed by a **P** are mainly political:

Chapter 1: Geography of the Middle East	**S**
Chapter 2: Ethnic groups in the Middle East	**S**
Chapter 3: The Middle East in antiquity	**S**
Chapter 4: The rise of Islam	**S/C**
Chapter 5: Arabic Language	**C**
Chapter 6: The Arab–Israeli Conflict	**P**
Chapter 7: Iraqi invasion of Kuwait	**P**
Chapter 8: Climate and environment	**S**
Chapter 9: Social Issues and Development	**S**
Chapter 10: Gender	**S/C**
Chapter 11: Popular culture	**C**
Chapter 12: Muslim Spain	**S/C**
Chapter 13: Arab nationalism	**P**
Chapter 14: Islamic fundamentalism	**P**
Chapter 15: Democracy	**P**
Chapter 16: Death and succession	**P**
Chapter 17: Arabic literature	**C**
Chapter 18: Economics	**S**
Chapter 19: Medicine	**S**
Chapter 20: Islamic heritage	**C**

Out of twenty topics, a rough balance is achieved between the three major categories of social, cultural and political topics. Seven chapters are purely social in orienation, seven are cultural (including three which also have a social aspect), and six are political. Chapters 1 to 10 of the course focus on more basic topics whose treatment requires relatively simple vocabulary and structures. Chapters 11 to 20 involve more complex and challenging material and build on the ideas presented in the first half of the course.

We have also been concerned to develop the sense of a 'storyline' between chapters where this is feasible. Chapters 1 to 5 form a general block. Chapters 1 and 2 provide general background to the Middle East, chapters 3 and 4 lead up to the rise of Islam, chapter five considers the Arabic language from the starting point of the normative effect of the canonical writings of Islam.

Chapters 6 and 7 deal with war and conflict, and introduce the student to the basic vocabulary of this area, as well as the specifics of the conflicts discussed. The environmental destruction associated with the Iraqi invasion of Kuwait (chapter 7) gives a lead into the topic of chapter 8, Climate and environment, while chapters 9 and 10 deal with other social topics of central importance in the Middle East.

Chapter 11 introduces aspects of Arab popular culture not typically treated in Arabic language courses. Chapter 12, Muslim Spain, gives a counterweight to the political material in chapters 13 to 16 (as well as providing a corrective to the impression of Arab/Islamic extremism that some readers might interpret these as portraying). Chapters 13 to 15 deal with the major political trends in the modern Arab world, while chapter 16 looks at an area in which political fragility and tensions within the Arab world are particularly manifest.

Chapters 17 to 20 deal with cultural and social themes. They emphasise the interdependence of the Arab world and the west, and focus on social and cultural rather than political responses to the challenge of the west. Chapter 20, in particular, brings out the fact that interchange has not simply taken place on the level of high culture – and rounds off the course on a fairly optimistic and non–controversial note.

All the chapters are laid out in sections according to a standard format, as follows:

1. Basic background material
This is material in English, often in the form of charts, whose purpose is to give students a basic background to the topic in question. The purpose of this is to provide general information and context for subsequent material in Arabic. More practically it provides students with information which they can re–use in essay writing and oral classes.

2. Additional reading
This section provides pointers to additional sources of information on the topic, particularly for keen students. These are not necessarily to be regarded as compulsory (this is obviously a matter for the individual teacher), but they would allow students to explore the topics further on their own. The additional reading could also be used to develop the topics to be discussed in the oral classes (section 12). Our intention is to limit references in the main to a small number of standard works (e.g. Albert Hourani *A History of the Arab Peoples*, Peter Sluglett and Marion Farouk-Sluglett (eds.) *The Times Guide to The Middle East: The Arab World and its Neighbours*), which students could either buy, or would at least have access to through university or departmental libraries.

3. Key vocabulary

This section presents lists of small and well–defined semantic fields within the topic of the chapter at hand for which students are to develop their own vocabulary lists in Arabic.

4. Written Arabic texts 1

Modern Arabic texts accompanied by exercises. These exercises include: comprehension in Arabic or English, paraphrasing in Arabic, synonym exercises, structure translations (this involves the identification of certain structures in the original text and the use of the structure to translate sentences from English to Arabic), translation into English. The texts in section 4 generally focus on one particular aspect of the chapter topic. Texts are taken from newspapers, magazines, academic journals, modern literature, essays, etc.

5. Written Arabic texts 2

As for section 4. However, these texts are generally more difficult than those of section 4. They either develop further the ideas presented in section 4, or focus on another aspect of the chapter topic.

6. Written Arabic texts 3 (classical)

One or two classical Arabic texts relating to the chapter topic. The main exercise associated with these texts is translation, however a small number of other exercises are used for some texts such as paraphrase and identification of place names.

7. Grammar/stylistics

This section provides detailed grammatical/stylistic notes. Given the topic–based structure of the course, grammatical/stylistic explanation occupies a subordinate position in the Course. This means that the only features of grammar and style which will be dealt with in detail are those which occur with reasonable frequency in the course, and which we are satisfied students have not in general mastered from their more elementary language studies. Additionally, no attempt is made to manipulate textual material by rewriting parts of it so that it is made to exhibit specific language features according to predetermined grammatical/stylistic criteria. This would in any case destroy the genuineness of the material; such genuineness is vital for the material to be accepted by students as 'real Arabic', and for the course to be regarded as providing real insights into the Arab world, rather than simply teaching the mechanics of the Arabic language at an advanced level.

Features of grammar and style are dealt with in two principle ways. The first is through practical exercises designed to focus on specific aspects of the language and to make students use these actively – principally through the structure translation exercises (e.g. chapter 1, section 9 iii; chapter 2, section 8 v; chapter 2, section 9 v, and many other places). The second is through the formal exposition of grammar/stylistics in section 7. Section 7 will make use of previously studied material where appropriate (this is obviously easier to achieve in later chapters). It will also, however, have a forward–looking aspect, and where appropriate relevant material will be quoted which appears later in the course. There will also be some cross–referencing from texts to grammar sections of relevant chapters where this is considered to be of use to the student.

Wherever Arabic examples are quoted in the grammar/stylistics section, English translations are given. These are provided solely to help with understanding of the original Arabic examples, and accordingly tend towards the literal. Sometimes the quoted examples are drawn from texts which students are asked to translate into Arabic. It is of course reasonable for students to make use of the quoted translations, but they should also bear in mind that in particular cases they may be able to find other more idiomatic English versions.

8. Aural Arabic texts 1
Aural text(s) from the BBC 'Pick of the Month' (حصاد الشهر) series (produced in the early 1980s for native speakers of Arabic as a kind of 'listener's digest'), BBC Arabic Service news, Yemeni radio, the Qur'an, and other sources. Various exercises are used including completing gapped transcriptions, structure translation, comprehension, translation, paraphrase. The exercises in this section start off fairly simply: in early chapters comprehension and gapped transcription predominates where students are required to fill in relatively few words in an otherwise complete text. Later on the number of gaps in the gapped transcription exercises are increased and eventually students are required to produce complete transcriptions of their own. This progression corresponds to our experience of teaching, where even students who have spent a year in the Middle East initially find aural work extremely difficult.

The aural texts are intended to be done by students in a language laboratory or equivalent where they have the opportunity to listen to the passage or to sections of the passage an unlimited number of times. As an introductory exercise, it may however prove useful in certain cases to allow the students to listen to the passage once without a break and ask them to note down and subsequently discuss as a group any general points which they are able to pick up from a single listening.

9. Aural Arabic texts 2
Second aural text; as for section 8 above.

10. Written English texts
English text(s) relating to the topic for translation into Arabic. In the early chapters notes are given to aid translation. Students are asked to translate using vocabulary and structures encountered in the written and spoken Arabic texts above as far as possible.

11. Précis

Longer Arabic text from which a précis is to be produced in Arabic. Teachers could also ask for précis in English. The teacher's handbook has guidelines for tackling the précis exercises and also gives questions for each précis exercise which provide possible structures for teaching précis. One teaching technique which we have found useful is to choose one student to present their précis to the class, and another to then ask questions of the class in Arabic about the précis piece. This yields maximum student involvement, and frees the teacher to act as monitor of progress, perhaps intervening to ask questions of their own when they feel that the student questioner is flagging, or has missed an interesting aspect.

12. Oral

Discussion of aspects of the topic in Arabic. One or two titles are provided for the oral. One of the standard problems in Arabic oral classes seems to be the lack of structure, and the tendency for conversation to break down (a problem we have come across in all eight Arabic–teaching British Universities which we have experience of whether as students or teachers). This section includes questions (in Arabic) around which a structured approach to the teaching of the particular oral topic can be built.

We recognise that there are widely differing views about the kind of oral Arabic which should be taught at the advanced level. These come down to three major positions: (i) that oral work should normally be conducted in colloquial Arabic (except in situations such as formal debates which are deliberately set up to mirror contexts where spoken Standard Arabic would be normal in the Arab world); (ii) that oral work should be conducted in a necessarily somewhat ill–defined middle register between colloquial and standard Arabic – known in Britain as Educated Spoken Arabic, and in America as Formal Spoken Arabic – which it is suggested is the nearest one can come to an educated spoken pan–Arabic, and which will therefore be of maximum use to the student in dealing with people from different parts of the Arab world; and (iii) that oral work is best conducted in a low–style Standard Arabic (without case endings, etc.), for one or more of the following reasons: (a) because this kind of low–style Standard Arabic, while not normally used by native Arabic speakers is perfectly acceptable coming from a foreigner; (b) because students in practice tend to have only a vague idea of colloquial dialect(s) even at the advanced stage; (c) because confidence in oral production gives students greater confidence and provides valuable reinforcement for other areas of language work, particularly aural comprehension (but also reading and writing).

It is clearly important that the course should be usable as a basis for oral work by proponents of all three approaches to oral Arabic teaching. We present material in section 12, and in oral comprehension exercises in other sections, in Standard Arabic. However, this could be adapted without difficulty by the individual teacher either to a particular dialect, or to Educated Spoken Arabic. If we were to present material in section 12 (and elsewhere) in a particular dialect, such as Egyptian, it is not the case that it could be similarly adapted by all teachers to another colloquial dialect, or to Educated Spoken Arabic, or Standard Arabic – if only because there is no dialect which is known by all teachers of Arabic. The use of Educated Spoken Arabic in section 12 (and elsewhere) would present even more problems. Not only is there no clear concensus about the precise linguistic features Educated Spoken Arabic should be deemed to have; many teachers of Arabic reject the notion of Educated Spoken Arabic altogether, regarding it as an unworkable linguistic fiction which fails to take into account the factors involved in register mixing in real contexts, and the effects which this achieves (or fails to achieve).

Our own position is that specifically oral classes are most profitably conducted in colloquial Arabic (with some allowance for the use of Standardisms, given the typical student's limited abilities in colloquial), while oral aspects of written–based classes (such as oral comprehension of written texts) are best conducted in Standard Arabic. In this latter case, the written text provides the register cue as well as the relevant linguistic material with which the student is required to work, and the oral work reinforces general learning. We would not wish to attempt to impose this position on teachers using the course.

13. Essay

An essay about the chapter topic in Arabic using vocabulary and structures encountered in the Arabic texts. One or two titles, and ordered questions relating to the title, are given in Arabic to facilitate a structured approach to the teaching of the particular essay topic. This could be oriented in particular to the pre–teaching of essay work through discussion in Arabic and development of skeleton essays in class.

This book is accompanied by a teacher's handbook, which contains a key to exercises, as well as some general suggestions for teaching the course, and a number of additional exercises.

Finally, there are no doubt shortcomings and certain errors in the current text of this book and the accompanying handbook. We would be very grateful for suggestions regarding ways in which any future edition of the book might be improved; we can be contacted via the publishers.

1
Geography of the Middle East

1. Basic background material
Political map of the Middle East

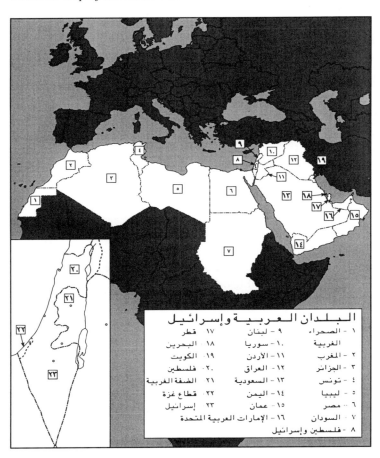

البــلدان الــعـربيــة وإسرائيـل		
١٧ قطر	٩ - لبنان	١ - الصحراء
١٨ البحرين	١٠. سوريا	الغربية
١٩. الكويت	١١- الأردن	٢ - المغرب
٢٠. فلسطين	١٢- العراق	٣ - الجزائر
٢١ الضفةالغربية	١٣- السعودية	٤ - تونس
٢٢. قطاع غزة	١٤- اليمن	٥ - ليبيا
٢٣ إسرائيل	١٥- عمان	٦ - مصر
١٦- الإمارات العربية المتحدة		٧ - السودان
٨ - فلسطين وإسرائيل		

2. Additional reading
(a) Albert Hourani, *A History of the Arab Peoples* (London: Faber & Faber, 1991), pp. 89–96.

3. Key vocabulary
Taking as your starting point the texts in this chapter, draw up basic lists of vocabulary in the following fields:
(a) Areas of land: e.g. desert, city, قطر vs. دولة vs. بلاد.
(b) Areas of water: e.g. river, straits, sea, ocean.
(c) Agricultural and animal husbandary: e.g. crops grown, processes used, people involved.

4. Written Arabic texts 1
(a) The following text gives a general background to the geography of the Arab world. As a preparatory exercise for this chapter, read this text at home. On the basis of your reading, draw a compass and provide basic compass points in Arabic. (This text is based on the text درس في الجغرافية in Karin C. Ryding, *Formal Spoken Arabic*, Georgetown University Press, 1990, p. 37).

يوجد في العالم العربي بحار وخلجان وأنهار ووديان وصحار وجزر وجبال. ويقع الخليج العربي في شرق شبه الجزيرة العربية ويقع خليج العقبة إلى الجنوب من الأردن. ويفصل البحر الأبيض شمال أفريقيا عن أوروبا ويفصل البحر الأحمر مصر عن المملكة العربية السعودية. أما قناة السويس فتقع في مصر وتربط البحر الأبيض بالبحر الأحمر، في حين أن البحر العربي فيقع جنوب شرقي شبه الجزيرة العربية، ويوجد بين البحر العربي والخليج العربي مضيق هرمز وخليج عمان.

وأهمّ الأنهار في العالم العربي هي نهر النيل في مصر والسودان ونهر الفرات في سوريا والعراق ونهر الأردن في الأردن.

وأهم وديان العالم العربي وادي النيل ووادي الملوك في مصر.

ويشمل العالم العربي صحاري عديدة منها صحراء سيناء في مصر وصحراء النفود في المملكة العربية السعودية والصحراء الكُبرَى في أفريقيا الشمالية. ويُعرف العالم العربي بصحاريه الكثيرة. ومن بين الجزر الموجودة في العالم العربي جزيرة البحرين

في الخليج العربي وجزيرة « مصيرة » في البحر العربي وجزيرة سقطرة الواقعة في خليج عدن.

وتوجد جبال كثيرة في الكثير من البلدان العربية مثل جبل الشيخ في لبنان وجبل عرفات في المملكة العربية السعودية وجبال الأطلس في أفريقيا الشمالية. ويقع بين المحيط الأطلسي والبحر الأبيض جبل اسمه باللغة العربية جبل طارق.

(b) The following three texts provide simple descriptions of three Arab countries – Saudi Arabia, Iraq and Sudan.

(i) Read the following text المملكة العربية السعودية and give oral answers in English to the questions which follow it.

المملكة العربية السعودية

المملكة العربية السعودية أكبر دولة في شبه الجزيرة العربية. ويحدّها من الشمال الأردن والعراق ومن الشمال الشرقي الكويت ومن الشرق البحرين والإمارات العربية المتحدة ومن الجنوب الشرقي عُمان ومن الجنوب الجمهورية اليمنية.

وكانت أغلبية السعوديين في الماضي بدوًا يسافرون من مكان إلى مكان في الصحراء بحثًا عن الغذاء لحيواناتهم. ولا يزال هناك بعض البدو في السعودية اليوم ولكنّ أغلبية الناس الآن يسكنون في المدن. وهناك عدد من المدن الكبيرة الحديثة مثل جدة والرياض. وفي السعودية أيضا مدينتان إسلاميتان هما مكة المكَرَّمة والمدينة المنَوَّرة.

إن أراضي المملكة العربية السعودية واسعة جدا إذ تبلغ مساحتها حوالى ثلث مساحة أوروبا ولكن عدد سكانها قليل جدا حيث أن قلة المطر جعلت الكثير منها صحراء ، وفي بعض المناطق قد لا تنزل قطرة مطر لمدة عشر سنين. وتتغطى مناطق كبيرة بكثبان يبلغ ارتفاعها ست مائة متر أو أكثر وطولها عدة

كيلومترات ، ويُعتبر الربع الخالي أكبر صحراء في المنطقة حيث تعادل مساحته مساحة فرنسا، وهناك منطقة أخرى اسمها النفود الكبير والتي تقع شمال الربع الخالي فتبلغ مساحتها أكثر من أربعين ألف ميل مربع ، وفي أماكن أخرى نجد حرات واسعة هي تراث من آثار نشاطات البراكين الموجودة هنا في العصور العابرة .

1. Where is the Kingdom of Saudi Arabia?
2. Name five countries which border Saudi Arabia.
3. What did most Saudis do in the past?
4. Where do most people live in Saudi Arabia today?
5. Which four Saudi cities are mentioned in the text?
6. What is the area of Saudi Arabia in relation to Europe?
7. How large are the dunes said to be in the desert?
8. Which region is the same size as France?
9. Where is Nafud located?
10. What is said to be a legacy of volcanic activity in the past?

(ii) Read the following text الجمهورية العراقية and give oral answers in Arabic to the questions which follow it.

الجمهورية   العراقية

يقع العراق في قارة آسيا. ويحده من الشمال تركيا ، ومن الجنوب المملكة العربية السعودية والكويت والخليج العربي ، ومن الغرب الأردن وسوريا ومن الشرق إيران. وتبلغ مساحة العراق حوالى ١٨١ ٦٠٠ ميل مربع. وأكثر الأراضي الواقعة في الغرب صحراء قاحلة لا ينبت فيها نبات ، ولا يوجد فيها ماء. أما الأراضي الواقعة في الشمال والشمال الشرقي فهي جبلية، هذا بالإضافة إلى بعض السهول المنتشرة في الأقسام المتبقية من البلاد.

١ – في أي قارة تقع الجمهورية العراقية؟
٢ – ما هي البلدان التي يحدها العراق؟
٣ – ما هي طبيعة الأراضي في غرب العراق؟
٤ – ما هي طبيعة الأراضي في شمال العراق؟
٥ – ما هي طبيعة الأجزاء الأخرى من البلاد؟

(iii) Read the following text السودان and give oral answers in Arabic to the questions which follow it.

السودان

السودان أكبر دولة في أفريقيا إذ تبلغ مساحته مليون كيلومتر مُربَّع تقريبًا. ويعتبر أقصى شمال السودان منطقة صحراوية وبعض الناس هناك بدو – وهم العرب الرُحَّل الذين يترحلون في الصحراء ويعيشون على تربية الماشية، وبعضهم مزارعون يسكنون على ضفتي نهر النيل ويزرعون البلح والقمح والخضروات. والمطر في هذه المنطقة قليل وقد لا ينزل مطر لسنين كثيرة. والمناطق الأخرى في شمال السودان ليست صحراوية مثل منطقة الشمال الأقصى. ففي هذه المناطق ينزل مطر لمدة شهرين أو ثلاثة أشهر كل سنة تقريبا. والناس هنا يزرعون القطن والسمسم والذرة بالإضافة إلى الخضروات. وأما جنوب السودان فيشمل غابات كبيرة وقد ينزل المطر كل يوم بهذه المنطقة لمدة تسعة أشهر في السنة. وأغلبية الناس في جنوب السودان رُحَّل يعيشون على تربية البقر.

١ – في أي قارّة يقع السودان؟
٢ – هل يُعتبَر السودان دولة كبيرة؟
٣ – هل السودان أكبر من الدول القريبة منه؟
٤ – أين تقع المنطقة الصحراوية في السودان؟
٥ – على ماذا يعيش البدو؟
٦ – من هم سكان شمال السودان غير البدو؟
٧ – هل المطر في هذه المنطقة كثير؟
٨ – هل المناطق الأخرى في شمال السودان صحراوية أيضا؟
٩ – ينزل المطر لمدة كم شهر كل سنة في هذه المناطق؟
١٠. – ما الذي يزرعه الناس في هذه المناطق؟
١١ – هل يُعتبَر جنوب السودان منطقة صحراوية؟
١٢ – هل ينزل مطر كثير في جنوب السودان؟
١٣ – على ماذا يعيش الناس في جنوب السودان؟

5. Written Arabic texts 2

(a) In class, read the following text from ٩١ عمان entitled جغرافية عُمان, then complete exercises i. and ii. which follow it.

من المعروف أن عُمان تقع في أقصى جنوب شرقي الجزيرة العربية، ويحدها من الشرق خليج عمان وبحر العرب، ومن الغرب المملكة العربية السعودية ودولة الإمارات العربية المتحدة، ومن الشمال مضيق هرمز، ومن الجنوب الجمهورية اليمنية. وقد أدى هذا الموقع إلى أن أصبحت لعُمان شخصيتها الجغرافية الخاصة، وأصبح اتصالها بالبحر من سماتها الواضحة، كما جعلها تتحكم في مضيق هرمز من الناحية الجنوبية، ذلك المضيق الذي كان منطلق التجارة الشرقية إلى حوض البحر المتوسط وأوروبا، كما هو الآن الشريان الرئيسي الذي يمد العالم بأكثر من ٦٠٪ من احتياجاته النفطية.

وهكذا كان موقع عُمان بالغ الأهمية في القديم والحديث، أما مساحتها فإنها تعتبر ثاني دولة عربية في منطقة شبه الجزيرة العربية، إذ تبلغ مساحة أراضيها حوالى ٣١٢ ألف كيلومتر مربع. وتتباين هذه الأراضي من منطقة لأخرى تباينا كبيرا، ويمكن تقسيمها من حيث مظاهر السطح (التضاريس) إلى أقسام عديدة. فهناك السهول الساحلية التي تمتد عبر أكثر من ١٧٠٠ كيلومتر من أقصى الجنوب الشرقي على بحر العرب إلى خليج رأس مسندم في الشمال. ومن أهم هذه السهول الساحلية، ساحل الباطنة الخصب الذي يقع في الشمال الغربي من مسقط ويمتد بطول ٢٧٠ كيلومتر، ثم السهل الساحلي في المنطقة الجنوبية الممتدة من ريسوت غربا إلى طاقة شرقا حيث سهل صلالة الأخضر اليانع.

يلي منطقة السهول الساحلية، المناطق الداخلية التي
تتميز بوجود سلسلة من الجبال يُطلَق عليها اسم
«الحجر»، وتمتدّ هذه السلسلة الجبلية بمحاذاة الساحل من
البريمي في الشمال حتى قرب صور في الجنوب، كما
توجد مناطق جبلية تطلّ على ساحل ظفر في المنطقة
الجنوبية، ويبلغ ارتفاع أعلى قمة جبلية في عمان نحو
٣.٧٥ مترا فيما يعرف بالجبل الأخضر .

i   Answer the following questions in English.

1.   Which countries border Oman?
2.   Which seas and stretches of water border Oman?
3.   What has Oman's link with the sea enabled it to do?
4.   What is the approximate area of Oman?
5.   How can Oman's territories be divided?
6.   How are the inner regions of Oman characterised?
7.   What is the height of the highest mountain in Oman?
8.   What is this mountain known as?

ii   At home, prepare an idiomatic translation of the text.

(b) As preparation for sections 7 and 8, read the following text on the Straits of
Hormuz. At home prepare an idiomatic translation of the text.

مضيق هرمز

إن مضيق هرمز ممرّ مائي عريض للغاية فلا يقلّ عرضه عن خمسة
وأربعين ميلاً من البرّ العماني إلى البرّ الإيراني ولكن هذا المدى
يضيق نوعًا ما إذا أخذنا بعين الاعتبار عددًا من الجزر المنتشرة في
تلك المنطقة فبين جزيرة «العنس» العمانية وجزيرة «لارك»
الإيرانية مسافة تبلغ حوالى خمسة وعشرين ميلاً. وهكذا فإنّ
المضيق أوسع بكثير مما يتصوره الناس.

وأما بالنسبة إلى النفط الذي يمرّ عبر مضيق هرمز في هذه
الأيام فيعادل ثمانية ملايين برميل يوميًا وهي كمية أدنى بكثير

مما كان يُنقل عبـر الخليـج قبـل بضـع سنوات، وكانت تُقدّر بـحـدود عشرين مليـون مليون برميل يومياً. ونتيجـة لهذا الهبوط انخفضت أهمية المضيق عمـا كانت عليـه زمـن الثـورة الإيرانيـة عام ألف وتسع مائة وتسعة وسبعين.

6. Written Arabic texts 3 (Classical)

(a) Read the following passage by the famous tenth–century geographer ابن حوقل about the extent of the original Arab lands, then complete exercises i. and ii. which follow it.

ديار العرب

فـابتدأتُ بديار العرب لأنّ القبلة بها ومكّة فيهـا وهي أمّ القـرى وبلد العرب وأوطانهم التي لم يشـركـهم في سكناها غيرهم.

والذي يحيـط بهـا بحـر فارس مـن عبّادان وهو مصبّ مـاء دِجلة في البحر فيمتدّ على البحرين حتّى ينتهـي إلى عُمان ثمّ يعطف على سواحل مهرةَ وحضرموتَ وعدن حتّى ينتهي على سـواحل اليـمـن إلى جُدّةَ ثمّ يمتدّ على البحـار ومَدْيَنَ حتّى ينتهي إلى أَيْلَةَ ثمّ قد انتهى حينئذٍ حدُّ ديار العرب مـن هذا البحـر وهذا المكان من البحـر لسـان ويعرف ببـحـر القُلْزُم والقُلْزُم مـدينة على طرفـه وسيفـه فـإذا استمرّ على تاران وجُبَيّلان وصل إلى القُلْزُم وينقطع حينئـذٍ وهو شـرقيّ ديار العرب وجنوبيهـا وشيءُ {من غربيّهـا، ثمّ يمتدّ عليها} من أَيْلَةَ على مَدائن قوم لوطٍ والبُحيرة الميتة التي تُعرف ببحيرة زُغر إلى الشراة والبلقاء وهي مـن عمل فلسطين واذرِعاتَ وحَوْران والبَثَنيّة وغُوطَة دمَشق ونواحي بَعْلَبكّ وهي مـن عـمـل دمشـق وتدمُر وسلمية وهمـا من عمل حمص ثمّ إلى الخُناصرة وبالس وهمـا من عـمل قنِسْرين، وقد انتهى الحدّ إلى الفُرات ثمّ يمتدّ الفُرات على ديار العرب حتّى ينتهـي إلى الرقّة وقرقيسيا والرَحبـة والدَاليـة وعانة والحديثـة وهِيتٍ والأنبـار إلى الكُوفة

ومستفرغ مياه الفُرات إلى البطائح، ثمّ تمتدّ ديار العرب على نواحي الكُوفة والحيرة على الخورنق وعلى سواد الكوفة إلى حدّ واسطٍ فتصاقب ما جاور دِجْلَةَ وقاربها عند واسط مقدار مرحلة ثمّ تستمدّ وتستمرّ على سواد البصرة وبطائحها حتّى ينتهي إلى عبّادان.

Vocabulary

سِيـف	shore; coast
عَمَل	district
سَواد	outskirts
صاقَب	to adjoin
بطائح	wide wadi beds

i   Answer the following comprehension questions based on ديار العرب in Arabic.

١ – لماذا ابتدأ المؤلف كتابه بديار العرب؟
٢ – ماذا يقول الكاتب عن عبّادان؟
٣ – أين ينتهي حد ديار العرب من بحر فارس؟
٤ – بما يُعرف هذا الجزء من البحر؟
٥ – ما اسم هذا الجزء من البحر اليوم؟
٦ – بما عُرفت البحيرة الميتة؟

ii Identify as many as possible of the places, rivers and seas given in this passage and give their English names.

(b) Read the following passage by the famous fourteenth–century Arab traveller ابن بطوطة from رحلات ابن بطوطة about Sana'a and Aden in Yemen, then translate the text into idiomatic English.

وأقمت في ضيافة سلطان اليمن أياما وأحسن إليّ وأركبني، وانصرفت مسافرا إلى مدينة صنعاء، وهي قاعدة بلاد اليمن الأولى، مدينة كبيرة حسنة العمارة، بناؤها بالآجرّ والجصّ، كثيرة الأشجار والفواكه والزرع، معتدلة الهواء طيبة الماء.

ومـن الـغـريـب أن المطر بـبـلاد الهـنـد واليمن والحبـشـة إنما يـنـزل
في أيـام القيـظ، وأكثر مـا يكون بـعـد الظهر مـن كلّ يوم في
ذلك الأوان، فالمسافرون يستعجلون عند الزوال لئلا يصيبهم
المطر، وأهل المدينـة ينصرفـون إلى منازلهم لأن أمطـارها وابلةٌ
متدفّقة.

ومدينـة صنعاء مـفـروشـة¹ كلّها، فإذا نـزل المطر غسل جميـع
أزقّتها وأنقاها. وجامـع صنعاء مـن أحسن الجوامـع، وفيـه قبـر
نبيّ مـن الأنبيـاء، عليهم السلام.

ثـمّ سـافـرت منـها إلى مـدينـة عَدَن مَرسى بلاد اليمـن على
ساحل البـحـر الأعظم، والجبـال تحفّ بـها، ولا مـدخل إليـها إلا مـن
جانـب واحد، وهي مـدينـة كبـيـرة، ولا زرع بـها ولا شجـر ولا مـاء،
وبها صهاريج يجتمع فيـها المـاء أيـام المطر، والماء على بـعـد منـها،
فربّما² مـنـعـتـها العـرب وحـالـوا بـين أهل المدينـة وبيـنـه حـتى
يصانعوهم بالمال والثياب. وهي شديدة الحرّ، وهي مـرسى أهـل
الهنـد تأتي إليـها المـراكـب العظيـمـة مـن كنبـايت وتانَه وكـولـم
وقـالقـوط وفنـدرايـنـه والشاليـات ومنجـرور وفـاكنـور وهنـور
وسنـدابـور وغيـرها، وتجـار الهنـد سـاكنون بـها، وتجار مـصـر
أيضا.

Notes

١ – مفروشة: أي بالبـلاط.

٢ – ربّما: أي كثيرا ما.

7. Grammar/stylistics

(a) *Countries and cities*

i Most countries are feminine in gender: these include مصر, سوريا ,اليمن,
الجزائر; a small number of Arab countries, however, are masculine. Masculine
Arab countries include: المغرب, الأردنّ ,لبنان ,العراق ,والسودان. Some
countries, e.g. اليمن, can be either masculine or feminine.

ii All cities are feminine. This is probably because city names, e.g. بيروت

'Beirut', فاس 'Fez', etc. are felt to be abbreviations of مدينة بيروت 'the city of Beirut', مدينة فاس 'the city of Fez', etc. where مدينة 'city; town' is feminine.

(b) بضع

There are two words for 'some' in Arabic: بعض and بضع. To say 'some X' both these terms occur as the first term in an إضافة phrase, as in: بعض الأيام 'some days' (بعض followed by a definite noun) and بضعة أيام 'some days' (بضع followed by an indefinite noun). The two words however differ in meaning. While بعض can be used to mean some of any number (including *one*, where the meaning would be, for example, 'some of it'; e.g. بعض الوقت 'some of the time'), بضع is used where the actual number is between 3 and 9. In modern Arabic another difference between بضع and بعض is due to the fact that بضع takes reverse agreement with the following noun in the same way as the numbers 3 to 10: the form بضع is used before nouns where the singular is grammatically feminine, while the form بضعة is used before nouns where the singular is grammatically masculine. Thus, 'some girls' is translated as بضع بنات, while 'some boys' is translated as بضعة أولاد. In Classical Arabic بضع is used before nouns of both genders. Examples of بضع include:

وهي كمية أدنى بكثير مما كان يُنقل عبر الخليج ... قبل بضع سنوات.

'It is an amount a lot less than that which used to be transported through the Gulf a few years ago.' (ch. 1, 5b)

ولا يقيم فيها سوى بضع مائات من السكان.
'Only a few hundred inhabitants live there.' (ch. 1, 9)

(c) شبه

The term شبه as the first term in an إضافة phrase expresses the notion of 'semi–' or 'almost'. The second part of the إضافة phrase can be a noun or an adjective. شبه commonly occurs in the phrase شبه جزيرة 'peninsula' (literally: semi–island). Examples include:

نحو ٥٥٠ مليون سيدة في الدول النامية يعشن في حرمان شبه كامل.

'... around 550 million women in developing countries living in almost total deprivation.' (ch. 10, 5c)

شبه الجزيرة العربية.   'The Arabian Peninsula'

لكن المأساة هي أن الخلاف بين السكان الزنوج تحول إلى مذابح

لكن المأساة هي أن الخلاف بين السكان الزنوج تحول إلى مذابح شبه يومية.

'But the tragedy is because the conflict between the black groups had turned into almost daily slaughter.' (ch. 6, 11)

The verb يُشبِه can also be translated into English as 'semi–', as in:

تمتع الأكراد بما يشبه الحُكم الذاتي.

'The Kurds enjoyed semi–autonomy [ما يُشبِه meaning literally 'that which resembles'].' (ch. 2, 5b)

(d) *'Semantically light' verbs*

Arabic prefers sentences which begin with a verb to sentences which do not begin with a verb, and therefore some verbs are often used where they do not appear to be strictly necessary, either for the grammar or for the meaning of a sentence: that is to say, such a verb could either be omitted or be replaced by a noun or adjective phrase, and the sentence would still be both grammatical and make sense; the verb is added mainly for stylistic reasons. Verbs which are used in this way for stylistic reasons can be called 'semantically light verbs'. These verbs are used predominantly in the imperfect aspect, and are generally found in descriptive texts; semantically light verbs include:

وقَع – يقَع – *to be located*

This verb is used to describe the location of a specific place, as in:

{يقع} العراق في قارة آسيا.

'Iraq is [situated] in the continent of Asia.' (ch. 1, 4bii)

The subject of وقع is usually definite, as in the above example. Occasionally, however, the subject of وقع is indefinite, as in:

و{يقع} بين المحيط الأطلسي وبين البحر الأبيض {جبل} اسمه باللغة العربية جبل طارق.

'Between the Atlantic Ocean and the Mediterranean there is a mountain whose name in Arabic is جبل طارق.' (ch. 1, 4a)

وُجِد – يُوجَد – *to be found*

When the location of an indefinite noun is described, the verb most commonly used is the passive of the verb وجد 'to find'. This is often translated into English as 'there is ...'. Examples include:

'There is no water in it.' (ch. 1, 4bii)   لا {يُوجَد} فيها ماء.

لا {يُوجَد} شعب اسمه الشعب الكردي في تركيا.

'There is no people called the Kurdish people in Turkey.' (ch. 1, 5a)

أعلى نسبة للأمية {تُوجَد} عادة في البلاد التي تعاني من أزمات اقتصادية حادة.

'The highest level of illiteracy is normally [found] in countries which suffer from severe economic crises.' (ch. 10, 4c)

وقيل إن على باب قبره {يُوجَد} قفل هائل.

'It is said that on the door of his tomb there is a huge lock.' (ch. 11, 4a)

Occasionally, the subject of يُوجد is definite, as in:

و{يُوجَد} بين البحر العربي والخليج العربي {مضيق هرمز} و{خليج عمان.}

'Between the Arabian Sea and the Persian Gulf there are the Straits of Hormuz and the Gulf of Oman.' (ch. 1, 4c)

بلغ – يبلغ – *to amount to; to reach; to cover*

This verb is used to describe amount or distance. The subject is usually definite:

تتغطى مناطق كبيرة بكثبان {يبلغ} ارتفاعها ست مائة متر.

'Large areas are covered by dunes whose height [reaches] is 600 metres.' (ch. 1, 4bi)

يتضاعف عدد سكان العالم خلال هذا القرن لـ{يبلغ} أكثر من خمسة مليارات نسمة في عام ١٩٨٥.

'The world's population will double this century to reach more than five billion in the year 1985.' (ch. 9, 5a)

فـ{تبلغ} مساحتها حوالى ثلث مساحة أروبا.

'Its area is approximately the size of Europe.' (ch. 1, 4bi)

Compare the following sentence where the verb بلغ is not used, but quite legitimately could be used:

فمساحته مليون كيلومتر مربع.

'Its area is one million square miles.' (ch. 1, 4biii)

زاد – يزيد + على – *to be more than*

This verb is generally used in the negative in the sense of ليس أكثر من and describes amount or distance:

{لا تزيد} رقعتها على خمسين مترا مربعا.

'Its area is no more than 50 m. sq.' (ch.1, 9)

The verb is less commonly used positively in the sense of أكثر من, as in:

يقدّرون نسبة الكلمات ذات الأصول العربية بما {يزيد عن} عشرة بالمائة.

'They estimate the percentage of words of Arab origin to be more than 10%.' (ch. 5, 9a)

عدد الأكراد الموجودين في هذه الدول اليوم {يزيد على} عشرين مليون نسمة.

'The number of Kurds in these countries today exceeds twenty million.' (ch. 2, 5a)

تجاوز – to exceed; to be more than
A verb which can occur in some of the same contexts as يزيد على is تجاوز 'to exceed'. This verb is used in particular in reference to age, as in:

فعمره الآن {تجاوز} الأربعة آلاف عام.

'Its age is now more than four thousand years.' (ch. 8, 5b)

This verb differs from most other semantically light verbs in that it is generally used in the perfect aspect.

قلّ + عن – to be less than
This verb has the opposite meaning to زاد على. It is also used negatively in the sense of ليس أقلّ من:

فـ{لا يقلّ} عرضه عن خمسة وأربعين ميلا.

'Its width is no less than forty–five miles.' (ch. 1, 5b)

أُعتُبِر – يُعتَبَر – to be considered
This passive verb is often translated into English simply as 'is'. It is often used before a prepositional phrase beginning with من which is used in the sense of 'one of the ... (e.g. largest, oldest, richest)'. يُعتَبَر is always followed by a subject complement (a phrase with the same referent as the subject) which is either a prepositional phrase, or a noun or adjective phrase in the accusative case, just as 'to be' and 'to be considered' in English require a complement in such sentences as:

The children are *rather young*.
He is considered *very clever*.
This is considered to be *one of the worst years of the drought*.

Examples of sentences with يُعتبر include:

أمــا مــساحتـها فـإنـها {تُـعتبـر} ثانـي دولـة عـربيـة فـي مـنـطقـة شبـه الجزيرة العربية.

'In terms of its area it is [considered to be] the second [largest] Arab state in the Arabian Peninsula.' (ch. 1, 5a)

ظاهرة تشغيـل الأطفال {تـعتبر} مـن أعقد الـمشاكل الاجتماعيـة.

'The phenomenon of child labour is [considered to be] one of the most complicated social problems.' (ch. 9, 4c)

{تُـعتبـر} الأمـيـة مـشكلة إنـسانيـة.

'Illiteracy is [considered to be] a human problem.' (ch. 10, 4c)

{تُـعتبـر} هذه البـقعـة الممتدة على مـساحة أربعة هكتارات اكتشافا بالغ الأهميـة.

'This place which occupies an area of four hectares is [considered to be] an extremely important discovery.' (ch. 3, 4a)

يُعَدّ – *to be considered*
A verb which is less common than يُعتبر, but which is used in the same contexts is يُعَدّ. Examples of this verb include:

هذا الكشف {يُعَدّ} إضافة هامة للتاريخ المصري القديم.

'This discovery is [considered to be] an important addition to ancient Egyptian history.' (ch. 3, 5)

(e) *Pause and liaison; high and low style*
There are two acknowledged styles in spoken Arabic: high style and low style (with gradations in between). High style is differentiated from low style by the pronounciation of final short vowels on nouns and verbs within the sentence (in liaison), and by *tanwin*. These vowels indicate case (nominative, accusative, genitive), mood (indicative, subjunctive, jussive – the latter taking no vowel), person in the perfect aspect of the verb (first singular versus second masculine singular), and gender in the second singular object pronouns – كَ 'you m.s.' versus كِ 'you f.s.'.

Short final vowels are not pronounced in low style – with the exception of the ــِ vowel for the second feminine singular in the perfect aspect of the verb – e.g. كتبتِ 'you f.s. wrote'. In the case of the second singular object or possessive pronouns, the final vowel is sometimes pronounced *before* the consonant, as in: درّستَك 'I taught you m.s.' and درّستِك 'I taught you f.s.', and أدرّسَك 'I am teaching/teach you m.s.', and بيَتِك 'your f.s. house' (this is a pronunciation which derives from colloquial forms rather than from standard Arabic). Notice that this transposed vowel is pronounced in place of the mood vowel of the imperfect, the person vowel of the perfect verb, or the case vowel of the noun. *Tanwin* is not pronounced in low style with the notable exception of adverbials such as خاصّةً 'especially', جداً 'very', مباشرةً 'directly' where the accusative ending اً is pronounced.

At the end of a sentence – or, more specifically, when the speaker takes a pause – final short vowels and *tanwin* are not pronounced irrespective of whether the speaker is using high or low style. Thus, there is no difference between 'you m.s. wrote' and 'I wrote' since both are pronounced as كتبْت. In most cases this is unproblematic, since there is little difference between low style and high style in pause. When the final vowel belongs to the third masculine singular object pronoun, however, it is easy to fail to hear the pronoun, in particular when the pronoun is attached to a preposition which ends in a vowelless consonant. Thus, عنْهُ 'about it m.s.' is pronounced as عنْه and منْهُ 'from it/him' is pronounced as منْه.

(f) *The use of pronouns to refer to place*
The English locatives 'here' and 'there' are used far more than the Arabic locatives هنا and هناك. English sentences such as 'I travelled to Syria, and from there continued to Kuwait' in which a specific location (Syria) is mentioned explicitly and is then referred to by the locative 'there', 'there' is best translated into Arabic, not by هناك, but rather by a pronoun which agrees in number and gender with the specific location, Syria. Other examples of the use of pronouns to refer to place include:

ثم سافرت {منها} إلى مدينة عدن.
'Then I travelled from there [i.e. the city of Sana'a] to the city of Aden.' (ch. 1, 6b)

فابتدأت بديار العرب لأن القبلة {بها} ومكة {فيها}.
'I began with the regions of the Bedouins because the *qibla* is there, and Mekka is there.' (ch. 1, 6a)

حجز هنالك قبائل من حمير فأقاموا {بها}.
'He kept Himyaritic tribes there and they stayed there.' (ch. 2, 6b)

... التي غزت مصر واستقرت {فيها}.
'... which invaded Egypt and stayed there.' (ch. 5, 4a)

فرغم أنها بلد فقير جدا إلا أن نسبة المتعلمين {فيها} عالية.
'Despite the fact that it is a poor country the percentage of educated people there is high.' (ch. 10, 4c)

8. Aural Arabic texts 1

Listen to the aural text from حصاد الشهر, no. 6, side 1, item 1, which deals with the Mandib Straits, مضيق باب المندب ١, then answer the comprehension questions below. This passage was produced before the unification of the Yemen Arab Republic (North Yemen) جمهورية اليمن العربية and the People's Democratic Republic of Yemen (South Yemen in 1990) جمهورية اليمن الديمقراطية الشعبية. Read the comprehension questions through before listening to the tape for the first time.

1. What is the length (طول) of the Red Sea?
2. What is the greatest width (أقصى عرض ...) of the Red Sea?
3. Where do the Mandib Straits lead to (يُفضي إلى) in the south?
4. What does the width of the Mandib Straits not exceed?
5. What destinations, to which ships make their way (المتَّجهة إلى) from the Indian Ocean, necessarily (لا بد) require passage through the Mandib Straits?
6. What African countries border the Red Sea to the west?
7. Where does the Suez Canal run to and from?
8. What Gulf lies to the east of the Sinai peninsula?
9. What are situated at the head of this Gulf?
10. Which countries are situated to the east of the Red Sea?
11. Where is the People's Democratic Republic of Yemen situated with respect to the Mandib Straits?
12. Where is the former French colony (مستعمَرة) of Djibouti situated?

9. Aural Arabic texts 2

Listen to the aural text from حصاد الشهر, no. 26, side 2, item 3, مضيق باب المندب ٢, on tape, then complete exercises i. – iii. below.

i   Fill in the gaps in the following text. You may find it useful to read through the gapped text a few times before you listen to the tape.

مضيق باب المندب ـــــــــــ Q1 الأهميـة ـــــــــــ لأنه منفـذ يـربط بـين

ـــــــــــ ـــــــــــ وـــــــــــ المحـيط الـهندي Q2 .

ومـعلوم أن ـــــــــــ ـــــــــــ ـــــــــــ يؤدي شـمـالاً إلى

ـــــــــــ ـــــــــــ وـــــــــــ

ـــــــــــ واتسـاع ـــــــــــ ـــــــــــ ـــــــــــ لا

يزيد على ـــــــــــ وـــــــــــ كيلومـترًا عند أضيق نقطة .

فالسفن المارّة يستطيع ملاّحوها أن يشاهدوا كلاً من _____ _____

و _____ و _____ . و _____ قريب من السواحل _____ _____ لا

يفصله عنها سوى _____ ضيّقة وقليلة العمق لا يسهل على

_____ أن تجتازها . Q3 وعندها _____ «مايم» التي لا

_____ _____ _____ _____ رقعتها على _____

ولا يقيم فيها سوى بضع مائات من السكّان _____ تفتقر

إلى _____ و _____ _____ . Q4 وهي بالرغم من

ذلك عظيمة _____ من الناحية الاستراتيجية . وقد أدرك

_____ أهميتها عام _____ و _____ _____ و _____

وتسعين فاحتلّوها يوم كان الجيش _____ في _____

بقيادة نابليون بونابرت Q5. فأراد _____ منعه من التوغل

في _____ _____ _____ خشيةً أن يكتسح الهند

. Q6 و _____ زال خطر نابليون جلا _____ عن

_____ «مايم» . لكنهم في _____ _____

و _____ و _____ و _____ احتلّوها مرة أخرى

كيلا يحتلّها _____ _____ .

ii Answer in English the following comprehension questions based on the text
مضيق باب المندب ٢.

1. Why are the Mandib Straits extremely important?
2. Where does the Red Sea lead to northwards?
3. How wide are the Mandib Straits at their narrowest point?
4. What can sailors see from passing ships?
5. What separates the Straits from the Arabian coast?
6. How large is the island of Mayum?
7. How many people live there?

8. Why is the number of inhabitants so few?
9. When did the British occupy it?
10. What did they hope to achieve by doing this?
11. When did the British reoccupy Mayum?
12. Why did they reoccupy Mayum?

iii Structure translations based on ٢ مضيق باب المندب.
Translate the following English sentences into Arabic using relevant constructions to be found in the text at the points indicated (e.g. Q1, Q2, etc.). This exercise is designed to help you identify and reuse specific grammatical constructions in Arabic.

1. This issue is extremely important.
2. The Suez Canal connects the Mediterranean with the Red Sea.
3. This problem will not be easy for the government to solve.
4. The present government lacks the necessary knowledge.
5. What were you doing on the day of the Iraqi invasion of Kuwait?
6. I didn't do anything for fear that you would get annoyed.

10. Written English texts

(a) Making use of constructions encountered in the Arabic texts above as far as possible, translate the following text adapted from *The Middle East and North Africa 1996, 1* (London: Europa Publications, 1996), p. 1023, into idiomatic Arabic. Give final vowels in all instances and translate numbers as words.

Republic of Yemen
Geography

On 22 May 1990 the Yemen Arab Republic[1] and the People's Democratic Republic of Yemen[2] merged to form the Republic of Yemen. The two former Yemeni republics had consisted of the south–west corner of the Arabian peninsula–the highlands[3] inland, and the coastal strip along the Red Sea; and the former British colony[4] of Aden (195 sq km) and the Protectorate[5] of South Arabia (about 333,000 sq km), in addition to the islands of Perim (13 sq km) and Kamaran (57 sq km). The Republic of Yemen lies at the southern end of the Arabian peninsula. Yemen is bordered by Saudi Arabia in the North and Oman in the East.[6] The capital of Yemen is Sana'a[7] which lies on the al-Jehal plateau.

Notes

1. الجمهورية اليمنية العربية
2. جمهورية اليمن الديموقراطية الشعبية

3. المرتفعات

4. المستعمرة

5. محمية

6. Translate as an active sentence with 'Yemen' as the object.

7. صنعاء

(b) Making use of constructions encountered in the Arabic texts above as far as possible, translate the following text adapted from Peter Mansfield, *The Arabs*, (London: Penguin Books, 1980), p. 48, into idiomatic Arabic.

Egypt: the centre of gravity

Egypt has 39 million people and is easily the most populous of the Arab countries. About one third of the Arab nation is Egyptian. Its inhabited areas are the most populated in the Arab world, because[1] although the area of Egypt is[2] the area of France and Spain, the Egyptians live only in the valley and delta of the Nile (with a few thousand in the oases of the western desert), which are no more than 4 per cent[3] of the total area (about the area of Holland). The consequence of this is that Egypt is one of the poorest Arab countries in terms of income per head, even though it is one of the most advanced.

Notes
1. There is no need to translate 'because' here.
2. Translate as 'equals'.
3. 'per cent' translates as في المائة.

11. Précis
Read the following text from الكاشف, 1963, then produce a précis in Arabic.

اليمن قطر عربي يقع في الجزء الجنوبي الشرقي من شبه جزيرة العرب ، وهو جزء من الوطن العربي الكبير ، وتسمى بلاد اليمن كذلك باليمن الخضراء ، لكثرة أشجارها وثمارها وزروعها ...

وبلاد اليمن ذات حضارة مجيدة تمتد في التاريخ آلاف السنين وقد ظهر في تاريخها قواد عظام ، عملوا على حماية بلادهم واتساع رقعتها ، وتتكون بلاد اليمن من ثمانية ألوية ، واللواء هناك يشبه المحافظة . ومن أهم الويتها تعزّ وصنعاء والحُدَيدة . وفي القطر اليمني الشقيق تنمو أشجار البنّ بكثرة على سفوح الجبال .

والبنّ اليمني من أجود أنواع البنّ في العالم ، وهو تجارة رابحة لكثير من السكان ، ويصدّر إلى كثير من أقطار العالم ، ويعتبر الثروة الأولى للبلاد . ومن أشهر مدن اليمن صنعاء ، وتعرف بطقسها الجميل ، ومناخها المعتدل ، في مختلف فصول السنة، وهي تقع على ارتفاع ألفين وثلاثمئة وخمسين مترا عن سطح البحر ، وتقع بالقرب منها عدّة قرى محاطة بالغابات الشاسعة .

والبلاد اليمنية تتميز بخصوبة أرضها ، وثروتها العظيمة الكامنة في البنّ وأشجار الفاكهة وغيرها من الزروع ، ففيها ينمو البرقوق والتفاح والبرتقال والكمثري واللوز والجوز .

ومن أروع المناظر التي يشاهدها الزائر لبلاد اليمن ، المزارع المدرجة التي يقام بعضها فوق بعض ، على أشكال هندسية بديعة . وهذه المزارع العجيبة موجودة بها منذ القدم ، من قبل أن تعرف في إيطاليا ، وتسمى بالحدائق المعلّقة ، ومن العجيب أنهم يعتمدون في زراعتها على الأمطار الموسمية والجداول والينابيع المتفرقة والآبار .

والعلم اليمني المرفوع على دور الحكومة ذو لون أحمر تزيّنه خمسة نجوم بيضاء . وقد وزّعت النجوم بحيث وضع نجم في كل زاوية من زوايا العلم ، أما النجم الخامس فيتوسط العلم فوق السيف تماما .

ومن أهم المدن اليمنية القديمة مدينة سبأ ، ولا تزال أنقاض هذه المدينة القديمة تحتفظ بأسرارها ، وكان أهلها قد بنوا فيها سدّا ، يعرف بسدّ مأرب ، كانت تتجمع خلفه مياه السيول والأمطار ، وذلك يدل على تفوّقهم في ذلك الزمن القديم في فنون الهندسة والبناء ، وبفضل هذا السدّ تحوّلت البلاد إلى جنّات وارفة الظلال ، وقد جاء ذكر هذه المدينة في القرآن ، فقال تعالى :

« لقد كان لسبأ في مسكنهم آية : جنّتان عن يمين وشمال » .

وقد شيّدوا في هذه المدينة القديمة القصور الشاهقة التي ما

زالت بقاياها قائمة للآن.

وقد ساهمت اليمن بقسط كبير في بناء صرح الوحدة العربية
فقد وقفت اليمن دائما إلى جانب الأقطار العربية الشقيقة ،
فآزرتها إذ هي جزء لا يتجزّأ من الوطن العربي الكبير .

12. Oral
جغرافية الوطن العربي: قطر عربي أعرفه
(a) Individual students to present a brief account in Arabic of an Arab country they
know (e.g. اليمن، مصر، لبنان، المغرب، الجزائر، السودان).
(b) The student presenter then asks the other students questions about the country.
The questions should include some which require factual answers and some
which require subjective, experiential or hypothetical answers. For example:

١ – ما هي البلدان المجاورة لهذه البلاد؟
٢ – هل هي بلاد جبلية أم صحراوية؟
٣ – أين تقع هذه البلاد، هل تقع في الجزيرة العربية أو خارجها؟
٤ – هل زرت هذه البلاد، ومتى زرتها؟
٥ – ماذا رأيت في البلاد؟
٦ – هل أعجبتك البلاد، ولماذا؟

(c) Open lecturer–led discussion on the geography of the Middle East.

13. Essay
Making use of the vocabulary and constructions encountered in this chapter, write
an essay (c. 150 words) in Arabic on the topic قطر عربي أعرفه. As far as
possible structure your essay around the following questions:

١ – ما اسم البلاد التي تصفها، وأين تقع هذه البلاد؟
٢ – كم مساحة البلاد؟
٣ – كم عدد السكان في البلاد؟
٤ – هل يعيش سكان البلاد بالزراعة أو بالصناعة أو بغيرها؟
٥ – ما هي أهم المدن والأقاليم في هذه البلاد، وما هي مهمتها؟

2
Ethnic groups in the Middle East

1. Basic background material
(a) *Ethnic and religious composition of the Arab world*

Total population of Arab world (including non-Arabs): 215 million.

Morocco	**Algeria**	**Tunisia**	**Libya**
Population: 24m	Population: 25m	Population: 8m	Population: 4.25m
ethnicity	*ethnicity*	*ethnicity*	*ethnicity*
Arabs: 60%	Arabs: 70%	Arabs: 97%	Arabs: 95%
Berbers: 40%	Berbers: 30%	Berbers: 3%	Berbers: 5%
religion	*religion*	*religion*	*religion*
Sunni Muslim	Sunni Muslim	Sunni Muslim	Sunni Muslim
small Jewish minority	small Khariji minority		small Khariji minority

Total Berber population across Maghrib and other states of northern Africa: 18m.

Egypt	**Sudan**
Population: 53m	Population: 23m
ethnicity	*ethnicity*
Arabs	Arabs: 60%
some Nubians in south	non–Arabs: 40%
religion	(non–Arab southerners: 25%)
Sunni Muslim: 90%	*religion*
Coptic Christian: 10%	Muslim: 70%
	Traditional tribal-based religions: 25%
	Christian: 4%

Israel

Population: 4.5m
ethnicity
Jewish Israelis: 82%
Palestinian Arabs
(Israeli citizens): 18%
religion
Jewish: 82%
Sunni Muslim: 15%
Christian (various sects): 3%

Israeli–occupied territories (West Bank, East Jerusalem, Gaza)

Population: 2.1m
ethnicity
Palestinian Arabs: 100%
religion
Sunni Muslim: 90%
Christian (various sects): 10%
(There are also at least 350,000
Israeli settlers in the Occupied Territories.
These are included within the population
figures for Israel.)

Jordan

Population: 4m
ethnicity
Palestinian Arabs: 65%
East Bank Arabs: 30%
Circassians: 2.5%
religion
Sunni Muslim: 94%
Druze (Muslim): 0.5%
Christian
    (various sects): 5%

Lebanon

Population: 3.5m
(excluding 750,000 who fled
country during Civil War
1975–1991)
ethnicity
Lebanese Arabs: 88%
Palestinian Arabs: 9%
Armenians: 3%
Kurds: 3%
religion
Shi'i Muslim (Twelver): 35%
Sunni Muslim: 23%
Druze (Muslim): 6%
Maronite Christian: 18%
Orthodox Christian: 8.5%
Greek and other
    Catholic Christian: 5%

Syria

Population: 11.75m
ethnicity
Syrian Arabs: 88.5%
Palestinian Arabs: 2.5%
Kurds: 8%
Turkomans: 1%
religion
Sunni Muslim: 70%
Shi'i Muslim
    (Alawis): 12%
Druze (Muslim): 4%
Christian (various
    sects): 14%

Total Palestinian population: 5.5 million, including 500,000 in the west or in Arab
states other than Israel, Israeli–occupied territories, Jordan, Lebanon, Syria.
Total Druze population: 750,000, including 100,000 living in the west.

Iraq
Population: 19m
(with over 2m migrant
workers prior to 1990)
ethnicity
Arabs: 73%
Kurds: 23%
Assyrians: 3%
Turkomans: 1%
religion
Sunni Muslim: 45%
Shi'i Muslim: 50%
Christian (various sects): 5%

Saudi Arabia
Population: 14.5m
(with over 3.5 m migrant
workers prior to 1990)
ethnicity
Arabs: 100%
religion
Sunni Muslim: 96%
Shi'i Muslim: 4%

Yemen
Population: 11.5m
ethnicity
Arabs
religion
Sunni Muslim: 50%
Shi'i Muslim (Zaydi): 43%
Shi'i Muslim (Ismaili): 7%

Total Kurdish population: 22.5 million, mainly in Turkey, Iran, Iraq, Syria, ex-USSR (Georgia and CIS), and Lebanon.
Total Christian population in Arab world: 9 million.

Oman
Population: 1.4m
(with 500,000
migrant workers)
ethnicity
Arabs: 92%
Baluchis: 8%
religion
Khariji Muslim (Ibadi): 75%
Sunni Muslim: 25%

United Arab Emirates
Population: 2m
(with 1.5 million
migrant workers)
ethnicity
Arabs
religion
Sunni Muslim

Qatar
Population: 420,000
(with 300,000
workers)
ethnicity
Arabs
religion
Sunni Muslim

Bahrain
Population: 420,000
(with 150,000
migrant workers)
ethnicity
Arabs
religion
Shi'i Muslim
   (Twelver): 60%
Sunni Muslim: 40%

Kuwait
Population: 2m
(with over 1.2 m migrant
workers prior to 1990)
ethnicity
Arabs
religion
Sunni Muslim: 70%
Shi'i Muslim
   (Twelver): 30%

Total Sunni Muslim population in Arab world: 182 million.
Total Shi'i Muslim population (all sects) in Arab world: 17 million.

(b) *Who are the 'Arabs'?*
Consider the following from *The Venture of Islam,* by Marshall G.S. Hodgson (University of Chicago Press, 1974), vol. I, pp. 62–3.

The term 'Arab' *'arab,* as noun and adjective, has been used on at least five levels. (1) It has referred – perhaps originally – expressly to the Bedouin, the nomads and especially the camel nomads of Arabia. (But careful usage has preferred a special term, *a'râb* [أَعْرَاب] sg.أَعْرَابِي] for them.) This has at times been the commonest usage of the term in Arabic. However, to render the Arabic *'arab* in such cases by our 'Arab', as some writers do when translating, is bound to be confusing and is to be avoided. The reader must be on the alert for such a usage in older translations. When a pre–Modern Arabic writer, such as Ibn–Khaldun, said something uncomplimentary about *'arabs,* he was usually speaking only of the Bedouin. (2) Then it has referred to all those claiming descent from or old cultural identification with the Bedouin or their language, including of course the 'settled Bedouin'. In this use, it has historically sometimes had an implication of 'Muslim', since the early Muslims were Arab in rather this sense; but the early jurist Abu–Yusuf, using it in this sense, included also some Christians and Jews. (3) The next extension was to all those peoples speaking Arabic–derived dialects, whatever their relations to Bedouin traditions or to Islam; in this sense, whole peasant populations can be called Arabs. (However, those among whom the literate have used some other than standard Arabic alphabet – for instance the Maltese and some other non–Muslim groups, especially Jews – have commonly, but not always, been excluded.) This latter sense is essentially a modern one. In using it in this work I am retrojecting it, for convenience's sake, upon a set of groups which might not have recognised that they formed a common category; it is analogous to having a common term, 'Latins', for all the Romance-speaking peoples. It must not, therefore, be lent any 'national' overtones: in this sense, 'the Arabs' have moved toward forming a nation only recently. However, it is the commonest modern usage and it must be remembered in this sense the Arabs are mostly neither Bedouin not tribal; they are, in large majority, peasants, living in villages and closely tied to the land. (4) It has further been used where the normal language of literacy was the classical Arabian, or Mudari [مُضَرِي], Arabic – whether the home vernacular was Arabic-derived or quite unrelated. Usually this usage has been restricted to the individual level. Persons who wrote in Arabic but whose own language was Persian or Spanish or Turkish or Kurdish have been included in what is collectively 'the Arabs'. Where whole peoples have possessed literacy only in Arabic – e.g. the Somalis – this usage has not usually applied. But even at best the usage is very dubious; it is sounder to say something like 'the Arabic writers'. (5) Finally, there are to be found authors who will seem to use the term for all peoples among whom Arabic is used at least in ritual. This is never done consistently; but it seems to be the implied definition when a book on the modern Arabs, for instance, includes, as illustrations of past Arab achievements, pictures of Taj Mahall in India or of illustrations to

Persian poetry. Such a usage is thoroughly confusing and unacceptable.

(c) The following is a saying from the Prophet on the subject of who is an Arab:

ليست العربية بأحدكم من أب ولا أم وإنما
هي اللسان، فمن تكلم بالعربية فهو عربي.

2. Additional reading
(a) Hourani, *A History of the Arab Peoples*, pp. 96–7; pp. 104–8; p. 434.

3. Key vocabulary
Taking as a starting point the texts in this chapter, draw up lists of vocabulary in the following fields:
(a) Names and terms used to describe ethnic groups.
(b) General terms for: people, race, migration, etc.

4. Written Arabic texts 1
(a) Read the following text, then give oral answers in English to the questions which follow it. You may find it useful to read through the questions first, in order to gain clues about the meanings of words used in the text.

يذكر علماء التاريخ أن العرب هم أحد الشعوب السامية التي
أنجبتها الجزيرة العربية. ويرى الباحثون أن أسلاف هذه الجماعات
كانوا يتمتعون بحضارة أصيلة، ويقطنون الطرف الجنوبي من
الجزيرة. ولكن بتزايد عدد السكان وتعرّض تلك المنطقة لتغييرات
مناخية سيئة، أُضطرّ سكّان الجنوب إلى الخروج من بلادهم على
شكل موجات متعاقبة. فاتّجه بعضهم شرقاً إلى بلاد الرافدين وكان
منهم الأكاديون والبابليون والأشوريون، ومنهم من توجّه شمالاً
وكان منهم الكنعانيون والفينيقون والأراميون والأنباط. وبقي في
وسط الجزيرة قبائل رحّل ورضيت بشظف العيش لكي تبقى
محافظة على كيانها واستقلالها وحريتها ولغتها.

1. Who say that the Arabs are a Semitic people?
2. According to researchers where did the ancestors of the Arabs live?
3. What forced these people to leave their country?
4. Did they leave all at once?
5. Which groups went to Mesopotamia?

6. Which groups went north?
7. Which groups remained in the peninsula?
8. What did their life of hardship enable them to do?

(b) Read the following text, then give oral answers in Arabic to the questions which
   follow it.

من الطبيعي في دولة كبيرة كالسودان أن يسكنها اجناس – أو
قبائل – كثيرة. ففي السودان مثلاً أكثر من مائتي قبيلة بعضها
كبيرة مثل قبيلة «الدينكا» – وهي قبيلة جنوبية يزيد عددها على
مليوني شخص – وبعضها صغيرة فمن الممكن أن تسكن القبيلة
كلها في قرية واحدة.

   ومن الطبيعي أيضا أن تختلف اللغات والعادات والأديان.
وأغلبية سكان شمال السودان مسلمون وأغلبية هؤلاء المسلمين –
سبعون في المائة منهم تقريبا – عرب. ولذلك يقول الإعلام الغربي
أحيانًا إن منطقة شمال السودان منطقة عربية إسلامية.

   أما جنوب السودان فإن أغلبية سكانه غير عرب وغير مسلمين.
ويتمسك معظم سكان الجنوب بالعادات التقليدية القديمة. وهناك
أيضًا عدد من المسيحيين أغلبيتهم كاثوليك وعدد قليل من
المسلمين. ولذلك يقول الإعلام الغربي أحيانًا إن منطقة جنوب
السودان هي منطقة أفريقية غير إسلامية.

paragraph one

١ – هل هناك أجناس كثيرة في السودان؟

٢ – كم عدد القبائل في السودان؟

٣ – هل تُعتبَر قبيلة «الدينكا» قبيلة كبيرة؟

٤ – كم عدد الناس في هذه القبيلة؟

paragraph two

٥ – هل هناك لغات كثيرة في السودان؟

٦ – ما هو الدين الرئيسي في شمال السودان؟

٧ – كم نسبة العرب في السودان؟

٨ – ماذا تقول الجرائد الغربية عن شمال السودان؟

paragraph three

٩ – هل أغلبية الناس في جنوب السودان مسلمون؟

١٠ – ما هي الأديان الموجودة في جنوب السودان؟

١١ – كيف تصف الجرائد الغربية منطقة جنوب السودان؟

5. Written Arabic texts 2

(a) Read the following text, then give oral answers in English to the questions which follow it.

الأكراد

الشعب الكردي شعب يعيش بصورة رئيسية في أربع دول في الشرق الأوسط ، هي تركيا وسوريا والعراق وإيران. يقول الخبراء إن عدد الأكراد الموجودين في هذه الدول اليوم يزيد على عشرين مليون نسمة يسكن منهم عشرة ملايين في تركيا ومليون في سوريا وستة ملايين في العراق وثلاثة ملايين في إيران.

يرجع تاريخ الشعب الكردي إلى الأزمان القديمة جدا فهم مذكورون في الروايات التاريخية الفارسية المكتوبة قبل ظهور الإسلام. وقد دخل معظم الأكراد الإسلام في عهد الخليفة عمر بن الخطاب إلا أنه هناك بعض الجماعات الكردية المسيحية في العراق حتى الآن.

للأكراد لغتهم الخاصة وهي قريبة من اللغة الفارسية ، ومعنى هذا أن اللغة الكردية تختلف في الأصل اختلافا كبيرا عن اللغة العربية إلا أنه قد دخلت إلى اللغة الكردية كلمات عربية كثيرة بسبب تأثير الإسلام في الحياة اليومية وانتشار الثقافة العربية في المناطق الكردية وخاصة في المدن الواقعة في شمال العراق. ومن الناحية الإقتصادية يعمل معظم الأكراد في الريف وهم رعاة أو فلاحون فقراء. ولكن هناك أيضا عدد كبير منهم هاجروا إلى المدن ويعملون الآن في المصانع. كما أن هناك أكراد آخرون سافروا

إلى أوربا – وخاصة أكراد تركيا – ووجدوا عملا في بلدان أوربية مختلفة مثل المانيا وبلجيكا. كما أن هناك طبعا بعض الأكراد المتعلمين وهم دكاترة ومهندسون وصحفيون ومدرسون إلى آخره.

وبالنسبة للوضع السياسي فيواجه الأكراد صعوبات في كل الدول التي يعيشون فيها. فالمعروف أن إيران مثلا جمهورية إسلامية ورأي هذه الدولة في الحركات الوطنية غير واضح حتى الآن. والنظام السوري نظام دكتاتوري لا يقبل الأحزاب السياسية غير العربية وغير الرسمية. وفي تركيا كانت اللغة الكردية لغة ممنوعة حتى بداية التسعينات عندما أعلنت الحكومة عن السماح باستعمالها رسميا في البيت وفي الشارع ولكنها لا تزال ممنوعة في المدارس فاللغة الوحيدة المستعملة هناك هي اللغة التركية. ورغم هذا فقد حصل في تركيا تحسين كبير في وضع الأكراد خلال السنوات الأخيرة. فكانت الحكومة التركية قد قالت حتى فترة قريبة إنه لا يوجد شعب اسمه الشعب الكردي في تركيا وإن الأكراد في الحقيقة أتراك قد نسوا اللغة التركية وبدأوا يتكلمون لغة غير لغتهم هي اللغة الكردية. وقد أطلقت الحكومة التركية على الأكراد اسم « أتراك الجبال » لأن وطن الأكراد الأصلي هو الجبال العالية الواقعة في شرق تركيا.

وأما في العراق فللأكراد مشاكل معروفة فقد حاربتهم حكومة البعث تحت رئاسة صدام حسين لمدة عشرين عاما. وفي عام ألف وتسع مائة وثمانية وثمانين استعمل الجيش العراقي الأسلحة الكميائية ضد الأكراد في شمال العراق ففي مدينة واحدة اسمها « حلبجة » قتل الجيش أكثر من خمسة آلاف شخص من الرجال والنساء والأطفال.

إذن، ما هو مستقبل الأكراد؟ لا يزال الوضع في إيران وسوريا كما قلنا غير واضح وتعتمد حالة الأكراد في العراق على الوضع السياسي العام في البلاد بعد الحرب السوداء التي دارت عام ١٩٩١

بـين الـعـراق والقـوات الـدوليـة تـحـت قـيـادة الـولايات المتـحـدة. أمـا فـي تـركـيـا فـيـبـدو أن المستقبل قد يكـون أحـسـن مـن الماضي. فـتـركـيـا دولـة ديموقـراطيـة فـيـها نـاس كثـيـرون يـؤيدون فكـرة حقـوق الإنـسـان ولا يقـبـلـون أن تـرفـض الحـكـومـة وجـود هذا الشـعـب داخل حدود الـبـلاد كـمـا عـمـلت فـي الماضي. وبـالإضـافـة إلى ذلك فـتـريد تـركـيـا أن تنضمّ إلى الـسـوق الأوروبـيـة المشتـركة وقـد قـال وزراء داخليـة الـسـوق أخـيـرا إنهم يـنـتـظـرون تـغـيـرات فـي وضـع الأكـراد فـي تـركـيـا فـي الـسـنـوات القادمـة – وسـيـتـحـقـق ذلك إن شاء الله.

1. Where do the Kurds live?
2. What is the total size of the Kurdish population?
3. When are the Kurds first mentioned in writing?
4. When did most of the Kurds embrace Islam?
5. What religion(s) do the Kurds profess today?
6. How similar is the Kurdish language to Arabic?
7. What do most Kurds work as?
8. What other jobs and professions do the Kurds have?
9. Why do the Kurds encounter problems in Iran?
10. Why do the Kurds encounter problems in Syria?
11. In what area of life is Kurdish still banned in Turkey?
12. What name did the Turkish government give the Kurds?
13. Why did it give them this name?
14. What problems have the Kurds experienced in Iraq over the past twenty years?
15. What happened in Halabja?
16. In which countries is the future of the Kurds not clear?
17. What does the future of the Kurds in Iraq depend on?
18. What is said about the future of the Kurds in Turkey?
19. What leads the writer to say this?
20. What is the EU ('Common Market') waiting for?

(b) Read the following text from الأهرام Mar. 20, 1990, then complete exercises i. – iii. which follow. You may find it useful to read through the questions first in exercise i, in order to gain clues about the meanings of words used in the text.

تاريخ الأكراد

دخل الاكراد في الاسلام في عهد الخليفة عمر بن الخطاب رضي الله تعالى عنه، بعد ان فتحت بلاد فارس، وذلك قبل ان يدخل في الاسلام جيرانهم من الفرس، وبقي الاكراد موالين للخلافة الاسلامية الى اواخر عهد بني امية، ثم انضووا تحت راية الدولة العباسية، ونجح ابو مسلم الخراساني في هزيمة نصر بن صبار والي بني امية في خراسان، وظل يتتبع فلول جيش بني امية حتى تم تقويض الخلافة الاموية وانتقل الامر الى بني العباس الذين غدروا بابي مسلم وقتلوه. وفي ظل الخلافة العباسية تمتع الاكراد بما يشبه الحكم الذاتي حتى انهم استطاعوا تأسيس دولة كبيرة هي الدولة المروانية على ان العبء الاكبر الذي اضطلع به الاكراد بعد ذلك كان هو مقاومة الصليبيين ولقد كان صلاح الدين الايوبي احد القواد البارزين في القوات الكردية التي كانت تحارب الصليبيين منذ عهد عماد الدين زنكي، ومن بعده ابنه نور الدين، وقد استطاع ان يؤسس دولة كبيرة شملت مصر والشام والحجاز واليمن والسودان والموصل، وقد تمكن من دحر الصليبيين في بيت المقدس واخراجهم منه وقضى على معظم قلاعهم على الساحل. وعندما تعرض المسلمون لغزو المغول وقف الاكراد وقفة مشرفة في وجه هذا الخطر، وحين وصلت قوات جنكيز خان الى مشارف همذان استدرجهم الاكراد الى ارض المعركة وهزموهم فاضطر المغول الى التقهقر، وكانت هذه هي المرة الاولى التي يتراجع فيها المغول وبذلك منع الاكراد تقدمهم نحو بغداد، ولكنهم عاودوا الكرة مرة اخرى في عهد هولاكو واضطر هولاكو الى تغيير خط سيره حتى لا يمر ببلاد الاكراد.

وحين اراد تيمـور لنك السيطرة على بلاد الكرد بعد انتصاره
على السلطان العثماني .. قاومـه الكرد فغزا بلادهم واحرق كثيـرا
من قراهم، ولكنه ادرك بغزيرته العسكرية ان التوغل في هذه البلاد
ليس في صالحه فرجع بجيوشه الى مقره في سمرقند وبخارى.

وفي ظل الخـلافـة العثـمانيـة تميـزت السـياسـة نحـو الاكراد
بالمرونة، واستغلت الخلافة العثمانية الاكراد كقوة عسكرية محاربة
فكانت شئون الجيش في ايديهم تقريبا، وكانوا هم فرسان الجيش.

وبعد الحرب العالمية الاولى اقتسم الغرب بموافقة روسيا تركة
الرجل المريض، وقسمت كردستان الى اربعة اقسام .. اقتطعت
روسيا جزءا وبقي القسم الاكبر تابعا لتركيا وخضع القسم الثالث
للانجليـز، وكان نصـيب فـرنسـا هذا الشـريط المتـاخم لتـركيا في
الجنوب .. وبدأت مأساة الاكراد المعاصرين.

i   Read the following questions in English. Then answer the corresponding
questions in Arabic below in section (b) ii:

1.   When did the Kurds embrace Islam?
2.   When did the Persians embrace Islam in relation to the Kurds?
3.   Until when did the Kurds remain clients of the Umayyad Caliphate?
4.   Which state succeeded the Umayyads?
5.   Who defeated the Umayyad governor of Khurasan?
6.   What then happened to this man?
7.   What sort of government did the Kurds enjoy under the successors to the
Umayyads?
8.   What was the name of the state the Kurds founded?
9.   Who was Salah al-Din?
10. Where were the Crusaders defeated?
11. How did the Kurds react to the Mongol attack?
12. How did the Kurds defeat the Mongols?
13. Under whose leadership did the Mongols return?
14. Who did the term « الرجل المريض » refer to at the end of the First World War?

ii Answer the following questions in Arabic.

١ –   متى أسلم الأكراد؟
٢ –   هل دخل الفرس الإسلام قبل الأكراد؟

٣ – متى كان الأكراد موالين للخلافة الإسلامية؟

٤ – ما هي الدولة التي تلت الدولة الأموية؟

٥ – من قتل أبو مسلم؟

٦ – من هو نور الدين؟

٧ – أين تم دحر الصليبيين؟

٨ – ماذا عمل الأكراد بالمغول قريبا من مدينة همذان؟

٩ – ما هي نتيجة معركة همذان؟

١٠ – من هو هولاكو؟

١١ – ما هي ميزة السياسة العثمانية نحو الأكراد؟

١٢ – ماذا يقصد الكاتب بلفظة «الرجل المريض»؟

iii Replace the words in brackets in questions 1–6 with synonyms. In 7–8, replace the existing underlined structures with different structures which give the same meaning.

١ – {اعتنق} الإسلام

٢ – نجح الأكراد في {هزم} المغول .

٣ – {قوّض} الأكراد جيوش المغول .

٤ – {غدر بـ}صديقه .

٥ – {تمتع} الأكراد بالحكم الذاتي .

٦ – كانت القوات الكردية {تقاتل} جيوش المغول .

٧ – كان عمر بن الخطاب {خليفة من خلفاء} بني أميّة .

٨ – استطاع الأكراد {أن يؤسّسوا} الدولة المروانية .

6. Written Arabic texts 3 (classical)

(a) Read the following passage by تاريخ العلامة from ابن خلدون, vol. II, pp. 505-6, then complete exercises i. and ii. which follow.

اعلم أنّ جميع العرب يرجعون إلى ثلاثة أنساب وهي عدنان وقحطان وقضاعة. فأما عدنان فهو من ولُد إسماعيل بالاتّفاق، إلا ذكر الآباء الذين بينه وبين إسماعيل فليس فيه شيء يرجع إلى يقينه، وغير عدنان من ولد إسماعيل قد انقرضوا فليس على وجه الأرض منهم أحد. وأما قحطان فقيل من ولد إسماعيل وهو ظاهر كلام البخاري في قوله: باب نسبة اليمن إلى إسماعيل ... والجمهور على أنّ قحطان هو يقطن[1] المذكور

في التـوراة في ولد عـابر، وأن حضـرمـوت من شـعوب قـحطان. وأمـا قـضـاعـة فـقيل إنهـا حِمْيَر قـاله ابن إسـحـاق والكلبي وطائفة، وقـد يحـتجّ لذلك بمـا رواه ابن لُهَيْـعَـة عن عُقْـبَـة بن عـامـر الجَهْني قـال: يا رسـول اللّه ممن نحن؟ قـال أنتـم من قـضـاعـة بن مـالك.

Note

١. الباب العاشـر لسفـر التكوين

i   Answer the following comprehension questions relating to the above text in Arabic.

١ – حسب الكاتب مـا هي الأنسـاب الثلاثة التي يعود العرب كلهم إليهـا؟

٢ – أي نسـب من هذه الأنسـاب أصله من ولد إسـمـاعيل؟

٣ – مـاذا حدث إلى هذا النسب؟

٤ – مـاذا قال البخاري عن النسب الثاني؟

٥ – مـاذا قيل عن النسب الثالث؟

٦ – من قال هذا؟

ii   Translate the text into idiomatic English.

(b)   Read the following passage, also by ابن خلدون from العلامة تاريخ, vol. II, pp. 16-17, out loud, providing all final vowels (some have been given for you). Then translate the text into idiomatic English.

من الأخـبـار الـواهيـة للمـؤرِّخين مـا ينقلونه كافّةً في أخـبـارِ التَبـابعَة[1] ملوك اليـمـن وجزيرة العـرب أنهم كـانـوا يغـزون من قـراهمْ باليـمـن إلى إفـريقـيـة والبـربر من بلاد المغـرب، وأنّ إفـريقش بن قـيس ابن صيـفيّ من أعـاظم ملوكـهم الأُوَل، وكـان لـعهد مـوسـى عليـه السـلام أوْ قـبله بقليل. غـزا إفـريقـيـة وأثخن في البـربر، وأنه سـمّـاهم بهـذا الاسم حين سـمـع رطانتـهم وقـال: مـا هذه البـربرة، فأُخـذ هذا الاسمُ عنه ودُعوا بـه من حينئذٍ، وأنه لمّا انصـرف من المغـرب حجَز هنالكَ قبـائلَ من حِمْيَرَ

فَأَقامُوا بِها واختَلطوا بِأَهلِها، ومِنهُم صِنهاجةٌ وكُتامةٌ ومِن هذا ذهبَ الطَّبَريُّ والجُرجانيُّ والمَسْعُوديُّ وابنُ الكَلبيُّ والبِيليُّ إلى أنَّ صِنهاجةَ وكُتامةَ مِن حِميَرَ وتَأْباهُ نَسّابةُ البَربرِ، وهو الصحيحُ.

Note

1. Plural of تُبَّع. A name for the ancient kings of Yemen.

(c) Read the following passage by المسعودي from مروج الذهب *Les Prairies d'Or*, (text and translation by C.B. de Meynard and P. de Courteille), vol. III, pp. 249-50, then translate the text into idiomatic English.

فَأَمّا أجناسُ الأكرادِ وأنواعِهم فَقد تنازعَ الناسُ في بدئِهم فمِنهُم مَن رأى أنهم مِن ربيعةَ بن نِزارِ ابنِ مَعدّ بن عدنانِ بن بكرِ بن وائلٍ انفردوا في قديمِ الزمانِ وانضافوا إلى الجبالِ والأوديةِ لأحوالٍ دعتهُم إلى ذلك وجاوروا مَن هنالكَ مِن الأمم الساكنةِ المدنَ والعمائرَ مِن الأعاجمِ والفُرسِ فحالوا عن لسانِهم وصارت لغتُهم أعجميةً ولكلّ نوعٍ مِن الأكرادِ لهم لغةٌ بالكرديةِ ومِن الناسِ مَن رأى أنهم مِن مُضَرِ بن نِزارِ وأنهم مِن ولدِ كردِ بن مَردِ بن صعصعةَ بن هَوازِنَ وأنهم انفردوا في قديمِ الزمانِ لوقائعَ كانت بينهم وبينَ غَسّانَ ومِنهُم مَن رأى أنهم مِن ربيعةَ ومُضَرِ اعتصموا بالجبالِ طلبًا للمياهِ والمراعى فحالوا عن اللغةِ العربيةِ لِمَن جاورهم مِن الأمم.

7. Grammar/stylistics

(a) *Basic sentential word order in Arabic*

i *Sentences with a verb*

The basic sentence in Arabic contains a verb, and as seen in chapter 1 (section 7d), in certain cases, where a sentence does not require a verb for it to make sense a 'semantically light' verb is inserted. The most common word order in a sentence with a verb is Verb–Subject–Object (VSO). However when an adverb or adverbial phrase (a word or phrase describing the place, manner or time of occurrence of the main event) occurs the adverbial phrase (A) may occur before the verb to give Adverb–Verb–Subject (AVS), less commonly between the verb and the subject to give Verb–Adverb–Subject (VAS), or after the subject to give

Verb–Subject–Adverb (VSA) word orders. One word order which was until recently fairly unusual, but which is becoming increasingly common since it tends to mirror the typical word order found in modern Arabic dialects, is Subject–Verb–Object (SVO) or Subject–Verb–Adverb (SVA). Finally, the object may precede the subject to give Verb–Object–Subject (VOS), but in this case usually translates, or is translated as, the English agentive passive. Essentially while, for different stylistic reasons, the subject, object and adverbial phrase can occur in any of first, second, third (or fourth) position within the sentence, the verb is restricted to either first or second position. Therefore word orders of the type ASVO giving a word–for–word translation of English sentences such as 'Yesterday the boy ate breakfast' are extremely rare: the correct Arabic translation of such a sentence has the word order AVSO, i.e. 'Yesterday–ate–the–boy–breakfast', or it begins with the verb and the adverbial is placed later in the sentence.

I have ordered the following examples into sentence types in which the verb comes in first position, and sentence types in which the verb comes in second position (the verb is bracketed in each example):

i.i *Verb in first position (VSO), (VSA), (VAS), (VOS)*
VSO

و{يشمل} العالم العربي صحارى عديدة.

'The Arab world has a large number of deserts.' (ch. 1, 4a)

إذ {تبلغ} مساحته مليون كيلومتر مربع.

'Its area is one million square kilometres.' (ch. 1, 4b)

{يذكر} علماء التاريخ أن العرب هم أحد الشعوب السامية.

'Historians say that the Arabs are one of the Semitic peoples.' (ch. 2, 4a)

VSA

و{توجد} جبال كثيرة في الكثير من البلدان العربية

'There are a lot of mountains in many Arab countries.' (ch. 1, 4b)

و{تقع} أهم وديان العالم العربي في مصر.

'The most important valleys in the Arab world are in Egypt.' (ch. 1, 4a)

{يقع} العراق في قارة آسيا.

'Iraq is in the continent of Asia.' (ch. 1, 4bii)

VAS

'There is no water there.' (ch. 1, 4bii)   ولا {يوجد} فيها ماء

'No plants grow there.' (ch. 1, 4bii)　　　　لا {ينبت} فيها نبات.

{كانت تجتمع} خلفه مياه السيول.
'The rains of the floods collected behind it.' (ch. 1, 11)

{يسكن} منهم عشرة ملايين في تركيا.
'Ten million of them live in Turkey.' (ch. 2, 5a)

'Many joined them.' (ch. 1, 8)　　　　{انضم} إليهم كثيرون.

VOS

{يلي} منطقة السهول الساحلية، المناطق الداخلية.
'Bordering the coastal plains are the inland regions. [lit: 'borders the region of the coast plains [object], the inner regions [subject]'].' (ch. 1, 5a)

i.ii *Verb in second position (SVO), (AVS)*
If there is any element other than the verb in first position, the first part of the sentence tends to be stressed. However, this does not always apply in modern Arabic, particularly with SVO, since this word order has come to mimic colloquial dialects where SVO is the usual word order for sentences with verbs. Both AVS and SVO are types of topic–comment (or subject–predicate) sentences (cf. ii. below) with the first element (the subject or the adverb) constituting the topic (i.e. the thing being talked about), and the second element (verb + subject or verb + object) the comment (i.e. the information provided about the topic) of the sentence. Both AVS and SVO can be accompanied by ف ... أما, as in the first two examples below, where أما introduces the topic, and ف the comment. A topic introduced by أما is always stressed:

SVO

وأما جنوب السودان فـ{يشمل} غابات كبيرة.
'The south of Sudan contains large forests.' (ch. 1, 4biii)

وأما البحر العربي فـ{يقع} جنوب شرقي شبه الجزيرة العربية.
'The Arabian Sea is in the south east of the Arabian peninsula.' (ch. 1, 4a)

وأهل المدينة {ينصرفون} إلى منازلهم.
'The people of the town set off for their houses.' (ch. 1, 6c)

AVS

وفي بعض المناطق قد لا {تنزل} قطرة مطر ...

'In some areas not a drop of rain may fall ...' (ch. 1, 4bi)

وفي مناطق أخرى {نجد} حرات واسعة.

'In other areas we find vast lava fields.' (ch. 1, 4bi)

وهكذا {كان} موقع عمان بالغ الأهمية.

'Thus the position of Oman was extremely important.' (ch. 1, 5a)

ii *Sentences without a verb: topic–comment sentences*
Although Arabic prefers sentences with a verb, within a text (more rarely at the beginning of a text) verbless sentences can be found. In this case the sentence usually has a definite subject topic followed by a comment providing information about the topic (cf. i. above); consider the English sentence 'the cat is on the mat': here 'the cat' constitutes the topic and 'is on the mat' the comment. In topic–comment sentences the comment can be realised by a noun or noun phrase (including noun + relative clause), an adjective or adjective phrase, a prepositional phrase, an entire clause, or, as seen above in i. above, a verb or verb phrase. Another term for topic–comment sentences is subject–predicate. Here I shall not consider topic-comment structures where the comment is a verb or verb phrase since these do not fall into the category of verbless sentences; however, students should note that the SVO word order is simply an instance of topic-comment structures. As noted above the topic of a topic-comment structure may be introduced by أما while the comment is introduced by ف. Consider the following examples (the topic is separated from the comment by a slash /):

comment = noun or noun phrase

إن مضيق هرمز / ممر مائي عريض للغاية.

'The straits of Hormuz are extremely wide.' (ch. 1, 5b)

و هي/ مرسى أهل الهند.

'It is the port for the people of India.' (ch. 1, 6c)

الشعب الكردي / شعب يعيش بصورة رئيسية في أربع دول في الشرق الأوسط.

'The Kurdish people are a people who live largely in four countries in the Middle East.' (ch. 2, 5a)

comment = adjective or adjective phrase

فإن المضيق/ أوسع بكثير مما يتصوره الناس.

'The straits are a lot wider than people imagine.' (ch. 1, 5b)

ومدينة صنعاء / مفروشة كلها.

'The town of Sana'a is all paved.' (ch. 1, 6c)

comment = prepositional phrase

وجامع صنعاء / من أحسن الجوامع.

'The mosque of Sana'a is one of the most beautiful mosques.' (ch. 1, 6c)

والماء / على بعد منها.

'The water is some distance from there.' (ch. 1, 6c)

comment = entire clause

أما عدنان / فهو من ولد إسماعيل بالاتفاق.

'Adnan is commonly acknowledged to be one of the sons of Ismail.' (ch. 2, 6a)

أما أجناس الأكراد وأنواعهم / فقد تنازع الناس في بدئهم.

'People have disagreed over the origins of the different groups of Kurds.' (ch. 2, 6c)

(b) *The coordination of adjectives*

Adjectives are coordinated (joined together) asyndetically – that is to say, they are linked with no conjunction such as و – when they refer to inseparable aspects of the noun, as in, for example, the English phrase 'the big, white house' where the noun, the house, is both big and white, and as in 'the Arab–Israeli dispute' where the dispute is necessarily both 'Arab' and 'Israeli'. In the following example, the string of adjectives 'short, pale, thin and in poor condition' are all inseparable attributes of the subject 'the boy':

وكان شيخنا الصبيّ {قصيرا نحيفا شاحبا زريّ الهيئة على نحو ما}.

'Our Sheikh the boy was short, thin, pale and generally in poor condition.' (ch. 4, 5b)

When near synonyms are coordinated they are linked asyndetically, as in:

لأن أمطارها {وابلة متدفقة}.

'Because its rains are very heavy and gushing.' (ch. 1, 6b)

Adjectives are also linked asyndetically when the second adjective modifies the whole of the preceding phrase – i.e. the noun plus the first adjective – as in:

$$\text{للتاريخ \{الإسلامي الأندلسي\}.}$$

'For Andalusian Islamic history.' (ch. 5, 9a)

Adjectives are linked syndetically – that is to say, by means of the conjunction و – when they refer to distinct, separable aspects of the noun. In the following example, three distinct types of security are described – political, economic and social:

$$\text{كل ما يتعلق بالأمن \{السياسي والاقتصادي والاجتماعي\}.}$$

'Everything connected to political, economic and social security.' (ch. 9, 4a)

And in the example below a single system (نظام) has three identifiable aspects – social, economic and political:

$$\text{بل هو نظام \{اجتماعي واقتصادي وسياسي\}.}$$

'Indeed it is a social, economic and political system.' (ch. 4, 4b)

In the following example three distinct periods of Islamic rule are described – Umayyad, Abbasid and Ayyubid:

$$\text{في فترات الحكم \{الأموي والعباسي والأيوبي\}.}$$

'In the periods of Umayyad, Abbasid and Ayyubid rule.' (ch. 3, 4b)

When adjectives refer to mutually incompatible aspects of the noun the noun may take dual or plural number (depending on the number of adjectives) while the adjectives each agree with the singular; in the following example the adjectives agree with the singular form منطقة 'region', but the noun is in the dual منطقتي آسيا 'the two regions of Asia':

$$\text{في منطقتي آسيا \{الغربية والجنوبية\}.}$$

'In the western and southern regions of Asia.' (More literally: 'In the two regions of Asia, the west and the south.') (ch. 3, 4a)

Finally, in the following example all the thoughts (أفكار) are Islamic, but they are described as falling into two groups: general and specific:

$$\text{الأفكار الإسلامية \{العامة والخاصة\}.}$$

'General and specific Islamic notions.' (ch. 4, 4b)

(c) *Subject clauses*

In Arabic, subjects are generally nouns or noun phrases, as in the English sentence 'the boy washed before going to bed' where the subject is 'the boy'. Subjects can, however, also be clauses. In the sentence 'that Alistair won the race is undeniable' the subject of the sentence is the clause 'that Alistair won the race' while the predicate is 'undeniable'. A more common way of expressing this in English is 'it is undeniable that Alistair won the race'; in this example, the predicate 'undeniable' comes before the subject 'that Alistair won the race'. In Arabic, sentences of this type are similar in terms of their parts to the English 'that Alistair won the race is undeniable' – i.e. the two parts are 'undeniable' and 'that Alistair won the race'; however, in terms of their word order, Arabic sentences of this type are more like 'it is undeniable that Alistair won the race': that is to say, the 'undeniable' element (the predicate) comes first, and 'that Alistair won the race' (the subject) comes second.

The initial predicate in this type of sentence can take one of four common forms: participle or adjective, participle preceded by الـ, participle preceded by مـن الـ, and verb. The predicative participle or adjective always takes the uninflected (masculine singular) form, just as the predicative verb always takes the third masculine singular (he) form. This is because clauses beginning with أنْ or أنّ can be regarded as masculine:

participle or other adjective

و{معلوم} أن البحر الأحمر يؤدي شمالا ...

'It is well known that the Red Sea leads north ...' (ch. 1, 9i)

In this example, the predicate is معلوم while the subject is the clause أن البحر الأحمر يؤدي شمالا ....

{صحيح} أن أعمال الحكومة العراقية في الأهوار تلكأت.

'It is true that the Iraqi government's works have been delayed.' (ch. 8, 11)

الـ + participle

فـ{المعروف} أن إيران مثلا جمهورية إسلامية.

'It is well known, for example, that Iran is an Islamic republic.' (or: 'What is well known is that ...') (ch. 2, 5a)

و{الظاهر} أنه لما اتسعت روما وأنشأت إمبراطورية استعملت كلمة بربر لجميع الشعوب التي تسكن إفريقيا.

'It appears that when Rome expanded and founded an empire it used the word Berber for all the peoples who lived in Africa.' (or: 'What is clear is that ...') (ch. 2, 8)

و{الأرجح} أن القادة المشاركين كانوا سينظرون إلى الموضوع المطروح كموضوع هامشي.

'It is probable that the participating leaders would have regarded the proposed subject matter as marginal.' (or: 'What is probable is that ...') (ch. 10, 5c)

من ال + *participle*

و{من الممكن} أن تسكن القبيلة كلها في قرية واحدة.

'It is possible for the whole tribe to live in one village.' (ch. 2, 4b)

و{من الطبيعي} أيضا أن تختلف اللغات والعادات والأديان.

'It is also natural for languages, customs and religions to differ.' (ch. 2, 4b)

و{من الغريب} أن المطر ببلاد الهند ... إنما ينزل في أيام القيظ.

'It is strange that rain in India ... only falls during hot periods.' (ch. 1, 6a)

و{من اللازم} أن يتزوج بالطريقة الإسلامية.

'It is necessary to marry in the Islamic way.' (ch. 4, 4b)

Where the predicate is a participle or adjective (optionally preceded by من and the definite article) the entire sentence is negated by adding ليس, and is put into the past by adding كان:

{ليس من الضروري} أن تكمل.

'It is not necessary for it to finish.' (ch. 10, 11b)

In this example, the subject is أن تكمل and the predicate is ليس من الضروري.

{ليس من المستحب} أن تأكل العسل بغير خبز.

'It is not right for you to eat honey without bread.' (ch. 11, 4b)

{كان من الطبيعي} أن تتنافس روما وقرطاجة.

'It was natural for Rome and Carthage to rival one another.' (ch. 3, 8)

Examples of initial verbal predicates include:

و{يبدو} أن هناك بشائر لطريقة جديدة فعالة تنفع لمواجهة هذا النوع من الكوارث.

'It appears that there are indications of a new effective means of combatting this type of disaster.' (ch. 8, 5c)

Again in this example, the subject is أن هناك بشائر لطريقة جديدة فعالة تنفع while the predicate is يبدو لمواجهة هذا النوع من الكوارث.

و{يمكننا} أن نتخيل أيضا انعكاسات هذا الواقع على تربية الأطفال.

'It is possible for us to imagine the repercussions of this state of affairs on the raising of children.' (ch. 10, 5c)

فهل {يجوز} أن نحمله شيئا فوق حمله إيانا.

'Is it right for us to make him carry anything more than us?' (ch. 11, 4biv)

{اتضح} أن بعض الإدارات لم يستدل فيها على سجلات منتظمة.

'It is clear that orderly records are not kept in some administrations.' (ch. 9, 5b)

فـ{اتفق} أنه اجتاز بذلك النهر صيادان.

'It happened that two fishermen crossed that river.' (ch. 11, 6b)

Verbal predicates are negated by adding لا:

إذ {لا يعقل} أن يعبر رجل عن تجارب كل الأجيال الزراعية، و{لا يمكن له} أن ينطق بلهجات جميع المناطق.

'For it is not reasonable for a man to express the experiences of all agricultural generations, nor is it possible for him to speak the dialects of all regions.' (ch. 11, 11)

{لا يمكن} التفريق بين الجماعتين عنصريا تاما ...

'It is not possible to distinguish the two groups on wholly racial grounds ...' (ch. 2, 8)

Finally, another common initial element in this kind of structure is the word معنى 'meaning' in an إضافة phrase with a following masculine singular demonstrative:

و{معنى هذا} أن اللغة الكردية تختلف ...

'This means that the Kurdish language differs ...' (ch. 2, 5b)

(d) *Active participles and verbal nouns taking objects*

In English, verbs and gerunds (verbal nouns which end in *–ing*) can take objects. In Arabic, active participles and definite verbal nouns can occasionally take objects, more commonly in Classical Arabic. In this chapter we have an example of an active participle taking an object:

الأمم {الساكنة} المدنَ والعمائرَ.

'The communities living in the towns and estates …' (ch. 2, 6c)

Verbal nouns can take objects, but are more commonly put as the first term in an إضافة phrase, as in: {استيطان} الضفة الغربية '[the] settlement of the West Bank'. Where verbal nouns do take objects in modern Arabic it is generally because a pronoun (or a noun) is required, and thus the verbal noun is made definite by adding a pronoun suffix, as in: {استيطانهم} الضفةَ الغربية 'their m. settlement of the West Bank' (or, 'their settling the West Bank'). Examples of definite verbal nouns taking objects include:

و{رفضها} جمعَ شمل العائلات الفلسطينية.

'… [Israel's] refusal to reunite Palestinian families.' (ch. 6, 4d)

لا يدركون العاصفة السياسية التي تحوط بـ{ـاستيطانهم} الضفةَ الغربيةَ.

'They do not realise the political storm which surrounds their settlement of the West Bank.' (ch. 6, 4c)

وانتقدت الولايات المتحدة لـ{ـفرضها} قيودا على دخول المهاجرين اليهود السوفيات.

'They criticised the United States for imposing restrictions on the entrance of Soviet Jewish immigrants.' (ch. 6, 4d)

8. Aural Arabic texts 1

Listen carefully to the aural text from حصاد الشهر من هم no. 26, side 2, item 6, البربر وما هو أصلهم؟, then complete exercises i. – v. below.

i Answer the following questions in Arabic orally in class.

١ – ما هو أصل كلمة «بربر»؟

٢ – لماذا أطلق اليونان هذا الاسم على الشعب البربري؟

٣ – على من أطلق العرب لفظة «أعاجم»؟

٤ – كيف استعمل الرومان لفظة بربر أول ما أخذوها؟

٥ – أين يسكن البربر اليوم؟

٦ – على قول المؤلف ما هو أصل البربر العنصري؟

٧ – في أية مناطق كان البربر يسكنون عندما فتح العرب شمال افريقيا؟

٨ – أي فريق من فروق البربر يتركز في الأطلس الأوسط؟

٩ - ما هو الفريق الذي يتحدث لغة الشلوح؟

١٠. -أين يوجد ارتكاز هذا الفريق؟

١١ -متى اختلط البربر في شمال افريقيا بالعرب؟

١٢ -متى اختلطوا بالقبائل الهلائلية؟

١٣ -في رأي الكاتب هل يوجد بربر أصلاء العنصر اليوم؟

١٤ -كيف تتبين الفروق بين البربر والعرب اليوم؟

١٥ -للبربر كم لغة؟

١٦ -ما هي اللغات البربرية المهمة؟

١٧ -متى يستخدم البربر اللغة العربية؟

١٨ -متى يستعمل البربر اللغات البربرية؟

ii Answer the following comprehension questions based on   من هم البربر وما
هو أصلهم؟ in written form in English.

1. Which word is the term بربر derived from?
2. Who did the Greeks describe by this term?
3. Who did the Arabs describe as أعاجم؟
4. At the time Rome established an empire, who were described as بربر؟
5. Who were ultimately described as بربر؟
6. According to some people, where do the Berbers originally come from?
7. If this is the case, the Berbers would belong to which race?
8. To which race do some legends link the Berbers?
9. According to researchers, where did the Berbers live at the time of the Arab conquest of North Africa?
10. How many groups of Berbers are there?
11. What are these groups?
12. Where can the first group be found?
13. Which language does the second group speak?
14. Who did the Berbers mix with?
15. According to the speaker, is it true that the Berbers can be divided into two groups: one which has maintained its original race, and a second which has become Arabised?
16. How can the Berber groups be distinguished?
17. Which languages do the Berbers speak?
18. For what purposes do the Berbers use Arabic?
19. How do the Berbers describe themselves?

iii Fill in the gaps in the following text. You may find it useful to read through the gapped text a few times before you listen to the tape.

كلمة ــــــــــ مأخوذة ــــــــــ ــــــــــ ــــــــــ
«بربروس» اليونانية ــــــــــ أطلقها اليونان ــــــــــ ــــــــــ
الشعوب ــــــــــ لم تكن ــــــــــ اللغة ــــــــــ على
غرار ما ــــــــــ ــــــــــ ــــــــــ بإطلاقهم ــــــــــ
«الأعاجم» على أولئك ــــــــــ لم يتكلموا ــــــــــ ــــــــــ. وأخذ
الرومان ــــــــــ نفسها و ــــــــــ على ــــــــــ
ــــــــــ تسكن الساحل الإفريقي ــــــــــ
لهم. و ــــــــــ أنه لما اتسعت ــــــــــ ــــــــــ وأنشأت
إمبراطورية ــــــــــ ــــــــــ ــــــــــ لجميع
ــــــــــ ــــــــــ بما
ــــــــــ ــــــــــ الصحراء. و
ــــــــــ ــــــــــ ــــــــــ صارت
ــــــــــ ــــــــــ ــــــــــ شعب ــــــــــ ــــــــــ واحة
سيوا في غرب مصر ونواكشوط ــــــــــ موريتانيا
و ــــــــــ ــــــــــ القبائل الجزائرية ــــــــــ جبال
جرجورة و ــــــــــ مناطق ــــــــــ الغربي الشمالية.
ــــــــــ ــــــــــ يقول ــــــــــ ــــــــــ
ــــــــــ من ــــــــــ ــــــــــ وإنهم جاءوا ــــــــــ
ــــــــــ في ــــــــــ سابق سحيق ــــــــــ القدم.
و ــــــــــ ــــــــــ أن ــــــــــ ــــــــــ
ــــــــــ سامـيا ــــــــــ ــــــــــ سامية.

و ———— ———— ———— اكتشف أساطير تربطهم بالحاميين

و ———— الرأي ———— يربط ———— العنصرين -

أي ———— ———— ———— و ———— ———— – أساسا

لتكوين ———— هو أقرب ———— ———— القبول.

والذي ———— ———— ———— ———— أنه لما

———— ———— إلى ———— ———— فاتحين

———— ———— ———— ———— المنطقة ————

والصحراء و ———— ———— ———— ————

الصحراء يسكنها ———— ———— وأنه ————

———— أقسام رئيسة ———— ———— هي زناتة ومصمودة

وصنهاجة. وكانت مواطن ———— ———— ————

زناتة تمتد ———— ———— إلى الريف ————

المغرب. وكان ———— الأوسط نقطة ارتكازهم. ومصمودة

و ———— ———— يتكلمون اللغة ———— تسمى

الشلوح يتركزون في سوس ———— ———— وينتشرون

———— ———— الريف و ———— المغرب.

———— صنهاجة فتشمل القبائل و ———— ————

من الأطلس ———— والطوارق ———— الطوارق.

و ———— اختلط ———— في ————

———— ———— المذكورة ———— الذين جاءوا ———— الفتح

———— ———— ثم مع ———— الهلاهلية في

الخامس ـــــــ ـــــــ أي الحادى عشر للميلاد، ثم مع الآخرين

ـــــــ جاءوا حتى ـــــــ الأندلس في ـــــــ

متأخر. و ـــــــ العادة أن يقال بأن ـــــــ

ـــــــ من لا يزالون يحتفظون بعنصرهم

وأن ـــــــ ـــــــ ـــــــ تعربوا.

و ـــــــ هذه المقولة شائعة فإنها ـــــــ

صحيحة إلى ـــــــ الذي تلقاه من البعض، فإن الاختلاط كان

ـــــــ بحيث أنه لا يمكن التفريق ـــــــ الجماعتين

عنصريا ـــــــ إلا في حالات محدودة ـــــــ

ـــــــ الأطلس الأوسط.

وإذا ـــــــ ثمة ـــــــ ـــــــ لتبيين ـــــــ

ـــــــ لغوي و ـــــــ عنصريا. فـ ـــــــ

يستعملون ـــــــ عددا ـــــــ اللغات ـــــــ

ـــــــ أهم لغاتهم ـــــــ – ـــــــ الأمازغ

ـــــــ المغرب و ـــــــ ـــــــ ـــــــ

وموريتانيا والتماشك للطوارق والزنقا في السنغال. فانتشار

ـــــــ البربر واستعمالهم ـــــــ

ـــــــ كتابةٍ وأدبٍ و ـــــــ

و ـــــــ وفقهٍ وما ـــــــ أزال

ـــــــ والعنصرية. و ـــــــ البربرية

المذكورة ـــــــ لها ـــــــ في ـــــــ

ــــــــــــــــــ و. ـــــــــــــ يشـــير ـــــــــــــ نفـــسـه

في ـــــــــــ بأنه «أماز غ» ومعناه ـــــــــــــ.

iv Compare your version of the complete text with the completed text below.

كلمــة بربــر مــأخــوذة أصــلا مـن كلمــة «بـربـروس» اليـونانيـة التـي أطلقها اليونان على الشعوب التي لم تكن تتكلم اللغة اليونانية على غـرار مـا عـمل العـرب بإطلاقـهم كلمـة «الأعـاجم» على أولـائك الذين لم يتكلمـوا العـربية. وأخذ الرومـان الكلمة نـفسـها وأطلقوها على الشعوب التي كـانت تسكن الساحل الإفـريقي المقابل لـهم. والظاهر أنه لما اتسعت روما وأنشأت إمبراطورية استعملت كلمة بربر لجمـيع الشعـوب التي تسكن إفريقيا بما في ذلك شعـوب الصحـراء. ومـع الزمـن صارت كلمة بربر تطلق على كل شعب يسكن بـين واحة سيوا في غرب مصر ونواكشوط عاصمة موريتانيا اليوم وبـين القبـائل الجزائرية في جبـال جرجورة وبـين مناطق السـودان الغـربي الشماليـة.

هناك مـن يقول إن أصل البـربـر من اليمن وإنهم جاءوا شمال أفـريقيا في زمن سـابق سحـيق في القدم. ومـعنى هذا أن البـربـر يكونون شعبا ساميا أو شعوبا سامية. وهناك من اكتشف أساطير تربطهم بالحـامـيـين ولعل الرأي الذي يربط بين العنصـرين – أي العنصـر السـامي والعنصر الحـامي – أسـاسـا لتكوين البـربـر هو أقرب إلى القبول.

والذي عليه الباحثون هو أنه لما جاء العرب إلى شمال إفريقيا فـاتحين كانت المنطقة التي تشمل الساحل والصحـراء ومـا إلى الجنوب من الصحـراء يسكنها البربر وأنه كانت هناك ثلاثة أقسام رئيسـة للبـربـر هي زنـاتة ومصمـودة وصنهاجـة. وكانت مـواطن القسم الأول أي زناتة تمتد من ليبيا إلى الريف في المغرب. وكان

الأطلس الأوسط نقطة ارتكازهم. ومصمودة وهم الذين يتكلمون اللغة التي تسمى الشلوح يتركزون في سوس في المغرب وينتشرون في الريف وفي جنوب المغرب. أما صنهاجة فتشمل القبائل والقسم الأوسط من الأطلس الكبير والطوارق أو الطوارق.

وقد اختلط البربر في جميع المناطق المذكورة بالعرب الذين جاءوا مع الفتح أولا ثم مع القبائل الهلاهلية في القرن الخامس للهجرة أي الحادي عشر للميلاد، ثم مع الآخرين الذين جاءوا حتى من الأندلس في وقت متأخر. وجرت العادة أن يقال بأن هناك من البربر من لا يزالون يحتفظون بعنصرهم الأصلي وأن هناك البربر الذين تعربوا. ومع أن هذه المقولة شائعة فإنها ليست صحيحة إلى الحد الذي تلقاه من البعض، فإن الاختلاط كان كبيرا بحيث أنه لا يمكن التفريق بين الجماعتين عنصريا تاما إلا في حالات محدودة المكان مثل الأطلس الأوسط.

وإذا كان ثمة مجال لتبيين الفروق فإن أساسها لغوي وليس عنصريا. فالبربر يستعملون الآن عددا من اللغات كبيرا لكن أهم لغاتهم أربع – هي الأمازغ في المغرب والشلوح في المغرب وموريتانيا والتماشك للطوارق والزنقا في السنغال. فانتشار الإسلام بين البربر واستعمالهم اللغة العربية لغةَ كتابةٍ وأدبٍ وشعرٍ وعلمٍ وفقهٍ وما إلى ذلك أزال الفروق الاجتماعية والعنصرية. واللغات البربرية المذكورة فوق لها وجود في الأدب الشعبي. والبربري يشير إلى نفسه خاصة في المغرب بأنه « أمازغ » ومعناه النبيل.

v Structure translations based on من هم البربر و ما هو أصلهم؟.
Translate the following English sentences into Arabic using relevant constructions to be found in the text at the points indicated.

1. The word 'qaamuws' in Arabic derives from the Greek word 'ökeanos'. (cf. para. 1, line 1)
2. This expression is normally used to refer to foreigners. (para. 1, line 2)

3. In the past the Berbers used to grow wheat. (para. 1, line 2)
4. What's that building opposite us. (para. 1, line 5)
5. It's clear that he's drunk. (para. 1, lines 4–5)
6. I want to buy the entire house, including the furniture. (para. 1, line 6)
7. Some people claim that the Irish originally came from North Africa. (para. 2, line 1)
8. This means that you haven't done the work. (para. 2, line 2)
9. What historians are agreed on is the following. (para. 3, line 1)
10. The Allies arrived in Eastern Europe as liberators. (para. 3, lines 1–2)
11. This region used to be inhabited by Armenians. (para. 3, lines 2–3)
12. He was born in the first century AH, i.e. the seventh century AD. (para. 4, lines 2–3)
13. It is claimed that most Turkmen in Iraq have forgotten their language. (para. 4, lines 4–5)
14. Despite the fact that he speaks good Arabic, he doesn't know many Arabs. (para. 4, line 6)
15. This is what some people say. (para. 4, line 7)
16. He owns a large number of businesses. (para. 5, line 2)
17. There are four key problems. (para. 5, line 3)
18. They use French as their written language. (para. 5, line 5)
19. She describes herself as an Arabised African. (para. 5, line 8)

9. Aural Arabic texts 2

Listen carefully to the oral text from حصاد الشهر no. 27, side 2, item 6, من هم الطوارق؟, then complete exercises i. – v. below.

i   Answer the following questions in Arabic orally in class:

1. What is distinctive about the Tuareg?
2. Why was the listener's question not answered the first time?
3. What is the profession of Nicola Ziadeh?
4. What is the skin colour of the Tuareg?
5. What larger ethnic group do they belong to?
6. Where do the Tuareg live?
7. How do the Tuareg make their living?
8. How many different groups of Tuareg are recognised?
9. How long have the Tuareg been around?
10. Why are the Tuareg called الملثمون?
11. When were they first given this name?
12. What do we know about Ibn Yasin?
13. When was the Almoravid state founded?
14. What was the capital of this state?
15. What is the origin of the name Tuareg?

ii Now produce written answers to the above questions in English.

iii Fill in the gaps in the following text. You may find it useful to read through the gapped text a few times before you listen to the tape.

الطوارق في ــــــــــــــــ ــــــــــــ اشـــتـــهـــروا بـغـطـاء

ــــــــــ الذي يرتدونه فيغطي ــــــــــــ بأكمله ولا يترك

سـوى ـــــــــ ـــــــــ هو ـــــــــ. ـــــــــــ

وهل ـــــــ ـــــــــ مـعـروفـين ـــــــــــ ـــــــــ الإسلام

ـــــــــــــــــــــــــــــــــ

مستمع ـــــــــ الجماهيرية ـــــــــ يعتب علينا لعدم

ـــــــــــ ولكنه لم يذكر ـــــــــ. على أية

ـــــــــــ أيـهـا ـــــــ الكريم ها ـــــــــ

ـــــــــ نيقولا الزيادة المؤرخ ـــــــــ يوافيك بجواب.

ـــــــ جمـاعـة ـــــــ ـــــــ البربر تغلب ـــــــ

الـبـشـرة ـــــــ ـــــــ ويقطنون ـــــــ ـــــــ

ـــــــ تـوات ـــــــ الجزائر وغدامس ـــــــ

ـــــــ ـــــــ الـفـزان وتمبكتـو. و ـــــــ

ـــــــ ـــــــ حيث ـــــــ و ـــــــ

قسـمـان - ـــــــ الشمـال وهم ـــــــ ـــــــ

وكـانت ـــــــ الصـحـراوية و ـــــــ الـقـوافـل

ـــــــ تجتاز منطقتهم ـــــــ ـــــــ للرزق

عندهم. والقـسـم ـــــــ ـــــــ ـــــــ

ـــــــ ـــــــ الذين ـــــــ في منطقة السهوب والسافانة

الإفريقية و ———— ———— رعاة يربون ———— ———— والإبل ويعملون

في ———— ———— ———— ———— و. ———— إبلهم وأبقارهم هي

عـادة ———— ———— ———— ———— ويطلق على

الشماليين تجمع الهقر ———— ———— الإقر فيما ————

الجنوبيون بتجمع ابسند وايفورة. و ———— ———— ———— أن

———— كانوا ———— ———— عصر الإمبراطورية

———— ———— إن ———— يكن ———— ———— .

و ———— ———— ———— وجوههم بلشام

———— ———— قمـاش مـصبـوغ ———— .

و ———— ———— يسمون ———— . و

أطلق هذا ———— ———— ————

———— إذ كانوا العنصر ———— ———— قيـام

———— المرابطين ———— ———— في أواسط

———— الخامس الهجري ————

———— عشر ———— . ———— أن ابن ————

المؤسس الروحي لهذه ———— ————

اعتـزل ———— جمـاعـة ———— ———— في

———— يرجح أنه كان يقوم على ———— ————

نهر السنغال. فلما ———— ———— ———— الاعتكاف والتأمل

———— مع جمـاعـتـه ———— ———— وهم

———— الرباط وانضم اليهم ———— . فأغاروا على

——————— مالي وجوارها و ——————— النتيجة ———————

لهـذه ——————— إنشـاء ——————— ——————— وكانت

عاصمتها ——————— مـراكش ونشروا ——————— في حوض

——————— النيـجـر عند منعـرجـه ——————— الاتجاه

——————— ——————— ——————— وبسـبب

——————— جماعة ابن ياسين ——————— فإن بعض المؤرخين

القدامى ——————— ——————— ——————— |

——————— دولة الملثمـين.

——————— أمـر ——————— :

تسـمـيـة هذه ——————— ——————— ،

و ——————— ——————— أصل ——————— ؟ الذين بحـثـوا

——————— غير متفقين ———————

——————— الأصل أو ——————— ، ولذلك

——————— ما يمكن ——————— ——————— : هو

أن ——————— كاسم لا يزال ينتظر ——————— أن

يميط ———————

iv Compare your version of the complete text with the completed text below.

الطوارق فـي شمـال إفـريقيا اشـتهروا بـغطاء الرأس الذي يـرتدونـه فيـغطي الوجه بأكمله ولا يترك سـوى العينين. ما هـو أصل الطوارق وهل كانوا مـعروفين قبل دخول الإسلام إلى شمـال إفريقيا؟ سؤال مـن مسـتمـع من الجماهيـرية الليبية يعتب علينا لعدم إجابة سؤالـه ولكنه لـم يذكر اسـمـه. على أية حـال أيهـا المسـتـمـع الكريم هـا هـو

الدكتور نيقولا الزيادة المؤرخ المعروف يوافيك بجواب.

هم جماعة من البربر تغلب عليهم البشرة البيضاء ويقطنون المنطقة الممتدة من توات في الجزائر وغدامس في ليبيا إلى الفزان وتمبكتو. وهم من حيث الاقتصاد والحياة الاجتماعية قسمان – أهل الشمال وهم سكان الصحراء وكانت التجارة الصحراوية وحماية القوافل التي تجتاز منطقتهم المصدر الرئيس للرزق عندهم. والقسم الثاني هم أهل الجنوب الذين يعيشون في منطقة السهوب والسافانة الإفريقية وهم رعاة يربون الأبقار والإبل ويعملون في الزراعة قليلا. وأسواق إبلهم وأبقارهم هي عادة عند أهل الشمال ويطلق على الشماليين تجمع الهقر أو الإقر فيما يعرف الجنوبيون بتجمع ابسند وايفورة. والمعروف هو أن الطوارق كانوا موجودين في عصر الإمبراطورية الرومانية إن لم يكن قبل ذلك.

ورجال الطوارق يغطون وجوههم بلثام من قماش مصبوغ باللون الأزرق. ومن هنا يسمون الملثمين. وقد أطلق هذا الاسم عليهم مرة في التاريخ إذ كانوا العنصر الأساسي في قيام دولة المرابطين في المغرب في أواسط القرن الخامس الهجري أي القرن الحادي عشر الميلادي. ذلك أن ابن ياسين المؤسس الروحي لهذه الدولة كان قد اعتزل مع جماعة من أصحابه في رباط يرجح أنه كان يقوم على جزيرة في نهر السنغال. فلما تمت فترة الاعتكاف والتأمل خرج مع جماعته من الملثمين وهم أهل الرباط وانضم اليهم كثيرون. فأغاروا على دولة مالي وجوارها وكانت النتيجة النهائية لهذه الحركة إنشاء دولة المرابطين وكانت عاصمتها الجديدة مراكش ونشروا الإسلام في حوض نهر النيجر عند منعرجه في الاتجاه من الشمال إلى الجنوب. وبسبب استعمال جماعة ابن ياسين للثام فإن بعض المؤرخين القدامى كانوا يطلقون على دولة المرابطين دولة الملثمين.

بقي أمر واحد: ما هو أصل تسمية هذه الجماعات الطوارق، وما

هو أصل الكلمة؟ الذين بحثوا في هذا الأمر غير متفقين على المعنى
أو الأصل أو التسمية، ولذلك فكل ما يمكن أن يقال هنا: هو أن
الطوارق كاسم لا يزال ينتظر من يمكن أن يميط اللثام عنه.

v   Structure translations based on من هم الطوارق؟.
Translate the following English sentences into Arabic using relevant
constructions to be found in the text at the points indicated.

1. He became famous for rearing camels. (para. 1, line 1)
2. This group existed before the arrival of Islam in India. (para. 1, line 3)
3. Can you provide me with the necessary information? (para. 1, line 6)
4. The women have generally got long hair. (para. 2, line 1)
5. In political terms there are two groups of Berbers. (para. 2, line 3)
6. Smuggling [التهريب] is their main source of money. (para. 2, line 5)
7. The northerners are called the Beni Amer [البني عامر]. (para. 2, line 9)
8. He is known as Abu Ahmad. (para. 2, lines 9–10)
9. What's known is [/it's known] that this man is a thief. (para. 2, line 10)
10. She was born in the 1920s [في العشرينات], if not earlier. (para. 2, line 11)
11. She was wearing a dress which had been dyed green. (para. 3, lines 1–2)
12. On account of this, he was known as 'the lion'. (para. 3, line 2)
13. The Almoravid state arose in the fifth century AH, i.e. the eleventh century AD. (para. 3, lines 4–5)
14. The reason for this is that he is mad. (para. 3, line 5)
15. The fortress was probably in the mountains of Kurdistan. (para. 3, lines 6–7)
16. He left with his friends, who are communists. (para. 3, line 8)
17. This man was betrayed [خان] by many people. (para. 3, line 9)
18. What was the ultimate result of your activity? (para. 3, lines 9–10)
19. They built the bridge where the river turns east. (para. 3, lines 11–12)
20. Because they use hashish [حشيش] we don't like them. (para. 3, lines 12–13)
21. What is the origin of the fact that these people are called foreigners? (para. 4, line 1)
22. Those who study such things are idiots. (para. 4, line 2)
23. I am waiting for someone who will be able to explain such things. (para. 4, line 4)

10. Written English texts

Using constructions and vocabulary encountered in the Arabic texts above as far as possible, translate the following text from Bernard Lewis, *The Arabs in History* (Oxford University Press, 1993), p. 3, into idiomatic Arabic.

The earliest account that has come down to us of Arabia and the Arabs is that of the tenth chapter of Genesis, where many of the peoples and districts of the peninsula are mentioned by name. The word Arab, however, does not occur[1] in this text, and makes its first appearance[2] in an Assyrian[3] inscription of 853 B.C., in which King Shalmaneser III records the defeat by the Assyrian forces of a conspiracy[4] of rebellious princelings[5]; one of them was 'Gindibu the Aribi' who appropriately contributed 1,000 camels to the forces of the confederacy[6].

Notes
1. Translate as 'is not used'.
2. Translate as 'first appears'.
3. Assyrian = أَشْورِيّ.
4. Conspiracy = مـؤامرة.
5. Translate as 'rebellious princes' = أمـراء مُتـمـرِّدون.
6. Confederacy = حلف or تحالُف.

11. Précis

Re-read the text تاريخ الأكراد (section 5b), then produce a précis in Arabic.

12. Oral

الأجناس في الوطن العربي

(a) Individual students to present a brief account in Arabic of an ethnic group in the Middle East (e.g. الأكراد، العرب، الطوارق، البربر، الدروز).

(b) The presenter then asks the other students questions about the particular ethnic group. The questions should include some which require factual answers and some which require more hypothetical or experiential answers. For example:

١ – أين يسكن الأكراد (أو البربر ...)، هل يعيشون في بلاد واحدة أو في عدد من البلدان؟

٢ – كيف يعيش الأكراد (أو البربر ...)؟

٣ – ماذا تعرف عن تاريخ الأكراد (أو البربر ...)؟

٤ – ماذا تعرف عن تقاليدهم؟

٥ – ما هي الصعوبات التي تواجه الأكراد (أو البربر ...) اليوم؟

٦ – في رأيك ما هو مستقبل الأكراد (أو البربر ...)؟

٧ – ما هو مستقبل لغة الأكراد (أو البربر ...)؟

(c) Open lecturer–led discussion on one or more ethnic groups in the Middle East.

13. Essay
Write an essay in Arabic of between 150 and 200 words around the title العرب
وغير العرب في الوطن العربي. In your essay address some of the following
questions:

١ – من هم العرب؟

٢ – ما هو الوطن الأصلي للعرب؟

٣ – ما هي الأجناس غير العربية في مصر، ما تعرف عن تاريخها وتقاليدها
ودينها؟

٤ – ما هي الأجناس غير العربية في شمال افريقيا، ما تعرف عن تاريخها
وتقاليدها ودينها؟

٥ – ما هي الأجناس غير العربية في فلسطين، ما تعرف عن تاريخها
وتقاليدها ودينها؟

٦ – من هم الأكراد، وأين يسكنون اليوم؟

3
The Middle East in antiquity

1. Basic background material

The Middle East to the rise of Islam

(a) *The Neolithic age to the Achaemenids*

c. 9000 BC	Transition from hunting and gathering to farming and herding.
8000–6000 BC	Gradual development of Jericho; regarded as first city in Middle East.
	Emergence of other urban centres in Syria, Iraq (Mesopotamia) and Iran.
c. 3000 BC	'Great Deluge' (probably series of floods and catastrophic events). Corresponding accounts in Bible and Mesopotamian Epic of Gilgamesh. Development of urban civilisations based around rivers, in Egypt (Nile) and Iraq/Mesopotamia (Tigris, Euphrates); also India (Indus). City states expand into empires.
c. 3000 BC	Egypt: Development and subsequent unification of two kingdoms of Upper and Lower Egypt.
2850–2052 BC	Egypt: Old Kingdom. Multiplicity of cults. Belief in many gods, judgement and life after death. Major pyramids built. Central power ultimately gives way to local rulers.
2800–2350 BC	Iraq: succession of Sumerian kingdoms.
2350–1800 BC	Iraq: Semitic Akkadians conquer Sumerians, establish state in southern Iraq.
2052–1570 BC	Egypt: Middle Kingdom. Reunification of state. Temple complexes erected at Karnak, shrine of new imperial God, Amon. Egypt conquered by Hyksos tribes migrating from Syria.
1800–1375 BC	Iraq: Old Assyrian Empire. Semitic Assyrians establish state in northern Mesopotamia.
1728–1100 BC	Iraq: Babylonian state in southern Iraq.
1570–715 BC	Egypt: New Kingdom. Hyksos defeated by Amosis. Egypt expands under Thutmosis III (1480–1448 BC) into Empire

stretching from Euphrates to Nubia (modern Sudan). Amenophis IV (1377–1358 BC), also known as Ikhnaton – introduces monotheistic worship of sun disk, Aton, with capital at Akhetaton (modern Tell El-Amarna). Return to older forms of worship after his death. By end of New Kingdom, Egyptian state reduced to Nile valley.

1375–1047 BC	Iraq: Middle Assyrian Empire based in southern Iraq.
c. 1250–587 BC	Palestine: Moses (c. 1250 BC) leads Israelite tribes out of Egypt back to Palestine. Jehovah established as only Lord; ark of covenant focal point of religious life. From c. 1200 BC coastal areas settled by Philistines. King David (1006–966 BC) captures Jerusalem, establishes major state in Palestine and Syria. Solomon (966–926 BC), son–in–law of Pharoah, consolidates state, but loses Syrian (Aramean) territories. State then splits into southern kingdom of Judah (Judea), and northern kingdom of Samaria. Samaria destroyed by Assyrian Sargon II (722 BC). Jerusalem destroyed by Babylonian Nebuchadnezzar II (587 BC). Portion of Jewish people exiled to Babylon.
909–626 BC	Iraq: New Assyrian Empire. Tiglathpileser III (745–727 BC) expands empire to include Babylon, Northern Syria, Damascus, Gaza. Sennacherib (704–681 BC) conquers Judea. Assurbanapal (668–626 BC) conquers Egypt (662 BC), but empire subsequently collapses.
835–550 BC	Iran: Median Empire becomes major power in western Iran.
715–332 BC	Egypt: Late Period. Egypt conquered by Ethiopians, then Assyrians (662 BC) and finally Persians (525 BC).
625–539 BC	Iraq: New Babylonian Empire. Nabopolassar (625–605) establishes state in Babylonia, Western Mesopotamia, Syria and Palestine. Empire flourishes under Nebuchadnezzar II (604–562), who occupies Jerusalem (598 BC). Babylon finally conquered by Persians (539 BC).

(b) *The Achaemenids to the Sassanians*

c. 650–550 BC	In Iran and Syria, Zarathushtra (Zoroaster) and Jeremiah and others develop ethically oriented views of cosmos and history; Thales and Pythagoras in Greek Anatolia and Italy pursue rational investigation of human and cosmic nature.
550–331 BC	Achaemenids overcome Medians, and establish a single tolerant and prosperous empire from the Aegean to the Indus. Return of exiled Jews to Palestine (539 BC).
433 BC	Nehemiah restores Jewish worship at Jerusalem on prophetic basis; Jewish community develops as a people based around

faith in scripture.

399 BC
Death of Socrates as martyr to philosphy at Athens. He becomes hero of Greek humanistic idealism in its many schools.

333–328 BC
Alexander the Great establishes Greek supremacy in former Achaemenid lands. Beginnings of long confrontation of Irano–Semitic prophetic tradition and Hellenic philosophic tradition.

c. 200 BC–200 AD
Mediterranean basin is dominated and then ruled by philhellenic Romans, under whom Hellenistic municipal culture is standardised, while philhellenic Parthians dominate Iranian highlands and Mesopotamian plain. Common cults offering personal salvation spread in all these areas.

30 AD
The Christian community founded in Syria, universalising appeal of Jewish divinity.

(c) The Sassanians to the death of Muhammad

226–642
Sassanian Empire replaces Parthians in Iran and Mesopotamian plain; fosters urban prosperity with relative centralisation.

273
Death of Mani, founder of otherworldly Manichean faith, and friend of Sassanian emperor.

285
After crises (235–268) in which Roman city loses its Mediterranean power, Roman Empire is bureaucratically reorganised with capital at Thracian straits (from 330, at Constantinople); Christianity persecuted as anti–social; rival cults encouraged.

275–292
Under Bahram II, Zoroastrian Mazdeism is given an official central organisation in Sassanian Empire, and is allowed to persecute dissenters.

324–337
Under Constantine I, Christianity gains an official position in the reorganised Roman Empire, and subsequently becomes legally enforced.

485–531
Under Qubad, Zoroastrianism and Sassanian aristocracy are torn by Mazdak's attempted egalitarian reform.

c. 525
Christian Abyssinians occupy Yemen, with the Romans, ending the Jewish kingdom (which had persecuted Christians).

527–565
Under Justinian, Roman power and cultural magnificence reach a peak, while the last Pagan school is closed (529) and Christian orthodoxy is enforced.

531–579
Under Nushirvan, Sassanian power and cultural magnificence reach a peak; heresies against Zoroastrian orthodoxy are stamped out.

c. 550
Final break of Ma'rib dam in Yemen, symbolising decline of

	south Arabian agricultural society and predominence of pagan Bedouin patterns in Arabian Peninsula.
603–628	Last great war between Roman and Sassanian Empires, in which forces of both are badly depleted, but political status quo is restored. Restoration of True Cross to Jerusalem (629) symbolises triumph of Christian over Zoroastrian empire – and over Jews and heretics.
622–632	Muhammad sets up religiously organised society in Medina and expands it over much of Arabian Peninsula to compete with and even replace Sassanian and Roman power.

2. Additional reading
(a) Hourani, *A History of the Arab Peoples*, chapter 1.

3. Key vocabulary
Taking as your starting point the texts in this chapter, draw up lists of vocabulary in the following fields:
(a) Nouns and adjectives related to ancient civilisations; e.g. civilisation, excavation, ancient, repair, etc.
(b) Verbs related to archeology.

4. Written Arabic texts 1
(a) Read the following text from مجلة الشرق الأوسط, then complete exercises i. and ii. which follow it.

اكتشاف آثار بلدة في الإمارات عمرها ستة آلاف سنة

يجري التنقيب في إمارة أم القيوين من الإمارات العربية المتحدة عن آثار بلدة تاريخية عريقة تعود إلى نحو ستة آلاف سنة وتضم برجاً جدارياً يرجح أن يكون الأضخم من نوعه في منطقة الخليج العربي.

فبدعم من حكومة أم القيوين وشركة جنرال موتورز، يقوم فريق من علماء الآثار يقودهم البروفسور الأسترالي دان بوتس من جامعة سيدني بكشف آثار تدل بوضوح على أن بلدة «تل أبرق» كانت مسكونة منذ ٣٨٠٠ سنة قبل الميلاد وحتى القرن الأول بعد الميلاد.

وقد صرّح البروفسور بوتس بقوله: «تعتبر هذه البقعة الممتدة

على مساحة أربعة هكتارات اكتشافا بالغ الأهمية، فهي أضخم وأقدم بلدة مأهولة يتم اكتشافها على السواحل الجنوبية للخليج العربي».

والبلدة المكتشفة كانت مركزا إقليميا يتبادل التجارة مع مدن مهمة في منطقتي آسيا الغربية والجنوبية. وقال البروفسور بوتس: «وجدنا قطعا من السيراميك المستورد، وأوعية حجرية، وأثقالا من الحجارة، وأختاما أسطوانية الشكل وأدوات معدنية متشابهة لتلك التي كانت مستخدمة في بلاد ما بين النهرين وإيران والبحرين ومنطقة الهند وباكستان.»

i Answer the following comprehension questions based on the text اكتشاف آثار بلدة in Arabic.

١ – أين تقع أم القيوين؟

٢ – في رأيك ما هي جنسية أكثرية الناس الذين يسكنون في أم القيوين ؟

٣ – كم عمر البلدة في هذا المكان؟

٤ – من يموّل الحفريات في أم القيوين؟

٥ – من يقود الفريق الآثاري؟

٦ – من أي جامعة هذا الرجل؟

٧ – ما هو اسم البلدة المكتشفة؟

٨ – متى اختفت البلدة؟

٩ – كم تبلغ مساحة البلدة؟

١٠ – ما هي الأهمية الآثارية للبلدة؟

١١ – ما هو النشاط الاقتصادي المذكور في هذا النص؟

١٢ – ما هو الدور الذي لعبته البلدة في هذا النشاط؟

١٣ – كيف يعرف قائد الفريق الآثاري أن هذه البلدة كانت لها علاقة مع منطقتي آسيا الغربية والجنوبية؟

١٤ – ما هي الأشياء الخمسة المكتشفة في البلدة؟

ii Now answer the following comprehension questions in written form in English.

1. Where is Umm al-Qaiwain?
2. How old is the settlement there?
3. What architectural feature does it possess?
4. What is noteworthy about this feature?
5. How is the archeological work on this settlement being financed?
6. Who is Dan Potts?
7. What is the name of the settlement?
8. When did it cease to be inhabited?
9. What is the area of the settlement?
10. How does Dan Potts rate the discovery of the settlement?
11. Why does he claim this to be the case?
12. What economic activity is mentioned?

(b) Read the following newspaper text from الشرق الأوسط Feb. 19, 1992, then complete exercises i. and ii. which follow.

كشف أثري في الأردن

تم الكشف عن كنيسة بيزنطية ثانية ذات أرض فسيفسانية تعود إلى القرن السادس الميلادي وتم استخدامها في فترات الحكم الأموي والعباسي والأيوبي وذلك في موقع البصيلة الأثري غرب مدينة الرمثا، شمال الأردن.

وقال الدكتور زيدون المحيسن رئيس فريق معهد الآثار والأنثروبولوجيا التابع لجامعة اليرموك والذي يقوم بأعمال التنقيب الأثري في الموقع، إن اكتشاف كنيسة ثانية في الموقع نفسه يدل على اتساع الموقع الأثري وأهميته الحضارية خلال الفترات الكلاسيكية والإسلامية.

وأضاف أنه تم الكشف أيضا عن أجزاء من مبنى إداري في الموسم الماضي، مما يدل على الاستقرار الحضاري لسكان الموقع، مشيرا أن فريق العمل يقوم بالوقت نفسه بإجراء دراسة توثيقية حول النظام المائي والزراعي في الموقع.

i   Structure translations based on كشف أثري في الأردن.
Translate the following English sentences into Arabic using relevant constructions to be found in the text at the points indicated.

1. The oldest building in the world was discovered in Jordan. (para. 1, line 1)
2. This story can be traced back to the fourth century AH. (in words). (para. 1, lines 1–2)
3. He is head of the department [قسم] attached to the United Nations [الأمم المتحدة]. (para. 2, lines 1–2)
4. She said that the Islamic manuscripts [مخطوطات] were discovered in the eighties [الثمانينات]. (para. 3, line 1)

ii   Translate the above text into idiomatic English.

5. Written Arabic texts 2
Read the following text from الأهرام 1990, then complete exercises i. – iv. which follow it. You may find it useful to read through the English comprehension questions in exercise i. first, in order to gain clues about the meanings of words in the text.

كشف أثري هام :

هرم تحت رمال سقارة .. وملكة لم تكن معروفة من قبل !

كشفت البعثة الفرنسية التي تجري حفائرها بمنطقة الشواف بصحراء سقارة برياسة عالم المصريات الفرنسي الكبير الدكتور ليكلان عن هرم لإحدى زوجات الملك بيبي الأول ثاني ملوك الأسرة السادسة وآخر أسرات الدولة الفرعونية القديمة (٤٣٠٠ سنة).

كما عثرت على لوحة بنفس الموقع عليها نقش بالهيروغليفية تأكد أنه اسم للملكة تسمى «نوب ونت» وأنها كانت إحدى زوجات الملك بيبي الأول ويمكن القول إن هذه الملكة قد نسيها التاريخ فلم ترد أي كلمة أو إشارة عنها في كتب التاريخ الفرعوني من قبل.

وقدم الدكتور زاهي حواس مدير عام آثار الجيزة تقريرا عاجلا إلى السيد فاروق حسني وزير الثقافة عن الكشف

الجديد وأعلن أن الهرم المكتشف توصلت إليه الأجهزة التكنولوجية المتقدمة التي استخدمتها البعثة مدفونة تحت رمال سقارة وقدر ارتفاعه بنحو ٣٠ مترا قبل تهدم أجزاء كبيرة منه وأنه فوق قاعدة مربعة من الحجر الجيري وبمدخله كتل من الجرانيت وما يشير إلى أن اللصوص قد دخلوه في عصر الاضمحلال الأول.

ويأتي هذا الهرم ليكون الهرم الثالث في مجموعة أهرامات الملكات زوجات الملك بيبي الأول والتي أعلن عن اكتشاف اثنين منها من قبل ولكن العلماء لم يجدوا حتى الآن اسم صاحبة كل هرم من زوجات الملك وإن كانت اللوحة التي عثر عليها اسم الملكة نوب- ونت والذي لم يكن معروفا للعلماء من قبل أنها صاحبة أحد الأهرامات خاصة أن النقش على اللوحة يقول « زوجة الملك المحبوبة منه » مما يؤكد أن أحد هذه الأهرامات بني لها .

وتبقى حيرة العلماء في تحديد صاحبتى الهرمين الآخرين محصورة بين ٣ زوجات أخرى للملك وهن « عنخ-نا-اس » و« مرى-ان-رع » الأولى « مرى-ان-رع » الثانية ولكن العلماء يستبعدون أن يكون الملك قد بنى للأولى أحد الهرمين لأنها - كما حكى أحد وزرائه قد تآمرت عليه أما الثانية والثالثة فكانتا ابنتى أمير أبيدوس ونجع حمادى وكان يحبهما الملك.

وقد رفعت البعثة تقريرا إلى الدكتور سيد توفيق رئيس هيئة الآثار بتفاصيل الكشف الهام وقد صرح الدكتور توفيق لمصطفى النجار مندوب الأهرام بأن هذا الكشف يعد إضافة هامة للتاريخ المصري القديم.

وقال الأثري محمود أبو الوفا مدير منطقة سقارة إن البعثة الفرنسية تضم مهندسين وإخصائيين في الترميم ويرافقهم الأثريان نبيل دانيال وعصام نبيل وقد بدأت أعمال

الترميم في الهرم المكتشف من الخارج وكذلك اللوحة التي
عليها اسم الملكة وتواصل حفائرها حول مدخل الهرم في
محاولة للوصول إلى حجرة الدفن التي ربما تفضي بأسرار أو
بنصوص تفيدنا في الكشف عن أسرار فترة حكم الملك بيبي
الأول .

i Answer the following comprehension questions in English.

paragraph one
1. Where have the French team carried out archeological investigations?
2. Who is heading the team?
3. What is the nationality of the team leader?
4. Whose pyramid has been discovered?

paragraph two
5. What confirms the name of the pyramid's owner?
6. How well known was this person historically?

paragraph three
7. What type of instruments were used in making this find?
8. Who is Mr Farouq Husni?
9. What is the pyramid's height estimated to have been?
10. From what type of stone is its base constructed?
11. What other stone was used in its construction?

paragraph four
12. How many pyramids have the archeological team found in all?
13. What does the inscription on this pyramid say?

paragraph five
14. Why do scholars reject the idea that the king would have built one of the pyramids for Ankh-na-as?
15. Who were the other two wives the daughters of?

paragraph six
16. Who is Dr Sayyid Taufiq?

paragraph seven
17. Who is the archeological team made up of?
18. Where are they now continuing their excavations, and what are they trying to do?

ii In pairs, construct and then ask each other questions in Arabic and in English about the remaining three paragraphs of the text.

iii In pairs, consider constructions of grammatical interest which occur in this text. Each pair should also consider one of:

1. Apposition.
2. Impersonal passive.
3. Active sentences which would be translated as passive in English.

iv Structure translations based on هرم تحت رمال سقارة.

Translate the following English sentences into Arabic using relevant contructions to be found in the text at the points indicated.

1. The German expedition came across a previously unknown village. (headline + para. 2, line 1)
2. It is possible to say that the Queen died in 4,000 BC. [in words] (para. 2, lines 3–4)
3. The Egyptian Ambassador issued a summary report. (para. 3, lines 1–2)
4. The depth of the lake (بحيرة) is estimated at circa 40 [in words] metres. (para. 3, line 5)
5. This discovery is an important addition to Yemeni history. (para. 6, lines 3–4)
6. The German expedition was accompanied by the famous Egyptian archeologist. (para. 7, line 3)
7. The old texts may reveal secrets about the British government. (para. 7, lines 6–7)

6. Written Arabic texts 3 (classical)

(a) Read the following passage by ابن بطوطة from رحلات ابن بطوطة pp. 41–2, ذكر الأهرام والبرابي¹, then translate the text into idiomatic English.

هي من العجائب المذكورة على مر الدهور، وللناس فيها كلام
كثير وخوض في شأنها وأولية بنائها. ويزعمون² أنّ جميع
العلوم التي ظهرت قبل الطوفان أُخِذت عن هُرمُس الأول
الساكن بصعيد مصر الأعلى، ويسمّى أخنوخ، وهو إدريس،
عليه السلام، وأنه أول من تكلم في الحركات الفلكية والجواهر
العلوية، وأول من بنى الهياكل ومجّد اللّه تعالى فيها، وأنه
أنذر الناس بالطوفان، وخاف ذهاب العلم ودروس الصنائع،
فبنى الأهرام والبرابي وصوّر فيها جميع الصنائع والآلات،
ورسم العلوم فيها لتبقى مخلدة.

ويقال إن دار العلم والملك بمصر مدينةُ منف، وهي على

بريد³ من الفسطاط، فلما بنيت الإسكندرية انتقل الناس إليها وصارت دار العلم والملك إلى أن أتى الإسلام، فاختطّ عمرو بن العاص، رضي اللّه عنه، مدينة الفسطاط، فهي قاعدة مصر إلى هذا العهد.

والأهرام بناء بالحجر الصلد المنحوت متناهي السموّ، مستدير، متسع الأسفل ضيق الأعلى، كالشكل المخروط، ولا أبواب لها، ولا تعلم كيفية بنائها.

ومما يذكر في شأنها أنّ ملكا من ملوك مصر قبل الطوفان رأى رؤيا هالته وأوجبت عنده أنّه بنى تلك الأهرامات بالجانب الغربي من النيل لتكون مستودعاً للعلوم ولجثّة الملوك، وأنّه سأل المنجّمين: هل يُفتحُ منها موضع؟ وأخبروه أنّها تُفتح من الجانب الشمالي، وعيّنوا له الموضع الذي تفتح منه، ومبلغ الانفاق في فتحه، فأمر أن يُجعل بذلك الموضع من المال قدر ما أخبروه أنّه ينفق في فتحه، واشتدّ في البناء فأتمّه في ستين سنة، وكتب عليها: بنينا هذه الأهرام في ستين سنة فليهدمها من يريد ذلك في ستمائة سنة فإنّ الهدمَ أيسر من البناء.

Notes
1. Sing. بربا : ancient Egyptian temple.
2. 'It is claimed'. Impersonal use of third masculine plural verbal form.
3. 'A mailpost away from …' [i.e. roughly twelve miles away from].

(b) Read the following passage by المسعودي from مروج الذهب, vol. II, pp. 378–80, then translate the text into idiomatic English.

وسئل عن بناء الأهرام فقال إنها قبور الملوك كان الملك منهم إذا مات وضع في حوض حجارة ويسمى بمصر والشام الجرون وأطبق عليه ثم يبنى له من الهرم على قدر ما يريدون من ارتفاع الأساس ثم يحمل الحوض فيوضع وسط الهرم ثم يقنطر عليه البنيان والاقبا ثم يرفعون البناء على هذا المقدار الذي

ترونه ويجمل باب الهرم تحت الهرم ثم يحفر له طريق في
الأرض ويعقد أزج فيكون طول الأزج تحت الأرض ماية ذراع
وأكثر ولكل هرم من هذه الأهرام باب مدخله على ما وصفت
قيل له فكيف بنيت هذه الأهرام الملسة وعلى أي شيء كانوا
يصعدون ويبنون وعلى أي شيء كانوا يحملون هذه الحجارة
العظيمة التي لا يقدر أهل زماننا هذا على أن يحركوا الحجر
الواحد إلا بجهد إن قدروا فقال كان القوم يبنون الهرم مدرّجا
ذا مراقى كالدرجة فإذا فرغوا منه نحتوه من فوق إلى أسفل
فهذه كانت حيلتهم وكان مع هذا لهم قوة وصبر وطاعة لملوكهم
ديانية.

7. Grammar/stylistics
(a) *Arabic active translated as English passive*
The passive is far more common in English than in Arabic. Apart from the fact that Arabic arguably lacks agentive passives (passive constructions in which the agent is mentioned, as in 'the snake' in the English sentence: 'John was bitten by the snake'), there are many other occasions in which an English passive would not be translated into Arabic by a passive construction. In this chapter we consider two types of active sentences in Arabic which are commonly translated into English by the passive. The first of these sentence types involves a specific construction – namely, the verb تم followed by a (usually definite) verbal noun; the second of these sentence types involves a specific word order – namely, the object precedes the subject.

i تم + *verbal noun*
When the subject of an English passive verb (or the logical subject) is inanimate (in the wider sense which includes non–human animals), and the verb describes the completion of something which takes some time and normally involves purposeful activity (Holes 1995: 258–9), the sense of the passive can be conveyed by the verb تم followed by the appropriate verbal noun. When the verbal noun is derived from a transitive verb it forms the first part of an إضافة of which the second part corresponds to the logical subject, as in:

... حتى تم {تقويض الخلافة الأموية}.
'... until the Umayyad Caliphate was destroyed.' (ch. 2, 5b)

قال إنه سيتم {توجيه الدعوة} لعدد كبير من علماء أوروبا وأمريكا.
'He said that the invitation would be sent to a large number of American
and European scientists.' (ch. 3, 11)

تم فيها {ترميم الجانب الأيمن} للتمثال.
'During [this time] the right side of the statue was repaired.' (ch. 3, 11)

In general, the verbal noun following تم is definite – either by virtue of taking the
definite article (see below), or by taking a definite annex (second term of إضافة) or
pronoun (see below). In a few cases, however, the verbal noun is indefinite by
virtue of taking an indefinite annex, as in:

كما تم {عملُ دراسة} مع هيئة اليونسكو.
'A study was also completed with the organisation UNESCO.' (ch. 3,
11)

The second part of the إضافة is often a pronoun which agrees with and refers back
to the previously mentioned logical subject.

فهي أضخم وأقدم بلدة مأهولة يتم {اكتشافها}.
'It is the largest and oldest inhabited place which has been discovered.'
(ch. 3, 4a)

وتم {استخدامها} في فترات الحكم الأموي والعباسي والأيوبي.
'It was used during the periods of Umayyad, Abbasid and Ayyubid
rule.' (ch. 3, 4b)

وجدنا أن هذه المدينة تم {إنشاؤها} سنة ثمان مائة وأربع عشرة
قبل الميلاد.
'We found that this building was completed in the year 814 BC.' (ch.
3, 8)

When the verbal noun following تم is derived from an intransitive verb which takes
a preposition, the verbal noun is defined by the definite article and the logical
subject is realised as the object of the preposition, as in:

تم {الكشف} عن كنيسة بيزنطية.
'A Byzantine church was discovered.' (ch. 3, 4b)

ii *Object precedes subject*
When the object (or, in some cases, prepositional phrase) precedes the subject the
Arabic active sentence is often translated into the English passive. This is

particularly, but not exclusively, the case when the subject is indefinite, as in:

فهو أكبر من أن يحله {عقل واحد}.
'It is too large to be solved by one brain.' (ch. 5, 11b)

... وعندما أضاءت وجه أبيك {سيارة عابرة}
'When your father's face was lit up by a passing car ...' (ch. 6, 5a)

يجيب على هذا السؤال {الدكتور نيقولا الزيادة}.
'This question is answered by Dr Nicola Ziadeh.' (ch. 3, 8)

The active verb may take a pronoun object which refers back to a noun phrase which precedes the verb, as in:

ويمكن القول ان {هذه الملكة} قد نسي{ـها} التاريخ.
'It may be said that this queen had been forgotten by history.' (ch. 3, 5)

As part of a more complex structure this type of structure is often translated by the English passive participle:

... تضم {مهندسين وإخصائيين في الترميم} ويرافق{ـهم} الأثريان نبيل دانيال وعصام نبيل.
'... it included engineers and renovation specialists *accompanied* by the two archeologists Nabil Daniel and Issam Nabil.' (ch. 3, 5)

تمثلت في تكاثر {السحب المتوسطة والمنخفضة والرعدية} صاحب{ـها} سقوط الأمطار الغزيرة.
'... it presented itself in the build up of medium, low and thunder clouds *accompanied* by the fall of heavy rain.' (ch. 8, 4c)

This type of structure often occurs within a relative clause:

في {مقابلة} نشرت{ـها} أمس الإثنين صحيفة «واشنطن بوست».
'... in an interview *published* yesterday (Monday) by the paper the Washington Post.' (ch. 8, 4d)

وشيد الجانب العراقي {قناة عريضة} نحف{ـها} سدود ترابية.
'The Iraqi side constructed a wide canal *bordered* by mud banks.' (ch. 8, 11)

لو لا {هذا التجمع} الذي استضافت{ـه} جنيف.
'If it were not for this gathering *hosted* by Geneva.' (ch. 10, 5c)

(b) *Dummy pronoun subjects*

Dummy pronoun subjects are not used in the same way in Arabic as in English (cf. ch. 2). There is, for example, no equivalent to 'it' in sentences such as '*it* is clear that he will go'. Dummy pronoun subjects are, however, often attached to أَنَّ or إِنَّ when أَنَّ or إِنَّ is otherwise followed by a verb or an adjunction. In all cases the dummy pronoun subject is the third masculine singular pronoun. Note that a dummy subject is *not* the subject of the following verb. The dummy subject has no formal translation equivalent in English. Examples include:

فاتفق أنَّ{ـه} اجتاز بذلك النهر صيادان.

'It happened that two fishermen crossed that river.' (ch. 11, 6b)

وأضـاف أنَّ{ـه} تم الكشف أيضـا عن أجـزاء مـن مـبـنـى إداري في الموسم الماضي.

'He added that parts of an administrative building had been found the previous season.' (ch. 3, 4b)

صـرح فـاروق حـسـني وزير الثقافـة المصـري لـ«الشـرق الأوسط» بأنَّ{ـه} سيتم تنظيم مؤتمر دولي في شهر فبراير (شباط) المقبل.

'Farouq Husni, Egyptian Minister of Culture told al-Sharq al-Awsat that an international conference would be held next February.' (ch. 3, 11)

وقـال الـوزير إنَّ{ـه} ستتم مناقشة نتائج جميـع هذه الدراسات.

'The Minister said that the results of all these studies would be discussed.' (ch. 3, 11)

والظاهـر أنَّ{ـه} لما اتسـعت رومـا وأنشـأت إمبـراطـورية اسـتـعمـلت كلمة بـربـر لجمـيـع الشـعـوب التي تسكن إفريقيا.

'It is clear that when Rome expanded and founded an empire it used the word Berber for all the peoples who lived in Africa.' (ch. 2, 8)

(c) *The use of* تابع *for association*

The word تابع 'subordinate لـ to; belonging لـ to; of' is often used when referring to groups which are subsidiary to or fall within the umbrella of a larger group or organisation, as in:

رئيس فـريق مـعـهد الآثار والأنـثـروبـولـوجـيا {التـابـع} لجامـعـة اليرموك.

'The Head of the Institute for Archeology and Anthropology *of* the University of Yarmuk.' (ch. 3, 4b)

ويولي المكتب التنفيـذي {التـابـع} لصندوق الأمم المتـحـدة لرعـاية
الأمـومة والطفـولة.

'The executive office *of* the United Nations fund UNICEF.' (ch. 9, 4b)

For different forces of the phrase تابع لـ and for further examples see Julia
Ashtiany, *Media Arabic* (Edinburgh University Press, 1993), p. 122.

8. Aural Arabic texts 1

Listen carefully to the following aural text from حصاد الشهر, no. 28, side 2, item
2, ما الفرق بين قرطاج وقرطاجنة؟ , then complete exercises i. – iv. below.

i   Answer the following questions in English. You may find it useful to read the
    questions before listening to the text.

1. Where does the person who asked the question come from?
2. What is the immediate origin of the form قرطاج?
3. Where is the form قرطاجنة found?
4. When was Carthage founded according to traditional sources?
5. What was the name of the Princess of Tyre?
6. What did the Princess's brother do?
7. What did she do as a result?
8. What is the original meaning of 'Carthage'?
9. When do archeologists suggest that Carthage was founded?
10. What were the main interests of the Carthaginians?
11. What were the eastern and western limits of the Carthaginian state?
12. How long did the wars between Rome and Carthage go on for?
13. When was Carthage destroyed?
14. Which is the most common Arabic form for 'Carthage'?
15. Who founded the other Carthage?
16. When did these people found this city?
17. Is it clear where the people who founded the other Carthage set out from?
18. Where is the other Carthage?

ii   Fill in the gaps in the following text. You may find it useful to read through the
    gapped text a few times before you listen to the tape.

ـــــــ ـــــــ اسـم ـــــــ ـــــــ قرطاج ـــــــ ـــــــ تـونس وأحيانا

تتحدث ـــــــ ـــــــ ـــــــ ـــــــ قـرطاجنـة. فـهل

ـــــــ وقـرطاجنـة لمدينة ـــــــ ـــــــ ـــــــ

هما ــــــــ ؟ سؤال ــــــــ ــــــــ ــــــــ ــــــــ ــــــــ ــــــــ

يجيب ــــــــ ــــــــ ــــــــ المستمع ادوا عراب أحمد

الزيادة نيقولا الدكتور السؤال ــــــــ ــــــــ

ـــــــــ .

ـــــــــ ــــــــ ــــــــ ــــــــ قرطاج ــــــــ

في الشائعة الصيغة أما . ــــــــ ــــــــ للفظ تعريب هو

ــــــــ ــــــــ وأما ــــــــ فهي للاسم

قرطاجة . ــــــــ ــــــــ فـ السؤال في

إنشاء ــــــــ الصوريون حفظه ما ــــــــ عدنا وإذا

تونس خليج ــــــــ ــــــــ قرطاجنة ــــــــ

أن ــــــــ ــــــــ ــــــــ الحاضرة

ــــــــ ــــــــ عشرة وأربع مائة ثمان ــــــــ إنشاؤها

أميرة إن ــــــــ الرواية وتقول . (م ق ٨١٤)

ــــــــ خشية ــــــــ ــــــــ فرّت « دودو » صور

انتزع ــــــــ ــــــــ أخوها بها يبطش ــــــــ

الفنيقيون سمّى ــــــــ و ــــــــ ــــــــ حقّها

« حدشت كرت » ــــــــ المنشأة ــــــــ الصوريون

ولكن . ــــــــ ــــــــ ــــــــ ومعناها

في ــــــــ به قام ــــــــ ــــــــ

أواخر ــــــــ أنشئت ــــــــ ــــــــ أن أظهر

أي ، ــــــــ ــــــــ ــــــــ ــــــــ

———— ———— ———— الرواية الصورية بقرن ————.

وقد سمّى ———— ———— ———— ———— «كرشدون»

تحريفا لـ«كرت حدشت» و ———— ———— جاءت

———— ———— ———— قرطاجة. واتّسعت

———— وعُني ———— بـ ———— و

أكثر ———— عنايتهم بالفن و ———— وسيطرت

قرطاجة ———— ———— ———— ————

———— حتى طنجة. ولما ———— روما

ووحّدت إيطاليا تطلّعت ———— حوض المتوسّط

الغربي فكان ———— ———— ———— تتنافس

———— وقرطاجة وأن يؤدّي ———— إلى ————

حروب بينهما ، ————— ————— ونصف ————

و ———— بانتصار ———— ———— هدّمت المدينة

———— ———— و ———— و ————

———— ———— (١٤٦ ق م). و ————

———— قرطاجة بـ ———— ———— ————

———— – أي قرطاجنة – وإن ————

———— هي الأغلب. لكن ———— ————

———— اسمه قرطاجنة وهذه ————

كانت ———— ———— إنشاء الفنيقيين ————

———— ———— ———— استوطنوا ————.

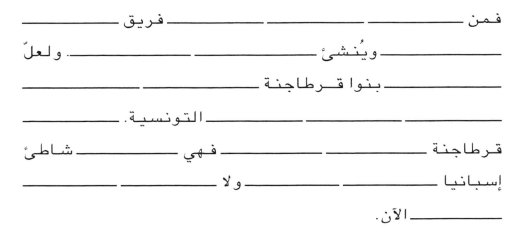

ــــــــــ ــــــــــ ــــــــــ ــــــــــ فريق ــــــــــ فـمن

ــــــــــ و لـعلّ ــــــــــ ــــــــــ ويُنشئ ــــــــــ

ــــــــــ ــــــــــ ــــــــــ بنوا قـرطاجنة ــــــــــ

ــــــــــ التونسية. ــــــــــ ــــــــــ ــــــــــ

شاطئ ــــــــــ فـهي ــــــــــ ــــــــــ قرطاجنة

إسبانيا و لا ــــــــــ ــــــــــ ــــــــــ

الآن. ــــــــــ

iii Compare your version of the complete text with the completed text below.

نـسمع اسم مـدينة قرطاج في تونس وأحيانا تتحدث كتب التاريخ عن قـرطاجنة. فـهل قرطاج وقرطاجنة اسمان لمدينة واحدة أم هما مـدينتان مـخـتلفتان؟ سؤال مـن المستمع ادوا عراب أحمـد مـن المغـرب. يجـيب على هذا السؤال الدكتـور نيقـولا الزيادة المؤرّخ المعروف.

الاسم قرطاج الوارد في السؤال هو تعريب للفظ الفرنسي. أمّا الصيـغـة الشائعة في المشرق للاسم فهي قرطاجـة وأمـا الصيـغـة الأخـرى الـواردة في السؤال فهي قرطاجنة. وإذا عدنا إلى مـا حـفظه الصـوريون عن إنشـاء مـدينـة قـرطاجـة في وسط خـليج تونس الحـاضرة وجدنا أن هذه المدينة تم إنشاؤها سنة ثمـان مـائة وأربـع عـشرة قبل الميلاد (٨١٤ ق م). وتقول الـروايـة التاريخـية إن أميـرة صـور «دودو» فرّت مـن مـدينتها خشـية مـن أن يبطش بها أخـوها بعـد أن انتزع حقّها في الحكم وقد سمّى الفنيقيون الصوريون هذه المنشأة الجديدة «كـرت حـدشت» ومـعناها البلدة الحـديثـة. ولكن التنقيب الأثري الذي قام به الباحثون في قرطاجـة أظهـر أن هذه المدينة أنشئت في أواخر القرن الثامن قبل الميلاد ، أي بعـد تاريخ

الرواية الصورية بقرن تقريبا.

وقـد سمّى اليـونـان هـذا المكان «كـرشـدون» تحـريفـا لـ«كـرت حدشت» ومن هنا جاءت مع الزمن لفظة قرطاجة. واتّسعت المدينة وعُني أهلها بالصناعة والتجارة أكثر من عنايتهم بالفن والأدب. وسيطرت قرطاجة على الساحل الأفريقي الممتدّ من ليبيا حتى طنجة. ولما قامت روما ووحّدت إيطاليا تطلّعت إلى حوض البحر المتوسّط الغربي فكان من الطبيعي أن تتنافس روما وقرطاجة وأن يؤدّي الأمر إلى قيام حروب بينهما دامت قرنا ونصف القرن وانتهت بانتصار روما التي هدّمت المدينة سنة مائة وست وأربعين قبل الميلاد (١٤٦ ق م). وقد ورد اسم قرطاجة بالصيغة الثانية الواردة في السؤال – أي قرطاجنة – وإن كانت الأولى هي الأغلب. لكن ثمة مكان آخر كان اسمه قرطاجنة وهذه البلدة كانت أيضا من إنشاء الفنيقيين بعد أن استوطنوا في شمال إفريقيا. فمن هناك كان يخرج فريق من الناس ويُنشئ مدينة جديدة. ولعلّ الذين بنوا قرطاجنة الثانية هم أصلا من قرطاج التونسية. أما قرطاجنة الثانية هذه فهي على شاطئ إسبانيا الجنوبي الشرقي ولا تزال قائمة إلى الآن.

iv Structure translations based on ؟ما الفرق بين قرطاج وقرطاجنة.
Translate the following English sentences into Arabic using relevant constructions to be found in the text at the points indicated.

1. Are these two words two names for a single idea? (para.1, line 2)
2. This question was answered by the prime minister. (para. 1, line 4)
3. This is an Arabisation of the English term. (para. 2, line 1)
4. What is the other form, which appears at the beginning of the book? (para. 2, lines 2–3)
5. The state was founded after the war. (para. 2, line 5)
6. They left their homes out of fear that the army would kill them. (para. 2, lines 5–6)
7. He got married three years after his father's death. (para. 2, lines 11–12)
8. They were more concerned with money than with honesty. (para. 3, line 3)
9. He owns the land extending from here to the sea. (para. 3, lines 4–5)

10. It's natural that you should get angry. (para. 3, line 6)
11. The first word is the more common. (para. 3, lines 10–11)
12. I know another woman called Miriam [مريم]. (para. 3, line 11)
13. Those who say this don't understand the problem. (para. 3, line 14)

9. Aural Arabic texts 2

Listen carefully to the following aural text from حصاد الشهر, no. 26, side 2, item 2, ما هي أقدم مدينة في العالم؟, then complete exercises i. – v. below.

i Answer the following questions in Arabic orally in class.

١ – هل توجد مدن تاريخية كثيرة في العالم؟

٢ – ما اسم المستمع الذي سأل السؤال في هذا البرنامج؟

٣ – ما هي مهنة الرجل الذي يجيب على السؤال؟

٤ – ما هي أقدم مدينة في العالم؟

٥ – أين تقع هذه المدينة؟

٦ – في أي بلاد تقع الضفة الغربية؟

٧ – بماذا اشتغل أول سكان أقدم مدينة في العالم؟

٨ – متى أصبحت هذه المدينة مدينة حقيقية؟

٩ – كم بلغت مساحتها في هذه الفترة؟

١٠ – بما بنى سكان المدينة بيوتهم؟

١١ – لماذا بنوا سوراً لمدينتهم؟

١٢ – ماذا بنوا بالإضافة إلى السور؟

١٣ – متى وصل الكنعانيون هذه المدينة؟

١٤ – من أين قدموا أصلا؟

١٥ – كيف دفنوا موتاهم؟

١٦ – متى أصبحت دمشق عاصمة بلاد آرام؟

١٧ – أين جاءت أقدم إشارة لمدينة دمشق؟

ii Answer the following comprehension questions in written form in English.

1. Are there a large number of historical cities worldwide?
2. What is the listener's name?
3. What is the name of the man who answers the question?
4. What is the oldest city for which there is archeological evidence in the world?
5. How old is this city?

6. Where is the city situated?
7. Who settled this city in the Mesolithic era?
8. When did this place acquire the characteristics of a city?
9. What did the inhabitants build their houses out of?
10. When did they build their city wall?
11. What did they build in addition to the wall?
12. When did the Canaanites arrive?
13. Where did the Canaanites originally come from?
14. Why have researchers got such a good idea about life at this time?
15. Where is Tell Al-Salihiyya?
16. How old is it?
17. When did Damascus become the capital of Aramea?
18. Where is Tell El-Amarna?
19. When did Tuhtamis the Third conquer Damascus?

iii Fill in the gaps in the following text. You may find it useful to read through the
gapped text a few times before you listen to the tape.

_____ _____ _____ _____ _____

تعود ــــــــ آثارا تضمّ ــــــــ ــــــــ والعديد

ــــــــ ــــــــ ولكن. خلت ــــــــ إلى

ــــــــ ــــــــ ــــــــ في التاريخ؟

يُجيب ــــــــ ــــــــ ــــــــ سرور أحمد سرور المستمع

.حدّاد فؤاد الأستاذ ــــــــ ــــــــ ــــــــ

ــــــــ ــــــــ أثرية ــــــــ ــــــــ إن

ــــــــ ــــــــ ــــــــ ــــــــ أريحا

الحفريات أثبتت وقد .الأردن ــــــــ ــــــــ

مأهولة ــــــــ ــــــــ ــــــــ ــــــــ

ــــــــ ــــــــ آلاف ثمانية منذ ــــــــ

الصيادين ــــــــ ــــــــ يسكنها وكان .ـ

لبثت وما .الميسوليثي العصر ــــــــ

——— بـحـوالى ——— ——— ——— أن أصبـحت لـها

——— ——— ——— وبـلغت مـسـاحـتـها ———

——— ——— سكانها ——— فـدادين. و

يظهر ——— أوّل ——— فـهي و ——— بـالأجرّ. و

——— ——— ——— انـتـقـال حـالة البـداوة

و ——— ——— ——— الثبـات والاسـتقرار .

و ——— ——— ———

——— ——— ——— بـنـى سكان

——— ——— لحماية ممتلكاتهم ——— لـمدينتـهم

——— ——— ——— و ومـزروعـاتـهم. و

——— و ——— الأحـجـار القـوية ———

البـرونزي ——— ——— الكنعـانيـون

——— ——— تَسَمَّت الحين ——— ——— و

. ——— ——— ——— بـاسـمـهم

و ——— ——— ——— ———

شبه الجزيـرة ——— ———

كانوا ——— و .———

——— حـوائج و ——— مـوتاهم و

ولـهـذا .——— ——— ——— ———

تَكوَّنت لدى ——— ——— ———

سـائـدا ——— ——— ——— عن

——————— ذلك الحين. وتُظهِر الحـفـريات ——————— تـل

الصالحية ——————— ——————— ——————— ——————— أنه

——————— ——————— ——————— مركز مدني ———————

——————— ——————— ——————— ———————

——————— ——————— و. ——————— دمشق في

——————— ——————— عاصمة ——————— ——————— آرام،

——————— ——————— إشارة لمدينة دمشق ——————— جـاءت وقـد

——————— ——————— تل العمارنة الفرعونية ———————.

——————— ——————— إحدى اللوحات الهيروغليفية ——————— فـقـد

——————— ——————— إنها إحدى ——————— و «دمـشـقـا»

——————— ——————— تهتميس ——————— التي أخضعها ———————

——————— ——————— ——————— ——————— إلى حكمه

———————

iv Compare your version of the complete text with the completed text below.

المدن التاريخية في العالم كثيرة والعديد من المدن تضمّ آثارا تاريخية تعود إلى قرون خلت. ولكن ما هي أقدم مدينة في التاريخ؟ سؤال من المستمع سرور أحمد سرور من القاهرة. يُجيب على هذا السؤال الأستاذ فؤاد حدّاد.

إن أقدم مدينة أثرية هي مدينة أريحا الواقعة على الضفة الغربية من نهر الأردن. وقد أثبتت الحفريات أن مدينة أريحا كانت مأهولة بالسكان منذ ثمانية آلاف عام قبل الميلاد. وكان يسكنها جماعات من الصيادين في العصر الميسوليثي. وما لبثت

بعد ذلك بحوالى ألف سنة أن أصبحت لها معالم المدينة وبلغت مساحتها حوالى عشرة فدادين. وبدأ سكانها يبنون بيوتهم بالأجرّ. ولذلك فهي أوّل مكان يظهر فيه انتقال الإنسان من حالة البداوة والصيد إلى حالة الثبات والاستقرار.

وفي عام ستة آلاف وثماني مئة قبل الميلاد بنى سكان أريحا لمدينتهم أول سور لحماية ممتلكاتهم ومزروعاتهم. وبنوا للسور برجا من الأحجار القوية للمراقبة. ودخلها الكنعانيون في أواسط العصر البرونزي ومنذ ذلك الحين تَسَمَّت البلاد كلها باسمهم أي بلاد كنعان. والكنعانيون هم قبيلة عربية دخلت أريحا قادمة من شبه الجزيرة العربية. ومن الطريف أنهم كانوا يدفنون موتاهم ومعهم حوائج وأشياء كثيرة من أمور البيت. ولهذا فقد تَكوَّنت لدى الباحثين فكرة جيدة عن أسلوب الحياة الذي كان سائدا في ذلك الحين. وتُظهر الحفريات في تل الصالحية الواقع جنوب شرقي دمشق أنه كان هناك مركز مدني مأهول منذ أربعة آلاف سنة قبل الميلاد. وأصبحت دمشق في القرن الحادي عشر قبل الميلاد عاصمة بلاد آرام ، وقد جاءت أقدم إشارة لمدينة دمشق من مكتبة تل العمارنة الفرعونية في مصر. فقد أشارت إحدى اللوحات الهيروغليفية إلى مدينة «دمشقا» وقالت إنها إحدى المدن الكبرى التي أخضعها الملك تهتميس الثالث إلى حكمه عام ألف وخمس مئة قبل الميلاد.

v   Structure translations based on ما هي أقدم مدينة في العالم؟.
Translate the following English sentences into Arabic using relevant constructions to be found in the text at the points indicated.

1. There aren't many beautiful cities in South Yemen. (para. 1, line 1)
2. These writings date back to the Pharoanic era. (para. 1, line 2)
3. What's the name of that village on the Nile which they visited last year? (para. 2, lines 1–2)
4. Do you mean the place where the Copts lived? (para. 2, lines 3–4)
5. Soon enough the Bedouin began to move into the towns. (para. 2, lines 4–5)

6. This village has come to exhibit some of the characteristics of a town. (para. 2, line 5)
7. The stadium occupies an area of three square kilometres. (para. 2, lines 5–6)
8. What did they make the statue out of bronze for? (para. 2, line 6)
9. Which was the first country in which capitalism appeared? (para. 2, line 7)
10. He bought an extremely expensive American car for his son. (para. 3, lines 1–2)
11. The strange thing is that they used to live in houses made of stone. (para. 3, line 6)
12. She lives in Stockport, which is south of Manchester. (para. 3, lines 9–10)
13. The first mention of this city appears in the Doomsday Book. (para. 3, line 12)
14. The entire region was subjugated by the Egyptians. (para. 3, line 15)

10. Written English texts

Making use of constructions encountered in the Arabic texts above as far as possible, translate the following text into idiomatic Arabic.

The sphinx

The most famous sphinx[1] in Egypt is the one at Giza, which is known in Arabic as 'the Father of Fear'. This sphinx was carved from a single rock and was constructed during the IVth dynasty[2]. According to an inscription of the XVIIIth dynasty in the shrine between the paws of the sphinx it represented the sun god Harmachis. The sphinx was completely excavated and its head restored in the early years of the twentieth century. The head of the sphinx is a royal portrait, and is apparently intended to represent the power of the reigning Pharoah. The sphinx was placed in its position in order to guard the entrance of the Nile valley, and the temples in the surrounding area.

Notes
1. Translate as 'lion man' رجل أسـد. This is an instance of nominal apposition (cf. chapter 11).
2. سلالة or أسـرة.

11. Précis

Read the following text from الشرق الأوسط Feb. 19, 1992, then produce a précis
in Arabic.

وزير الثقافة المصري لـ«الشرق الأوسط»

علماء أوروبا وأمريكا يشاركون في المؤتمر الدولي لترميم أبو الهول

القاهرة: مكتب «الشرق الأوسط»

صرح فاروق حسني وزير الثقافة المصري لـ«الشرق الأوسط» بأنه
سيتم تنظيم مؤتمر دولي في شهر فبراير (شباط) المقبل لمناقشة
مراحل ترميم تمثال أبو الهول . وقال إنه سيتم توجيه الدعوة لعدد
كبير من علماء أوروبا وأمريكا في جميع التخصصات الأثرية
والعلمية والتاريخية للمشاركة في المؤتمر الدولي الذي سيبحث
على مدى ثلاثة أيام ، نتائج أعمال ترميم المرحلة الأولى للتمثال ،
وخطة العمل للمرحلة القادمة التي تستغرق ثلاث سنوات ،
والاقتراحات المطلوبة لأعمال الصيانة الدورية.

وأكد فاروق حسني نجاح أعمال ترميم المرحلة الأولى للتمثال
والتي استغرقت عاما كاملا ، تم فيها ترميم الجانب الأيمن للتمثال.
وقال إن الترميمات تمت على أسس علمية وفنية دقيقة يشارك
فيها فريق متكامل من الأثريين والمرممين والمهندسين والفنانين
التشكيليين ، يهدف إلى إعادة التمثال إلى صورته التي كان عليها
منذ إزاحة الرمال من حوله عام ١٩٢٦.

وقال الوزير إن أعمال الترميم بدأت بين تسجيل شامل لحالة
التمثال كما هو عليه وجمع كل الدراسات التي تمت عن التمثال
في الفترة الماضية. وجمع جميع الصور التي نشرت لأبو الهول
منذ القرن ١٨ حتى الآن. وقد أكدت جميع الدراسات الأولية أن
الجانب الأيمن للتمثال يتعرض لمخاطر أكثر من الجانب الشمالي.
ولذلك تقرر البدء في ترميم التمثال من الناحية اليمنى لحين

انتهاء جميع الدراسات العلمية عن التمثال لوضع خطة العلاج طويلة الأمد وسبل الصيانة الدورية. وشملت هذه الدراسات مشكلة المياه الجوفية، والظروف البيئية ووضع رقبة التمثال والصدر.

وتم التعاقد مع هيئة الإرصاد الجوية لإنشاء محطة إرصاد أعلى الربوة بجوار التمثال. كما أقام معهد بول جنين الدولي للترميم محطة مشابهة فوق التمثال نفسه. وتوفر المحطتان قراءات متتابعة على مدى ٢٤ ساعة للظروف المناخية التي يتعرض لها التمثال بالنسبة لدرجات الحرارة والرطوبة واتجاهات الرياح. كما تم التعاقد مع معهد الدراسات الجيوفيزيقية لدراسات منسوب المياه الجوفية، والعيوب الجيولوجية في الصخرة الأم، ودراسة تأثير الذبذبات والحركة حول التمثال. كما تم عمل دراسة مع هيئة اليونسكو لإجراء دراسة بالموجات فوق الصوتية لدراسة صلابة الرأس والرقبة.

وقال الوزير إنه ستتم مناقشة نتائج جميع هذه الدراسات وكذلك نتائج أعمال الترميم التي تمت في المرحلة الأولى في المؤتمر الدولي المقبل من خلال مجموعات عمل متخصصة. كما سيقوم أعضاء المؤتمر بزيارات ميدانية لمناقشة المشاكل على الطبيعة.

ومن أهم الموضوعات المطروحة على المؤتمر إنشاء مظلة حول التمثال كإجراء وقائي في أعمال الصيانة الدورية. يتم إغلاقها عليه خلال فترة الليل أو أثناء حدوث أمطار غزيرة.

12. Oral
الحضارات القديمة في الشرق الأوسط
(a) Individual students to present brief accounts in Arabic of an ancient civilisation in the Middle East (e.g. المصريون القدماء، الكنعانيون، الصوريون، الفنيقيون).

(b) The student presenter then asks the other students questions about the particular civilisation. The questions should include some which require factual answers and some which require subjective, hypothetical or experiential answers. For example:

١ – ماذا نعرف عن هذه الحضارة؟

٢ – كيف نعرف هذا؟

٣ – ما هي أهم المدن في هذه الحضارة؟

٤ – متى بُنيت هذه المدن؟

٥ – بماذا عُني أهل هذه المدن/المدينة؟

٦ – هل قامت هذه الحضارة بالتجارة؟

٧ – هل زرت بلاد هذه الحضارة (مصر، تونس، دمشق)؟

٨ – هل رأيت آثار هذه الحضارة؟

٩ – في رأيك ما الذي سبب اختفاء هذه الحضارة؟

(c) Open lecturer–led discussion on one or more ancient civilisations in the Middle East.

13. Essay

Write an essay in Arabic on the following title الحضارات القديمة في الشرق الأوسط. In writing your essay address at least some of the following questions:

١ – ما هي الحضارة القديمة في مصر؟

٢ – ماذا تعرف عن هذه الحضارة؟

٣ – ما هي أقدم مدينة في العالم، وماذا تعرف عنها؟

٤ – من هم الكنعانيون؟

٥ – كيف تم الكشف عن الحضارات القديمة في الشرق الأوسط؟

4
The rise of Islam

1. Basic background material
(a) *Chronology of the life of the Prophet*

c. 570	Birth of Muhammad (his father died a few months earlier).
576	Death of his mother Amina.
595	Marriage to Khadija.
c. 610	Beginning of Call.
615	Flight of his followers to Ethiopia.
619	Death of Khadija.
620	Muhammad's reputed 'Night Journey' from Mecca to Jerusalem, and from there to the Seventh Heaven.
622	The *Hijra* (Flight or Migration) of Muhammad and his followers to Medina, and the beginning of the Muslim Era.
624	Battle of Badr: the Quraysh defeated by the Muslims.
625	Battle of Uhud: the Muslims defeated.
626	The Jewish tribe of al-Nadhir crushed and expelled.
627	'The War of the Ditch' – the Meccans' expedition against the Muslims in Medina. Attackers driven off.
627	The Jewish tribe of Qurayza raided by Muhammad; some 800 men beheaded (only one Jew abjuring his religion to save his life) and all the women and children sold as slaves.
628	The Treaty of Hudaybiyya: truce with the Quraysh, who recognise Muhammad's right to proselytise without hindrance.
629	The Jews of Khaybar put to the sword.
630	Truce broken by the Quraysh. Mecca taken by Muhammad – the entire population converted, and the Ka'ba established as the religious centre of Islam.
631	'The Year of Embassies' – Islam accepted by Arabian tribes.
632	Muhammad's Farewell Pilgrimage to Mecca.
632, 8 June	Death of Muhammad, three months after his return to Medina.

(b) *The Islamic state and main developments in Islam to the fall of the Abbasids*

632–634   Caliphate of Abu Bakr. Arab tribes who had apostasised from Islam following death of Muhammad defeated in Ridda wars. Single state established in Arabia.

634–644   Caliphate of Umar. Most of Fertile Crescent and Egypt conquered from Byzantines, where Arabs are generally welcomed as liberators from intolerant Byzantine rule. Much of Iran conquered from Sassanians.

644–656   Caliphate of Uthman. Continuation of conquests eastwards and northwards in Iran, where last Sassanian emperor, Yazdagird, is killed (651); also westwards into North Africa from Egypt, with decisive defeat of principal Byzantine fleet (655).

656–661   Murder of Uthman, civil wars with Ali at first recognised as Caliph. Bases himself at Kufa. Challenged for caliphate by Umayyad Mu'awiyah. Unsuccessful arbitration over caliphate leads to split in Ali's supporters between the 'Party of Ali', who support arbitration, and the Kharijis, who reject it. Ali eventually murdered by Kharijis. Kharijis continue as minor strand within Islam. Shi'ism begins to develop on basis of succession of divinely inspired line caliphs (some of whom had no real political power). Subsequently splits into three major branches: Zaidis, Twelvers and Ismai'ilis. Sunnism develops around notion of central legitimacy of Islamic law, rather than individual leader.

661–680   Mu'awiya generally accepted as caliph, with base in Damascus.

680–683   Mu'awiya succeeded by son, Yazid. Ali's son, Husayn killed at Kerbala during anti–Umayyad uprising – becomes symbol of martyrdom for Shi'ites.

683–692   Period of upheaval with Umayyads challenged by family of Ali and others for caliphate.

685–705   Rule of Umayyad, Abd al-Malik; regains control of all Islamic provinces.

705–743   Conquest of most of Spain, and Sind. Conquest of Transoxania. Islamic state stretches from Atlantic in west to borders of China in east.

744–750   Period of civil war. Eventual triumph of Abbasids over Umayyads, except in Spain, where Umayyads continue to rule until 1031. Abbasids base themselves in Iraq.

750–861   More-or-less unified Islamic state (except Spain) under Abbasids.

c.8–c.9   Development of four Sunni schools of law, under Abu Hanifah (d. 767), Malik ibn Anas (715–795), al-Shafi'i (d. 820), and Ibn Hanbal (d. 855).

873   Disappearance of the twelfth imam of 'Twelver' Shi'ite thought, Muhammad al-Muntazar, the alleged son of eleventh imam Hasan al-

Askari. Believed to be waiting in hiding until the end of the world. Followed in 'Twelver' Shi'ism by four *wakils*, the last of whom died in 940 refusing to name a successor. End of direct divine guidance of Twelver leaders.

861–945   Breakup of Abbasid power, with provinces increasingly becoming independent of central government. Abbasid caliphate nominally continues until 1258, when Mongols sack Baghdad (Mongols subsequently turned back in Syria having wreaked havoc in Middle East).

901   Zaydi state established in Yemen. Continues until modern era.

909–1171   Rise of Isma'ili Fatimids in Maghrib, and subsequent conquest and rule of Egypt. Development of complex Isma'ili cosmological ideas, which are subsequently carried further east.

2. Additional reading

(a) Hourani, *A History of the Arab Peoples*, pp. 14–21 'Muhammad and the Appearance of Islam'; pp. 147–57 'Ways of Islam'.

(b) Chart on the spread of early Islam: *Penguin Atlas of World History*, (Middlesex/New York: Penguin Books, 1974 (1977)), vol. I, p. 134.

(c) Chart on the spread of Islam: Malise Ruthven, *Islam in the World*, (Middlesex/New York: Penguin Books, 1984 (1985)), pp. 16–17, 'Worldwide distribution of Muslims today'.

3. Key vocabulary

Taking as your starting point the texts in this chapter, draw up lists of vocabulary in the following fields. Include plurals of nouns where relevant – checking in the dictionary where necessary:

(a) General religious terms: e.g. دين

(b) Key Islamic terms: e.g. نبي، رسول (الله)، نبي، القرآن، سورة، آية

(c) Key Islamic epithets: e.g. بسم الله الرحمن الرحيم، صلّى الله عليه وسلم، مكة المكرمة

4. Written Arabic texts 1

(a) Read the following passage, then give oral answers in Arabic to the questions which follow.

أركان الإسلام

١ – الشَّهَادَة   أَشْهَدُ أَنْ لا إِلَهَ إِلا اللّه

وَأَشْهدُ أَنَّ مُحَمَّدًا رَسُولُ اللّه

٢ – الصَّلاة

أ – أوْقاتُ الصَّلاة   ١ – الفَجْر

٢ – الظُّهْر

٣ – العَصْر

٤ – المَغْرِب

٥ – العِشَاء

ب – فَرائِض الوُضُوء   ١ – غَسْل الوَجْه

٢ – غَسْل اليَدَينِ إلى المِرْفَقَينِ

٣ – مَسْح الرَأْس

٤ – غَسْل الرِجْلَينِ إلى الكَعْبَينِ

ج – الأذان   اللّهُ أَكْبَرُ اللّهُ أَكْبَرُ

اللّهُ أَكْبَرُ اللّهُ أَكْبَرُ

أشْهَدُ أَنْ لا إله إلا الله   (مَرَّتَانِ)

أشْهَدُ أَنَّ مُحَمَّدًا رَسُولُ الله   (مَرَّتَانِ)

حَيٍّ عَلَى الصَّلاة   (مَرَّتَانِ)

حَيٍّ عَلَى الفَلاح   (مَرَّتَانِ)

اللّهُ أَكْبَرُ اللّهُ أَكْبَرُ

لا إله إلا اللّه

د – الرَكْعَة   فــــــي كُلِّ رِكْعَةٍ يَقُومُ المَسْلِمُ ثُمَّ يَرْكَعُ ثُمَّ يَسْجُدُ ثُمَّ يَجْلِسُ ثُمَّ يَسْجُدُ

١ – صَلاةُ الفَجْرِ رَكْعَتان

٢ – صَلاةُ الظُّهْرِ أَرْبَعُ رَكَعَاتٍ

٣ – صَلاةُ العَصْرِ أَرْبَعُ رَكَعَاتٍ

٤ – صَلاةُ المَغْرِبِ ثَلاثُ رَكَعَاتٍ

٥ – صَلاةُ العِشَاءِ أَرْبَعُ رَكَعَاتٍ

يَوْمَ الجُمْعَةِ في وَقْتِ صَلاةِ الظُّهْرِ خُطْبَةٌ ثُمَّ رَكْعَتَانِ

٣ – الزَّكاةُ   يَجِبُ عَلَى كُلِّ مُسْلِمٍ أَنْ يُعْطِيَ لِلْفُقَرَاءِ كُلَّ سَنَةٍ.

٤ – الصَّوْمُ   يَجِبُ عَلَى كُلِّ مُسْلِمٍ أَنْ يَصُومَ في شَهْرِ رَمَضَانَ مِنَ الفَجْرِ إِلَى المَغْرِبِ.

٥ – الحَجُّ   يَجِبُ عَلَى كُلِّ مُسْلِمٍ أَنْ يَذْهَبَ إِلَى مَكَّةَ لَلْحَجِّ مَرَّةً وَاحِدَةً فِي حَيَاتِهِ.

القُرآن

١ – التَّنْزِيلُ الأَوَّلُ الَّذِي جَاءَ إِلَى رَسُولِ اللّه

بِسْمِ اللّهِ الرَّحْمَنِ الرَّحِيمِ

اِقْرَأْ بِاسْمِ رَبِّكَ الَّذِي خَلَقَ . خَلَقَ الإِنْسَانَ مِن عَلَقٍ .

اِقْرَأْ وَرَبُّكَ الأَكْرَمُ . الَّذِي عَلَّمَ بِالقَلَمِ . عَلَّمَ الإِنْسَانَ مَا لَمْ يَعْلَمْ .

٢ – الكَلِمَاتُ الأُولَى مِنْ سُورَةِ الفَاتِحَةِ

بِسْمِ اللّهِ الرَّحْمَنِ الرَّحِيمِ

الحَمْدُ لِلّهِ رَبِّ العَالَمَينَ . الرَّحْمَنِ الرَّحِيمِ . مَالِكِ يَومِ الدِّينِ .

١ – ما هي أركان الإسلام؟

٢ – كم مرّة يصلّي المسلم في اليوم؟

٣ – بماذا يشهد المؤذّن في الأذان؟

٤ – كيف يقوم المسلم بالركعة؟

٥ – بكم ركعة يقوم المسلم خلال صلاة العصر؟

٦ – ماذا يحصل في يوم الجمعة؟

٧ – ما هي الزكاة؟

٨ – متى يصوم المسلم؟

٩ – من الواجب على المسلم أن يحجّ كم مرّة في حياته؟

١٠ – حسب الآية القرآنية ممّا خُلق الإنسان؟

١١ – من هو مالك يوم الدين؟

(b) Read the following passage, then give oral answers in English to the question which follow.

الإسلام والحضارة الإسلامية

الإسلام دين ظهر في بداية القرن السابع للميلاد في منطقة الحجاز في الجزيرة العربية. أصل الإسلام هو التوحيد ويعني هذا أنه يجب على المسلم أن يصدّق أن الله واحد لا اثنان أو ثلاثة كما يدّعي بعض الناس. يقبل الإسلام الدين المسيحي والدين اليهودي ويعترف المسلمون ببعض الرسل المذكورين في الكتب الدينية اليهودية والمسيحية ولكن الإسلام يرفض أن عيسى ابن مريم – يعني المسيح – هو ابن الله فهذا لا يتّفق مع فكرة التوحيد المعروفة في الإسلام. وبالإضافة إلى الرسل الموجودين عند اليهود والمسيحيين هناك رسول آخر خاص بالإسلام واسمه محمد بن عبد الله وهو الذي جاء بالرسالة الإسلامية.

قضى الرسول محمد معظم حياته في مدينتين هما مكة والمدينة وكان في بداية الأمر تاجرا. ثم أصبح رجلا دينيا يدعو الناس إلى الإسلام وفي نفس الوقت زعيما سياسيا يبني دولة إسلامية في المناطق التي يسكن فيها العرب. وبعد وفاة الرسول توسّعت الدولة

الإسلامية وأصبحت إمبراطورية تمتدّ من إسبانيا في الغرب إلى الهند والصين في الشرق. وكانت هذه الإمبراطورية أكبر دولة شهدها التاريخ حتى ذلك الحين. وتطورت في هذه البلدان حضارة جديدة هي الحضارة الإسلامية وأخذ المسلمون كل الأشياء الجيدة التي وجدوها في الحضارات القديمة وتركوا الأشياء الرديئة.

وأصبح الإسلام نظاماً كاملاً يعاون المسلم في كل أموره فلا يفصل الإسلام بين الدين ووجوه الحياة الأخرى. فالله ملك كل شيء. ولذلك لا يشمل الإسلام الأمور الدينية فقط بل هو نظام اجتماعي واقتصادي وسياسي أيضاً. فعندما يتزوج المسلم من اللازم أن يتزوج بالطريقة الإسلامية، فيمكن للمسلم مثلاً أن يتزوج امرأة غير مسلمة ولكنه لا يمكن للمسلمة أن تتزوج رجلاً غير مسلم. وعندما يقوم المسلم بمشروع صناعي من اللازم أن يوافق تنظيم هذا المشروع الشريعة الإسلامية وعندما تقرّر حكومة إسلامية شيئاً من اللازم أن يتّفق هذا القرار مع الأفكار الإسلامية العامة والخاصة. وهكذا يسهّل الإسلام أمور الضعيف والفقير ويوضّح الطريق الصحيح ويؤدي إلى مجتمع مبني على الأمن والسلام والسعادة.

1. When precisely did Islam appear?
2. Where precisely did Islam appear?
3. What is the fundamental principle of Islam?
4. Do Muslims accept the validity of Christian and Jewish prophetic figures?
5. Why do Muslims not accept that Jesus is the son of God?
6. What is the Islamic Prophet's association with Mecca and Medina?
7. What was Muhammad's original profession?
8. What were the two aspects of his religious mission?
9. What were the borders of the Islamic empire?
10. How did this empire compare in size with previous empires?
11. Where did Islamic civilisation develop?
12. On what basis did the Muslims select those aspects of other civilisations which were to be part of their civilisation?
13. Why may Islam be regarded as an integral system?
14. What does Islam involve in addition to the purely religious?

15. What is the basis for this wide scope?
16. What are the Islamic rules regarding marriage?
17. How are industrial enterprises to be organised in the Islamic world?
18. What restrictions does Islam place on political decision making?
19. What are the results of Islamic practice for those without wealth or power?
20. What is the basis of the resulting Islamic society?

(c) Translate the following text into idiomatic English.

الإسلام

الإسلام كلمة مشتقة من «أسلم» ومعناها الخضوع التام لله ولما
يأمر به وما ينهى عنه، والإسلام نوعان: النوع الأول إجباري وهذا
يشمل كل ما هو موجود في هذا الكون – الشمس والقمر والكواكب
والإنسان والحيوان والنبات، كل هذه الأشياء تسلم لله تعالى بمعنى
أنها تخضع للقوانين التي وضعها سبحانه وتعالى في هذه
الطبيعة، من هذه القوانين بالنسبة للإنسان مثلا الحاجة إلى الطعام
والشراب والنوم إلى آخره. وكذلك الشمس والقمر والكواكب كلها
تسير حسب نظام دقيق معين لا تخرج عنه. أما النوع الثاني
فيُسمى الإسلام الاختياري وهو أن يختار الإنسان أن يخضع لله
في كل ما يفعل باختياره. وهذا النوع خاص بالإنسان وحده. ويبدأ
هذا النوع بأن يعتقد الإنسان ويؤمن أولا بالله، ثانيا بملائكته، ثالثا
بكتبه، رابعا برسله، خامسا بالقدر خيره وشره من الله تعالى،
سادسا باليوم الآخر، وأن يلتزم الإنسان بأركان الإسلام الخمسة،
وهي أولا الشهادتان: أشهد أن لا إله إلا الله وأشهد أن محمدا
رسول الله، ثانيا الصلاة، ثالثا الزكاة، رابعا صوم رمضان، وخامسا
الحج، وأن يتبع الإنسان كل ما أمر الله به وأن يبتعد عما نهى عنه.

5. Written Arabic texts 2
(a) Translate the following text from the introduction to المفصل في علم اللغة by
الزمخشري, edited by محمد عز الدين السعيدي into idiomatic English.

أمـا بعـد، إن القـرآن الكـريم هـو مـعجـزة الإسـلام العـظمـى لمـا حـوى مـن فصـاحـة وبـلاغـة وأحـكام وحكم. وكانت فصـاحـتـه السـبب الأول لإيمان الكثـيرين من العرب الجاهلـيين الذيـن رأوا فـيه مـا لم يروه مـن أعظم بلـغائهم وفصحـائهم، فـهو كـما وصـفه أحـد صناديـد قريش (فإن فـيه لحلاوة وإن عليه لطلاوة وإنـه يعلو ولا يعلى عليه).

وقـد اسـتمـرت مـعجـزة القـرآن البـلاغـيـة واضحـة المعالم للأجيـال المسلمـة العـربيـة الأولى والتي تلتهـا، حتى إذا اختلط العرب بالعجم وبدأ اللحن والعجمـة يدبان إلى ألسنـة العرب شيئـا فشيئـا، دعت الضـرورة إلى قيـام العلمـاء الأفـذاذ إلى اسـتنبـاط قـواعـد اللغـة العـربيـة وابتكار العلوم التي تساعد على تقويم الألسنـة وفهم القرآن الكريم فهمـاً يماثل فهم الذين عاصروا نزوله.

(b) Read the following text by طه حسين from الأيام, pp. 37–8, then answer the questions which follow in English.

منذ هذا اليوم أصبح صبيُّنا شيخـا وإن لم يتجاوز التـاسعـة: لأنه حفظ القرآن، ومن حفظ القرآن فهو شيخ مهما تكن سنُّه. دعاه أبـوه شيخـا، ودعته أمّه شيخـا، وتعوّد سيّدنا أن يدعوه شيخـا أمام أبويه، أو حين يرضَى عنه، أو حين يُريد أن يترضّاه لأمـر من الأمـور. فـأمّـا فـيمـا عدا ذلك فقد كان يدعوه باسمـه، وربما دعاه «بالواد». وكان شيخنا الصبيُّ قصيرا نحيفا شاحبا زريَّ الهيئة[1] على نحو مّا، ليس له من وقار الشيوخ ولا من حسن طلعتهم حظٌّ قليلٌ أو كثيـر. وكان أبواه يكتفيان من تمجيده وتكبيره بهذا اللفظ الذي أضافاه إلى اسمـه كِبرًا منهما وعُجبا لا تلطفا به ولا تحبُّبا إليه. أمّا هو فقد أعجبه هذا اللفظ في أوّل الأمـر، ولكنه كان ينتظر شيئـا آخر من مظاهر المكافأة والتشجيع: كان ينتظر أن يكون شيخا حقّا، فيتّخذَ العمّة ويلبس الجبّة والقفطان، وكان من العسير إقناعُه بأنه أصغرَ من أن يحمل العمّة، ومن أن يدخل في القفطان... وكيف السبيل

إلى إقناعه بذلك وهو شيخ قد حفظ القرآن! وكيف يكون الصغير
شيخاً! وكيف يكون من حفظ القرآن صغيراً! هو إذن مظلوم ... وأيُّ
ظلمٍ أشدّ من أن يُحال بينه وبين حقّه في العمّة والجُبّة والقفطان! ..
ما هي إلا أيام حتى سئم لقب الشيخ، وكرِه أن يُدْعى به،
وأحسّ أنّ الحياة مملوءة بالظلم والكذب، وأنّ الإنسان يظلمه حتى
أبوه، وأنّ الأبوّة والأمومة لا تعصم الأب والأُمَّ من الكذب والعبث
والخداع.

Note

١ – زري الهيئة: حقيرها.

1. Why did the boy become a sheikh?
2. How old was the boy when he began to be called 'sheikh'?
3. On what occasions did the sayyid call the boy 'sheikh'?
4. What did he call him on other occasions?
5. How is the boy's physical appearance described?
6. Why is a description of his appearance relevant at this point in the story?
7. What did the boy think about being called sheikh?
8. What was he waiting for?
9. What would he wear when this event took place?
10. How did he feel about this period of waiting?
11. What were his subsequent feelings about being called sheikh?
12. How did he then feel about life?

6. Written Arabic texts 3 (Classical)

Translate the following text by ابن هشام into idiomatic English (مبعث النبي
(صلعم) in Brünnow and Fischer (eds.), *Arabische Chrestomathie* (Leipzig: Veb
Verlag Enzyklopädie, 1966), pp. 41–3). This passage deals with the revelation of
the Qur'an to the Prophet Muhammad by the Archangel Gabriel (جبريل) in a cave
on the hill of Hira a few miles north–east of Mecca.

قال رسول الله (صلعم) فجاءني وأنا نائم بنمط من ديباج فيه
كتابٌ فقال اقرأ قال قلت ما أقرأ قال فغَتَّني به حتى ظننتُ
أنّه الموت ثم أرسلني فقال اقرأ قال قلت ما أقرأ قال فغتّني
به حتى ظننت أنّه الموت ثم أرسلني فقال اقرأ قال قلت ماذا

أقرأُ مـا أقول ذلك إلا افـتداءً مـنـه أن يـعـودَ لـي بمثل مـا صنع بي
فقال ¹ اقـرأ باسم ربّك الذي خلق الإنسان مـن عـلق اقـرأ
وربُّك الأكـرمُ الذي علّم بـالقلم علّم الإنسان مـا لـم يَـعلم قـال
فـقـرأتـها ثمّ انتهى فـانصرف عنّي وهببتُ من نومي فكأنما
كُتبت في قلبي كتابًا قال فخرجتُ حتى إذا كنت في وسط من
الجبل سمعتُ صوتا من السماء يقول يـا محمّد أنت رسول الله
وأنا جبريل قال فرفعت رأسي إلى السماء أنظر فإذا جبريل
في صورة رجل صافّ قدمَيْه في أُفُق السماء يقول يا محمّد
أنت رسول الله وأنا جبريل فوقفتُ أنظر إليه فما أتقدّم وما
أتأَخّر وجعلتُ أصرف وجهي عنه في آفاق السماء فلا أنظر في
ناحية منها إلا رأيته كذلك فما زلتُ واقفا ما أتقدم أمامي وما
أرجـع ورائي حتى بعثت خديجةُ رسلها في طلبي فبلغوا أعلى
مكّة ورجعوا إليها وأنا واقف في مكاني ذلك ثم انصرف عنّي
وانصرفتُ عنه راجعا إلى أهلي حتى أتيتُ خديجةَ فجلست
إلى فخذها مُضيفا إليها فقالت يا أبا القاسم أين كنت فوالله
قد بعثتُ رسلي في طلبك حتى بلغوا أعلى مكّة ورجعوا إليّ ثم
حدثتُها بالذي رأيت فقالت أبشر يابنَ عَمِّ واثبُتْ فوالذي نفسُ
خـديجـة بيـده إنّي لأرجـو أن تكون نبيّ هذه الأمّة ثم قـامت
فجمعت عليها ثيابها ثم انطلقت إلى ورقة بن نوفل وهو ابن
عمها وكان ورقة قد تنصّر وقرأ الكُتُب وسمع من أهل التَوْراة
والإنجيل فأخبرته بما أخبرها رسول الله صلعم أنّه رأى وسمع
فـقـال ورقـة قُدُّوس قُدُّوسُ والذي نفسُ ورقة بيـده لئنْ كُنْتَ
صدقتيني يا خديجة لقد جاءه الناموسُ الأكبرُ الذي كان يأتي
مُوسى وإنّه لنبيّ هذه الأمة فقولي له فَلْيَثبتْ.

Note

١ – القرآن ٩٦:١–٥

7. Grammar/stylistics

(a) *Affirmative* لَ

The affirmative particle لَ intensifies or emphasises the truth value of a statement. It is especially common in Classical Arabic and in religious writing where a classical style is imitated. Unlike prepositional لِ it does not put a noun into the accusative case: a following noun is always nominative; as a result لَ can be followed by one of the independent pronouns, as in لَهو 'certainly he is', لأَنتـم 'certainly you m.pl. are'. Similarly, it does not alter the mood of an imperfect verb: an imperfect verb after لَ remains in the indicative. (For more examples and for further explanation of لَ see Wright I: 282–3.) There are four common contexts in which لَ occurs:

i   Oaths – such as وَاللّه 'by God' require a complement. If the complement is an affirmative nominal clause it is introduced either by إنّ or by لَ:

وَاللّه {لـ}مَحمدٌ رسولٌ.

'By God, verily Muhammad is His apostle.' (Wright I: 175)

ii   The apodosis (main clause) of a hypothetical conditional clause beginning with لو or لو لا often begins with لَ. This is common in modern as well as in Classical Arabic:

لو لا فضل الله عليكم ورحمته {لـ}اتّبعتم الشيطان.

'If it had not been for the goodness of God towards you and his mercy, verily ye would have followed Satan.' (Wright I: 283)

ولو لا الأهوار {لـ}هلك هؤلاء الناس.

'If it were not for the marshes, those people would perish.' (ch. 8, 11)

When the apodosis consists of a form of كان followed by the imperfect, it is often the imperfect which is preceded by لَ, as in:

.. إلى مشكلة ما كانت {لـ}تقفزُ إلى الصفحات الأولى في الصحف
... لو لا هذا التجمع الذي استضافته جنيف.

'... to a problem which would not have leapt to the front pages of the papers ... were it not for this gathering called by Geneva.' (ch. 10, 5c)

iii   Affirmative لَ is often prefixed to the predicate of إنّ, as in:

إنّي {لـ}أَرجو أَنْ تكون نبي هذه الأمة.

'I really hope that you will become Prophet of this community.' (ch. 4, 6a)

كلا إنّ الإنسان {لـ}يَطْغَى.

'Nav. but man doth transgress all bounds.' (ch. 4, 8a)

فإن فيه {لـ}حلاوةٌ وإن عليه {لـ}طلاوةٌ.
'There is certainly refinement and beauty in it.' (ch. 4, 5a)

i v Affirmative لَ often occurs before the particle قد and the perfect aspect, particularly, but certainly not exclusively, in the apodasis of a conditional clause, as in:

لَئِن كنت صدقتيني يا خديجة {لـ}قد جاءه النامُوس الأكبر.
'If you have told me the truth, Khadija, it was certainly the Archangel Gabriel who came to him.' (ch. 4, 6a)

This usage is common in modern Arabic:

{لـ}قد درسنا مشكلة الشرق الأوسط دراسةً شاملةً.
'We have indeed made a comprehensive study of the Middle East.' (EMSA I: 539)

(b) لَ *of command*
In classical texts لَ is often prefixed to the third person singular of the jussive to give an imperative sense. This would usually be translated into English as 'let him/her …'. When لَ is preceded by وَ or فَ, the vowel of لَ is generally dropped. Examples include:

فَـ{لـ}يَدْعُ ناديه.
'Then, let him call [for help] to his council [of comrades].' (ch. 4, 8a)

فقولي له فَـ{لـ}يَثْبَتْ.   'Tell him he should persevere.' (ch. 4, 6a)

(c) وَ *as a preposition*
وَ is most commonly used as a conjunction meaning 'and'. In oaths and exclamations it also has a prepositional use similar to بـ, however, and in this case is often translated as 'by'. وَ as a preposition is most common in classical and religious texts. Examples include:

فَـ{ـو}الذي نفسُ خديجة بيده.
'By the One in whose hands lies the soul of Khadija…' (ch. 4, 6a)

{و}رَبِّي   'By my Lord!'

{و}اللّه   'By God!'

(d) *'Too small to do X'*
The idea of 'too', as in 'too small to do X' or 'too old to do X', is expressed by the elative followed by مِن أنْ يفعلَ. Examples include:

وكان من العسير إقناعه بأنه {أصغر من أنْ يحملَ العمة} و{من أنْ
يدخُلَ في القفطان}.

'It was difficult to convince him that he was too small to wear a turban
or to get into a caftan.' (ch. 4, 4b)

فهو {أكبر من أنْ يحله عقل واحد}.

'It is too big to be solved by one mind.' (ch. 5, 11b)

(e) *Use of* الذي / *with no* راجع

The relative clause almost always takes a pronoun which agrees with the relative
pronoun (or preceding noun where one exists). This pronoun is called a راجع or
عائد in Arabic. In classical texts, however, relative clauses can occasionally lack a
راجع.

ثم حدثتها بالذي رأيت.

'Then I told her about what I had seen.' (ch. 4, 6a)

8. Aural Arabic texts 1

(a) Qur'anic suras. Listen to the following suras from the Qur'an read first in
Arabic and then in English: سورة العلق ، سورة الإخلاص.

(٩٦) سورة العلق

بِسمِ اللَّهِ الرَحْمَنِ الرَحِيمِ

(١) اقْرَأْ بِاسْمِ رَبِّكَ الَّذِي خَلَقَ

(٢) خَلَقَ الإِنْسَانَ مِنْ عَلَقٍ

(٣) اقْرَأْ وَرَبُّكَ الأَكْرَمُ

(٤) الَّذِي عَلَّمَ بِالقَلَمِ

(٥) عَلَّمَ الإِنْسَانَ مَا لَمْ يَعْلَمْ

(٦) كَلا إِنَّ الإِنْسَانَ لَيَطْغَى

(٧) أن رَّءَاهُ اسْتَغْنَى

(٨) إِنَّ إِلَى رَبِّكَ الرُّجْعَى

(٩) أَرَءَيْتَ الَّذِي يَنْهَى

(١٠) عَبْدًا إِذَا صَلَّى

(١١) أَرَءَيْتَ إِن كَانَ عَلَى الهُدَى

(١٢) أَوْ أَمَرَ بِالتَّقْوَى

(١٣) أَرَءَيْتَ إِن كَذَّبَ وَتَوَلَّى

(١٤) أَلَمْ يَعْلَمْ بِأَنَّ اللَّهَ يَرَى

(١٥) كَلَا لَئِن لَّمْ يَنتَهِ لَنَسْفَعَا بِالنَّاصِيَةِ

(١٦) نَاصِيَةٍ كَاذِبَةٍ خَاطِئَةٍ

(١٧) فَلْيَدْعُ نَادِيَهُ

(١٨) سَنَدعُ الزَّبَانِيَةَ

(١٩) كَلَا لَا تُطِعْهُ وَاسْجُدْ وَاقْتَرِبْ

(١١٢) سورة الإخلاص

بِسم اللَّه الرَّحْمَن الرَّحيم

(١) قُلْ هُوَ اللَّهُ أَحَدٌ

(٢) اللَّهُ الصَّمَدُ

(٣) لَمْ يَلِدْ وَلَمْ يُولَدْ

(٤) وَلَمْ يَكُنْ لَّهُ كُفُوًا أَحَدٌ

(b) Listen to the whole of the following text from حصاد الشهر, no. 8, side 1, item
1, which introduces and includes a recording by the late شيخ محمد رفعة of
سورة مريم, then complete exercises i. and ii. below which relate to the
introductory section of the text.

i   Listening to the text, fill in the gaps in the following transcription.

ـــــــــ نستهل بتلاوة ـــــــــ ـــــــــ ـــــــــ اَية ذكر

الكريم، ـــــــــ ـــــــــ ـــــــــ رفعة، ـــــــــ تُوفي

ـــــــــ ـــــــــ يزيد ـــــــــ ـــــــــ

ـــــــــ ـــــــــ يزال ـــــــــ ـــــــــ ،

ــــــــ المُقرئ ــــــ ــــــ ــــــ إذ ، ــــــ شيخ المُقرِئين ــــــ

ــــــ ــــــ لم نادرا ــــــ ــــــ حباه الكفيف

ــــــ ــــــ إنه و ، ــــــ ــــــ قارئ به يحْظى

ــــــ ومن ــــــ في ــــــ ــــــ ــــــ

في حوزة ــــــ في ــــــ ــــــ ــــــ تسجيلاته

من آيات ــــــ و سيداتي .ــــــ ــــــ الإذاعة ــــــ

محمد ــــــ ــــــ يتلو ــــــ ــــــ الله

ــــــ ــــــ له يتيسر ــــــ ــــــ ــــــ

.ــــــ

ii Answer the following questions relating to the text in English.

1. When did Shaikh Muhammad Rif'at die?
2. What is he still considered to be?
3. What disability did he have?
4. What did God bless him with?
5. What is he said to have recorded in Cairo?
6. What is in the possession of the BBC?

9. Aural Arabic texts 2

Listen to the following text from حصاد الشهر مساعدة, no. 12, side 2, item 4, الغرب على فهم الإسلام, then complete exercises i. and ii. below.

i Answer the following questions based on the first paragraph of the passage beginning مكارم الأخلاق في القرآن الكريم and ending دور النشر في لندن.

1. Who is Yahya al-Mu'allim?
2. How many times was his book مكارم الأخلاق في القرآن الكريم printed in the Arab world?
3. What has he decided to do now?
4. What is the name of the radio programme in which he discusses this project?
5. What did Yahya al-Mu'allim's English–speaking friends suggest?
6. What was his response?
7. Where is Tariq Ihsan from?

8. Where is Hala al-Sulh from?
9. What did Yahya al-Mu'allim do with the results of their endeavours?
10. Where is the new book being printed?

ii Produce a transcript in Arabic of the remainder of this passage from ما سبب to
the end. You may find the following words put in the order in which they occur
in the text useful.

تأليف	composition
طُبع	to be printed (passive)
أجاد لغة	to be proficient in a language
لخّص	to summarise, condense
نسخة	manuscript
بصفة عامة	in a general way
سواء ... أو	either ... or
الدين الحنيف	the True (i.e. Islamic) Religion

10. Written English texts
Making use of constructions encountered in the Arabic texts above, as far as
possible, translate the following texts into idiomatic Arabic. The texts are from
E.A. Bawany (ed.) *Islam–our choice* (Cairo: Dar al-kitab al-masri), p.7 and p.11.

(a) **A complete way of life**
Islam is not a religion in the common distorted meaning of the word,
confining its scope to the private life of man. It is a complete way of
life, catering to all the fields of human existence. Islam provides
guidance for all walks of life – individual and social, material and
moral, economic and political, legal and cultural, national and
international. The Qur'an enjoins man to enter the fold of Islam,
without any reservation and follow God's guidance in all fields of life.

(b) **Simplicity, rationalism and practicalism**
Islam is a religion without any mythology. Its teachings are simple and
intelligible. It is free from superstitions and irrational beliefs. Unity of
God, Prophethood of Muhammad (peace be upon him) and the
concepts of life–after–death are the basic articles of its faith. They are
based on reason and sound logic. All the teachings of Islam follow
from these basic beliefs and are simple and straightforward. There is no
hierarchy of priests, no far–fetched abstractions, no complicated rites
and rituals. Everybody is to directly approach the Book of God and
translate its dictates into practice.

11. **Précis**

Read the following text from الثقافية Issue 4, Oct. 1994 (published by the Saudi Cultural Bureau, London) and produce a précis in Arabic.

محاميات وطبيبات وباحثات في العلوم والآداب
١٠ آلاف بريطانية دخلنا دين الاسلام

لندن – «الثقافية»:

أكد تقرير – نُشِر مـؤخّـراً – أن حـوالي عـشـرة آلاف امـرأة بـريطانيـة دخلن الدين الإسلامي في السنوات القليلة الماضية، بعد تعرُّفِهن عن قُرب قواعـد الشـريعـة الإسلامـيـة السـمـحـة التي تحمي الأسـرة وتُكـرم المرأة وتُعلي من قيم الفضيلة والأخلاق.

إن قـيـم الإسلام تبـرز شـامـخـةً تُقـدِّم الحلول الصـحـيـحـة لأزمـة مجتمعات حَرَّفها تيّار المادة وألقى بها في محيط الرغبات المُهْلِكة، التي تهدم البنيـة الأسـاسيـة للحيـاة، وتخـرب الشعـور الإنسـاني وتُلْقِي بالعائلة في محيط هائج من الانقسام والضياع.

ومع العـودة إلى حقـائـق الإسـلام بعـد قـرون من التشـوه والعـداء يزداد عدد الداخلين في دين الله يبـحثون عن الحق والفضيلة، ويرون «بـوصلة» تهـديهم ونُخْرجـخـن من ظلمـات الجـهـل إلى أفـق نور الإسلام.

وأشار التـقـريـر أن النسـاء البـريطانيـات يجـدن في الدين الحل لأمراض المادية التي تفترس الغرب منذ سنوات، لذلك تزداد نسبة المعتنقات للإسلام كل يوم، مع اهتمام واضح في بريطانيا بالعقيدة الاسلامية وتشريعاتها لكل أوجه الحياة البشرية.

وتردّ هذه النسبة المرتفعة لنساء بـريطانيات دخلن الإسلام على بـعض افتراءات في الفكر الغربي تروِّج عن جهلٍ وغرضٍ بأن الإسلام يحرم المرأة من حقوقها ويسلبها العديد من حريتها ويضعها في خانة ثانية في سلّم المجتمع.

وهذا التـقـريـر يقـول العكس تمـامـاً، ويوضِّح أن نسـاء غـربيـات

متعلمات بعد معرفةٍ بحقائق الدين الحنيف قَرَّرْن دخول خيمة الإسلام والتمتّع بكل ما يمنحه للمرأة من كرامة أولاً تستحقّها بعيداً عن كل ما يمسّ وجودها أو يقترب من شخصيتها.

إن الشريعة السَمْحة العادلة تحدّد وظائف كل عضو في المجتمع الإسلامي، وعندما تتحدّث عن المرأة وضعت كل الضوابط التي تسمح لها بممارسة دورها الطبيعي في الحياة تحت مظلّة القيم وداخل بناء الأسرة وفي قلب خلايا المجتمع.

محاميات وطبيبات

ويقول تقرير نشرته صحيفة « الصنداي تايمز » البريطانية، إن مُعْتنقي الإسلام من النساء البريطانيات يشغلن درجات عالية من السلّم الأكاديمي والحياة العملية .. وهن من نخبة المجتمع، ويُميِّزهن التحصيل العلمي الواسع والعميق ونجاحهن في الحصول على شهادات عالية. فمن بينهن مَن لديه درجات الدكتوراه في القانون أو الآداب أو العلوم التطبيقية والعلمية.

ومن بين هذه النسبة المعْلَنة لنساء دخلن دين الله محاميات وطبيبات وباحثات في ميدان الأسرة والعلوم الاجتماعية.

ويشير تقرير « الصنداي تايمز » أن النساء البريطانيات يتّجهْن إلى الإسلام في وقت تعاني فيه الأسرة الغربية من عوامل تحلّل اجتماعي نتيجة ارتفاع نسبة الطلاق، وزيادة عدد الأسر التي تعتمد على عائل واحد هو الأم دائماً.

ويُضيف التقرير أن توجُّه البريطانيات نحو الإسلام خصوصاً مَن ينتسبن إلى الطبقة الوسطى المتعلمة يتمّ في وقت تحدث فيه إغراءات شديدة تقوم بها جماعات نسائية تطالب المرأة بالتمرُّد على قيم الأسرة والخروج على مجتمع الرجال، وتدعيم الاتّجاهات التي تسمّيها تحرراً من سيطرة القيود أو ما تُطْلِق عليه سمات المجتمع الأبوي.

12. Oral

ظهور الإسلام

(a) One or two students to present a brief account of the emergence of Islam and its
early history.

(b) The presenter(s) then ask(s) the other students questions about Islam. The
questions should require mainly factual answers but could also include some
which require subjective or hypothetical answers. For example:

١ – متى ظهر الإسلام؟

٢ – ما هو أصل الإسلام؟

٣ – ماذا يعني هذا؟

٤ – لماذا أصبح محمد رسول الله؟

٥ – ما هي أركان الإسلام؟

٦ – كيف يصلي المسلم؟

٧ – كم مرة في اليوم يصلي المسلم؟

٨ – ما هي الفروق المهمة بين الإسلام والمسيحية؟

(c) Open lecturer–led discussion on Islam including the principles of Islam, the
early history of Islam and differences between Islam and other religions.

13. Essay

Write an essay in Arabic of between 150 and 200 words on the title ظهور الإسلام.
In writing your essay address at least some of the following questions:

١ – كيف صار محمد رسول الله؟

٢ – كيف بدأ دين الإسلام؟

٣ – ما هي أركان الإسلام؟

٤ – كيف يختلف الإسلام عن الدينين المسيحي واليهودي؟

٥ – كيف توسعت الدولة الإسلامية قبل وفاة محمد وبعدها؟

5
Arabic language

1. Basic background material

(a) *Arabic as a Semitic and Afro–Asiatic language*

Arabic is a Semitic language (Shem or Sem being one of the sons of Noah in the Bible), and is related genetically to a number of other languages in the Middle East and Ethiopia. The Semitic language group includes not only Arabic, but also ancient languages such as Biblical Hebrew, Akkadian (formerly spoken in Iraq), Aramaic and its descendent Syriac (formerly spoken in much of Iraq and Greater Syria), ancient South Arabian languages (formerly spoken in southern Arabia, and also known as Himyaritic languages), and Ge'ez (formerly spoken in Ethiopia). Among the modern Semitic languages are Modern Hebrew, Modern Aramaic languages (with pockets of speakers in Syria, Iraq and Iran), Amharic and Tigriniya (both spoken in Ethiopia), Maltese (which is basically a dialect of Arabic), and a number of South Arabian languages (descendents of the ancient South Arabian languages, and spoken in parts of Oman, Saudi Arabia, and Yemeni island of Socotra).

More distantly, Arabic forms part of the Afro–Asiatic language family (also known as the Hamito–Semitic language family, Ham being another son of Noah). This family includes Ancient Egyptian, the Berber languages (spoken in parts of north Africa), Hausa (spoken in Nigeria and other parts of west Africa and in Sudan), and Somali. It is strongly suspected that the Afro–Asiatic language family is ultimately related to the Indo–European language family (which includes English, almost all the languages of Europe, Persian, Kurdish, Sanskrit, Hindi, and most other languages of north India). However, nobody has as yet been able to convincingly demonstrate the nature of this relationship.

(b) *Varieties of Arabic: the relationship between standard and colloquial Arabic*

The following definitions of dialect, standard language, and diglossia provide a background account in modern linguistic terms of aspects of the relationship between classical or standard Arabic (فصحى), and colloquial Arabic (عامّية).

Dialect

A regionally or socially distinctive variety of a language, identified by a particular set of words and grammatical structures. Spoken dialects are usually also associated with a distinctive pronunciation or accent. Any language with a reasonably large number of speakers will develop dialects, especially if there are geographical barriers separating groups of people from each other, or if there are divisions of social class. One dialect may predominate as the official or standard form of the language, and this is the variety which may come to be written down (Crystal 1985: 92).

Standard language

'Standard languages/dialects/varieties' cut across regional differences, providing a unified means of communication, and thus an institutionalised norm which can be used in the mass–media, in teaching the language to foreigners, and so on (Crystal 1985: 286).

Diglossia

A term used in sociolinguistics [i.e. that branch of linguistics which studies the relationship between language and society] to refer to a situation where two very different varieties of a language co–occur throughout a speech community, each with a distinct range of social function. Both varieties are standardised to some degree, are felt to be alternatives by native–speakers and usually have special names. Sociolinguists usually talk in terms of a high (H) variety and a low (L) variety, corresponding broadly to a difference in formality: the high variety is learnt in school, tends to be used in church [also mosque], on radio programmes, in serious literature, etc., and as a consequence has greater social prestige; the low variety in family conversations, and other relatively informal settings. Diglossic situations may be found in Greek (High: Katharevousa; Low: Dhimotiki), Arabic (High: classical; Low: colloquial), and some varieties of German (H: Hochdeutsch; L: Schweizerdeutsch, in Switzerland) (Crystal 1985: 93).

The following is an account of the relationship between types of فصحى and عامية in Egypt, as proposed by the modern Egyptian linguist El-Said Badawi (forms in transcription in the original have been replaced by Arabic script in the text as given here). The situation in most other Arab countries is similar to the one described here, the most important exceptions being the countries of North Africa المغرب – Tunisia, Algeria and Morocco – in which French is widely spoken in addition to Arabic (and in some areas Berber). To describe the situation in Egypt, Badawi establishes a general scheme which distinguishes two levels of standard Arabic – فصحى – and three levels of فصحى التراث which he terms – فصحى العصر and فصحى

عامية and – which he terms عامية الإميين, عامية المتنوّرين colloquial Arabic عامية المثقّفين. Badawi describes his overall scheme in the following terms:

> This scheme distinguishes two levels of فصحى and three levels of
> عامية. The older of the two levels of فصحى, which may be termed
> فصحى التراث, is specifically the linguistic vehicle of the legacy of
> Islamic high culture and religion, while contemporary فصحى which
> may be termed فصحى العصر, is the vehicle of modern culture and
> technology. In Egypt, فصحى التراث varies only minimally from the
> classical descriptions of فصحى as might be expected in what is now
> in effect a liturgical language. فصحى العصر, on the other hand, as
> the vehicle of today's intellectual needs, exhibits features which
> contrast with the usual classical conventions – notably a marked
> preference for nominal, rather than verbal, sentences; moreover, when
> employed orally in Egypt, فصحى العصر displays other departures
> (phonological, morphological and syntactic) from the norms of فصحى
> التراث, and these departures for the most part occur in more
> pronounced forms in the various levels of عامية. ...
>
> Three levels of عامية can usefully be distinguished ... The mother
> tongue of any Egyptian child is one of only two of these, the principal
> distinction here being whether the family background of the child is
> characterized by literacy or illiteracy. By the time the child reaches
> school age, he will have acquired a type of mother tongue which can be
> broadly classified as the عامية either of the 'enlightened' (المتنوّرون)
> or of the illiterate (الأمّيون), the latter being predominant. If the child
> then goes to school, he is made to function not on his own linguistic
> level but on the level of فصحى العصر (in secular schools) or of
> فصحى التراث (within the Azhar الأزهر system). It is here, in
> respect of the individual – rather than in the broader frame of the
> totality of Egyptian language variation – that the phenomenon of
> diglossia can usefully be recognized and studied, for from this time the
> child advances (or fails to advance, as the case may be) simultaneously
> on two separate language levels, advance in one being linked with
> advance in the other. What may be regarded as a fruitful culmination of
> this process – in the form of mastery of the third, acquired, level of
> عامية, namely that the highly educated (المثقّفون) – is restricted to a
> small percentage of the population. This level of عامية is in effect the
> spoken counterpart of the written فصحى العصر and is used only in
> appropriate contexts of interaction between مثقّفون or would–be
> مثقّفون; their language in more mundane contexts is ordinarily عامية
> المتنورين, although some may also initially have been speakers of
> عامية الأميين. (Hinds and Badawi, 1986: viii–ix)

2. Additional reading

(a) Clive Holes, *Modern Arabic: Structures, Functions and Varieties* (London and New York: Longman, 1995), pp. 7–45.

3. Key vocabulary

On the basis of the texts in this chapter, draw up a list of Arabic grammatical terms: include terms such as رفع، نصب، جرّ: اسم، فعل، حرف. e.g. لحن 'grammatical mistake'.

4. Written Arabic texts 1

(a) Read the following text by طه حسين from من تاريخ الأدب العربي pp. 201–2, then complete exercises i. – iv. which follow.

فقد رأيت في الكتاب الثاني أنا نستعمل ألفاظ مضر وربيعة
وعدنان وقحطان وحمير لا نريد بها معانيها التي كان يفهمها
النسابون، وإنما هي ألفاظ شاعت: وألفها الناس فنحن
نستعملها ونريد بها المواطن الجغرافية فنحن لا نعرف عدنان
ولا قحطان ولا مضر ولا ربيعة، وإنما نعرف الحجاز ونجداً
واليمن والعراق، نعرف هذه المواطن التي كانت مستقر هؤلاء
العرب، ونعرف أن هذه اللغة القرشية كانت قبل الإسلام ظاهرة
في الحجاز ونجد. فإذا ذكرنا مضر فإنما نريد هؤلاء العرب
الذين كانوا يتكلمون هذه اللغة ويتخذونها مظهراً لحياتهم
الأدبية. ومن الذي يستطيع أن يزعم أنه يعرف اتصال
الرومانيين بأهل طروادة اتصالا تاريخيا صحيحا؟ ومع ذلك
فقد كان الرومانيون يزعمون أنهم هاجروا من طروادة إلى
إيطاليا. وقل مثل ذلك في كل هذه الأحاديث التي تنتحلها
الشعوب لتصل أنسابها بالشعوب القديمة، فقد زعم بعض
اليونان أنهم من سلالة الفينيقيين، وزعم بعضهم الآخر أنهم
من سلالة المصريين. ونحن الآن عرب من الوجهة الأدبية مهما
يكن نسبنا في حقيقة الأمر، لنكن متصلين بالمصريين القدماء
أو اليونان أو بالترك أو بمن شئت من الشعوب التي غزت

مصــر واستقـرت فيها . فذلك كلـه لا يغيـر حقيقـة علميـة واقـعة،
وهي أن لغتنـا هي اللغة العربيـة القرشيـة . لا نعـرف غيـرها لغـة
طبيـعيـة لنـا مـنذ قـرون .

i   Answer the following questions based on the above text in English.

1. According to the writer, how are the terms Mudar, Rabi'a, Adnan, Qahtan and Himyar now used?
2. Before Islam, where was the language of the Quraysh spoken?
3. What is meant when Mudar is mentioned?
4. What did the Romans use to claim?
5. What descent did some Greeks claim for themselves?
6. Why does the author claim that 'we are now Arabs from the cultural point of view whatever our lineage may be in reality'?

ii   Answer the following questions based on the above text in Arabic.

١ – ما هو المعنى الأصلي لألفاظ مضر وربيعة وعدنان وقحطان وحمير ؟
٢ – ماذا يعني العرب اليوم بألفاظ مضر وربيعة وعدنان وقحطان وحمير ؟
٣ – أين تكلم الناس اللغة القرشية قبل ظهور الإسلام ؟
٤ – من زعموا أنهم هاجروا من طروادة إلى إيطاليا ؟
٥ – أين طروادة ؟
٦ – من أين الفينيقيون ؟
٧ – ما هي الشعوب التي غزت مصر ؟
٨ – ما هي لغة المصريين الطبيعية اليوم ؟

iii Explain the meaning of the following words in Arabic.

1. ألفاظ (line 1)
2. نسابون (line 2)
3. مَوَاطن (line 3)
4. يزعَم (line 8)
5. هاجروا (line 10)
6. الأحاديث (line 11)
7. سلالة (line 12)

iv Translate the text into idiomatic English.

(b) Read the following text by عبد العزيز المقالح from شعر العامية في اليمن, (Beirut: دار العودة, 1978), p. 26, then answer the comprehension questions which follow.

ومن المفيد بعد هذا أن نعلم أن عرب عصور الازدهار الحضاري لم يكونوا كلهم يتكلمون الفصحى. فقد ظل الالتزام اللغوي مقصوراً على لغة الكتابة دون الحديث. وبقيت اللهجات الإقليمية في البوادي والحواضر تضيق بضوابط الإعراب وتميل إلى التخفف منها. فتحددت بذلك ملامح الازدواجية اللغوية. لقد صارت اللغة الفصيحة أداة الكاتب والشاعر. في حين بقيت اللهجة الدارجة لغة الحديث غير المكتوب. يستخدمها الناس في حياتهم اليومية دون التزام بالتركيب النحوي والصرفي. وكان التفاوت الاجتماعي والثقافي يزيد من شقة الخلاف بين اللغتين، ويضاعف حدة هذه الازدواجية اللغوية، حتى وصلت – أي الازدواجية اللغوية – إلى الكتابة الأدبية.

1. What period of Arab history is mentioned in this passage?
2. Why was it the case that not everyone spoke فصحى during this period?
3. Who came to use the classical language?
4. In what situations was the vernacular language used?
5. What served to increase the disparity between the two languages – classical and colloquial?

5. Written Arabic texts 2

(a) Read the following text, also by عبد العزيز المقالح from شعر العامية في اليمن, pp. 17–18, then complete exercises i. and ii. which follow.

واللغة العربية – أو لغة الضاد كما تدعى – واحدة من أقدم اللغات الإنسانية وأكثرها عراقة، وقد خضعت عبر تاريخها الطويل لما تخضع له كل لغة تحرص على أن تكون أداة للاتصال والتفكير والتأمل، فهي في الجاهلية غيرها في العصر

الإسلامي، غـيـرهـا في العـصـرين الأمـوي والعـبـاسـي، بـعـد أن
اتسعت لمفردات جديدة في المجالات الدينية والاجتماعية
والفنـيـة، وبـعـد أن أفـادت مـن مـجـازات القـرآن والحـديث ومـن
معجم المتصوفة ومصطلحات الفلسفة الإسلامـية، لقد تزودت
من ذلك كله بزاد رومي خـفف من خشـونة بـعض مـفـرداتـهـا
واستعاضت عن بـعض هذه المفردات بأخرى أيسـر نطقا وأكثر
جريانا على الألسنة. كما أضفت عليها أسبـاب الحضارة نعومة
ظهرت في شـعـر المحبين والغـزليين في حواضر الشام والـعـراق،
وفي بـوادي نجـد والحـجـاز، ثم التـوت بـهـا بـعـض الألسـنـة – كـمـا
يقولون – التواءً يسيرا أو كثيرا، فصدر عنها ذلك النوع من
الأشعار والأغاني الموسومة بالعامية.

والعـامـيـة اسم أو مـصـطـلح لغـوي لمسـتـوى مـعـيـن من الكلام
يصدر عن العامة – وهم الغالبية الساحقة من أي شعب – دونما
تقـيـد بـالقـواعـد النحـوية والصـرفـيـة، ودونما التـزام بضـوابط
الإعراب المتبعة في المستوى الرسمي أو الخاص من اللغة. وقد
اشـتـق هذا الاسـم من العـامـة أو العـوام ثم تحـول مـع الـزمـن إلى
دلالة اصطلاحية على المستوى اللغوي الذي يستخدمه العامة أو
الغـالبية العظمى من الناس. ولم يأخذ لفظ «العـامـيـة» شكل
اصطلاح علمي إلا في العصـر الحـديث حين ظهرت الجـامـعـات،
وصار تحديد مفهوم الألفاظ ودلالتها مهمة علمية.

i In Arabic, discuss orally what عبد العزيز المقالح considers to be the main differences between فصحى and عامية.

ii Translate the above text into idiomatic English.

(b) Read the following text by نوال السعداوي from امرأة عند نقطة الصفر, p. 19, then translate it into idiomatic English. Also give your opinion in English of the grammar of the phrase which ends the passage في البـحـر لم فتكم، في البـر فتوني.

ولم يكن عمي صغيراً. كان أكبر مني بسنين كثيرة، يسافر وحده
إلى مصر ويذهب إلى الأزهر ويتعلم، ولم أكن إلا طفلة لم تفك الخط
بعد. يضع عمي بين أصابعي قلم الرصاص ويجعلني أكتب فوق لوح
الاردواز: أ . ب . ج . د . ... وأحياناً يجعلني أردد وراءه: الألف لا
شيء عليها، والباء نقطة تحتها، والجيم نقطة وسطها، والدال لا
شيء عليها. ويهز رأسه وهو يتلو ألفية ابن مالك كما يتلو القرآن،
وأهز رأسي أنا الأخرى وراءه وأردد بالحرف الواحد ما يقول.

وتنتهي الإجازة ويركب عمي الحمارة وأحمل فوق رأسي
« السبت » الكبير مليئاً بالبيض والجبن والفطير ومن فوقه كتبه
وملابسه، وأسير وراءه حتى محطة قطار الدلتا. ويحدثني عمي
طوال الطريق عن حجرته في القلعة في نهاية شارع محمد علي،
والأزهر، والعتبة الخضراء، والترام، والناس في مصر، ويغني
بصوت عذب وهو يهتز فوق الحمارة: «في البحر لم فتكم، في
البر فتوني ».

(c) Read the following text by سعد الدين وهبة from the play سكة السلامة, pp.
8–9, then, as far as possible, paraphrase the colloquial elements in standard
Arabic.

(يرفع الستار والمسرح مضيء بضوء الغروب وخال
تماما. مقدمة موسيقية هادئة جدا لمدة دقيقتين. والمسرح
خال. تتوقف الموسيقى فُجاءة أي أن اللحن لا ينتهي
نهايته الطبيعية ثم يسمع صوت سيارة من الناحية
اليسرى للمسرح. يظهر من الصوت أن السيارة تسير في
طريق غير معبد. فحركة صعودها وهبوطها واضحة من
صوت السوست.

وصوت المارش واضح وواضح كذلك أنها سيارة كبيرة
.. يستمر الصوت مع خلو المسرح تماما. وفجاءة يسمع

صوت سقوط السيارة في حفرة ... ويختلط صوت
السقوط بصوت صراخ حاد .. وزعيق .. أصوات مختلفة ..
استغاثات وبكاء ..

وأثناء ذلك يندفع بعض الغبار إلى المسرح من
الناحية اليسرى مختلطا بدخان السيارة.

تسكن الأصوات. صوت نحيب ضعيف يأخذ في
الخفوت حتى يصمت تماما. تمر عدة ثوان وكل شيء صامت
والمسرح خال، وفجاءة يدخل من الناحية اليسرى ركاب
السيارة متتابعين على الوجه التالي:

يدخل الأستاذ فكري الصحفي ... وجهه ممتقع ... يعرج
وهو يسير ويحدث نفسه وهو يقطع المسرح ثم يجلس
على مكان مرتفع)،

فكري: آه ... آه يا جنبي ... يعني لو كنت مت دلوقت
ولا رحت في داهيه كان يبقى كويس ... آدى شورتك يا
استاذ عبد السميع ... شورتك المهببه ... آه ... آه ...

(يدخل العمدة الشيخ عثمان رافعا اصبعه إلى
السماء واضعا يده الاخرى على صدره.)

عثمان: يا لطيف ... يا لطيف ... يا لطيف الطف يا رب
يا رب ارفع مقتك وغضبك عنا يا رب ...

(يشاهد الصحفي فيتجه اليه ويقف قبالته)

عثمان: احنا فين يا ابني ... ؟ هه ... احنا فين ...

فكري: احنا فين؟؟ في الجنه ...

عثمان: الجنه؟ بسم الله الرحمن الرحيم ... جنه ايه يا
ابني الهى لا يسيئك ...

فكري: ودا سؤال تسأله يا حضرة ... ما انتاش شايف
احنا فين ؟

عثمان: ما انا شايف كل حاجه ... بس يعني الحته دي ...

الحته دي اسمها ايه؟

فكري: اسمها صحرا ... وبالنحوي صحراء ...

6. Written Arabic texts 3 (classical)

(a) Read the following text by القفطي from أنباه النجاة على أنباه الرواة, إنباه الرواة على أنباه النجاة
(Cairo, 1950), p. 4, then complete exercises i. and ii. which follow.

الجمهور من أهل الرواة على أنّ أولَ من وضع النحو أمير المؤمنين
عليّ بنُ أبي طالب كرم اللّه وجهه قال أبو الأسود الدُوَليّ رحمه
اللّه:

دخلت على أمير المؤمنين عليّ عليه السلام فرأيته مُطرقاً مفكّراً،
فقلت: فيمَ تفكّر يا أميـر المؤمنين؟ فقال: سمعت ببلدك لحناً،
فأردت أن أصنع كتاباً في أصول العربية. فقلت له: إن فعلتَ هذا
أبقيتَ فينا هذه اللغة العربية، ثم أتيتُه بعد أيام، فألقى إليّ
صحيفةً فيها:

«بسم اللّه الرحمن الرحيم. الكلام كلّه اسم وفعل وحرف[1]، فالاسم
ما أنبأ عن المسمّى، والفعل ما أنبأ عن حركة المسمّى، والحرف ما
أنبأ عن معنى ليس باسم ولا فعل».

Note

1. Traditional Arabic grammar recognises only three parts of speech: nouns (which
   includes what are from an English point of view both nouns and adjectives),
   verbs, and 'particles' (this last category covering everything which is not a
   noun or a verb).

i   Make a note of the epithets used in this text.
ii Translate the text into idiomatic English.

(b) Translate the following text by أبو الفرج الإسفهاني from كتاب الأغاني, vol.
XII, (Cairo, 1950), p. 298, into idiomatic English.

إنّ أبا الأسود الدوَلي دخل إلى ابنته بالبصرة فقالت له: يا أبت ما
أشدُّ الحرّ! (رَفَعتْ أشدّ) فظنّها تسأله وتستفهم منه: أيُّ زمان الحرّ

أشدُّ؟ فقال لها: شهر ناجر، (يريد شهر صفر. الجاهلية كانت تسمى شهور السنة بهذه الأسماء). فقالت: يا أبتِ إنما أخبرتك ولم أسألك. فأتى أمير المؤمنين عليُّ بن أبي طالب عليه السلام فقال: يا أمير المؤمنين، ذهبتْ لغة العرب لمّا خالطت العَجَم، وأوشك إن تطاولَ عليها زمان أن تضمحلَّ، فقال له: وما ذلك؟ فأخبره خبر ابنته، فأمره فاشترى صحفاً بدرهم، وأملّ عليه: الكلام كله لا يخرج عن اسم وفعل وحرف جاء لمعنى. (وهذا القول أول كتاب سيبويه[1])، ثم رسم أصول النحو كلّها، فنقلها النحويّون وفرّعوها. قال أبو الفرج الأصبهاني: هذا حفظته عن أبي جعفر وأنا حديث السنّ، فكتبتُه من حِفْظي، واللفظ يزيد وينقص وهذا معناه.

Note

1. سيبويه أبو بشر عمرو ابن قنبر was of Persian stock and is the first Arab grammarian whose work is extant. His book, كتاب سيبويه, is perhaps the most well known and most frequently cited work on Arabic grammar.

7. Grammar/stylistics

(a) تمييز

The accusative case is often used for تمييز 'specification'. When used in this way it can be glossed as 'in regard to', 'as', or 'in terms of'. The accusative of specification occurs after a verb or an elative and serves to delimit or specify the scope of that verb or elative. It is frequently used after the elative أكثر 'more' when the following noun cannot be made into an elative to give the sense of 'more *in terms of* …' or 'more *with regard to* …', as in:

تعتبر من أعقد المشاكل الاجتماعية، وأكثرها {تشابكا} مع غيرها من مشاكل الواقع الاقتصادي والاجتماعي.

'It is [considered] one of the most complicated social problems and one of the most intrinsically bound up with other economic and social problems.' (ch. 9, 4c)

واستعاضت عن بعض هذه المفردات بأخرى أيسر نطقا وأكثر {جريانا على الألسنة}.

'Some of these words were replaced by others [which were] easier to pronounce and more fluid on the tongue.' (ch. 5, 5a)

واحدة من أقدم اللغات الإنسانية وأكثرها {عراقة}.
'One of the oldest human languages and one of the most deep rooted.'
(ch. 5, 5a)

The accusative of specification is used after other elatives when the speaker wants
to say 'more X in terms of Y', as in:

واستعاضت عن بعض هذه المفردات بأخرى {أيسر نطقا} وأكثر
جريانا على الألسنة.
'Some of these words were replaced by others [which were] easier to
pronounce [i.e. more easy in terms of pronunciation] and more fluid on
the tongue.' (ch. 5, 5a)

Examples of the accusative of specification preceded by a verb include:

خاصة وأن الحياة تزداد {صعوبة} بالنسبة للأمي.
'Especially since life is more difficult [i.e. increases in terms of
difficulty] for the illiterate.' (ch. 10, 4c)

والنبط من جانب الجزيرة والموصل ما لا يُحصى {كثرة وتنوعا في
العصبية}.
'The Nabateans from the Peninsula and Mosul are innumerable in terms
of number and type of tribal group.' (ch. 6, 6a)

'Zayd is cheerful in [terms of] spirit.' (Wright II: 122) .طاب زيدٌ نفسًا

طاب الوردُ لونًا.
'The flower is charming in [terms of] colour.' (Wright II: 122)

In this last example, the noun لونا limits the application of the verb طاب to colour.
We can see that it would not be contradictory to say that the flower was charming
in colour but not, for example, in shape.

(b) غَيْر
A very common word in Arabic is the word غَيْر which is used both as a noun and
as a preposition. In the first instance we shall consider its use as a noun. As a noun
غَيْر can be used singly preceded by ليس or لا generally at the end of a sentence to
mean 'nothing else' or 'only this', and in this sense functions as a synonym to
حسب or فحسب. غير can also be used singly preceded by the definite article, as
in الغير to mean 'the others', 'neighbours' or 'fellow men' (cf. Wehr). However,
it is more commonly used as the first term of an *idafa* phrase in which the genitive
term can be either an adjective or a noun. In an *idafa* phrase it usually means 'other

than', 'differing from' or 'opposite to' the object or objects expressed by the genitive. Where the genitive is an adjective, غير can also be glossed as 'non–', 'un–' or 'in–'. Insofar as غير is most commonly used as the first term in an *idafa* phrase it is similar to the nouns شبه and مثل which often translate as 'semi–' and 'like' respectively. (For other common first terms of *idafa*s cf. Wright II: 210–11) Examples of غير as the first term in an *idafa* phrase include:

i غير + *indefinite adjective*
غير + indefinite adjective is often used as the predicate of a sentence, as in the first two examples below. As in other subject–predicate structures, the indefinite adjective following غير agrees with the subject in number and gender:

وهكذا نرى أنّ علي بن زايد {غير معروف الجد والبيت ولا المولد} أيضا.

'Thus we see that it is not known who Ali ibn Zayid's grandfather was, nor what his tribe was [بيت = 'tribe' here], nor where he was born.' (ch. 11, 11)

و٤٨٦ التجهيزات المكتبية {غير متوفرة}.

'486 pieces of office equipment is insufficient.' (ch. 9, 5b)

غير + indefinite adjective is also used as the attribute to an indefinite noun. Where a غير + adjective construction functions as an attribute the adjective following غير agrees with the noun in definiteness, number and gender (just as it would were it not preceded by غير). Consider the following two examples:

والأمطار الغزيرة في هذا الشتاء على نحو {غير مألوف}.

'The torrential rains this winter [fall] in an unaccustomed manner.' (ch. 8, 11)

يظهر من الصوت أن السيارة تسير في طريق {غير معبد}.

'It appears from the noise that the car was travelling along an unpaved road.' (ch. 5, 5c)

ii غير + *definite adjective*
Where غير + adjective functions as an attribute to a definite noun the adjective following غير is definite, as in:

في حين بقيت اللهجة الدارجة لغة الحديث {غير المكتوب}.

'While the colloquial language remained the language of unwritten speech.' (ch. 5, 4b)

iii غير + *pronoun*

غير + pronoun is often used in the sense of 'others' or 'other', where the pronoun refers back to a (usually immediately) preceding noun, as in:

وأشار على والدي أن يضم إليها {غيرها}.

'He suggested to my father that he add others to them.' (ch. 11, 6a)

منذ أيام الإمام محمد عبده وجمال الدين الأفغاني و{غيرهما} ...

'From the days of the Imam Muhammad Abdu, Jamal al-Din al-Afghani and others...' (ch. 10, 5a)

هذه الأسئلة و{غيرها} ما تزال محل بحث الحكومة المصرية.

'These and other [related] questions remain a subject of discussion for the Egyptian government.' (ch. 9, 4c)

إلا أنها لم تستطع استخدام طائرة الهليكوبتر و{غيرها} منذ أغسطس في العام الماضي.

'... however, she [Iraq] had been unable to use helicopters and the like from August last year.' (ch. 8, 11)

... أو أنه شخصيات متعددة نسبت إليه أقوال {غيره}.

'... or that he was several personalities and the sayings of others were attributed to him.' (ch. 11, 11)

وهي أن لغتنا هي اللغة العربية القرشية. لا نعرف {غيرها} لغةً طبيعةً لنا منذ قرون.

'... and this is that our language is the Arabic language of the Quraysh. We have known no other as a natural language for centuries.' (ch. 5, 4a)

غير + pronoun can also be used in the sense of 'not the same as' or 'different from', as in:

فهي في الجاهلية {غيرها} في العصر الإسلامي و{غيرها} في العصرين الأموي والعباسي.

'In the Jahiliyya era it was not the same as in Islamic times, and it was different in the Umayyad era from in the Abbasid era.' (ch. 5, 5a)

غير + pronoun is frequently followed by من + definite plural noun. In this case, it usually means 'other' things expressed by the noun following من. Examples include:

ونتيجة لهذا التلوث تكثر الإصابة بالكوليرا والتيفود و{غيرهما
من الأمراض المتوطئة في القارة}.

'As a result of this pollution there has been a rise in the number of
instances of cholera and typhoid and other diseases indigenous to the
continent.' (ch. 9, 4a)

... وأكثرها تشابكا مع {غيرها من مشاكل الواقع الاقتصادي
والاجتماعي}.

'... and the most bound up with other economic and social problems.'
(ch. 9, 4c)

Also consider the following example where an *in*definite noun phrase follows the
preposition من:

إلى جانب الحق في التعليم و{غير ذلك من حقوق لم تحظ بها المرأة
في كثير من المجتمعات العالمية المعاصرة}.

'Apart from the right to education and other rights which women do not
enjoy in many societies in the world today.' (ch. 10, 4b)

iv غير + *noun*
Less commonly غير takes a *noun* in the genitive followed by من + (usually)
definite noun. This construction is sometimes translated as '[quite] apart from', as
in:

... {غير مئات الألوف من الأطفال العاملين في الريف}.

'... quite apart from the hundreds of thousands of children working in
the countryside.' (ch. 9, 4c)

Preceded by a negative verb phrase غير can be translated as 'only', as in:

وليس بجميع مكة شجر مثمر {غير شجر البادية}.

'In the whole of Mekka the only fruitful tree is the tree of the steppe.'
(ch. 8, 6b)

v بغَير *and* من غير
As the object of the prepositions ب and من, غير is translated as 'without' and
functions as a synonym of بدون. Consider the following example:

ليس من المستحب أن تأكل العسل {بغير خبز}.

'It is not right for you to eat honey without bread.' (ch. 11, 4b)

vi غير *as a preposition*

غير can also function as a preposition (cf. Wehr). In this case it is followed by a clause beginning with أنّ, and usually translates as 'however'. Consider the following examples:

{غير} أنّ العاقل لا ينقط من منافع الرأي.

'However, the intelligent person does not despair of the benefits of opinion.' (ch. 11, 6b)

وأتمت الحكومة سدودا ترابية مماثلة في يوليو الماضي على طول الأنهر التي تغذي أهوار الحويزة ... {غير} أنّ تأثير هذه السدود محدودا تماما.

'The government completed similar mud dams last July along the length of the rivers which fed the marshes of Huwayza ... however, the effect of these dams was very limited.' (ch. 8, 11)

(c) *Tense subordination in Arabic*

In main clauses in Arabic the time reference of the verb or verbal participle is relative to the moment of utterance:

يرفع الستار والمسرح مضيء بضوء الغروب.

'The curtain opens and the stage is lit with the light of sunset.' (ch. 5, 5c)

ولم يكن عمي صغيرا. كان أكبر مني بسنين كثيرة.

'My uncle was not young. He was several years older than me.' (ch. 5, 5b)

In subordinate clauses, however, the past, present or future reference of a verb is relative to the moment to which the verb in the main clause applies. Thus the bracketed imperfect verbs in the following sentences have a past time reference because of the time reference of the initial perfect verb:

ظنّها {تسأله} و{تستفهم} منه.

'He thought she was asking him and enquiring of him.' (ch. 5, 6b)

كان أكبر مني بسنين كثيرة، {يسافر} وحده إلى مصر و{يذهب} إلى الأزهر و{يتعلم}.

'He was several years older than me, and used to travel on his own to Cairo and go to Al-Azhar and learn.' (ch. 5, 5b)

فيما أكد مسؤولون أردنيون وفلسطينيون أن إسرائيل {تعمد} إلى تهجير مئات من النساء والأطفال إلى الأردن.

'While Jordanian and Palestinian officials confirmed that Israel was intending to deport hundreds of women and children.' (ch. 6, 4b)

When a subordinated verb is in the perfect aspect the past reference of the subordinated verb again is relative to the moment to which the verb in the main clause applies and is translated by the English *plu*perfect when the main verb is in the perfect, as in:

وأفادت مصادر فلسطينية أن سبعة فلسطينيين {أصيبوا} أمس برصاص الإسرائيليين.

'Palestinian sources said that seven Palestinians had been shot yesterday by the Israelis.' (ch. 6, 4b)

And by the future past when the main verb is in the imperfect:

'He will have gone.'   يكون قد {سافر}.

In some writing, particularly modern literary prose, initial كان can be followed by several sentences or even paragraphs in which the time reference of the (usually) imperfect verb is subordinated to the initial verb. For an example of this see ch. 5, 5b from line 2, and other works by نوال السعداوي. When translating into English the habitual or continuous aspect of the imperfect verb is maintained but the tense is translated as past. For further discussion of tense subordination in Arabic with particular reference to Yemeni Arabic see (Watson 1993: 85–91).

8. Aural Arabic texts 1

Listen to the aural text from حصاد الشهر, no. 36, side 2, item 6, أصول اللهجات العربية then complete exercises i. – iii. below. You may find it useful to read through the comprehension questions before listening to the text.

i Answer the following questions in English.

1. What is the standard Arabic meaning of وبس؟
2. Dialects of Arabic are said to have arisen from a linguistic conflict between Arabic and which other language/s?
3. The dialect of which country is taken as an example in this passage?
4. When was Arabic introduced into this country?
5. Which were the predominant languages in the country at that time?
6. Which language was the official language of the ruler?
7. Which language came to be restricted to the church and Christian families?

8.   When did elements of Turkish enter this dialect?
9.   Elements of which other languages entered this dialect at a later stage?
10. Who is said to speak عامية قاع المجتمع؟

ii Fill in the gaps in the text below.

نشــأت _____ _____ المحليــة المعروفــة باسم _____ _____ فــي البـلاد

العـربيــة المخـتـلفــة نتـيـجــةً للصــراع اللـغـوي بـين اللغـة العـربيــة

لـهـذه _____ _____ _____ _____ _____

_____ من ناحية واللغات التي كانت _____ _____ فيها في

ذلك _____ _____ من _____ _____ كـالـرومـي أي

الـيـونـانيــة أو الـرومــانيــة الـقـديمة و _____ و _____ والـقـبـطيــة

و _____ والرومـانثيـة المتطورة عن اللاتينيـة. وهكذا، وإذا

أخذنا _____ _____ _____ لما نقول فسنجد أن _____

_____ _____ _____ العربيـة _____ مع _____

_____ _____ _____ أحدث صراعًا _____ _____ بـينـها وبـين

_____ _____ الرئـيـسـيـتين _____ _____ وهمـا _____

_____ _____ _____ و _____ _____ التي هـي

امـتـداد للغـات _____ _____ القـديمة. وهي لغـة _____

والكنـيـسـة. وهكذا _____ _____ خليط _____ _____ يضمّ

_____ _____ وتـراكـيـب و _____ _____ من _____

_____ _____ والـرومـانيــة والقـبطيــة يسـتـعـمـله

_____ _____ بنسب متفاوتة _____ بدأ سُلّم _____

في الصـعود على المستوى _____ _____ وانحصار سُلّم _____

و _____ التي أصبحت مقـصورة على _____ _____ وبـعض

الأسر المسيحية المحافظة على التمسك بها.

ثم أُتيح لهذه ———— ———— ———— المزيدُ من التفاعل

والاحتكاك والثراء والغنى من ———— ———— ————

———— ———— وافدة على مصر أهمها ———— من

خلال السيطرة ———— لعدة ———— ثم ————

التي حملها المماليك المجلوبون إلى ———— من بلاد وسط

آسيا فاللغة الفرنسية ———— فالإيطالية. وعبر التركية

———— ———— الفارسية التي انتقلت

أولا إلى التركية، وأصبحت ———— ———— في مصر

الآن مزيجاً من هذا كله ———— أن نحلله وأن نردّه إلى

عناصره الأولية ———— ———— ————

———— وأن ———— فيه ———— ———— من

———— نسباً متباينة من ———— ———— الأخرى،

وهذا هو ما يُفسّر لنا وجود ———— في ————

———— مثل « أورمة » و « ———— » و « ———— » و « أسطة »

و « ———— » و « أجزخانة » و « ———— » و « ———— » و « ————»

و « بنسوار » و « ———— » و « نجريت » و « هنسبول » و « جورن »

و « ماجور » و « ———— » و « تليس » و « أليت » و « ————»

و « ———— » و « ———— » و « شفخانا » و « ضلمه »

و « سبداك » و « زيّك » و « ———— » و « ———— » وغيرها

من ألوف ———— التي تتردد ———— على ————

ـــــــ . ويبقى أن نُشير إلى ـــــــ ـــــــ ـــــــ ـــــــ في

هذا المجال وهي أنه ـــــــ ـــــــ كـان المتكلم على درجـة من

ـــــــ و ـــــــ ـــــــ كلما شاعت في ـــــــ ـــــــ أي لغته

في الحديث اليومي نسبة أكبر من ـــــــ ـــــــ ـــــــ

ـــــــ ، وكلما حُرم هذا ـــــــ ـــــــ من التعليم والثقافة

ـــــــ ـــــــ ـــــــ كانت ـــــــ تماماً عن التأثر

ـــــــ ـــــــ وانطبق عليها ما يُسمّى بعامية

ـــــــ ـــــــ أو ـــــــ قاع المجتمع .

iii Translate the first paragraph of the above text into idiomatic English.

9. Aural Arabic texts 2

(a) As a preparatory exercise for aural Arabic text 2, read the following short text from مجلة الشرق الأوسط, Feb. 3, 1993 at home.

لعلّ أبرز التأثيرات المعاصرة للتاريخ الاسلامي الأندلسي في إسبانيا هي تلك الكلمات ذات الأصول العربية التي يتحدّث بها المواطن الإسباني يومياً، وتعيش مع حياته العادية وممارساته في عمليات البيع والشراء بعد أن صارت جزءًا مهمًا من ثقافته، فالخبراء يقدّرون نسبة الكلمات ذات الأصول العربية بما يزيد عن عشرة بالمائة من مجموع اللغة الإسبانية المعاصرة .

(b) Listen to the following aural text from حصاد الشهر, no. 5, side 1, item 7, كلمات عربية في اللغة الإسبانية, then fill in the gaps in the text below.

الأندلس: ـــــــ ـــــــ ـــــــ أن سماع اسمها يدغدغ

ـــــــ ـــــــ ـــــــ بعظمة ـــــــ

أسلافـه. ولا تقتصـر ———— ———— ———— فـيـها على

———— المعماري بل تشمل ———— ———— ————

———— . فوجود ———— ———— ———— من

———— ما يزال ماثلاً، ———— في اللغة ———— بل

———— في أسـمـاء ———— و ————

و———— . وقـد أكـد ذلك في ———— « ————

———— ———— » جرير أبو حيدر فحلّل

لمستمعي ———— ———— أسماء كثيرة من بينها ————

———— يمرّ ———— قرطبة ————

اشبيلية ويجعل من الأخيرة ميناء ———— ———— ————

———— Guadalquivir والاسم ———— ———— من

———— ———— ———— هما على ———— «وادي» أو

«الوادي» و«الكبيـر». وهكذا يكون ———— ————

———— «الوادي الكبير». و———— «وادي» هذه ما تزال

———— في أسماء ———— ———— و ————

في ———— ، فهناك ———— في إسبانيا ————

بـاسـم Guadalajara و———— تُعـرف بنفس

———— . وهذا ———— بدوره ————

في ———— هما «واد» أو «وادي الحجارة». و————

يجـدر بنا أن ———— ———— أن ————

———— بين مدن المكسيك في أميركا الوسطى ————

_____ _____ _____ Guadalajara.

و _____ _____ _____ _____ من _____ التي يمكن أن نستدلّ

على _____ _____ _____ في اللغة الإسبانية لأنها تبتدئ

_____ وهي al _____ « الـ _____ » _____

_____ . ومن هذه _____ على _____ المثل almacen

_____ من _____ « مخزن » _____ . وهذه كلمة

_____ _____ طريقها _____ _____

_____ أيضًا في _____ magasin التي تعني

« _____ » كما نجد _____ لها في _____

_____ _____ في فعل immagazzinari

_____ « خَزَنَ » أو « _____ » . و _____ alferez وهي رتبة

_____ _____ _____ في _____ الإسباني

كلمة « الفارس » العربية . و _____ _____ الذي أدخله

_____ _____ في _____ كما يبدو إلى إسبانيا

_____ algodon . والزيت و _____ في اللغة الأسبانية

_____ aceitunas أو aceituna و aceite على التوالي

_____ الإسبان _____ وإنْ تكن _____

_____ _____ _____ مأخوذة من _____ لاتيني وهي

كلمة oliva أو olivas . و _____ أن الكلمات الإسبانية من

_____ _____ فإن تُعدّ _____

قد سقط _____ من الاستعمال وإن كانت

ـــــــــــ ما تزال تُثبِته وتُشير إلى مصدره.

10. Written English texts

Making use of constructions encountered in the Arabic texts above, as far as possible, translate the following text from Richard Hudson, *Sociolinguistics,* (Cambridge University Press, 1980), p. 54, into idiomatic Arabic.

> In an Arabic–speaking diglossic community, the language used at home is a local version of Arabic (there may be very great differences between one 'dialect' of Arabic and another, to the point of mutual incomprehensibility), with little variation between the most educated and least educated speakers. However, if someone needs to give a lecture at a university, or a sermon in a mosque, he is expected to use Standard Arabic, a variety different at all levels from the local vernacular, and felt to be so different from the vernacular that it is taught in schools in the way that foreign languages are taught in English–speaking societies. Likewise, when children learn to read and write, it is the standard language, and not the local vernacular, which they are taught.

11. Précis

(a) Listen to كلمـات عـربيـة فـي اللغـة الإسبانيـة (section 9 above) again, then produce a written précis in Arabic.

(b) Read the following text by the Lebanese writer ميـخـائـيل نعيمة, then produce a written précis in Arabic.

الرواية التمثيلية العربية

لكن أكبر عقبة صادفتها في تأليف «الآباء والبنين» – وسيصادفها كل مـن طرق هـذا البـاب سـواي – هـي اللغـة العـاميـة والمقـام الذي يـجب أن تـعطـاه فـي مــــثل هـذه الروايـات. فـي عــــرفـي – وأظنّ الكثيــرين يوافـقـونني على ذلك – أن أشخـاص الروايـة يـجب أن يخـاطبـونا باللغـة التـي تعـودوا أن يعبـروا بهـا عن عـواطفـهم وأفكارهم وأن الكاتب الذي يحـاول أن يجعل فلاحا أمّيا يتكلم بلغة الدواويـن الشعريـة والمؤلفـات اللغـويـة يظلم فلاحـه ونفسـه وقارئـه وسـامـعـه، لا بل يظـهر أشخـاصـه في مظهر الهـزل حيث لا يقصد الهـزل، ويقتـرف جرمـا ضد فنّ جمـالـه في تصـويـر الإنسان حسبـما نراه في مـشاهد الحيـاة الحقيقيـة. هناك أمـر آخـر جدير بالاهتمام

متعلق باللغة العامية - وهو أن هذه اللغة تستر تحت ثوبها الخشن كثيرا من فلسفة الشعب واختباراته في الحياة، وأمثاله واعتقاداته التي لو حاولت أن تؤديها بلغة فصيحة لكنت كمن يترجم أشعارا وأمثالا عن لغة أعجمية. وربما خالفنا في ذلك بعض الذين تأبطوا القواميس وتسلّحوا بكتب الصرف والنحو كلها قائلين: إن «كل الصيد في جوف الفرا»، وأن لا بلاغة أو فصاحة أو طلاوة في اللغة العامية لا يستطيع الكاتب أن يأتي بمثلها بلغة فصحى. فلهؤلاء ننصح أن يدوسوا حياة الشعب ولغته بإمعان وتدقيق.

الرواية التمثيلية، من بين كل الأساليب الأدبية، لا تستطيع أن تستغني عن اللغة العامية. إنما «العقدة» هي أننا لو اتبعنا هذه القاعدة لوجب أن نكتب كل رواياتنا باللغة العامية، إذ ليس بيننا من يتكلم عربية الجاهلية أو العصور الإسلامية الأولى. وذلك يعني انقراض لغتنا الفصحى. ونحن بعيدون عن أن نبتغي هذه الملمة القومية. فأين المخرج؟

عبثا بحثتُ عن حل لهذا المشكل، فهو أكبر من أن يحله عقل واحد. وجلّ ما توصلت إليه بعد التفكير هو أن أجعل المتعلمين من أشخاص روايتي يتكلمون لغة معربة. والأميين اللغة العامية. لكني أعترف بإخلاص أن هذا الأسلوب لا يحل «العقدة» الأساسية. فالمسألة لا تزال بحاجة إلى اعتناء أكبر رجال اللغة وكتّابها.

12. Oral

(a) Preparatory oral exercises: Re–read the passage by نوال السعداوي and سعد الدين وهبه above (section 5), and discuss i. and ii. below in Arabic.

i Why has نوال السعداوي placed the two expressions, which we have highlighted in **bold**, in brackets (قَوس dual قوسان)?

ii Comment on سعد الدين وهبه's use of language as illustrated in the passage from سكة السلامة.

(b) الفصحى والعامية

i One or two students to present a brief account in Arabic of the usage differences between standard and colloquial.

ii The presenter(s) then ask(s) the other students questions about standard versus colloquial Arabic. The questions should require both factual and subjective answers. For example:

١ – في أي مناسبات تستعمل الفصحى عادة؟

٢ – في أي مناسبات تستعمل العامية عادة؟

٣ – هل يستخدم الكاتب العامية، ولماذا؟

٤ – ما هي أهم الفروق النحوية بين الفصحى والعامية؟

٥ – ما هي اللهجة العربية المحبوبة لك؟

٦ – لماذا تُفضل هذه اللهجة على غيرها من اللهجات؟

٧ – هل هناك اختلافات كثيرة بين اللهجات العربية الحديثة؟

٨ – ما هي الكلمات الأصلية في اللهجة المصرية (اليمنية، المغربية) في
معنى « أراد »، « نقود »، « ذَهَبَ »، « نعم »، « لا »، « ليس »؟

(c) Open lecturer–led discussion on the usage of standard versus colloquial Arabic, and on differences between Arabic dialects spoken in the Middle East.

13. Essay
Write an essay in Arabic of around 200 words on the title الفصحى والعامية. In writing your essay address the following questions:

١ – ما هي مظاهر الفصحى اللغوية؟

٢ – في أي مناسبات تُستخدم الفصحى؟

٣ – ما هي مظاهر العامية اللغوية الرئيسية؟

٤ – متى تُستخدم العامية؟

٥ – هل تُستعمل العامية كتابةً، ولماذا؟

6
The Arab–Israeli conflict

1. Basic background material

Chronology of the Arab–Israeli dispute.

pre–1881   Palestine mainly Arab and Muslim with some Christians and small Jewish community (approximately 24,000 out of total population of 500,000).

1881–1903   Beginning of Russian pogroms against Jews. First wave of Jewish immigration to Palestine.

1896   Publication of Theodor Herzl's *The State of the Jews*, advocating the establishment of a Jewish state in Palestine.

1897   First Zionist congress meets at Basel, Switzerland. Demands establishment of Jewish state in Palestine.

1914–1918   World War I.

1917   Balfour Declaration in which the British government declares itself favourable towards the establishment of national home for Jews in Palestine, on condition that this should not harm the civil and religious rights of existing non–Jewish communities in Palestine.

1922   Beginning of British mandate in Palestine.

1933   Hitler comes to power in Germany. Persecution of Jews in Germany and other states in central Europe greatly increases Jewish emigration to Palestine.

1936–1939   First Arab revolt (*intifada*).

1939–1945   World War II. Nazis murder vast majority of Jews (c. 6,000,000 people) in areas under their control.

1947   UN General Assembly Resolution 181 on partition of Palestine proposes Jewish state in almost all areas of Palestine with significant Jewish populations; accepted by Zionists, rejected by Palestinians and Arab states.

1948–1949   Internal war in Palestine followed by internal and international war after Israel declares independence. Approximately 750,000 Palestinians displaced.

1948–1958   Massive Jewish immigration to Israel from Europe, North Africa and Asia. Jews leave Arab countries – in some cases forced out by governmental or popular hostility, or both – as opposition to Zionism gives rise to anti–Jewish sentiment in Arab world.

1956   Suez War. Israel with British and French support attacks Egypt. UN, under American leadership, forces subsequent removal of British and French troops from Egyptian soil, and pull–back of Israelis.

1964   Establishment of Palestine Liberation Organisation (PLO).

1967   June War. Israel launches lightning strike against Arab states, occupying Sinai, Gaza Strip, Golan Heights and West Bank. UN Security Resolution 242 calling on Israel to withdraw from occupied territories in exchange for peace with Arab states. Israel begins moving Jewish settlers into areas occupied during war.

1970   Jordanian civil war between government forces and Palestinians. Palestinian forces defeated. Palestinian political and military groupings move to Lebanon.

1971   'Pacification' of Gaza by Ariel Sharon.

1973   October War. Egypt and Syria attack Israel to regain territories lost in 1967, with limited success for Egyptians. Non–Aligned Movement recognises PLO as representative of the Palestinian people.

1974   Arafat addresses UN. PLO granted observor status at UN.

1975   Civil war in Lebanon, in which Palestinians are involved on side of Muslim–based groups against Maronite Christians.

1976   Pro–PLO candidates sweep municipal elections in West Bank. Israel subsequently annuls results.

1977   Right–wing Likud grouping wins Israeli elections. Menachem Begin becomes PM. Sadat visits Jerusalem and addresses Knesset.

1978   Israeli invasion of South Lebanon in attempt to destroy PLO political and miltitary base. Begin, Sadat and Carter sign Camp David Accords.

1979   Begin and Sadat sign Israeli–Egyptian Peace Treaty in Washington, DC.

1980   Israel officially annexes all of East Jerusalem. UN Security Council condemns action.

1981   Israeli attack against Iraqi nuclear reactor. Israeli annexation of Golan Heights.

1982   Massive Palestinian protests against civil administration. Israel completes evacuation of Sinai. Israeli invasion of Lebanon in second attempt to destroy Palestinian political and military base. Massacre of 1,000 civilians at Sabra and Shatilla Palestinian refugee camps in Beirut by Lebanese Christian militiamen, invited in to 'clean up' camps by Israeli army.

1984   Early Israeli election creates Labour–Likud Unity goverment.

1985   Israeli withdrawal from most of Lebanon. Israel bombs Tunisian headquarters of PLO.

Dec. 1987   Beginning of Palestinian popular uprising *(intifada)* against Israeli occupation.

1989   Shamir plan calling for limited Palestinian elections. International peace demonstration in Jerusalem. Start of increased Jewish emigration from Soviet Union to Israel.

Aug. 1990   Iraq invades Kuwait.

1991   US–led coalition defeats Iraq. International Arab–Israeli peace conference in Madrid.

1992   Labour party wins plurality in Israeli elections. Yitzhak Rabin becomes PM.

1993   Israel and PLO sign Oslo Accords on interim self–government arrangements. Early Palestinian enthusiasm gives way to popular disillusion as Israel greatly increases Jewish settlement in East Jerusalem and West Bank in what Palestinians regard as violation of Oslo Accords.

1994   Massacre of Palestinians in Hebron by Israeli settler damages peace process. Militant Islamist groups switch from attacking Israeli military targets to suicide attacks against Israeli civilians. Palestinian police force arrives in Jericho and Gaza Strip.

1996   Right–wing coalition government brought to power in Israel, stating that it will not be bound by agreement signed between previous Israeli government and PLO. Recommences settlement on massive scale in Jerusalem and West Bank (with settler population 200,000 in East Jerusalem and 150,000 in West Bank by 1996). Attempt to decisively alter demography in occupied territories (with settler population of 350,000 planned over next five years in West Bank). Intention to expand Israeli control, enclosing Palestinians within fragments of territory, and thwarting attempts to establish Palestinian state. Increasing support among Palestinians for militant Islamist groups, with continuing suicide attacks, and concomitant growth in support for extremist policies towards Palestinians amongst Israelis.

2. Additional reading

(a) Peter Sluglett and Marion Farouk–Sluglett (eds.), *The Times Guide to the Middle East: The Arab World and its Neighbours,* (London: Times Books, 1993), pp. 108–27; pp. 209–24; pp. 307–9.

(b) Hourani, *A History of the Arab Peoples,* pp. 288–9; pp. 315–32; pp. 358–69; pp. 411–21; pp. 426–33; p.477.

(c) Maxime Rodinson, *Israel and the Arabs,* (New York: Penguin Books, 1982).

3. Key vocabulary

On the basis of the texts in this chapter, draw up lists of vocabulary in the following fields:

(a) Emigration, etc.

(b) Nationalism (Zionism/Palestinians).

(c) Violence/demonstrations.

(d) Negotiations

4. Written Arabic texts 1

(a) Read the following definition of انتفاضة from المعجم العربي الأساسي (Larousse Dictionary), 1989, p. 1217.

انتفاضة: ... حـركـة فـيـهـا قـوة وسـرعـة وهيـجـان
«انتفاضة الشعب» «انتفاضة العمّال».

(b) Read the following newspaper text from النهار Jan. 25, 1990, then answer the questions which follow in Arabic.

قتيل و١٨ جريحاً في الضفة والقطاع
وإسرائيل تبعد النساء والأطفال

قتل الجنود الإسرائيليون فلسطينيا وجرحوا ١٨ في مواجهات مخـتلفة في الضـفـة الـغـربيـة وقطاع غـزة المحتلين في اليـومين الأخـيـرين، فـيـمـا أكد مـسؤولون أردنيـون وفلسطينيـون أن إسرائيل تعمـد إلى تهجيـر مئـات من النسـاء والأطفـال إلى الأردن.

وأفادت مصادر فلسطينية أن سبعة فلسطينيين أصيبوا أمس برصاص الإسرائيليين في مـواجهـات متـفرقـة في قطاع غـزة، بعـدما كان ثمـانيـة أصـيبـوا أول من أمس بينهم أربـعـة تراوح أعمارهم بين ١٣ و١٥ عاما. كذلك جرح فتى في السابعة فـي مخـيم عسكر في الضفـة الـغربيـة وأصيب شابان بالرصاص أيضا.

وقتل الجنود الإسرائيليون أول من أمس موسى سعيد (٢٤ عـامـا) بسـبع رصـاصـات في مطـاردة بحـثـا عن مناضلين

فلسطينيين في نابلس. وأوضحت مصادر فلسطينية أن
سعيد كان ينتمي إلى «القوات الضاربة». وقالت مصادر
عسكرية إسرائيلية إن الجنود أمره بالوقوف ولما لم يمتثل
أطلقوا الرصاص في الهواء قبل أن يوجهوه إليه.

وفي بلدة عرابة شمال الضفة عثر على جثة الفلسطيني
أحمد سعد الله موسى (٢٨ عاما) داخل منزله. وقال السكان إنه
قضى بطعنات سكين لـ«تعاونه» مع الإسرائيليين.

١ -   كم عدد القتلى في المواجهات؟

٢ -   كم عدد الجرحى؟

٣ -   متى حدثت المواجهات؟

٤ -   إلى أين تريد إسرائيل أن تهجّر الأطفال والنساء حسب قول الأردنيين؟

٥ -   كم عدد المصابين الفلسطينيين في قطاع غزة أمس؟

٧ -   كم عدد المصابين أمس الأول؟

٨ -   كم عمر المصاب في مخيم عسكر؟

٩ -   كم عمر موسى سعيد؟

١٠ - أين قُتل موسى سعيد؟

١١ - أين توجد بلدة عرابة؟

١٢ - أين وُجد جسد أحمد سعد اللّه موسى؟

١٣ - كيف قُتل؟

١٤ - لماذا قُتل؟

(c) Read the following text from النهار, Jan. 1990, then complete the structure
translations which follow.

بدأت مشكلة تدفق المهاجرين اليهود السوفيات إلى المستوطنات
الإسرائيلية في الضفة الغربية المحتلة، تثير غضب الفلسطينيين
وقلق منظمة التحرير الفلسطينية ودول عربية.

وأعلن الرئيس المصري حسني مبارك معارضته التامة لتوطين
اليهود السوفيات في الأراضي العربية المحتلة، فيما اعتبرت

الحكومـة الأردنيـة أن هذا التطور مـن شـأنـه أن يعرقل عمليـة السلام في الشرق الأوسط .

وفي تحقيق لوكالة « رويتر » من الضفة الغربيـة أن نحـو ١٠٠ مـهاجر من الاتحاد السوفيـاتي وأوروبا الشرقيـة وصلوا في الأشهر الثلاثة الأخيرة إلى مستوطنة أريئيل شمال القدس ، وهذا العدد يفوق عدد المهاجرين الذين قدموا في السنتين الأخيرتين . ومعظم هؤلاء المهاجرين لا يدركون العاصفة السياسية التي تحوط باستيطانهم الضفة الغربية ولا الانتفاضة الفلسطينية ضد الاحتلال الإسرائيلي .

ونقلت « رويتر » عن بنحاس مندلون الذي يشرف على مؤسسة استشارية خاصة لمساعدة المهاجرين أن «المستوطنين بدأوا ينظمون أنفسهم واعتقد أننا سنرى زيادة كبيرة في عدد المهاجرين السوفيات الذين ينضمون إليهم» . وتكهن بأن اليهود السوفيات سيشغلون قريبا كل المساكن الخالية في مستوطنة أريئيل علما أن مستوطنة معالي أدوميم شرق القدس تستقبل ٣٠ مهاجر شهريا .

زيادة كبيرة

ويبدو أن نسبة صغيرة من اليهود السوفيات المتوقع وصولهم هذه السنة والذين يراوح عددهم بين ٥٠ ألفا و١٠٠ ألف يهودي سوفياتي ، قد تشكل زيادة كبيرة في عدد المستوطنين الـ٨٠ ألفا الذين يعيشون بين ١,٨ مليون فلسطيني .

وقد وصل معظم المهاجرين إلى مطار بن غوريون في تل أبيب من دون أي فكرة واضحة عن المكان الذي يريدون العيش فيه . ويشير مسؤولون في المطار إلى أنهم يحاولون منع دعاة العيش في المستوطنات من استقطاب القادمين الجدد الذين يكونون غالبا في حيرة من أمرهم . لكن مهاجرين كثيرين أعلنوا أن مثل هؤلاء الدعاة قابلوهم في المطار وحاولوا إقناعهم بالإقامة في

مستوطنات . وقال إيغال بلكان الذي وصل إلى أريئيل مع زوجته وولديه في العاشر من كانون الثاني «في روسيا يقولون إن هناك حرب شوارع في إسرائيل لكن الجو هادئ للغاية هنا ولم نسمع طلقة واحدة». وقال جيرالد باستور الذي وصل إلى أريئيل قادما من رومانيا «لا أعرف أي شيء عن الموقف السياسي هنا ، وعليّ أن أدرس الموقف أولا ثم أفكر فيه ».

ويتوقع مسؤولون إسرائيليون أن يهاجر ما يصل إلى ٧٥٠ ألف يهودي سوفياتي إلى إسرائيل على مدى السنوات الخمس أو الست المقبلة . وصرح رئيس الوزراء الإسرائيلي إسحق شامير هذا الشهر أن إسرائيل تحتاج إلى الاحتفاظ بالأراضي المحتلة لاستيعاب القادمين الجدد من اليهود السوفيات .

Structure translations based on بدأت مشكلة تدفق المهاجرين اليهود.
Translate the following English sentences into Arabic using relevant constructions
to be found in the text at the points indicated.

1. The refugees poured into the Sudanese capital Khartoum. (para.1, line 1)
2. His comment roused my anger. (para. 1, line 2)
3. She expressed her total opposition to the plan. (para. 2, lines 1–2)
4. These concessions will tend to help the peace process. (para. 2, line 3)
5. They all arrived in the last three months. (para. 3, lines 2–3)
6. Damascus is south of Aleppo. (para. 3, line 3)
7. Most of the immigrants don't understand the problem. (para. 3, lines 4–5)
8. He was quoted by al-Nahar as saying, 'There will be a big increase in the price of oil.' (para. 4, lines 1–2)
9. Who is the man who is expected [use متوقع] to resign? (para. 5, line 1)
10. He arrived this year. (para. 5, line 2)
11. She arrived from Russia [use a form of قادم in the accusative]. (para. 6, lines 10–11)
12. You have [use على] to think about it. (para. 6, lines 11–12)
13. I'm meeting the newly arrived foreign tourists [use a construction containing امن]. (para. 7, line 5)

(d) Translate the following text from النهار Jan. 25, 1990 into idiomatic English.

قلق عَميق بِسَبَب الهجرة السوفياتية
زعماء فلسطينيـون حَضّوا العَرب عَلي مَنع توطين
المهَاجرين   الجدد

دعـا أمـس زعمـاء فلسطينيـون مـن الأرَاضي المحتلة الدول العـربيـة إلى العـمل على مـنع إسرائيـل مـن توطين الألـوف من المهاجرين اليهود السوفيات في الضفة الغـربيـة وقطاع غـزة المحتلين.

وكـشـفت وكـالـة «رويتـر» نـص مـذكـرة أرسلت إلى القنصليات العـامـة الغـربيـة في القدس يعـرب فـيهـا ٢٦ من زعمـاء الضفة وقطاع غـزة والقدس الشرقيـة عن مشاعر قلق عميقة بـسبب الهجرة الجماعية المتوقعة لليهود السوفيات إلى إسـرائيـل. ووقـع المذكـرة الزعيـم الفلسطيني البـارز فـيصل الحسيني ومـفتي القدس الشيخ سعد الدين العلمي و٢٤ من الأطبـاء والأكـاديميين ورجـال الأعمـال والصـحافيين وزعمـاء نقابات العمال.

وأشارت المذكـرة إلى تصريح رئيس الوزراء الإسرائيلي إسـحق شـامـيـر في شـأن الحـاجـة إلى «إسرائيل الكبـرى» لاستقبـال اليهود السوفيات، داعيـة إلى اتخاذ خطوات عملية لضمان عدم توطين أي مهاجر إلى إسرائيل في الأرَاضي المحتلة بما في ذلك القدس الشرقيـة. وانتقدت الولايات المتحدة لفرضها قيودا على دخول المهاجرين اليهود السوفيات مما يجبـر الراغبين منهم في الهجرة على التوجه إلى إسرائيل. ولاحظت أن هذه الهجـرة الجمـاعيـة تأتي في وقت تـواصل إسـرائيـل سـياسـتهـا ومسـاعيهـا لإفرَاغ الأرَاضي المحتلة من سكانها عن طريق عمليات الإبعاد وطرد الفلسطينيين غير المسجلين في

سـجـلات الـتـعـداد الإسـرائـيـلـيـة ورفـضـهـا جمـع شمـل الـعـائـلات الـفـلسطـيـنـيـة.

5. Written Arabic texts 2

(a) Read the following text by غـسان كنـفانـي from الـحـزيـن أرض الـبـرتقال, pp. 372–3, then complete exercises i. – iii. which follow.

وأتى يوم « ١٥ أيار » بعد انتظار مـر ... وفي الـساعـة الـثانـيـة عشرة تمامـا لكزنـي أبـوك بقـدمـه وأنـا مـسـتـغـرق في نـومي قـائـلا بصـوت يـهـدر بالأمـل الـبـاسـل : قـم . . فـاشـهـد دخـول الـجـيـوش الـعـربـيـة إلى فلسطـين ... وقـمـت كالمـسـعـور ... وانحـدرنـا عـبـر الـتـلال حفـاة في منتصف الـليل إلى الـشارع الـذي يبعد عن الـقـريـة كيلومـترا كامـلا ... كنا كلنـا ، صغـارا وكبـارا، نلهـث ونحـن نركـض كالمجـانـين ... وكانـت أضـواء الـسيـارات تبـدو مـن بعيـد ، صاعـدة إلى رأس الـناقـورة . وحيـن وصلنـا إلى الـشارع أحـسـسنـا بالـبـرد . ولكـن صيـاح أبـيـك كـان يملـك علينـا وجـودنـا ... لقـد أخـذ يركـض وراء الـسـيـارات كطفـل صغـيـر ... إنـه يـهـتـف بهـم . . إنـه يصيـح بصـوت أبـح ... إنـه يلهـث ... لكنـه مـا زال يركـض وراء رتـل الـسـيـارات كطفـل صغـيـر ... كنـا نركـض بجـواره صائـحـين مـعـه ، وكـان الـجنـود الـطيـبـون ينـظـرون إليـنا مـن تحـت خـوذهـم بجـمـود وصمـت ... كنا نلهـث ، فـيـما كان أبـوك يخـرج مـن جيبـه ، وهـو يركـض بأعـوامه الخمسـين ، لفـافات الـتبـغ يرميها للجنـود ، كان لا يـزال يهتـف بهـم وكنـا نحـن لا زلنا نركـض إلى جـواره كقطيـع صغيـر مـن المـاعـز ...

وانـتـهـت الـسـيـارات فجـاءة ... وعـدنا إلى الـدار منـهـوكين نلهـث بصفـيـر خـافـت ... كان أبـوك صامـتـا لا يتكلـم ، وكنـا نحـن أيـضـا لا نقـوى على الكـلام ... وعنـدمـا أضـاءت وجـه أبـيـك سيـارة عابـرة كانـت دمـوعـه تملأ وجـنتـه ...

i Answer the following questions in Arabic.

١ – ما هو تاريخ هذا الحادث؟ وفي أي سنة في رأيك؟

٢ – في أي ساعة لكز الكاتبَ أبو صديق الكاتب؟

٣ – ما هو حال الكاتب في هذا الوقت؟

٤ – ماذا أراد أبو صديق الكاتب أن يشاهدوه؟

٥ – أين يوجد الشارع؟

٦ – كيف وصلوا إليه؟

٧ – إلى أين صعدت السيارات؟

٨ – بماذا أحسوا عندما وصلوا إلى الشارع؟

٩ – ماذا عمل أبو صديق الكاتب عندما وصلوا إلى الشارع؟

١٠ – ماذا عمل الكاتب والآخرون الذين كانوا معه؟

١١ – ما هو رد فعل الجنود؟

١٢ – ماذا رمى أبو صديق الكاتب للجنود؟

١٣ – ما هو حالهم عندما رجعوا إلى الدار؟

١٤ – ما هو حال أبي صديق الكاتب عند رجوعه؟

١٥ – ماذا شاهدوا في وجه أبي صديق الكاتب؟

١٦ – ما هو معنى رد الفعل هذا في رأيك؟

ii Structure translations based on أرض البرتقال الحزين.
Translate the following English sentences into Arabic using relevant
constructions to be found in the text at the points indicated.

1. She spoke in a voice which simmered with rage. (lines 2–3)
2. The soldiers behaved like madmen. (line 4)
3. We walked barefoot through the town. (line 4)
4. The town is several kilometres from the Nile. (line 5)
5. All of them, rich and poor, were feeling tired. (line 6)
6. She was seized with strong feelings for the president. (line 8)
7. Your mother, mourning with [all] her sixty years, handed us handkerchiefs.
   (lines 13–14)

iii Translate the above text into idiomatic English.

(b) Read the following poem by the well–known Palestinian poet, محمود درويش,
then answer the questions which follow in Arabic.

نسافر   كالناس

نسافرُ كالناس، لكننا لا نعودُ إلى أي شيءٍ. كأنَّ السفرْ

طريقُ الغيوم. دَفَنّا أحبتنا في ظلامِ الغيوم وبين جذوعِ الشجرْ

وقُلنا لزوجاتِنا: لِدْنَ مَنا مئاتِ السنينَ لنكملَ هذا الرَحيلْ

إلى ساعةٍ من بلادٍ، ومترٍ من المستحيلْ.

نسافرُ في عرباتِ المزامير، نرقدُ في خيمةِ الأنبياء، ونخرجُ من

كلماتِ الغجرْ.

نقيسُ الفضاءَ بمنقارِ هُدْهُدة أو نغني لِنُلهي المسافةَ عنا، ونَغسلَ

ضَوءَ القمرْ.

طويلٌ طريقكَ فأحلم بسبعِ نساءٍ لتحمل هذا الطريقَ الطويلَ على

كتفيكَ. وهزَّ لهن النخيل لِتَعْرِفَ أسماءَهُنَ ومن أي أم سيولدُ طفلُ

الجليلْ

لنا بلدٌ من كلامٍ. تَكلم تكلمْ لأَسنِدَ دربي على حجرٍ من حجرْ

لنا بلدٌ من كلامٍ. تَكلم تكلم لنعرفَ حداً لهذا السفرْ!

١ – ما هي الأفكار الرئيسية في هذه القصيدة؟

٢ – ما هي أهمية السفر في القصيدة؟

٣ – في رأيك، لماذا يقول الشاعر إننا «نقيس الفضاءَ بمنقار هُدْهُدَة»؟

٤ – هل السفر قصير أم طويل، وكيف نعرف هذا؟

6. Written Arabic texts 3 (classical)

Translate the following text by ابن خلدون from تاريخ العلّامة ابن خلدون, vol.
I, pp. 290–1, into idiomatic English.

قال ابن أبي زيد: ارتدّت البرابرةُ بالمغرب اثنتيْ عشرةَ مرّةً.

ولم تستقرَّ كلمةُ الإسلام فيهم إلا لعهد ولايةِ موسى بن نُصَير

فما بعدَه. وهذا معنى ما يُنقَّلُ عن عُمَر أنّ إفريقيةَ مفرّقةٌ

لقلوبِ أهلِها، إشارةً إلى ما فيها كثرةِ العصائبِ والقبائلِ

الحاملة لهم على عدم الإذعان والانقياد. ولم يكن العراقُ لذلك
العهدِ بتلك الصفةِ ولا الشامُ، إنّما كانت حاميتُها من فارسَ
والرومِ، والكافّةُ دهماءُ أهلِ مــدنٍ وأمــصارٍ. فلمــا غلبــهم
المسلمون على الأمرِ وانتـزعوه من أيديهم لم يبقَ فيها مُمانعٌ
ولا مُشاقٌّ. والبربرُ قبائلُهم بالمغربِ أكثرُ من أن تُحصى، وكلهم
باديةٌ وأهلُ عصائبَ وعشائرَ. وكلما هلكت قبيلةٌ عادتِ الأخرى
مكانَها وإلى دينِها من الخلافِ والردّةِ، فطال أمرُ العربِ في
تمهيدِ الدولةِ بوطنٍ إفريقيةَ والمغربِ. وكذلك كان الأمرُ بالشامِ
لعهدِ بني إسرائيلَ: كان فيه من قبائلَ فلسطينَ وكنعانَ وبني
عيصـو وبني مَدْيَنَ وبني لوطٍ والرومِ واليونانِ والعمالقةِ
وأكريكشَ، والنبطِ من جانبِ الجزيرةِ والموصلِ ما لا يُحصى
كثرةً وتنوُّعاً في العَصبيةِ. فَصعُب على بني إسرائيلَ تمهيدُ
دولتِهم ورسوخُ أمرِهم واضطرب عليهم الملكُ مرّةً بعد أخرى.
وسرى ذلك الخلافُ إليهم فاختلفوا على سلطانِهم وخرجوا
عليــه، ولم يكن لهم مُلكٌ مُوطَّدٌ سائرَ أيامِهم إلى أن غلبــهم
الفرسُ ثم اليونانُ ثم الرومُ آخرَ أمرِهم عند الجلاءِ. واللّهُ غالبٌ
على أمرِهِ.

7. Grammar/stylistics

(a) حال clauses

حال clauses, or circumstantial clauses, are subordinate clauses which describe the circumstance or situation in which a given act or event takes place (cf. also EMSA I: 535–7). They are often translated into English as 'while', and/or by a gerund (a word which ends in –ing). The tense of the verb (the imperfect) or participle (usually the active) in the circumstantial clause is subordinated to the time reference of the verb in the main clause (see Tense Subordination in ch. 5, 7). The *italics* part of the following English sentence is a circumstantial clause:

he fell over *while crossing the road*

since this part of the sentence tells us what the subject was doing at the time he fell over. Circumstantial clauses in Arabic take the form of either (a) و + nominal clause in which the predicate is a participle, or (b) و + nominal clause in which the predicate is an imperfect verb.

(a) is exemplified by:

رجعوا إليها {وأنا واقف في مكاني}.

'They returned while I stood in my place.' (ch. 4, 6)

لكزني أبوك بقدمه {وأنا مستغرق في نومي}.

'Your father kicked me with his foot while I was deeply asleep.' (ch. 6, 5a)

(b) is exemplified by:

كنا كلنا ... نلهث {ونحن نركض كالمجانين}.

'We were all panting while running like madmen.' (ch. 6, 5a)

The subordinating particle و is often omitted in circumstantial clauses. Where this happens the independent pronoun will also be omitted, as in:

وعدنا إلى الدار ... {نلهث بصفير خافت}.

'We returned to the house ... gasping with a faint whistle.' (ch. 6, 5a)

فيما كان أبوك يخرج من جيبه ... لفافات التبغ {يرميها للجنود}.

'While your father took from his pocket ... tobacco roll–ups, throwing them to the soldiers.' (ch. 6, 5a)

سمعتُ صوتا من السماء {يقول يا محمد أنت وسول الله}.

'I heard a voice from heaven saying, "Muhammad, you are the messenger of God."' (ch. 4, 6)

Where a noun or adjective remains after the particle و and an independent pronoun have been omitted, the noun or adjective predicate will be put in the *accusative* case, as in:

لكزني أبوك بقدمه {قائلا} (={وهو قائلٌ}) ..

'Your father kicked me with his foot, saying ...' (ch. 6, 5a)

كنا نركض بجواره {صائحين معه}.

'We ran beside him, shouting with him.' (ch. 6, 5a)

انحدرنا عبر التلال {حفاةً}.

'We went down the hill barefoot.' (ch. 6, 5a)

وانصرفتُ عنه {راجعا إلى أهلي}.

'I left him, returning to my family.' (ch. 4, 6)

(b) *Word order: the use of nominal sentences in news headlines and summaries*

In general, verbal sentences – that is to say, sentences which begin with a verb – are preferred over nominal sentences – sentences which begin with a noun or an adjective. One notable exception to this order is found in journal headlines and news summaries where the usual order is for the noun to precede the verb. This is not surprising, since headlines and news summaries often have their own peculiar syntax: English headlines are very abbreviated, and often constitute a concatenation of nouns without articles, such as 'Charles naked pictures fury'. Examples of nominal sentences in Arabic headlines include:

معظم سكان أفريقيا يعيشون تحت حد الفقر.

'Most of population of Africa live below poverty line.' (ch. 9, 4a)

علماء أوروبا وأمريكا يشاركون في المؤتمر الدولي لترميم أبو الهول.

'European and American scientists take part in international conference to repair Sphinx.' (ch. 3, 11)

الحسين يحذر من مخاطر حرب في الخليج.

'Hussein warns of dangers of war in Gulf.' (ch. 8, 4dii)

(c) *Aspect: the use of the imperfect aspect in news headlines and summaries*

In English headlines and news summaries the present tense of the verb is used although the event discussed has probably already taken place. Headlines such as 'Queen opens parliament', and 'al-Jihad release hostages' are found in place of *'Queen opened parliament' and *'al-Jihad released hostages'. In Arabic we see the same pattern: with very few exceptions (one of these exceptions is seen in ch. 6, 4d) زعماء فلسطينيون {حضّوا} العرب 'Palestinian leaders *urged* the Arabs ...'), the imperfect aspect of the verb is used in the headline or in the news summary even when the event under discussion has already taken place. Examples include the last of the three headlines given above (the first two refer to events which either are taking place, in the case of the first, or will be taking place, in the case of the second), and the following:

... وإسرائيل {تبعد} النساء والأطفال.

'...and Israel banishes women and children.' (ch. 4, 4b)

باحث أمريكي {يؤكد}: تلوث القاهرة يعجل بنهاية أبو الهول ...

'American researcher confirms: Cairo pollution speeds up end of Sphinx.' (ch. 8, 5b)

مـؤتمر إحـلال الـسـلام في الشـرق الأوسط {يبـدأ} يومـه الثـاني في مادريد.

'The Middle East peace conference begins its second day in Madrid.'
(ch. 6, 9)

Note that where a news summary gives the same information as the opening lines of the news details, the details are given in a verbal sentence with the verb in the perfect aspect. Compare the last example above with the following sentence taken from the news details:

إلى تفاصيل الأنباء مـن لندن: {بـدأ مـؤتمر إحـلال السـلام في الشرق الأوسـط يومـه الثـاني في مادريد}.

'Here is the news in detail: the Middle East peace conference began its second day in Madrid.' (ch. 6, 9)

8. Aural Arabic texts 1

Listen to the following BBC Arabic Service news broadcast from Sept. 26, 1988, nine and a half months after the start of the *intifada*, then complete exercises i. and ii. below.

i Answer the following questions in Arabic.

١ – كم عدد الأشخاص المصابين بالاعيرة البـلاستيكية في قطاع غزة؟

٢ – هل هناك قتلى في الضفة الغربية؟

٣ – ما هو هدف الإضراب العام؟

٤ – ما هو مـوقـف وكالة غـوث وتشغيل اللاجئين الفلسطينيـين من ارتفاع عدد المصابين الفلسطينيين؟

٥ – ما هو الشيء الذى يُقلق الوكالة؟

٦ – متى بدأت القوات الاسرائيلية تستعمل العيارات البـلاستيكية؟

٧ – مـا هو حـجم الازديـاد في عـدد الذين يتم مـعـالجـتـهـم من الاصـابـات بالعيارات؟

٨ – ما هو موضوع الشكوى التي قدّمتها الوكالة الى الاسرائيليين؟

ii Fill in the gaps in the text below.

أنبـاؤنا ـــــــــــــ سـيـداتي سـادتي تأتيكم ـــــــــــــ
ـــــــــــــ :ـــــــــــ

اندلعت اشتباكات _____ _____ _____ _____

الأمن _____ _____ و _____ الأراضي المحتلّة

_____ _____ _____ يُنفّذ إضراب _____ .

_____ _____ أُصيب شخصان بأعيرة _____

_____ _____ . وتفيد الانباء _____

_____ _____ جُرحوا _____

_____ _____ جرت _____

_____ _____ فرض _____ حظر

التجوُّل _____ _____ _____

ومخيمات اللاجئين _____ _____ . ويُنفّذ

_____ _____ لمساندة السجناء _____

المحتجزين _____ معسكر الاعتقال _____

_____ النقب.

_____ وكالة غوث وتشغيل _____

التابعة للامم المتحدة _____ عدد _____

_____ برصاص _____

ارتفع _____ _____ _____

مستويات _____ _____ القبول

_____ _____ _____

_____ _____ . وعبّرت _____ قلقها بشأن

السماح رسميا _____ العيارات _____

المتظاهرين ——————— الاجراء ——————— أعلن —————

————— مسؤول ————— /آب. ————————————————

————————— إنّ ——————————————————————

——————— يتمّ معالجتهم ——————— ———————

والحيـة ——————— ——————— ———————

اضـعـاف ——————— المتـوسـط عمّا ——————— ———————

———————— وقـدّمـت ——————— شكوى ———————

————— السلطات ——————— بشـأن سلوك احدى وحدات

——————— ——————— ——————— ————————

9. Aural Arabic texts 2
Listen to the following BBC Arabic Service news broadcast from Oct. 31, 1991 on the Madrid peace conference between Israel and the Arabs, then complete exercises i. and ii below.

i   Fill in the gaps in the text below. These relate to the first portion of this passage, from the beginning to جنوب لبنان.

مـؤتمر إحلال ————— ——————— ———————

يبـدأ يـومـه ——————— ——————— مـادريد و——————— ألقى

إسـحـاق شـامـيـر ——————— ——————— ——————— كلمـة

و——————— ——————— إن ——————— ملتـزمـة

بالتـفـاوض للتـوصل ——————— ——————— و———————

——————— بـأنـه حـدث ——————— ومنـاسـبـة

يرقبها ——————— بـلـهفة وتـوقـع. ——————— ——————— كامـل

أبو جابـر ——————— ——————— ——————— دعا

كامل وعادل. ـــــــــ ـــــــــ ـــــــــ ـــــــــ ـــــــــ

هذا وسـيـسـتـمـع ـــــــــ ـــــــــ حـوالى نصف

حيدر عبد ـــــــــ ـــــــــ ـــــــــ ـــــــــ

الشـافي ـــــــــ الوفـد ـــــــــ ـــــــــ المشـترك

كمـا ـــــــــ ـــــــــ ـــــــــ ـــــــــ

ـــــــــ الوفـد ـــــــــ ـــــــــ ـــــــــ

ولم تتـفّـق ـــــــــ ـــــــــ . ـــــــــ ـــــــــ

الوفـود المشـتـركة ـــــــــ ـــــــــ ـــــــــ على

إجـراء المحـادثـات الثنـائيـة للمـرحلة ـــــــــ ـــــــــ

ـــــــــ ـــــــــ

تـواصل قـصف ـــــــــ ـــــــــ ـــــــــ ـــــــــ

جنوب لبنـان. ـــــــــ

ii Answer the following questions which are based on the second portion of this text from الوفـد الأردني إلى تفـاصـيـل الأنبـاء من لنـدن to the end, الفلسطينـي المشترك.

1. According to Shamir what does the conference provide an opportunity to end?
2. According to Shamir what does the conference provide an opportunity to begin?
3. According to Shamir what would be a cause for regret (أمـر مـؤسـف)?
4. Why?
5. According to the BBC's Jerusalem correspondent what changes had Shamir hinted at regarding his opposition to the idea of land for peace (الأرض مـقـابـل السلام)?
6. What did Shamir call on Arab leaders to renounce?
7. According to Shamir what is the basic reason for the continuation of the Arab–Israeli conflict?
8. Where did Shamir suggest to Arab leaders that the next round of peace talks be held?
9. Where else did Shamir say Israel would be ready to hold negotiations?

10. Where did Ronny Milo say Israel would be ready to hold negotiations if circumstances so dictated?

11. Which specific city did he suggest?

12. How did the BBC correspondent in Madrid describe the speech by Kamel Abu Jaber?

13. How did the BBC correspondent describe Jordanian policy in the region?

14. How did Kamel Abu Jaber describe the principle of land for peace?

15. What did Kamel Abu Jaber say the Palestinians should be allowed to do on the land of their forefathers?

10. Written English texts

(a) Making use of constructions and vocabulary encountered in the Arabic texts above as far as possible, translate the following text from *Middle East International*, Feb. 2, 1990, into idiomatic Arabic.

Arabs express their fears[1]

The Palestinians and the Arab governments are beginning to express their real anxiety and indignation over the large–scale exodus of Jews from the Soviet Union into Israel. They could hardly do less when the latest of Israel's exaggerated and expanding estimates is that 100–120,000 immigrants will enter Israel every year for the next five to seven years. Shamir declared, on 15 January, that the immigrants would have the right to settle anywhere, in Israel proper or in the territories[2].

The Arab, and especially the Jordanian, fear is that Israel might use the large influx as an excuse to push the West Bankers out, mainly to Jordan, so as to make room for the new arrivals. The first official expression of Arab opposition came from the Jordanian foreign minister, Marwan al-Qasim, and on 30 January Jordan and Syria jointly called for an Arab summit to discuss Israel's 'expansionism'. Egypt, Israel's only Arab 'friend', has also condemned the settlement of Soviet Jews in Palestine.

Notes

1. Translate headlines as nominal sentences. Also put the verb in the imperfect aspect.
2. Translate this phrase as إمّا ... وإمّا.

(b) Making use of constructions and vocabulary encountered in the Arabic texts above as far as possible, translate the following text from *Middle East International*, 1991, into idiomatic Arabic.

Amnesty International accuses[1,2]

In a report published on 3 January, Amnesty International accused the Israeli government of actively encouraging the killing of Palestinians by its security forces in the West Bank and Gaza Strip. Amnesty's report calls for an urgent review of the guidelines under which troops are permitted to open fire and for a judicial enquiry into 'extensive and serious' human rights violations committed by Israeli security forces since the *intifada* began.

The report, citing a figure of 560 Palestinians shot dead during the *intifada*, a figure rather lower than other independent estimates, questions both the high percentage of children killed and the number of abuses of official guidelines for opening fire and their inadequate investigation. In an 'alarmingly high number' of cases, Amnesty said, Palestinians were killed when not engaging in violence and furthermore the report doubted whether children throwing stones at troops are enough of a threat to justify shooting them.

Notes
1. See note 1. in (a) above.
2. Amnesty International is translated as منظمة العفو الدُوَليّ.

11. Précis
Read the following newspaper passage from الشرق الأوسط, Sept. 11, 1993, which is a preview of the Oslo Accords (Gaza–Jericho Agreement) two days before their signing in Washington, then complete exercises i. and ii. which follow.

بداية النضال وليست نهايته
قبول أو رفض الاتفاق الفلسطيني - الاسرائيلي
لا يعني رأيا مع عرفات أو ضده،
فالقضية ليست قضية زعامات بل مصير شعب

عثمان ميرغني

تبادل الاعتراف بين منظمة التحرير الفلسطينية واسرائيل ليس نهاية للصراع، لكنه خطوة صغيرة في الطريق الطويل الشاق نحو ذلك الهدف. وتوقيع الاتفاق الفلسطيني - الاسرائيلي للحكم الذاتي على غزة واريحا، في واشنطن بعد غد، لن يكون ايضا هو نهاية الحل، بل بداية لعملية - لكى تنجح - يجب ان تنتهي

بالحصول على الحقوق والتطلعات المشروعة للشعب الفلسطيني، وبالحلول على الجبهات الاخرى السورية واللبنانية والاردنية. وما تم حتى الآن ما يزال بعيدا عن تلك الغايات، لكنه يبقى بداية تحتاج الى كفاح طويل من نوع جديد حتى تصل الى نهاياتها.

ان السلام ليس سهلا، بل قد يكون في بعض الاحيان اصعب من الحرب، خصوصا في قضية بعمر القضية الفلسطينية وبحجمها وابعادها التاريخية والانسانية. ولذلك من المنطقي الا يقلل المرء من العقبات التي ستعترض هدف السلام، وهو هدف مطلوب حتى من جانب غلاة المعارضين للاتفاق الفلسطيني – الاسرائيلي الحالي.

ومن مصلحة الفلسطينيين ان يكون هناك حوار بل حتى جدل حول الاتفاق الذي حصل بالفعل وينتظر فقط التوقيع، فقرار السلام لا يمكن ان يكون قرارا فرديا، ويجب الا يبقى داخل غرف الاجتماعات، بل من حق كل فلسطيني في اي بقعة من الارض ان يقول رأيه، ان يجادل، ان يؤيد او يعارض، لكن من المهم ان يبقى الحوار سلميا وديمقراطيا والا يتحول الى مقارعة بالرصاص، والا ستكون الفاجعة الحقيقة.

وعلى الفلسطينيين ان ينظروا الى جانب افريقيا ويتعلموا. فهناك ايضا مأساة انسانية انتهت بعد صراع دام وطويل، الى توقيع اتفاقات من اجل السير في طرق السلام والتعايش الشاق. لكن المأساة هي ان الخلاف بين السكان الزنوج تحول الى مذابح شبه يومية يقتل فيها العشرات واحيانا المئات، بينما يقترب شبح الحرب الاهلية الشاملة مع اقتراب هدف حكم الاغلبية السوداء. ان اكثر الناس تطرفا في تأييد الاتفاق الفلسطيني – الاسرائيلي لا يستطيع ان يقول انه الاتفاق الامثل او انه الحل للقضية. مثلما ان اكثر الناس غلوا في معارضته لا يستطيع ان يزعم انه يملك حلا افضل يستطيع ان يحقق به دفعة واحدة كل الطموحات الفلسطينية، اليوم قبل الغد. ان الاتفاق ليس مثاليا، بل ابعد ما

يكون عن ذلك، وهو قطعا ليس النهاية بقدر ما هو خطوة صغيرة في بداية الطريق نحو الحل، وهي خطوة تحتاج الى المثابرة والكفاح حتى تصل الى غاياتها.

لقد رفض الفلسطينيون والعرب عموما مشروع التقسيم عام ١٩٤٧ من اجل الحصول على كامل حقوقهم المشروعة وليس على نصفها. وخاضوا من اجل تلك الحقوق ثلاث حروب كبرى ومئات المعارك الصغرى، ودفعوا الكثير الكثير. ورفضوا اتفاقية كامب ديفيد عام ١٩٧٩ التي كانت تنص على حكم ذاتي فلسطيني على الضفة والقطاع، واتهموا الرئيس المصري الراحل انور السادات بالخيانة وبيع القضية وقاطعوا مصر سنوات طويلة وقعت خلالها الكثير من الاحداث والخطوب.

ان مقارنة بسيطة تجعل المرء يخرج بنتيجة مريرة. فلو قبل العرب التقسيم لكانوا حتما فازوا باكثر مما عرض عليهم في كامب ديفيد. ولو كانوا قبلوا بحكم كامب ديفيد الذاتي، لما وجدوا انفسهم اليوم يوقعون على نصف ما كان معروضا عليهم قبل ١٤ عاما. والخوف هو ان الرفض اليوم ربما يعني القليل غدا، مع استمرار المعاناة والخسائر، ومن غير ضمان شيء افضل، خصوصا انه لا يبدو في الافق ما يشير الى ان الظروف الدولية يمكن ان تساعد في تحقيق حل افضل مستقبلا.

لذا فإن قبول اتفاق غزة – اريحا اليوم، ليس خيانة او تفريطا كما قد يسميه البعض، لكنه قراءة واقعية للظروف الحالية والمستقبلية على الاقل في المدى المنظور. صحيح ان الاتفاق لا يحقق للفلسطينيين استقلالا ولا حتى حكما ذاتيا على كل الضفة والقطاع، لكنه على الاقل بداية يجب ان تتركز كل الجهود الفلسطينية من اجل الدفع بها الى الامام للحصول على المزيد، وهي مهمة لن تكون سهلة في كل الاحوال.

وقبول او رفض هذا الاتفاق يجب الا يعني رأيا مع عرفات او

ضده، لان القضية ليست قضية افراد او زعامات، بل مصير شعب عانى طويلا وتعلم من معاناته ان كل القرارات الدولية قد لا تنجح في اعادة شبر من الارض، وان الشعارات وحدها لا تحقق الاحلام ولا تحرر الاوطان.

والواقع ان الاعتراف الفلسطيني باسرائيل و«نبذ الارهاب» لم يحدثا مع تبادل الرسائل الموقعة بين عرفات ورابين، فقد نبذ المجلس الوطني الفلسطيني في جلسته التاريخية في الجزائر عام ١٩٨٨ التي اعلن فيها قيام الدولة الفلسطينية المستقلة، «كل اشكال الارهاب»، كما وافق على القرار ٢٤٢ الذي يعترف ضمنا بوجود اسرائيل. وقالها عرفات صراحة من على منبر الامم المتحدة عندما انتقلت اليه بكاملها من نيويورك الى جنيف في اواخر عام ١٩٨٨ عندما تحدث عن «التخلى الكامل عن الارهاب» ثم اعترف خارج القاعة «بحق اسرائيل بالعيش في امن وسلام». وحتى بالنسبة للميثاق الوطني الفلسطيني الذي يدور الآن الجدل بشأن الغاء بعض فقراته، فإن عرفات سبق واعلن في مايو (ايار) ١٩٨٩ ان الميثاق اصبح «كادوك» اي لاغيا.

اما من جانب اسرائيل فإنها كانت تعرف انها تجلس مع منظمة التحرير الفلسطينية عبر طاولة المفاوضات في مؤتمر مدريد حتى وان احتجت على كوفية صائب عريقات. وكانت تعرف ايضا ان اعضاء الوفد الفلسطيني في واشنطن لا يمثلون فلسطينيي الداخل بل كل الفلسطينيين، ولا يتصرفون من تلقاء انفسهم بل بأوامر منظمة التحرير.

ان الجديد ليس هو الاعتراف وان تم تبادله رسميا، بل الجديد هو اتفاق الحكم الذاتي الذي سيوقع في واشنطن بعد غد، وهو الاتفاق الذي يجب ان تتركز عليه الانظار والجهود من اجل دفعه نحو تحقيق هدف الدولة الفلسطينية المستقلة. فالذي يرفض الاتفاق الحالي – باعتباره غير كاف – عليه ان يوجه جهوده نحو

كيفية دفعه نحو مراحله الاخرى الموعودة، بدلا من توجيه الرصاص نحو صفوف الفلسطينيين. والذي يؤيد عليه ان يبرز تأييده بالعمل من اجل ان يصل الاتفاق الى غاياته.

تبقى كلمة اخيرة وهي ان السلام الذي يلوح في الافق اليوم، ولو عن بعد، ما كان سيتحقق لولا تضحيات الكثيرين الذين يغيب بعضهم عن هذه اللحظات التاريخية.

وعلى الكثيرين ان ينصفوا السادات، وان يتذكروا ابو جهاد، وكل شهداء ثورة الحجارة ومسيرة القضية الفلسطينية منذ بروزها وحتى اليوم، والى الغد. فالحلم لم يتحقق بعد، والنضال لم ينته، والعطاء لن يتوقف وكذلك مسيرة الذين يقدمون من غير حساب من اجل القضية والشعب. وهناك كثيرون آخرون يجب الا تغيب ذكراهم في اللحظات الراهنة او المقبلة، وان كان يصعب حصرهم كلهم او الاتفاق على ادوارهم.

i Answer the following questions relating to the above text in English.

1. Which historical events does the writer mention? List the events in the order given in the text.
2. How does the writer justify his view that the Palestinians should accept the Oslo Accords (Gaza–Jericho Agreement)?
3. Which country does the writer say the Palestinians should look to and why?
4. What does the writer say is new about the Accords?
5. Which political figures are mentioned in the text and why?

ii Write a précis in Arabic of the above text.

12. Oral
النزاع العربي – الإسرائيلي

(a) One or two students to present a summary in Arabic of significant events in the Arab–Israeli dispute since the early twentieth century.
(b) The presenter then asks questions about some of these events. Again some of the questions should require simple factual replies while others will require more subjective or hypothetical answers. For example:

١ – ما هي أهم الحروب في النزاع العربي-الإسرائيلي؟

٢ – متى أُنشِئت منظمة التحرير الفلسطينية؟

٣ – متى أصبح مناحم بيغن رئيس الوزراء في إسرائيل؟

٤ – من هو السادات وما هي أهميته في النزاع العربي-الإسرائيلي؟

٥ – ما الذي حدث في الانتفاضة؟

٦ – في رأيك، من هم اللاعبون الرئيسيون في النزاع العربي-الإسرائيلي اليوم؟

٧ – ما هو اتفاق أوسلو؟

٨ – على أي أساس يقوم السلام بين الفلسطينيين والإسرائيليين؟

٩ – هل سوف نرى السلام في فلسطين في المستقبل القريب؟

(c) Open lecturer–led discussion on the future of the Arab–Israeli conflict.

13. Essay

Write an essay of around 200 words on the title: النزاع العربي-الإسرائيلي أسبابه وحلّه. Structure your essay around the following questions:

١ – ما هي الأحداث في أوروبا التي جعلت اليهود يهاجرون إلى فلسطين؟

٢ – ما هي الصهيونية، وماذا حدث نتيجةً للهجرة الصهيونية حتى عام ١٩٤٨؟

٣ – ماذا حدث في حرب ١٩٦٧ وبعدها؟

٤ – ماذا حدث في ١٩٧٣، وإلى ماذا أدّت؟

٥ – ما هي الانتفاضة، وماذا حدث فيها؟

٦ – ما هو دور منظمة التحرير الفلسطينية في حرب الخليج ١٩٩٠ – ١٩٩١، وما هي نتائج هذه الحرب بالنسبة للنزاع العربي – الإسرائيلي؟

٧ – ماذا حدث أخيرا في فلسطين، وفي رأيك ماذا سيحدث في المستقبل؟

7
Iraqi invasion of Kuwait

1. Basic background material

(a) *The Iran–Iraq war: 1980–1988*

1980   Following Iranian revolution of 1978–1979, Iraq under dictator Saddam Hussein unilaterally abrogates 1975 agreement with Iran over Shatt al-Arab waterway in Gulf, which he had originally signed with Shah of Iran in order to end Iranian support for Kurdish rebels in northern Iraq. Iraq declares war on Iran, hoping for quick military victory against apparently disorganised revolutionary Iranian regime. Some initial Iraqi success.

1982   Iranian forces expel Iraqis from Iranian territory and advance into Iraq.

1986   Iranians take Fao, and advance to within forty miles of Basra. Saudi Arabia increases oil production in attempt to cripple economy of Iran, which is dependent on oil exports, and to raise funds for Iraq.

1987   Iran and Iraq try to destroy each other's oil facilities. Iran launches attack on Basra. Iraq attempts to internationalise war by drawing in USA and USSR, and put pressure of Iran to reach a settlement. Iraq attacks Iranian tankers, Iran attacks Iraqi and Kuwaiti tankers. With Iranians now close to Kuwaiti border, Kuwait appeals to Soviet Union and United States for support. Fearing increased Soviet influence in region, and possibility that Iran will 'export' its revolution to Arab world, United States adopts policy of strong support for Iraq, supplying it with military intelligence including satellite photographs of Iranian troop concentrations. July 1987, UN Security Council Resolution 598 calls for end to war; accepted by Iraq, rejected by Iran.

1988   With support from Iraqi Kurds, Iranians capture Halabja in Iraqi Kurdistan. On following day, Iraqi air–force bombs Halabja with chemical weapons, killing 5,000 civilians (out of up to 100,000 Kurds murdered by Iraqi regime in 1988–1989). No significant action against Iraq by west (shortly after, Britain doubles Iraq's Export Credit Rating). Subsequent use of chemical weapons by Iraq against Iranian forces in Iraqi recapture of Fao and Mehran. On July 18, Iran accepts Resolution

598; Iranian forces then driven out of southern and central Iraq. Aug. 20, Iran and Iraq agree to ceasefire.

The Iran–Iraq war cost around 300,000 Iranian and 100,000 Iraqi dead, with perhaps 750,000 wounded. The financial cost has been estimated at $644.3 billion for Iran and $452.6 billion for Iraq, much of the Iraqi war costs being paid by Saudi Arabia and Kuwait, to which Iraq emerged from the war massively in debt. In the period following the war, Iraq attempted to recoup some of its debts by persuading OPEC to cut overall production and raise oil prices, and by pressurising Kuwait in particular to cancel some war debts. Meanwhile, peace negotiations with Iran dragged on inconclusively.

(b) *1991 Gulf war and aftermath*

July 17, 1990	Iraq threatens military action against Kuwait for exceeding OPEC quotas and allegedly siphoning off Iraqi oil from border Rumalia oil fields.
July 31, 1990	Talks between Iraq and Kuwait break down.
Aug 2, 1990	Iraq invades Kuwait. UN Security Council passes Resolution 660, condemning invasion, demanding withdrawal, and calling for immediate Iraq–Kuwait negotiations.
Aug. 6, 1990	US sends first troops to Saudi Arabia. Begins to put together international coalition against Iraq.
Aug. 15, 1990	Iraq accepts Iran's peace terms, including restoration of 1975 agreement over Shatt al-Arab waterway, in apparent attempt to neutralise residual threat of Iran.
Aug. 29, 1990	UN passes resolution 676 setting Jan. 15 deadline for Iraqi withdrawal from Kuwait.
Aug. 1990 – Jan. 1991	Various negotiations, all of which fail. Massive build–up of American, British and other troops in Saudi Arabia. Coalition against Iraq includes not only traditional western allies of United States, but also Saudi Arabia, Egypt, Syria, and Morocco from Arab world. As American willingness to use massive force against Iraq becomes clear, Algeria, Jordan, Libya, Sudan, Tunisia, Yemen and PLO adopt increasingly anti–American position. Emergence of popular support in poor Arab countries for Saddam Hussein, who is seen to be standing up against the west.
Jan. 16, 1991	Bombing of Iraq begins.
Feb. 24, 1991	Land war begins.
Feb. 25, 1991	Saddam Hussein orders withdrawal of Iraqi troops from Kuwait. Tens of thousands of fleeing Iraqi troops massacred in allied ambushes.
Feb. 27, 1991	Iraq accepts allied terms. US ceases hostilities.
March 1991	Popular insurrections break out against Iraqi regime in Kurdish

north and Shiite south of Iraq. Despite rebel appeals and
previous encouragement by Americans, allied forces offer no
assistance, Americans apparently fearing downfall of Saddam
Hussein would lead to independent Kurdish state in northern
Iraq, and pro–Iranian government in south. Insurrections put
down by Iraqi government with indiscriminate brutality.

April 1991   Sulaimaniyya, last major Kurdish city in rebel hands, falls to
Iraqi government troops. Exodus of 2.5 million Iraqi refugees to
Turkey and Iran (with Kurdish refugees fearing Halabja–style
chemical attacks) leads to outcry in mainland Europe in
particular. Bowing to public pressure, America and Britain
establish military exclusion zone north of 36th parallel, with de
facto establishment of Iraqi Kurdish state.

1992   Free elections for Kurdish National Assembly held in Iraqi
Kurdistan, with apparent agreement between two main Iraqi
Kurdish factions led by Mas'ud Barzani and Jalal Talabani.

1996   Final collapse of Kurdish agreement, with conflict over control
of tax revenues from trans–border trade with Turkey (main
source of income for Kurdish groups). Talabani obtains Iranian
military support. Fearing defeat at hands of Talabani and Iran,
Barzani enters into agreement with Saddam Hussein and obtains
military support from Iraq.

1990–1997   Allied sanctions, first imposed against Iraq following invasion
of Kuwait, have catastrophic effect on civilian population (see
below). The severity of continuing western actions against Iraq
causes disquiet even among erstwhile Arab allies such as Saudi
Arabia (cf. Section 11).

(c) *Deaths in war and aftermath*

100,000–200,000 Iraqi troops killed in war; minimal allied casualties. Several
thousand Kuwaitis killed during and after Iraqi invasion of Kuwait (many
apparently random victims of torture by Iraqi forces).

40,000 Iraqis die in failed rebellions against Saddam Hussein following end of
war.

Between 750,000 and 1,500,000 Iraqi civilians, mainly children and old people,
die as result of allied sanctions in six years (up to 1997) following war.

(d) *Other human cost of war: forced migration*

1,000,000 Iraqis flee country in wake of war.

700,000 Yemenis expelled from Saudi Arabia in Sept. 1990, following 'soft'
Yemeni line against Iraq.

350,000 Egyptians forced to leave Iraq when Egypt joins anti–Iraqi coalition.

150,000 Egyptians forced to leave Kuwait by Iraqi invasion.

600,000 Asians forced to leave Kuwait by Iraqi invasion.

300,000 Palestinians forced to leave Kuwait and Saudi Arabia following Iraqi
invasion, and following liberation from Iraqi occupation.

(e) *Environmental cost of war*
Iraqi burning of oil fields leaves huge slicks in Kuwait. Kuwait itself wrecked by Iraqi soldiers.

(f) *Economic cost of war*
Damage to Iraq estimated at $175 billion.
Damage to Kuwait estimated at $60 billion.
Allied war costs: $100 billion – mainly paid by Saudi Arabia, and Kuwait, leaving Saudi Arabia in particular with relative economic crisis.
Economy of Jordan seriously damaged, with influx of Palestinians from Kuwait, and economic sanctions against Iraq, Jordan's main trading partner.
Economy of Yemen seriously damaged by expulsion of Yemenis from Saudi Arabia.

2. Additional reading
(a) *The Times Guide to the Middle East*, pp. 311–12, 'The Gulf War: key UN resolutions'; p. 306 'Defence spending'.
(b) Hourani, *A History of the Arab Peoples*, pp. 426–33, 'Arab unity and disunity (since 1967)' .

3. Key vocabulary
On the basis of the texts in this chapter, draw up lists of vocabulary in the following fields:
(a) Military (any not covered in Arab–Israeli dispute).
(b) Diplomatic.
(c) Economic (sanctions, etc.).
(d) Human rights.

4. Written Arabic texts 1
(a) Read the following text from العلم, Aug. 3, 1990, then complete exercises i. and ii. which follow.

القوات العراقية تهاجم الكويت وتحتل القصر الأميري

القوات الكويتية تقاوم وتطلب من الأصدقاء التدخل لحماية الكويت

مجلس الأمن والولايات المتحدة يطلبان من العراق الانسحاب

تميز المشهد العربي في الساعات الأولى ليوم الخميس بتدخل

القوات العراقية في الكويت، وإعلان العراق الإطاحة بنظام الشيخ جابر الأحمد الصباح الذي تضاربت المعلومات حول مصيره، وتعويضه بحكومة مؤقتة.

وإلى غاية زوال الخميس التزمت الدول العربية الصمت تجاه الحادث، وتكثفت الاتصالات بين بعض القادة العرب، وبالمقابل حركت الإدارة الأمريكية أساطيلها البحرية في المنطقة معلنة في نفس الوقت تجميد الودائع العراقية والكويتية في المصارف الأمريكية، كما دعت إدارة بوش العراق إلى سحب قواته فوراً واتخذت موسكو نفس الموقف كما ندد مجلس الأمن الدولي بالتدخل العراقي.

أعلن بيان لمجلس قيادة الثورة العراقية أنه تمت الإطاحة بالحكومة الكويتية. وأشار البيان أن مجلس قيادة الثورة قرر «الاستجابة لطلب حكومة الكويت الحرة المؤقتة والتعاون معها».

وأضاف البيان أن القوات العراقية ستنسحب من الأراضي الكويتية «حالما يستقيم الحال وتطلب منه حكومة الكويت الحرة المؤقتة ذلك» مشيراً إلى أن مدة تواجد القوات العراقية بالأراضي الكويتية قد لا تتعدى «بضعة أيام أو بضعة أسابيع».

ومن جهة أخرى أعلن مصدر في مطار الكويت الدولي أن المطار أغلق يوم الخميس أمام الملاحة الجوية، وذلك بعد بضع ساعات على دخول القوات العراقية أراضي الكويت.

وكانت وزارة الدفاع الكويتية أعلنت أن القوات العراقية عبرت الحدود الشمالية للكويت، واحتلت مواقع في الأراضي الكويتية.

وذكرت وكالة فرانس بريس أن «حكومة مؤقتة للكويت الحرة» أعلنت الإطاحة بنظام الأمير الشيخ جابر وحل البرلمان.

i   Answer the following questions in English.

1. When did Iraqi forces invade Kuwait?
2. What did Iraq announce that day?

3. How did the Arab states react immediately to the Iraqi invasion of Kuwait?
4. How did the United States react?
5. Who condemned the Iraqi invasion?
6. The Iraqi Revolutionary Command Council said that it responded to a call from which government?
7. When did the Council say that Iraqi forces would withdraw from Kuwaiti territory?
8. What did France Press report?

ii   Translate the above text into idiomatic English.

(b) Read the following newspaper text from الحياة, Feb. 27, 1991, then translate the first half of the text (upto حاكما عرفيا) into idiomatic English. This text reports the end of the Gulf war.

الكويت   حُرِّرت

دخلت امس قوات الحلفاء مدينة الكويت التي بقيت تحت الاحتلال العراقي منذ ٢ آب (اغسطس) الماضي، وقال شهود عيان ان الاعلام الكويتية ارتفعت على سطوح الابنية، فيما عبر المواطنون عن فرحهم على رغم الوضع الذي تعانيه المدينة لجهة افتقادها اي نوع من الخدمات العامة.

وعلى رغم اعلان الرئيس صدام حسين سحب قواته من الكويت، الا ان التحالف اعتبر ذلك « غير مقبول » واعلن الرئيس جورج بوش ان « الحرب مستمرة » وافادت تقارير عسكرية ان قوات فرنسية وامريكية وبريطانية اجتازت نهر الفرات ووصلت الى مدينة الناصرية شمال البصرة لتقطع بذلك كل الجسور والطرق امام انسحاب قوات الحرس الجمهوري المرابطة جنوب العراق وبقية القوات المنسحبة من الكويت.

واستسلم الوف امس من الجنود العراقيين في الكويت تاركين آلياتهم ومعداتهم من دون مقاومة تذكر، باستثناء معركة بالدبابات في مطار الكويت بين قوة عراقية وقوات حليفة. وقد وصلت طليعة قوة مصرية الى المطار.

واعلن امير دولة الكويت الشيخ جابر الاحمد فرض الاحكام

العرفية في بلاده لمدة ثلاثة اشهر ابتداء من امس وعين ولي العهد الشيخ سعد العبد الله حاكما عرفيا.

الوضع العسكري

ومن الرياض كتب *المحرر العسكري* انه يمكن تلخيص الموقف العسكري بعد مضي ثلاثة ايام على الحرب البرية بناء على المعلومات الرسمية الصادرة عن القيادة الحليفة وكذلك استنادا الى المعلومات المتعددة المنسوبة الى مصادر عسكرية عربية ودولية ان الحلفاء عازمون على مواصلة عملياتهم الهجومية على القوات العراقية سواء داخل الكويت او في العراق نفسه، وذلك الى حين تحقيق هدفين اساسيين هما:

اولا – القضاء على اي وجود عراقي قتالي منظم في الكويت وتجريد هذا الوجود من اسلحته ومعداته خصوصا الثقيلة منها كالدبابات والمدرعات والمدفعية الميدانية.

ثانيا – ازالة اي مصدر تهديد للقوات المتحالفة في مسرح العمليات الكويتي قد تشكله الوحدات العراقية العاملة على الجانب العراقي من الحدود، ولا سيما منها قوات الحرس الجمهوري.

ولذلك كان من الملاحظ تشديد جميع الناطقين العسكريين باسم القوات الحليفة في الرياض على القول ان الحرب لم تنته بعد، وانه لن يكون كافيا ان تنفذ القوات العراقية قرار الرئيس صدام حسين القاضي بمجرد انسحاب هذه القوات من الكويت.

واشارت المصادر العسكرية الى ان هناك فارقا بين التراجع والانسحاب وان ما تقوم به القوات العراقية في الكويت حاليا هو من الزاوية العسكرية مجرد تراجع تكتيكي سيكفل لهذه القوات في حال اتمامه الاحتفاظ بمعداتها وقدراتها، وهو ما لن تسمح به القوات الحليفة.

5. Written Arabic texts 2

Translate the following text by غسان كنفاني from رجال في الشمس, pp. 71–2, into idiomatic English. In your translation take account of the author's use of metaphor.

خرج مروان من دكان الرجل السمين الذي يتولى تهريب الناس من البصرة إلى الكويت، فوجد نفسه في الشارع المسقوف المزدحم الذي تفوح منه رائحة التمر وسلال القش الكبيرة ... لم تكن لديه أية فكرة محددة عن وجهته الجديدة ... فهناك، داخل الدكان، تقطعت آخر خيوط الأمل التي شدت، لسنوات طويلة، كل شيء في داخله ... كانت الكلمات الأخيرة التي لفظها الرجل السمين حاسمة ونهائية، بل خيّل إليه أنها كانت مصبوبة من رصاص:

– خمسة عشر ديناراً ... ألا تسمع؟

– ولكن ...

– أرجوك! أرجوك! لا تبدأ بالنواح! كلكم تأتون إلى هنا ثم تبدأون بالنواح كالأرامل! ... يا أخي، يا روحي ... لا أحد يجبرك على الالتصاق هنا، لماذا لا تذهب وتسأل غيري، البصرة مليئة بالمهربين!

طبعاً سيذهب ويسأل غيره، لقد قال له حسن – الذي اشتغل في الكويت أربع سنين – أن تهريب الفرد الواحد من البصرة إلى الكويت يكلف خمسة دنانير فقط لا غير، وأنه يجب أن يكون – حين يمثل أمام المهرب – أكبر من رجل وأكثر من شجاع وإلا ضحك عليه وخدعه واستغل سنيه الست عشرة وجعل منه ألعوبة.

6. Written Arabic texts 3 (classical)

Read the following text by ابن قتيبة from كتاب الحرب in عيون الأخبار, pp. 107–8, then translate the first two paragraphs into idiomatic English. This text is concerned with the morals of war.

حدثنا القاسم بن الحسن عن الحسن بن الربيع عن ابن المبارك عن حَيَوة بن شُرَيح قال: كان عمر بن الخطاب رضي الله عنه إذا

بعث امراء الجيوش اوصاهم بتقوى الله العظيم، ثم قال عند عقد
الالوية: بسم الله وعلى عـون الله وامضُوا بتـأييـد الله بالنصـر
وبلزوم الحق والصبـر، فـقـاتِلوا في سبيـل الله من كـفر بالله ولا
تعتدوا إن الله لا يحب المعتدين. لا تجبنوا عند اللقاء ولا تمثِّلوا عند
القدرة ولا تسرفوا عند الظهور ولا تقتلوا هَرِما ولا امرأة ولا وليدا.
وتوقُّوا قـتـلهم إذا الـتـقى الـزَّحْفان وعند حُمَّة النَهَضاتِ¹ وفي شنّ
الغـارات. ولا تغُلُّوا عند الغنائم ونزِّهوا الجهـاد عن عـرَض الدنيـا
وأبشروا بالرِّبَاح في البيع الذي بايعتم به وذلك هو الفوز العظيم.

استشار قوم اكثم بن صَيْفِيّ في حرب قوم أرادوهم وسألوه أن
يوصيهم فقال: أقلُّوا الخلاف على أمرائكم، واعلمـوا أن كثرة الصِّيا ح
من الفشل والمرء يَعجز لا محالة. تثبّتوا فإن أحزم الفريقين الرَّكين،
ورُبَّتَ عَجَلة تُعقب رَيْثا، واتّزروا للحرب وادّرعوا الليل فإنه أخفى
للويل، ولا جماعة لمن اختُلف عليه.

وقال بعض الحكمـاء: قـدْ جمع الله لنا أدب الحرب في قوله تعالى
«يَأَيُّهـا الَّذِينَ آمَنُوا إِذَا لَقِيتُمْ فِئَةً فَاثْبُتُوا وَاذْكُرُوا اللَّهَ كَثِيرًا لَعَلَّكُمْ
تُفْلِحُونَ وَأَطِيعُوا اللَّهَ وَرَسُولَهُ وَلَا تَنَازَعُوا فَتَفْشَلُوا وَتَذْهَبَ رِيحُكُمْ
وَاصْبِرُوا إِنَّ اللَّهَ مَعَ الصَّابِرِينَ ».

Note

١ – أي شدتها ومعظمها.

7. Grammar/stylistics

(a) *The use of deictics*

The pronouns ذلك and, to a far lesser extent هذا, are used not only before definite
nouns, as in: هذا البيت 'this house' or as the subject of a sentence, as in: هذا
رجل 'this is a man', but also as clausal anaphoric deictics: that is to say, they occur
after a clause or sentence and refer back to that particular clause or sentence. In
general the deictics occur after a comma followed by a conjunction (و or ...ف) and
take no verb; this is particularly relevant for translation purposes since ذلك is often
used to translate 'this happened' or 'this took place' in sentences such as: 'the man
leapt from the roof and broke his leg; *this happened* a few minutes before the police
arrived.' Consider the following examples:

دخل الأكراد في الإسلام في عهد الخليفة عمر بن الخطاب، رضي الله
تعالى عنه، بعد أن فتحت بلاد فارس، {وذلك} قبل أن يدخل في
الإسلام جيرانهم من الفرس.

'The Kurds embraced Islam during the era of Umar ibn al-Khattab, may
God be pleased with him; this happened before their neighbours the
Persians embraced Islam.' (ch. 2, 5b)

تم الكشف عن كنيسة بيزنطية ثانية ذات أرض فسيفسانية ...
{وذلك} في موقع البصيلة الأثري غرب مدينة الرمثا، شمال
الأردن.

'A second Byzantine church was discovered with a faince floor. This
[discovery] took place in the archeological site of Basila to the west of
the city of Ramtha in the north of Jordan.' (ch. 3, 4b)

Often ذلك and وذلك is best left untranslated in the English, as in the example
below where the literal translation 'and that' is sectioned off in square brackets:

ومن جهة أخرى أعلن مصدر في مطار الكويت الدولي أن المطار
أُغلق يوم الخميس أمام الملاحة الجوية {وذلك} بعد بضع ساعات على
دخول القوات العراقية أراضي الكويت.

'Meanwhile a spokesman for Kuwait International Airport announced
that the airport had been closed to international air–traffic on Thursday
[and that] a few hours after the entry of Iraqi troops on Kuwaiti soil.'
(ch. 7, 4b)

ذلك often occurs deictically as the object of a preposition, usually ـبـ، ـكـ or ـل. In this
context it still functions as a clausal anaphora but usually translates as an English
adverb or adverb phrase, as: بذلك 'thus' or 'therefore', كذلك 'similarly' or
'likewise', and لذلك 'therefore', 'because of this'. Examples include:

كانت هذه هي المرة الأولى التي يتراجع فيها المغول {وبذلك} منع
الأكراد تقدمهم نحو بغداد.

'This was the first time that the Mongols retreated, and thus the Kurds
prevented them from advancing on Baghdad.' (ch. 2, 5b)

وأما قضاعة فقيل انها حمير قاله ابن اسحاق والكلبي وطائفة،
وقد يحتج {لذلك} بما رواه ابن لهيعة عن عقبة بن عامر الجهني.

'The Quda'a were said to be Himyaritic. This was said by Ibn Ishaq, al-
Kalbi and Ta'ifa, and evidence for this is given in what Ibn Luhay'a
said on the authority of 'Uqba ibn Amir al-Jahni.' (ch. 2, 6a)

الذين بحـثـوا في هذا الأمـر غيـر متـفـقين على المعنى أو الأصل
للتسمـية، {فلذلك} كل ما يمكن أن يقال هنا: هو أن الطوارق كاسم
لا يزال ينتظر من يمكن أن يميط اللثام عنه.

'Those who study this matter do not agree on the meaning or the origin
of the name, thus all that can be said at the moment is that 'Tuareg' as a
name is still awaiting someone to remove the veil [i.e. mystery] from
it.' (ch. 2, 9)

... وقـد بدأت أعـمـال التـرمـيـم في الهـرم المكتـشف من الخـارج
{وكذلك} اللوحة التي عليها اسم الملكة.

'The restoration works on the discovered pyramid began from the
outside, and also the tablet which bears the name of the queen.' (ch. 3,
5b)

... انفردوا في قديم الزمان وانضـافـوا إلى الجبـال والأودية لأحوال
دعتهم إلى {ذلك}.

'They separated a long time ago and set out for the mountains and
valleys because of circumstances which impelled them to do so.' (ch. 2,
6c)

وكان يسكنها جماعات من الصيادين في العصر الميسوليثي. وما
لبث بعد {ذلك} بحوالى ألف سنة أن أصبـحت لها معالم المدينة.

'Groups of hunters lived there during the Mesolithic age, and only a
thousand years after this it began to acquire the characteristics of a
town.' (ch. 3, 9)

... ويختلط صوت السقوط بصوت صراخ حاد .. وزعيق .. أصوات
مـختلفة .. استـغاثات وبكاء وأثناء {ذلك} يندفع بعض الغبار إلى
المسرح.

'The sound of falling is accompanied by the sound of shrill screams,
yelling, different sounds, cries for help, weeping, and at the same time
dust falls onto the stage.' (ch. 5, 5b)

ذلك can occasionally be the subject of a preceding or following verb, as in:

إذ ليس بيننا من يتكلم عـربيـة الجاهليـة أو العصـور الإسـلامـيـة
الأولى. {وذلك} يعني انقراض لغتنا الفصحى.

'There is no-one amongst us who can speak the Arabic of pre–Islamic
times of the early Islamic eras, and that would mean the end of our
classical language.' (ch. 5, 11b)

وحول ملاحظة البعض أن الأمطار كانت « غامقة » اللون أي ملوثة،
حيث ظهر {ذلك} بشكل كبير على زجاج السيارات.

'Regarding the fact that some people had seen that the rain was dark in colour, i.e. polluted, since that [i.e. the dark coloured rain] had appeared in large measure on the window screens of cars ...' (ch. 8, 4c)

The deictic هذا is used less commonly than ذلك and is usually followed by معنى or preceded by a verb (usually يعني), as in:

ارتدت البرابرة بالمغرب اثنتى عشرة مرة. ولم تستقر كلمة
الإسلام فيهم إلا لعهد ولاية موسى بن نصير فما بعده. {وهذا}
معنى ما يُنقَل عن عمر أن إفريقية مفرقة لقلوب أهلها.

'"The Berbers in North Africa apostacised twelve times and the message of Islam did not become firmly established amongst them until the rule of Musa ibn Nusayr and after him." This means, as related by Umar, that Africa is divided according to the hearts of its people.' (ch. 6, 6b)

وهناك من يقول إن أصل البربر من اليمن .. ومعنى {هذا} أن
البربر يكونون شعبا ساميا أو شعوبا سامية.

'There are people who say that the Berbers originate from Yemen, and this would mean that the Berbers are a Semitic race.' (ch. 2, 8)

أصل الإسلام هو التوحيد ويعني {هذا} أنه يجب على المسلم أن
يصدّق أن الله واحد لا اثنان أو ثلاثة.

'Islam is based on belief in the unity of God, and this means that Muslims must believe that there is only one God, and not two or three.' (ch. 4, 4b)

تمادت إسرائيل فوق تحدياتها ونفت أكثر من أربعمائة فلسطيني
من بلادهم، وتركتهم يموتون من البرد، كل {هذا} لم يحرك الدول
الثلاث ولم يغضبها.

'Israel overstepped the marks in its defiance, expelled more than 400 Palestinians from their country and left them to die of cold. None of this moved or angered the three states.' (ch. 7, 11)

هذا can also occur in the same context as ذلك, i.e. on its own or as the object of a preposition, but in fewer instances:

فـإذا فـرغـوا مـنـه نـحـتـوه مـن فـوق إلى أسـفل فهـذه كانـت حيـلـتـهم وكـان
مـع {هذا} لـهم قـوة وصـبـر وطـاعة لمـلـوكهم ديـانـية.

'When they finished they carved it from top to bottom. This was their
technique, and in addition [to this] they had strength, patience and a
devout obedience to their kings.' (ch. 3, 6c)

فـقـال: سـمـعت بـبـلدك لحنـا، فـأردت أن أصـنـع كـتـابـا في أصـول
العـربـية. فقـلت لـه: إن فعـلتَ {هذا} أبـقيت فينـا هذه اللغة العـربـية.

'He said, "I heard a grammatical error in your village, and I would like
to write a book on the basic rules of Arabic." I said to him, "If you do
that then you will establish the Arabic language for us."' (ch. 5, 6c)

Finally, one common deictic use of هذا today is in news broadcasts where it is
used as an anaphoric pronoun not to a previous clause or sentence but to a previous
set of clauses or related news chunk. In this case هذا is not preceded by a
conjunction, but is *followed* by the conjunction و. Its purpose appears to be simply
to provide a link between and within news items. Depending on the context هذا و
can be translated as 'also', 'however', or in some cases is best left untranslated in
English. Examples include:

وصرّح المبعوث السوفياتي لصحيفة النيو يورك تايمز بانه يعتقد
ان الرئيس صدام حسين يفكّر الآن بطريقة اكثر واقعية واذا امكن
ايجاد تحرك ما بشأن مطالبته بربط مشاكل الشرق الاوسط معا
فان ذلك سيسمح له باتخاذ قرار بالانسحاب من الكويت. هذا
وتفيد الانباء بأن الولايات المتحدة اطلقت قمرا صناعيا جديدا
للتجسس لرصد تحركات القوات العراقية.

'The Soviet envoy expressed his belief that President Saddam Hussein
was now thinking more realistically to the New York Times, and that if
it was possible to find anyway forward in regard to his [SH's] demand
of linking the problems of the Middle East, this would enable him to
withdraw from Kuwait. The news also reports that the USA has
launched a new spy satellite to monitor Iraqi troop movements.' (ch. 7,
8)

ثم ألقى كامل أبو جابر وزير الخارجية الأردني كلمة دعا فيها إلى
إحلال سلام كامل وعادل. {هذا و}سيستمع المؤتمر بعد حوالي نصف
الساعة إلى كلمة الدكتور حيدر عبد الشافي من الوفد الأردني
الفلسطيني المشترك كما سيستمع بعد ذلك إلى كلمة الوفد
اللبناني ثم إلى كلمة الوفد السوري. {هذا و} لم تتفق الوفود
المشتركة في مؤتمر مادريد على مكان المحادثات الثنائية للمرحلة

الثانية من المؤتمر.

'Then Kamil Abu Jaber, the Jordanian Minister of Foreign Affairs gave
a speech in which he called for a full and just peace. In half an hour the
conference will listen to a speech by Dr Haydar Abd al-Shafi from the
Jordanian–Palestinian delegation. After that it will listen to a speech by
the Lebanese delegation, and then to a speech by the Syrian delegation.
[However] The delegations have not yet decided on the venue for the
bilateral talks in the next stage of the conference.' (ch. 6, 9)

(b) *Compound adjectives*

When a noun can only be described by two adjectives, neither of which is more
important than the other, the two adjectives both agree with the head noun and the
order of the adjectives is immaterial. Compound adjectives are used particularly in
political and diplomatic texts in the description, for example, of wars which cannot
be described as belonging to one side and not another, talks, and diplomatic or
trade relations. An example from English would be 'Sino–British relations' where
the 'relations' described are both 'Sino' and 'British' and thus neither adjective can
be omitted, and syntactically (though not necessarily stylistically) the order could
be either 'Sino–British' or 'British–Sino'; indeed in some cases the translation of
compound adjectives may alter the word order for stylistic reasons peculiar to the
target language. In this regard consider the second example below. This type of
equal adjective combination can be compared to non–equal combinations where the
second adjective describes a type of the noun plus first adjective and therefore the
second adjective cannot be placed before the first adjective without altering the
meaning: consider 'the Arab Islamic world' where 'Arab' describes a sub–type of
'Islamic world' and thus compares the '*Arab* Islamic world' with the '*non–Arab*
Islamic world'. Orthographically compound adjectives of the type 'Sino–British
relations' may be linked by a hyphen (–) or by nothing at all in Arabic. The use of
a hyphen in Arabic is a relatively recent phenomenon and has probably arisen as a
result of the influence of western journalistic writings. Examples include:

خلال الحرب {العراقية – الإيرانية}.

'During the Iraqi–Iranian war' (ch. 8, 11)

توقيع الاتفاق {الفلسطيني – الاسرائيلي}.

'The signing of the Palestinian–Israeli Agreement' (ch. 6, 11)

ونشاط شركة الهند {الشرقية الإنجليزية}.

'The activity of the Indian Anglo–Eastern company' (ch. 18, 5b)

النزاع {الاسرائيلي – الفلسطيني} هو اساس النزاع {العربي – الاسرائيلي}.

'The Israeli–Palestinian conflict is the basis of the Arab–Israeli conflict.'

This use of (usually) hyphenated compound adjectives can be compared to the use of hyphenated, and hence syntactically equal, second parts of the إضافة, as in:

'The Gaza–Jericho Agreement' (ch. 6, 11)   اتفاق {غزة – أريحا}.

It is also possible to find other kinds of compound adjective in Arabic. Examples are the neologism شرق أوسطي for 'Middle Eastern'. The feminine of this is شرق أوسطية, and the form with the definite article is الشرق أوسطي (masculine), with the feminine الشرق أوسطية. Arabs who take a purist attitude towards the Arabic tend to reject forms of this kind, since they represent a grammatical innovation. A slightly different type of compound adjective is حِزْبيٌّ تَعَدُّدِيّ 'multi–party', as in:

تبدو مصر الآن مجتمعا شبه حزبي تعددي.
'Egypt today appears to be a quasi–multi–party society.' (ch. 13, 5c)

The feminine of حزبي تعددي is حزبية تعددية, and the form with the definite article is الحزبي التعددي (masculine), الحزبية التعددية (feminine).

8. Aural Arabic texts 1
Listen to the following BBC Arabic Service news broadcast from Nov. 16, 1990, then complete exercises i. – iii. below. This broadcast relates to the post–invasion / pre–war period.

i   Answer the following questions in English.

1. Who is Yevgeny Primakov?
2. What does he call for?
3. What would this enable President Hussein to do?
4. Why did the Americans launch a new satellite?
5. How was this new satellite carried?
6. How many American satellites are observing the area?
7. Iraq condemned the military exercises conducted by American and Saudi forces as what?
8. How did the Iraqi Thawrah newspaper describe the military exercises?
9. What did it accuse the United States of?
10. What were the military exercises called?
11. How long will the exercises last?
12. How many planes took part in the exercises?
13. What was the function of these planes?

ii Answer the following questions in Arabic.

١ – من هو يذغيني بريماكوف؟

٢ – إلى ماذا دعى؟

٣ – ما رأي بريماكوف في حالة عدم انسحاب عراقي من الكويت؟

٤ – هل يلاحظ بريماكوف تغييرا في موقف صدام حسين؟

٥ – ما هو هدف القمر الصناعي الأمريكي الجديد؟

٦ – ما هو السبب الرسمي في تأخير إطلاق القمر الصناعي؟

٧ – ما هو السبب غير الرسمي؟

٨ – لماذا ندد العراق بالتدريبات العسكرية الأمريكية؟

iii Listen to the tape and fill in the gaps in the text below. This relates to the last two thirds of the text, beginning الأنباء بالتفاصيل.

الأنبـاء ————————— ————————— . —————————

يذغيني بريماكوف ————————— ————————— الخاص —————————

————————— إلى ————————— التمهل —————————

أن يُقدِم مجلس ————————— ————————— على التخويل باستخدام

————————— ————————— لإخراج ————————— من ————————— .

و————————— إن هذه المهلة ————————— أن تُستغَل —————————

إيجاد صيغة تحفظ ماء الوجه تمكّن ————————— —————————

————————— من سحب قواته . و————————— ————————— قال إنه

إذا لم ————————— ————————— ————————— لذلك فسيتعيّن على

————————— ————————— الموافقة على —————————

إجـراء ————————— ————————— سـينبـغي تنفـيـذه على

————————— ————————— ————————— . و————————— المبـعوث

النيـو يورك تايمز بأنه ————————— ————————— الرئيس

————————— ————————— يفكّر ————————— بطريقة —————————

ــــــ وإذا أمكن إيجاد ــــــ ــــــ ــــــ بشأن

مطالبته بربط ــــــ ــــــ ــــــ ــــــ

ــــــ فإن ذلك سيسمح له باتخاذ ــــــ بالانسحاب

ــــــ ــــــ . ــــــ وتفيد ــــــ ــــــ بأن

الولايات ــــــ أطلقت قمرا صناعيا ــــــ للتجسس

لرصد ــــــ ــــــ ــــــ . وذُكر أن

ــــــ ــــــ حُمل على ــــــ مكوك الفضاء

« ــــــ » و ــــــ في آخر مهمة ــــــ له ، إذ

ستحل محله في ــــــ صواريخ غير مأهولة .

و ــــــ ــــــ الجوية ــــــ إن تأخير

ــــــ المكوك في ــــــ ــــــ يرجع إلى

ــــــ تقنية . ولكن ــــــ هيئة ــــــ

ــــــ ــــــ للشؤون ــــــ ــــــ

يُعتقد أن تعديلات قد أُجريت على ــــــ

لتمكينه من جمع ــــــ من ــــــ التي تتعلق

ــــــ ــــــ . ومن ــــــ أنه يوجد

ــــــ أقمار ــــــ أخرى ــــــ ــــــ .

ــــــ ــــــ العراق ــــــ التي تجريها

ــــــ ــــــ و ــــــ في

باعتبارها ــــــ يمكن أن ــــــ المنطقة في

ــــــ . فقد قالت ــــــ ــــــ البغدادية

Sell your books at
World of Books!
Go to sell.worldofbooks.com
and get an instant price
quote. We even pay the
shipping - see what your old
books are worth today!

Inspected By: Gicels_Bello

00091237526

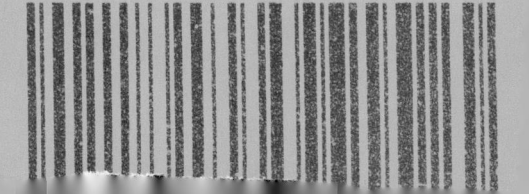

—————— بلسان حزب —————— —————— —————— بالعراق أن

هذه —————— التي ستستغرق —————— —————— إنما

هي استفزاز يهدف إلى —————— —————— من الضغط على

—————— —————— —————— . واتهمت —————— ——————

بتلفيق الذرائع من أجل شن حرب . وتشترك في هذه التدريبات

التي أطلق عليها اسم —————— —————— —————— ألف ——————

توفر غطاءا —————— —————— وهم يقومون بهجوم من ——————

على —————— —————— —————— قرب —————— —————— .

9. Aural Arabic texts 2

Listen to the following BBC Arabic Service news broadcast from Jan. 21, 1991, then complete exercises i. and ii. below. This broadcast relates to the period of the Gulf war.

i Answer the following questions in Arabic.

١ – يهدّد العراق بنقل طياري القوات المتحالفة الأسرى إلى أماكن معينة مذكورة . ما هي؟

٢ – ما هو التبرير العراقي لهذا الإجراء؟

٣ – حسب إذاعة بغداد كم عدد الأسرى لدى العراقيين الآن؟

٤ – ماذا سلمت وزارة الخارجية الأمريكية إلى القائم بالأعمال العراقي في واشنطن؟

٥ – ماذا عمل دوغلاس هارد؟

٦ – كيف وصف هارد معاهدة جينيف؟

٧ – كم عدد الصواريخ من طراز «اسكاد» المطلقة على الرياض أمس؟

٨ – ماذا عمل سكان الرياض عند الهجوم؟

٩ – كم عدد المصابين في الهجوم؟

١٠- كم عدد الصواريخ المطلقة على المنطقة الشرقية من المملكة العربية السعودية؟

١١ – أين سقطت هذه الصواريخ؟

١٢ –هل حملت الصواريخ العراقية المتفجرات الكيميائية؟

ii Fill in the gaps in the text below.

قالت : ـــــــــــ ـــــــــــ ـــــــــــ ـــــــــــ إلى

إذاعة ـــــــــــ ـــــــــــ طياري ـــــــــــ المتحالفة

الأسرى سيُنقلون ـــــــــــ ـــــــــــ ما سمّته بمنشآت علمية

ـــــــــــ ـــــــــــ ـــــــــــ ـــــــــــ .

ـــــــــــ إن ـــــــــــ القرار اُتّخِذ ـــــــــــ ـــــــــــ قصف

ـــــــــــ ـــــــــــ ـــــــــــ لأهداف

ـــــــــــ أحدث اصابات

ـــــــــــ ـــــــــــ ـــــــــــ المدنيين وأضافت قائلة

الطيّارين ـــــــــــ أسروا ـــــــــــ ـــــــــــ ـــــــــــ

ـ. أعربت ـــــــــــ ـــــــــــ الولايات

ـــــــــــ ـــــــــــ قلقهما ـــــــــــ ـــــــــــ و

معاملة ـــــــــــ للأسرى . ـــــــــــ استُدعى القائم

بالأعمال ـــــــــــ ـــــــــــ

ـــــــــــ وسُلّم مذكّرة احتجاج تضمّنت شكوى

ـــــــــــ سوء ـــــــــــ ـــــــــــ ما يبدو

وذُكّر بأن ـــــــــــ يُعدّ جريمة ـــــــــــ بموجب معاهدة

جينيف. ـــــــــــ ـــــــــــ دعا

دوغـــلاس هـورد ـــــــــــ ـــــــــــ

ـــــــــــ ـــــــــــ مراعاة

ـــــــــ وُجـدت ـــــــــ ـــــــــ ـــــــــ ـــــــــ ـــــــــ

لضـمـان حسـن ـــــــــ ـــــــــ ـــــــــ ـــــــــ دون

تحفّظات.

ـــــــــ ـــــــــ ـــــــــ ـــــــــ ـــــــــ

ـــــــــ إنها سوف ـــــــــ ـــــــــ

ـــــــــ إليها ـــــــــ ـــــــــ. وجاء

ـــــــــ بيـان صـادر عن ـــــــــ أنـه سـيُبلّغ بـأن

ـــــــــ تتتوقع ـــــــــ ـــــــــ يطبّق

بنود ـــــــــ بحـذافـيـرها. ـــــــــ

ـــــــــ تمكّنت ـــــــــ صد

هجـمـات صـاروخـيـة ـــــــــ ـــــــــ

ـــــــــ ـــــــــ ـــــــــ باستعمال

صـواريخ «بـاتريوت». ـــــــــ المتـحـدّثون الرسـمـيـون

ـــــــــ ـــــــــ أطلِقت ـــــــــ

ـــــــــ طراز «اسكاد» ـــــــــ

ـــــــــ الرياض ـــــــــ دُمّرت

ـــــــــ ـــــــــ بـوابل ـــــــــ.

ـــــــــ ـــــــــ يشنّ

ـــــــــ هجـومًا صـاروخـيًا ـــــــــ

ـــــــــ ـــــــــ ـــــــــ

الانفجارات ـــــــــ

هزّت أجواء المدينة حيث ———— ———— ———— الدفاع الجوّي

———— ———— ———— . ———— ———— لاعتراض

سكّان ———— ———— ———— الملاجئ وارتدوا الأقنعة الواقية

———— ———— ———— انفجر ———— الغاز

———— ———— ———— ———— ———— ما يبدو

———— بأحد ———— الأرض وألحق أضرارا ————

تحدث إصابات ———— ———— إلا ، ————

المسؤولون ———— الأفراد . ————

———— ———— ———— ————

———— ———— ———— ————

———— ———— ———— ————

———— صُوّب نحو ———— ———— موجتين

———— ———— ———— ———— الظهران .

———— ———— أُسقطت ————

———— ———— . ———— ———— يظهر

———— أي ———— يدلّ ———— ————

———— ———— ———— متفجرات

ثاني ———— ———— كميائية .

———— ———— تتعرّض ————

———— ———— قد أسقطِ ———— إذ ————

———— ———— ———— ————

الماضي. _____

10. Written English texts

(a) Making use of constructions and vocabulary encountered in the Arabic texts above as far as possible, translate the following text from the *Guardian Gulf Special Report* into idiomatic Arabic.

> The invasion of Kuwait has its roots in the Iran–Iraq war. Saddam wanted to regain control of the Shatt al-Arab waterway which he had been forced to surrender to the Shah at the 1975 Algiers conference. He failed and incurred huge debts of between £16bn–£21bn to rich states like Kuwait and Saudi Arabia. The invasion of Kuwait gave him access to the disputed islands of Warbah and Bubyan and hence better access to Gulf waters, while allowing him to write off his Kuwaiti debts.

(b) Making use of constructions and vocabulary encountered in the Arabic texts above as far as possible, translate the following text from *Middle East International*, Aug. 31, 1990 into idiomatic Arabic.

> **1 August:** Talks between Iraq and Kuwait collapse; Iraqi troops mass on Kuwaiti border. The US expresses its 'concern'.
>
> **2 August:** Iraqi forces cross the border into Kuwait at 2am local time and quickly gain control of the country. The amir and his extended family flee to Saudi Arabia. A new 'Provisional Free Government' closes all ports and the airport, bans foreign travel, imposes a curfew, and cuts off telecommunications with outside world. President Bush condemns Iraq's invasion as 'naked aggression', freezes Iraqi and Kuwaiti assets in the US and sends extra warships to the Gulf. He told reporters he was not contemplating military intervention. Britain freezes Kuwaiti assets in the UK worth billions of dollars. The Iraqi army announces the mobilisation of all reserves. The UN Security Council, summoned by Kuwait, passes resolution 660 calling for an immediate Iraqi withdrawal. Iran and Syria join in the condemnation, with the latter calling for an emergency Arab League summit; the rest of the Arab world conveys a stunned silence.

11. Précis

Read the following newspaper editorial from الشـرق الأوسـط Jan. 16, 1993, which was writtten following a large–scale attack by the western Gulf allies on an Iraqi rocket installation, then produce a précis in Arabic summarising the major points. The text was written during the war in Bosnia; there was strong Arab support for Muslim Bosnians.

مائة طائرة للهجوم على العراق! انها اشبه بمئة فيل تقرر الهجوم على ناموسة! لم تكن امريكا وانجلترا وفرنسا في حاجة الى هذه القوة الهائلة لضرب اربع قواعد للصواريخ، وأغلب الظن ان المقصود بهذا العدد الكبير تخويف الجيران وعلى رأسهم ايران.

ولقد كان في امكان الحلفاء ان يحصلوا على التأييد الاجماعي لو انهم عاملوا اسرائيل والصرب بما عاملوا به العراق ولكنهم كالوا بكيلين.

ان الهجوم العسكري على العراق سببه رفض العراق تنفيذ قرارات مجلس الامن، واسرائيل والصرب رفضتا قرارات مجلس الامن، وكل واحدة منهما تحدت الامم المتحدة وسخرت منها، وتمادت اسرائيل فوق تحدياتها ونفت اكثر من اربعمائة فلسطيني من بلادهم، وتركتهم يموتون من البرد، كل هذا لم يحرك الدول الثلاث ولم يغضبها، ذلك ان اسرائيل هي الدولة المدللة من الحلفاء، اذا اخطأت سامحوها، واذا اجرمت غفروا لها واذا اخرجت دولة عربية لسانها لاسرائيل قامت الدنيا ولم تقعد، او سمعنا كلاما كثيرا عن اننا دول ارهاب غير متمدنة واننا وحوش ومعتدون.

ولهذا استنكرت بعض الدول العربية العدوان الثلاثي بينما قالت دول اخرى بأن الحلفاء لقنوا العراق درسا لن ينساه، ولن ينسى صدام حسين هذه الضربة طالما هو يحكم العراق .. والوسيلة الوحيدة للتخلص من خطر صدام حسين ان يخرج صدام حسين.

ونحن نعترض على ان يقوم الحلفاء بضربة جديدة قبل خروج بوش من منصبه ونعترض على ارساله قوات برية لمحاربة العراق، فإن هذا يفيد صدام حسين اكثر مما يضره، ويصوره امام بعض العرب بصورة البطل الذي يحارب ثلاث دول عظمى تماما كما اعجب هؤلاء بالرئيس عبد الناصر بعد هزيمته المروعة في ٥ يونيو.

اننا ضد استعمال القوة، ونرى ان العالم يكسب بالسلام اكثر مما يكسب بالحرب ونعتقد انه كان من الممكن تسوية الخلاف مع العراق بغير قنابل وصواريخ، ونرى اننا اذا استعملنا القوة مع العراق فإنه يجب ان نستعمل نفس القوة مع اسرائيل والصرب وكل دولة معتدية لا ان نقسم العالم الى اصدقاء مَرْضى عنهم واعداء مغضوب عليهم.

12. Oral

الغزو العراقي للكويت

(a) One or two students to present a brief account of events leading up to the Gulf War.

(b) The presenter(s) then ask(s) the other students questions about events leading up to the Gulf War, major players in the war, and consequences of the war. These questions should require both factual answers and subjective answers. For example:

١ – ما هي الحوادث الرئيسية التي أدت إلى حرب الخليج؟

٢ – كيف استجابت الحكومة الكويتية الملكية لغزو العراق الكويت؟

٣ – ما هو رد فعل الوطن العربي للغزو العراقي؟

٤ – ما هو رد فعل أمريكا للغزو العراقي؟

٥ – ماذا كان دور بريطانيا في حرب الخليج؟

٦ – ما هي نتائج الحرب الرئيسية على الصعيد السياسي؟

٧ – هل هناك كاسبون في الحرب؟

٨ – في رأيك هل استجابت أمريكا للغزو العراقي استجابة مناسبة أم لا؟

٩ – ما هي عواقب الحرب البيئية؟

١٠. –ما هي عواقب الحرب الاجتماعية؟

(c) Open lecturer–led discussion on the Gulf War. Within the discussion consider the causes of the war, the events of the war, the aftermath and consequences of the war, and the winners and losers.

13. Essay

Write an essay in Arabic of around 200 words on the title حرب الخليج: أسبابها ونتائجها Structure your essay around the following questions:

١ – كيف ابتدأت حرب الخليج؟

٢ – من هم اللاعبون الرئيسيون في حرب الخليج؟

٣ – كيف أثرت حرب الخليج على البيئة في المنطقة وخارجها؟

٤ – ماذا كانت عواقب حرب الخليج الاقتصادية والاجتماعية في العراق؟

٥ – كيف تغيرت العلاقات السياسية في المنطقة بعد حرب الخليج؟

٦ – كيف أثرت حرب الخليج على قضية السلام في الشرق الأوسط؟

٧ – إلى أية درجة كانت حرب الخليج معرض أسلحة؟

8
Climate and environment

1. Basic background material

Energy use, water use and forest coverage in the Arab countries and Israel. (Figures for Japan, Netherlands, United Kingdom and United States are given separately below for comparison.)

	Energy use (Oil equiv.) per cap. (kg) 1993	Water use /a per cap. (cubic m) 1970–1994	Forest coverage /b Total area (000 sq km) 1990	As % of total land area 1990	Annual av. change (%) 1990
Algeria	955	160	41	2	-0.8
Bahrain	11,925	–	0	1	0.0
Egypt	576	956	0	0	0.0
Iraq	1,103	4,575	19	4	-0.1
Israel	2,607	408	1	6	0.3
Jordan	922	173	1	1	1.1
Kuwait	4,217	–	0	0	0.0
Lebanon	727	271	1	8	-0.6
Libya	1,883	692	7	0	1.4
Morocco	299	427	90	20	1.5
Oman	2,408	564	41	19	0.0
Qatar	16,196	–	0	1	-0.2
Saudi Arabia	4,552	497	12	1	0.0
Sudan	68	1,091	430	18	-1.1
Syrian Arab Rep.	798	435	7	4	4.5
Tunisia	576	317	7	4	1.9
UAE	16,878	884	0	0	0.0
Yemen, Rep.	285	335	41	8	0.0

Japan	3,642	735	238	63	0.0
Netherlands	4,533	518	3	10	0.3
United Kingdom	3,718	205	24	10	1.1
United States	7,918	1,870	2,960	32	-0.1

Note: '–' means not available; the number 0 or 0.0 means zero or less than half the unit shown, or not known precisely. Figures for water use in the West Bank are included in Jordan; no figures are given for water use in Gaza.

2. Additional reading
(a) Hourani, *A History of the Arab Peoples*, pp. 98–104; pp. 333–6.

3. Key vocabulary
Taking the texts in this chapter as a starting point, draw up lists of vocabulary in the following fields:
(a) Weather/climate.
(b) Pollution.
(c) Desertification.
(d) Oil–specific.
(e) General environmental: ozone layer, global warming, etc.

4. Written Arabic texts 1
The following texts provide general background to weather vocabulary. As a preparatory exercise for classwork on this chapter, read the following texts at home.

(a) From a radio weather broadcast

حالة الطقس ليوم غد:

سيكون الجو حسنًا مع تصاعُد غبار محلّي والرياح شمالية شرقية. درجات الحرارة المتوقّعة ليوم غد: درجة الحرارة العظمى ٤٢، درجة الحرارة الصغرى١٩.

كانت درجة الحرارة العظمى البارحة ٤٠، والصغرى ١٨.

(b) A Gulf newspaper weather forecast. Read this forecast, then complete exercises
   i. – iii. which follow.

الطقس لدول مجلس التعاون

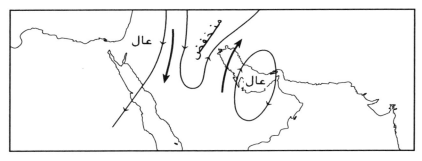

خارطة الطقس المتوقع اليوم ٨٨/١١/١٠.

تبين الدوائر درجة الحرارة العظمى المتوقعة أما الأسهم فتشير إلى اتجاه
الرياح والسرعة (كم/الساعة) أما الضغط الجوي فيظهر بالبكتوباسكال
«ميليبار».

الطقس المتوقع لعواصم مجلس التعاون

الكويت: طقس معتدل والرياح متقلبة إلى جنوبية شرقية خفيفة إلى
معتدلة السرعة.

المنامة: طقس معتدل والرياح جنوبية غربية خفيفة إلى معتدلة السرعة.

الدوحة: طقس معتدل والرياح جنوبية قربية خفيفة السرعة.

أبو ظبي: طقس رطب والرياح شمالية شرقية خفيفة السرعة.

مسقط: طقس غائم جزئيا والرياح متقلبة خفيفة السرعة.

الرياض: طقس غائم جزئيا والرياح شمالية غربية خفيفة إلى معتدلة
السرعة.

درجات الحرارة في عواصم دول مجلس التعاون الخليجي

الطقس	درجة مئوية	العاصمة
صحو	٣٣	الكويت
صحو	٢٩	المنامة
غائم	٣٠.	الدوحة
صحو	٣٠.	أبو ظبي
صحو	٣٠.	مسقط
صحو	٣٢	الرياض

i   Draw up a list of weather terms from this chart. Include adjectives.

ii   Explain what the map shows.

iii Write a description in Arabic of the weather in your town or village today. Take
the additional vocabulary you require from standard dictionaries and lexicons.

(c) Read the following text from الأهرام, Mar. 23, 1991, then complete exercises
i. and ii. which follow.

بعد «صدمة» المطر والبرق والرعد ..
الارصاد «تتوقع» تحسن الجو اليوم

بعد أن تناول سكان القاهرة وجبة إفطارهم أول أمس (الخميس) وأثناء
مشاهدتهم لبرامج التليفزيون بدأت الأمطار تهطل بغزارة لم يعهدوها من
قبل. وسمعوا لأول مرة في هذه الشتاء أصوات الرعد مع البرق الشديد،
ولكن التحسن في الجو أصبح متوقعا من اليوم.

وليس سكان القاهرة فقط هم الذين تأثروا بتلك الأمطار بل مصر كلها
منذ أمس الأول حتى ما قبل ظهر أمس (السبت).

ولكن ما هو السبب العلمي الذي جعل تلك الأمطار تهطل بتلك الصورة
في مثل هذا الوقت من السنة بل وبشكل استمر أكثر من ١٢ ساعة متواصلة
في بعض المحافظات.

يقول السيد أحمد مختار المصري رئيس الهيئة العامة للأرصاد الجوية
إن حالات عدم الاستقرار الشديدة منذ مساء أول أمس (الخميس) تمثلت في
تكاثر السحب المتوسطة والمنخفضة والرعدية صاحبها سقوط الأمطار
الغزيرة على معظم المناطق من أقصى الشمال وحتى أقصى الجنوب نتيجة
وجود منطقة تخلخل على الخرائط السطحية تشمل الجمهورية والجزء
الشرقي من البحر المتوسط، وصاحب ذلك في طبقات الجو العليا منخفض
جوي عميق مصحوب بكتلة هوائية باردة، أدت إلى هذه الحالة.

وأضاف رئيس الهيئة في تصريحات لخالد عز الدين مندوب الأهرام أن
الأمطار في الإسكندرية استمرت ١٢ ساعة متواصلة، وفي مرسى مطروح ١١
ساعة، ووصلت مدينة القاهرة مع غروب الشمس أمس الأول مصحوبة
بسحب رعدية ثم توجهت إلى مصر الوسطى ومصر العليا والتي بدأت فيها
الأمطار أمس (الجمعة) مثل الأقصر وأسوان وباقي محافظات الوجه القبلي.
وكانت الأمطار هناك غزيرة والسحب منخفضة وحدث رعد في أسوان.

وفي سوهاج تسببت الرياح الشديدة في اقتلاع الأشجار من جذورها وتحطيم نوافذ العمارات، وفي البحيرة قطعت المواصلات بين القرى والمدن واقتلعت بعض العشش والأكشاك، ووقعت حادثتان على الطريق السريع مصر - الإسكندرية.

ومن ناحية أخرى صرح اللواء سيد النبوي مدير أمن جنوب سيناء بأن الأمطار استمرت طوال الـ٤٨ ساعة الماضية وارتفعت المياه في بعض الأماكن إلى نحو المتر وتسببت في سقوط كميات كبيرة من الصخور.

وقد أمر محافظ جنوب سيناء بتكريس الجهود لربط المحافظة بالمحافظات الأخرى في أقرب وقت بعد أن تسببت السيول في غلق طريق نويبع - نفق الشهيد أحمد حمدي وغلق كل الطرق المؤدية إلى منطقة أبو رديس ورأس النقب.

وحول ملاحظة البعض أن الأمطار كانت «غامقة» اللون أي ملوثة، حيث ظهر ذلك بشكل كبير على زجاج السيارات، قال رئيس الهيئة: اطمئن بأننا في مصر بعيدون كل البعد عن تأثر منطقة الخليج بالسحب السوداء، وأن ما شهده سكان القاهرة وبعض المحافظات من سقوط أمطار سوداء يرجع إلى الشوائب العالقة في الجو، والتلوث الموجود من أدخنة المصانع وليس بسبب اشتعال الآبار في الخليج.

وعن حالة الجو اليوم (السبت) يقول رئيس الهيئة: إننا «نتوقع» تحسنا سريعا في الأحوال الجوية يبدأ غربا ويتقدم تدريجيا نحو المناطق الداخلية في حين تظل هذه الحالة متأثرة في المنطقة الشرقية، وإن هذا التحسن يشمل قلة كميات السحب من حيث النوعية ويقتصر وجود السحب على المنخفضة فقط وتكثر أثناء الظهيرة مع فرصة لسقوط أمطار خفيفة على بعض المناطق وتظل درجات الحرارة أقل من معدلاتها.

i Answer the following questions in Arabic.

١ - متى سقطت الأمطار في القاهرة؟

٢ - ما هو الغريب في هذه الأمطار؟

٣ - كم ساعة استمرّ نزول الأمطار؟

٤ - في أي مناطق سقطت هذه الأمطار؟

٥ - ماذا أدّى إلى الأمطار الشديدة؟

٦ - ماذا صاحب نزول الأمطار في القاهرة؟

٧ - في أي مدينة اقتلعت الرياح أشجارًا؟

٨ – ماذا تسبّب في سقوط الصخور في بعض المناطق؟

٩ – ما سبب لون الأمطار الغامق؟

١٠. –على قول رئيس الهيئة العامّة للأرصاد الجويّة ما هي العلاقة بين هطول أمطار سوداء واشتعال العراق الآبار في الخليج؟

١١ –كيف أثّرت الأمطار على درجة الحرارة في مصر؟

ii   Answer the following questions in English.

1. What happened in Cairo the day before yesterday?
2. During which Islamic month did this occurrence take place?
3. What did the population of Cairo hear for the first time this winter?
4. What is now expected?
5. Who has been affected?
6. Which areas of Egypt were affected?
7. According to the head of the meteorological office, what had caused this occurrence?
8. How long did it continue in Alexandria and Mersa Matruh?
9. Who is Khalid Izz al-Din?
10. When was Cairo hit by rain?
11. Which areas were then affected?
12. How are the clouds described in these areas?
13. What did strong winds cause in Sohag?
14. What happened in al-Buhayra?
15. What happened on the Alexandria–Cairo road?
16. What did Said Nabawi say about the rains?
17. What did the governor of South Sinai province order?
18. What happened to necessitate this order?
19. What colour is the rain said to have been?
20. What did some people think this colour could be due to?
21. What did the head of the meteorological office consider the colour due to?
22. How does he then describe the predicted improvement in weather – give details?

(d) Read the following texts (i) from صوت العرب, Oct. 7, 1990, and (ii) from الحياة, Sept. 25, 1990, then paraphrase them in Arabic:

(i) الحسين يحذر

الحسين يحذر من مخاطر حرب في الخليج
«ستكون كارثة على البيئة»!
جنيف – الأمم المتحدة – ا.ف.ب.
وصل العاهل الأردني إلى جنيف ضمن جولة أوروبية يقوم بها في

عدة عواصم. وركز الحسين في جولته الأوروبية على قضايا البيئة في محاولة منه لجذب أحزاب الخضر الأوروبية لموقف العاهل الأردني المؤيد للعدوان العراقي على الكويت.

قال العاهل الأردني: إن الحرب إذا اندلعت في الخليج ستكون كارثة بيئية لم يعرف العالم لها مثيلا منذ حادثة مفاعل تشرنوبيل النووي.

وقال الملك حسين: إنه قرر المجيء إلى جنيف رغم التوتر المتصاعد في الشرق الأوسط ليذكر بأن التسخين الخطير لجو الأرض يقع ضمن سياق سياسي وإنساني شامل.

وقال: إن التصعيد العسكري المتمثل في وجود مليون جندي وجها لوجه والتوتر السياسي لا يكفان عن التصاعد، مضيفا أن هناك احتمالات كبيرة في حال اندلاع الحرب في الخليج كأن تستخدم الأسلحة الكيميائية والجرثومية مع ما يعنيه التدمير للحقول النفطية ومخزونات النفط.

وتابع، أن ثاني أوكسيد الكربون المنبعث سيؤدي إلى زيادة حرارة جو الأرض وهي الظاهرة التي اعتبرت في المؤتمر المسؤول الرئيسي عن تسخين الجو ولاحظ المراقبون، أن العاهل الأردني الذي انضم إلى أنصار البيئة، لم يذكر كلمة واحدة عن احتلال العراق للكويت.

(ii) وزير النفط الكويتي

وزير النفط الكويتي:
الجيش العراقي لغم آبار النفط في الكويت

واشنطن – أ.ف.ب. – أكد وزير النفط الكويتي السيد رشيد سالم العميري في مقابلة نشرتها أمس الاثنين صحيفة «واشنطن بوست» أن الجيش العراقي لغم معظم آبار النفط في الكويت التي يبلغ عددها ألفا.

وأوضح العميري واثنان من أقرب مساعديه لم تكشف هويتهما وأجريت المقابلة معهم في السعودية أن آبار النفط لغمت بمتفجرات من نوع «سي-٤». وعبروا عن خشيتهم من أن يشعل العراق حرائق هائلة في حقول النفط في المنطقة.

وكان الوزير الكويتي أعلن تلغيم آبار ومنشآت النفط في

الكويت أثناء توقف قصير له في سنغافورة في ٣٠ آب (أغسطس) الماضي.

وقال المسؤولون الكويتيون إن انفجار الآبار يؤدي إلى حرائق قد تمتص من الجو المحيط كل الأوكسيجين تقريبا.

وكانت الحكومة العراقية هددت أول من أمس بتدمير المنشآت النفطية في الشرق الأوسط وضرب إسرائيل في حال توجيه «ضربة دموية».

5. Written Arabic texts 2

(a) Translate the following newspaper text from الأهرام Mar. 21, 1990 into idiomatic English.

بسبب ضوضاء القاهرة :

٦٢٪ يتعاطون المهدئات و٣٣٪ ضغطهم مرتفع والإنتاج يهبط ١٤٪

سمات مرورية تنفرد بها القاهرة عن كل مدن العالم وتخرج على كل المعايير المرورية بما لديها من كباري تتمدد في شوارع ضيقة مثل شارع الأزهر وكوبري ١٥ مايو بالزمالك وحركة المشاة والسيارات التي اختلط فيها الحابل بالنابل بالإضافة إلى سلوكيات المشاة التي تأبي أن تعترف بأية قواعد مرورية، وقائدي السيارات الذين يستخدمون آلات التنبيه بطريقة عشوائية بالإضافة إلى أصوات المحركات التي تصرخ بأعلى صوتها لتعلن انتهاء عمرها الافتراضي منذ سنوات.

وهذا الأسبوع ظهرت دراسة تتضمن قياسات فعلية عن الضوضاء في شوارع القاهرة الكبرى والصادرة عن نحو مليون سيارة. نتائج الدراسة تؤكد أن الضوضاء قد تجاوزت مرحلة دق ناقوس الخطر، والأرقام تقول إن ٦٢٪ من السكان يتعاطون العقاقير المهدئة والمنومة والمسكنة بسبب الضوضاء وإن ضغط الدم ارتفع لدى المعرضين للضوضاء بنسبة ٣٣٪ في

حين انخفضت الإنتاجية بنسبة ١٤٪ سنويا وقد تجاوزت بعض مواقع الدراسة النسبة المسموح بها دوليا بمعدل ١٠ مرات.

ويقوم بتنفيذ هذه الدراسة علماء المركز القومي للبحوث كجهة رئيسية بتمويل من أكاديمية البحث العلمي بالاشتراك مع فريق من معهد بحوث البناء برئاسة الدكتور عادل الملواني رئيس قسم الصوتيات وتشرف هندسة القاهرة على الجزء الخاص بربط الضوضاء بتلوث الهواء من العادم، ويستعين الفريق البحثي بفريق استشاري يضم اللواء عواض الكردي مدير الإدارة العامة للمرور واللواء مصطفى بيلي مدير مرور القاهرة واللواء لطفي أيوب مدير مرور الجيزة.

(b) Read the following newspaper text, then complete exercises i. – iii. which follow.

باحث أمريكي يؤكد : تلوث القاهرة يعجل بنهاية أبو الهول الذي وصل لمرحلة الشيخوخة

رولا «ولاية ميسوري الأمريكية» – ي . ب . أ – أعلن البروفسور الأمريكي الان هيثواي الخبير الجيولوجي بجامعة رولا الأمريكية والذي شارك علماء مصر جهودهم من أجل إنقاذ أبو الهول من محنته أن تلوث القاهرة الذي فاق كل حد يؤثر تأثيرا مباشرا على حالة أبو الهول التي تدهورت بعد أن دخل مرحلة الشيخوخة ، فعمره الآن تجاوز الـ٤ آلاف عام وقال إن الأبحاث المصرية الأمريكية التي أجريت وما زالت تجري على التمثال أثبتت بما لا يدع مجالا للشك أن التمثال أصبح في حالة مريضة متدهورة وأنه لا بد من الإسراع بإنقاذه .

وقال البروفسور الأمريكي لقد تجمعت عوامل الطبيعة والإنسان لكي تضعف من قدرة أبو الهول بمرور الزمن على مقاومة عوامل التعرية ومن ثم فقد التمثال – الذي بني ليمثل

جسد أسد ووجه إنسان هو وجه الفرعوني خفرع – كثيرا من هيئته وشكله الأول .

وقد انتهى البروفسور هيثواى مؤخرا من إعداد دراسة عن طريق المشاهدة على الطبيعة للنواحي الجيولوجية المتعلقة بحماية أبو الهول وقال إن جزءا من المشكلة هو أن أبو الهول يقع في نفس المكان الذي نحت منه حيث تعود أحجار هذا المكان وهي أحجار جيرية إلى نحو ٧٠ مليون سنة إلى الوراء!! ويقف التمثال الآن فوق مستوى المياه الجوفية بأربعة أمتار فقط .

ويضيف الباحث الامريكي انه كنتيجة مباشرة لذلك يرتفع الماء الى جسم التمثال عن طريق الخاصية الشعرية لتؤدي الى ذوبان الملح الموجود في الحجر الجيري وتحول هذا الملح الى بلورات تتجمع على سطح التمثال الامر الذي يؤدي بدوره الى تفتيت وتكسير السطح بسبب عوامل التعرية الناتجة عن التغيرات المناخية.

i   Answer the following questions in English.

1. Who is Professor Heathway?
2. Who is the Professor working with in Egypt?
3. What project has this team been working on?
4. What does the Sphinx represent?
5. When was the Sphinx built and by whom?
6. What is the state of the Sphinx today?
7. What are the key factors which have caused the Sphinx to be in its present condition?
8. Where was the stone quarried from which the Sphinx was sculptured?
9. How old is this stone?
10. What effect does the level of ground water have on the state of the Sphinx?

ii   Structure translations based on باحث أمريكي. Translate the following English sentences into Arabic using relevant constructions to be found in the text at the points indicated.

1. He met the ministers in order to sign the agreement. (para. 1, lines 3–4)
2. My brother is a member of the American–Yemeni Institute. (para. 1, line 7)
3. The historic monument has to be saved this year. (para. 1, line 9)
4. The new professor completed his book recently. (para. 3, line 1)
5. The level of ground water is only 5 metres below the house. (para. 3, lines 6–7)

iii Using fewer words than the original text, paraphrase the contents of text (b) orally in Arabic.

(c) Read the following text from مجلة الشرق الأوسط, April 1–7, 1992, then complete exercises i. – iii. which follow.

التجميد:

علاج للماء من التلوث

مرة أخرى نعود إلى كوارث تدفق النفط الخام إلى مياه البحر، والكل يعرف أن إزالة أثر النفط من المياه أمر صعب جدا. هذا على الرغم من إنتاج عدد من المحاليل الكيمياوية المضادة. من أسباب تعذر التنظيف أن النفط مادة سائلة يصعب احتواؤها في مياه المحيطات. ويبدو أن هناك بشائر لطريقة جديدة فعالة تنفع لمواجهة هذا النوع من الكوارث.

تشير المصادر المتخصصة بصناعة النفط إلى توصل أحد الباحثين في مركز « لانجلي » للأبحاث إلى استنباط طريقة سريعة وسهلة لإزالة تلوث النفط. تتلخص هذه الطريقة باستخدام بخات النايتروجين السائل لتجميد النفط في المياه وتحويله إلى حبيبات وكريات صلبة. بهذه الطريقة يتمكن رجال الإنقاذ من جرف النفط المتسرب وفصله عن مياه البحر. ويعتقد المتخصصون بمكافحة تلوث المياه أن بالإمكان استعمال سائل النايتروجين لتجميد شتى أشكال النفايات الكيمياوية التي يمكن أن تتسرب إلى مياه البحر.

يرى صاحب هذه الفكرة وهو الباحث دانيال سنو أن

أسلوب التنفيذ يستوجب الاعتماد على سفن خاصة
تحتوي على تقنيات تمكنها من رش سائل النايتروجين
عبر خراطيم تستقر فوهاتها تحت طبقة البترول الطافية.
أي أن عملية الرش تتم تحت سطح الماء الملوث مباشرة.
بناء على ذلك يقتصر الانجماد على طبقة التلوث بالذات.
وطريقة التجميد هذه تضع حدا للانجراف المتواصل لسموم
الكيمياويات إلى مساحات واسعة أو تجمعات أخرى
للمياه، أما كتل النفط المتجمدة فيمكن جرفها أو ضخها
عبر خراطيم واسعة إلى سفن ذات مستودعات وصهاريج
كبيرة. يلي ذلك إعادة ضخ المياه المصفاة إلى البحر. يضاف
إلى ذلك أن بالإمكان إعادة تكرير كتل النفط المجروفة
للحصول على مستحضرات بتروكيماوية مناسبة.

i   Answer the following questions in English.

1. What is said to be common knowledge about oil and water?
2. What makes cleaning up oil from the sea a difficult operation?
3. Who has claimed that there is a new method for cleaning up oil pollution?
4. Who invented this new method?
5. Where do they work?
6. What chemical solution is used in this new cleaning method?
7. How does this cleaning method work?
8. What will salvage teams be able to do using this new method?
9. What do specialists in water pollution believe it will be possible to do with this new cleaning method?
10. What does the inventor believe the method will require in order to be effective?
11. Describe how the cleaning–up operation will remove oil from the sea.
12. How will the oil be removed from the sea?
13. How could the salvaged oil then be used?

ii Paraphrase the contextual meanings of the following words and phrases in Arabic from the above text.

1. تجميد
2. محاليل كيمياوية مضادة

٣. يرى

٤. رجال الإنقاذ

٥. صاحب هذه الفكرة

٦. بناء على ذلك

٧. استوجب

٨. إعادة ضخ المياه المصفاة

iii Translate the above text into idiomatic English.

6. Written Arabic texts 3 (classical)

Read the following text by ابن حـوقل, from *Opus geographicum*, vol. I, pp. 29–30 aloud, providing all case and mood endings (a few are already provided for you); then translate the text into idiomatic English.

وليس بمكّة ماء جار إلا شيء أُجري إليها من عين قد كان عمل فيها بعضُ الولاة فاستتمّ في أيّام المُقْتَدِر ويُمْنَح إلى مسيل قد جُعِل لـه إلى باب بنـي شَيْبَة في قناة قـد عُمِلَتْ هناك وكانت أكثـر ميـاهِهـم من السمـاء إلى مـواجِنَ وبركٍ كانت بـها عامـرةً فخرجت باستيلاءِ المتولّين على أمـوال أوقـافِـها واستئثارِهم بـها وليست لهم اَبْآَرُ يُشـرب منهـا وأطيبُـها زَمْزَمُ ولا يمكن الإدمـان على شُرب مائـها، وليس بجميع مكّة شجرٌ مُثْمِر غير شـجـر البـادية وإذا جُزْتَ الحرم فـهناك عيـون وأبْآر وحـوائط كـثـيـرة وأودية ذات خُضَر ومـزارع ونخـيـل ويقـال إنّ بفخّ نخيلات يسيرة متفرقة وهي من الحرم ولم أرها.

7. Grammar/stylistics

(a) *The use of* إعادة + *verbal noun*

A common way of expressing the idea of doing something again, or re–, is to use إعادة (the verbal noun of أعاد) in a genitive construction with the appropriate verbal noun. Examples include:

يلي ذلك {إعادة ضخ المياه المصفاة} إلى البحر.

'This is followed by pumping the purified water back into the sea.' (ch. 8, 5c)

يضاف إلى ذلك أن بالإمكان {إعادة تكرير كتل النفط المجروفة} ..
'In addition to that, it is possible to re–refine the body of oil which has
been scooped up ...' (ch. 8, 5c)

(b) *Impersonal passives*
An impersonal passive in Arabic is a passive in which the logical subject is the
object of a preposition which 'goes with' the verb. Although the impersonal
passive may be difficult conceptually, it is very easy to construct since it only takes
the third masculine singular ('he') inflectional form irrespective of the gender and
number of the logical subject. Examples of the impersonal passive include:

... في مجموعة إهرامات الملكات زوجات الملك بيبي الأول والتي
{أُعْلِنَ عن اكتشاف اثنين منها} من قبل.
'... in a group of pyramids of the wives of King Bibi the First, the
discovery of two of which has been announced before.' (ch. 3, 5)

In the above example the object of the verbal preposition, اكتشاف اثنين منها, is
the *logical* subject of the verb, but not the *grammatical* subject. Other examples
include:

كانت اللوحة التي {عُثِرَ عليها}.
'The tablet, which was stumbled across ....' (ch. 3, 5)

وليست لهم آبَارُ {يُشرَب منها}.
'... they had no wells which could be drunk from.' (ch. 8, 6b)

اتضح أن بعض الإدارات {لم يُستدَلُ فيها على سجلات منتظمة}.
'It is clear that some organisations do not have orderly records.' (ch. 9,
5b)

.. إلا أن العمل {بوشِرَ فيه} في العام الماضي.
'...however, work was carried out last year.' (ch. 8, 11)

Impersonal passive participles are also common. Again the passive takes the
uninflected masculine singular form irrespective of the gender and number of the
preceding noun. Examples include:
النسبة {المسموح بها} دوليا.
'...the internationally permitted level.' (ch. 8, 5a)

وقال لي طبيب السجن أن هذه المرأة {حُكِمَ عليها بالإعدام} ..
'The prison doctor told me that this woman had been condemned to

نوال السعداوي by امرأة عند نقطة الصفر (from '...death, p. 5)

(c) *Asyndetic coordination of sentences in news summaries*

In chapter 6 we mentioned that journal headlines and news summaries have their own peculiar sentence–level syntax: nominal sentences prevail over verbal sentences, and the imperfect aspect of the verb is used to describe events which have already taken place. The peculiarity of news summary syntax extends beyond the sentence and also affects linkage of sentences: it is usual for most, if not all, sentences of a text to be linked syndetically – that is to say, by a conjunction such as و, ف, or ثم. In news summaries, however, linkage of sentences is almost wholly asyndetic – that is to say, sentences are linked without a conjunction. Asyndetic linkage serves to give the text a sense of urgency and immediacy, and helps to isolate one news item from another. As an example, consider the BBC Arabic Service news summary from Nov. 16, 1990:

الثالثة بتوقيت غرينيتش ، هنا لندن سـيـداتي وسادتي إلى حضراتكم نشرة الأخبار تقرأها سلوى أبو سـعـود . في هذه النشرة مبعوث سوفياتي يقول إنه يجب إمهال العراق مزيدا من الوقت كي يسـحب قـواتـه من الكويت قـبـل أن يوافق مـجلس الأمن على استعمال القوة ضده . الرئيس السوفياتي ميخائيل غورباتشوف يلقي خطابا في جلسة استثنائية يعقدها البرلمان السوفياتي يتّهم فيها بعض الجمهوريات السوفياتية بالتشجيع على الانفصال . ورئيس جمهورية روسيا الاتحادية يردّ على ذلك مطالبا بحجب الثقة عن الحكومة الاتحادية . الصين تعلن عن تخفيض جديد في عملتها . وزير خارجية إيران يقول إن تبادل أسرى الحرب التي دارت بين العراق وإيران سيُستأنف في الأسبوع القادم.

In this broadcast, the only sentence which begins with و is the third sentence from the end which begins: ورئيس جمهورية روسيا الاتحادية يردّ على ذلك 'and the president of the United Russian Republic replies to that …'. All other sentences begin with nouns or prepositions.

Consider also the BBC Arabic Service news summary from Jan. 16, 1990:

استمرار الاشتباكات ذات الطابع القومي في جمهورية آذربيجان السوفيتية. ولم يبد حتى الآن ما يدل على وصول وحدات من الجيش وهو ما كانت الحكومة السوفياتية قد تعهدت به في وقت سابق. وزير الخارجيـة المصري يصل الى واشنطن بعـد قليل للتفاوض بشأن احياء جهود السلام في الشرق الاوسط . الرئيس الصومالى يقيل مزيدا من المسؤولين وقد شمل قرار له هذه المرة

رئيس بلدية مقاديشو ورئيس احد اكبر البنوك الصومالية. مئات من لاجئي القوارب الفيـاتنامـيـين في هونغ كـونغ يتظاهرون احتجـاجـاً على قـرار الحكومـة البـريطانيـة القاضي بإعادتهم الى بلادهم بالقوة.

In this broadcast the second sentence is linked to the first by و, while all other sentences are linked asyndetically. Linkage of the second sentence to the first by و is employed because the two sentences deal with the same event, while other sentences refer to unrelated events.

8. Aural Arabic texts 1

Listen to the following BBC Arabic Service news broadcast from Jan. 22, 1991 which relates to Iraq's mining and burning of the Kuwait oil wells, then complete exercises i. and ii. below.

i Transcribe from بالأزمة القائمة في الخليج until الرابعة بتوقيت غرينيتش.

ii Fill in the gaps in the following text (from قال متحدث عسكري أميريكي).

قــال ———— ———— ———— في ———— ————

يقـــوم ———— ———— ————

———— ———— في ———— المحتلة .

وقــال ———— ———— التي التُقطت

———— ———— أن العـراق فـجـر

في ———— وصـهــاريج ————

———— الوفـرة ———— ————

———— على ———— مع ———— ————

———— ولم ———— المتـحـدث ————

———— وجـدير بـالذكـر أن ———— ————

«تيكساكو» ———— تقـوم ———— حقل ————

نيابة ———— ———— ، وهـو ————

في ———— أجنبية ———— الذي تقوم ————

. ————

وكان ———— ———— ———— في السابق

وتعتقد ———— ———— ———— ————

بأنه جرى ———— ————

———— ويقول مراسل ————

———— في ———— لشؤون ————

مخاوف ———— من ———— إن من

منشآت ———— ———— ———— قيام

———— ———— إنه بصرف النظر ويقول

فإن ———— في حد ذاتها ————

من الناحية ———— له ————

———— ———— نظرا لأن انبعاث

———— يمكن أن يعيق ————

———— ———— المتحالفة.

———— علماء البيئة ————

———— من بصورة ———— ————

———— ———— يمكن أن

———— ———— سطح ———— يؤدّي

رد فعل ———— وقد اتسم ———— المتأثرة

———— ———— بالتحفظ لما ذُكر من

_____ _____ _____ المنشآت _____ _____

نيران _____ _____ _____ وقال . _____ _____

_____ _____ _____ _____ ربما

_____ _____ ولكن إشعال _____ _____ _____

يكون _____ الكويتية _____ _____ _____

_____ _____ _____ لانسحاب _____ _____

التي _____ _____ أو محاولة لإعاقة _____ _____

تشنها _____ _____ ..

9. Aural Arabic texts 2

Listen to the following text from حصاد الشهر, no. 7, side 1, item 2, مشاريع التنمية الاقتصادية الكبرى في العالم: الري which discusses the transfer of water resources from the south of Libya to major population areas in the north, then complete exercises i. and ii. below.

i   Answer the following questions in English. You may find it useful to read through the questions before listening to the text.

1. Who is Dr Tony Allan?
2. According to Tony Allan, what is extraordinary about Libya's attitude to the project discussed in this passage?
3. In general, what does the project aim to do?
4. What does John Wright suggest the project might at first glance appear to contradict?
5. Where is the most dramatic water source discovered?
6. What is the somewhat poetic assessment of the amount of water potentially available here?
7. When did the Libyan government start these projects?
8. What problems did the project face?
9. What is described as illogical?
10. What has happened to the water table in Tripoli and its outskirts in recent years?
11. According to John Wright, where will the water be collected from?
12. Where is Srir located?
13. How will the water travel through the pipes?
14. What is the diameter of the pipes?

ii Fill in the gaps in the following text (from (واستهلّ هذه السلسلة).

واستهلّ هذه السلسلة ـــــــــــ ـــــــــــ ـــــــــــ ـــــــــــ

أنابيب الماء ـــــــــــ الجماهيرية ـــــــــــ، و ـــــــــــ

ـــــــــــ الحالي ـــــــــــ ـــــــــــ ـــــــــــ

ـــــــــــ ـــــــــــ Tony Allan ـــــــــــ ـــــــــــ

ـــــــــــ ـــــــــــ ـــــــــــ بقوله: «لا

ـــــــــــ مستعداً ـــــــــــ ـــــــــــ ـــــــــــ

ـــــــــــ ـــــــــــ ـــــــــــ لإنفاق ما

إنه» ـــــــــــ ـــــــــــ ـــــــــــ بأكملها ـــــــــــ

ـــــــــــ ـــــــــــ استنباط ـــــــــــ ـــــــــــ

ـــــــــــ إليه ـــــــــــ تشتدّ حيث ـــــــــــ ـــــــــــ وضخه

وقد ـــــــــــ الكبرى ـــــــــــ ـــــــــــ ذات الشمالية ـــــــــــ

وصفه John Wright ـــــــــــ ـــــــــــ ـــــــــــ

قد ـــــــــــ، وطموح ـــــــــــ ـــــــــــ بأنه البريطانية

ففي ـــــــــــ ـــــــــــ لقانون مناقضاً لأول وهلة ـــــــــــ

من ـــــــــــ ثروات ـــــــــــ ـــــــــــ ـــــــــــ

ـــــــــــ ـــــــــــ لم يتمّ وإن العذبة ـــــــــــ

ـــــــــــ أُكتشفت وقد، ـــــــــــ ـــــــــــ ـــــــــــ

ـــــــــــ ـــــــــــ قصية ـــــــــــ في ـــــــــــ

وُصف وقد، الكُفرى واحة ـــــــــــ هذه أروع ولعل

شعرياً وصفاً البقعة ـــــــــــ ـــــــــــ ـــــــــــ

بأنه ـــــــــــ ـــــــــــ دقيقاً

_____ _____ _____ تدفّق _____

_____ _____ _____ قرنين _____، ثم مضى برنامجنا

«أضــواء» _____ _____ لســان John Wright «إن

قد _____ _____ _____ الحكم _____

_____ _____ في _____ العمل في _____

استغـلال _____ _____ طمـوحـة _____

_____ وإن _____ تلك، _____

وجـهـة نظرية _____ سليمـة _____ _____

_____ تقنية _____ صادفت إلا أنها _____

_____ العـامـلة _____ جمـة في إيجـاد الإيدى _____ و

ومن _____، في بقاع _____ والعمل على _____ _____

صعـوبة تذليلها _____ لا _____ _____ _____

المنطقي _____ _____ فـمـن _____، و _____

في بقعة _____ _____ من _____ _____

_____ _____ ثَمـة ومن _____ _____

_____ _____ عـبـر _____ _____

_____ لتـسـويقـه الطرق الصحـرويـة _____

المنتجات بكُلفـة أكبـر من سـائـر _____

في _____ _____ «.

يخطط _____ _____ _____ جلب

_____ _____ مصادرها _____ _____

———————— الصحارى الجنوبية ————————

———— ———— ———— الرئيسية ————

———— ———— ، ولا سيما ————

وضواحيها ———— بلغ انخفاض منسوب ————

———— ———— ———— ————

حداً يدعو ———— الفزع، ولكن ————

تنطوي عليه ———— ————

عمق ———— إلى سواحل ———— على ————

———— ، John Wright ————: ————

» ———— تجميع ———— ————

———— بئر أرتوازي ———— تزربو،

———— ———— ———— و

———— الشمال الشرقي ———— الكفرى و ————

———— ———— ———— ————

———— وجياله و ————

———— ضخ ————

———— بقوة الجاذبية ———— ————

الفلاذ والأسمنت المسلّح ———— قطرها ————

———— ما يُساوي قطر نفقٍ للسكك الحديدية

———— لقطار ————، و ———— من

الآبار ———— تزربو و ————

إجدابية لمسافة ــــــــــــ ــــــــــــ ــــــــــــ ــــــــــــ

ــــــــــــ ــــــــــــ ــــــــــــ ومن ، ــــــــــــ ــــــــــــ

شمالاً ــــــــــــ ــــــــــــ ــــــــــــ ــــــــــــ

والمناطق ــــــــــــ ــــــــــــ ــــــــــــ ــــــــــــ

ــــــــــــ ــــــــــــ ــــــــــــ ــــــــــــ ــــــــــــ

سرت ــــــــــــ ــــــــــــ على ــــــــــــ ــــــــــــ

ــــــــــــ «.

10. Written English texts

(a) Making use of constructions and vocabulary encountered in the Arabic texts used in this chapter, in particular the Arabic précis text below (section 11), translate the following text from Wilfred Thesiger, *The Marsh Arabs* (Harmondsworth: Penguin Books, 1983), p. 13, into idiomatic Arabic.

Introduction

I lived in the marshes of Southern Iraq from the end of 1951 until June 1958, sometimes for as long as seven months on end. 1957 was the only year when I did not go there. Although I was almost continuously on the move this is not properly a travel book, for the area over which I travelled was restricted. Nor does it pretend to be a detailed study of the Marshmen among whom I lived, for I am not an anthropologist nor indeed a specialist of any kind. I spent these years in the Marshes because I enjoyed being there. During this time I lived among the Marshmen as one of themselves, and inevitably over the years I became to some extent familiar with their ways. From my recollections, helped by my diaries, I have tried to give a picture of the Marshes and of the people who live there. Recent political upheavals in Iraq have closed this area to visitors. Soon the Marshes will probably be drained; when this happens, a way of life that has lasted for thousands of years will disappear.

(b) Making use of constructions and vocabulary encountered in the Arabic texts used in this chapter as far as possible, translate the following English weather forecast into idiomatic Arabic.

British Isles

Wet and windy conditions will spread across the British Isles in the morning, rain will push into Ireland and Wales with near gale force winds from the south or south–west. However, England and Scotland will start dry with isolated sunny spells. Clearing skies will move in from the west, reaching Ireland around noon. Meanwhile, rain will spread into England and Scotland and push eastward. Skies are not expected to clear before sunset. Late in the afternoon, near gale force winds from the south will develop in England and Scotland.

11. Précis

Read the following text from الشرق الأوسط, April 17, 1993, then complete exercises i. and ii. which follow.

كارثة إنسانية وبيئية تهدد سكان الأهوار بسبب خطط بغداد لتجفيف المياه في المنطقة

لندن: من الن جورج

بدأ نظام حكم الرئيس العراقي صدام حسين حملة مخططة لتجفيف قطاعات واسعة من أهوار العراق كوسيلة لحرمان المتمردين في الجنوب من أي غطاء، ولإجبار سكان الأهوار أنفسهم على الخضوع لسيطرة النظام في بغداد.

إن مشروع التجفيف الذي ألبس زورًا رداء مشروع لاستصلاح الأراضي، سيؤدي إلى إحداث كوارث بيئية وبشرية كبرى. وجاءت خطط بغداد هذه إثر التمرد الدامي، الفاشل، الذي اندلع في مناطق جنوب العراق، ذات الأغلبية الشيعية، في أعقاب تحرير الكويت. ورغم سحق المتمردين عموماً، فإن مجموعات منهم لجأت مع أعداد هائلة من المدنيين الأبرياء إلى الأهوار.

وواصل المتمردون بمساعدة من إيران المجاورة، شن الغارات على القوات العراقية التي تقصف مناطق الأهوار بصورة روتينية، إلا أنها لم تستطع استخدام طائرات الهليكوبتر وغيرها منذ اغسطس (آب) في العام الماضي، عندما أعلنت الأمم المتحدة منطقة الجنوب منطقة حظر جوي على الطائرات العراقية.

١٢٠ ألف نسمة

إن الأهوار تأوي قرابة ١٢٠ ألف نسمة، وتمتد على رقعة شاسعة في منطقة

تقارب دجلة والفرات، وتؤلف مثلثاً تمتد أضلاعه بين مدينة العمارة شمالاً، والناصرية في الجنوب الغربي، والبصرة جنوباً. أما الحواف الشرقية للأهوار فتنطلق تقريباً مع الحدود العراقية مع إيران.

بدأت أولى الأعمال الهندسية الكبرى في منطقة الأهوار خلال الفترة من عام ١٩٨٠ إلى عام ١٩٨٨، أي خلال فترة الحرب العراقية-الإيرانية. وشيد الجانب العراقي قناة عريضة تحفها سدود ترابية من قلعة صالح (على نهر دجلة، جنوب مدينة العمارة) إلى الهوير، على الفرات قرب نقطة التقائه بنهر دجلة عند بلدة القرنة. وأتاح ذلك القيام بأعمال التجفيف، واستقرار الناس للزراعة في منطقة واسعة على الضفة الشرقية من نهر دجلة، وحرم القبائل المتمردة والهاربين من الخدمة العسكرية من أي غطاء يحميهم.

قناة جديدة

وهناك رسوم هندسية استولى عليها المتمردون الشيعة من الحكومة تبين أن هناك قناة جديدة قيد البناء منذ أزمة الخليج، وتقع جنوب شرقي بلدة السلام، لتلتقي بالطرف الشمالي من القناة الأولى التي انجزت في سبتمبر (أيلول) الماضي، وحدت بساتر ترابي ارتفاعه ٦ أمتار، مما يمنع الماء عن التدفق شمالاً، ويدفع به ليصب في الفرات.

وهناك علاوة على ذلك، مشروع آخر أنجز في يوليو (تموز) الماضي، يمنع مياه النهيرات التي تغذي المنطقة شمال القناة الجديدة بسدود مانعة.

وأتمت الحكومة سدودا ترابية مماثلة في يوليو الماضي على طول الأنهر التي تغذي أهوار الحويزة، جنوب شرقي العمارة. غير أن تأثير هذه السدود محدود تماماً نظراً لأن قرابة ٦٥٪ من مياه هذه الأهوار تأتي من إيران، ولا تقع في متناول يد أجهزة السلطات العراقية.

وهناك عنصر آخر مهم في خطة بغداد وهو ما يسمى بـ«النهر الثالث» وهذا كناية عن قناة بين الفرات ودجلة. وكان الغرض الأصلي منها شطف الملوحة من الأراضي السبخة وتحويلها إلى الأهوار، ويعود تاريخ المشروع إلى الخمسينات من القرن الحالي. إلا أن العمل بوشر فيه في العام الماضي بعد أن أحيا صدام المشروع بهدف الانتقام، واكتمل شق القناة في نهاية العام نفسه.

«النهر الثالث»

إن القناة تعبر الفرات عبر سداده قرب سوق الشيوخ (جنوب شرقي الناصرية) وتمتد جنوب هور الحمّار لتصب في الخليج قرب الحدود العراقية-الكويتية. واكتمل بناء السدادة في يوليو من العام الماضي

ليتحول مجرى مياه الفرات شمال هور الحمار وصولاً إلى «النهر الثالث».

ومنذ إتمام أعمال التحويل هذه، بدأ العمل في بناء سد على طول الضفة الجنوبية للفرات ابتداءً من سوق الشيوخ فصعوداً باتجاه الشرق. وحين يكتمل هذا السد في الصيف، إذا سارت الأمور حسب الخطة المقررة، فإن النهر سيعاد إلى مجراه الطبيعي، لكن السد، وهو بعرض ٢٥ متراً عند القاعدة و ٦ أمتار عند القمة، وبارتفاع ٥ أمتار، سيوقف وصول المياه إلى اهوار الحمار.

وهناك عملية أخرى، من المقرر لها أن تكتمل في الصيف، تتوخى بناء سلسلة من السدود حاليا، وستتيح هذه السدود تجفيف منطقتين مربعتين كبيرتين، تؤلفان معاً ما مساحته ١٥٠٠ كيلومتر مربع، وتقعان إلى الغرب من المنطقة التي جففت خلال الحرب العراقية-الإيرانية.

إن خطط التجفيف، بالنسبة لبغداد، تتصف بأولوية كبرى، رغم أن هناك ٣ عوامل أبطأت سير التنفيذ:

نشاط المتمردين لضرب الأعمال الترابية، والأمطار الغزيرة في هذا الشتاء على نحو غير مألوف، ونشاطات الأكراد في شمال العراق، ففي مسعى الأكراد لإحباط خطط صدام حيال الأهوار، أطلقوا كميات هائلة من المياه الحبيسة وراء سد دوكان لتتدفق على نهر دجلة.

صحيح أن أعمال الحكومة العراقية، في الأهوار تلكأت إلا أنها لم تتوقف. فسكان الأهوار في الجنوب، شأن الأكراد في الشمال، يتعرضون أصلا لحصار اقتصادي من جانب بغداد مقروناً بقصف مستمر. ولولا الأهوار لهلك هؤلاء الناس، فالأهوار تقدم لهم الحماية، وتشكل أساس حياتهم بأسرها، مأكلاً ومشرباً. ولذلك فإن كارثة إنسانية بيئية تتفتح أمام الأبصار.

i Answer a selection of the following questions in Arabic.

Part One: from beginning to على الطائرات العراقية

١ – ما هي الأهوار وأين تقع؟
٢ – ماذا يهدد سكان الأهوار؟
٣ – ماذا تخططه الحكومة العراقية؟
٤ – ما هو هدف هذه الخطة؟
٥ – ما هو هدف هذه الخطة الرسمي؟
٦ – إلى أي شيء ستؤدّي الخطة العراقية؟
٧ – متى جاءت خطة بغداد؟

٨ – ما هو الدين الرئيسي في جنوب العراق؟
٩ – من لجأ إلى الأهوار؟
١٠ –أي دولة ساعدت المتمردين؟
١١ –ماذا عملت القوات العراقية؟
١٢ –لماذا لم تستعمل القوات العراقية طائرات الهليكوبتر؟

Part Two: from ١٢٠ ألف نسمة (part title) to من أي غطاء يحميهم

١ – كم عدد سكان الأهوار حالياً؟
٢ – ما هما النهران اللذان تقع الأهوار بالقرب منهما؟
٣ – ما هي المدن الثلاث التي تشكّل حدود الأهوار؟
٤ – أين تقع الحدود الشرقية للأهوار؟
٥ – متى بدأت الأعمال الهندسية الكبيرة في الأهوار؟
٦ – حاربت العراق أي دولة في هذه الفترة؟
٧ – من بنى القناة في هذه الفترة؟
٨ – أين تقع قلعة صالح؟
٩ – أين يلتقي نهر الفرات بنهر دجلة؟
١٠ –ما هو الشيء الأول الذي أتاح به بناء القناة؟
١١ –أين تم استقرار الناس للزراعة؟
١٢ –من الذي حرمته القناة من أي غطاء يحميهم؟

Part Three: from قناة جديدة (part title) to في نهاية العام نفسه

١ – من استولى على الرسوم الهندسية؟
٢ – ماذا تُبِّين الرسوم الهندسية؟
٣ – أين تُبنَى القناة؟
٤ – متى أُنجز بناء القناة الأولى؟
٥ – كم ارتفاع ساتر القناة الترابي؟
٦ – ماذا يمنع هذا الستار؟
٧ – أين يصبّ الماء؟
٨ – ماذا يمنع المشروع الآخر؟
٩ – متى أُنجز هذا المشروع؟
١٠ –ماذا أتمّت الحكومة في يوليو الماضي؟
١١ –أين تقع أهوار الحويزة؟
١٢ –من أين تأتي أغلبية مياه أهوار الحويزة؟
١٣ –كم في المائة؟
١٤ –ما هو «النهر الثالث»؟

١٥ -ما هو الهدف الأصلي من النهر الثالث؟

١٦ -إلى متى يعود تاريخ هذا المشروع؟

١٧ -متى بدأ العمل بهذا المشروع

١٨ -متى شُقَّت القناة؟

Part Four: from «النهر الثالث» (paragraph title) to تتفتح أمام الأبصار

١ – أين تعبر القناة الفرات؟

٢ – أين تصبّ القناة في الخليج؟

٣ – متى تمّ بناء السدادة؟

٤ – ما هو هدف السدادة؟

٥ – متى بدأ العراقيون ببناء سد على طول الضفة الجنوبية للفرات؟

٦ – أين يبدأ هذا السد؟

٧ – متى سيكتمل هذا السد حسب الخطة المقررة؟

٨ – كم عرض السد عند القاعدة؟

٩ – وعند القمة؟

١٠ -كم ارتفاع السد؟

١١ -ما سيكون تأثير السد؟

١٢ -متى ستكتمل العملية الأخرى؟

١٣ -ماذا ستتيح هذه السدود؟

١٤ -كم مساحة المنطقتين المذكورتين؟

١٥ -أين تقع هاتان المنطقتان؟

١٦ -ما هو العامل الأول الذي أبطأ سير تنفيذ خطط التجفيف؟

١٧ -ما هو العامل الثاني؟

١٨ – ما هو العامل الثالث؟

١٩ -ماذا عمل الأكراد لإحباط خطط صدام حيال الأهوار؟

٢٠ -ما هو تأثير هذه العوامل الثلاثة؟

٢١ -لأي شيء يتعرّض سكان الأهوار أصلا؟

٢٢ -ماذا تقدّم الأهوار لهؤلاء الناس؟

ii Provide a précis in Arabic of the first two parts of this text.

12. Oral
مشاكل البيئة في العالم العربي
(a) Individual students to present a brief account of environmental problems in one
   country in the Middle East.
(b) The presenter then asks the other students questions about environmental
   problems in that country. These questions should include some which require

factual answers and some which require hypothetical or subjective answers. For example:

١ – في رأيك، ما هي أخطر مشكلة بيئية في الوطن العربي/في هذه البلاد؟

٢ – ما هو سبب هذه المشكلة؟

٣ – هل لهذه المشكلة حل؟

٤ – ما هي العوامل الرئيسية التي تؤثر على البيئة؟

٥ – هل من الممكن أن نعالج المشاكل البيئية على الصعيد السياسي؟

٦ – هل من الممكن أن نعالج المشاكل البيئية على الصعيد الاجتماعي؟

٧ – إذا أصبحت أنت رئيس هذه الدولة فكيف تتناول المسائل البيئية فيها؟

(c) Open lecturer–led discussion on climate and the environment in the Middle East. Consider the interplay of climate and man–made causes of environmental problems in the discussion.

13. Essay

Write an essay in Arabic of around 200 words on the following title مشاكل البيئة في العالم العربي. Structure your essay around the following questions:

١ – ما هي المشاكل البيئية الرئيسية في الوطن العربي اليوم؟

٢ – ما هي أسباب هذه المشاكل؟

٣ – هل تختلف المشاكل البيئية في الشرق الأوسط عن تلك الموجودة في الغرب؟

٤ – ما هي العلاقة بين الحرب والمشاكل البيئية؟

٥ – ما الذي سببته حرب الخليج الثانية من مشاكل بيئية؟

٦ – في رأيك ما هو الحل للمشاكل البيئية في الوطن العربي؟

9
Social issues and development

1. Basic background material
(a) Poverty and wealth: population and per capita incomes in the Arab world.

	Population	*GNP per capita in US dollars*
Algeria	25.36m (1990)	2,450 (1988)
Bahrain	486,000 (1990)	6,610 (1987)
Egypt	50.74m (1989)	650 (1988)
Iran	53.92m (1988)	1,690 (1986)
Iraq	17.06m (1988)	2,140 (1986)
Israel	4.82m (1990)	8,650 (1988)
Jordan	3.17m (1989)	1,500 (1988)
Kuwait	2.04m (1990)	13,680 (1988)
Lebanon	2.8m (1988)	NA
Libya	4m (1990)	5,410 (1988)
Morocco	24.5m (1989)	750 (1988)
Oman	2m (1990)	4,200 (1989)
Qatar	371,863 (1987)	11,610 (1988)
Saudi Arabia	12m (1988)	6,170 (1988)
Sudan	25.56m (1987)	340 (1988)
Syria	11.3m (1988)	1,670 (1988)
Tunisia	7.75m (1988)	1,230 (1988)
UAE	1.6m (1988)	15,720 (1988)
Yemen	12m (1987)	540 (1988)

(b) Population, population growth, life expectancy and illiteracy rates in the Arab world.

	Population (000) 1994	Pop. growth rate (% p.a.) 1993	Life expectancy (years) 1993	Illiteracy rate (%) 1990
Algeria	27,325	2.5	67	43
Bahrain	548	3.1	72	23
Egypt	57,556	2.0	64	52
Iraq	19,951	2.9	66	40
Israel	5,420	2.7	77	5
Jordan	4,217	5.2	70	20
Kuwait	1,651	-0.5	75	27
Lebanon	3,930	2.7	69	20
Libya	5,222	3.6	64	36
Morocco	26,488	2.2	64	51
Oman	2,073	4.4	70	–
Qatar	537	4.5	72	24
Saudi Arabia	17,498	3.6	70	38
Sudan	27,361	2.7	53	73
Syrian Arab Rep.	14,171	3.5	68	36
Tunisia	8,815	2.3	68	35
UAE	1,855	3.3	74	–
West Bank + Gaza	2,063	–	–	–
Yemen, Rep.	13,873	4.1	51	62

(c) Infant mortality rates per 1,000 births in the Arab world.

	1990–5	1995–2000	2000–5
Bahrain	18.0	16.0	13.0
Egypt	67.0	54.0	43.0
Iraq	58.0	47.0	39.0
Jordan	34.0	28.0	24.0
Kuwait	18.0	14.0	12.0
Lebanon	34.0	29.0	25.0
Oman	30.0	25.0	21.0
Palestine – West Bank	36.0	30.0	25.0
Palestine – Gaza Strip	42.0	32.0	24.0
Qatar	20.0	17.0	14.0
Saudi Arabia	29.0	23.0	18.0
Syrian Arab Rep.	39.0	33.0	28.0
UAE	19.0	15.0	12.0
Yemen, Rep.	119.0	109.0	98.0

(d) Predicted population growth in the Arab world.

	1990	1995	2000	2005
World	5,284,816	5,716,407	6,159,030	6,594,379
Asia	3,186,446	3,457,957	3,735,846	4,003,212
Arab countries	228,653	257,073	291,462	325,031

2. Additional reading
(a) Hourani, *A History of the Arab Peoples*, pp. 373–9; pp. 384–8; pp. 436–9.
(b) Unni Wikan, *Life Among the Poor in Cairo*, (London and New York: Tavistock Publications, 1980).

3. Key vocabulary
Taking the texts in this chapter as a starting point, draw up lists of vocabulary in the following fields:
(a) Development: poverty and wealth.
(b) Population.

4. Written Arabic texts 1
(a) Read the following newspaper text from الأهرام, Mar. 20, 1990, then answer the questions which follow in English.

معظم سكان افريقيا يعيشون تحت حد الفقر

نقص المياه وزحف الصحراء ومياه الشرب الملوثة .. مشاكل تواجه افريقيا

حول تلوث البيئة في القارة الافريقية وتأثيره على القوى البشرية يعقد بالقاهرة يوم الاربعاء القادم مؤتمر تلوث البيئة والأمن الافريقي وذلك بمقر جامعة الدول العربية.

ويشترك في المؤتمر كما يقول الدكتور عصام الدين جلال رئيس جماعة باجواشي الافريقي وهي الجمعية المنظمة للمؤتمر حوالى ٢٥ دولة افريقية وذلك لمناقشة كل ما يتعلق بالأمن السياسي والاقتصادي والاجتماعي للقارة السوداء وأهمها المشكلات البيئية التي تؤكد تقارير الأمم المتحدة انها تلعب دورا « خطرا » في تهديد الامن الداخلي والخارجي للعديد من الدول الافريقية.

وسوف يتناول المؤتمر الذي يستمر لمدة اربعة ايام العديد من المشكلات البيئية في افريقيا ومن بينها الانفجار السكاني وازالة الغابات ونقص المياه والتصحر ودفن النفايات الذرية والخطرة في ارض افريقيا.

ويقول الدكتور احمد عبد الوهاب استاذ علم تلوث البيئة بزراعة مشتهر واحد المشتركين في هذا المؤتمر عن الجانب المصري ان مشكلة الانفجار السكاني قد لا يتصور انها مشكلة بيئية ولكن عندما نعرف انه طبقا لتقارير الامم المتحدة ان عدد سكان افريقيا عام ١٩٥٠ كان ٢٢٤ مليونا زاد الى ٥٥٥ مليونا عام ١٩٨٥ ومن المتوقع ان يصل الى ٨٧٢ مليونا عام ٢٠٠٠ وان معظم هؤلاء السكان تحت حد الفقر حيث ان الزيادة في انتاج الغذاء لا تتعدى ٢.٥٪ فسوف يتضح ان الانفجار السكاني واحد من اهم المشكلات البيئية التي تواجه القارة فمن بين ٨٥ دولة افريقية هناك ١٩ دولة معدل زيادة سكانها ٣٪ وهذا يعني ان عدد سكان القارة سوف يتضاعف خلال ٢٣ سنة او اقل والاخطر من كل هذا ٨٦٪ من سكان العالم يعيشون في الدول النامية.

ويصاحب هذه المشكلة زيادة متوسط عمر الفرد من ٤٥ سنة عام ١٩٥٥ الى ٥٨ سنة عام ١٩٨٥ ومن المتوقع ان يصل متوسط عمر الفرد عام ٢٠٠٠ الى ٧٠ سنة.

اما مشكلة ازالة الغابات فهي مشكلة متفاقمة فالغابات هي الغطاء السحري الذي يحمي التربة ويساعد على تحسن الظروف البيئية والحفاظ على خصوبة التربة والاحتفاظ بالماء وكذلك الحفاظ على الكائنات الحية من نباتات وحيوانات وكذلك الكائنات الدقيقة .. والتقارير تؤكد ان نصف سكان القارة يستخدمون اخشاب الغابات كمصدر للوقود.

وان ١٥ مليون فدان من الغابات تزال كل عام ويمكن القول ان حوالى ثلثي غابات القارة ازيلت. هذا في الوقت الذي تضم فيه القارة ٦٥٪ من غابات العالم.

ونقص المياه من ناحية اخرى واحدة من اهم المشكلات فالجفاف مشكلة تهدد كثيرا من دول القارة اما تلوث المياه سواء عن طريق مخلفات المصانع او الصرف الصحي فهو مشكلة تهدد الاحياء البشرية والنباتية والحيوانية وطبقا لتقارير الامم المتحدة فان ٦١٪ من سكان القرى و٢٦٪ من سكان المدن في الدول النامية لا يجدون مياه نقية صالحة للشرب ونتيجة لهذا التلوث تكثر الاصابة بالكوليرا والتيفود وغيرهما من الامراض المتوطنة في القارة.

اما اذا تناولنا مشكلة التصحر والتي تهدد القارة الافريقية نتيجة لسوء استعمال الارض وازالة الغابات والرعي الجائر ونقص المياه فنجد انها السبب الرئيسي في تهجير ١٠ ملايين مواطن من مواطنهم الاصلية كما وصل ١٥٠ مليون مواطن افريقي الى مرحلة الفقر المدقع كنتيجة مباشرة للتصحر.

ودفن المواد الخطيرة في افريقيا مشكلة تهدد القارة بأكملها فعلى سبيل المثال وفرت اربعة آلاف طن من هذه المواد القادمة من ايطاليا في نيجيريا و١٥ الف طن من امريكا دفنت في جزيرة كاسا ولقد تنبهت منظمة الدول الافريقية الى هذا الخطر وطالبت الدول الافريقية بفسخ عقود دفن النفايات الخطيرة في اراضيها.

1. What will take place in Cairo next Wednesday?
2. Where exactly will it take place?
3. Which organisation will convene the conference?
4. According to the head of this party, who will participate in the conference?
5. What will they discuss in general?
6. What does the UN say about environmental problems in Africa?
7. How long will the conference last?
8. What are the five major problems which will be discussed?
9. Who is Dr Ahmad Abd al-Wahhab?
10. What nationality is he?
11. According to him, is the population explosion generally seen as an environmental problem?
12. What do UN reports say about the size of the population?
13. Why does this, in fact, make the population explosion an environmental problem?
14. How many African countries have an average population increase of 3%?
15. What does this mean in terms of the overall size of the continent's population?
16. Where do 86% of the world's population live?
17. What is the average life span of people in Africa predicted to be in the year 2000?
18. How is the disappearance of the forests described?
19. What do the forests do?
20. According to reports, how do half the continent's population use the forests?
21. How much of the forests is disappearing each year?
22. How much of the forests has already disappeared?
23. What does the lack of sufficient water lead to?
24. How is water polluted?
25. What does water pollution threaten?
26. What percentage of people in developing countries cannot find clean water to drink?
27. What is the result of water pollution?
28. What is the principle reason behind the emigration of 10m. people from their home countries?
29. What other problem threatens the entire continent?
30. How much of this came from Italy to Nigeria?
31. Which organisation took notice of this danger?

32. What does it now demand?

(b) Read the following newspaper text from الوطن, 1988, then complete exercises
    i. and ii. which follow.

العالم يحتفل اليوم بعيد الطفولة المعذبة

تحتفل مصر والعالم اليوم بعيد الطفولة وهو اليوم الذي
يوافق ذكرى اعلان حقوق الطفل الذي اعلنته الامم المتحدة
منذ ٢٦ عاما.

وتجري الاحتفالات بعيد الطفولة وسط ظروف صعبة
يمر بها اطفال العالم النامي فهناك اكثر من ٤٠ الف طفل
في دول العالم النامي يموتون من قهر الجوع يوميا في
حين تؤكد تقارير اليونيسيف ان مئات الملايين من
الاطفال الافريقيين الذين يعانون الجفاف ولا يزالون على
قيد الحياة لن يكونوا في حالة صحية جيدة عندما يكبرون
نتيجة ما تعرضوا له من هزال ومرض وضعف في البنية.

كما ان حقوق الطفل تنتهك في عالمنا بسبب الاوضاع
السياسية .. ففي ايران نجد الاطفال يزجون الى صفوف
القتال في حربها مع العراق .. والطفل الفلسطيني يعاني
الاهمال والتشتت في الارض المحتلة .. والطفل اللبناني
يعاني التمزق النفسي ..

وهناك مظهر آخر لهدر حقوق الطفل في عدد من دول
آسيا وامريكا اللاتينية حيث يسخر الاطفال في سن
صغيرة للعمل في المهن الشاقة.

ومما يزيد الصورة قتامة للطفل في العالم وجود
ظاهرة بيع الاطفال وخاصة الفتيات للعمل في الخدمات
المنزلية ووجود عصابات لاختطاف الاطفال بالهند
والبرازيل لبيعهم كرقيق.

كما نجد الطفل في العالم المتقدم يعاني من الاهتزاز النفسي بسبب مشاكل الوالدين الشخصية.

ويولي المكتب التنفيذي التابع لصندوق الامم المتحدة لرعاية الامومة والطفولة «يونيسيف» اهتماما بالام من اجل الابناء فقد خصص اكثر من ٤٨ مليون ونصف مليون دولار لهذا العام للنهوض بالام.

كما خصص «يونيسيف» اعانة للاطفال المتضررين من النزاعات المسلحة في العالم وظروف اخرى مقدارها ٢٨٥ مليون دولار.

وبذلك اصبحت الحاجة ماسة الآن الى عقد مؤتمر دولي لصياغة اعلان عالمي يصون حقوق الطفل على غرار الاعلان العالمي لحقوق الانسان والاعلان العالمي لحقوق المرأة.

i Paraphrase the following terms orally in Arabic.

١ – العالم النامي

٢ – على قيد الحياة

٣ – هدر

٤ – الأرض المحتلة

٥ – مهن

٧ – الخدمات المنزلية

٨ – سخّر

٩ – نهوض

١٠ – صان (و)

١١ – على غرار ما

ii Answer the following questions in English.

1. What did the United Nations announce twenty–six years ago?
2. How many children are dying each day from hunger?
3. According to UNICEF reports, why will hundreds of millions of children in

Africa not be healthy when they grow up?
4. Why are the rights of children being infringed?
5. What do Iranian children have to do?
6. What do Palestinian children suffer from?
7. What do Lebanese children suffer from?
8. What makes the picture of children in the world worse?
9. What do children in the developed world suffer from?
10. For what purpose has UNICEF set aside $48m. this year?
11. What has $285m. been set aside for?
12. What is there now a pressing need for?

(c) Read the following newspaper text from الحوادث, 1988, then complete
exercises i. and ii. which follow.

مليون طفل في سوق العمل الأسود

رجل ... قبل الأوان

«الطفل البروليتاري» تعبير غريب ..لكنه يلخص واقعا
اجتماعيا وعالما غريبا يقترب في تفاصيله من المأساة. هو
عـالـم مليء بالتعب والاحزان والافراح المجهضة .. انه عـالـم
الاطفال الذين يخرجون للعمل قبل ان يكملوا تعليمهم، بل
وقبل ان يعيشوا احلام الطفولة.

وفـي مـصـر كـمـا فـي بلدان الـعـالـم الـفـقـيـرة تظهـر
«بروليتاريا الطفولة» وتلعب دورا مؤثرا في كل الانشطة
الاقتصادية، لكن عمالة الطفل في مصر تأخذ ابعادا هامة
وخطيرة تقلق الحكومة والمعارضة والرأي العام، فقد وصل
عدد الاطفال العاملين أقل من ١٢ سنة الى (١,٠١٤) مليون
طفل يمثلون (٧٪) من اجمالي قوة العمل في البلاد، غـيـر
مـئـات الالوف من الاطفال العاملين في الريف، والذين لا
تصل اليهم الاحصاءات ولا تعرف عنهم الحكومة شيئا ...

لماذا يخـرج الاطفـال الى العـمـل؟ ولماذا يـؤيـد بـعـض
الخبراء تشغيل الاطفال رغم اعترافهم بان ذلك قد يعرضهم
لحوادث العمل ولتشوهات نفسية لا حصر لها؟

هذه الاسئلة وغيرها ما تزال محل بحث الحكومة
المصرية وخبراء مراكز البحوث والجامعات .. وقد يطول
البحث كثيرا لانهم يعترفون بان ظاهرة تشغيل الاطفال
تعتبر من اعقد المشاكل الاجتماعية، واكثرها تشابكا مع
غيرها من مشاكل الواقع الاقتصادي والاجتماعي، بل انها
برأي الكثيرين نتاج هذه المشاكل.

i   Paraphrase, provide synonyms for, or explain the following terms in Arabic.

١ – الطفل البروليتاري

٢ – يلخص

٣ – مأساة

٤ – الافراح المجهضة

٥ – الرأي العام

٦ – اجمالي قوة العمل

٧ – الاحصاءات

٨ – تشوهات نفسية

٩ – ظاهرة تشغيل الاطفال

ii   Translate the second paragraph of this text into idiomatic English.

5. Written Arabic texts 2
(a) The following texts provide differing views of the 'population explosion'. As a
preparatory exercise for work on texts (b) and (c) section 5, read texts (i) and
(ii) at home. When you are satisfied that you have achieved a good command of
the texts, record them onto a tape for assessment by the lecturer.

(i) يشهد العالم اليوم

يشهد العالم اليوم أزمة كبرى تُسمّى بالانفجار السكّاني.
فلأول مرّة يتضاعف عدد سكّان العالم خلال هذا القرن ليبلغ
أكثر من خمسة مليارات نسمة في عام ١٩٨٥، فالأمر الذي
يدعو العلماء والحكومات والهيئات الدولية إلى القلق أن
هذا الرقم في تزايُد مستمرّ وسريع خاصّةً في دول العالم

الثالث إذ يتوقّع الدارسون أن يتضاعف عدد سكّان العالم بحلول عام الفين ليصبح ستة آلاف مليون نسمة أي ستة مليارات نسمة ممّا يهدّد بانفجار ما يُسمّى بالقنبلة السكانية وما سيتلو ذلك من مشاكل وتغيّرات.

(ii) إن الضجة

إن الضجة التي أثيرت حول موضوع الانفجار السكاني – أو قُل كثيرًا منها – تبنّى وجهات نظر وافتراضات ليست بالضرورة دقيقة. كما أنه إذا كان ثمة قلق عالمي من تزايد سكاني ضخم فإن القلق يجب أن يوجَّه نحو موضوع آخر، هو توزيع ثروات العالم بالعدل على هذا العدد من السكان، أو على الأَقلّ منع إهدار هذه الثروات من قبل قلة من البشر وعدد قليل من البلدان التي اصْطُلِح على تسميتها «الغنية».

(b) Read the following newspaper extract from الوطن, then complete the paraphrase exercise which follows.

«الوقت من ذهب» عند الدول المتقدمة وفي مجتمعاتنا «الوقت من صفيح» واحيانا «من تراب» وبالارقام هناك اربعة ملايين ساعة تضيع من المصريين شهريا في: زحام المواصلات، والتسكع في الشوارع، والتزويغ من ساعات العمل الرسمية، والجلوس في المقاهي، والثرثرة وحضور الحفلات، ومشاهدة دور العرض، ومتابعة الشاشة الصغيرة، بخلاف الوقت الضائع في: النوم والاكل واللبس والحمام!!

اضافة الى ذلك هناك «٧٢٪» من ساعات العمل «مفقودة» في: دواوين الحكومة والاجهزة المركزية و«٨٧٪» من التجهيزات المكتبية غير متوفرة و«٦٤٪» من موظفي الحكومة يعملون بالتجارة اثناء الدوام الحكومي، و«٨٣٪» من العاملين والموظفين يتعمدون اتلاف المباني وادوات العمل. وهناك دراستان خطيرتان .. احداهما اعدها الجهاز المختص بوظائف العاملين في الدولة – التنظيم والادارة –

والاخرى اجـراها بـاحـث اجتمـاعي وعـالـم نفس. الاولى تـرصـد عـدد سـاعـات العـمـل «المفقـودة» في الـدواويـن والقطاعـات الحكـومـيـة، والثانية تبحث عن القيم الاجتماعية «المفقودة» في الحياة المصرية اليومية.

وتوصلت الدراستان – دون اتفاق مسبق بينهما، وبالرغم من تبـاعـد واختلاف مجـالات البحث – الى نتيجة واحدة، عنوانها، ومضمونها هو «الوقت الضائع».

ومـن واقـع سـجـلات الموظفين والعـامـلين بالدواوين، اتضح ان بعض الادارات لم يستـدل فيهـا على سـجـلات منتظمـة، وبالتالي فـهنـاك عـدم انتظـام في تسجيل الاجازات، خاصة اجازات الادارات العليا، وبجوارها يأتي الكتبة وموظفو الارشيف على رأس القائمة في استنفاد كافة انواع الاجازات – الاعتيادية والعرضية والمرضية – اضافة الى الاجازات الرسمية والقومية والاسبوعية، اما في شهر رمضان ينخفض العمل الى ساعتين ونصف الساعة يوميا، فالعمل لا يبدأ قبل «الحادية عشرة» صباحاً، وبدلا من تضييع الوقت في الاكل والشرب يكون البديل لقتل الوقت الطويل – اثناء الصيام – هو الكلام والاحاديث وقراءة الصحف، وحل الكلمات المتقاطعة، وسمـاع الراديو، والتـردد على الجمعيات الاستهـلاكيـة داخل مبـاني الوزارات والهيئات وخارجها.

يقـول خبـراء التنظيم والادارة ان نحـو «۲۷٪» من الموظفين يتأخرون عن مـواعيد العمل الرسمـية و «۲٤٪» منهم ينصرفون قبل انتهـاء المواعيد الرسمـية و .. بدون اذن و«۳۳٪» منهم يستقبلون الزائرين و«۲۷٪» من العاملين يتحدثون أثناء العمل في امور وقضايا ومشاكل لا علاقة للعمل بها.

ويحـلل عـالـم النفس د. ملاك جرجس مسـألة «المواعيد» عند المصـريين اجتمـاعيـا فيـقـول ان ٥٠٪ من الافراد لا يحترمون المـواعيد لا في العمل ولا في المنزل ولا حتى مع الاصدقاء. و۱٥٪

يحافظون ويحرصون عليها. و٢٥٪ لا يحضرون في الموعد المحدد. او يحضرون بعد الميعاد بساعات. و٧٥٪ لا يحضرون في مواعيدهم على الاطلاق!! وبالطبع يتعلل الكثيرون بالمثل الشعبي القائل: «الغايب حجته معاه» ولهذا اصبح عدم الحرص على المواعيد سمة مميزة عند المصريين.

واستكمالا لقواعد العمل واصوله ومدى الالتزام بها كشفت الدراسة عن «٥٥٪» من رؤساء العمل المباشرين يتركون ويبعدون عن اماكن عملهم و«٣٣٪» من الالات الكتابية والادوات المكتبية مكدسة في حجرة واحدة و«٢١٪» من الادوات الفرعية متداخلة في اختصاصاتها و«٤٤٪» من الموظفين تتشابه وتتداخل اختصاصاتهم لدرجة التكرار والصدام، ومع ذلك يجتمعون في حجرة واحدة. بالرغم من تبعيتهم لاكثر من ادارة.

وترتفع الارقام الى اعلى معدلاتها فتسجل ان نسبة حث الزملاء في العمل على مخالفة الرؤساء تصل الى «٧١٪» «٨٣٪» من العمال والموظفين يتعمدون اتلاف المبنى وادوات العمل «٢٧٪» يتكاسلون عن اداء اعمالهم «٣٠٪» يلهون مع الزملاء في مكان العمل. «٢٩٪» يتعمدون تعطيل العمل دون مبرر «٢٦٪» يصطحبون ابناءهم الى اماكن عملهم.

ويتفق الباحث الاجتماعي مع خبراء التنظيم والادارة في ان حجم العاملين يتناسب مع اعباء العمل لكن العمل لا يسير وفق انضباط معين، لان الفاقد الناتج عن الزيارات يمثل «٦١٪» من اجمالي ساعات التشغيل اليومي.

ويوضح د. ملاك جرجس ان المصريين يتفننون في قتل الوقت، بالجلوس في المقاهي لساعات طويلة، التسكع في الشوارع، في اوقات العمل الرسمية، والثرثرة و«المغالاة» في اتباع التقاليد، المجاملات، وما يلاحظ بصورة واضحة ان الغالبية العظمى من الناس – في المدينة والريف على السواء، يستهلك ساعات طويلة

من التزاور في البيوت او زيارة المستشفيات او مواساة الآخرين.

Write a brief explanation in Arabic of the meaning of each of the following phrases, in the sense in which it is used in the text.

١ – الوقت من ذهب

٢ – الوقت من صفيح

٣ – هناك اربعة ملايين ساعة تضيع من المصريين

٤ – التزويغ من ساعات العمل الرسمية

٥ – متابعة الشاشة الصغيرة

٦ – بخلاف الوقت

٧ – دواوين الحكومة

٨ – التجهيزات المكتبية

٩ – الدوام الحكومي

١٠ –يتعمدون إتلاف المباني

١١ –الجهاز المختص بوظائف العاملين في الدولة

١٢ –عدد ساعات العمل «المفقودة»

١٣ –القيم الاجتماعية «المفقودة»

6. Written Arabic texts 3 (classical)

Translate the following text into idiomatic English. The text is by ابن قتيبة from عيون الأخبار in كتاب السؤدد, p. 245.

وقال زيد بن جَبَلة : لا فقير أفقر مِن غنيٍّ أمِنَ الفقرَ . وروى عن على بن أبي طالب كرم اللّه وجهه أنه قال : ما دون أربعة آلاف درهم نفقةٌ ، وما فوقها كنزٌ . ويقال : القبرُ ولا الفقرُ . ويقال : ما سبق عيالٌ مالاً قطّ إلا كان صاحبه فقيرا . وقيل لرجل من البصريين : مالكَ لا يَنمي مالُكَ ؟ قال : لاني اتخذتُ العيالَ قبل المال واتخذ الناسُ المالَ قبل العيال . ويقال : العيالُ سوسُ المال . وقيل لمدينيّ : كيف حالُك ؟ قال : كيف يكون حال من ذهب مالُه وبقيت عادته . ويقال : الغنَى في الغربة وطنٌ والفقرُ في الوطن غربةٌ .

حدّثني محـمـد بن يـحـيي بإسناد ذكره قـال : شكا نبيّ من
الأنبياء إلى اللّه شدّةَ الفقر فأوحى اللّهُ إليه : هكذا جرى أمرُك
عندي أفتريد من أجلك أن أُعيد الدنيا .

قـال أبو حـاتم قال حدّثني العُتبيّ قال سـمـعت يونس بن
حبيب يقول : مـا أجدب أهلُ البادية قطّ حتى تسوّيهم السّنّةُ[1]
ثم جاءهم الخِصْب إلا عاد الغنى إلى أهل الغنى .

قـال الأصـمـعـيّ رأيت أعـرابيـة ذات جمـال رائـع تسـأل بمنًى
فـقلت: يا أمـة اللّه تَسْألينَ ولك هذا الجمال ! قالت : قدّر اللّهُ فما
أصنعُ؟ قلت : فـمـن أين مـعـاشُكم ؟ قالت : هذا الحاجُّ نتقممُهُم
ونغسلُ ثيـابهم . فـقلت : فـإذا ذهب الحاجُّ فـمـن أين ؟ فنظرتْ
إلىَّ وقـالت : يا صُلْبَ الجبـين ! لو كنا إنما نعيشُ من حيث نَعلمُ
لما عِشْنا .

Note
1. سَنَة unfruitfulness, barren land

7. Grammar/stylistics
(a) *Relative clauses without an antecedent noun phrase*
In this section, familiarity is assumed with the construction of relative clauses which
have an antecedent noun phrase, of the type {من هو الرجل {الذي اشترى البـيت
'Who is the man who bought the house', and {رأيت رجلا {اشترى بيتا جديدا} 'I
saw a man who bought a new house'.

Relative clauses without an antecedent noun phrase are relatively common, and
are found either when the identity of the head of the relative clause is not known or
when the identity is immaterial. When there is no antecedent noun phrase one of five
relative pronouns must be used: مَن or مـا، التي ، الذين ، الذي. Of these الذي
'what; that; that which; who; he who; whoever' takes the place of a singular noun
phrase; الذين 'those; those who; those which' takes the place of a plural noun
phrase; التي 'what, etc.' is used very occasionally in place of an inanimate (i.e.
non–human) plural or feminine singular noun phrase; مـا 'what; whatever', takes the
place of an inanimate singular or plural noun phrase; and مَن 'who; he who;
whoever' takes the place of an animate (i.e. human) singular or plural noun phrase.
Consider the following examples:

الذي and الذين can be used in place of animate or inanimate nouns, as in:

وأن {الذي تشعر به} هذا ليس انتقاما.

'...and that what she feels is not revenge.' (ch. 10, 11b)

ثم حدثتُها {بالذي رأيت}.

'Then I told her about what I had seen.' (ch. 4, 6a)

ما {الذي تسأل منه}. (ch. 11, 4bii) '?What is it you are asking about'

.. ومن {الذي يستطيع أن يزعم} ..

'...and whoever can claim ...' (ch. 5, 4a)

وربما خالفنا في ذلك بعض {الذين تأبطوا القواميس}.

'Perhaps some of those who carry dictionaries under their arms would disagree with us.' (ch. 5, 11b)

وفهم القرآن الكريم فهما يماثل فهم {الذين عاصروا نزوله}.

'...and an understanding of the Holy Qur'an which is similar to the understanding of those who lived at the time of its revelation.' (ch. 4, 5a)

Where it is clear that the relative pronoun takes the place of an inanimate plural or feminine singular noun phrase التي can be used, as in:

للأجيال المسلمة العربية الأولى و{التي تلتها}.

'... for the first Arab Muslim generations and those which followed them.' (ch. 4, 5a)

However, الذي will be used in place of a feminine singular noun when it is not immediately obvious that the replaced noun phrase is feminine singular, as in:

و{الذي قال للناس هو الزوجة}.

'... and the one who told the people was his wife.' (ch. 10, 11b)

الذي can be used to describe God, particularly in classical and religious texts, as in:

فو{الذي نفس خديجة بيده}.

'By the One in whose hands lies the soul of Khadija.' (ch. 4, 6a)

أرَءَيتَ {الذي يَنْهَى}. 'Seest thou the One who forbids.' (ch. 4, 8a)

الذين can similarly be used to describe people being addressed by God, and is translated as 'those of you' or 'those' according to the context, as in:

يا أيها {الذين آمنوا} ..   'Oh those of you who believe...' (ch. 4, 6a)

ما is used in place of an inanimate noun, irrespective of whether the replaced noun is singular or plural, as in:

أعجبني {ما رأيت}.   'What I saw pleased me.'

أُعْجِبْتُ بـ{ما رأيت}.   'I liked what I saw.'

من is used in place of an animate noun, irrespective of whether the replaced noun is singular or plural, masculine or feminine, as in:

رأيت {من دخل البيت}.   'I saw who came into the house.'

أعجبني {من رأيت}.   'Those/He] who I saw pleased me.'

أحببت {من رأيت}.   'I loved [those/who] I saw.'

Unlike in relative clauses with a noun phrase antecedent, when the relative pronoun ما or من refers to the same thing as the object of the verb in the relative clause, an object pronoun which is co–referential with the relative pronoun (an عائد or راجع) is *optional*, but is most commonly omitted (cf. Hayward and Nahmad, 1979: 284–5). In the above examples, object referential pronouns have been omitted. In the following examples, object referential pronouns have been included:

{ما شهده سكان القاهرة}.
'What the population of Cairo saw'. (ch. 8, 4c)

و{ما يكتنفه من تعبير صادق}.
'... what it embraces in way of true expression'. (ch. 11, 5c)

بـ{ما يحمله من ميزات}.
'... with the characteristics it bears'. (ch. 11, 5c)

كان سبب وضعه لها {ما حكاه ولده}.
'The reason behind his codification of them [the *maqamat*] was what his son related'. (ch. 11, 6c)

(b) ما ... من

A very common construction involving the pronoun ما is ما ... من where ما is followed by a verb or prepositional phrase, and من is followed by a [usually indefinite, but see below] noun phrase. Literally this construction can be translated as 'what *verb* in terms of X'. More idiomatically, the construction is translated as 'the X which *verb*'. Consider the following examples:

إن القرآن الكريم هو معجزة الإسلام العظمى لـ{ما حوى من فصاحة وبلاغة وأحكام وحكم}.

'The Holy Qur'an is the miracle of Islam for the purity, eloquence and wisdom which it contains.' (ch. 4, 5a)

و{ما سيتلو ذلك من مشاكل وتغيرات}.

'... and the problems and changes which follow from that.' (ch. 9, 5ai)

وأن {ما شهده سكان القاهرة وبعض المحافظات من سقوط أمطار سوداء} يرجع إلى الشوائب العالقة في الجو.

'... the black rain which the people of Cairo and some of the provinces have seen can be attributed to particles in the air.' (ch. 8, 4c)

و{ما يكتنفه من تعبير صادق}.

'... and the true expression which it embraces.' (ch. 11, 5c)

وهذا النوع من الأدب – بـ{ما يحمله من ميزات}.

'... and this type of literature – with all its peculiarities [/with the peculiarities it bears].' (ch. 11, 5c)

The pronoun ما may be followed by a prepositional phrase rather than a verb phrase, as in:

وملأ جحا معدته بكل {ما أمامه من خبز وجبن}.

'Juha filled his stomach with all the bread and cheese in front of him.' (ch. 11, 4b)

Usually the noun phrase following من is indefinite, as in the examples above; it may, however, be definite, as in:

فيصيدا {ما فيه من السمك}.

'... and catch [dual] the fish that were there [lit: in it].' (ch. 11, 6b)

قد سمعت مقال زوجتك فـ{ما عندك من الجواب}.

'You have heard what your wife has said, so what do you have in way of an answer.' (ch. 10, 6a)

على قدر {ما يريدون من ارتفاع الأساس}.

'... to the height they wanted the foundation [to be].' (ch. 3, 6b)

(c) مَن ..... مِن

A construction related to مِن ... ما is مِن ... مَن, which is used to describe animate objects rather than inanimate objects. مَن...مِن is markedly less common than ما مِن .... This construction can be translated literally as '[those] who *verb* in the way of X', and more idiomatically as 'the X who *verb*'. As with the ما ... مِن construction considered above, مَن is followed either by a verb or by a prepositional phrase or locative pronoun (هنا or هناك, etc.), and مِن is followed by a noun phrase. Unlike with the ما ... مِن construction, however, the noun phrase following مِن is usually definite. Consider the following examples:

وجاوروا {من هنالك من الأمم الساكنة المدن والعمائر من الأعاجم والفرس}.

'They lived beside the Persians and non–Arabs who inhabited the towns and settlements.' (ch. 2, 6b)

فحالوا عن اللغة العربية لـ{من جاورهم من الأمم}.

'They deviated from Arabic towards [that spoken by] their neighbouring communities.' (ch. 2, 6c)

أو بـ{من شئت من الشعوب التي غزت مصر}.

'[related to] whoever you wish of those who conquered Egypt.' (ch. 5, 4a)

(d) مما *and relative clauses with a clausal antecedent*

Relative clauses can have either a noun phrase antecedent, or no antecedent, as we have seen in (a) above, or a clause antecedent, in which case the relative clause relates to the *entire preceding clause*, or even in some cases to a series of clauses, a sentence, or a series of sentences. A relative clause which relates to a clause antecedent may begin with مما (from مِن ما) (for other means of introducing relative clauses of this type, cf. ch. 13, 7d). مما in this context is usually translated into English as 'which', and is often separated from its clausal antecedent by a comma. Consider the following examples:

تم الكشف أيضا عن أجزاء من مبنى إداري في الموسم الماضي {مما يدل على الاستقرار الحضاري لسكان الموقع}.

'Last season, parts of an administrative building were also found, which indicates that the inhabitants of the area were settled/the settled nature of the inhabitants of the area.' (ch. 3, 4b)

خاصة أنّ النقش على اللوحة يقول «زوجة الملك المحبوبة منه» {مما يؤكد أن أحد هذه الأهرامات بنى لها}.

'Particularly since the inscription on the tablet reads, 'The King's beloved wife', which confirms that one of the pyramids was constructed for her.' (ch. 3, 5)

وانتقدت الولايات المتحدة لفرضها قيودا على دخول المهاجرين اليهود السوفيات {مما يجبر الراغبين منهم في الهجرة على التوجه إلى إسرائيل}.

'It criticised the United States for imposing restrictions on the immigration of Soviet Jews, which has forced those of them who wish to emigrate to head for Israel.' (ch. 6, 4d)

وحدت بساتر ترابي ارتفاعه ٦ أمتار، {مما يمنع الماء عن التدفق شمالا، ويدفع به ليصب في الفرات}.

'It is delineated by a mud curtain 6 metres high, which prevents the water from flowing North, and directs it into the Euphrates.' (ch. 8, 11)

إذ يتوقع الدارسون أن يتضاعف عدد سكان العالم بحلول عام ألفين ليصبح ستة آلاف مليون نسمة أي ستة مليارات نسمة {مما يهدد بانفجار ما يُسمّى بالقنبلة السكانية وما سيتلو ذلك من مشاكل وتغيّرات}.

'Researchers expect the world's population to double by the beginning of the year 2,000 to 6,000,000,000 – i.e. six billion – which will threaten an explosion of the so–called human time bomb with all the problems and changes which will ensue from that.' (ch. 9, 5ai)

أزواج الكثير من النساء الريفيات يهاجرون إلى المدن بحثا عن لقمة العيش {مما يعني عمليا مضاعفة المسؤوليات الملقاة على عاتق المرأة}.

'The husbands of many rural women migrate to the towns in search of a living, which means in practice the doubling of responsibilities borne by the women.' (ch. 10, 5a)

(e) *Logical versus grammatical agreement: number phrases from 11–99, 100s and 1,000s*
There is often a discrepancy between logical agreement and grammatical agreement in Arabic. This discrepancy is perhaps shown most clearly in structures involving the cardinal numbers above 11.

i In modern Arabic, when a number from the number classes 11–99, 100s or 1,000s takes a following singular noun, a following adjective will show *grammatical* agreement, and will agree with the singular noun in case, number, gender and definiteness, as in:

ما يصل إلى ٧٥٠ ألف يهودي {سوفياتي}.

'... to what amounts to 750,000 Soviet Jews.' (ch. 6, 4c)

بين ٥٠ ألفا و ١٠٠ ألف يهودي {سوفياتي}.

'... between 50,000 and 100,000 Soviet Jews.' (ch. 6, 4c)

...كما وصل ١٥٠ مليون مواطن {إفريقي}...

'... also 150 million Africans have reached ...' (ch. 9, 4a)

١٥ مليون سيدة {جديدة}.   '15 million new women...' (ch. 10, 4c)

ii When, however, a verb phrase or relative clause follows the noun, the verb and relative pronoun take *plural* and not singular agreement: in other words, the verb reflects *logical* agreement as opposed to *grammatical* agreement:

الـ ٨٠ ألف {الذين يعيشون} بين ١.٨ مليون فلسطيني.

'... the 80,000 who live among 1.8 million Palestinians.' (ch. 6, 4c)

أكثر من ٤٠ ألف طفل في دول العالم النامي {يموتون} من قهر الجوع.

'... more than 40,000 children in the developing world die of hunger.' (ch. 9, 4b)

فقد وصل عدد الأطفال العاملين أقل من ١٢ سنة إلى ١.١٤ مليون طفل {يمثلون} ٪٧ من إجمالي قوة العمل.

'The number of children working under the age of twelve years has reached 1.14 million which makes up 7% of the total workforce.' (ch. 9, 4c)

نحو ٥٥٠ مليون سيدة في الدول النامية {يعشن} في حرمان شبه كامل.

'Around 550 million women in the developing countries live in almost total deprivation.' (ch. 10, 5c)

When the noun following the number is inanimate, the verb takes feminine singular agreement to agree with the inanimate plural:

وأن ١٥ مليون فدان من الغابات {تزال} كل عام.

'... and that 15 million feddans of forest are disappearing every year.' (ch. 9, 4a)

و١٥ ألف طن من أمريكا {دفنت}.

'... and 15,000 tons from America were buried...' (ch. 9, 4a)

8. Aural Arabic texts 1

Listen to the following text from حصاد الشهر no. 12, side 2, item 1, in which طه حسين responds to a question about animosity between wives and their mothers–in–law, then complete exercises i. and ii. below.

i Listening to the tape, fill in the gaps in the following transcription.

ثم ـــــــ ـــــــ الندوة ـــــــ في ـــــــ ـــــــ ـــــــ

أسئلة ـــــــ، ـــــــ، ـــــــ لم تخلو في ـــــــ

ـــــــ من سؤال ـــــــ ما ـــــــ ـــــــ إلى

ـــــــ هذا ـــــــ الحيرة في ـــــــ

ـــــــ منا، ـــــــ سؤال ـــــــ ـــــــ

في ذلك ـــــــ:

ما ـــــــ ـــــــ بين ـــــــ ـــــــ وأم

ـــــــ وهل ـــــــ عند ـــــــ ـــــــ أم

ـــــــ ـــــــ ـــــــ العالم؟ هذا

ـــــــ ـــــــ ورد ـــــــ ـــــــ من السيد عبد الله

صادق ـــــــ ـــــــ ـــــــ ولعلّه ـــــــ

ـــــــ الحماة. ـــــــ يُريد أن ـــــــ

ـــــــ العداء بين ـــــــ وـــــــ وهل هذا

ـــــــ على ـــــــ الذي هو ـــــــ أم

ـــــــ جميع بلاد ـــــــ الدكتور ـــــــ

ـــــــ:

أظن أن هذا ـــــــ ـــــــ على ـــــــ

بعينه، ــــــ نعرفه في ــــــ ـــــــ، قد

عـرفنـاه عنـد ــــــ ـــــــ، وفي ــــــ ـــــــ المروي

في الحماسة قالت له ــــــ يوم لتسمعني مثلا فإن لنا في

أمـنا أربـة ولو ... ــــــ ـــــــ في نارٍ مـؤجـجـة ثم استطاعت لا

ــــــ فـوقـهـا حطبـة . ونـعـرف ـــــــ أن في

ــــــ ـــــــ عظيما ـــــــ هو François Mauriac

قـد ــــــ ـــــــ من ـــــــ مـا كُتب في هذا

ــــــ ـــــــ أو ـــــــ وهي ـــــــ ،

فـيهـا مـا ــــــ من ـــــــ بـين أم ـــــــ

و ــــــ ـــــــ، وأكبـر ـــــــ أن

ــــــ ـــــــ بـين ـــــــ وزوجة ـــــــ

أو ــــــ ـــــــ يأتي من أن ـــــــ تحب ـــــــ أن

ــــــ بحب ـــــــ وأن ـــــــ لهـا نفسـه

وحيـاتـه، و ــــــ ـــــــ وحدهن هـن ـــــــ

ــــــ ـــــــ ويقـرّرن في ـــــــ أن الحب

ــــــ استئئارا وإنما هو ـــــــ ، وهذا ـــــــ

إلى مـا ــــــ ـــــــ فـيـه ـــــــ من

ــــــ والقلب والعقل فـفي هذا ـــــــ

ــــــ عنصـر ـــــــ الذي ـــــــ من

ــــــ وعنصـر ـــــــ والحكم ـــــــ

ــــــ من ـــــــ فـالأم التي تؤثر ـــــــ على

_____ تتركـه _____ بحـياتـه _____ دون أن

_____ ولا من _____ تنـغّـص عليـه من _____

شيئـا ولكن _____ التي _____ بالخير

_____ _____ بكل شيء، هي _____ أن وتريد

على _____ أو على _____ _____ لأنّهـا لا

_____ لها من دون _____ أنّ ابنها _____ .

ii Answer the following questions relating to the aural text in English.

1. What are the two parts of the question put to Dr Taha Hussein?
2. Where does the questioner come from?
3. What evidence does Taha Hussein bring to bear to demonstrate that this problem is not restricted to one part of the world?
4. According to Taha Hussein what is the most probable reason for animosity between a man's mother–in–law and her daughter–in–law?
5. How do sensible mothers view love?
6. What was Taha Hussein talking about earlier?
7. Which element stems from the heart?
8. Which elements stem from the mind?

9. Aural Arabic texts 2

Listen to the following text from حصاد الشهر no. 19, side 1, item 2, المجاعة in which the causes of drought and starvation in Ethiopia are discussed, then complete exercises i. – iii. below.

i Listening to the tape, fill in the gaps in the following transcription.

_____ في _____ التي ضربت _____ المجاعـة

_____ لها حركت من شـدتها _____ _____ و

النـاس _____ أن _____ ومن . _____

_____ انصبّ _____ المناطق _____

وفـي . _____ _____ وليس على

ـــــــــ ــــــــــ ـــــــــ ما ــــــــــ فـيـه ـــــــــ ـــــــــ

ـــــــــ ــــــــــ عـن ـــــــــ دون وقـوع الـزلازل والأعـاصـيـر

والـبـراكـيـن لأنـه يـعتبـرها ـــــــــ ـــــــــ نجـد علمـاء

ـــــــــ بأنّـه يجب على ـــــــــ ـــــــــ يـنظر إلى

ـــــــــ مـن ـــــــــ ـــــــــ و ـــــــــ عـلى

أنها ـــــــــ ـــــــــ ـــــــــ. فهنـاك ـــــــــ

هـو Lloyd Timberlake ألَّـف ـــــــــ عـن ـــــــــ

تسـاءل فـي ـــــــــ «هل هـي من صنـع ـــــــــ أم من

الإنسـان؟». هاكـم ـــــــــ على سـؤاله ـــــــــ بـعـد أن

ـــــــــ إلـى ـــــــــ برنامـجنا «عـلى ـــــــــ

ـــــــــ».

إن المجاعـة الرهيـبـة ـــــــــ في إثيوبيا أحد ـــــــــ

على أن ـــــــــ مـن ـــــــــ الـتـي ـــــــــ فـي

ـــــــــ مـن صنـع ـــــــــ إنما هـي في ـــــــــ مـن

ـــــــــ. و ـــــــــ قائـلا إنه ـــــــــ

شُـحّ فـي ـــــــــ فـي ـــــــــ ،

ولكن ـــــــــ هنـاك ـــــــــ ـــــــــ

أكـثـر مـن ـــــــــ كمـا قامـوا ـــــــــ ـــــــــ مـن

ـــــــــ فـي ـــــــــ فـي ـــــــــ ممـا

تـسبب في ضيـاع ـــــــــ المطر ـــــــــ وعدم امتصـاص

التـربـة ـــــــــ ـــــــــ، وبالتـالي لـم

—————— أي محصول على ——————. ثم مضى ——————

—————— إن تآكل التربة يحصل بفعل عوامل التعرية من

—————— ورياح و —————— عالية طبيعية ويحدث هذا

التآكل —————— —————— درجاته في ——————

—————— تفقد تربتها الفوقية —————— أكبر

من —————— التي تغطيها نباتات —————— فهذا الغطاء

النباتي —————— يحتفظ برطوبة بدرجة ——————، ولكنّ

تآكل —————— وفقدها —————— مرتفعات ——————

شكّل كارثة —————— أن التربة —————— في ——————

وصلت —————— مائتي طن للهكتار ——————

—————— وذلك في —————— أحد —————— طنا للهكتار

وهو المعدَّل —————— عالميا، إلا أن —————— وجهة

—————— رأي —————— : ——————، ولكن

لم تثبت صحته —————— ——————، إن —————— أو

إزالة غطاء النباتات —————— في —————— الشبه القاحلة

—————— يمكن أن يؤثر —————— المناخ حيث

أنه —————— نقص في هبوب الرياح ——————

—————— ولكن —————— تآكل ——————

إلى درجة معينة فإن —————— لو جاء لن يقضي ——————

القحط أو —————— فقد هطلت في —————— ——————

غزيرة لحوالى —————— ، كل ما —————— هذه ——————

هو أنها كسحت المزروعات والتربة ــــــــ ــــــــ في ــــــــ

المرتفعة إلى الحقول الأكثر انخفاضا على ــــــــ التل ، كما

أن ــــــــ ــــــــ ــــــــ أخرى ــــــــ ــــــــ : في

ــــــــ هذا ــــــــ تم تشجيــر ــــــــ

ــــــــ مـن ــــــــ ، ــــــــ مسـاحتها إلى

ــــــــ ، أمـا ــــــــ فهذه المساحات لا

ــــــــ عن اثنين ــــــــ ، ولكن ــــــــ لا يقتصر

على ــــــــ ففي الثلاثينيات ــــــــ ــــــــ

ــــــــ حدث تآكل في السهول الشمالية من

ــــــــ الأمريكية ــــــــ في إفقار ملايين

ــــــــ ، ــــــــ إنه دفع ببعــضهم إلى حـافـة

جوعا.

ــــــــ Roy Morgan ــــــــ ــــــــ

ــــــــ إن ما ــــــــ في ــــــــ ما

هو إلا ــــــــ ــــــــ ــــــــ لما

ــــــــ في ــــــــ على مــر ــــــــ ، لقد

ــــــــ الرئيسي فيه هو ــــــــ الزحف

الزراعي إلى ــــــــ مناسـبة للزراعة

و ــــــــ إذا ــــــــ أراض لا تصلـح إلا للـري

ــــــــ . لقد ــــــــ ذلك في زيادة ــــــــ التعرية

و ــــــــ تلك ــــــــ ــــــــ الرياح.

ii Provide a paraphrase or simple explanation in Arabic for the following words and phrases which occur in the aural text.

١ – المجاعة

٢ – ضربت أطنانها في إثيوبيا

٣ – الضمير العالمي

٤ – الكوارث الطبيعية

٥ – من صنع الطبيعة

٦ – في مقابل

٧ – تشجير

٨ – القحط

٩ – خبير البيئة

١٠. –عوامل التعرية

iii Using between 100 and 150 words, summarise the main points of this text in English.

10. Written English texts
Using constructions encountered in the Arabic texts above, translate the following newspaper passage adapted from the *Guardian*, May, 1988 into idiomatic Arabic. Note that even the spoken sections should be translated into Standard Arabic, in accordance with the normal rules of formal newspaper writing in Arabic.

Cairo poor swell in former land of plenty
Two years ago, Ahmad's father lost his job at the factory. Now he rents a little kiosk where he makes about 30 Egyptian pounds (£12 on the black market) a month selling cigarettes, soap and biscuits. 'It keeps a little money coming in,' Ahmad said. 'But my father smokes at least two packets of cigarettes a day from the shop, which reduces profits by a lot.'

Ahmad works as a cleaner twice a week. His wages more than treble the family income and allow him to go to college at the local technical school. 'If it wasn't for the money I bring home, my father wouldn't let me go to school,' he said.

Ahmad, who sees education as the only chance of finding a job abroad and marrying the girl he has been engaged to for more than a year, lives in the capital's northern district of Shobra. With four million inhabitants, it is one of the most densely populated areas in the world – the result of Egypt's enormous population explosion which is the chief reason for today's economic crisis.

11. Précis

The following text from مجلة الشرق الأوسط, Mar. 7, 1995 describes the findings of a study of young people who had made suicide attempts. Read the text, then produce a précis in Arabic summarising the major findings of the study.

دراسة علمية عربية تنصح الشباب
تزوج حتى لا تموت

القاهرة: « مجلة الشرق الاوسط »

دون ادنى مسؤولية على « مجلة الشرق الاوسط » وعلى مسؤولية البحث العلمي في مصر، عليك ان تتزوج حتى لا تلجأ الى الانتحار لتنهي حياة العزوبية .. فقد اكدت دراسة علمية اجريت حديثا في القاهرة ان الزواج يمثل خط الدفاع الاول ضد محاولات الانتحار خاصة اذا كان الزواج مدعما بوجود اطفال.

شملت الدراسة التي اعدها الدكتور سامي عبد القوي الاستاذ في قسم علم النفس بجامعة عين شمس ٢٠ حالة من محاولي الانتحار بينهم ٤ ذكور و١٦ فتاة وكان متوسط اعمارهم ٢١ عاما وجميعهم لم يسبق لهم الزواج. ورغم ان الارقام تؤكد ارتفاع معدلات الانتحار حيث بلغت ٣٨ حالة انتحار بين كل عشرة آلاف شخص في مدينة القاهرة بينما كانت ٢٨ حالة بين كل مائة الف شخص عام ١٩٥٩ الا ان الباحث وجد صعوبة في ايجاد عدد كبير من محاولي الانتحار كعينة للدراسة لان اسرهم يرفضون الحديث عن هذه المحاولات بالاضافة الى ان كثيرا من الحالات اثارت شكوكا في كونها محاولة انتحار حيث يصفونها بأنها حالات تسمم غير مقصودة وليس فيها شبهة وعلى الجانب الاخر تأكد الباحث من ان ٥٠ في المائة من افراد العينة حاولوا الانتحار اكثر من مرة سابقة.

اكدت الدراسة ان فترة المراهقة والشباب هي اكثر مرحلة تزداد فيها معدلات الانتحار وان العوامل الشخصية التي ترتبط بأزمة سن المراهقة والشباب والضغوط التي تمارسها الاسرة على

ابنائها في تلك الفترة هي الدافع الاساسي لانتحارهم.

كما ان للتعليم دورا في حماية الشاب من الانتحار حيث اكدت الدراسة ان معظم افراد العينة من متوسطي التعليم وانهم يلجأون الى الانتحار كوسيلة للتخلص من مشاكلهم. كما ان للمشاكل الاسرية دورا كبيرا في زيادة حالات الانتحار حيث تبين ان ٤٥ في المائة من افراد العينة عكست مشاكلهم الاسرية المتمثلة في سوء واضطراب علاقة الشاب بأسرته وذاته سببا مباشرا في الانتحار.

وان اضطراب العلاقة بين الاباء والابناء في تلك المرحلة من العمر بكل ما تحمله من ازمات مع سوء التوافق الاسري يؤدي الى افتقاد الشاب الاستقرار داخل اسرته التي تعتبر التنظيم الاجتماعي الذي يمده بهويته واحساسه بقيمة ذاته.

واشارت الدراسة الى ان المشاكل الدراسية المتمثلة في الفشل في الامتحانات وضعف القدرة على الانجاز والتحصيل الدراسي بالاضافة الى تطلعات الاباء وتوقعاتهم نحو ابنائهم دون النظر لامكانيات وقدرات هؤلاء الابناء يؤدي الى خلق مجموعة من الضغوط والصراعات التي تعوقه عن تحقيق هدفه حيث تحدث في نفسه عدم الثقة وعدم الكفاءة في الحياة فيواجه الشاب حياته بطريقة غير سوية ويحاول حلها بشكل سلبي لانه عاجز عن مواجهتها بشكل ايجابي فيلجأ الى الانتحار.

وعن السمات الشخصيات لمحاولي الانتحار اشارت الدراسة الى انهم اتسموا بالاضطراب الوجداني وعدم الاستقرار الانفعالي وسرعة الاستثارة وعدم القدرة على ضبط النفس وارتفاع درجة العصابية والاضطراب الذهني كما انهم تميزوا بالانطوائية والافتقار الى الصحة النفسية واحساسهم الدائم بالظلم والتوجس والريبة تجاه الاخرين بالاضافة الى تميزهم بالاعتمادية والسلبية في حل مشكلاتهم، وحاجتهم الدائمة الى مساعدة الاخرين كما انهم يتمتعون بقدر كبير من العدوانية التي تنعكس على الذات في هذا

السلوك المدمر لها والمتمثل في محاولة الانتحار.

وتشير هذه الدلائل الى مدى ما يعانيه هؤلاء الافراد من صراعات وتوترات وقلق وعدم القدرة على تحمل الاحباط ومواجهة المشاكل بشكل سلبي حيث انهم يتميزون بالاندفاعية وسوء القدرة على التكيف مع الميل الى التفريغ الانفعالي بشكل انفجاري يظهر في سلوك الانتحاري.

الا ان الباحث توصل من خلال دراسته لهذه الحالات الى ان محاولة الانتحار لا تتعدى مجرد صرخة استغاثة من هؤلاء الشباب لان معظمهم قاموا بالانتحار في حضور الاخرين.

12. Oral

الفقر والمشاكل الاجتماعية

(a) One or two students to present a brief account of poverty and social problems in the Arab world. You may wish to concentrate on the problems of a specific country.

(b) The presenter(s) then ask(s) the other students questions relating to social problems. These questions should include some which require factual answers and some which require more subjective or speculative answers. For example:

١ – في رأيك، ما هو سبب الفقر في هذه البلاد/في الوطن العربي؟

٢ – ما هي المشاكل الاجتماعية الرئيسية في الوطن العربي؟

٣ – ما هي العوامل التي ادت الى هذه المشاكل؟

٤ – هل يوجد حل لهذه المسائل؟

٥ – ما هي المشاكل الاسرية الموجودة في الوطن العربي؟

٦ – كيف تختلف المشاكل الاسرية في الوطن العربي عن التي في الغرب؟

٧ – ما هي العلاقة بين المشاكل البيئية والمشاكل الاجتماعية؟

٨ – في نظرك، ما هي المشاكل التي ستواجهها المجتمعات العربية بعد عشر سنوات؟

(c) Open lecturer–led discussion on social problems in the Arab world and how to solve them.

13. Essay
Write an essay in Arabic of around 200 words on the following title المشاكل الاجتماعية في العالم العربي. Structure your essay around the following questions.

١ – ما هي المشاكل الاجتماعية الرئيسية في الوطن العربي ؟

٢ – كيف يؤثر الانفجار السكاني على غيره من المشاكل الاجتماعية؟

٣ – كيف تؤثر المشاكل البيئية على المجتمع في الوطن العربي ؟

٤ – ما هي اسباب تسخير الاطفال في الوطن العربي ؟

٥ – لماذا يرى البعض تسخير الاطفال مشكلةً اجتماعيةً ؟

٦ – هل الفقر مشكلة كبيرة في الدول العربية، وما هي اسباب الفقر في الوطن العربي ؟

10
Gender

1. Basic background material
Female labour force as a percentage of the total in the Arab countries and Israel in 1994.

	Female labour force % of total 1994
Algeria	10
Bahrain	10
Egypt	11
Iraq	23
Israel	34
Kuwait	16
Lebanon	27
Libya	10
Morocco	22
Oman	9
Qatar	8
Saudi Arabia	8
Sudan	23
Syrian Arab Rep.	18
Tunisia	25
UAE	7
Yemen, Rep.	14

2. Additional reading
(a) Nawal Al-Sa'dawi, *The Hidden Face of Eve: women in the Arab world*, (London: Zed Books, 1980).

(b) Fatima Mernissi, *Beyond the Veil*, (London: Al-Saqi Books, 1985).

(c) Hourani, *A History of the Arab Peoples*, pp. 439–42.

3. Key vocabulary

Taking the texts in this chapter as a starting point, draw up lists of vocabulary in the following fields:

(a) Gender.

(b) Family and home economics.

(c) Literacy.

4. Written Arabic texts 1

(a) Read the following text, منظمة الصحة العالمية, then complete exercises i. and ii. which follow.

منظمة الصحة العالمية ومنظمة رعاية الطفولة (اليونسكو) أصدرتا تقريرًا جاء فيه أن النساء في سوريا والأردن يعبّرن عن رغبتهن في إنجاب أطفال ذكور وتزداد هذه الرغبة في كوريا الجنوبية وبنغلادش ثم تزداد أكثر في باكستان ونيبال. أما في كثير من بلاد الغرب وفي الفلبين وبيرو فإنّ الرغبة في إنجاب بنت أو ولد متساوية تقريبًا وإن كانت النساء يرغبن في أن يكون الوليد الأول ذكرًا.

i   Paraphrase the following expressions in Arabic orally, in the sense which they have in the text.

١ – رعاية (line 1)

٢ – جاء فيه (line 2)

٣ – إنجاب أطفال (line 3)

٤ – تزداد (line 4)

٥ – متساوية (line 7)

٦ – الوليد الأول (line 8)

ii   Answer the following questions in Arabic.

١ – ما هما المنظمتان اللتان أصدرتا التقرير المذكور في النص؟

٢ – ما هو موضوع التقرير؟

٣ – ما هما الدولتان اللتان توجد فيها الرغبة في ولادة الذكور أكثر من أي دول أخرى؟

٤ – ما هي الدول التي تتساوى فيها الرغبة في إنجاب الذكور والرغبة في إنجاب البنات؟

٥ – في رأيك لماذا ترغب النساء في بعض البلدان في إنجاب الأطفال

الذكور؟

٦ - في رأيك ما هو السبب في الاختلافات بين البلدان والمجتمعات المختلفة في هذا الصدد؟

(b) Read the following text from الشرق الأوسط May 2, 1992, then complete exercises i. and ii. which follow.

المرأة المسلمة تعيش عصر الصحوة الإسلامية

أكّدت الدكتورة زينب عصمت راشد رائدة تعليم البنات في الأزهر وأول عميدة لكلية البنات الإسلامية في مصر ... أن الإسلام قد رفع مكانة المرأة، ومنحها حقوقا إنسانية ومدنية واقتصادية واجتماعية، لم تحظ بمثلها في شرع سماوي سابق، ولا في تشريع وضعي، حيث أعطاها الإسلام الحق في الحياة والحق في الميراث والحق في التملك، وحرية التصرف في أموالها والحق في الإبداء رأيها في من تتّخذه شريكًا لحياتها، إلى جانب الحق في التعليم وغير ذلك من حقوق لم تحظ بها المرأة في كثير من المجتمعات العالمية المعاصرة.

i Paraphrase the following expressions in Arabic orally, in the sense which they have in the text above.

١ - عصر الصحوة الإسلامية

٢ - رائدة

٣ - شرع سماوي

٤ - تشريع وضعي

٥ - حرية التصرف

ii Answer the following questions orally in English.

1. Who is Dr Zeinab Ismet Rashid?
2. According to Dr Rashid, in what general areas has Islam given women rights?
3. Dr Rashid refers to Islam as a شرع سماوي. According to Islam, what are the other شروع سماوية؟
4. In what specific areas has Islam given women rights according to Dr Rashid?
5. According to Dr Rashid, how do the rights of women in Islamic societies compare with those of women in other contemporary societies?

(c) In English paraphrase the main points of the following text.

تُعتبر الأمية مشكلة إنسانية يُعاني منها الملايين في جميع أنحاء العالم لا فرق في ذلك بين الدول النامية أو الصناعية. وترجع أهمية القضاء على الأمية إلى ارتباطها بالفقر والمرض والجهل فقد أعلنت منظمة الأمم المتحدة عام ١٩٩٠ عاماً دولياً لمحو الأمية بين شعوبها خاصةً وأن الحياة تزداد صعوبةً بالنسبة للأمي.

وحسب إحصائيات اليونسكو فإن واحداً من بين كل أربعة من البالغين في العالم أُمي، وهذه نسبة كبيرة. ومع أنها مُوزعة على مختلف بلاد العالم – النامية والصناعية – إلا أن معظمها يتركز في العالم الثالث خاصةً في القارة الإفريقية حيثُ تعتقد اليونسكو أن أكثر من نصف عدد السكان في إفريقيا لا يعرفون القراءة والكتابة. وتمثل النساء الأُميات نسبة الثلثين تقريباً من عدد الأميين الكُلي وهذا دليل على أن النساء يحصلن على القليل من الاهتمام والفرص في الكثير من البلاد.

وتشير اليونسكو إلى أن الأمية مرتبطة بالفقر، والدليل على ذلك أن أعلى نسبة للأمية توجد عادةً في البلاد التي تعاني من أزمات اقتصادية حادة. ولكن هناك أيضاً بعض الاستثناءات ... كما في سريلنكا مثلاً، فرغم أنها بلد فقير جداً إلا أن نسبة المتعلمين فيها عالية.

وكما في العالم الثالث فإن العالم الصناعي أيضاً يعاني من الأمية ولكنها أمية من نوع مختلف ... فمن كان متعلماً أصبح أمياً يعرف الأرقام ويقرأ الحروف ولكن لا يستطيع أن يستخدم المهارات الأساسية في القراءة والكتابة في حياته اليومية.

5. Written Arabic texts 2

(a) Translate the following book announcement into idiomatic English.

المرأة   العربية

دعوة   إلى   التغيير

منذ أكـثـر مـن مـئـة سنة، لا يزال الحـوار ســاخناً حـول دور المرأة العـربـيـة في المجـتـمـع ولا تزال الأسـئـلة تتـردد على ألسنة العلمـاء والمصلحين الاجتماعيين منذ أيام الإمام محـمد عبده وجمال الدين الأفغاني وغيرهما.

وفي هذا الكتاب، تستعرض الكاتبة ناديا حجاب الأسبـاب التي تحـول حتى الآن دون حسم قضيـة دور المرأة العربيـة وفعاليتها في المجـتـمـع كأم وكعضـو منتج وتنتـهي إلى القـول بأن دور المرأة في المجـتـمـع العـربـي، مـثل غيـره من القـضـايا، ينتظر حسم النقـاش المفتوح حول دور الإسلام في المجتمع العربي.

وفي القسم الثاني من الكتـاب تستـعـرض المؤلفة الانعكاسـات الاقتصـادية التي قـد تطرأ على تركيبـة المجتمع العربي، في حـال مشاركة المرأة العربيـة للرجل في مجالات العمل.

وتخلص ناديا حجـاب إلى القـول بأن تحـرر المرأة العـربـيـة وانطلاقها مرتبط بتحرير المجتمع من التقاليد الموروثة وأن على المصلحين الاجتمـاعـيين أن يركّزوا جهـودهم على تغيـيـر البنيـة الاجتماعية والسياسية والاقتصادية للمجتمع العربي.

(b) Translate the following text by the Egyptian feminist writer نوال السعداوي from مذكرات طبيبة, p. 32, into idiomatic English. In this text, the writer describes the liberating effect her scientific education had on her.

وانفـتـح أمـامي عـالم واسـع جـديد ... وشـعـرت بالرهبـة أول الأمـر ولكني سرعان ما أوغلت فيه بنهم وقد استولى علي جنون المعرفة ... كـشف لي العلم سـر الإنسـان وألغى تلك الفـروق الهـائلة التي حاولت أمي أن تضعها بينـي وبين أخي.

أثبت لي العلم أن المرأة كالرجل والرجل كالحيوان ... المرأة لها قلب ومخ وأعصاب كالرجل تماماً ... والحيوان له قلب ومخ وأعصاب كالإنسان تماماً ... ليست هناك فروق جوهرية بين أحد منهم وإنما هي فروق شكلية تتفق جميعاً في الأصل والجوهر.

المرأة تحتوي في أعماقها على رجل والرجل يخبئ في أعماقه امرأة ... المرأة لها أعضاء الرجل بعضها ظاهر وبعضها ضامر والرجل تجري في دمائه هرمونات مؤنثة.

الإنسان يغلق قفص صدره على وحش غابة كاسر والحيوان في داخله إنسان ...

الإنسان له ذيل ... ذيل قصير مبتور في فقرة صغيرة في مؤخرة عموده الفقري، والحيوان له قلب يدق وله دموع تسيل ...

وفرحت بهذا العالم الجديد الذي يضع المرأة إلى جوار الرجل إلى جوار الحيوان.

فرحت بالعلم وأحسست أنه إله قوي جبار عادل يعرف أسرار كل شيء فآمنت به واعتنقته ...

(c) Read the following text from مجلة الشرق الأوسط, Mar. 17, 1992, then complete exercises i. and ii. which follow.

القمة النسائية واقناع الغائبين

تبقى القمة النسائية التي عقدت في جنيف وشاركت فيها قرينات ٦٤ حاكما من مختلف انحاء العالم حدثا ملفتا في هذه الايام المليئة بالاحداث. وتنبع اهمية هذه القمة من اعتبارات عديدة تبدأ اولا بالموضوع الذي دعيت للبحث فيه وهو سبل مكافحة تزايد فقر النساء في المناطق الريفية في العالم الثالث. وهذا يعني ان الموضوع يمس مصير نحو ٥٥٠ مليون سيدة في الدول النامية يعشن في حرمان شبه كامل وتنضم اليهن سنويا ١٥

مليون سيدة جديدة.

ولا حاجة ابدا لسوق الادلة على ضرورة التصدي لهذه المشكلة المأساة. ولنا ان نتخيل الآثار الكارثية التي يرتبها على وضع الاسرة برمتها كون المرأة تعيش في حالة من الفقر والاحباط واليأس.

ويصعب الحديث عن عيش صحي تتوافر فيه الحدود الدنيا من الشروط الانسانية اذا كانت شروط حياة المرأة على هذا النحو. ويمكننا ان نتخيل ايضا انعكاسات هذا الواقع على تربية الاطفال الذين تضطلع الام، خصوصا في هذه المجتمعات، بدور كبير في تربيتهم في غياب المدرسة التي تستحق التسمية. وعلاوة على قابلية انتقال مشاعر القلق من الام الى اطفالها فان الفقر يؤدي وبصورة اكيدة الى الحاق ضرر واسع بفرص الابناء في التعلم والتقدم. والاخطر من الضرر اللاحق بالمستوى التعليمي ذلك الذي يلحق بالمستوى التربوي ككل. وهل من غرابة اذا كبر الطفل في مثل هذه الشروط وجنح لاحقا الى العنف والسلبية نظرا لافتقاره كشاب ورجل الى مفاتيح الاندماج السوي في مجتمعه.

يضاف الى ذلك ما يؤكده الخبراء من ان الاوضاع التي تعيشها المرأة الريفية في العالم الثالث تشكل عائقا امام خطط التنمية. ونجاح هذه الخطط يتوقف قبل كل شيء على درجة وعي السكان لاهميتها وضرورة المساهمة في انجاحها. ومن المتعذر انتظار رد ايجابي في مجتمع يخيم عليه الفقر وترتفع فيه نسبة الامية. وترتدي هذه المشكلة طابعا بالغ الالحاح اذا اخذنا في الاعتبار ان ازواج الكثير من النساء الريفيات يهاجرون الى المدن بحثا عن لقمة العيش مما يعني عمليا مضاعفة المسؤوليات الملقاة على

عاتق المرأة ودون اي زيادة في قدراتها على مواجهة هذه الاعباء. واذا اخذنا في الاعتبار ما تشير اليه الارقام من ان النساء يؤمن ما بين ٥٠ في المئة و ٧٠ في المئة من انتاج الغذاء في مختلف مناطق العالم الثالث يصبح انقاذ الغذاء مرهونا فعلا بتحسين شروط حياة المرأة الريفية.

لا شك ان الصندوق الدولي للتنمية الزراعية، وهو وكالة متخصصة تابعة للامم المتحدة، احسن صنعا حين اختار الدعوة الى قمة نسائية للبحث في موضوع المرأة الريفية في العالم الثالث. فلو اختار الصندوق دعوة الحكام لا الزوجات لكان ادخل نفسه في ملف يصعب اغلاقه ويصعب التقدم فيه. فبالدرجة الاولى كان لا بد من الانتظار طويلا لتوفير موعد ملائم للحكام ذوي الارتباطات المتراكمة في مفكرات مواعيدهم. ومن الطبيعي ان يستلزم الامر ايضا بحثا طويلا ومسهبا في اعداد جدول الاعمال وتوزيع الكلمات اضافة الى تكاليف امنية باهظة لضمان سلامة الوافدين. والارجح ان القادة المشاركين كانوا سينظرون الى الموضوع المطروح كموضوع هامشي ولذلك سيطلبون من مستشاريهم الافادة من المناسبة لترتيب سلسلة من اللقاءات الثنائية على هامش المؤتمر وهكذا تنتقل الاضواء من القاعة الرئيسية الى الصالونات الجانبية والكواليس. ولا مبالغة في القول ان المؤتمر كان سيتحول في حضور الحكام لا الزوجات الى مؤتمر تهيمن على اعماله قضايا انهيار الاتحاد السوفياتي والمساعدة المطلوبة للجمهوريات التي ولدت من الزلزال اضافة الى شؤون الحد من التسلح والملفات الاقليمية المعقدة ومعها مشاكل الحماية التجارية واغلاق الاسواق. وعلاوة على ذلك فان من الصعب اصلا

تصور زعيم دولة يجلس مستمعا الى تقارير عن اوضاع المرأة الريفية في وقت سيواجه فيه قريبا انتخابات حاسمة تقرر مستقبله او ينشغل مساعدوه بانباء فضيحة تتسابق الصحف على اصطياد اخبارها.

طبعا لا بد من الاعتراف ان القمة النسائية لا تستطيع الخروج بنتائج عملية من نوع قطع التعهدات والدخول في التزامات مالية لا يمكن ان يبادر الى التعهد بها الا من اوكلت اليه المؤسسات الدستورية مثل هذه المهمة. لكن القمة النسائية تبقى حدثا اذ انها لفتت العالم بأسره الى مشكلة ما كانت لتقفز الى الصفحات الاولى في الصحف وتتصدر انباء التلفزيون لو لا هذا التجمع الذي استضافته جنيف. وربما راهن الصندوق قبل كل شيء على قدرة السيدة الاولى خصوصا لجهة اقناع زوجها بادراج ملف المرأة الريفية في العالم الثالث بين اهتماماته ولو في موقع متواضع في سلم الاولويات. ومن يدري فقد تنجح القمة النسائية في ما فشلت فيه قمم كثيرة.

i   Answer the following questions in English.

1. Where was the women's summit held?
2. Who took part in the summit?
3. How is the summit described?
4. What was discussed at the summit?
5. How is poverty said to affect children?
6. How does poverty affect young people?
7. How does the situation of rural women affect development?
8. What do husbands of rural women tend to do?
9. What actual effect does this have on women?
10. How are women involved in food production?
11. Detail what would have happened at the summit had the UN invited world leaders to the summit instead of women.
12. What matters would have been discussed?

13. What does the writer consider to be the main importance of the women's summit?

ii Draw up a list of the phrases used to link paragraphs and sentences in this passage.

6. Written Arabic texts 3 (classical)

(a) Read the following text by شاكر البتلوني from كتاب تسلية الخواطر out loud, pronouncing all case and mood endings, then translate the text into idiomatic English.

حُكِيَ أنَّ امرأة تخاصمت مع زوجها في ولد عند بعض الحكام فقالت المرأة أيّدك اللّه تعالى هذا ولدي كان بطني له وعاء وحجري له فناء وثديي له سقاء ألاحظه إذا قام وأحفظه إذا نام فلم أزل كذا مدّة أعوام فلمّا كمل فصاله واشتدّت أوصاله وحسنت خصاله أراد أبوه أخذه منّي وإبعاده عنّي فقال الحاكم للرجل قد سمعت مقال زوجتك فما عندك من الجواب قال صدقت ولكنّي حملته قبل أن تحمله ووضعته قبل أن تضعه وأريد أنْ أعلّمه العلم وأفهّمه الحكم فقال الحاكم ما تقولين في جواب كلامه أيّتها المرأة فقالت صدق في مقاله ولكنّه حمله ضعيفاً وحملته ثقيلاً ووضعه شهوة ووضعته كرهاً فتعجّب الحاكم من كلامها وقال للرجل ادفع لها ولدها فهي أحقّ به منك.

فِصال weaning
خِصال qualities

(b) Translate the following text by ابن قتيبة from كتاب النساء in عيون الأخبار, pp. 77–8, into idiomatic English.

عيسى بن يونس قال حدثنا شيخ لنا قال: سمعت سمرة بن جندب يقول على منبر البصرة: قال رسول اللّه صلى اللّه عليه وسلم: إنما المرأة خُلقت من ضلع عوجاء[1] فإن تحرص على إقامتها تكسرها فدارِها تعشْ بها.

وقال بعض الشعراء:

هي الضلع العوجاء لست تقيمها

* ألا إنّ تقويم الضلع انكسارها

أتجمع ضلعًا واقتدارًا على الفتى

* أليس عجيبًا ضعفها واقتدارها

عن الحسن قال: قال عمر بن الخطاب رضي الله عنه: النساء عَوْرَة فاستروها بالبيوت، وداووا ضعفهن بالسكوت.

في حديث آخر لعمـر: لا تُسكنوا نسـاءكم الغـرف²، ولا تعلّموهن الكتاب، واستعينوا عليهن بالعُرَى، وأكثروا لهن من قول « لا »، فإنّ «نعم» تُغَرِّيهن على المسألة. قال الأصمعي: قيل لعُقيل بن علفة وكان غَيـورًا: مـن خَلَّفْتَ فـي أهلك؟ فـقـال: الحـافـظَيْن، العُرَى والجُوع. يعني أنّه يُجيـعـهن فـلا يَمْزَحن، ويُعرّيهن فلا يَمُرَحن.

Notes
1. ضلع 'rib' is masculine in modern Arabic.
2. غرفة pl. غرف here used in the sense of 'high room', 'room at the top of the house'.

7. Grammar/stylistics
(a) *Linking phrases and textual cohesion*
A text is not simply made up of a series of sentences and clauses, but of sentences and clauses which are linked by appropriate conjunctions (such as 'and', 'but'), conjuncts (such as 'yet', 'so') and adverbial phrases which serve to produce textual cohesion. Common linking phrases in Arabic used in the texts in this course book include بناء على ذلك 'according to that', علاوة على ذلك 'in addition to that', إضافة إلى ذلك 'in addition to that', بالتالي 'consequently', طبعا 'of course'. A number of linking phrases are expressed by absolute negation: لا شك أنّ 'there is no doubt that', لا مبالغة في القول أن 'it is no exaggeration to say that', لا حاجة لـ 'there is no need to'. Other phrases are verbal, such as: ويصعب الحديث عن 'it is difficult to talk about', يضاف إلى ذلك 'in addition to that'. These phrases do not serve to add any factual information to the text, but rather to express the writer's or speaker's attitude about the subject under discussion and to provide a means of linking a sentence or clause with previous and following sentences in the text.

(b) *The use of the function words* (أَنّ) لا إِ *and* فإِنّ *as resumptive particles*

Many function or grammatical words are used in Arabic which are not translated into English. One of the most common of these is the word إِ لا or إِنّ often introduced by the conjunction فـ, and used to introduce a main clause after an adverb or an adverbial clause. Particles used in this manner may be termed resumptive particles, since they mark the resumption of the clause, and the start of its main part, following an introductory element. Consider the following examples:

وهكذا {فإِنّ} المضيق أوسع بكثير مما يتصوره الناس.

'Thus, the straits are much wider than people imagine.' (ch. 1, 5b)

وحسب إحصائيات اليونسكو {فإِنّ} واحدا من بين كل أربعة من البالغين في العالم أمي.

'According to UNESCO statistics, one out of every four adults in the world is illiterate.' (ch. 10, 4c)

ولهذا {فإِنّ} معظم النصوص الأدبية ... قيلت في مناسبات مختلفة.

'Thus, most of the literary texts ... have been recited on different occasions.' (ch. 11, 5c)

وكما في العالم الثالث {فإِنّ} العالم الصناعي أيضا يعاني من الأمية.

'As in the third world, the industrialised world also suffers from illiteracy.' (ch. 10, 4c)

وعلاوة على ذلك {فإِنّ} من الصعب أصلا تصور زعيم دولة يجلس مستمعا إلى تقارير عن أوضاع المرأة الريفية.

'In addition to that, it is difficult to imagine a head of state who would sit and listen to reports about rural women.' (ch. 10, 5c)

فإِنّ is often used to introduce a main nominal clause of a conditional sentence as a means of emphasising the main clause:

كما أنّه إذا ثمة قلق عالمي من تزايد سكاني ضخم {فإِنّ} القلق يجب أن يوجه نحو موضوع آخر...

'Also if there is worldwide concern over a huge population increase this concern should be directed to another issue....' (ch. 9, 5aii)

إذا كنت أنا ألهو وألعب {فإِنّ} هذه الفتاة جادة.

'Even if I am messing around playing, this girl is serious.' (ch. 10, 11b)

The word الا is usually used before إن to introduce a main clause after a concessive adverbial clause of the type رغم (أن) or مع (أن). It is often preceded by ف as in the first example below.

ومع أنّ هذه المقولة شائعة {فإلا أنّها} ليست صحيحة إلى الحد الذي تلقاه من البعض.

'Despite the fact that this view is widely held, it is not as true as some people would have you believe.' (ch. 2, 8)

ومع أنّها موزعة على مختلف بلاد العالم – النامية والصناعة – {إلا أنّ} معظمها يتركز في العالم الثالث.

'Although it can be found in many countries throughout the world – developing and industrialised – it is concentrated in the third world.' (ch. 10, 4c)

فرغم أنّها بلد فقير جدا {إلا أنّ} نسبة المتعلمين فيها عالية.

'Despite the fact that it is a very poor country there are a high number of educated people there.' (ch. 10, 4c)

(c) *The generic use of the definite singular*
Generic nouns are nouns which refer to the genus, type or class of something, but do not refer to a particular entity within that class. In English, generic nouns are usually marked by having no article (definite or indefinite), and may be singular or plural. Generic nouns are used when the speaker or writer wants to say something general about the species. Examples of generic nouns in English include the italicised nouns in the following sentences:

Tigers are fierce animals.
Man is the most dangerous animal.
Men can't be trusted.

When the generic noun does take an article, the noun is always singular:

The tiger is a fierce animal.

When the generic noun refers to an abstract concept, the noun is singular with no article:

Poverty is a political issue.

In Arabic, generic nouns are always definite and usually singular (cf. EMSA I: 153–4). This generally affects translation into or out of English, because the

English will usually (in the case of concrete and animate nouns) be plural with no article. Consider the following examples and their translations:

{الطفل الفلسطيني} يعاني {الإهمال والتشتت}.

'Palestinian children suffer from neglect and displacement.' (ch. 9, 4b)

{الطفل اللبناني} يعاني {التمزق النفسي}.

'Lebanese children suffer from psychological trauma.' (ch. 9, 4b)

{المرأة العربية}

'Arab women' (ch. 10, 5a)

وهذا النوع من {الأدب} ..

'And this type of literature ...' (ch. 11, 5c)

{فالأديب} يجد فيه لذته من سمو الخيال وجمال الإبداع.

'The man of letters finds his pleasure in it from the loftiness of imagination and the beauty of creativity.' (ch. 11, 5c)

Verbal nouns are often used generically in Arabic, and may be translated as gerunds with no article in English:

ثم يذكر أنه كان يحب {الخروج}.

'Then he remembered that he used to love going out.' (ch. 11, 5d)

هناك أربعة ملايين ساعة تضيع من المصريين شهريا في {زحام المواصلات} و{التسكع} في الشوارع ...

'There are 4m. hours lost by Egyptians each month in traffic jams, loitering on the streets ....' (ch. 9, 5b)

8. Aural Arabic texts 1

Listen to the following text from a Yemeni radio programme entitled برنامج الأسرة, then complete exercises i. and ii below.

i Fill in the gaps in the text below.

_____ _____ _____ _____ بأنه _____ يقال _____ _____

_____ الضيق _____ يُبعد ، _____ _____ _____

_____ _____ _____ ضغطه _____ _____ عزيزتي ربة

حاولتما _____ _____ _____ _____

_____ _____ _____ _____ استقطاع

أن _____ _____ مكان _____ _____

تتّفقا _____ _____ _____

، _____ إلا _____ _____

_____ _____ _____ ، الضرورية _____

كاحتياطي _____ _____ ظروف _____ تأتي مما

_____ ، فمثلاً _____ _____

_____ _____ لا قدر _____ تعرض

لمرض _____ فهو _____ _____ لمصاريف

_____ تعطل _____ ، _____

وأنتم ، _____ _____ _____

، _____ _____ لأن _____

فبالتالي _____ _____ _____

. عنه _____ غنى _____

ii Transcribe the remainder of this passage in Arabic. You may find the following
vocabulary items of use.

حُسْبان	account, consideration
رِفاهية	comfort, luxury

غَسّالة	washing machine
قَضاء	spending (time) (verbal noun of قضى)
حَيَوية	vitality
عَوائِد	benefit, profit, advantage (pl. of عائدة)

9. Aural Arabic texts 2

Listen to the following BBC Arabic Service news broadcast from Mar. 5, 1990, then answer the following questions in Arabic.

١ – ما هو موضوع المؤتمر؟

٢ – ماذا يُقال عن حجم المؤتمر؟

٣ – أين يُعقد المؤتمر؟

٤ – ما هي مشكلة الأطفال المئة مليون المذكورين في النص؟

٥ – هل يتمّ حل هذه المشكلة حاليا؟

٦ – ما هي نسبة الأمّيين التي يشكلها الرجال في العالم؟

10. Written English texts

(a) Making use of constructions and vocabulary encountered in the Arabic texts above as far as possible, translate the following text from the *Middle East*, Nov. 1986, into idiomatic Arabic.

> Egypt's first feminist organisation was founded in 1923 and its leader, until her death in 1947, was Huda Shaarawi. For a generation she was a familiar and respected public figure.
>
> During the first forty years of her life Shaarawi led the secluded existence customary for Egyptian women of the upper classes, but unlike most such women she left a record of these 'hidden years' in the memoirs she dictated to her secretary in later life.
>
> Margot Badran, an American historian researching women's history in Egypt, discovered the existence of these memoirs in the early 1970s, and in close collaboration with Huda's cousin, Hawa Idris, has edited and translated them into English.

(b) Making use of constructions and vocabulary encountered in the Arabic texts above as far as possible, translate the following extract about نوال السعداوي from the *Guardian*, June 1, 1988, into idiomatic Arabic.

> She was born on the Nile delta in a village where her father was the first person to be educated. A generation later, she was the first girl to go to college. She would have loved to study literature, but with her high

grades, was persuaded to go to medical school. In the end she did both successfully. Despite being a women, and coming from a poor and unconnected family, she rose to become director of education in Egypt's ministry of health, a post she held from 1966 to 1972. From her clinic days, she knew it was poverty, not disease, she would have to fight.

11. Précis

(a) Re–read and produce a précis in Arabic of القمة النسائية (section 4 (c)).

(b) Read the following short story قصة خيوط by انيس منصور, from his collection بقايا كل شيء, then produce a précis in Arabic.

خيوط قصة

البطل شاب في السابعة والعشرين من عمره .. طويل أسمر وطبيب، تخرج حديثا ويتمرن في عيادة طبيب كبير .. وهو طبيب القلب .. فيه رجولة وشهامة .. وله مبادىء يتمسك بها .. والبطلة سيدة في الأربعين من عمرها لها أولاد .. وزوجة الطبيب الكبير .. وكانت زوجة قبل ذلك .. وأحبت هذا الطبيب الكبير .. وتركت من أجله زوجها الأول .. وهي سيدة جميلة .. رأت هذا الشاب التفتت إليه، بعقلها وقلبها وأحبته .. وأحبها الطبيب الشاب.

أما الأسباب التي أدت إلى هذا الحب أو هذا الميل .. فهي أن الطبيب الكبير قد أصبح مشغولا عن زوجته .. ليس مشغولا بعمله، ولكنه مشغول عنها بنساء أخريات، ولا يخجل هو أبدا من ذكر هذه الحقائق ولكن الزوجة تحبه، وتعرف نزواته، وتعرف أنه مرهق وأن التغيير أمر ضروري للزوج، وأن الزوجة التي تريد أن تغير طبيعة الرجل وخصوصا إذا كان طبيبا فنانا، كزوجها، فإنها تطلب المستحيل.

وأحست الزوجة شيئا آخر .. إن زوجها حريص على إهانتها أيضا أمام أصدقائه وأمام صديقاتها .. وأن الغرض من هذه الإهانة هو لذة تعذيبها .. فهذه لذة شاذة عند الزوج، قد ظهرت أخيرا ولم تكن تعرفها من قبل .. لقد كانت تجد هذه اللذة على صورة بخل

شديد .. فهو حريص على أن يتلذذ لصراخها وهي تطلب منه المال لشراء الملابس والسفر وتغيير أثاث البيت .. وكان يجد لذة في الرفض.

فإذا رآها بملابس ممزقة، وكذلك أولاده .. كانت هذه لذة تفوق لذة الجنس عنده.

ولاحظت أيضا أن زوجها يدفعها إلى أشياء أخرى ليست كريمة .. إنه يعرضها على أصدقائه ويغريهم بها .. فإذا صدقوه ثار على الزوجة، وتلذذ بعذابها وأمعن في تعذيبها .. وأحست الزوجة أن الطبيب زوجها – كما كانت تراه – فهو كبير عندما يجري عملية جراحية وهو يتقدم الأطباء جميعا في غرفة العمليات .. ولكن عندما يجيء البيت، فليس طبيبا ولا ممرضا، بل هو مريض، ومرضه لا علاج له .. إنه ليس كبيرا في نظرها .. وإن كان هو عظيما ومشهورا في عيون الناس.

إنه ليس كبيرا عندما يأكل وعندما يجلس إليها وإلى أولاده.

إنه إنسان عادي جدا، بل أحط من الإنسان العادي.

ورأت هذا الشاب .. إنه شيء آخر.

إنه شاب، هو الآخر مخدوع في الطبيب الكبير .. إنه يراه كبيرا.

وأخذت الزوجة تروي للشاب كيف أن زوجها هذا ليس شيئا إطلاقا .. وإنه سافل وإنه منحط وإنه بخيل وإنه مريض وإن فيه وحشية الجراثيم الفتاكة. وبدأ الشاب هو الآخر يتحرك .. في هذه القصة.

إنه يحب هذه السيدة الجميلة .. إنه هو الآخر بلا تجارب .. إنه خجول ويتهيب الزواج من أي فتاة شابة، تقرأ المجلات وتذهب إلى السينما وتعرف الرقص وأحبت قبله عشرات الشبان.

أما الآن فهو أمام السيدة .. هذا أفضل وأحسن.

وهي سيدة معروفة عظيمة .. إن عشرات من مشاهير الرجال

يطمعون فيها ويتمنونها لأنفسهم .. وهو يكره أستاذه هذا فهو رجل أناني .. وهو لا يطلعه على كل أسراره .. وحبه لزوجته انتقام منه وانتقام لها أيضا .. وزواجه من هذه السيدة هو انتصار وانتقام معا.

إن هذه السيدة قد فتحت حواسها جميعا .. لقد تحولت حواسه إلى أكف ضارعة .. تنتظر ما يملؤها .. وكانت هذه السيدة تملأ حواسه .. إنها امرأة قد جربت الحياة وعرفت الرجال .. لعلها هي الأخرى قد قررت أن تتزوج هذا الشاب.

وبدأ الشاب يفكر، أو يتراجع ..

وكان تفكيره على صورة ندم .. لأن ضميره قد صحا.

فهو يتساءل: لماذا قررت الزواج منها؟ لأنها قررت الانتقام من زوجها .. فدفعها الانتقام إلى أن تتزوج أحد تلامذته.

إنه الانتقام إذن، وليس الحب .. وجعل يقول أيضا: ولكنني سأكون خائنا وجبانا، إن الرجل قد ائتمنني على زوجته، فإذا بي أخونه وأخونها .. نعم أخونها أيضا فإن ابنتها الكبرى تحبني وقد وعدتها بشيء كصداقة أو كالزواج .. ولا بد أن الفتاة الصغيرة قد صدقتني .. وإذا كنت أنا ألهو وألعب فإن هذه الفتاة جادة، ولا أريد أن أكون هذا الخادع الخائن وفي بيت واحد .. وفي بيت أستاذي الطبيب الكبير.

ولكن الزوجة تبكي وتقسم أنها تحبه، وأن الذي تشعر به هذا ليس انتقاما .. ولا هي رغبتها في فضيحة الزوج ولا في أن يتحدث عنه الناس .. ولكنها تريد أن تكون زوجة للشاب الذي أحبته، وأنها ستضحى بالطبيب العظيم وشهرته ومجده، ومن أجل حبها.

ولكن الشاب يسأل نفسه: أليس هو نفس الكلام الذي قالته يوم تزوجت الطبيب العظيم .. أليست هي نفس الكلمات؟ وماذا كانت النتيجة؟!

وأحس الشاب كأنه ثعبات كبير، وكأن خيطا صغيرا قد دخل
فمه ثم كسر أسنانه كلها .. وأصبح ثعبانا بلا أسنان .. ثعبان لا
يلدغ ولا يقتل .. لقد فوجيء الشاب بأن قصته هذه قد عرفها كل
الناس والذي قال للناس هو الزوجة .. لقد تحققت الفضيحة إذن ..
وعرف الطبيب الكبير ذلك .. وتحقق الانتقام أيضا .. وعرفت الفتاة
الصغيرة خداع الطبيب الشاب .. وحدثت النذالة أيضا.

وكاد الثعبان الشاب أن يمضغ الخيط الذي تكسرت به أسنانه ..
وأن يلزم جحره .. وينتظر الأبطال الآخرين لكي يكملون قصته ..
فقد قرر هو أن يختفي عند النصف الأول منها.

ولكن الانتقام والانتصار والعطف والشماتة، ما تزال تتردد في
أذنه عند كل مرة تتحدث إليه هذه الزوجة في التليفون في
الساعات الصغيرة من الليل.

ولم تكمل القصة بعد

وليس من الضروري أن تكمل.

12. Oral

(a) Preparatory oral exercise: listen to the aural Arabic text 1 again and provide an oral answer in Arabic to the question ؟ ما هي فوائد التوفير وعوائده.

(b) المرأة العربية

i   One student to produce an account in Arabic of the typical daily work carried out by Arab women living in rural communities.

ii A second student to produce an account in Arabic of the typical daily work carried out by poor Arab women living in urban communities.

iii The two presenters then ask the other students questions about the life of Arab women in towns and in the country. These questions should include some which require factual answers and a large proportion which require speculative or subjective answers. Do not avoid controversial questions or answers! For example:

١ – كيف تقضي المرأة العربية الريفية الفقيرة حياتها اليومية؟

٢ – ما هي التجهيزات التي تستخدمها في البيت؟

٣ – ما هي التجهيزات التي تستخدمها في الزراعة؟

٤ – كيف تقضي المرأة العربية المدنية حياتها اليومية؟

٥ – ما هي التجهيزات التي تحتاج اليها في شغلها المنزلي؟

٦ – كيف تقضي المرأة العربية الغنية حياتها في المدينة؟

٧ – ما هي الفروق الرئيسية بين حياة المرأة العربية الفقيرة والمرأة العربية الغنية؟

٨ – ما هي المشاكل التي تعاني منها المرأة العربية؟

٩ – ما هو تأثير التعليم على حياة المرأة العربية؟

(c) Open lecturer–led discussion on the role of women in Arab society. Include within this a discussion of women's work, and work–related and leisure activities.

13. Essay

Write an essay in Arabic of around 200 words on the title دور المرأة في المجتمع العربي. Structure your essay around the following questions.

١ – دور المرأة العربية في البيت، وما هي واجباتها الرئيسية في البيت؟

٢ – ما هي فوائد تعليم المرأة في العالم العربي؟

٣ – ما هي العوائق الرئيسية لتعليم المرأة في العالم العربي؟

٤ – ما هي الانعكاسات التي قد تطرأ على المجتمع العربي الإسلامي في حال مشاركة المرأة للرجل في مجالات العمل؟

٥ – كيف تعاني المرأة العربية من الفقر؟

٦ – كيف يختلف دور المرأة في الوطن العربي عنه في الغرب؟

11
Popular culture

1. Basic background material
(a) *High culture and popular culture*

There is a long tradition of high culture in the Arab world. Much of this high culture relates to Islam, and includes not only the Qur'an and Hadith, but all the related scholarly activities of the Islamic sciences. It also includes poetry, going back to the pre–Islamic era, and the high forms of poetry and prose which developed in Islamic times. More widely, this high culture includes various forms of high art, from calligraphy to architecture, as well as the philosophy, science and medicine which developed as part of this culture.

In addition to this high culture, however, there existed in the Islamic world various forms of more–or–less localised popular culture. These included local traditions and beliefs, styles of dress, designs of household objects, jewellery, and so on. Such popular culture is a feature not only of the Middle East or the Islamic world, but was found in all societies, including western societies, prior to the advent of mass production, mass mobility and instant communication which are the hallmarks of the modern world.

With the coming of the modern world to the Middle East, this traditional popular culture has begun to disappear from everyday life, just as it has now virtually disappeared in the west. People in the Middle East now buy mass–produced clothing and household objects, which may have been manufactured thousands of miles away; they watch television soap–operas, most of which are produced in Egypt, and typically present a glamourised image of westernised, middle–class urban life in Cairo or Alexandria.

Traditional popular culture, however, persists in two ways. Firstly, it remains in areas of the Middle East which are as yet relatively untouched by modernity – typically the poorer and more remote parts of the region. Secondly, it survives by being more or less consciously revived, and intellectualised. From the end of the nineteenth century onwards, scholars began to collect folk–stories and artefacts from the Middle East. Initially, these were western scholars, but increasingly in the twentieth century Arab scholars, and other interested individuals began to take an interest in traditional popular culture – recording stories, both in written form and later on tape, and collecting traditional material objects.

Today, in many Arab countries, there are folklore and popular heritage museums, as well as archives in university departments dedicated to the preservation of popular culture. Sometimes the main motive for these is simply to preserve some aspects of the past before it disappears. In other cases, there is a nationalistic element involved – an attempt to maintain and define traditions which make manifest a specific ethnic identity (as in the case of the Palestinians, for example).

(b) *Story–telling*

Story–telling is one of the most prominent aspects of popular culture in the Middle East. Stories were, and are, told for many purposes – from moral instruction through to pure entertainment. Sometimes the characters involved are found throughout the Middle East, as for example Juha, the wise fool, who is the hero of stories from Turkey, where he known as Nasreddin Hoca, all the way through to Morocco, where he known as Si Djeha. In other cases, figures may more localised. A good example is Ali ibn Zayed, who is known throughout Yemen, where he fulfills something of the same role as Juha elsewhere, but does not appear in the wider Arab world.

Stories were told in many environments and by many people. In the home, where women and children gathered, they were often told to the children by a grandmother, or other older woman. Outside the home, where men met together in tea–houses, as well as chatting to one another they would sometimes listen to the tales told by the *rawi*, the professional itinerant story teller.

Traditional tales are set in a world of half–reality; they are not literally true, but there may be some 'truth' to be gleaned from them. This is emphasised by the 'Once upon a time' rubric with which they are introduced. Typically this runs something like:

$$كان ما كان$$
$$في قديم الزمان$$

There was, there was not
In ancient time

Similar formulas are encountered not only in Arabic, but in other Middle Eastern languages, such as Turkish and Armenian.

Nowadays, the tradition of story–telling still continues in the home, just as it does in the west, although the *rawi* virtually disappeared. With the advent of mass literacy, however, some folk stories are preserved. It is possible, for example, to pick up cheap editions of Juha stories from almost any bookshop in the Middle East, and although the language used is normally a form of standard Arabic, rather than the colloquial in which the stories would previously have been told, many of the stories are recognisably the same as those which were formerly passed on as part of the oral tradition.

Other Juha tales to be found in these collections, however, are unambiguously set in the modern world. Some of these may be reworkings of traditional stories, but many seem entirely new, and involve a Juha character who could not have existed in previous times – Juha as a student, for example, or a car–driver. The Juha stories also become supplemented by shorter anecdotes, which are in effect Juha jokes, as elements of traditional popular culture are influenced by other cultural changes, and slowly transform themselves into part of modern popular culture.

2. Additional reading
Arab Folktales, translated by Inea Bushnaq, (Harmondsworth: Penguin Books, 1986).

3. Key vocabulary
Taking the texts in this chapter as a starting point, draw up lists of vocabulary in the field of folktale vocabulary.

4. Written Arabic texts 1
(a) Read the following text about the Middle Eastern folk hero جحا, then answer the questions which follow in Arabic.

ترجمة حياة جحا

الشيخ نصر الدين جحا الرومي هو تركي الأصل من الأناضول تلقى العلوم الدينية وبرع فيها حتى ولي الخطابة ونصب إماماً ومدرساً في بعض المدن وكان رحمه الله واعظاً يأتي بالموعظة في أسلوب النوادر والأمثال، وكان له جرأة على الأمراء والقضاة والحكام وكان عفيفاً زاهداً يحرث أرضه ويحتطب بيده وكانت داره ملجأ للواردين من الغرباء والفلاحين ومما يذكر أن وساطته أنقذت بلدة من ظلم الطاغية تيمورلنك سنة ٦٧٤هـ، وعاش من العمر ستين وله ضريح عظيم في بلدته (آق شهر) وفوقه قبة قائمة على أربعة أعمدة وقيل إن على باب قبره يوجد قفل هائل أما جهاته الثلاث فخالية، ولعله أوصى بذلك وأراد بها النكتة، ولأهل تلك البلاد اعتقاد بكرامات الشيخ وهم يربطون على بابه الخرق استشفاعاً من الحمى والتماساً للبركة ويكثرون من الضحك عند قبره ويعتقدون

أن من زاره ولم يضحك لم يسلم من نائبة تصيبه ومن عاداتهم حين الزواج أن يبدأ العريسان بزيارة ضريح الشيخ ويدعوانه إلى حفلة الزواج ويقولان له « شـرفنا مـع تلامـيذك » وعندهم اعتـقاد أن من تزوج ولم يقم بهذا الواجب لا يوفق بزواجه.

١ – ما هي جنسية جحا الأصلية؟

٢ – بماذا اشتغل جحا؟

٣ – كيف تصرف جحا عند القائمين على الأمور؟

٤ – من لجأ إلى بيته؟

٥ – أين تقع بلدته؟

٦ – لماذا يربط سكان هذه البلاد خرقا على باب قبر جحا؟

٧ – ماذا يفعل العريسان حين الزواج عند ضريح جحا؟

(b) Individual students to read the following short anecdotes about جحا at home. In class students individually paraphrase the vocabulary given below each anecdote in Arabic, read out the anecdotes, then ask comprehension questions variously in English and in Arabic. The comprehension questions are to be answered orally.

(i) ذهب جحا

ذهب جحـا لتناول الغذاء عند صديق له كان مـشهوراً عنه البـخل وقدم الصديق لجحا خبزاً وجبناً وعسلاً وملأ جحا معدته بكل ما أمامـه من خبـز وجبن ثم أمسك بوعاء العسل رغم أنه لم يبق هناك خبز يأكل به العسل.

عندئذ أسرع صاحب البيت يحذر جحا قائلاً: « ليس من المستحب أن تأكل العسل بغير خبز سيزعجك هذا جداً » لكن جحا رفع وعاء العسل إلى فمه وبعد أن تناول آخر نقطة منه قال لصديقه ضاحكاً « اللّه عـز وجل يعرف وحده من الذي سينزعج في النهاية ».

بُخْل

وِعَاء

عِنْدَئِذٍ

أزْعج
انزعج

(ii)   ذات يوم

ذات يوم سمع رجل أن جحا رجل كريم جداً، فترك بلدته، وبدأ
في سفر طويل ليقابله.

وعندما وصل أخيراً إلى جحا قال له: «أرجو أن تجيبني
على سؤال احترت طويلاً في الإجابة عليه» قال جحا: «ما
الذي تسأل عنه؟!» قال الرجل «ما هي الأشياء التي يجب أن
يتذكرها الإنسان، وما الأشياء التي يجب أن ينساها؟»

استغرق جحا لحظةً في التفكير ثم أجاب: «إذا قدم
أحدهم خدمة لك فيجب أن تتذكرها دائماً، أما إذا قدمت أنت
خدمة لأحد فيجب أن تنسى هذا في الحال!!»

احتار في
استغرق في

(iii)   الورقة معي

اشترى يوماً معلاقاً. فصادفه أحد أصدقائه وسأله كيف يطبخ
المعلاق فعلمه كيفية طبخه فقال له الشيخ اكتب لي إياها
بورقة حتى لا أنسى فكتب الورقة وسار جحا إلى بيته وهو
يفكر في كيفية طبخه وإذا بباز انقض عليه وخطف منه
المعلاق فلم يغضب جحا وصاح في الباز قائلاً لا فائدة لك منه
فلا تعرف أن تطبخه لأن الورقة معي.

باز
انقض عليه
خطف

(iv)   نركب عليه ونحمله أثقالنا

ذهب يوماً إلى السوق ليشتري لوازمه ووضعها في الخرج
ووضع الخرج على كتفه وركب الحمار فصادفه الناس في
الطريق فقالوا له لماذا لا تضع الخرج أمامك على الحمار

وتركب براحة؟ فأجاب الشيخ: «انصفوا يا أخوان إن هذا الحمار يريحنا بركوبنا فهل يجوز أن نحمله شيئاً فوق حمله إيانا؟ »

لوازمه
الخرج

(٧) أطعموا ضيوفكم المآكل الطيبة

أقام جحا في بعض رحلاته في قرية عدة أيام فكانوا يُطعمونه الخبز والملح فقط، فصلّى بهم يوماً الصبح فقرأ في الركعة الأولى وبعد الفاتحة «يا أيها الذين آمنوا لا تطعموا ضيوفكم الملح بل لحماً فإن لم تجدوا لحماً فعسلاً فإن لم تجدوا عسلاً فبيضاً ومن لم يفعل ذلك فقد ضلّ ضلالاً بعيداً وخسر خسراناً وقرأ في الركعة الثانية بعد الفاتحة وإن لم تجدوا بيضاً فسمكاً فإن لم تجدوا سمكاً فلبناً ومن لم يفعل ذلك منكم فقد افترى إثماً عظيماً ومأواه جهنّم وساءت مصيراً، فلما فرغ من الصلاة جاؤوا إليه واعتذروا من التقصير في حقه وأنهم لم يكن عندهم علم بأن اللّه أنزل هذه الوصية وسألوه «في أي سورة هذه الآيات؟ » فقال لهم «في سورة الأكل! »

ضلّ ضلالاً بعيدا
خسر خسرانا
افترى إثما
الوصية

(vi) جئت إن شاء الله

كان يتسامر مع امرأته ذات ليلة فقال لها سأذهب غداً للاحتطاب وإذا كان الجو رائقاً أروح إلى المزرعة فقالت له امرأته «قل إن شاء اللّه» فأجابها «لا لزوم لذلك» وفي الصباح خرج من البلد فصادف سرية من الفرسان ينادونه «يا عم من أين الطريق إلى القرية؟ » فقال «لا أعلم» فنقموا عليه وأخذوا يسبونه ويصفعونه قائلين له «امش أمامنا

وخذنا إلى القرية التي نريدها وكانت بعيدة عن قريته فما
أوصلهم إليها حتى سال العرق من رأسه إلى قدميه وعاد
مريضاً إلى داره وطرق الباب فقالت امرأته: « من الطارق؟ »
فأجابها: « أنا يا عزيزتي، إن شاء اللّه! »

سرية من الفرسان
نقموا عليه
يسبّونه

5. Written Arabic texts 2
The first three passages in this section deal with sayings, proverbs and gnomic
poetry, folk dance, and colloquial poetry.

(a) Read the following introduction to أقوال علي ابن زايد: دراسة ونصوص, p.
   5, then complete exercises i. and ii. which follow.

الأدب هو تعبير عن حقيقة وواقع إنسانيين، وهذا ما جعله
سجلاً لما نلاحظه ونختبره ونفكر فيه أو نشعر به، ولهذا فإن
معظم النصوص الأدبية – شعراً ونثراً – قيلت في مناسبات
مختلفة، ينضوي تحت هذا الحكم جميع الفنون الأدبية، ومنها
الشعر الحكمي الذي هو نتيجة تأمل الشاعر في نظام الوجود
وأخلاق البشر، واستخلاصه الفكر والعبر والمواعظ.

فإذا أصبحت تلك الفكر والمواعظ أقوالاً يرددها الناس في
مناسبات تحاكي المناسبات التي قيلت فيها سميت أمثالاً.

عرف الأدب العربي الشعر الحكمي والأمثال في كل عصوره.
حيث جاء في البدء على صورة خواطر ترد في البيت والبيتين
موزعة في قصائد الشعراء، ثم تطور إلى أن أصبح يرد في
قصيدة كاملة، جمعت نصائح ووصايا في الأخلاق والسلوك.

والحكم والأمثال عبارة عن أقوال مأثورة يطلقها صاحبها
ليعبر فيها عن رأي أو مبدأ، أو ليظهر حقيقة تتصل بحياة
الإنسان وسلوكه في حياته الاجتماعية.

i Answer the following questions in English.

1. How does the writer define أدب؟
2. What is gnomic poetry the result of?
3. When do sayings become proverbs?
3. How did proverbs and gnomic poetry develop?
4. What does the originator of a proverb intend?

ii Translate the first paragraph of the text into idiomatic English.

(b) Read the following text by محمد السقاف from لمحات عن الأغاني والرقصات الشعبية في محافظة حضرموت, p. 19, then answer the question ما هو الرقص الشعبي؟ in Arabic using different words and structures to those given in the text.

الرقص الشعبي هو اللغة المفهومة لدى كل الشعوب بطريقة الإشارة والرمز تساعدهما الملابس المميزة والصورة، فهو يعبر بالحركة ويشرح العادات والحرف السائدة في المجتمعات، وبالتالي هو وسيلة إعلام وإفهام غريزي، ولعل الطفل اهتدى في الأشهر الأولى من عمره إلى الرقص قبل أن يهتدي للكلمة.

(c) Read the following introduction to الطرائف المختارة من شعر الخفنجي والقارة edited by أحمد شرف الدين, p. 5, then summarise in English the writer's description of colloquial poetry in the Arab world.

في كل قطر عربي نقرأ ونسمع من هذا الشعر الملحون الذي ما نكاد نلمّ به إلمامةً يسيرةً حتى يستهوينا بخصائصه الإبداعية وبراعته التصويرية وما يكتنفه من تعبير صادق عما تجيش به المشاعر وتفيض به العواطف ويختلج في النفوس من أفراح وأتراح في خضم الحياة.

وهذا النوع من الأدب – بما يحمله من ميزات – قد روّض الأفهام على تقبّله وجعلها تنساق طواعية للتعلق برومانسيته الخلابة وواقعيته الجذّابة ولغته السهلة المبسّطة التي أتاحت له الخلود على مرّ العصور، فهو لم ينحدر إلى حضيض التفاهة

والابتذال حتى تعافه الأذواق الرفيعة، ولم يرتفع إلى مستوى
التصنع والتحذلق حتى تمجه مدارك العامّة، بل هو لدى الجميع
عذب مستمراً يَعلق بالنفوس ويأخذ بمجامع القلوب، فالأدب
يجد فيه لذّته من سموّ الخيال وجمال الإبداع، والعامّي يدرك
فيه سلوته من سهولة التعبير وروعةِ الإيقاع.

(d) Read the following text by طه حسين from الأيام, p. 5, then complete exercises
i. and ii. which follow.

ثم يذكر أنه كان يحب الخروج من الدار إذا غربت الشمس
وتعشّى الناسُ، فيعتمدُ على قصب هذا السياج مفكراً
مُغرقاً في التفكير، حتى يَرُدَّه إلى ما حوله صوت الشاعر
قد جلس على مسافةٍ من شماله، والتفّ حوله الناس وأخذ
يُنشدهم في نَغمةٍ عذبةٍ غريبةٍ أخبارَ أبي زيد وخليفةَ
ودياب، وهم سكوتٌ إلا حين {يـستـخـقّـهم} الطربُ أو
{تستفزُّهم} الشهوة، فيستعيدون و{يتمارَون}
ويختصمون، ويسكتُ الشاعرُ حتى يفرُغوا من {لغطهم}
بعد وقت قصيرٍ أو طويل، ثم يستأنفُ إنشادَه العَذْبَ
بنَغمته التي لا تكاد تتغيَّر.

i   In Arabic, paraphrase the words given in {curly brackets}.

ii Translate the text into idiomatic English.

6. Written Arabic texts 3 (classical)

(a) Translate the following text by ابن خلكان from كتاب وفيات الأعيان وأنباء
أبناء الزمان (1054–122), the الحريري with مقامة into idiomatic English. The
author who is regarded as having brought to a peak of development the literary
form of the مقامة, the مقامة being 'a sequence of narratives written in rhymed
prose (saj'), in which a narrator tells stories of a trickster or vagabond
encountered in a variety of situations' (Hourani 1991: 52).

الحريري صاحب المقامات

أبو محمد القاسم بن عليّ بن محمد بن عثمان الحريري البصري الحَرامي صاحب المقامات كان أحد أئمة عصره ورزق الحظوة التامة في عمل المقامات واشتملت على شيء كثير من كلام العرب من لغاتها وأمثالها ورموز أسرار كلامها ومن عرفها حق معرفتها استدلّ بها على فضل هذا الرجل وكثرة اطلاعه وغزارة مادته وكان سبب وضعه لها ما حكاه ولده أبو القاسم عبد الله قال كان أبي جالساً في مسجده ببني حرام فدخل شيخ ذو طمرين عليه أهبة السفر رث الحال فصيح الكلام حسن العبارة فسألته الجماعة من أين الشيخ فقال من سَرُوج فاستخبروه عن كنيته فقال أبو زيد فعمل أبي المقامة المعروفة بالحَرامية وهي الثامنة والأربعون وعزاها إلى أبي زيد المذكور واشتهرت فبلغ خبرها الوزير شرف الدين أبا نصر أنوشروان بن خالد بن محمد القاساني وزير الإمام المسترشد بالله فلما وقف عليها أعجبته وأشار على والدي أن يضم إليها غيرها فأتمها خمسين مقامة.

(b) Translate the following anecdote from كليلة ودمنة, reproduced in نصوص أدبية, (Tunis, 1968), p. 11, into idiomatic English.

السمكات الثلاث

زعموا أن غديراً كان فيه ثلاث سمكات: كيسة، وأكيس منها وعاجزة. وكان الغدير بنجوة من الأرض، لا يكاد يقربه أحد وبقربه نهر جار. فاتفق أنه اجتاز بذلك النهر صيادان، فأبصرا الغدير، فتواعدا أن يرجعا إليه بشباكهما، فيصيدا ما فيه من السمك. فسمعت السمكات الثلاث قولهما. فأما أكيسهن لما سمعت قولهما ارتابت بهما، وتخوفت منهما، فلم تعرج على شيء حتى خرجت من المكان الذي يدخل فيه الماء من النهر إلى

الغدير. وأما الكيسة فإنها مكثت مكانها حتى جاء الصيادان
فلما رأتهما وعرفت ما يريدان ذهبت لتخرج من حيث يدخل
الماء فإذا بهما قد سدّا ذلك المكان. فحينئذ قالت: فرطت، وهذا
عاقبة التفريط، فكيف الحيلة على هذه الحال؟ وقلما تنجح
حيلة العجلة والإرهاق. غير أن العاقل لا يقنط من منافع الرأي،
ولا ييأس على حال، ولا يدع الرأي والجهد، ثم انها تماوتت.
فطفت على وجه الماء منقلبة على ظهرها تارةً، وتارةً على
بطنها فأخذها الصيادان فوضعاها على الأرض بين النهر
والغدير، فوثبت إلى النهر فنجت. وأما العاجزة فلم تزل في
إقبال وإدبار حتى صيدت.

7. Grammar/stylistics

(a) *Apposition*

Appostion is a fairly common structure in Arabic in which a definite noun is defined more closely by a following (usually definite) noun or noun phrase. Apposition most commonly occurs with names and titles of people, things or places, and is exemplified in English in phrases such as: 'London, capital of England' where 'capital of England' more closely defines the main noun 'London'. In English the two parts of an apposition phrase are often separated by a comma, as here, and as in: 'Diana, Princess of Wales'. In Arabic the two parts of an apposition phrase take the same case, as with noun–adjective phrases of the type البيتُ الكبيرُ 'the large house'. In the following examples of apposition I bracket the entire apposition phrase with curly brackets, and separate the two (in multiple apposition, more) parts of the phrase with a slash /. The examples are considered in terms of: titles/relationships and names; names and occupations/locations (in case of place names); occupations and relationships; and multiple apposition. This section is concluded by considering one instance of embedded apposition:

i *Titles/relationships and names*

في عهد {الخليفة / عمر بن الخطاب}.
'In the era of the Caliph Umar ibn al-Khattab.' (ch. 2, 5a)

ومن بعده {ابنه / نور الدين}.
'And after him his son, Nur al-Din.' (ch. 2, 5b)

وقد صرح {البروفسور / بوتس} بقوله ...
'Professor Potts explained, saying ...' (ch. 3, 4a)

{الملك / بيبي الأول}.   'King Bibi the First.' (ch. 3, 5)

ii *Names and occupations/locations*

ونجح أبو مسلم الخراساني في هزيمة {نصر بن صبار / والي بني
أمية في خراسان}.

'Abu Muslim al-Khurasani succeeded in defeating Nasr ibn Sabbar, the Umayyad governor in Khurasan.' (ch. 2, 5b)

و{نواكشوت / عاصمة موريتانيا}.

'And Nuakchott, the capital of Mauritania.' (ch. 2, 8)

وذلك أن {ابن ياسين / المؤسس الروحي لهذه الدولة} كان قد
اعتزل مع جماعة من أصحابه.

'That is because Ibn Yasin, the spiritual founder of this state, had separated with a group of his supporters.' (ch. 2, 9)

iii *Occupations and relationships*

وأحبت الزوجة أن {الطبيب / زوجها} ...

'The wife wanted the doctor, her husband to...' (ch. 10, 11b)

وكاد {الثعبان / الشاب} أن يمضغ الخيط الذي تكسرت به أسنانه.

'The fox youth almost swallowed the thread with which he broke his teeth.' (ch. 10, 11b)

iv *Multiple apposition*

ها هو {الدكتور / نيقولا الزيادة / المؤرخ المعروف}.

'Here is Dr Nicola Ziadeh, the well–known historian.' (ch. 2, 9)

وقال {الدكتور / زيدون المحيسن / رئيس فريق معهد الآثار
والأنثروبولوجيا التابع لجامعة يرموك} ...

'Dr Zaydun Muhaysan, head of the Institute for Archeology and Anthropology attached to the University of Yarmuk, said ...' (ch. 3, 4b)

...لإحدى زوجات {الملك / بيبي الأول / ثاني ملوك الأسرة
السادسة}.

'... of one of the wives of King Bibi the First, second king of the Sixth Dynasty.' (ch. 3, 5)

يدخل {الأستاذ / فكري / الصحفي} ...
'Enter Ustadh Fikri, the journalist ...' (ch. 5, 5c)

يدخل {العمدة / الشيخ / عثمان} ...
'Enter the Chief, Sheikh Uthman ...' (ch. 5, 5c)

وقال {الأثري / محمود أبو الوفا / مدير منطقة سقارة} ...
'The anthropologist, Mahmoud Abu al-Wafa, Head of the Saqqara region, said... ' (ch. 3, 5)

In some cases one apposition phrase can be embedded within another apposition phrase, as in:

في مجموعة إهرامات {الملكات / زوجات {الملك / بيبي الأول}}.
'In a group of pyramids for the queens, wives of King Bibi the First.' (ch. 3, 5)

(b) *Presentative particles*
Arabic is fairly rich in presentational particles which function as *exclamatory* or *imperative* demonstratives. These are particles which translate, or are translated, as English 'here is ...!', 'there is ...!', or 'suddenly ...'. The main presentational particles are ها + *pronoun*, or إذا + بـ... + *pronoun* or *noun*. For example:

{ها هو} الدكتور نيقولا الزيادة.
'Here is Dr Nicola Ziadeh.' (ch. 2, 9)

إن الرجل قد ائتمنني على زوجته فـ{إذا بـ}ي أخونه وأخونها.
'The man entrusted his wife to me, and here I am betraying him and her as well.' (ch. 10, 11b)

وهو يفكر في كيفية طبخه و{إذا بـ}باز انقض عليه.
'As he was thinking about how to cook it, a falcon suddenly swooped down at him.' (ch. 11, 4biii)

ذهبت لتخرج من حيث يدخل الماء فـ{إذا بـ}هما قد سدا ذلك المكان.
'It made to get out from where the water came in, but they had blocked that place!' (ch. 11, 6b)

إن الرجل قد ائتمنني على زوجته، فـ{إذا بـ}ي أخونه وأخونها ..
'... the man had trusted me with his wife, and here I am betraying him and betraying her ...' (ch. 10, 11)

8. Aural Arabic texts 1

Listen to the following text about جحا from حصاد الشهر, no. 33, side 2, item 2,
هل جحا شخصية حقيقية أو أسطورية؟, then complete exercises i. – iii. below.

i Answer the following questions orally in Arabic.

١ – أين يشتغل الذي يجيب على السؤال؟

٢ – من يقرأ الإجابة؟

٣ – من قال إن جحا له اسم نوح الفزاري؟

٤ – ما هي كنية جحا؟

٥ – متى وُلد جحا؟

٦ – من قال «دلّهت عقلي وتلاعبت بي حتى كأني من جنون جحا»؟

٧ – كم سنةً عاش جحا تقريباً؟

٨ – متى مات جحا؟

٩ – من أدرك جحا؟

١٠ –كيف يظهر جحا للناس؟

١١ –كيف يعتبره المؤلفون؟

١٢ –من هو نصر الدين خوجا؟

١٣ –ماذا تشمل الكتب المنشورة عن نوادر جحا؟

١٤ –في رأي المتحدث هل نصر الدين خوجا أسطورة أم شخصية حقيقية؟

١٥ –هل كل الناس يوافقون على هذا الرأي؟

١٦ –أين تعلم نصر الدين؟

١٧ –ماذا اشتغل نصر الدين؟

١٨ –هل خاف من الحكام؟

١٩ –بما عُرف نصر الدين؟

٢٠ –متى عاش نصر الدين؟

٢١ –كم عُمّر نصر الدين؟

٢٢ –ما هما الدولتان اللتان أدركهما نصر الدين؟

٢٣ –أين يقع ضريح نصر الدين؟

٢٤ –بما عُرف ضريحه؟

٢٥ –مما تتكون نوادر جحا المدونة والمتداولة على ألسنة الناس؟

ii Provide written answers in English to the following questions.

1. Who is Muhammad Radwan Daya?
2. According to the writer, what other names does Juha have?
3. What is Juha's kunya?
4. When was Juha born?
5. When did he die?
6. Who is Mahdi?
7. How does Juha come across in his anecdotes?
8. What is the relationship between Juha and al-Khawja Nasr al-Din?
9. Does everyone believe that al-Khawja Nasr al-Din was a real person?
10. What did Nasr al-Din work as?
11. What sort of life was he known for?
12. What is his tomb renowned for?

iii Transcribe the passage in Arabic. You may find the following vocabulary items of use.

دلّه	to rob someone of their senses
تلاعب ب	to mock someone
تكيُّف	adaptation
تحامُق	pretence of being stupid
مُغَفَّل	simple, stupid
الشائع بين أيدى الناس من كتب	books in mass circulation
زُهْد	piety
نزاهة	honesty
جُود	goodness

9. Aural Arabic texts 2

Listen to the following text from حصاد الشهر, no. 17, side 2, item 3, موسم التـين في الفلكلور الشعبي, then complete exercises i. and ii. below.

i Answer the following questions based on the aural text in English.

1. In what respects is man felt to be suffering from a cultural crisis today?
2. What plants play a role in Palestinian folklore?
3. When is the fig season in Palestine?
4. What do the farmers call this season, and why?
5. What do young men hope to be able to do around sunset during the fig season?
6. What is said about the سـوادي fig?
7. Why is the بيـاضي fig so called?

8. Why is the سماوي the most common fig in the country?
9. Why is the عسالي fig so called?
10. What is said about the خضاري fig?
11. How does the speaker suggest that القيسي got its name?
12. What is said about the عديسي fig?
13. Which fig is as yellow as a banana?

ii Complete the following gapped text.

لن ———— بموضوعنا ———— ———— ————

ولو أننا ———— نتناوله ———— ———— آخر

———— الشعبي وهو ———— ———— ————

حياة ———— ———— وفق المقومات الحياتية المتوفرة

———— ———— ———— وفي ———— واجتماعية

نشهد ———— ———— ، وبناءا ————

———— ———— وثبة هائلة ————

———— ———— ———— . فعلم ———— الفلكلورية

غيره ———— العلوم الاجتماعية ———— جعل حياة

———— في ———— ، و ———— أكثر

———— ———— الذي ———— إنسانه ————

———— التوازن ———— تتبين ظواهرها في ————

———— و ———— التقني ———— ————

ويرى ، ———— ———— في ———— البطيء

———— ———— عيسى المصو أن ————

———— ثقتها ———— إلى ———— ما

———— مرتكزا تمثّل ———— والمثل العليا

——————— المرتكزات ——————— ——————— عليها

——————— ———— زخـر الفلكلور ———————

—————— بـثـروة ——————— بـالنبـات

——————— أنـواعـه كـالزيتـون و ———————

و ———— و ———— و ——————، ومنذ ————

——————— الإنسـان بشجـرة ———————

——————— تراثها ———— ومأثوراتها القولية

لا يتـجـزأ ——————— واقـعـهـا، وكـان لموسم

في ——————— ——————— أسهب

——————— ——————— المصو

——————— لبـرنامـجنا «ركن الثـقـافـة» ————

——————— العدد سنبدأ بتقديم الجزء ————

————— :

——————— ——————— آب (————) (————)

——————، ويطلق عليه ——————— اصطلاح

القيظ لشدة ——————، ومـعناه ———— ————

التـمـوين إذ يستكفي ——————— ————

——————— ثمار ———— ، ومن

——————— «في ———————

فيش ———— ——————— » كان القُطَّين يبادل

——————— ——————— السلع التـمـوينـية، و

‫———— ———— من ———— ———— ———— ———— يترقبه‬

‫———— ———— وصغارا بفارغ الصبر و ————‬

‫يتمشورون في ———— ———— ———— في زرافات‬

‫———— ———— كروم ———— أملاً في‬

‫اقتناص نظرة ———— فتيات أحلامهم ———— عودتهن‬

‫———— سلال ———— والعنب‬

‫———— ———— ———— ، ويعبّر ————‬

‫بصدق عن ———— ———— في ————‬

‫———— ————: «سقى ————‬

‫والتين ———— من الحلوى تصير تلاقيني ————‬

‫———— لزراعة القطين ———— تمرقي بتذكرينا».‬

‫وللتين ———— ———— ———— منتزعة‬

‫———— صميم ———— ———— وقد ————‬

‫———— مختلفة للنوع ———— في المناطق المختلفة، وهي‬

‫———— العموم ———— اصطلح‬

‫———— عليها ———— أشهرها السوادي ويُسمّى‬

‫بسلطان ———— لحُلو ———— ، البياضي سمّي‬

‫———— لبياض ———— يميل ————‬

‫———— ، السماوي وهي ———— شيوعا ————‬

‫———— ———— لتحمله‬

‫———— قسوة ———— يتحمله غيره ———— أنواع‬

——— ، العسالي وسُمِّي ——— ——— ——— لأنه

عسلي ——— ولأنه ——— ——— ——— ———

——— ومن خصائصه ——— نقطة ———

——— ——— ——— الحلو ——— الثمرة الناضجة ،

الشحيمي وتتميز ——— بسمكها وكأن ———

——— الشحم تعلوها، الخضاري و——— يميل إلى

——— وطعمه ——— بطعم السماوي، القيسي وهو

——— ——— و——— أطلق

——— القبلي

——— القيسية واليمنية ، المُلَّيَـسي وتنزلق ———

——— ——— ——— ——— قطفها لرقة

——— ——— ، العديسي ويشبـه ———

——— ——— العدس كما ——— باستدارته،

الموازي وثمـرته ——— ولونه ——— كـالموز .

——— ——— ——— الشنّيري والأصبيعي

والقراعي والمواني وغيرها، ——— ——— مخصص

لأكل ——— لكونه ——— أجود ——— ——— القطين.

——— ——— فقد لا تزال تُزرَع في

——— ولكن لا يُزرع إلا ——— منها لكي

يُؤكل ثمـرها ——— ——— فـتُسَمَّى «أطعَام»

——— للطعام.

10. Written English texts

(a) Making use of constructions and vocabulary encountered in the Arabic texts above as far as possible, translate the following text from *Arab Folktales*, p. 252, into idiomatic Arabic.

The Moroccans claim Si' Djeha as an inhabitant of Fez. They call him Si' Djeha el Fasi and have named a street for him in his hometown. The history of Djuha in the east, however, is more complicated. A Djuha is mentioned in Arab writing of the middle ages as having lived to be one hundred years old in eighth–century Kufa (Iraq). In 1880 the first modern collection of Djuha stories was printed in Cairo under the title *The Anecdotes of the Khodja Nassreddin called Djuha Al Rumi* [the Turk]. A tomb of supposedly historical Nassreddin Khodja at Akshehir in Turkey is still visited by Djuha fans. This Djuha is said to have once lived at the court of Tamerlane, the Mongol conqueror, who invaded Asia Minor and Baghdad in the fourteenth century.

(b) Translate the following text from *Arab Folktales*, p. 266, into idiomatic Arabic.

Si' Djeha and the Qadi's coat

One day Si' Djeha was strolling on the outskirts of the town when he came upon the *qadi* snoring under a tree, working off his last wine–drinking bout. So deeply sunk in sleep was the judge that Si' Djeha was able to pull his fine new woolen cloak off him without making him stir.

When the *qadi* woke up and saw that he had been robbed of his costly coat, he sent his men to search for it. They soon recognised it on Si' Djeha's back and dragged him to court. 'How did you come to possess so fine a cloak?' demanded the *qadi*. 'I saw an unbeliever grossly drunk with the stink of wine upon him lying asleep under a tree. So I spit on his infidel beard and took his coat. But if your honour claims the cloak, it is only just that you should have it back.' 'I have never seen this coat before in my life,' hissed the *qadi*. 'Now be off with you, and take the coat along too.'

11. Précis

Read the following text from أقوال علي بن زايد: دراسة ونصوص, pp. 7–9, then produce a précis in Arabic. This passage describes the Yemeni folk character علي ابن زايد.

وهكذا نرى أن علي بن زايد غير معروف الجد والبيت ولا المولد

أيضـا، بالرغم مـن شـهـرته الـواسـعـة ، حـيـث ذكـره عـلـى كل لـسـان ، وأمثاله تتردد في كل المناطق والبيوت اليمنية . ولا نعرف إن كان علي بن زايد شخصاً واحداً أو أنه شخصيات متعددة نسبت إليـه أقوال غيره ، كما نُسبت إلى شخصيات تاريخية أخرى ، حتى ازداد التسـاؤل حـوله ، هل هو شـخـص تاريخي فـعـلاً ، أو أنه أسطوري مـن صنع الخيال الشعبي .

إن تسميـة عـلي بـن زايد واتفاق جمـيـع الناس حول هذا الاسم يجعله شخصية حقيقية ، أما من حيث وفرة أمثاله وكثرة حكمه وأقـواله فـهـو شـخـصـيـة أسطورية ، إذ لا يُعقل أن يعـبـر رجل عن تجارب كل الأجيال الزراعية ، ولا يمكن له أن ينطق بلهجات جميع المناطق ، وبما أن هذا خارج عن نطاق المعـقـول ، فـأغـلب الظن أن الرواة نسبوا إليه أقـوالاً وأمثالاً ليست له في الأساس ، حتى غدا وكأنه مجموع الشعب، أو الموروث الفكري والزراعي لهذا الشعب.

أمـا مـن حيث العصر الذي عـاش فـيـه علي بن زايد ، فلا نستطيع الـوقـوف عـلى تاريخ مـحـدد لذلك ، وهل عـاش في العصر الجاهلي أم في العصر الإسلامي . لقد اعتبره بعض المؤرخين جاهلياً ، مستدلين على ذلك بما ورد في بعض أشعاره ، كذلك اعتبره آخرون إسلامياً ، مستدلين بتسميته ، هذا أيضاً لا يكفي ، فاسمه واسم أبيه معروفان في الجاهلية والإسلام .

لقد كانت أقوال علي بن زايد وأعرافه مقدسة في مجتمعه قداسة الشريعة لدرجة أن أحداً لا يستطيع مـخالفتها أو الخروج عليها ، لأن ذلك يعتبر عاراً عليه ، سيما وأن جل أمثاله تتطابق مع احكام الشريعة الإسلامية ، فهو يرى أن الوفاء بالدّين ، والمحافظة على العهد، من القوانين المرعية في الجاهلية والإسلام ، فمن نكث وعداً ، أو أنكر دينا نبذته قبيلته ، وتخلت عنه ، وخلعته من عهدتها ، وأجبرت قومه على قضاء دينه . وهكذا كان حكم علي بن زايد (الدَّين

قبل الوراثة) يتفق مع الشريعة ومع كل القوانين النافذة .

وكذلك كانت له أقوال مطابقة لما كان سائدا في الجاهلية ثم جاء الإسلام ورفضها ، وحرم التعامل بها ، فهو يدعو لما كانت القبائل تفعله في الجاهلية ، حين كانت تتربص لأخذ ثأرٍ ، فتحرم على نفسها اللذات في أوقات معينة .

ومن أمثلته التي تتعارض مع الشريعة المحمدية قوله : (بين إخوتك مخطي ولا وحدك مصيب) ، لأن الشريعة تعاقب على الخطأ وتكافئ المصيب ، كما كان يطلب من القبيلة كلها أن تنصر فرداً منها عندما يطلب هذا الأخير البحث ، كما في هذا العرف: « من صاح صبيان قومي ، حمّل بني عمّه اللوم » .

وواضح أن هذا القول يطابق العرف الذي كان سائداً في العصر الجاهلي وهو : « أنصر أخاك ظالماً أو مظلوماً » .

12. Oral
من هو جحا؟
(a) One or two students to produce in Arabic an account of Juha as a person.
(b) Individual students to compose possible Juha jokes or anecdotes in Arabic.
(c) The presenter(s) of the account of Juha then ask the other students questions about Juha and the type of jokes and anecdotes relating to him.
(d) Open lecturer–led discussion on the role of Juha and Juha–like characters in Middle Eastern society.

13. Essay
Write an essay in Arabic of around 200 words on the title الأدب الشعبي في الشرق الأوسط. Structure your essay around the following questions:

١ – ما هو الفرق بين الأدب الشعبي والأدب غير الشعبي؟

٢ – ما هي أنواع الأدب الشعبي؟

٣ – من هو الراوي، وما هو دوره في المجتمع العربي؟

٤ – من هو جحا؟

٥ – في رأيك لماذا يُعتبر الأدب الشعبي أهم في الوطن العربي منه في الغرب؟

12
Muslim Spain

1. Basic background material

(a) *Chronology*

711	Under Umayyad Caliph al-Walid, Islamic army crosses from N. Africa to Spain; victory of Tariq ibn Ziyad (from whom the name Gibraltar) over Visigoth King Roderic in southern Spain.
718	Greater part of peninsula occupied by Islamic armies. Arab rule established in Spain.
756	Following overthrow of Umayyads by Abbasids elsewhere, Umayyad emirate established by Abdurrahman in Spain.
961–976	Umayyad al-Hakam II fosters science and letters at Cordova.
978–1008	Umayyad vizier al-Mansur and later his son effective rulers in Spain; peak of Muslim power.
1031	Fall of Umayyads.
1031–1090	Period of 'party kings' (Spanish: *reyes de taifas*); numerous small dynasties rule parts of southern Spain. Peak of Spanish poetry, with development of new poetic forms esp. the *muwashshahah*, which appeared by the end of the tenth century, and was strophic (i.e. not every line ended in the same rhyme). Later development of *zajal* form, also strophic, but composed in colloquial Arabic of Andalusia.
1085	Christian Spaniards capture Toledo.
1086–1147	Intolerant Berber–based Almoravids under spiritual leadership of Ibn Yasin summoned from N. Africa to combat Christian threat initiated by King Alphonso VII of Castile. Halt Christian advance in Spain.
1130–1269	Almoravids succeeded by intolerant N. African Berber–based Almohades who introduce violent religious persecution into Islamic Spain, during which Spanish Jews in particular flee north to Christian Toledo and elsewhere.
1236	Fall of Cordova to Christian Spaniards.
1248	Fall of Seville to Christian Spaniards.
1260–1492	Granada: last Arab state in Europe under Nasrid dynasty.

1492   Fall of Granada to Christian Spaniards.

(b) *Ethnic and religious composition*
C.8 onwards Islamic conquest and immigration of Berbers and Arabs from N. Africa and Middle East.
C.10   Muslim immigration and conversion of Christians and Jews to Islam result in majority Muslim population in Spain by end of century.
C.11   Arabic becomes language of majority of population, including Christians and Jews. Mixed ethnic population of indigenous Spaniards, Arab elite, Berbers, and soldiers of fortune (originally enslaved) from western and eastern Europe (the Slavs).
C.15   Following renewal of Inquisition in 1481, increasing Christian fanaticism. Persecution of Muslims and Jews, forced conversion to Christianity.
C.16   Royal edict in 1500 decreeing expulsion of all non–Catholics from Iberian peninsula. Most Jews flee to N. Africa and Middle East. Muslims flee to N. Africa.
C.17   Deportation in 1609 of remaining Arabic–speakers to N. Africa (forced converts to Christianity, who secretly maintained their Islamic faith).

(c) *Major intellectual figures*
Ibn Hazm, 994–1064
Vizier, poet and theologian. Author of *Dove's Neck Ring* collection; translated into most western languages.

Ibn Zaydun, 1003–1071
Poet, whose wistful love poems reflect his own personal history of imprisonment in his native city of Cordova and subsequent political exile in Seville.

Ibn Tufayl, 1110–1185
Philosopher; author of philosophical treatise in form of story, *Alive Son of Awake*, concerning a young man who appears on an island as a baby, either having emerged through spontaneous generation (in one account in the story), or, Moses–like, having been previously abandoned in a basket to the sea by his mother. Isolated on his island the boy is able, solely through the exercise of reason, to rise through the various stages of understanding the universe, until he reaches the highest stage of philosophical awareness.

Averroes, 1126–1198
Arab philosopher and physician in Spain, pupil of Ibn Tufayl. Noted particularly for his attempts to reconcile Aristotelian philosophy with Islamic religion, which profoundly influenced Christian scholasticism. His works include *The Incoherence*

of the Incoherence, a reply to Al-Ghazali's attack on philosophy in his *The Incoherence of the Philosophers*.

Moses Maimonedes, 1135–1204
Jewish philosopher, physician, and jurist; greatest figure of medieval Judaism. Born in Spain; moved to Egypt to avoid religious intolerance of Al-Mohades. His best known work *Guide of the Perplexed*, written in Arabic (in Hebrew script), provides a philosophical interpretation of the Jewish religion.

(d) *1492 and after: the wider world*
Setting out from south–west Spain in 1492, a few months after the fall of Grenada, Columbus becomes probably the first European to reach America since Icelander Leif Ericsson (c. 1000 AD). Catastrophic decline in indigenous Indian population (from 100 million in 1492, to 10 million in 1600, to 5 million in 1700), due to epidemics (lack of resistance to European diseases), slaughter by European invaders, economic destruction and resultant famine, enslavement, and cultural devastation (forced Christianisation, etc.). West European states left with unconstrained power to exploit resources of double continent (gold, silver, sugar, other cash crops, etc.). Atlantic slave trade (20 million African slaves shipped to Americas between early 1500s and middle of nineteenth century) produces massive pool of forced labour in Americas. Ensuing European economic advantage over Middle East and Far East is major factor in fuelling inexorably increasing scientific and technological advantage, leading ultimately to industrial revolution, 'triumph of the west', and 'Europeanisation of the earth'. The modern world begins.

2. Additional reading
(a) Lewis, *The Arabs in History*, pp. 120–30.
(b) Hourani, *A History of the Arab Peoples*, pp. 189–98; pp. 462–71.
(c) Hans Koning, *Columbus: his Enterprise*, (London: Latin America Bureau, 1991).

3. Key vocabulary
Taking as your starting point the texts in this chapter, draw up lists of vocabulary in the following fields:
(a) Various arts and sciences (including the religious sciences) practised in Islamic Spain.
(b) Names of practitioners of these arts and sciences; e.g. فِقْه ,جَرَّاح – جِراحة – فقيه.
(c) Verbs related to arts and sciences. Differentiate these from any obvious near synonyms; e.g. شَرَح 'to interpret (esp. of philosophical and literary texts)' v. فسّر 'to interpret (esp. of religious texts).

4. Written Arabic texts 1
(a) Read the seven short texts below, then complete the exercise which follows.

(i) الأندلس [from] المنجـد فـي اللغـة والإعـلام [المنجـد فـي الإعـلام] (Beirut: دار المشرق, 1986), p. 76).

اسم عُرف به جنوب اسبـانيا بعـد أن احتلها الڤانـدال فـأخذ عنهم اسمـه: واندالوسيـا. ثم أطلقه العـرب على شبـه جزيرة ايبيريا عامةً بعـد أن دخلوها. استقلت الأندلس عن العبّاسيـين وكونت إمارة قرطبـة في عهـد الخليفة الأمـوي عبـد الرحمن أ ٧٥٢. تلاشت الإمارة فـعقبها دويلات حكمها ملوك الطوائف ١٠٣١ ومن بعـدهـم «المرابطون» ثم «الموحّدون». هـزمـهـم الإسبـان في وقـعة العقاب ١٢١٢. وبعـد ذلك انحصـر سلطان العـرب في مملكة غـرناطة (١٢٣٦–١٤٩٢) فـعُرفت بـالأندلس في المعنى المحصور. والأندلس اليوم ولاية في إسبـانيا الجنوبية تتـألـف من ثمانية أقضية. فيها جبـال سيـيرا نيڤادا (٤٧٨، ٣ م.) منطقة زراعية.

(ii) طارق بن زياد [from] المورد السنوي [معجم الإعلام] (p. 83,).
قائـد مسلم. اجتاز المضيق الذي عُرف بعدُ بـاسمه (مضيق جبل طارق) وفتح الأندلس (عام ٧١١ م.).

(iii) ابن حزم [from] المنجد في اللغة والإعلام [المنجد في الإعلام] (p. 9,).
فـقيه وشاعر وفيلسوف ومـؤرخ ومـتكلم أندلسي مـن أصل مسيـحي. ولد في قرطبـة. اشتـرك في حرب غـرناطة وصار وزيـرًا للمـستظهـر ١٠٢٣ وبعـد مقـتله اعتـزل السيـاسـة وانصـرف إلى التـأليـف. لـه «طوق الحمـامـة» الذي يتـأثر بـأفلاطون و«الفصل في الملل والأهواء والنحل» ويـعتبـر أول تاريخ مقارن للأديان.

(iv) ابن زيدون [from المنجد في الإعلام] المنجد في اللغة والإعلام (p. 10,).
ولد في قرطبة وتوفي في إشبيلية. وزير من شعراء
الأندلس. اشتهر شعره بولّادة بنت المستكفي. أخباره معها
ومع منافسه فيها الوزير ابن عبدوس كثيرة. كان له بين
الأمراء منزلة عالية لمواهبه الأدبية ومعرفته بأحوال
المسلمين في الأندلس. له «ديوان».

(v) ابن طُفيل [from المنجد في الإعلام] المنجد في اللغة والإعلام (p. 11,).
عالم موسوعي عربي ولد في مقاطعة غرناطة وتوفي في
مراكش. اهتم بالطب والرياضيات والفلك والفلسفة
والشعر. له قصة «حي بن يقظان» يحاول فيها التوفيق بين
الفلسفة والدين.

(vi) ابن رشد [from المنجد في الإعلام] المنجد في اللغة والإعلام (p. 10,).
فيلسوف عربي ولد في قرطبة وتوفي في مراكش. درس
الكلام والفقه والشعر والطب والرياضيات والفلك
والفلسفة. قدمه ابن طفيل لأبي يعقوب يوسف خليفة
الموحدين ١١٨٢، فعيّنه طبيبًا له ثم قاضيًا في قرطبة. سماه
الغرب «الشارح» نظرًا لشروحه الكثيرة والممتازة لأرسطو.
حاول التوفيق بين الشريعة والفلسفة في «فصل المقال فيما
بين الحكمة والاتّصال» كما دافع عن الفلسفة ضد الغزالي في
كتاب «تهافت التهافت».

(vii) ابن ميمون [from المنجد في الإعلام] المنجد في اللغة والإعلام (p. 13,).
ولد في قرطبة ودفن حسب رغبته في طبرية (فلسطين).
فيلسوف يهودي. هجر الأندلس وأقام بالقاهرة حيث انصرف
إلى ممارسة الطب فاشتهر حتى أصبح طبيب صلاح الدين
الأيوبي. له عدة مؤلفات طبية ودينية وفلسفية منها: «دلالة
الحائرين» وكان له أثر كبير عند مفكري القرون الوسطى
في الغرب.

Exercise: Making use of information from section 1 *Basic background material*
where appropriate, give the Arabic for the following, plus a single–sentence Arabic
description.

1. Umayyad
2. Straits of Gibralter
3. the Abbasids
4. Cordova (Spanish *Córdoba*)
5. 'party kings'
6. Al-Moravids
7. Al-Mohades
8. Seville
9. Granada
10. theologian
11. Dove's Neck Ring (title of book)
12. Plato
13. encyclopedic
14. to reconcile, reconciling (noun)
15. Averroes
16. Aristotle
17. Alive Son of Awake (title of book)
18. The Incoherence of the Incoherence (title of book)
19. Maimonedes
20. Saladin
21. The Guide of the Perplexed (title of book)

(b) Read the following text from المعجم العربي الأساسي (Tunis: Larousse, 1989), pp. 112–3, then explain the contextual meanings of the words and phrases listed below the text orally in Arabic.

الأَنْدَلُسُ: اسم أطلقه العرب المسلمون على شبه جزيرة إيبيريا (إسبانيا والبرتغال) وهي اليوم إحدى مقاطعات إسبانيا الجنوبية. وكانت الفترة العربية هي العهد الذهبي لها بعد أن أسس الأمويون فيها خلافة توازي الخلافة العباسية في بغداد. واستقرّ العرب فيها حوالى ثمانية قرون.

مقاطعات
العهد الذهبي
توازي
استقرّ

5. Written Arabic texts 2

(a) As a preparatory exercise for subsequent materials, read the following text from مجلة الشرق الأوسط, Feb. 3, 1993, at home.

استقرّ المسلمون من عرب وبربر في الأندلس لمدة ثمانية قرون، فاستطاعوا خلال تلك الفترة، وهذا طبيعي عند تزاوج الحضارات، إحداث الكثير من التغييرات لدى سكان البلاد الأصليين واكتساب الكثير منها. ولم يغادر المسلمون الأندلس كما دخلوها لا من الناحية العسكرية ولا الاقتصادية ولا الحضارية. فمقاتلو جيش طارق بن زياد (١٢ ألف مقاتل بربري تقريباً)، الذين شاركوا طارق الانتصار على الملك القوطي لذريق، وجيش موسى بن نصير (عام ٧١٢ ميلادية) العربي المكون من ثمانية ألف مقاتل، استقر أغلبهم في البلاد التي فتحوها، وتزوج قسم كبير منهم بنساء من أهل البلاد، الأساس الذي كون وعلى مدى القرون المقبلة هوية المجتمع الأندلسي. لذلك ليس صحيحاً التفكير بأن المسلمين الذين دخلوا الأندلس هم أنفسهم الذين غادروها.

(b) Read the following text from مجلة الشرق الأوسط, Feb. 3, 1993, then complete exercises i. and ii. which follow.

كان المجتمع الأندلسي فريداً من نوعه، فإلى جانب العرب والبربر، كان هنالك سكان البلاد الأصليون، فمنهم من اعتنق الإسلام وأُطلق عليهم أولاً اسم «المسالمة» وعلى الذين نشأوا في ظل الإسلام وربوا بتربيته اسم «المولّدين». ومنهم من بقي على الدين المسيحي وأطلق عليهم اسم العجم أو المستعربين (موزاراب). ومن بين هؤلاء المولدين من كان حراً تماماً ومنهم من كان عبداً، كما احتفظ قسم منهم بأسمائهم الإسبانية القديمة. وقد أصبحت العلاقات بين المسلمين الجدد والقدماء وثيقة بمرور الأيام نتيجة الاختلاط والتزاوج. ولقد كان لهذا التمازج أثره الكبير في التكوين العنصري للمجتمع الأندلسي. وقد ظهر في القرن العاشر عنصر جديد من الموالين، أطلق عليهم اسم «الصقالبة» وأصولهم من

الأسرى الذين يؤتى بهم من الشمال. وكان في المجتمع أيضاً قسم كبير من غير المسلمين من النصارى واليهود الذين قدموا للمسلمين عند فتحهم شبه الجزيرة مساعدات جمة.

i   Answer the following questions orally in Arabic.

١ – ما هي الأجناس الثلاثة التي كوّنت المجتمع الأندلسي؟

٢ – من هم «المسالمة»؟

٣ – من هم «المولدون»؟

٤ – من هم العجم أو المستعربون؟

٥ – من هم «الصقالبة»؟

٧ – متى وكيف تكوّنوا؟

٨ – ما هما الدينان غير الدين الإسلامي الموجودان في الأندلس؟

ii   Translate the text into idiomatic English.

(c) Read the following text from مجلة الشرق الأوسط, Feb. 3, 1993, then complete exercises i. and ii. which follow.

ارتبط اسم الأندلس بعدد من الفنون العربية التي {سادت} في تلك المنطقة وانتقلت منها إلى باقي العالم العربي، فقد استطاع فنانو الأندلس {مزج} الفنون العربية الأصيلة القادمة من الشرق ومزجوها بفنون الأرض التي {استقروا} فيها مما نتج عنها العديد من {أنماط} الفنون الجديدة التي أضافت إلى الشرق العربي المزيد من {الألق}، فقد شهدت أرض الأندلس مولد فنون الموشحة والزجل في الشعر وشهدت الموسيقى إضافة الوتر الخامس إلى {العود} وتطور الأداء الموسيقي بظهور الموشحة أيضاً كفن عربي أندلسي خالص.

i   Explain the contextual meaning of the words and phrases given in {curly brackets} in Arabic.

ii   Paraphrase the text orally in Arabic.

6. **Written Arabic texts 3 (classical)**

(a) Translate into idiomatic English the following text by ابن طفيل from حي بن. The text relates two versions of how حي came to grow up on a small island without a father or a mother, from edition by Léon Gauthier (Algiers, 1900), p. 17 and pp. 20–2.

ذكـر سلفنا رضي الله عنهم أن جـزيرة من جـزائر الـهند الـتي تحت خط الإستـواء وهـي الجـزيرة الـتي يتـولد بـها الإنسان من غيـر أم و لا أب ....

.... ومنـهم مـن أنكر ذلك وروى مـن أمـره خبـرًا نقـصـه لك فـقال إنه كان بإزاء تلك الجزيرة جزيرة عظيمة متّسعة الأكنـاف كثيـرة الفـوائد عامـرة بالنـاس يملكها رجل منهم شديد الأنفـة والغيـرة. وكانت لـه أخت عضلها ومنـعها من الأزواج إذ لـم يجد لـها كفؤًا وكان لـه قريب يسمى يقظان فتزوجها سرًا على وجه جائز في مذهبـهم المشهـور عندهم وفي زمنهم. ثم أنها حملت منـه ووضعت طفـلاً فلمـا خـافت أن يفتـضح أمـرها وينكشف سرها وضعتـه في تابـوت زمّه بعد أن روته مـن الرضـاع وخرجت بـه في أول الليل في جملة من خدمـها وثقاتها إلى سـاحل البـحر وقلبـها يحـترق صبابةً بـه وخوفًا علـيـه ثم إنها ودعتـه وقالـت اللهم إنك أنت خلقت هذا الطفل ولـم يكن شـيئًا مذكورًا[1] ورزقتـه فـي ظلمـات الأحشـاء وتكفلت بـه حـتى تم واستوى وأنا قـد أسلمتـه إلى لطفك ورجوت لـه فـضلك خـوفًا من هذا الملك الغشوم الجبار العنيد فكن لـه ولا تسلمـه يا أرحم الراحمـين ثم قـذفت بـه في اليم فـصـادف ذلك جريـة المـاء بقـوة فاحتمله من ليلته إلى ساحل الجزيرة المتقدم ذكرها وكان المـد يصل في ذلك الوقت إلى موضع لا يصل إليـه إلا بـعد عام فأدخلـه الماء إلى أجمـة ملتفة الخمـر عذبة التـربـد مستورة عـن الريـاح والمطر مـحـجـوبـة عـن الشـمس تزور عنهـا إذا طلعت وتميـل إذا غربت[2] ثم أخـذ المـاء في الجَـزر وبقـي التـابـوت في ذلك الموضع

وعلت الرمال بعد ذلك حتى سدت مدخل الماء إلى تلك الأجمة
فكان المد لا ينتهي إليها وكانت مسامير التابوت قد قلقت
وألواحه قد اضطربت عند رمي الماء إياه في تلك الأجمة فلما
اشتدّ الجوع بذلك الطفل بكى واستغاث وعالج الحركة فوقع
صوته في إذن ظبية فقدت طلاها فتبعت الصوت وهي تتخيل
طلاها حتى وصلت إلى التابوت وفحصت عنه بأظلافها وهو
ينوء من داخله حتى طار عن التابوت لوح من أعلاه فحنت
الظبية ورانت به وألقمته حلمتيها وروته لبناً سائغاً وما
زالت تتعهده وتربيه وتدفع عنه الأذى.

Notes

1. cf. سورة الإنْسَان, Qur'an LXXVI, 1–2: هَلْ أَتَى عَلَى الإِنْسَانِ حِينٌ لَمْ يَكُنْ
شَيْئًا مَذْكُورًا إِنَّا خَلَقْنَا الإِنْسَانَ مِنْ نُطْفَةٍ أَمْشَاجٍ نَبْتَلِيهِ فَجَعَلْنَاهُ سَمِيعًا
بَصِيرًا.

2. cf. سورة الكَهْف, Qur'an XVIII, 16: وَتَرَى الشَّمْسَ إِذَا طَلَعَت تَزُورُ عَنْ
كَهْفِهِم ذَاتَ الْيَمِينِ وَإِذَا غَرَبَتْ تَقْرِضُهُمْ ذَاتَ الشِّمَالِ وَهُمْ فِي فَجْوَةٍ مِنْهُ
ذَلِكَ مِن أَيَاتِ اللَّهِ مَنْ يَهْدِ اللَّهُ فَهُوَ الْمُهْتَدِ وَمَنْ يُضْلِلْ فَلَنْ تَجِدَ لَهُ وَلِيًّا
مُرْشِداً.

(b) Translate into idiomatic English the following text, which is an extract from a
مُوَشَّحَة from the ديوان of ابن زيدون.

سلام على تلك الميادين

قال وهو في السجن يذكر قرطبة وايام صباه فيها

أَقُرطُبَةُ الْغَرَّاء هَلْ فِيكِ مَطْمَعُ

وَهَلْ كَبِدٌ حَرَّى لِبَيْنِكِ تُنْقَعُ

وَهَل لِلَيَالِيكَ الْحَمِيدَةِ مَرْجِعُ

إِذِ الْحُسْنُ مَرْأَى فِيكِ وَاللَّهْوُ مَسْمَعُ

وَإِذْ كَنَفُ الدُّنْيَا لَدَيْكِ مُوَطَّأَ[١]

أَلَيْسَ عَجِيبًا أَنْ تَشُطَّ[٢] النَّوَى بِكِ

فَأَحْيَا كَأَنْ لَمْ أَنْسَ نَفْحَ جَنَابِكِ

وَلَمْ يَلْتَئِمْ شَعْبِي[٣] خِلَالَ شِعَابِكِ[٤]

وَلَمْ يَكُ خَلْقِي بَدْوُهُ مِنْ تُرَابِكِ

وَلَمْ يَكْتَنِفْنِي مِنْ نَوَاحِيكِ مَنْشَأُ

نَهَارُكِ وَضَّاحٌ وَلَيْلُكِ ضَحْيَانٌ

وَتُرْبُكِ مَصْبُوحٌ[٦] وَغُصْنُكِ نَشْوَانٌ

وَأَرْضُكِ تُكْسَى حِينَ جَوُّكِ عُرْيَانُ

وَرَيَّاكِ رَوْحٌ لِلنُّفُوسِ وَرَيْحَانُ

وَحَسْبُ الأَمَانِي ظِلُّكِ المُتَفَيَّأُ[٧]

وَلَا يُغْبِطُ الأَعْدَاءَ كَوْنِيَ فِي السِّجْنِ

فَإِنِّي رَأَيْتُ الشَّمْسَ تُحْضِنُ بِالدَّجْنِ[٨]

وَمَا كُنْتُ إِلَّا الصَّارِمَ الغَضْبَ فِي جَفْنٍ

أَوِ اللَّيْثَ فِي غَابٍ أَوِ الصَّقْرَ فِي وَكْنٍ[٩]

أَوِ العِلْقَ يُخْفَى فِي الصِّوَارِ[١٠] وَيُخْبَأُ

Notes

١ – مُوَطَّأ　　　　=　　ميسر مذلل

٢ - تشط   =   تبعد

٣ - يلتئم شعبي   =   نجتمع بعد التفرق

٤ - شعابك   =   الناحية = واحدها شعب

٥ - ضحيان   =   بارز ظاهر

٦ - مصبوح   =   ممطور صباحًا

٧ - المتفيأ   =   الذي يستظل به

٨ - الدجن   =   الغيم

٩ - الوكن   =   عش الطائر

١٠ - الصوار   =   وعاء المسك

7. Grammar/stylistics

(a) *Coordination of attributives, and elements in predicate*

The principles of both syndetic and asyndetic coordination of adjectives were discussed in chapter 2 (ch. 2, 7c). Such coordination can occur with all attributives, i.e. any phrases which function to define a noun. The category of attributives covers not only simple one–word adjectives, but also compound phrases consisting of at least one adjective plus another element or elements (cf. ch. 7, 7b), including participles, both active (cf. ch. 2, 7d) and passive (cf ch. 9, 7a), and relative clauses (cf. ch. 9, 7a). The following are examples of coordinated attributives.

فقال إنه كان بإزاء تلك الجزيرة جزيرة {عظيمة} {متّسعة الأكناف} {كثيرة الفوائد} {عامرة بالناس} {يملكها رجل منهم شديد الأنفة والغيرة}.

'He said that there was opposite that island, a huge island, with far–flung areas, full of beneficial things, and crowded with people, which was owned by a man who was very proud and jealous.' (ch. 12, 6a)

فأدخله الماء إلى أجمة {ملتفة الخمر} {عذبة التربد} {مستورة عن الرياح والمطر} {محجوبة عن الشمس} ..

'The water carried him into a thicket of reeds, which closed in around, and was sweetly shaded, which was protected from the winds and rain, and sheltered from the sun ...' (ch. 12, 6a)

لا شك أن أهداف «البعث العربي» التي لخصناها في «الحرية والاشتراكية والوحدة» هي أهداف {أساسية} {متساوية في الاهمية} {لا يجوز فصل او تأجيل بعضها عن البعض الآخر}.

'There is no doubt that the goals of the Arab Ba'th [Renaissance] Party which we have summarised as 'Freedom, Socialism and Unity' are goals which are fundamental and equal in importance, none of which may be separated from or deferred after any of the others.' (ch. 13, 11a)

The same kind of coordination can occur between elements in a predicate, which may be adjective phrases or verb phrases, or both. Thus:

شـاي الكمـون {طـارد للـريح} {مـضـاد لـسـمـوم البـدن وسـوء الـهـضـم} {وتخمر المعدة} ..

'Cumin tea gets rid of wind, counters the poisons of the body and indigestion, and causes fermentation in the stomach ...' (ch. 19, 4b)

.. وهو {مـهدئ للاعصاب} {خافض للحرارة} {ينـفع لسوء الـهـضـم}.

'... it calms the nerves, reduces fever, and helps with indigestion.' (ch. 19, 4b)

The following is an example where the coordinated adjectival is the second object of the verb اعتبر. (The verb اعتبر takes two objects; e.g. أعتـبـر ذلك الـرجلَ صـديقاً 'I consider that man a friend', where ذلك الـرجلَ is a first object, and صـديقاً is a second object.)

هذه امـراض يعتبـرها عدد كبيـر مـن الـنـاس {بـسـيطة} {لا تستـحق مراجعة الطبيب}.

'These are illnesses which many people consider trivial and undeserving of an examination by a doctor.' (ch. 19, 5c)

(b) Definiteness and indefiniteness, الـ and الذي

There is a close relationship between the definite article الـ and the relative pronoun الذي (f. الـتي, m.pl. الذين, etc.). This is suggested by the way in which the word الذي is made up: ذي + الـ (which is an ancient emphatic particle) + ل (cf. ذو 'possessor of'). More importantly, الـ and الذي function in rather similar ways. So, just as an attributive adjective following a definite noun takes the definite article الـ, so an attributive clause following a definite noun takes the relative pronoun الذي, الـتي, الذين, etc; similarly an attributive adjective following an indefinite noun does not take the definite article, while an attributive clause following an indefinite noun does not take the relative pronoun. So:

الأفكار الـتي تمتـاز 'the ideas which excel' and الأفكار المتـازة 'the excellent ideas'

أفكار تمتـاز 'ideas which excel' and أفكار ممتـازة 'excellent ideas'

Just as it is possible to have adjective phrases which are compound in various ways (see 7a, above), so it is possible to have verb phrases which are compound in various ways, including ways which parallel compound adjective phrases. So:

'ideas which are excellent above others'	أفكار ممتازة عن غيرها
'the ideas which are excellent above others '	الأفكار الممتازة عن غيرها
and	
'ideas which excel above others'	أفكار تمتاز عن غيرها
'the ideas which excel above others'	الأفكار التي تمتاز عن غيرها

In Arabic there is an obvious parallelism between a verb phrase functioning attributively, i.e. as a relative clause (whether this verb phrase is simple as in تمتاز or complex as in تمتاز عن غيرها), and an adjective phrase functioning attributively (whether this adjective phrase is simple as in ممتازة, or complex as in ممتازة عن غيرها); in all cases the attributive (verb phrase or adjective phrase) immediately follows the noun. In English attributive verb phrases, i.e. relative clauses (whether simple as in 'an idea {which excels}', or complex as in 'an idea {which excels above others}'), and complex adjective phrases (as in 'an idea {excellent above others}') follow the noun. A simple adjective (as in 'an {excellent} idea'), by contrast, precedes the noun.

The fact that simple adjectives in English precede the noun but complex adjectives follow the noun sometimes makes it difficult for native English speakers to identify an adjective followed by a prepositional phrase as an adjectival phrase and not as two separate phrases. For instance, a chunk هذه الاتجاهات الجديدة على كافة الاصعدة includes the adjective phrase الجديدة على كافة الاصعدة, where جديد على means 'new to/for/in respect of'. The whole phrase should therefore be translated along the lines, 'These trends which were/are (etc.) new on all levels'. It is easy for an English speaker, however, to mistake الجديدة for a simple Arabic adjective phrase, and to translate the whole chunk incorrectly as something like, 'These new trends on all levels'. Similarly, a chunk اهداف متساوية في الأهمية includes a compound adjective phrase متساوية في الاهمية, and will need to be translated along the lines, 'goals which are equal in importance', rather than 'equal goals in importance'.

A related problem for English speakers translating into Arabic is that they are tempted to translate a phrase such as 'These trends which were new on all levels' using an Arabic relative pronoun; thus: * هذه الاتجاهات التي جديدة على كافة الاصعدة* (an asterisk is used here and below to mark putative forms which are grammatically unacceptable). This is incorrect; before the adjective phrase ال must always be used.

Similar examples are:

النسبة {المسموح بها} دولياً

'levels which are permitted internationally'/'internationally permitted
levels.' (ch. 8, 5a)

وبالكاد يوجد منها سجن في عاصمة كل مديرية مخصص {للمحكوم
عليهم} بالحبس أو السجن من المديرية نفسها

'There's virtually no more than one prison in the capital of every
province specifically for those who are condemned to detention or
imprisonment in the province itself.' (ch. 17, 5b)

In the above two examples constructions involving forms involving الذي, التي,
الذين, etc. are not acceptable. One cannot therefore have forms in Arabic such as
the following:

النسبة {التي} مسموح بها دوليا

*وبالكاد يوجد منها سجن في عاصمة كل مديرية مخصص {للذين}
محكوم عليهم} بالحبس أو السجن من المديرية نفسها*

Normally where what follows the noun is a clause, and not simply an adjectival
phrase, الذي (etc.) is used. When what follows the noun is an adverbial, الذي etc.
is also used. For example:

.. جزيرة من جزائر الهند التي تحت خط الإستواء ..

'... one of the islands of India which is below the equator ...' (ch. 12,
6a)

There is, however, one case in which an adjectival clause following a definite noun
is preceded by the definite article. Consider the following:

.. فاحتمله من ليلته إلى ساحل الجزيرة {المتقدم ذكرُها} ..

'... it carried him off that very night to the shore of the island which has
been previously mentioned ...' (ch. 12, 6a)

Here the adjectival clause متقدم ذكرها consists of two elements, ذكرها which is
the subject, and متقدم which is the predicate (cf. ch. 2, 7a; ch. 13, 7aii, 7aiii).
This is one of the relatively rare cases in which the predicate precedes the subject
(corresponding to structures of the type in English 'Blessed are the peacemakers',
'Tender is the night'). The same basic notion, with the same basic
subject–predicate structure, could also be expressed by متقدم ذكرها. In this case,
however, the whole phrase would be الجزيرة التي ذكرها متقدم. The use of ال,
rather than التي, in the phrase المتقدم ذكرها is clearly motivated by the fact that

the phrase starts with an adjective. Logically, however, the definiteness of the الـ could be regarded as applying to the whole adjectival clause متـقدم ذكرها, just as the definiteness of الذي (etc.) applies to the entire clause with which الذي (etc.) goes.

In attributive clauses which involve a noun subject and an adjective predicate and where the adjective comes first (as in المتقدم ذكرها), the adjective agrees in gender and number with the subject (ذكر is masculine, singular), but agrees in case with the preceding noun (thus إلى ساحل الجزيرة المتقدم ذكرها, not * إلى ساحـل, and *الجزيـرة المتقدمُ ذكرها). This is counter to the normal situation, where the noun phrase subject and adjective phrase predicate agree with one another in case, as well as in number and gender, in accordance with the normal rules of agreement in Arabic.

Another example of the same type as الجزيرة المتقدم ذكرها is:

مـع الرجالِ المعروفةِ أسماؤُهم

'with the men whose names are known'

(c) *Relative clauses with clausal antecedent*
As discussed in chapter 9 (ch. 9, 7d), it is possible in English to have relative clauses whose antecedent – i.e. what they describe – is not the information given by a noun, but that given by a clause, series of clauses, sentence, or even series of sentences. For example:

'He admires John Smith, which I find extraordinary.'

Here what the writer finds extraordinary is the whole clause, or rather the information expresed by the whole clause, 'he admires John Smith'. As is evident, English uses 'which' to express this relationship.

In Arabic it's possible to use مما to refer back to a clausal antecedent (as discussed in ch. 9, 7d). It is also possible in Arabic to use a definite noun which summarises the relevant previous information, and then follows this with the relative clause introduced with الذي (etc.). The noun which is normally used is الأمر. So:

تجددت الاسبوع الماضي حوادث الشغب في بعض مدن صعيد مصر «سـوهاج، بنـي سـويف، اسـيـوط» بصدامـات بـين بعض عناصـر الجماعات الاسلامية المتطرفة وعدد من المسيحيين {الامر الذي} ادى الى صدامـات بـين الطرفـين مـن جهة ورجـال مكافـحـة الشغب «الامن المركزي»

'There were renewed riots last week in some of the cities of Upper Egypt – Sohag, Bani Suef, Asyut – with clashes between certain extremist Islamic groups and a number of Christians, {which} led to

clashes between the two sides on the one hand, and members of the riot
police, the Central Security [on the other] ...' (ch. 14, 4d)

وانطلقت جماعة الإخوان المسلمين في دعوتها من التراث الديني
المقدس الذي يصعب على الاتجاهات الفكرية الأخرى أن تنافسه كما
اعتمدت في تحليلاتها للأحداث على رؤية بسيطة تتفق مع فطرة
الغالبية العظمى من الجماهير والتي اعتمدت على تحليل كل ما
يدور من صراعات في مختلف المجالات وعلى كافة الأصعدة المحلية
والعالمية باعتبارها أشكالاً متعددة لرغبة أعداء الإسلام في تحطيم
الإسلام والمسلمين {الأمر الذي} ساعد على توسيع عضوية جماعة
الإخوان المسلمين بصورة لم يسبق لها مثيل بالنسبة لحزب
عقائدي في مصر ..

'The Muslim Brotherhood based itself in its propaganda on the holy
religious heritage which it was difficult for other ideological tendencies
to compete with. It also relied on a simplistic vision which accorded
with the simple nature of the great majority of the people, and which
relied on the analysis of all the surrounding conflicts in various areas
and all levels as so many forms of the desire of the enemies of Islam to
destroy Islam and the Muslims, {which} helped to increase the
membership of the Muslim Brotherhood in a manner unprecedented in
relation to any ideologically based party in Egypt.' (ch. 14, 11b)

As these two examples show, the tendency for Arabic sentences to be much longer
than English ones often means that phrases beginning with الأمر الذي are better
translated into English as separate sentences. Thus in the first example above one
might replace ', which led to clashes' with '. This led to clashes', and in the second
example, one might replace ', which helped to increase' by '. This helped to
increase'. From the point of view of Arabic grammar, however, the الامر الذي
phrase is part of a single sentence. Another alternative in English would be to
substitute for 'which' the phrase 'something which'; this usage bears a close
resemblance to the Arabic الامر الذي.

Occasionally, one comes across other nouns than أمر used as the antecedent to
the relative clause. In the following, for instance, أساس is used:

.. وتزوج قسم كبير منهم بنساء من أهل البلاد، الأساس الذي كون
وعلى مدى القرون المقبلة هوية المجتمع الأندلسي.

'... a large group of them intermarried with the womenfolk of the
existing population, which formed over the coming centuries the
identity of Hispano–Arabic society.' (ch. 12, 5a)

As in the previous two examples, in a more elegant translation one might replace ', which formed over the coming centuries ...' by a separate sentence, beginning along the lines, 'Over the coming centuries, this formed ...'. Alternatively, another type of subordinating structure might be used such as '..., thus forming over the coming centuries'. Note that الأساس here means 'the basis' (as might be expected), i.e. the fact that a large group of them intermarried with the womenfolk of the existing population is summed up as the 'basis' for the identity of Hispano–Arabic society, rather than simply a 'thing' or 'matter' (أمر). This is important for the meaning of the Arabic, although it is difficult to convey in an English translation.

(d) إذ

The word إذ is given in the dictionary as meaning 'as', 'when', 'since', 'because'. It is typically followed by a verb. For example:

الا ان ثمـة 6 احـزاب اخـرى سـيكون مـن حـقـهـا ممارسـة الدعـاية الانتخابية لبـرامجها ومرشحيها عبر وسائل الاعلام الرسـمية وفقاً لقانـون الانتخـابـات، {اذ} تقدمـت بـأكثر مـن 15 مرشـحـا.

'There are, however, six other parties which will have the right to put out electoral propaganda regarding their programmes and candidates via the official media in accordance with the electoral law, since they have put forward more than fifteen candidates.' (ch. 15, 4b)

وذلك الاختـيـار هـو مـايتكرر التـأكيد عليـه ... ، {اذ} لا يـخلو خطـاب او حديث من احاديثه من الاصرار على المضي في هذا التـوجه ..

'This choice is repeatedly emphasised ..., such that no speech or interview of his omits to insist on the pursuance of this orientation ...' (ch. 15, 11)

.. أن نصيب ابن البيـطار كان عظيمـا في الفقرات التـي احتـواها كتابه، {اذ} نجد مائتي دواء جديد ..

'... that Ibn al-Baytar's own contribution to the sections included in his book was enormous; for we find two hundred new remedies ...' (ch. 19, 11)

وتلا الفتح العسكري فتح لغوي {اذ} انتشرت العربية في أنحائه ..

'The military conquest was followed by a linguistic conquest; [for] Arabic spread in the conquered areas ...' (ch. 20, 4b)
to Arabic.' (ch. 20, 4b)

Occasionally إذ is followed by a noun. For example:

ولا يصدُقُ دفاعُهم وذيادُهم إلا إذا كانوا عصبيّةً ... {إذ} نُعْرةُ كلِّ
واحدٍ على نَسَبه وعصبيّته أهمُّ ..

'They can only be properly defended and protected if they are a group possessing social solidarity ... For the clamour which each one of them makes in battle on account of his lineage and tribal solidarity is more important ...' (ch. 13, 6a)

Normally, when a noun follows immediately, the form إذ أنَّ is used rather than إذ on its own. The form إذ أنَّ is, predictably, also used with a following pronoun suffix. Examples are:

.. يتعلق بالموقف الذي سيتخذه حسني مبارك المرشح الأوحد
لخلافة السادات إزاء إسرائيل، {إذ} أنه لم يقم قط بزيارة للكيان
الصهيوني.

'... is dependent on the attitude which will be taken towards Israel by Husni Mubarak, the sole candidate to succeed Sadat. Mubarak has not yet paid a visit to the Zionist entity.' (ch. 16, 4b)

وقد أسفرت عملية الهبوط الاضطراري عن مقتل افراد طاقم
الطائرة الثلاثة {إذ} ان الطائرة هبطت على جسمها بينما كانت
عجلاتها غير مفرودة .

'The emergency landing operation led to the death of the three–man crew of the aircraft, as the aeroplane was forced to land on its body while the wheels were not lowered [lit: 'not detached'].' (ch. 16, 11)

The existence of إذ أنَّ would suggest the possibility of using this form in order to give a subsequent emphatic nominal clause (cf. ch. 2, 7a; ch. 13, 7aii). The three above examples do not, however, seem to display emphatic function for the noun or pronoun suffix following إذ أنَّ, and, in some cases at least, the form إذ أنَّ is perhaps best regarded as a stylistic variant of إذ followed by the verb.

At the start of this section, إذ was glossed as meaning 'as', 'since', 'because'. In the various examples involving إذ discussed in this section, however, إذ is translated into English in different ways: 'since', 'such that', 'for', 'thus', 'as', 'and'. In the example .. يتعلق بالموقف الذي سيتخذه حسني مبارك المرشح الأوحد لخلافة السادات إزاء إسرائيل، إذ أنه لم يقم قط بزيارة للكيان الصهيوني., there is no lexical (word) translation of إذ; the English translation starts a new sentence, in effect translating the words إذ أنه by the proper name 'Mubarak'.

In other cases an appropriate English translation may seem even more distant from the Arabic. For example, the most obvious English translation of إذ in the following is the word 'where':

.. بينما يعد حزب الرابطة المنافس الاقوى في محافظتي شبوة
وحضرموت {اذ} يواجه المؤتمر الشعبي، والاشتراكي، والاصلاح
بنحو 20 مرشحًا، حيث يتمتع بنفوذ قوي.

'... while the League Party is regarded as the most powerful contender
in the Provinces of Shabwa and Hadramawt where it faces the Popular
Congress, the Socialist Party and the *Islah* with around twenty
candidates ...' (ch. 15, 4b)

The variety of English translation equivalents of the word اِذ might give the
impression that اِذ has a rather vague and extended range of uses in Arabic. In fact
this impression of variety is more a function of the different usages of English and
Arabic than a demonstration that اِذ has a large variety of meanings. A closer
examination of the examples involving اِذ quoted in this section shows that in all
these cases اِذ serves the same function; in all cases the statement after اِذ provides a
logical justification for the statement which precedes it.

(e) حيث

Somewhat similar to اِذ is حيث. In fact, حيث is more problematic than اِذ partly
because حيث does have a variety of different meanings. One usage of حيث is as
the second element in a compound phrase. Forms include من حيث 'in terms of',
'in respect of' (as a preposition), 'from where (as a conjunction), بحيث 'inasmuch
as', 'in such a manner that' (conjunction), الى حيث 'to where' (conjunction). For
example:

والاستفادة من جميع الدروس السابقة، {من حيث} تطوير
الايجابيات مثل وقف الحرب ..

'... to make use of all previous lessons in terms of developing positive
features such as putting an end to the war ...' (ch. 16, 5c)

وقد وضعت وزارة السياحة السورية خطة لتطوير المناطق
السياحية والاثرية في الجمهورية العربية السورية {بحيث} تشمل
مناطق الاصطياف الجبلية والساحلية والاثرية ..

'The Syrian Ministry of Tourism has drawn up a plan to develop the
touristic and historical regions in the Syrian Arab Republic, in such a
way as to include mountainous, coastal and historical summer resorts
...' (ch. 18, 11)

ثم ذهب إلى أصحابه فرافقهم {إلى حيث} كان يذهب معهم في كلّ
يوم ..

'Then he went to his friends and accompanied them to the place where
he used to go with them every day ...' (ch. 19, 5d)

Fairly commonly, حيث is used on its own to express an essentially non–logical place relationship, 'where':

هجر الأندلس وأقام بالقاهرة {حيث} انصرف إلى ممارسة الطب ..

'He left Spain and settled in Cairo where he took up the practice of medicine ...' (ch. 12, 4avii)

.. وبعد رحلة طويلة استقر في مصر {حيث} انصرف الى خدمة سلطانها الايوبي الملك الكامل ..

'After a long journey, he settled in Egypt where he went into the service of its ruler, King al-Kamil ...' (ch. 19, 11)

وكان اثناء اقامته في مصر يقوم برحلات علمية عديدة انتهى في احداها الى الاستقرار في دمشق، {حيث} واصل نشاطه العلمي حتى وفاته سنة 646 هـ – 1248 م.

'During his stay in Egypt, he undertook a number of scientific journeys, during one of which he came to settle in Damascus, where he continued his scientific studies until his death in 645 AH / 1248 AD.' (ch. 19, 11)

More typically حيث has the logical sense of 'as', 'since', 'because'. The usage of حيث is very similar to that of إذ, in that the statement introduced by حيث substantiates the previous statement. حيث in the logical sense is also normally followed by a verbal clause:

فلا عجب أن تترك آثارها في تلك البلاد بعد أن انتهت دولة الأندلس، وربما قبل ذلك {حيث} كانت الممالك المسيحية في شمال إسبانيا تقتدي بملوك الأندلس الإسلامية وتضم إلى قصورها وعروشها مئات من المطربين ..

'... it is not surprising that it should leave its influence on that country after the end of the Spanish Islamic state, and possibly before that, such that the Christian kingdoms in northern Spain copied the Spanish Islamic kings and attracted to their castles and thrones hundreds of singers ...' (ch. 12, 11)

كانت محافظات الصعيد الثلاث ... قد تحولت الى نيران مشتعلة، {حيث} تم احراق كنيسة وجامع ..

'.. the three provinces of Upper Egypt ... had been transformed into a raging inferno; [for] a church and a mosque had been burnt down ...' (ch. 14, 4c)

وقد فاز حزب جبهة القوى الاشتراكية الذي يتزعمه حسين اية
احمد بالمركز الثاني في الانتخابات بعد جبهة الانقاذ الاسلامية
{حيث} احرز ٢٦ مقعدا فقط .

'The Socialist Forces Front led by Hocine Aït-Ahmed was second in the
elections after the Islamic Salvation Front, gaining only 26 seats.' (ch.
15, 5c)

ويبدو ان رحلته كانت علمية تطبيقية {حيث} كان ينصرف في كل
بلد يزوره الى دراسة اعشابه ونباتاته ..

'It appears that his visit was scientific and practical, since in every
country he visited, he turned his attention to a study of its herbs and
plants ...' (ch. 19, 11)

Sometimes it is not particularly clear whether the relationship expressed by حيث is
logical or locational. For example:

.. بينما يعد حزب الرابطة المنافس الاقوى في محافظتي شبوة
وحضرموت اذ يواجه المؤتمر الشعبي، والاشتراكي، والاصلاح بنحو
20 مرشحًا، {حيث} يتمتع بنفوذ قوي.

'... while the League Party is considered the most powerful contender
in the Provinces of Shabwa and Hadramawt, where it faces the Popular
Conference, the Socialist Party and the *Islah*, with around twenty
candidates, where/such that it enjoys significant influence.' (ch. 15, 4b)

وهذا يعكس الواقع السياسي في الجزائر {حيث} تشكل جبهة
القوى الاشتراكية قوة في ارضية الجزائر منذ زمن بعيد .

'This reflects the realities of the political situation in Algeria,
where/such that the Socialist Forces Front has represented a force in its
area of Algeria for a long time.' (ch. 15, 5c)

Sometimes the English translation may even suggest a sense other than 'where' or
a logical relationship (although this is properly to be regarded as feature of the way
English works, rather than what is actually expressed in the Arabic). For example:

كما ان طبيعة العلاقات التجارية في المنطقة قد تغيرت نسبيا بعد
استقلال دول شبه القارة الهندية عام ١٩٤٧، {حيث} دخلت هذه
الدول مرحلة جديدة ..

'... the nature of commercial relations altered somewhat following the
independence of the states of the Indian sub–continent in 1948, when
these states entered a new phase ...' (ch. 18, 5b)

تقع الجمهورية العربية السورية على الساحل الشرقي للبحـر
الابيض المتوسط، {حيث} يحدها من الشمال تركيا ..

'The Syrian Arab Republic lies on the west coast of the Mediterranean,
and is bounded/being bounded to the north by Turkey ...' (ch. 18, 11)

As a conjunction, حيث may also be followed by a nominal clause. The following
are examples in which حيث means 'where':

.. وأنه كانت تقـام حفـلات مـن تلك القصـور في مكان يُعد لذلك
{حيث} الأمير والملك في ديوانه بينمـا يكون المطربون والموسيقيـون
في المقابل تفصل بينهما ستارة خفيفة ..

'... and parties used to be held in those castles in a place prepared for
that purpose, where the king was in his *diwan* while the singers and
musicians were opposite, with a light curtain separating them ...' (ch.
12, 11)

.. هربوا إلى الداخل {حيث} الطرقُ الوعرةُ والجبالُ ..

'... they fled into the interior, where there were rough tracks and
mountains ...' (ch. 12, 11)

This last example is particularly interesting because what follows حيث is a
noun–phrase (in fact a complex noun phrase consisting of a noun and an adjective
الطرق الوعرة plus a second noun الجبال conjoined to the first noun and adjective
with و). This noun phrase, however, is functioning as a clause. This can be seen
from the fact that حيث is not a preposition, and that the following nouns and
adjectives الجبالُ and الطرقُ الوعرةُ are in the nominative not the genitive.

The following are examples of حيث followed by a simple nominal clause in
which حيث is a substantiates the previous statement:

ما بقي هو الآلات التي ظلت تحتفظ بطابعها الأندلسي لوقت طويل
مـثل العـود والماندولين {حيث} هناك مـخطوطات ... تضم رسـومـًا
لهذه الآلات ..

'... what remains is these instruments which continued to preserve their
Andalusian character for a long time, such as the Oud and the mandolin;
for there are manuscripts ... which contain pictures of these instruments
...' (ch. 12, 11)

فإنها لم تتوان في إعلان رفضها لكافة المؤسسات السياسية
الأخرى كالدستور والبرلمان والأحزاب {حيث} لا دستور إلا القرآن
كما أن البرلمان مخصص للصراع الحزبي ..

'... it was not slow to announce its rejection of all other political institutions such as the constitution, the parliament and the political parties; for there is no constitution but the Qur'an, and the parliament is devoted to political struggle ...' (ch. 14, 11b)

The phrase حيث أنَّ followed by a nominal sentence is also used as a substantiator. Thus:

وفي الوقت نفسه ندد حزب الطليعة الاشتراكي بنتائج الانتخابات ودعا الى الغائها فورا {حيث انها} تتعارض ... مع المصالح العليا للجزائر .

'At the same time, the Socialist Vanguard Party criticised the results of the elections and called for their immediate annulment on the basis that they conflict with the supreme interest of Algeria.' (ch. 15, 5c)

As with إذ, in these examples at least, there does not seem to be a particular sense of emphasis associated with the use of حيث أنَّ or حيث followed by a nominal clause (cf. ch. 2, 7a; ch. 13, 7aii).

8. Aural Arabic texts 1

Listen to the following conversation between Dr Mu'nis and Dr Arafat about Muslim Spain from the BBC programme معرض الرأي, then complete exercises i. and ii. below. (Note that the quality of the original recording is not as good as most of the other aural texts.)

i Answer the following comprehension questions in Arabic.

١ – أين يعمل الدكتور وليد عرفات؟

٢ – ما هو بالتحديد الموضوع الذي يناقشه الأستاذان؟

٣ – لا يقبل الدكتور مؤنس أن العرب حكموا إسبانيا. فكيف يصف الوجود العربي في الأندلس؟

٤ – متى انتهى الوجود العربي في إسبانيا؟

٥ – ما هو بالتحديد الموضوع الذي يناقشه الدكتور عرفات؟

٦ – ما هي المقارنة التي يقدّمها الأستاذ عرفات بين الطلاب الغربيين في العصور الوسطى والطلاب العرب اليوم؟

٧ – أين تأسست أول مدرسة للدراسات الشرقية؟ ومتى؟

٨ – ما هي الموادّ التي درسها الغربيون في الأندلس؟

٩ – ماذا ترجم « Adelard of Bath »؟ – وإلى أي لغة؟

١٠. –ماذا ترجم « Gerard of Cremona »؟

١١ –بماذا تتعلق كلمة « الجيب » في الرياضيات؟

١٢ –متى تُوفي الغافقي؟

١٣ –ماذا جمع الغافقي؟ في أي لغات؟

١٤ –في أي موضوعين كتب ابن البيطار؟

١٥ –إلى أين ذهب الفيلسوف اليهودي ابن ميمون بعد أن أُضطرّ إلى الخروج
من الأندلس؟

١٦ –من هو ابن العربي؟

١٧ –ماذا ترجم « Robert of Chester »؟ وإلى أي لغة؟

ii Transcribe Dr Mu'nis's initial comments in Arabic, from the first instance of يا
دكتـور مـؤنـس تفضـل until, and including, بنهاية القصـة (note that the
broadcaster interrupts twice with the word لطيف. You do not need to include
this in your transcription).

9. Aural Arabic texts 2

(a) Listen to the following text from حصـاد الشهر, no. 7, side 2, item 3, دين
الغرب للعرب في الموسيقى, then complete exercises i. and ii. below.

i   Answer the following questions in English.

1. How many instruments introduced by the Arabs into Spain are listed in the text?
2. What was Seville the centre of?
3. What was Cordoba the centre of?
4. Who presided over the debate mentioned in the passage?
5. According to Averroes (Ibn Rushd), what happened if a scholar died in Seville?
6. According to Averroes, what happened if a musician died in Cordoba?
7. When, according to the text, did the Arabs conquer Spain?
8. What activity is mentioned as having been pursued in Toledo?
9. When did 'Villancico' singing become widespread in Spain?
10. What was the musical achievement of the Arabs of Granada?
11. What, according to the text, are the emotional characteristics of Fado music?
12. How does Dr Husayn Mu'nis describe Fado music?

ii   Fill in the gaps in the following text.

أدخـل ـــــــــــ ـــــــــــ ـــــــــــ إلى ـــــــــــ ـــــــــــ

إيبـيـريا ـــــــــــ ـــــــــــ مـن الآلات الموسـيـقـيـة

ـــــــــــ ـــــــــــ ـــــــــــ ـــــــــــ .

———————— ———— و ———— التي ———— ————

أسـمـاؤهـا ———— في ———— المشتقات من تصنيف

اسـيـدور ———— ———— ————

———— والتي ———— تُعْرَف ————

———— بـ———— الآتيـة: «الدوف» ————

———— الدف، «الجبابة» ———— ———— الشبابة،

«البـوغند» البـوق، «النفيل» النفيـر، «التبل» ————،

«كنون» ———— ————، «اندرت» البندير أو الطنبور، «سوناخس

دي السوفار» سنوج ———— أو ———— ————، «نكير» نقارة،

«لـوت» ————، «ريبك» ———— ———— و.

———— ———— ———— ———— إشبيليا

———— ———— كما ———— قرطبة ———— ————

———— ———— ابن سعيد: «وجرت ————

يدي منصور بن عبد المؤمن ————

———— أبي الوليد ابن رشد و———— أبي

بكر ابن زهر»، فـ———— ابن رشد لابن زهر ————

———— ———— ———— «مـا ————

———— إذا ———— بـ

———— فأُريدَ بيعُ ———— حُملت ———— قرطبة

وإذا ———— ———— مطرب

بـقـرطـبـة ———— تركـتـه ————

‫إشبيليا ». إن ــــ الأندلس ــــ ــــ‬

‫يُدخلوا معهم ــــ‬

‫زالت تحمل في ــــ ــــ أسماءها ــــ‬

‫ــــ بـل ــــ جلبـوا ــــ‬

‫في الموسيقى ــــ و ــــ‬

‫إلى ــــ ــــ‬

‫طليطلة ــــ ــــ منها‬

‫في ــــ ــــ. وثمـة أوجـه شبـه ــــ‬

‫الأزجال ــــ و ــــ‬

‫الذي ذاع في ــــ‬

‫و ــــ « فيلانجيكو » ــــ جعل بعض‬

‫النـوعين ــــ ،‬

‫أن ــــ‬

‫مـا يوحي بأن ــــ في‬

‫غرناطة ــــ أيدي‬

‫النصارى ــــ و ــــ‬

‫و ــــ و ــــ‬

‫الهجائية ــــ‬

‫على ــــ الإصبع من القيـثار. إن‬

البــرتغال ــــــــــــــــ ـــــــــــ ـــــــــــ ــــــــ ـــــــــ

ـــــــــــ ــــــــــ ـــــــــ يحرص على ـــــــــ ـــــــــ ــــــــ

البــرتغـالي ـــــــــــ ــــــــــ ـــــــــ من ـــــــــــ ـــــــــ

ـــــــــ القيثارة وهو ـــــــــ عــازف ـــــــــ ـــــــــ

يشوبه ـــــــــ ـــــــــ ويُعرف بالبرتغالية ـــــــــ ـــــــــ

« فــادو » و ـــــــــ ـــــــــ تحريف للفظ ـــــــــ

ـــــــــ إن. ـــــــــ ـــــــــ ـــــــــ ـــــــــ

البرتغالي ـــــــــ ـــــــــ ـــــــــ

هو ـــــــــ ـــــــــ ـــــــــ حسين مؤنس حداء

ـــــــــ والعصور ـــــــــ ـــــــــ ـــــــــ

ـــــــــ غلاف ـــــــــ ـــــــــ.

(b) Listen to the following piece of music from حصــاد الشــهر, no. 2, side 2, item 2, مقطع من موشـح أندلسي.

10. Written English texts

Using constructions and vocabulary encountered in the Arabic texts above as far as possible, translate the following text from Lewis, *The Arabs in History*, pp. 140–1, into idiomatic Arabic.

> The Arabs left their mark on Spain – in the skills of the Spanish peasant and craftsman and the words with which he describes them, in the art, architecture, music and literature of the peninsula, and in the science and philosophy of the mediaeval West which they had enriched by the transmission of the legacy of antiquity faithfully guarded and increased. Among the Arabs themselves the memory of Muslim Spain survived among the exiles in North Africa, many of whom still bear Andalusian names and keep the keys of their houses in Cordova and Seville hanging on their walls in Marrakesh and in Casablanca. In more recent times visitors to Spain from the East, like the Egyptian poet Ahmad Shawqi and the Syrian scholar Muhammad Kurd Ali, have reminded the Arabs of the Orient of the great achievements of their Spanish

brothers and restored the memory of Spanish Islam to its rightful place
in the national consciousness of the Arabs.

11. Précis
Read the following piece about the music of Islamic Spain from مجلة الشرق
الاوسط Feb. 3–9, 1993, then produce a précis in Arabic.

إذا كانت تلك المنطقة استوعبت تلك الفنون وأعادتها إلى الوطن
الأم في ثوب جديد، فلا عجب أن تترك آثارها في تلك البلاد بعد أن
انتهت دولة الأندلس، وربما قبل ذلك حيث كانت الممالك المسيحية
في شمال إسبانيا تقتدي بملوك الأندلس الإسلامية وتضم إلى
قصورها وعروشها مئات من المطربين والمطربات والموسيقيين
الذين ذاعت شهرتهم، وكان أكثرهم عربًا أو تتلمذوا على يد العرب،
وقد التقينا الباحثة الاسبانية مانويلا كورتيس التي تحاضر في
هذه المادة في العديد من المؤتمرات التخصصية في الموسيقى بشكل
عام والاندلسية بشكل خاص، وتعد حاليًا بحثًا متخصصًا في
التأثيرات الأندلسية في الموسيقى الإسبانية المعاصرة.

تقول مانويلا كورتيس إنه بداية من القرن التاسع وطوال
القرن العاشر الميلادي بدأت تأخذ الموسيقى طريقها إلى قصور
الأندلس وبشكل خاص في عهد عبد الرحمن الأول الذي كانت
قصوره تضم جواري مطربات تعلَّمْن في مدارس الطرب الحجازية
وفي الحيرة والموصل، وكن يحيين الأعياد الرسمية للأسرة الحاكمة.
ثم جاء عبد الرحمن الثاني فرفع من قيمة الطرب والموسيقى بعد
أن استضاف أشهر موسيقي في تاريخ الموسيقى العربية
«زرياب» الذي كان أول من تجرأ على تطوير الموسيقى العربية
التي كانت تعتبر آلة العود من أهم الآلات، فقام بإضافة الوتر
الخامس إليه ليطور إمكانيات أدائه بعد أن كانت هذه الآلة تقتصر
فقط على أربعة أوتار لعصور طويلة.

وكما يقول المؤرخ العربي الأندلسي أن وصول زرياب إلى

الأندلس كان نقطة انطلاق في فنون الموسيقى والغناء، فقد جاء بآلات التخت الموسيقي الشرقي وأكثر من ألف أغنية شرقية كان يحفظها. ومن ذلك الوقت بدأ تدريس الموسيقى والغناء في الأندلس بعد أن كانت الجواري يتم تدريبهن في مدارس الشرق العربي. وكانت قرطبة هي مدينة المدارس الموسيقية التي وصلت شهرتها إلى الممالك المسيحية التي كانت تستدعي مطربي وموسيقيي تلك المدارس لإحياء أعيادها واحتفالات قصورها. وفي عصر ملوك الطوائف كان الملوك في الممالك الإسلامية يهدون إلى أصدقائهم من ملوك الممالك المسيحية الجواري المغنيات والموسيقيين كنوع من التفاخر. وكان ملوك الطوائف لهم مطربوهم وكانت بعض قصورهم تضم أكثر من مئة مطرب في الوقت نفسه، وبعض المؤرخين يؤكدون أن بعض القصور كان بها أكثر من مئتين، وأنه كانت تقام حفلات من تلك القصور في مكان يُعد لذلك حيث الأمير والملك في ديوانه بينما يكون المطربون والموسيقيون في المقابل تفصل بينهما ستارة خفيفة تخفي أو تفصل بين المطربين والأمير.

لكن بعد سقوط غرناطة، هجر الموسيقيون الأندلس إلى المغرب والجزائر وتونس بحثًا عن أغنياء الأندلس الذين هاجروا إلى تلك البلاد، وحملوا معهم الموسيقى الكلاسيكية الرسمية، ونظرًا لعدم وجود نوتة موسيقية مكتوبة فقد ذهبت الموشحة بموسيقاها إلى شمال أفريقيا وتوزعت الموسيقى الأندلسية في المغرب بينما استقر الغناء الغرناطي في الجزائر واستقبلت تونس المالوف فيما احتفظت مصر بالموشحة وأشهر مقاطعها الوصلة، وكذلك في سوريا التي احتفظت بالموشحة أيضًا.

وتقول مانويلا كورتيس إن البحث عن الموسيقى الأندلسية يتكون من شقين: الشعر والموسيقى، الشعر لا يزال في المخطوطات محفوظًا، بينما طريقة العزف والموسيقى تناقلها المطربون والموسيقيون جيلاً عن جيل وبقيت في شمال أفريقيا، لذلك تعتقد

الباحثة الإسبانية أن الموجود منها حاليًا لا نستطيع أن نتعامل معه على أنه الموسيقى الأندلسية كما كانت قبل خمسة قرون.

وتتساءل الباحثة عن ما بقي من الموسيقى العربية في الممالك المسيحية وتجيب على التساؤل بأن ما بقي هو الآلات التي ظلت تحتفظ بطابعها الأندلسي لوقت طويل مثل العود والماندولين حيث هناك مخطوطات تعود إلى زمن الفونسو العاشر العلامة الذي تميز بعشقه للعلوم، وهذه المخطوطات تضم رسومًا لهذه الآلات وطرق العزف عليها، وكلها محفوظة في عدة مكتبات منها «الاسكوريال» والمكتبة الوطنية بمدريد وكذلك بمكتبة مخطوطات طليطلة. وهناك أكثر من ٧٥ ألف مرسومة بطرق أدائها.

أما البحوث التي جرت حول اكتشاف تأثيرات الموسيقى العربية في الموسيقى الإسبانية في ما بعد عصر الأندلس والموسيقى المعاصرة بشكل خاص الفلامنكو والموسيقى الشعبية تقول مانويلا كورتيس إن هناك العديد من الدراسات التي تؤكد هذه التأثيرات توصل إليها باحثون معاصرون مثل باتروثينيو غارثيا باريوسيو وخرمان ذي فالدارما حللوا هذه الموسيقى وقارنوها بالموسيقى الأندلسية في المغرب بحثًا عن أوجه التشابه. فيما قام الباحث الأب باريا ببحث نوبة إصبهان. وتشير الباحثة إلى أنه ربما كانت التأثيرات في موسيقى الفلامنكو أكثر وضوحًا رغم عدم خضوع هذه الموسيقى للبحث المتأني الذي يحلل ويتوصل إلى نتائج حاسمة، لكنها تقول إن ما بقي من المورسكيين بعد سقوط غرناطة هربوا إلى الداخل حيث الطرق الوعرة والجبال وأقاموا على هامش المجتمع وهو ما جمعهم على هذا الهامش مع الغجر وكانوا يقيمون معا احتفالاتهم حتى أنه صدرت قوانين تمنع هؤلاء من إقامة احتفالات في القرى تقلق السكان بل أن بعض هذه القرارات الرسمية منعت العزف على آلات معينة مثل الرباب والدف لأنها تثير ضجيجًا. لكنها تؤكد أن هناك تشابهًا بين

الاحتفالات الشعبية المعاصرة المتوارثة عن تلك الموسيقى مثل لعبة التحطيب في قادش الأندلسية المعاصرة وكذلك الفلامنكو الذي تعتبره الباحثة خليطًا من الثقافة الإسلامية والمسيحية.

12. Oral

الأندلس

(a) Individual students to present brief accounts in Arabic of i. الأندلس, ii. ابن زيدون .vii ,ابن حزم .vii ,ابن ميمون .iii ,رشد

(b) The presenters then ask the other students questions about their topic. The questions should be mainly, but not exclusively, factual. For example:

١ – ما هي الاندلس؟

٢ – متى فتح العرب الاندلس؟

٣ – كم سنة استقر العرب في الاندلس؟

٤ – ماذا فعل العرب بعد ان فتحوا الاندلس؟

٥ – ما هو اصل كلمة الاندلس؟

٦ – من الذي سماه الغرب «الشارح»، ولماذا؟

٧ – اين تقع طبرية ومَن من سكان الاندلس دُفن فيها؟

٨ – ماذا كونت الاندلس بعد استقلالها عن العباسيين؟

٩ – ما هي الاندلس اليوم؟

١٠ –لو ظل العرب يستقرون في الاندلس فكيف يا تُرى تطورت المنطقة؟

١٢ –هل زرت اسبانيا، وهل رأيت الآثار العربية فيها؟

١٣ –ماذا تعرف عن جغرافية الاندلس؟

(c) Open lecturer–led discussion on Islamic Spain.

13. Essay

Write an essay in Arabic of 200 words on the title تأثيـر العـرب علـى الحضـارة الإسبانية. Structure your essay around the following questions:

١ – متى فتح العرب الاندلس؟

٢ – ماذا فعلوا بعد فتحهم الاندلس؟

٣ – ماذا اسّس العرب من مدارس في الاندلس؟

٤ – ماذا احدثه العرب في مجال الطب في الاندلس؟

٥ – ما هي الموشحة وما هو الزجل؟

٦ – ماذا شهدت الموسيقى في الاندلس من احداث وتغييرات؟

٧ – الى اي درجة اثرت اللغة العربية على اللغة الاسبانية؟

13
Arab nationalism

1. Basic background material

(a) *Origins of Arab nationalism*

1798   Napoleon invades Egypt. Start of European colonialism in Arab world.

C19   Beginnings of modern education system in Arab world. Start of printing in Arabic on a wide scale. Development of periodicals and journals. Emergence of Islamic modernists such as Jamal al-Din al-Afghani, and the Egyptian Muhammad Abduh.

1908–1918   Young Turks, under leadership of nationalistic Turkish army officers, emerge as dominant element in Ottoman government. Arab elements begin to demand greater autonomy for Arab Ottoman provinces. Appearance of nationalist groups in Arab world on lines of Young Turks, such as Young Tunisians in Tunisia.

Early C.20   Opposition to British colonial rule in Egypt, and French rule in Tunisia and later Algeria and Morocco. Localised to particular country, rather than pan–Arab, and committed to achieving better access to education etc. within colonial framework, rather than political independence.

(b) *Arab independence and the rise of pan–Arabism*

1918   Following formal end of Ottoman sovereignty (north) Yemen achieves independence. Britain subsequently extends its rule in southern Arabian peninsula to Aden (south Yemen).

1919   With defeat of Ottoman Empire Britain gains control over Iraq and Palestine, and France over Syria and Lebanon under mandate established by Treaty of Versailles. France also controls most of N. Africa.

1919–1922   Nationalist uprising against British rule in Egypt. Uprising suppressed, but leads to creation of the nationalist Wafd party.

1923   Treaty of Lausanne establishes Turkish republic in Anatolia (and

	small adjoining part of Europe). Subsequent success of Atatürk has profound effect on Arab nationalists.
1924	Wahhabi Saudi ruler of Najd defeats Sherif Hussein of Mecca, ruler of Hijaz and establishes rule over both areas. (Kingdom of Saudi Arabia officially established, 1934).
1932	Iraq obtains full independence.
1933	Establishment of Young Egypt youth movement working for patriotic goals by paramilitary methods. Successor to Socialist Party of Egypt.
1934	Italian Fascist government conquers whole of Libya.
1936	Egypt obtains full independence; Britain keeps troops in Suez Canal Zone.
1941	Syria and Lebanon obtain full independence from France (although French troops remain in Syria until 1946).
1944, 1945	Conferences at Alexandria and Cairo result in formation of League of Arab States, by founder members Egypt, Syria, Lebanon, Transjordan, Iraq, Saudi Arabia, and (north) Yemen.
1947–1949	Palestine War leads to creation of state of Israel.
1951	Libya becomes independent.
1952	Following Britain's refusal to withdraw from Suez Canal, popular uprising in Cairo during which British installations are destroyed. In 23rd July Revolution, Free Officers' group seizes power, ousts King Farouk, and declares Egypt a republic. Nasser (Gamal Abd al-Nasir) emerges as leader, with pan–Arabist ambitions.
1956	Sudan, Morocco and Tunisia achieve independence.
1956	Egypt nationalises Suez Canal. Under secret agreement between Britain, France and Israel, Israel invades Egypt to Canal Zone. Britain and France occupy Canal Zone under pretext of forcing both Israel and Egypt to withdraw from Canal Zone. The 'tripartite aggression' foiled by American insistence on withdrawal of British, French and Israelis. Invading troops replaced by UN peacekeepers. Height of pan–Arabism in Arab world.
1958	Establishment of United Arab Republic (UAR) comprising Egypt and Syria. Emergence of Ba'th Party as significant force in Syria, and in Iraq following revolution there.

(c) *Arab disunity and the decline of pan–Arabism*

1961	Collapse of UAR following coup in Syria.
1962	Following bloody eight–year war Algeria obtains independence from France.
1963	Ba'th Party seizes power in Syria.
1962–1967	Egyptian army intervenes indecisively in civil war in Yemen.
1967	People's Democratic Republic of Yemen (Aden) achieves

	independence from Britain following guerilla war. New government closely allied to Soviet Union.
1967	Israel attacks Egypt, Syria and Jordan. Occupies remainder of Palestine, Golan Heights and Sinai. PLO emerges as significant force in Arab politics.
1968	Military coup brings Ba'th Party to power in Iraq.
1970	Death of Nasser. Succeeded by Sadat (Anwar al-Sadat), who is at first regarded as Nasser's spiritual heir.
1970	Domination of Syrian Ba'th party (which had held power since 1960s) by Alawi Shi'ite military, led by President Hafez al-Asad. Syrian Ba'th becomes widely viewed as an expression of factional interest.
1970	Civil war in Jordan between forces loyal to King Hussein (ethnic Jordanians), and Palestinian nationalists (refugee Palestinians) won by King Hussein.
1973	Egypt and Syria attack Israel. Despite failure to achieve military victory, war perceived as successful in Egypt in particular. Differences in aims between Syria and Egypt quickly emerge.
1975–1990	Civil war in Lebanon divides Arabs.
1975–present	Moroccan invasion and annexation of Western Sahara (formerly Spanish Sahara) brings Morocco into confrontation with Algeria.
1977	Sadat concludes separate peace with Israel (ratified in 1979). Egypt expelled from Arab League; felt to have abandoned pan–Arab cause. Increasing disunity between 'conservative' and 'radical' Arab regimes.
1979	Saddam Hussein becomes President of Iraq following internal Ba'th Party coup. Saddam executes all potential opponents and inaugarates reign of terror. Iraqi government increasingly becomes dominated by Saddam Hussein's immediate family and clan. Like Syrian Ba'th, Iraqi Ba'th becomes widely viewed as an expression of factional interest.
1979–1982	Virtual civil war in Syria between government and Muslim Brotherhood; culminates in Hamah massacre in which government troops kill between 10,000 and 30,000 inhabitants of city.
1980–1988	War between Iran and Iraq divides Arabs, with Saudi Arabia and Gulf states supporting Iraq and Syria supporting Iran.
1982	Israeli invasion of Lebanon. Impotence of Arab states in face of Israeli military power.
1985–present	Civil war in Sudan between Muslim mainly Arab north, and animist and Christian south. Increasing isolation of Sudanese regime from West, and most Arab states from late 1980s.
1989	Egypt readmitted to Arab League.
1990	North and South Yemen unite to form single state.

1991	Iraqi invasion of Kuwait. Arab disunity reflected in failure to find peaceful 'Arab solution'.
1992	American–led war against Iraq causes profound divisions in Arab world. Populations of most poor Arab countries side with Iraq against what is seen as Western imperialism. People and governments of Gulf states and Saudi Arabia back American–led anti–Iraqi forces. Governments of Egypt and Syria back Americans but without evident public support.
1994	Following breakdown of unity government in Yemen, army of former N. Yemen invades south, and occupies southern capital, Aden.

(d) *Trends in Arab nationalism*

(i) *Ba'thism*

Pan–Arab movement. Founded by Syrian Christian, Michel 'Aflaq (1910–1989). According to Ba'thism, Islam belongs not only to Arab Muslims but to all Arabs, who have the right to establish a single unified state. From 1950s onwards, Ba'thism became more explicitly socialist, appealing to intellectuals but also some parts of urban working class. Influential in Syria, Lebanon, Jordan, Iraq and Arabian Peninsula. By 1990s, appeal of Ba'thism severely damaged by association between Ba'th party and military regimes and Alawite and Tikriti minorities in Syria and Iraq.

(ii) *Nasserism*

Pan–Arab movement. Grew out of Nasser's experience of power. Incorporated reformist vision of Islam compatible with modernisation. Existing Egyptian nationalism expanded to incorporate view of Egypt as natural leader of entire Arab world. State ownership and redistribution of income used to generate mass support for regime. By 1990s and abandonment of Nasserist principles by Egyptian government, Nasserism virtually defunct.

(iii) *Other movements and parties*

Most other nationalist movements and parties in the Arab world are localised. Some are the party of government in an authoritarian set–tup, such as the National Liberation Front (FLN) in Algeria (until 1992), or the Neo–Destour in Tunisia. Some have local historical roots, such as the Wafd in Egypt, and others represent distinct sectional, including ethnic, interests, such as the Popular Forces Front in Morocco, which is in effect a Berber party. Most localised parties (if they are of Arab orientation), are mainly nationalist in the restricted sense of supporting the national interests of the state.

There are two major movements in the Arab world, which are in essence not nationalist. The first is the Communists. There have been moderately strong Communist parties in a number of Arab countries, including Sudan, Iraq and Lebanon, but since the fall of the Soviet Union in particular, Communism has tended to be eclipsed, and like the Communists of Eastern Europe a number of former Communist parties have renamed themselves and adopted policies more like those of the social–democratic parties of western Europe.

The other major non–nationalist movement is Islamic fundamentalism. The main Islamic fundamentalist group is the Muslim Brotherhood, which is active in almost all countries in the Arab world (although banned in many). Other groups include the outlawed Nahda in Tunisia, the Islamic Salvation Front (FIS) in Algeria, and the Shi'ite Hizbullah in Lebanon. (cf. ch. 14).

2. Additional reading

(a) Consider the following explanation of Ibn Khaldun's concept of عصبية, or social solidarity, by Charles Issawi, *An Arab Philosophy of History*, (London: John Murray, 1958), pp. 10–11.

> The core of Ibn Khaldun's general and political Sociology is his concept of *'asabia*, or Social Solidarity. Society is natural and necessary, since the isolated individual could neither defend himself against the more powerful beasts nor provide for his economic wants. But individual aggressiveness would make social life impossible unless curbed by some sanction. This sanction may be provided by a powerful individual's imposing his will on the rest – in this Ibn Khaldun anticipates Hobbes – or – and here he shows deeper insight than Hobbes – it may be provided by Social Solidarity. The need for a common authority generates the State, which is to Society as Form is to Matter, and as inseparable from it. Ibn Khaldun traces the origin of this Solidarity to the blood ties uniting the smaller societies, but is careful to point out that blood ties mean nothing unless accompanied by proximity and a common life, and that living together may generate as powerful a solidarity as kinship. Moreover, the relations between allies, between clients and patrons, and between slaves and masters, may all lead eventually to a wider solidarity.

(b) F. Gabrieli, *asabiyya*, in *Encyclopaedia of Islam*, new edition, (Leiden: Brill/London: Luzac & Co., 1960), p. 681.

(c) Hourani, *A History of the Arab Peoples*, pp. 308–10; pp. 340–5; pp. 401–11; pp. 453–8.

3. Key vocabulary

Taking the texts in this chapter as a starting point, draw up a list of vocabulary in the following fields:

(a) Colonialism.

(b) Nationalism.

(c) Revolution.

4. Written Arabic texts 1

(a) Read the following definitions of قوميّ and قوميّة, from المنجد في اللغة, p. 664, and قوميّة from المنجد العربي الأساسيّ, p. 1016; then, without looking at the original text, answer the question ما هي القومية العربية؟.

القَوميّ: المنتمي إلى مبدأ القومية

القَوميّة: مبدأ سياسي اجتماعي يُفضل معه صاحبه كل ما يتعلق بأمّته على سواه مما يتعلق بغيره.

قوميّة ج قوميّات: ١ صلة اجتماعية عاطفية تنشأ من الاشتراك في الوطن واللغة والتاريخ، ٢ دعوة إلى توحيد العرب تحت شعار «القومية العربية».

(b) Read the following text by عبد الله عبد الشكور from دراسات يمانية, p. 80, then complete exercises i. and ii. which follow. The September revolution referred to in the text was the revolution of 22nd September, 1962, which overthrew the last Yemeni Imam (theocratic ruler), محمد البدر, and led to the establishment of the Yemen Arab Republic in the northern part of Yemen.

إن كل ثورة ضد ظلم أو طغيان إنما هي أخت لكل ثورة ضد ظلم أو طغيان كائناً ما كان موقعها أو أرضها التي اشتعلت فيها فالظلم هو الظلم، قاساه أبيض أو عاناه أسود، ونحن حين نقدر ثورة قامت من أجل صالح الشعب، وحريته وحقه في الحياة، ليس ذلك الموقف سياسة وإنسانية، وإنما هو دين كذلك، ومن هنا فإنني أود أن يكون واضحاً أن كلمتي هذه ليست بحثاً بالمعنى المنهجي، وإنما هي تحية إلى كل ثوراتنا العربية، بل الإفريقية التي كانت ثورة ٢٣ يوليو[1] لها السند القوي والتأييد الأخوي، والتضحية الصادقة، خاصة ثورة سبتمبر اليمنية التي أصبحت هي الأخرى آية على جهد الأحرار، وجهاد هؤلاء الذين قدموا كل شيء في سبيل أن يكون لشعبهم حياته وحاضره وغده.

Note
1. The revolution of 23rd July refers to the Egyptian revolution of 23rd July, 1952.

i Paraphrase the following phrases in Arabic, giving the sense intended in the text.

١ – كائناً ما كان موقعها

٢ – قاساه أبيض أو عاناه أسود

٣ – هي الأخرى

٤ – الأحرار

ii In Arabic, explain the writer's argument from the beginning of the text until
وإنما هو دين كذلك.

(c) Read the following text by قسطنطين زريق from معنى الوعي القومي, pp.
36–7, which describes what it is to be a nationally conscious Arab, then
translate the text into idiomatic English. قسطنطين زريق was an early
intellectual proponent of pan–Arabism, along with ساطع الحصري and ميشال
عفلق. معنى الوعي القومي was written in 1939.

يقــوم الوعـي القـومـي أولاً عـلى مـعـرفـة مـاضي الأمـة مـعـرفـة
صحيـحـة، وفـهم العـوامـل الطبـيـعـية والتاريـخـيـة التي كـونتـها
حتى جعلتـها في حالتها الحاضرة، والكشف عـن مصادر قـواها
الروحية الخاصة التي تمتـاز بها عـن غيـرها مـن الأمم. فالعـربي
الـواعي قـوميًا يعـرف من أين أتى، وكيف تحدّرت أمـته، ومـن أي
جـذور نبـتـت حـيـاتـه الحـاضـرة. يضـع يده على أصل الجنس
العـربي، ويتـابـعـه في شيـوعـه من الجزيرة إلى مـا حـولها مـن
البلـدان، ويسـايره في سيـادته على الأجناس الأخـرى وامتـزاجـه
بهـا، وفي مـا تكوّن من هذا الامـتـزاج من أمـة مـخـتلطة الدم
والجنس، مـوحّدة في مـا هـو أهم من هذا كـثـيـرًا في الارتبـاط
القـومـي، الا وهـو: اللغـة، والتقـاليـد، والجهـاد الماضي، والمصالـح
الحاضـرة والمقبلة. وهـو يعـرف، مـع هذا كله، مـا يقـولـه العلمـاء
الحديثـون عـن معـنى «الجنس» وعـن مـقدار مـا للوراثة مـن جهـة
والمحيـط مـن جهـة أخـرى مـن أثـر في تكوينـه، وعـن نوع عـلاقتـه
بـالقـومـيـة، وعـن الحركـات السـيـاسـيـة والمذاهـب الاجـتـمـاعـيـة
والفكريـة التي أثارتـها مشاكل «الجنس» في الشرق والغـرب.

5. **Written Arabic texts 2**

(a) Read the following newspaper text from الوطن May 8, 1988, which was
written during a period of rapprochement between North and South Yemen
before their apparently successful merger into a single state in 1990. Then
complete exercises i. and ii. which follow.

اتفاق اليمنين .. قوة للعرب

الاتفـاق الذي تم التـوصل اليـه بـين شطري اليمن لحل المسـائل
الحدودية المعلقة والاستثمار للنفط بين البلدين هو خطوة هـامة في
مسـيرة اليمـن بشطريه، وهو انتصـار لارادة العقل على الجـهل،
ولارادة المحبة على الكراهية، فـأهل عدن وأهل صنعـاء بحـاجة الى
العمل الوحدوي المشترك وبحـاجة ماسـة الى امـوال النفط من اجل
بناء وطنهم الذي قاسى الكثير وعانى الامـرين طيلة سنوات طويلة
من الحاجة والفاقة.

والجبهـة العربية لم تكن بحـاجـة الى نزف جـديد يضـاف الى
النزف العربي المستمر. لذلك قـوبل اتفـاق شطري اليمن بالتفـاؤل
والفرح مـن اقطار العروبة ومن الشعوب العربية التي قاست وتقاسي
كما قاسى اليمن من الفرقة والتناحر والاقتتال العدمي بين الاشقاء.

ان نفط اليمن هو قوة للعرب. وهو خير لشعب اليمن ولا يجوز
ان يكون الخير عامل فرقة وتناحر بين ابناء الوطن الواحد. بل ان
الاستثمار المشترك للنفط في المناطق المتنازع عليها سيضيف قوة
للروح الوحدوية التي يعيشـها ابناء اليمن، والذين يرون في وجـود
شطرين لوطن واحد كارثة وطنية وقومية.

ان يمنـاً فقيراً هو افضل الف مرة من وطن غني متقاتل، فدم ابناء
اليمن اغلى من النفط ووحدتهم وكرامتهم اهم من الدولارات. فكيف
اذا اتفق ابناء اليمن على الاستثمار المشترك لخيراتهم ووظفوا هذه
الخيرات لصالح شـعبهم ولاقامة تنمية وطنية ترفع من مسـتوى
معيشة الناس وتوفر لهم الحد الادنى من متطلبات الحياة الكريمة.

لذلك كله قـوبل اتفـاق شطري اليمن بالفرحـة والاغتبـاط في

صفوف الشعب اليمني والشعوب العربية وعلى امل ان يكون هذا الاتفاق فاتحة لاتفاقيات اخرى بين الشطرين تعيد للوطن اليمني المجزأ وحدته وللشعب اليمني شروط حياة كريمة ونظيفة .

i Divide the text up into its consituent sentences. Identify all the nominal sentences, i.e. all the sentences which begin with a noun, or a noun–equivalent (such as a nominal clause). Consider the rhetorical purposes of the use of nominal sentences in this text. Finally convert all the nominal sentences to equivalent verbal sentences.

ii Translate the text into idiomatic English.

(b) Read the following text by غالي شكري from مواويل الليلة الكبرى, p. 44, then complete exercises i. and ii. which follow. The fire of Cairo took place in Ismailiyya on 'Black Saturday', January 1952 following a massacre by the British army of over twelve auxiliary policemen. During the riots which took place on this day much of Cairo went up in flames. These riots eventually led to the seizure of power in July 1952 by a secret society of middle–rank Egyptian officers.

كم كتب عن « حريق القاهرة » وكم سيكتب. اتهم فيها جميع الناس، بمن فيهم أنا. ليكن، فأنا لست أبرئ نفسي مما وقع، ولكن على نحو آخر ومختلف عن التفسير البوليسي « للمؤامرة » كما دعوها. إذا كان المقصود بالاشتراك في حريق القاهرة يوم ٢٦ يناير ١٩٥٢ هو المشي في المظاهرات أو التحويض عليها أو الإمساك بالمواد المتفجرة وتحطيم دور السينما والملاهي، فأنا بريء من ذلك كله، ولا علاقة لي به. أما إذا كان المقصود هو اشتراك شعب كامل في تقويض نظام كامل للحكم، فإنني بالطبع أحد أبناء هذا الشعب.

ولكن الشعرة رفيعة جداً بين « الجريمة » و« الثورة ». وفي حريق القاهرة اختلطت الجريمة بالثورة، للدرجة التي تعذر معها على المؤرخين والأكاديميين والقانونيين

أن يحددوا بشكل نهائي من هو المسؤول أو المسؤولون عن
حريق القاهرة.

الوطنيون قالوا إن السراي والإنجليز هم الذين
أحرقوا عاصمة مصر. الشيوعيون أضافوا الإخوان
المسلمين وأحياناً « مصر الفتاة ». والبعض قال إن « الوفد »
متواطئ. وبعض البعض قال إنهم الضباط الأحرار.
وأجدني أقول مرة أخرى، ليكن. فالأهم من ذلك كله هو
وضع الحدود بين الجريمة والثورة. فليست هناك شرارة
واحدة لحريق القاهرة، بل أكثر.

وكنت مع الرجال في أواخر صيف ١٩٤٩ بدأنا ننفض
عنا رداء المصادفات والانفعالات والتشرذم، وشرعنا في
تكوين الخلية الرئيسية لتنظيم الضباط الأحرار حيث
اختاروني رئيساً كما سبق أن أشرت. وكنا نتابع
« الشرارات » التي راحت تندلع منذ نهاية الحرب في
فلسطين. تابعنا مثلاً انقلاب حسني الزعيم في سوريا،
وكان قد نجح في مارس من ذلك العام. كما تابعنا
إخفاقات فاروق المتتالية في تنصيب إحدى حكومات
الأقلية الدستورية، كذلك تابعنا موجة الاغتيالات الفردية
التي شاركت شخصياً في إحداها.

i Referring back to the original text, translate the following phrases and clauses into idiomatic Arabic.

1. I was accused of it (para. 1, line 1)
2. including me (para. 1, line 2)
3. so let it be (para. 1, line 2)
4. what is meant by (para. 1, line 4)
5. I have no connection with it (para. 1, line 7)
6. responsible for (para. 2, line 4)
7. it was the Palace and the English who burnt the capital of Egypt (para. 3, lines 1–2)
8. what is more important than all of that/this (para. 3, line 5)

9. in the latter part of the summer of 1949   (para. 4, line 1)
10. the Free Officers (para. 4, line 3)
11. as I have previously mentioned (para. 4, line 4)
12. minority constitutional governments (para. 4, line 8)

ii Translate the text into idiomatic English.

(c) Read the following text from الشرق الاوسط, July 23, 1994, then answer the
    questions which follow in English.

افلام للمناسبة ويوم عطلة
23 يوليو المصري:
يوم عادي واحتفال باهت
القاهرة: من محمد حربي

ربما باستثناء عرض بعض الافلام الخاصة بالمناسبة، يمكن القول ان
يوم 23 يوليو، وهو يوم ذكرى ثورة يوليو (تموز) يمر مثله مثل أي
يوم عادي آخر في حياة المصريين، لكن يظل، بالطبع، يوم عطلة
رسمية.

والملاحظ ان القاهرة احتفلت مبكرا هذه السنة بالذكرى الثانية
والاربعين لثورة 1952 التي تصادف اليوم، وذلك عندما دشن
الرئيس المصري الاحتفال بخطاب سياسي يوم اول من امس ركز
فيه على «اهمية الثورة في كتابة تاريخ سياسي جديد لمصر».

ويقتصر الاحتفال الرسمي بالثورة، التي قادها جمال عبد
الناصر، على منح المصريين يوم عطلة وعرض عدة افلام سينمائية
صنعت خصيصا لكتابة تاريخ الثورة فنياً ومنها «رد قلبي» الذي
اذاعه التلفزيون المصري على القناة الثالثة – والتي يقتصر البث
فيها على دائرة القاهرة الكبرى فقط – والذي كتب قصتة يوسف
السباعي الضابط الذي تولى منصب وزير الثقافة في العهد
الثوري. وكذا فيلم «في بيتنا رجل» الذي لعب بطولته النجم
المصري العالمي عمر الشريف، فيما تهتم أحزاب المعارضة في

سياق احتفالها بالمناسبة باقامة الندوات.

ولا يظهر المحللون السياسيون في القاهرة اندهاشا ازاء خفوت صوت الثورة في احتفالات ذكراها. فقد اعتادت مصر على مدى 20 عاما على احتفال بسيط للذكرى يضم المثلث التقليدي: خطاب الرئيس، والفيلم السينمائي، والعطلة.

فمنذ سنوات اختفت اغاني عبد الحليم حافظ (المطرب الراحل) الوطنية، خاصة بعد انتهاء حرب اكتوبر (تشرين الأول) 1973، وصدور السياسة الاقتصادية المعروفة بسياسة الانفتاح الاقتصادي ايام حكم الرئيس (الراحل) انور السادات.

وبعد 42 عاما من ثورة يوليو التي رفعت شعار الاشتراكية، والغت الاحزاب السياسية، تبدو مصر الآن مجتمعا شبه حزبي تعددي، عادت الى مسرحه السياسي قوى قديمة مثل «الوفد» الذي صار حزباً، و«الاخوان» الذين يعانون عدم الاعتراف الرسمي حتى الآن رغم دخولهم البرلمان، و«مصر الفتاة» الذي أصبحت حزبا باسم «العمل».

كما ان الاحتفال الباهت بذكرى الثورة المصرية يعكس نمو توجهات مغايرة لتلك التي طرحتها الثورة ازاء قضايا كثيرة، لاسيما قضية الصلح مع اسرائيل، إذا شهد هذا العام دخول الرئيس الفلسطيني ياسر عرفات الى غزة واريحا من القاهرة، في اطار الصلح الذي كانت ترفضه الثورة رغم قبول عبد الناصر لمبادرة روجرز.

1. What was the date of the Egyptian revolution?
2. What was the title of the Egyptian President's speech in commemoration of the revolution?
3. Where can the Third Channel be received?
4. Who is Yusuf al-Siba'i?
5. How was the event commemorated by opposition groups?
6. How has the revolution been traditionally celebrated over the past twenty years?
7. Who introduced the 'Open Door' economic policy?
8. Why is Egypt now describable as a 'quasi multi–party' society?

9. Which three opposition groups and parties are mentioned?
10. What is odd about the constitutional position of the Muslim Brothers?
11. What is the major current trend which the text says is opposed to the principles of the Egyptian revolution?
12. What seems slightly odd about Nasser's acceptance of the Roger's peace plan of 1970?

6. Written Arabic texts 3 (classical)

Read the following text by ابن خلدون from المقدّمة, (Beirut, 1956), pp. 229–30, then complete exercises i. and ii. which follow.

وأمّا أحياءُ البدو فيَزَعُ بعضهم عن بعض مشايخُهم وكبراؤُهم بما وقَرَ في نفوس الكافّة لهم من الوقار والتجلّة، وأمّا حلالهم فإنّما يذود عنها من خارج حاميةِ الحيّ من أنّجادهم وفتيَانهم المعروفينَ بالشجاعة فيهم، ولا يصدُقُ دفاعُهم وذيادُهم إلاّ إذا كانوا عَصبيّةً وأهل نسبٍ واحد، لأنهم بذلك تشتدُّ شوكتُهم ويُخشي جانبُهم، إذ نُعْرةُ كلّ واحدٍ على نَسَبه وعصبيّته أهمُّ، وما جعل اللّهُ في قلوب عباده من الشفَقَة والنُعرة[1] على ذوي أرحَامهم وأقربائهم موجودةً في الطبَائعِ البشريَّة، وبها يكونُ التعاضدُ والتناصُرُ وتعظُمُ رهبةُ العدوِ لهم، واعتبر ذلك فيمَا حكاهُ القرآنُ عن إخوة يوسف عليه السلام، حين قَالوا لأبيه لئن أكلهُ الذئبُ ونحنُ عصبةٌ إنا إذاً لَخاسرون[2] والمعنى أنه لا يُتوَهَّمُ العُدوانُ على أحدٍ مع وجود العِصبةِ له.

Notes

١ - النعرة والنعار بالضم فيهما والنعير: الصراخ والصياح في حرب أو شرّ كما في القاموس.
٢ - من سورة يوسف، آية ١٤.

i   How does the Qur'anic quotation reinforce Ibn Khaldun's argument?
ii   Translate the text into idiomatic English.

7. Grammar/stylistics

(a) *Word order in Arabic: clause–initial emphasis*

The issue of word order in Arabic was discussed in chapter 2 of this book (cf. ch. 2, 7a). In this section, the ideas laid down in chapter 2 will be developed further.

The most common types of word order in Arabic can be summarised as follows:

1. V–first   i.e. Verb–first (verb in first position; ch. 2, 7ai), followed by other elements, if there are any, such as subject, object, adverbial(s) or combinations of these. Sentences in which the verb comes first are traditionally known in Arabic grammar as verbal sentences; clauses in which the verb comes first can be termed verbal clauses; the abbreviation *Vc* will be used for a verbal clause. An example of a verbal clause is: هَنَّأ زيدٌ عمروا 'Zayd congratulated Amr'. A verbal clause may also contain no explicit subject; i.e. the subject is expressed in the verb, as in هَنَّأ عمروا '[he] congratulated Amr'. This latter kind of verbal clause is also a verb phrase; see category 2.2 below. The former kind of verbal clause, which contains an explicit subject, is not, however also a verb phrase.

2. Non–V–first i.e. anything other than the verb first (cf. ch. 1, 7ai, 7aii). Non–V–first sentences can also be termed topic–comment sentences; that is to say, the first element, can be regarded as the topic (i.e. 'what is being talked about') and the elements following this topic can be regarded as the comment (i.e. 'what is being said about this topic').

Category 2. can be subdivided as follows:

2.1 A–Vc   i.e. Adverbial followed by a Verbal Clause (see category 1. above). Examples of an adverbial followed by a verbal clause are: في الصباح هَنَّأ زيدٌ عمروا 'In the morning Zayd congratulated Amr', and في الصباح هَنَّأ عمروا 'In the morning he congratulated Amr'.

2.2. S–P   i.e. Subject–Predicate. The subject of such a sentence is always a noun, while the predicate may be a verb phrase (symbolised *Vp*) – i.e. a verb on its own (such as ضحك '[he] laughed'), a verb plus an object (such as أضحكني '[he] made me laugh'), or a verb plus a dependent prepositional phrase (such as ضحك عليّ '[he] laughed at me'); or it may be something else (categories 2.2.2.–2.2.6. below). A clause which consists of a subject and a predicate can be termed a subject–predicate clause; the abbreviation (S–Pc) will be used for subject–predicate clause. Another term for subject–predicate clause is nominal clause.

Category 2.2 can itself be subdivided as follows:

2.2.1.   S–Vp   i.e. a Subject followed by a Verb phrase. An example of such a sentence is زيدٌ هَنَّأَ عمروأً 'Zayd congratulated Amr'.

2.2.2.   S–Np   i.e. Subject–Noun phrase; e.g. زيدٌ مـهـندسٌ 'Zayd is an engineer'.

2.2.3.   S–Ap   i.e. Subject–Adjective phrase; e.g. زيدٌ طيـبٌ 'Zayd is good natured'.

2.2.4.   S–Adv   i.e. Subject–Adverbial; e.g. زيد هنا 'Zayd is here' (with the adverb هنـا), زيدٌ في البـيت 'Zayd is in the house' (with the prepositional phrase في البـيت).

2.2.5.   S–(S–Pc) i.e. Subject–(Subject–Predicate clause); e.g. زيدٌ أخوه في البيت 'Zayd's brother is in the house' (lit. 'Zayd, his brother is in the house').

2.2.6.   S–Vc   i.e. Subject–Verbal clause (where the verbal clause is not a verb phrase; cf. category 1); e.g. زيدٌ دَخَلَ أَخوه البـيتَ.

Categories 2.2.5 and 2.2.6 are relatively rare in Standard Arabic. Many writers would also reserve the term 'subject' for the initial noun in categories 2.2.1, 2.2.2, 2.2.3, and 2.2.4. The term 'preposed topic' might be used by some writers for the initial noun in categories 2.2.5 and 2.2.6.

The subject–predicate order can be reversed in the case of categories 2.2.2, 2.2.3, and 2.2.4. That is to say, it is possible to have word orders Np–S (i.e. Noun Phrase–Subject), Ap–S (i.e. Adjective Phrase–Subject), and Adv–S (Adverbial–Subject). Examples of these are as follows:

Np–S   مـهندسٌ زيدٌ 'An engineer is Zayd'

Ap–S   طيـبٌ زيدٌ 'Good is Zayd'; cf. متقدمٌ ذكرُها (ch. 12, 7a); also the common phrases with ممنوعٌ, e.g. ممنـوعٌ التدخينْ 'no smoking' (lit: 'prohibited [is] smoking'), ممنـوعٌ الدخولْ 'no entry'.

Adv–S   في البـيت زيدٌ 'In the house is Zayd'; cf. في البـيت رجلٌ 'In the house is a man'/'There is a man in the house'. Where the subject is indefinite, this is the only acceptable word order.

The order of words at the start of the sentence in Arabic, as in English, is closely related to what can be called in general terms sentence–initial emphasis (the notion of sentence–initial emphasis is discussed in more detail below). One basic general principle can be established regarding the relationship between word order and sentence–initial emphasis, namely that: *Any sentence which does not begin with a verb has the potential to display sentence–initial emphasis.*

So, a sentence which has the word order A–Vc (Adverbial–Verbal clause) such as في الصباح هَنَّأَ زيدٌ عـمـرواً 'In the morning Zayd congratulated Amr' will potentially display sentence–initial emphasis (in this case the phrase في الصباح 'in the morning' is potentially emphatic). The same is true of a sentence in which the subject comes first and the verb second, such as زيدٌ هَنَّأَ عـمـرواً 'Zayd congratulated Amr'; in this case the word زيد 'Zayd' (the subject of the sentence) is potentially emphatic. Similarly any sentence which does not contain a verb is potentially emphatic, e.g. زيدٌ مـهـندس 'Zayd is an engineer'; here the subject زيد 'Zayd' is again potentially emphatic. Inverted word orders in which the predicate precedes the subject are also potentially emphatic (although examples of the type في البـيت رجل, where this is the only possible word order are typically not emphatic).

The notion of emphasis

The best way to consider what is meant by the notion of emphasis is to look at examples of sentences which contain potentially emphatic word orders. These are divided in the following section into the following main types: i. Adverbial–Verbal clause, ii. Subject–Verb phrase. The Adverbial–Verbal clause type is sub–divided in terms of the following sub–types of emphasis: i.i. stress, i.ii. contrast or parallelism, i.iii. scene–setting and organisation of material, i.iv. long adverbial , i.v. other. The Subject–Verb phrase type is sub–divided into the following types of emphasis: ii.i. stress, ii.ii. contrast or parallelism, ii.iii linkage, and ii.iv. other.

i *Adverbial–Verbal clause*

Stress is probably the easiest form of emphasis to identify. In translation into English, stress in Arabic is relayed either as intonational stress (in spoken English), or through non–standard word order, or through the use of 'additional' words. An example of a stressed initial Arabic adverbial is the following:

i.i *Stress*

ولا يظهر المحللون السياسيون في القاهرة اندهاشا ازاء خفوت صوت الثورة في احتفالات ذكراها. فقد اعتادت مصر على مدى 20 عام على احتفال بسيط للذكرى يضم المثلث التقليدي: خطاب الرئيس، والفيلم السينمائي، والعطلة. {فمنذ سنوات} اختفت اغاني عبد الحليم حافظ (المطرب الراحل) الوطنية ...

'Analysts in Cairo are not surprised at the dying away of the revolutionary spirit [voice] in its anniversary celebrations ...

'It is many years since the disappearance of the patriotic songs of Abd-al-Haleem Hafez (the late singer) ...' (ch. 13, 5c)

Here the English form 'It is many years since ...' provides the same kind of stress as is provided in the Arabic by the preposing (placing first in the sentence) of the adverbial phrase.

A similar example is provided by the following:

ودخلت أحد الكباريهات . . وقد امتلأ بالبوليس وعيونهم تتجه
إلى من يدخل من المدنيين ولكنهم حريصون على أن يضيقوا
اتصالهم بالناس إلى الحد الأدنى . . و{في هذا المكان منذ سنتين}
ظهرت فتاة يونانية ..

'I went into a cabaret. It was full of policeman, who stared at any civilians who entered, although they were keen to restrict their contacts with other people to the minimum. In this very place, two years ago, a Greek girl appeared ...' (ch. 13, 11b)

Here the stress of the Arabic is echoed in the use of 'very' ('In this very place') in the English translation. (The Arabic example is also interesting because of the unusual use of a double adverbial at the start of the sentence – an adverbial of place في هذا المكان, followed by an adverbial of time, منذ سنتين, before the verb.)

i.ii *Contrast or parallelism*
Contrast may be of time or place or manner. The easiest to illustrate and the most common in texts is time contrast. Consider the following extracts from a text about the assassination of the Lebanese President René Mouawad in 1989 (ch. 16, 4d). The first two paragraphs deal with the general lessons to be drawn from Mouawad's assassination. The next three paragraphs begin as follows, establishing a contrast (and parallels) between the assassination of 1. President Kennedy, 2. Indira Ghandi, and 3. Mouawad:

{بعد اغتيال كيندي الديمقراطي} خلفه نائبه جونسون ..
'After the assassination of the Democrat Kennedy, he was succeeded by his deputy Johnson.'

و{لدى اغتيال انديرا غاندي} خلفها ابنها راجيف واستمر حزب
المؤتمر بحكم البلاد.
'When Indira Ghandi was assassinated, she was succeeded by her son Rajiv, and the Congress Party continued to govern the country.'

و{بعد اغتيال رينيه معوض} يجب ان يخلفه « ابنه » السياسي او
نائبه المفترض ..
'Following the assassination of René Mouawad, he must be succeeded by his political "son", or his designated deputy.'

Another example of contrast occurs in the use of time expressions in a text describing the life of the Egyptian writer طه حسين (ch. 17, 4b). The second paragraph of this reads as follows (date expressions are put in curly brackets):

ولد طه حسين علي سلامة {في الرابع عشر من نوفمبر (تشرين الثاني) سنة ١٨٨٩} بقرية الكيلو في مركز مغاغة محافظة المنيا بصعيد مصر. بدأ {في طفولته} تعلم القراءة والكتابة وحفظ القرآن الكريم في كُتَّاب القرية، وفقد بصره {في طفولته} نتيجة اصابته بالرمد، وكانت المحنة الاولى التي لازمته طوال مشواره الطويل. و{بعد ان أتم حفظ القرآن الكريم} التحق بالجامع الازهر في القاهرة ودرس علوم اللغة العربية والفقه الاسلامي وتاريخ الادب العربي ثم التحق بالجامعة المصرية القديمة وحصل على درجة الدكتوراة {عام ١٩١٤} ليكون أول مكفوف توفده الدولة الى فرنسا لاستكمال دراسته. {وفي عام ١٩١٨} حصل على درجة الدكتوراة في فلسفة ابن خلدون بالفرنسية من جامعة السوربون وعاد الى مصر {عام ١٩١٩} ليعمل استاذا بالجامعة المصرية ثم عميدا لكلية الآداب {عام ١٩٣٠} ثم وزيرا للمعارف «التربية والتعليم» {عام ١٩٥٠}. {وفي عام ١٩٦٣} تولى رئاسة المجمع اللغوي خلفا لاحمد لطفي السيد وظل في هذا المنصب حتى وفاته.

The text starts with a verbal sentence ولد طه حسين علي سلامة {في الرابع عشر من نوفمبر ... سنة ١٨٨٩ ... بصعيد مصر. Here the information about the time of his birth has no contrastive function, and therefore is not preposed. The next two sentences also contain the time information في طفولته. This is not treated in the text as contrastive, perhaps because it is vague (contrast requires some degree of specificity to be contrastive) and proceeds predictably from the idea of birth. The next sentence begins with the preposed adverbial phrase بعد ان أتم حفظ القرآن الكريم, which links back to the previous sentence (see *linkage* below) but also introduces a new phase in Taha Hussein's life, describing his move from the village to the Azhar. The next time phrase عام ١٩١٤ is not preposed, because it links directly to the following information – i.e. the fact that by virtue of finishing his doctorate at this time he was the first disabled Egyptian person to be sent to France to complete his studies. The next time phrase وفي عام ١٩١٨ is, however, preposed, and is used to pick out a new and important phase in Taha Hussein's life (obtaining his doctorate from France). The next time phrase عام ١٩١٩ occurs mid–sentence (after وعاد); the information conveyed is thus treated as less important than that conveyed by the previous time phrase, and the phrase عام ١٩١٩ is not preposed. The next two time phrases عام ١٩٣٠ and عام ١٩٥٠ are also in subordinate structures (following ثم in each case, which expresses the time progression) and as minor elements are not preposed. The final time phrase وفي

عام ١٩٦٣ is, however, preposed. It begins a new sentence and serves to introduce
what the writer chooses to treat as an important new phase in Taha Hussein's life.
It is also striking that the preposed phrases giving years all start with في, e.g. في
عام ١٩١٨, while the non–preposed year phrases all use the shorter and less
emphatic form without the preposition, i.e.عام ١٩١٩, etc.

A good example of a non–preposed time phrase is also to be seen in the text
ثورية الوحدة العربية (ch. 13, 11a). The second paragraph of this begins:

كان « البعث العربي » عند تأسيسه عام ١٩٤٠ أول حزب اشتراكي
في العالم العربي.

'When it was founded in 1940, the Arab Ba'th Party was the first
socialist party in the Arab world.'

The text then explains that despite this fact, the Ba'th did not choose to call itself
the Socialist Party, and goes on to discuss why it also didn't call itself the
Democratic Party, despite its deep commitment to freedom, etc. It would have been
possible for the author to have preposed the time phrase in this sentence and written
something like:

عند تأسيس « البعث العربي » عام ١٩٤٠ كان [هو] أول حزب
اشتراكي في العالم العربي.

Although the English translation of this might be no different from that of the
sentence which actually occurred, the Arabic sentence with the preposed adverbial
عند تأسيس « البعث العربي » عام ١٩٤٠ would tend to suggest a contrast; and
the text might be expected to go on to describe how the Ba'th now has altered from
the party it was when it was founded in 1940.

i.iii *Scene–setting and organisation of material*
Sometimes a preposed adverbial is used to set the scene for a passage or part of a
passage. The following is the first sentence of the short story حفنة تراب, for
which Port Said constitutes the entire setting:

{في بور سعيد} قابلت كثيراً من الناس جاءوا من الشمال
والجنوب ..

'In Port Said I met many people who came from both north and south
...' (ch. 13, 11b)

The following is from the start of Naguib Mahfouz's acceptance speech for the
Nobel Prize for Literature:

{في البدء}، أشكر الأكاديمية السويدية ولجنة نوبل التابعة لها على

التفاتها الكريم لاجتهادي المثابر الطويل.

'Firstly, I would like to thank the Swedish Academy and the Nobel Committee which is affiliated to it for their gracious interest in my long and persistent efforts.' (ch. 17, 11)

Here the phrase في البدء does not so much set the scene as serve to organise the material which is being delivered, by defining it as a preliminary statement.

i.iv *Linkage*

Adverbials may be preposed in order to provide a link between what is going to be said in the sentence which begins with the adverbial, and what has been said in the previous sentence or sentences. Such linkages may involve place, time, manner, or a logical connection. An example of place linkage is the following:

وكثيراً ما ينبت عندهم في جبل ماكوص، و{من هناك} جمعته أيام كنت هناك.

'It frequently grows in their part of the world on Mount Makus; and I collected it [from] there when I was there.' (ch. 19, 11)

The following is an example of time linkage:

فلما كان أوّلُ الليل عاد وقضى ساعةً في ضحك وعبث مع إخوته . و{في هذه الليلة} زعم لأهل البيت جميعاً أنَّ في أكل الثّوم وقايةً من الكوليرا ..

'At the start of the night he came back and spent an hour laughing and joking with his brothers. That night he told all the people of the house that eating garlic warded off cholera ...' (ch. 19, 5d)

The following is an example of manner linkage:

وكانت طيبة القلب ، وبهذه الطيبة خربت بيت أعز أصدقائي ..

'She was good natured; and with her good nature she destroyed the house of one of my closest friends ...' (ch. 13, 11b)

The following is an example of logical linkage:

بُعيد وفاة الرسول صلى الله عليه وسلم بدأ العرب فتوحهم التي وضعت تحت تصرفهم خلال قرن واحد جميع المنطقة الشاسعة الممتدة من أواسط آسيا وحوض السند شرقًا إلى شمال إسبانيا غربًا. و{بذلك} أقاموا دولة الخلافة ..

'Shortly after the death of the Prophet Muhammad the Arabs began their conquests which within one century placed under their control all of the vast area stretching from central Asia and the Indus Basin in the east, to northern Spain in the west. They thus [i.e. by doing this] set up the Caliphal state ...' (ch. 20, 4b)

i.v Long adverbial
Sometimes adverbials are put at the start of a sentence before the verbal clause, because they are long. For example:

في اول اختـبـار جدي لمحافظها السـابق الذي عـين اخيـرا وزيرا للداخلية، كانت مدينة اسيـوط في جنوب مصر، الاثنين، مـسرحا لصدامات بين مسلمين اصوليين والشرطة ..

'In the first serious test for its former governor, who was recently appointed Minister of the Interior, the city of Asyut in the south of Egypt was the scene of disturbances on Monday, between fundamentalist Muslims and the police ...' (ch. 14, 4b)

في الاحتفال المرتقب عالميا لاستلام أول كاتب عربي لجائزة نوبل، استمعت لجنة الأدب بالأكاديمية السويدية إلى خطاب عميد الرواية العربية الكاتب الكبير نجيب محفوظ بهذه المناسبة.

'In the ceremony which had been awaited throughout the world for the first Arab writer to receive the Nobel Prize, the Swedish Academy of Literature listened to the speech of the founder of the Arab novel, the major writer, Naguib Mahfouz, in relation to this occasion.' (ch. 17, 11)

بُعيد وفاة الرسـول صلى الله عليه وسلم بدأ العرب فتوحهم ..

'Shortly after the death of the Prophet Muhammad, the Arabs began their conquests ...' (ch. 20, 4b)

It is possible to regard the preposing of a long adverbial as a particular form of stress. Stress involves drawing more attention to one part of a sentence – the stressed part – than other parts. If an adverbial is long, it will contain a relatively large amount of information. Accordingly the reader has to pay more attention to it than he or she must to a part of the sentence which is less long and contains less information. It is therefore not surprising that long adverbials should be placed at the start of a sentence, where stressed information generally can be placed.

i.vi Other
There are a number of other reasons why an adverbial may be preposed before a verbal clause. Some adverbial phrases typically occur at the start of sentences, particularly those which involve the form ما. Examples are كَثيراً ما 'often,

frequently' and سُرْعَانَ مَا 'how quickly ...!; soon, before long', also رُبَّمَا
'sometimes', 'perhaps', 'máybe', 'possibly' (definitions from Hans Wehr). Thus:

و{كثيراً ما} ينبت عندهم في جبل ماكوص ..

'It frequently grows in their part of the world on Mount Makus ...' (ch. 19, 11)

و{سرعان ما} أصبحت مدينة فاس قبلة أنظار العلماء والأدباء ..

'Before long, the city of Fes became a point of attraction for scholars and men of letters.' (ch. 20, 4c)

It is noteworthy here that the first dictionary definition of سرعان ما 'how quickly ..!' suggests an exclamatory, and therefore emphatic, sense.

Other cases of adverbials preposed before a verbal clause may have nothing to do with emphasis. Sometimes writers may use a preposed adverbial because they are trying to produce a piece of Standard Arabic, which has the 'feel' of colloquial Arabic, for instance in cases of dialogue in a novel or short story. Sometimes preposed adverbials may reflect the influence of English or another language, as when a journalist draws on a news agency report written in English to produce his own Arabic article (even where the Arabic is not a direct translation of the English). There may also be a tendency in modern Standard Arabic to use more preposed adverbials than in older forms of Standard (or Classical) Arabic, such that the association between preposing of adverbials and emphasis is becoming less strong.

ii *Subject–Verb phrase*
Of the various types of Subject–Predicate structures in Arabic (cf. category 2.2. above), the one which is both commonly used and displays an obvious potential for emphasis is the Subject–Verb phrase structure, i.e. the structure in which the subject comes first followed by a verb phrase (category 2.2.1). There is an obvious parallelism between the Adverbial–Verbal Clause structure and the Subject–Verb phrase structure; in both cases the verb comes second in the overall sentence structure preceded by one other element.

The emphatic uses of the subject in Subject–Verb phrase structures can be analysed using some of the same heads as those for the Adverbial–Verbal Clause structure: i.e. stress, contrast or parallelism, linkage, and other.

ii.i *Stress*
An example of the use of Subject–Verb phrase word order for stress is the following:

تسعة عشر عاما مضت على رحيل عميد الادب العربي الدكتور طه
حسين ..

'Nineteen years have [now] passed/It is [now] nineteen years since the death of the doyen of Arabic ...' (ch. 17, 4b)

ii.ii *Contrast or parallelism*
As an example of contrast/parallelism, consider the following section of text which discusses who was responsible for the fire of Cairo.

{الوطنيـون} قـالـوا إن الـسـراي والإنجليـز هم الذيـن أحرقـوا عـاصمـة
مصـر. {الشيـوعيـون} أضافـوا الإخـوان المسلمـين وأحيـاناً «مصـر
الفتـاة». و{البـعض} قال إن «الوفد» متـواطئ. وبعض البـعض قال
إنهم الضبـاط الأحـرار.

'The Nationalists said ... The Communists added ... Some said ... Some of those said [lit: Some of the some said] ...' (ch. 13, 5b)

Here there is a contrast and parallelism between the three groups which claim various people to have been responsible for the fire of Cairo.

A similar example of contrast combined with parallelism occurs in the following:

وتكتظ مـداخل البيـوت بالنـساء، {هذه} تخـرط الملوخيـة، و{تلك}
تقشر البصل، و{ثالثة} توقد النار ..

'Women crowded in the doorways of the houses, one chopping moulukhiyya, another peeling onions, a third lighting the fire.' (ch. 17, 5a)

ii.iii *Linkage*
Examples of linkage, where a preposed subject picks up a phrase or notion introduced in a previous section of text, are the following:

وكان الليل باردا في بـور سـعيـد ، و{البـرودة} تعلـن حـالة الطوارئ
في كل الشوارع ..

'The night was cold in Port Said, and the cold announced the state of emergency throughout the streets ...' (ch. 13, 11b)

وأي شيء أيسـر مـن أن تأخذ مـا اتفقت عليـه كثرة الرواة على أنـه
حق لا شك فيـه ؟ و{كثرة الرواة} قد اتفقت على أن اسمـه حندج ابن
حجـر ..

'And what is easier than accepting that what the majority of reciters are agreed is the indubitable truth? The majority of reciters are agreed that his name is Handaj ibn Hujr ...' (ch. 17, 4c)

{كل هذه العوامل} ادت الى عودة الثقة الى القطاع التجاري ..

'All these factors led to a return of confidence in the commercial market
...' (ch. 18, 4b)

This example is taken from the start of a paragraph in a newspaper article. The
phrase كل هذه العوامل refers back to the factors mentioned in the previous
paragraph.

{هذه جميعها} انتقلت إلى الحضارة العربية بالواسطة، أي عبر
التوارث الاجتماعي.

'All these features became transferred to Arabic culture indirectly, i.e.
by being passed on down the generations.' (ch. 20, 4b)

In this case, the phrase هذه جميعها refers back to features discussed in the
previous sentence.

ii.iv *Other*

There are a number of other reasons why a subject may be preposed before a verb
phrase. Sometimes the reason is stylistic. Newspaper headlines, as already seen,
standardly have S–Vp word order (ch. 6, 7b). Since colloquial Arabic dialects have
a standard word order in which the subject precedes the verb, writers may use
S–Vp word order, for instance in dialogue, to suggest colloquial Arabic, even
where the grammar is entirely in conformity with standard Arabic. An example of
the use of S–Vp word order to give the sense of an informal style is the following,
from a 'Your stars today' column in an Arabic newspaper:

{الحكمة} تقول ما استحق ان يولد من عاش لنفسه فقط.

'The saying goes: he who lives only for himself does not deserve to
have been born.' (ch. 20, 5b)

All the sentences involving a verb phrase and a subject in this passage have the
word order S–Vp.

Holes (1995: 265–6) proposes that word order may also reflect the nature of the
message in other ways. In a travel article about Brazil, he shows that the parts of
the text which describe the journey undertaken by the writer typically have
sentences which start with a verb; and since the writer is describing things which
happened in the past, he typically uses perfect verbs. In the sections which make
more general comments about the environment in Brazil, however, the sentences
typically begin with a noun followed by a verb phrase. In this case, the verbs are in
the imperfect (representing the present) since what are being described are general
truths, habitual actions, etc. The following two paragraphs are from the article
described by Holes (from مجلة الشرق الأوسط, July 15–21, 1992):

{الدراسات} الحديثة تؤكد بأن قطع الأشجار وتشويه مساحات من الغابة باشعال الحريق لا يدمر الأشجار والأحياء فقط بل يحرم الاجيال المقبلة من النباتات التي تصنع منها الأدوية ومن الغذاء والاكسجين، بالاضافة الى اضطراب أحوال الطقس في بعض انحاء الكرة الارضية فتزداد {الفيضانات} فتغرق {بعض الناطق}، وينعدم {المطر} في بعض الانحاء الاخرى فتشكو من الجفاف. واذا اختصرنا كل تلك العناصر الى واحدة لقلنا ان العنصر الأساسي هو فقدان التوازن بين الانسان والطبيعة. {هذا الخلل} ينتشر على جميع الاصعدة ويؤدي الى انتشار الفقر والمرض.

لم يحد {مارتشلو ماركويز، وزير الاقتصاد البرازيلي} عن الحقيقة عندما قال ان الفقر هو اسوأ انواع التلوث. ولكن البرازيل ليست دولة فقيرة. و{الفقر السائد} لم يحدث بين يوم وليلة. فهي دولة هائلة جغرافيا، غنية بثرواتها الطبيعية، تجري فيها الانهار ولا تتعرض لتقلبات ارضية كالزلازل والفيضانات والأعاصير والبراكين، ولا تعاني من الثورات الأهلية ولم تدخل في حروب منذ ١٠٠ عام او اكثر. وفي عداد الدول الصناعية يأتي ترتيبها في المرتبة الحادية عشرة. ولكن الفقر نتج عن سياسات اقتصادية محورها الحصول على الثروة، لا توزيعها.

In considering this extract I shall ignore clauses beginning with the particles أنّ, إنَّ and لكنّ. The reason is that these particles require a clause beginning with a noun to follow them (cf. ch. 15, 7a; also ch. 20, 7aii); it is therefore not independently significant that the clauses concerned should have the word order S–Vp (subject–verb phrase). Here the first sentence of the first paragraph has S–Vp word order .. تؤكد {الدراسات الحديثة} and introduces a major general statement. The next clause expressing a major general statement ينتشر على جميع {هذا الخلل} الاصعدة ويؤدي الى انتشار الفقر والمرض. also has S–Vp word order. In the first sentence of the second paragraph, لم يحد {مارتشلو ماركويز، وزير الاقتصاد البرازيلي} عن الحقيقة عندما قال ان الفقر هو اسوأ انواع التلوث. a specific statement is made by someone at a specific time in the past; accordingly the verb is placed first. The next sentence, while also in the past, expresses a more general fact and the subject is placed first: و{الفقر السائد} لم يحدث بين يوم وليلة.

Interestingly, minor statements, even of a general nature, do not have preposed subjects. So in the first paragraph: فتزداد {الفيضانات} فتغرق {بعض الناطق}، وينعدم {المطر} في بعض الانحاء الاخرى. These facts are presented as consequences of other phenomena, and not as major notions in their own right. This use of the non–emphatic word order mirrors the situation in the text about Taha Hussein (ch. 17, 4b) discussed above (section 7i.ii). There, preposing of the adverbial time phrases before the verb was used to signal dates and events treated as particularly important by the writer. Where the information being conveyed was treated as being of less importance, the time phrase was not preposed.

Another interesting feature of this text is the relationship between nominal sentences in which a subject is followed by a verbal clause, and those in which it is followed by some other element. The following is an example: لم {الفقر السائد}و يحـدث بـين يـوم وليـلة. فـهي دولة هائلة جـغـرافيـاً. Here the S–Vp structure of لم يحـدث بـين يـوم وليـلة. is followed by an S–Np (subject–noun phrase) structure فـهي دولة هائلة جـغـرافيـاً. It would seem that one factor motivating the use of S–Vp structures (rather than Verb–first structures) to express general truths, etc., is that they parallel in terms of word order S–Np structures and other subject–predicate structures without a verb, which may also express general truths, etc., and which are therefore likely to occur in close proximity.

The above remarks are not meant to be conclusive, and different interpretations even of some of the material quoted might be offered. For instance in the case of ولكن و{الفقر السائد} لم يحـدث بـين يـوم وليـلة., the previous sentence reads البـرازيـل ليـست دولة فـقـيـرة. One might argue that the preposing of the phrase دولة الفقر السائد in the second sentence is a form of linkage with the mention of فقيرة in the previous sentence.

The influence of English word order is also important in some styles of modern Arabic. Many Arabic newspaper articles for example are either direct translations of reports originally written in English, or draw on reports produced by Reuters or other news agencies which are originally written in English. Such articles may well contain S–Vp word orders which do not appear to have anything to do with emphasis, and simply reproduce the English word order.

Modern Arabic typically makes greater use of S–Vp structures than Classical Arabic, also suggesting that not all uses of S–Vp structures in modern Arabic can be regarded as emphatic. Some may be the result of idiosyncratic usage on the part of a particular author, or even a desire to vary word order for stylistic effect, as, perhaps, in the following.

و{الأطفال الحفاة أشـباه العـرايا} يلعبـون فـي كل ركن، ويملأون الجو بصراخهم والأرض بقاذوراتهم. و{تكتظ} مداخل البيـوت بالنساء ..
'Half–naked, barefoot children filled the air with their screams and the earth with their filth. Women crowded in the doorways of the houses ...' (ch. 17, 5a)

Here there seems no particular reason why the clause beginning و{الأطفال الحفاة أشـباه العـرايا} يلعبـون .. has S–Vp word order but the clause beginning و{تكتظ} مداخل البيـوت بالنساء .. should have Verb–first word order.

iii *Other types of subject–predicate clause*
In the case of other types of simple nominal clause – i.e. Subject–Noun phrase, Subject–Adjective phrase, Subject–Adverbial – the emphatic function is less

pronounced than in the case of Subject–Verb phrase structures. This is because it is only in the case of sentences containing a main verb that it is possible to vary the word order (either verb–first, or subject–first). Where there is no verb, the only possible orders are subject–first, or much more rarely predicate–first (cf. section 7a above).

Nonetheless, there remains a potential association between nominal sentences (regardless of whether they contain verbs or not) and emphasis. This can be seen from the wide use of nominal sentences (both with and without main verbs) in the text اتفاق اليمنين (ch. 13, 5a), for example, where the writer adopts a rather exclamatory style in order to get his message across.

Conversely, writers may opt to avoid nominal sentences by using verbal sentences with semantically light verbs (ch. 1, 7a)

8. Aural Arabic texts 1
Listen to the following aural text from حصاد الشهر, no. 7, side 1, item 3, جمال عبد الناصر يؤمم قناة السويس, which is taken from a speech made by Nasser in Alexandria announcing the nationalisation of the Suez Canal on July 26, 1956; then, using the vocabulary given below, transcribe the text in Arabic. You may find it useful to study the vocabulary before listening to the text.

تأميم	nationalisation
مادة	article
مساهمة	participation
شركة مساهمة	joint stock company
التزام	commitment
هيئة pl. هيئات	board
لجنة pl. لجان	committee
عوض .... عن	to compensate .... for
حامل pl. حملة	holder
حصة pl. حصص	share (in a company)
تأسيسي	founding, establishment
سهم pl. أسهم	share
سعر	price
سعر الإقفال	= closing price
بورصة	stock market
ممتلكات	property, estates, possessions

9. Aural Arabic texts 2

Listen to the following text from 'Extracts of speeches by Gamal Abdul Nasser', side 1, item 1, أَيُّها المُواطنون. Then produce a translation in English. You may find it useful to study the vocabulary before listening to the text.

اسْتَبَدّ	to rule despotically
مُسْتَبِدّ	despot, tyrant, autocrat
هَدَم	to knock down, tear down
صَرْح	castle, palace, fortress
سِيادة	sovereignty
عِزَّة	might, power, glory, honour
مُساهَمة	participation
مُؤامَرة	plot, conspiracy
مَنْفَعة	use, value
مَنْبَع	source
اسْتَنْزَف	to drain off
امْتَصّ	to suck
عَضّ	to bite
نَواجِذ .pl ناجِذ	molar
ذِلّة	humiliation
مَسْكَنة	poverty, misery

10. Written English texts

Using constructions and vocabulary encountered in the Arabic texts above as far as possible, translate the following text from Heather Bleaney and Richard Lawless, *The Arab–Israeli Conflict 1947–67*, (London: B.T. Batsford Ltd, 1990), p. 22, into idiomatic Arabic.

Gamal Abdul Nasser (1918–1970)

Gamal Abdul Nasser was born on 15 January 1918 in Alexandria, where his father worked as a post office clerk. Gamal was the eldest of 11 children. He grew up during Egypt's struggle for national independence from Britain and became involved in nationalist agitation while still at school. He started to study law at Cairo University but then joined the army in 1937, where he soon distinguished himself. He served in the Palestine war of 1948.

In 1949, Nasser founded the Society of Free Officers, a secret underground group within the Egyptian army, to plan for a revolution in Egypt. The Free Officers successfully mounted a coup on 23 July 1952 and sent King Farouk into exile. Nasser had clearly been the

strong–man of the new ruling group and in November 1954 he became
President of the Republic of Egypt.

11. Précis

(a) Read the following extract by ميشيل عفلق from معركة المصير الوحيد,
(Beirut: دار الادب, 1963), pp. 18–20, then produce a précis in Arabic.

ثورية

الوحدة   العربية

لا شك أن أهداف «البعث العربي» التي لخصناها في «الحرية
والاشتراكية والوحدة» هي أهداف أساسية متساوية في الاهمية لا
يجوز فصل او تأجيل بعضها عن البعض الآخر. ولكن الشيء الذي لا
شك فيه أيضاً هو ان للوحدة (وهي ما تعبر عن الصفة العربية
الشاملة) تقدماً ورجحاناً معنوياً يجب ان لا يغفل عنه البعثيون
لئلا ينساقوا مع تيارات فكرية وسياسية هي أبعد ما تكون عن
فكرة «البعث العربي».

كان «البعث العربي» عند تأسيسه عام ١٩٤٠ أول حزب
اشتراكي في العالم العربي. ومع ذلك لم يختر لنفسه اسم الحزب
الاشتراكي. وكان فهمه للحرية وفعلها الخطير الاساسي في بعث
الأمة العربية فهماً لم تسبقه اليه حركة أخرى من حيث العمق
والنضج والوضوح، ومع ذلك لم يتسم بالحزب الديمقراطي. ولئن
كان قد تسمى بالبعث العربي، فليس ذلك لأنه أول حزب آمن
بالوحدة العربية فكراً وعملاً، وجعل تنظيمه على أساس عربي
شامل فحسب، بل لأنه آمن منذ البدء أن كل نظرة ومعالجة لمشاكل
العرب الحيوية في أجزائها ومجموعها لا تصدر عن هذه المسلّمة:
«وحدة الامة العربية»، تكون نظرة خاطئة ومعالجة ضارّة. فليس
إذن الفرق بين «البعث العربي» وبين الأحزاب الأخرى التي تنشأ
في الأقطار العربية والتي منها ما ينادي بالاشتراكية، ومنها ما
ينادي بالديمقراطية، ومنها ما ينادي بالاثنين معاً في حدود القطر

الذي تنشأ فيه، وكثيرها يقول بالوحدة العربية وكنتيجة وهدف أخير سيصل اليه كل قطر عندما يكتمل تطوره وتنضج الشروط اللازمة لتحقيق الوحدة، نقول إن الفرق بين حزبنا وهذه الاحزاب ليس فرقاً في الكم بل في النوع. ان الحرية التي يطلبها حزب مصري او لبناني، والاشتراكية التي يعمل لها حزب عراقي او سوري، هما غير الحرية والاشتراكية اللتين تحتاجهما وتقدر على تحقيقهما الأمة العربية كأمة واحدة ذات تراث حضاري، واستعدادات وامكانيات لنهضة جديدة أصيلة. فالحرية التي يسعى اليها كل قطر عربي على حدة لا يمكن ان تبلغ من العمق الشمول والمعنى الايجابي ما تبلغه الحرية التي تنزع اليها الأمة العربية عندما تضع مصيرها ومصير الانسانية موضع التساؤل، كما ان الاشتراكية التي تتقلص وتتشوه – في حدود القطر الواحد – حتى تقتصر على إصلاحات جزئية خادعة، تأخذ كل مداها النظري والتطبيقي عندما يكون مجالها العالم العربي كوحدة اقتصادية وكوحدة شعبية نضالية. وهذا الفرق أيضاً بين الحرية والاشتراكية كما تُفهمان في حالة التجزئة (وفي عقلية التجزئة) وبينهما في عقلية الوحدة، هو فرق في النوع وليس في الكم. فلم يعد إذن عمل الأحزاب القطرية مرحلة توصل الى الوحدة، بل اتجاهاً جديداً وطريقاً مختلفاً يبعد عنها ويضعف امكانياتها، وهو الفرق نفسه بين الجامعة العربية التي تجمع العجز الى العجز، والاستثمار والاحقاد والمصالح الخاصة بعضها الى بعض، وبين الوحدة العربية التي تخلق العرب خلقاً جديداً. وليس ما يمنع اتحاد او انصهار الأحزاب القطرية ذات الاهداف الواحدة الحواجز والعراقيل التي تضعها الحكومات أو ضعف الوسائل في سبيل ذلك بقدر ما هي طبيعة هذه الاحزاب وطبيعة اهدافها، المستمدة مباشرة من وضع التجزئة، وعقليتها والتي تستعصي على كل توحيد.

(b) Read the following short story by انيس منصور from بقايا كل شيء, pp. 47–9, then produce a précis in Arabic.

حفنة   تراب

في بور سعيد قابلت كثيراً من الناس جاءوا من الشمال والجنوب .. كلهم ليروا ماذا فعل العدوان بهذه المدينة الآمنة .. إن كل شيء هادئً فيها ، الناس والحياة ، والانقاض ترتفع من الشوارع ، ودخان البارود قد طغت عليه رائحة البحر ، والناس ينزلون من القطار يبحثون عن تمثال دي لسبس .. لقد تحطم التمثال وسقط فوق زورق صغير وانكفأ على وجهه .. إنه غارق على سطح الماء .. وتمثال الجندي المجهول قد انفصل حصاناه . وألقى أحدهما في الشارع وامتطاه الناس .. والتقطت لهم صور ، والآخر في منزّه صغير.

والشوارع امتلأت بالبيريهات الزرقاء يتحرك تحتها جنود وضباط .. إنهم الكنديون أبناء عم الإنجليز والأمريكيون ليسوا صغار السن كالدنماركيين والسويديين، بل معظمهم على أعتاب الأربعين والخمسين .. وهم لا يتحدثون إلى أحد من الناس .. ولكنهم يداعبون الباعة والمتجولين.

وكل شيء سيتغير في هذه المدينة .. فالشوارع تنظفها السيارات والفؤوس تعمل على إزالة الأنقاض .. ولن يكون هناك خراب ولا دمار .. سيختفي التراب الذي أغمض العيون وسد النفوس .. تماماً كما اختفى من المدن الألمانية .. لقد رأيت ميونيخ ودسلدورف ورأيت هانوفر وهمبورج ، كلها ضربت بمئات الألوف من القنابل، ولكن اذهب إليها الآن وأرني أثراً واحداً لقنبلة أو طوربيد .. لا شيء ، قامت البيوت ، أو على الأصح قام الناس فقامت البيوت !

وستمتلئ محلات بور سعيد بالزبائن ، والشوارع بالسائحين من كل بلد في أوربا وآسيا .. ولن تقف طويلاً زوارق الصيادين ،

ولن يطول تثاؤب عمال الأرصفة سيكون هناك بحر – كما يقول
أبناء بور سعيد – وهم يعنون بذلك الحركة والتجارة، فإذا كانت
هناك حركة وتجارة فهذا هو البحر . . وإذا لم يكن هناك حركة
فالبحر أرض يابسة . . إذن فليس هناك بحر .

وكان الليل باردا في بور سعيد ، والبرودة تعلن حالة الطوارئ
في كل الشوارع حتى البوليس الدولي قد توارى في البارات . .
إنهم وحدهم يشربون ويضحكون . . ولا توجد بينهم ولا معهم امرأة
واحدة . . والتعليمات صريحة بأن يلتزموا الأدب والوقار حتى إذا
شربوا . . إلا إذا ذهبوا إلى الصحراء فهم أحرار أن يفعلوا ما
يريدون . . وقد سألت ضابطاً دولياً رأيته يتطلع إلى السماء : كيف
الحال ؟ فأجاب : لا شيء هناك . . وإنما ننتظر سقوط الجليد ! .

وتركني ومضى يضحك واحتفظ بالمعنى في بطنه أو ربما كان
كلاماً بلا معنى أو هي إجابة تقليدية أو أنه كلام دولي ! .

ودخلت أحد الكباريهات . . وقد امتلأ بالبوليس وعيونهم تتجه
إلى من يدخل من المدنيين ولكنهم حريصون على أن يضيقوا
اتصالهم بالناس إلى الحد الأدنى . . وفي هذا المكان منذ سنتين
ظهرت فتاة يونانية كانت جميلة الصوت والشكل ، وكانت طيبة
القلب ، وبهذه الطيبة خربت بيت أعز أصدقائي . . إنني أستطيع
أن أروي قصته هنا وأنا آمن . . فهو غاضب مني ، وقد أقسم ألا
يقرأ شيئاً مما أكتب ، وخسرت قارئاً مستنيراً صادق الإدراك
والنقد . . كانت تربطه بهذه المطربة اليونانية واسمها « ميراندا »
صلة الحب العنيف . . وكان يسافر يوماً بعد يوم من القاهرة إلى
بور سعيد ليجلس إليها حتى الصباح ويعود إلى مصر . . ولم أكن
أعرف هذه العلاقة .

وفي يوم تلقيت دعوة من زوجته لحضور عيد ميلادها . .
وذهبت ولم أفطن إلى أن مجيئي إلى بيت هذا الصديق كان
مفاجأة كبرى لي . . وبعد وصولي بدقائق استدرجتني الزوجة إلى

البلكونة وفتحت مظروفاً كبيراً وسألتني إن كنت أعرف واحدة من هؤلاء . . والمظروف مليء بصور الفتيات . . ولم أكن أعرف . إلا « ميراندا » هذه ومددت يدي إليها . . وسقطت الصور من يدي الزوجة . . بل سقطت الزوجة من حياة هذا الرجل وانفصلت عنه حتى هذا اليوم .

وكان الزوج قد أكد لها أنه لا يعرف صاحبة هذه الصورة ولا يدري من الذي دسها في جيبه ، وقاطع الزوج أصدقاءه القدماء وصديقاته القديمات . . وهو اليوم متصوف لا يقرأ إلا القرآن وإلا الأحاديث النبوية . . ويعيش في أرضه التي يملكها بعيداً عن كل إنسان وكل زوجة وكل ميراندا .

إن هذا الصديق كأنه مات . . يكفي أنه قرر ألا يكون له مستقبل.

والإنسان الحي هو الذي له مستقبل ، والميت هو الذي لا مستقبل له.

ونحن وبور سعيد أحياء . . سيكون لنا شأن . . وسنعيش وننهض لأن الحياة تستحق أن نعيشها وأن نمدها بنا والناس بعدنا . . وما دام هناك بحر ستكون حياة .. ليس هذا كل ما أحسسته في بور سعيد وإنما هذه حفنة من تراب الأرض التي تلقت عنا الفزع والنار والدمار . . وبقيت وستبقى وتعيش بنا وبعدنا .

12. Oral
القومية العربية
(a) One student to present a concise definition of القومية.
(b) A second student to present an account of القومية العربية as it has manifested in an Arab state.
(c) The presenters then ask the other students questions about nationalism. These should include questions which require factual answers and others which require speculative or subjective answers. For example:

١ – ما هي القومية؟

٢ – ما هي العلاقة بين القومية والاشتراكية في الوطن العربي؟

٣ – ما هي الاحداث المهمة التي ادت الى نشوء القومية في مصر في عهد جمال عبد الناصر؟

٤ – كيف ظهرت القومية العربية في دول غير مصر؟

٥ – في رأي قسطنطين زريق، من هو العربي الواعي قوميا؟

٧ – كيف تختلف القومية العربية عن القومية في بريطانيا وغيرها من الدول الغربية، مثلا؟

٨ – في نظرك، ما هي فضائل القومية وما هي مساويئها؟

(d) Open lecturer–led discussion on the future of Arab nationalism.

13. Essay

Write an essay in Arabic of 200 words on the title القومية العربية ماضيها وحاضرها ومستقبلها؟. Structure your essay around the following questions:

١ – ما هي القومية العربية؟

٢ – ما هو اصل القومية في مصر وغيرها من الدول العربية في القرن العشرين؟

٣ – من هم القوميون الرئيسيون في الوطن العربي من الثلاثينات حتى الآن؟

٤ – الى اي حد تتعلق القومية العربية بالاشتراكية؟

٥ – ما هي حالة الاشتراكية في الوطن العربي اليوم؟

٦ – ما هي فوائد القومية للشعوب العربية؟

٧ – الى اين القومية العربية؟

14
Islamic fundamentalism

1. Basic background material
(a) *Beginnings of Islamic fundamentalism*
The roots of modern Islamic fundamentalism lie in nineteenth–century Islamic reformers such as Jamal al-Din al-Afghani and Muhammad Abduh, who were themselves attempting to formulate an Islamic response to the pressures of western colonialism.

The first major fundamentalist grouping in the Middle East was the Muslim Brotherhood. This was founded in 1928 in Egypt by Hasan al-Banna, a schoolteacher by training, and quickly attracted support from all social groups, with a strong base among the urban working class. Members were organised into 'families', families into 'clans', clans into 'groups', and groups into 'batallions', creating a structure with strong internal discipline and cohesion. The Muslim Brotherhood has continued to spread throughout the Middle East. However, by the late–1970s, other, more extreme Islamic groups had begun to appear, particularly in Egypt. Here the grinding poverty of the mass of the population, widespread economic corruption, and the failure of education to bring about economic progress for large sections of the population provided fertile ground for proposed radical solutions to the problems of life and society.

(b) *Major tenets of Islamic fundamentalism*
Islamic fundamentalists advocate a return to what they regard as the pristine form of Islam before it became corrupted (the demand for a return to the pristine form of the religion being effectively a definition of fundamentalism in any religion). Islamic fundamentalists typically regard Islam as having been corrupted by Western influence, while some would see the corruption as having begun much earlier in Islamic history.

Fundamentalist groups differ in their attitude to the state. Some, like the Muslim Brotherhood, regard the current states of the Middle East as potentially reformable. In addition to a general 're–Islamisation' of social values and behaviour, all that is required is the reform of government and law, and in particular the replacement of imported European codes of law by the Islamic Shari'a. By implication, Western–style multi–party democracy is not necessarily inconsistent with Islam.

More radical Islamic groups regard the current states of the region as properly speaking un–Islamic. This attitude finds some support in the Kharijis, who withdrew their support from the Caliph Ali, when he agreed to arbitration following the battle of Siffin (cf. ch. 4, 1). Interestingly, the Egyptian press dubbed the Society of Muslims (الجماعة الإسلامية), which assassinated President Sadat, the 'Excommunication and Emigration' group (التكفير والهجرة), because of their deeming un–Islamic (تكفير, from كافر) the Egyptian state, and their withdrawal (هجرة) from it, pending its revolutionary overthrow by themselves.

Within Sunni Islam, however, there is only relatively marginal support for this attitude to the state. The Islamic jurist Ibn Taymiyya, for instance, issued a *fatwa* declaring as falling outside the Abode of Islam (دار الإسلام) the city of Mardin (in the south of present–day Turkey); at the time this city was ruled by a Muslim, who was, however, subject to Mongol control, and had adopted Mongol symbols of power in recognition of this fact. Support for this notion can also be found in the Qur'an commentary of Ibn Kathir, who specifically declared as un–Islamic nominally Muslim rulers who ruled according to Ghengis Khan's codification of Mongol traditional law, known as the *yasaq* or *yasa* (Kepel 1993: 195–6; cf. also section 6b).

Elsewhere, however, even Ibn Taymiyya quotes with approval the well–known Islamic saying: ستّون سنة من إمام جائر أصلح من ليلة واحدة بلا سلطان 'Sixty years with an unjust ruler is better than a single night without any authority' (cf. section 6), implying that even a bad Muslim ruler is still to be regarded as Islamic.

Inasmuch as radical Islamic groups regard present–day society as unreformable, they have much in common with Marxist groups, who regarded – and still do regard, to the extent that these groups still exist – revolution as the only way of achieving progress. To some extent Islamic fundamentalist groups in the Middle East have drawn support from disillusioned former Marxists.

(c) *Chronology of Islamic fundamentalist groups in Egypt*

1928	Foundation of the Muslim Brotherhood (Society of Muslim Brethren) by Hassan al-Banna in Ismailiyya, Egypt.
1933	First congress of the Muslim Brothers in Cairo.
1948	Dissolution of Muslim Brotherhood by government on charges of 'attempts to overthrow the existing order, terrorism, murder'.
1949	Hasan al-Banna assassinated by Egyptian police.
1951	Legal reconstitution of Muslim Brotherhood.
1954–1970	Extreme repression of Muslim Brotherhood under Nasser regime.
1971	Sadat releases Islamists imprisoned by Nasser
1979	All Islamist groups oppose Sadat's peace treaty with Israel
1981	Assassination of Sadat by Khalid Islambuli of the Society of Muslims

(جماعة المسلمين) group (dubbed by the Egyptian press the
'Excommunication and Emigration' group (التكفير والهجرة).

present   The Muslim Brotherhood currently functions semi–legally in Egypt
             and has representatives in parliament, who are officially classed as
             independents. More radical Islamic groups are banned, and carry out
             sporadic armed attacks (particularly against Western tourists). There
             are also relatively frequent clashes between Islamic fundamentalists
             and Coptic Christians.

(d) *Major fundamentalist movements in some other Arab countries*
Algeria
Major Islamist group the National Salvation Front (FIS). Since the unilateral
annulling of the 1991 election results by the Algerian authorities and the outlawing
of the FIS in March 1992, the FIS and other more radical Islamic groups, such as
the Islamic Armed Group (GIA), have fought a de facto civil war with the Algerian
government (cf. also ch. 15, 1).

Iraq
Main Islamic group underground Shi'ite Da'wa (الدَّعْوة). This has been more or
less wiped out inside Iraq by government repression, and is now based in Iran.

Jordan
Main Islamic fundamentalist grouping Muslim Brotherhood attracts high level of
support, is represented in parliament, and abides by democratic norms.

Lebanon
Most important group Hizbullah (حزب الله); backed by Iran, pursues guerilla war
against Israeli occupation forces in southern Lebanon.

Palestine
Growing support for Islamic Jihad (الجهاد الإسلامي) and Hamas (حماس)
movements with growing Palestinian disillusionment and despair at percieved
failure of peace process. Both groups committed to armed struggle; responsible for
numerous suicide attacks against Israeli civilians.

Saudi Arabia
Committee for the Defence of Legitimate Rights established in early 1990s as
Islamic–based dissenting group. Suppressed by government.

Sudan
Current military regime dominated by Muslim Brotherhood elements, who lack mass support, but are well organised and influential among educated. Situation extremely unstable, with civil war in much of country and neighbouring states opposed to current regime.

Syria
Muslim Brotherhood almost wiped out following virtual civil war in late 1970s, early 1980s.

Tunisia
The major Islamic fundamentalist group, the Nahda (النَهْضـة), stood as independents in 1990 general elections, officially winning 13% in somewhat rigged vote, which the Nahda bitterly denounced. Since 1991, the Nahda has been severely repressed, and some of its members have taken to violence against the state.

Yemen
Main Islamic grouping is the *Islah* (الإصلاح); represented in parliament, where it constitutes the official opposition.

2. Additional reading
(a) Hourani, *A History of the Arab Peoples*, pp. 345–9; pp. 397–400; pp. 442–58.
(b) Gilles Kepel, *Muslim Extremism in Egypt: The Prophet and Pharaoh*, (University of California Press, 1993).

3. Key vocabulary
Taking the texts in this chapter as a starting point, draw up a list of vocabulary in the following fields:
(a) General Islamic vocabulary (not covered in chapter 4).
(b) Specific vocabulary related to fundamentalism.

4. Written Arabic texts 1
(a) Read the following newspaper text from الوطن Oct. 7, 1988, then give oral answers in English to the questions which follow.

الأصوليــون هاجمــوا مكتبة
للأقبـاط في مصـر

ذكرت مصادر امنية مصرية ان ١٥ مسلما اصوليا هاجموا امس الاول
مكتبة تابعة لجمعية المسيحيين الاقباط قرب كنيسة سان جورج في

مدينة اسيوط التي تبعد ٣٨٠ كم جنوب القاهرة .

وابلغت المصادر وكالة «اسوشيتدبرس» ان الاصوليين قاموا عقب صلاة الجمعة بالهجوم على المكتبة ومزقوا محتوياتها وخربوا الاشرطة المسجل عليها الاناشيد الكنائسية بالاضافة الى تحطيم مقاعد المكتبة قبل وصول قوات الشرطة .

واضافت المصادر ان قوات الشرطة المصرية اعتقلت الاصوليين وتواصل البحث عن سبعة اشخاص شاركوا في الهجوم على المكتبة .

وفي وقت لاحق نفت وكالة «انباء الشرق الاوسط» المصرية صحة الخبر . وقالت انه «خبر غير صحيح».

1. Which sources does the report quote first?
2. What did the fundamentalists attack?
3. Where did the attack take place?
4. Where is this city in relation to Cairo?
5. Which agency does the report go on to quote?
6. When did the attack take place?
7. What did the fundamentalists tear up?
8. What was on the tapes?
9. What did the fundamentalists do to the chairs?
10. What did the police do to the fundamentalists?
11. Who are the police still looking for?
12. What did the Egyptian 'Sons of the Middle East' news agency claim?
13. Why do you think the Egyptian news agency may have made this claim?

(b) Read the following newspaper text from النهار, Jan. 25, 1990, then complete the structure translations which follow. Nicolai Caecescu was the Communist dictator of Romania who was overthrown by a popular revolution in Dec. 1989.

الشعب: التغيير أو تشاوشيسكو
مقتل متظاهر واعتقال ١٢ في مصر
في صدامات بين الشرطة واصوليين

في اول اختبار جدي لمحافظها السابق الذي عين اخيرا وزيرا للداخلية، كانت مدينة اسيوط في جنوب مصر، الاثنين، مسرحا لصدامات بين مسلمين اصوليين والشرطة انتهت بمقتل شخص واعتقال ١٢ آخرين.

وافادت وكالة "انباء الشرق الاوسط" المصرية الرسمية "ان بعض الجماعات المتطرفة في مدينة اسيوط حاولت الخروج في تظاهرة مساء (اول من) امس من مسجد خشبة في شارع الجمهورية فتصدت لها قوات الشرطة الموجودة خارج المسجد ووجهت اليها انذارا بالتفرق وعدم التجمهر او التظاهر. وقد رفضت هذه الجماعات الامتثال للاوامر والقت الحجارة على قوات الشرطة". واضافت ان الشرطة اضطرت الى اطلاق النار مما اسفر عن مقتل زعيم الجماعة عبد الصبور محمد حسنين العريني الذي يعمل بقالا في مدينة منفلوط.

وقالت مصادر امنية ان نحو ٢٠٠ شخص اشتركوا في احتجاجات اسيوط التي تعد مركزا رئيسيا للجماعات الاسلامية المعارضة للحكومة، وطالبوا بتطبيق احكام الشريعة الاسلامية وبتوقيف وزير الداخلية السابق السيد زكي بدر المعروف بمواقفه المتشددة من الجماعات المتطرفة بسبب ما وصفته بتجاوزات قام بها اثناء توليه مسؤولياته.

ويذكر ان بدر اعفي من منصبه في ١٢ كانون الثاني بعدما نشرت صحيفة "الشعب" الناطقة باسم حزب العمل الاشتراكي المعارض قائمة بشتائم كان الوزير السابق يستخدمها لاهانة شخصيات عامة ومن هؤلاء رجال سياسة ومفكرون اسلاميون وكتاب.

وكان حادث الاثنين الاخطر الذي يواجه اللواء محمد عبد الحليم موسى الذي كان محافظا لاسيوط الى حين تعيينه وزيرا للداخلية خلفا لبدر، علما ان مصادر معارضة كانت تحدثت عن اعتقال الشرطة ٣٠ مسلما اصوليا في اثنين من احياء القاهرة يوم السبت.

في غضون ذلك، حذرت صحيفة "الشعب"، في هجوم هو الاعنف تشنه صحيفة معارضة على الحكومة، من انهيار النظام السياسي على غرار ما شهدته دول اوربا الشرقية ما لم يتفق على مبادئ

الاصلاح السياسي في البلاد. وقال رئيس تحرير الصحيفة السيد عادل حسين في مقال رئيسي عنوانه: "التغيير او تشاوشيسكو" في اشارة الى الانتفاضة الشعبية في رومانيا: "ان الاتفاق على مبادئ الاصلاح السياسي وعلى صوغها في دستور جديد هو الذي يعيد الحيوية الى المجتمع وهو الذي يفتح الطريق السلمي للاصلاح وهو الذي يجنّبنا الانهيارات والانفجارات العنيفة على النحو الذي اجتاح الدول الشيوعية الاوربية".

Translate the following sentences into Arabic.

1. The government appointed him head of the committee. (para 1, line 1)
2. The army ordered them not to demonstrate. (para 2, lines 4–5)
3. There was a recession leading to further economic problems. (para 2, line 7)
4. She worked as an engineer. (para 2, line 8)
5. They arrested the former minister, who was suspected of corruption. (para 3, line 4)
6. The paper talked about the army killing a number of demonstrators. (para 5, lines 3–4)
7. Democracy is what the people demand. (para 6, lines 7–8)
8. These reforms will allow the government to avoid a revolution. (para 6, line 9)

(c) Read the following newspaper text from النهار, Jan. 27, 1990, then in Arabic briefly paraphrase the contents of the text orally.

غداة تحدي "الجماعة الاسلامية" للحكومة
القاهرة: الشرطة قتلت متطرفاً في اشتباك في
عين شمس

افادت مصادر امنية مصرية ان الشرطة قتلت مسلما اصوليا مطلوبا بتهمة ممارسة نشاطات مناهضة للحكومة في اشتباك وقع امس في احد احياء القاهرة.

واضافت ان القتيل، واسمه احمد كامل، اطلق النار من مسدس غير مرخص على رجال الشرطة الذين كانوا يحاولون القبض عليه

في حي عين شمس تنفيذا لمذكرة اتهمته بحيازة متفجرات وتوزيع منشورات مناهضة للحكومة. وقد ردت الشرطة على النار بالمثل فاصابت المتهم بجروح بالغة توفي متأثرا بها في احد مستشفيات القاهرة.

وكامل هو ثاني متشدد اصولي يقتل برصاص الشرطة المصرية هذا الاسبوع. وكان الاول قتل في اشتباك مساء الاثنين الماضي في مدينة اسيوط في صعيد مصر.

وادانت منظمة اسلامية اصولية محظورة تطلق على نفسها اسم "الجماعة الاسلامية" الاشتباك الذي وقع في اسيوط وجاء في بيان وزعته الاربعاء الماضي ان اعضاءها سيتحدون وزير الداخلية الجديد اللواء محمد عبد الحليم موسى الذي "يحاور بالرصاص".

وكشفت انباء ان الشرطة اعتقلت عشرات من المسلمين الاصوليين في انحاء متفرقة من مصر في الايام السبعة الاخيرة في اطار حملة على النشاط الاصولي.

(d) Read the following newspaper text from الوطن, 1988 at home and give your opinion of the writer's attitude in Arabic.

الوطن تنشر تفاصيل احداث الصعيد
السفير الأميركي زار أسيوط قبل « أعمال الشغب »
والأزهر حذر من الإمبريالية و« الإخوان » من الأصابع الخفية

القاهرة : من احمد رجب

* تجددت الاسبوع الماضي حوادث الشغب في بعض مدن صعيد مصر «سوهاج، بني سويف، اسيوط» بصدامات بين بعض عناصر الجماعات الاسلامية المتطرفة وعدد من المسيحيين الامر الذي ادى الى صدامات بين الطرفين من جهة ورجال مكافحة الشغب «الامن المركزي» الذين حاولوا احتواء الازمة التي بدأ يخفت ضجيجها في

اعقاب حملة اعتقالات واسعة في جنوب مصر بين صفوف التيار الديني المتطرف ومثيري الشغب من المسيحيين .

وقد بدأت الازمة عقب انتشار اشاعة بين طلاب الجماعات الاسلامية مفادها ان بعض الشباب المسيحي يقومون برش مادة سائلة على ملابس الفتيات المحجبات تظهر بعد جفافها علامة صليب مطبوع على ملابسهن ، وقام احد طلاب كلية الحقوق في بني سويف من اعضاء الجماعات الاسلامية بدعوة زملائه لمؤتمر لبحث صحة هذه الاشاعة ، واظهر لزملائه غطاء رأس لفتاة محجبة ، مطبوع عليها علامة الصليب .

ونتيجة لذلك اندفع الطلاب في مظاهرة ضخمة طافت شوارع مدينة بني سويف ، وسرعان ما انتقلت الى المدن والمراكز والقرى المحيطة ، وبعد لحظات كانت محافظات الصعيد الثلاث «بني سويف – اسيوط – سوهاج » قد تحولت الى نيران مشتعلة ، حيث تم احراق كنيسة وجامع ، وقامت بعض العناصر المتطرفة من الجماعات الاسلامية بالاعتداء على عدد كبير من المتاجر والصيدليات التي يمتلكها مسيحيون ، ومع تفاقم الازمة ، اضطرت قوات الامن الى طلب تعزيزات اضافية من قوات مكافحة الشغب للسيطرة على الموقف .

* وعلى مدى عشرة ايام – تقريبا – واصلت الشرطة حصارها لمناطق الشغب ، وقامت باعتقال عدد كبير من اعضاء الجماعة الإسلامية ، وفي مقدمتهم أمير الجماعة الاسلامية في بني سويف ، وكذلك بعض المسيحيين الذين اشتركوا في اعمال الشغب .

*زيارة مريبة

* ومن الغريب ان السفير الاميركي بالقاهرة «فرانك ويرنر » قام بزيارة سرية لاسيوط – قبيل احداث الشغب الاخيرة ، وعقب زيارته «المعلنة » لبني سويف لافتتاح بعض المشروعات الجديدة .

* ومن المعروف ان السفارة الاميركية بالقاهرة قامت مؤخرا بعمل

مسح اجتماعي شامل لمحافظات الصعيد ، كما انها تعد مشروعا لانشاء قرية نموذجية هناك .

* السكرتير الخاص لشيخ الازهر رفض التعليق على الاحداث وقال لـ *الوطن* ان بيانا سيصدر في وقت لاحق ، تعليقا على هذه الاحداث .

* وفي تصريح خاص لـ *الوطن* قال جابر رزق المتحدث الرسمي لجماعة الاخوان المسلمين ان الاضطرابات التي شملت مدن الصعيد الثلاث تدل دلالة قاطعة على ان هناك اصابع خفية ومشبوهة تريد اثارة الفتنة بين عنصري الامة ، المسلمين والاقباط ، تحقيقا لمخطط معروف للجميع يستهدف « لبننة » المنطقة ، وتفجير الصراعات الطائفية التي لم تعرفها مصر من قبل ، ويكفي للدلالة على ذلك ان الاحداث الاخيرة اندلعت عقب زيارة السفير الاميركي لبعض مدن الصعيد .

وحذر جابر رزق من الوقوع في هذا الفخ الذي تنصبه الامبريالية الاميركية لتمزيق الوحدة الوطنية ولمزيد من السيطرة والهيمنة على مقدرات الشعب المصري .

5. Written Arabic texts 2

(a) Read the following newspaper text from الأهرام, Mar. 20, 1990, then complete exercises i. – iii. which follow.

الاهالي

ليس اسلاما وليسوا مسلمين!

ازعم انني اعرف كمواطن مصري عربي الاسلام كما يعرفه كل مسلم مستنير . وازعم انه يشكل مع الحضارة الاسلامية الجانب الاساسي من ثقافتنا بعد ان استوعب كل العناصر الايجابية من الحضارات غير الاسلامية التي ساهمت في تشكيل وجداننا .

ولذلك ازعم بضمير مستريح ان كل ما حدث ويحدث في المنيا و« ابو قرقاص » وبني مزار وغيرها من البؤر المشابهة لا علاقة له

بالاسلام ولا يقوم به مسلمون.

وكل الآيات القرآنية الكريمة والاحاديث الصحيحة او المكذوبة التي توجهها تلك الجماعات الشريرة الى جماهير البسطاء لا تغير من هذه الحقيقة الثابتة.

فهل هناك مسلم يمكن ان يحرق بيت او محل جاره المسيحي ويعتدي على حياته لان هناك إشاعة او «حقيقة» تتهم احد المسيحيين بالفسوق ؟ !

منذ عامين او يزيد سرت إشاعة بأن في بلدتنا «طما» بصعيد مصر اخترع «عالم» صعيدي قبطي جهازا به سائل ملون إذا وجهته الى ملابس الفتيات المسلمات يطبع عليها علامة الصليب !!

ورغم ان العلماء الامريكيين والسوفييت لم يصلوا الى مثل هذا الاختراع المذهل الا انه .. كم ذا بمصر من « المعجزات » ؟!

وبدأت فتنة طائفية ساهمت فيها للأسف صحف في القاهرة تدعي الدفاع عن الاسلام عندما اخذت تناقش في جدية شديدة : احتمالات ارتكاب بعض الاقباط لمثل هذا السخف ، وتبحث عن الجهاز الذي « يرش » الصلبان ولا يرسم هلالا واحدا !!

ولم يتحرك احد في اسيوط او سوهاج من العلماء الاجلاء « المعتدلين » من اساتذة الجامعة او نادي هيئة التدريس الذين ينسبون انفسهم الى الحركة الاسلامية ليشرح لتلاميذه تناقض مثل هذه الخرافات مع الاسلام ومع ابسط قواعد العلم .

وفي الاحداث الاخيرة يحدث نفس الشيء بحذافيره . يتقاسم صغار رجال الامن في « ابو قرقاص » وغيرها سلطة الدولة مع صبية يدعون التفقه في شئون الدين والدنيا وينصبون الفاعل ويرفعون المفعول به .

ويخضع مسئولون للابتزاز في تراجع مهين امام اي قاطع طريق او جهول ما دام يرفع لافتة دينية حتى لو كانت زائفة او مهلهلة.

والحزب الوطني الديمقراطي يحتكر كل الاجهزة السياسية
والتنفيذية والاعلامية لكنه لا يعمل بالسياسة . ولا يسمح للآخرين
بان يعملوا بها . وهو لا يريد ان يعرف ان ما يحدث في تلك الاماكن
لا علاقة له بالدين من قريب او بعيد . انها حركات سياسية في
احط درجاتها . وهدفها الوحيد هو تمزيق اوصال مصر . ومن ثم ما
تبقى من الوطن العربي . وليس هذا اكتشافا . انها خطة معلنة
ومطبقة منذ اعوام وعلى رؤوس الاشهاد.

والجانب الامني رغم اهميته البالغة ليس وحده الحل حتى لو
شعر الناس بالفزع كما يقول مندوبنا في المنيا « وترحموا » على
ايام زكي بدر !

والاهم من ذلك هو ان يكون هناك حـــزب وطني يحكم لانه
يحصل على اغلبية حقيقية دون تزوير . وان يعمل اعضاؤه
بالسياسة بعض الوقت بدلا من ان يكون همهم الوحيد هو الاقتصاد
او الاثراء .

وفي ظل وضع اكثر ديموقراطية ستنكشف كل الاوراق دون ان
يهتز الامن او الاستقرار .

وسيبدو مدعو الاعتدال او المتواطئون على حقيقتهم . حيث
يتوارون الآن في الظل لكي يتقدموا الصفوف كمنقذين بعد ان
تستهلك المعركة قوات النظام وقوات المتطرفين.

i Answer the following questions in English.

1. What is the nationality of the writer?
2. Can the religion of the writer be inferred from the text?
3. What role does the writer claim Islam plays in 'our' culture?
4. According to the writer, what relation do recent events in al-Minya, etc. bear to Islam?
5. What can you infer happened in these places? (see para. 4)
6. What rumour circulated in Tama two years ago or more?
7. What was amazing about this rumour?
8. How did the newspapers react to the rumour?
9. How did 'moderate' university professors then respond?

10. What has been happening recently in Abu Qarqas and other places?
11. In what circumstances have people in authority been robbed?
12. What does the National Democratic Party control?
13. What does the National Democratic Party fail to do, according to the writer?
14. Whose sole aim is to tear Egypt apart?
15. What would they then do?
16. What do members of the National Party concern themselves with now?
17. When will proponents of moderation be seen as they really are?

ii Compare the accounts of the 'cross–spraying' incident in paragraphs 5–8 of this passage with the account of this incident in paragraph 2 of the written Arabic texts 1 (d) السفير الأميركي زار أسيوط. Consider in English how the two accounts differ in terms of the details they present, and their general assessment of the incident. What linguistic features (words, structures) are used by the two writers to reinforce the particular view of the incident?

iii Translate the first seven paragraphs of this passage (down to ولا يرسم هلالا واحدا) into idiomatic English.

(b) Read the following piece of academic writing by أحمد كمال ابو مجد from الباحث العربي no. 31, Nov. 1992, in التطرف الديني ... أم أزمة مجتمع (pub. The Arab Research Centre), then translate the text into idiomatic English.

ولقد تطورت ظاهرة التطرف الديني تطوراً سريعاً خلال
السنوات الأخيرة ... فامتدت من قطر عربي إلى قطر
عربي آخر، واتسعت قاعدتها – خصوصاً بين الشباب –
داخل أكثر الأقطار العربية ... وتحولت في بعض الأقطار
العربية من ظاهرة هامشية قليلة التأثير على التيار
العام للحياة إلى ظاهرة نشطة تمتد عمقاً ومساحةً.
ويمارس أصحابها تأثيراً متعاظماً على المسيرة السياسية
والاجتماعية للعديد من الشعوب العربية والإسلامية كذلك
سجلت السنوات الخمس الأخيرة إخفاق الوسائل الأمنية
الخالصة التي اعتمدت عليها كثير من الحكومات في
مقاومة الجماعات العديدة التي تحمل شعارات إسلامية
والتي تمارس صوراً عديدة من العنف السياسي

والاجتماعي ... بدلاً من أن يؤدي هذا الضغط الأمني الذي
تجاوز الحدود في بعض البلاد العربية إلى اختفاء هذه
الجماعات أو تغييرها لأساليبها أو تنفير القواعد
الجماهيرية والشعبية منها، فقد أدت الوسائل الأمنية إلى
نمو تيار من العنف المتبادل سقط بسببه مئات من
القتلى والجرحى وازداد الأمن اختلالاً واهتز الاستقرار
السياسي والاجتماعي. وأخطر من ذلك كله أن المقولات
الفكرية والسياسية لكثير من تلك الجماعات بدأت تأخذ
سبيلها إلى المزيد من الدوائر الشبابية ... وأن درجة
التوتر العام في المجتمع قد زادت زيادة كبيرة، حتى بدت
مشكلة «التطرف الديني» وكأنها المشكلة الوحيدة التي
تواجه الشعوب والحكومات العربية والإسلامية دون أن
يبدو لها حل في الأفق...

(c) The following text is from the novel أولاد حارتنا by نجيب محفوظ, p. 5.
It is possible to interpret this book in religious terms: الجبلاوي can be seen as a
God figure, and other major characters are interpretable as Prophets in the
Islamic line; أدهم can be identified with Adam, جبل with Moses, رفاعة with
Jesus, and قاسم with Muhammad. When the book was first published in Egypt
in serial form in the Egyptian newspaper الأهرام in 1959, it was severely
criticised by Islamic leaders and caused major public disturbances. It was
subsequently banned, and was only finally published in book form in Lebanon
in 1976.
Read the text, then complete the vocabulary identification exercise which
follows.

هذه حكاية حارتنا، أو حكايات حارتنا وهو الأصدق. لم أشهد من
واقعها إلا طوره الأخير الذي عاصرته، ولكني سجلتها جميعاً كما
يرويها الرواة وما أكثرهم. جميع أبناء حارتنا يروون هذه
الحكايات، يرويها كل كما يسمعها في قهوة حيّة أو كما نقلت إليه
خلال الأجيال، ولا سند لي فيما كتبت إلا هذه المصادر. وما أكثر

المناسبات التي تدعو إلى ترديد الحكايات. كلما ضاق أحد بحاله، أو ناء بظلم أو سوء معاملة، أشار إلى البيت الكبير على رأس الحارة من ناصيتها المتصلة بالصحراء وقال في حسرة: «هذا بيت جدّنا، جميعنا من صلبه، ونحن مستحقو أوقافه، فلماذا نجوع وكيف نضام؟!» ، ثم يأخذ في قصّ القصص والاستشهاد بسير أدهم وجبل ورفاعة وقاسم من أولاد حارتنا الأمجاد. وجدّنا هذا لغز من الألغاز. عمّر فوق ما يطمع إنسان أو يتصور حتى ضُرب المثل بطول عمره. واعتزل في بيته لكبره منذ عهد بعيد، فلم يره منذ اعتزاله أحد. وقصة اعتزاله وكبره مما يحير العقول، ولعل الخيال أو الأغراض قد اشتركت في إنشائها. على أيّ حال كان يدعى الجبلاوي وباسمه سميت الحارة.

Identify the words or phrases in the Arabic text which correspond to the following in English (N.B. the English words and phrases are listed in the same order of occurrence as the corresponding Arabic words and phrases in the original text).

lines 1–5
1. to be more precise
2. how many they are/they are so many/who are extremely numerous
3. across the generations
4. how many occasions there are/there are so many occasions
lines 6–10
5. anyone
6. he felt depressed
7. we are entitled to his endowments
lines 11–15
8. a total mystery/one of life's mysteries
9. his longevity became proverbial
10. since he secluded himself he has been seen by no–one
11. our quarter was named after him

6. Written Arabic texts 3 (classical)

(a) Read the following text by ابن تيمية from إصلاح في السياسة الشرعية
(Cairo: الراعي والرعية مكتبة دار الشعب), pp. 184–8, then translate the text into idiomatic English.

أهمية الولاية

يجب أن يُعْرَف أنَّ ولاية أمر الناس من أعظم واجبات الدين ، بل لا قيامَ للدين إلاّ بها ، فإن بني آدم لا تَتم مصلحتهم إلاّ بالاجتماع لحاجة بعضهم إلى بعض ، ولا بد لهم عند الاجتماع من الحاجة إلى رأس حتى قال النبي صلى الله عليه وسلم « إذَا خَرَجَ ثَلاَثَةٌ في سَفَرٍ فَلْيُؤَمِّروا أحَدَهُمْ ». رواه أبو داود ، من حديث أبي سعيد، وأبي هريرة.

وروى الإمام أحمد في المسند ، عن عبد الله بن عمرو أن النبيَّ صلى الله عليه وسلم قال : « لاَ يَحلُّ لثَلاَثَةٍ يَكُونُونَ بفَلاةٍ منَ الأرْض إلاّ أمَّروا عَلَيهمْ أحَدَهُمْ » فأوجب صلى الله عليه وسلم تأمير الواحد في الاجتماع القليل العارض في السفر ، تنبيها بذلك على سائر أنواع الاجتماع ، ولأن الله أوجب الأمر بالمعروف والنهي عن المنكر ؛ ولايتم ذلك إلاّ بقوة وإمارة . وكذلك سائر ما أوجبه من الجهاد والعدل ، وإقامة الحج والجمعة والأعياد ، ونصر المظلوم ، وإقامة الحدود ، لاتتم إلاّ بالقوة والإمارة.

ولهذا روي : « أنَّ السُّلْطَانَ ظلُّ الله في الارْض » . ويقال : « ستُّونَ سَنَةً من إمامٍ جائرٍ أصلَحُ منْ لَيْلَةٍ واحدَةٍ بلاَ سُلْطَانٍ » . والتجربة تبين ذلك ؛ ولهذا كان السلف كالفُضَيْلِ بن عياضٍ ، وأحمد بن حنبل ، وغيرهما ، يقولون : « لو كان لنا دعوة مجابة لدعونا بها للسلطان ». وقال النبي صلى الله عليه وسلم : « إنَّ اللهَ يَرْضَى لَكُمْ ثَلاَثَةً : أنْ تَعْبُدُوهُ ولاَ تُشْركُوا به شَيْئاً ، وأنْ تَعْتَصمُوا بحَبْل الله جَميعاً ولاَ تَفَرَّقُوا ، وأن تُنَاصحُوا مَنْ ولاَّهُ اللهُ أمْرَكمْ » . رواه مسلم ، وقال : « ثَلاَثَةٌ لايُغلُّ(١) عَلَيْهنَّ قَلْبُ مُسْلمٍ : إخْلاَصُ

الــعَمَل لــه ، وَمُنَاصَحَةُ وُلاَةِ الأَمْرِ ، وَلُزُومُ جَمَاعَةِ الْمُسْلِمِين ، فَإِنَّ دَعْوَتَهُمْ تُحِيطُ مِنْ وَرَائِهِمْ » . رَواهُ أَهْلُ السُّنَن ، وفي الصَّـحِـيـحِ عنه أنَّهُ قال : « الدِّينُ النَّصِيـحَةُ ، الدِّينُ النَّصِيـحَةُ ، الدِّينُ النَّصِيـحَةُ . قَالُوا : لِمَنْ يا رَسُولَ اللَّـهِ ؟ قَالَ : لـلَّـهِ وَلِكِتَابِهِ وَلِرَسُولِهِ وَلأَئِمَّةِ الْمُسْلِمِينَ وَعَامَّتِهِمْ » .

فَالـوَاجِب اتخَاذ الإمارة دِينًا وقربة يتقرَّبُ بها إلى الله ، فإن التَّقرُّب إليه فيها بطاعته وطاعة رسوله من أفضل القربات ، وإنما يفسد فيها حال أكثر الناس لابتغاء الرياسة أو المال بها .

......

وغاية مُريد الرِّياسة أن يكون كفرعون ، وجامع المال أن يكون كقارون ، وقد بين الله تعالى في كتابه حال فرعون وقارون ، فقال تعالـى : (أَوَلَمْ يَسِيـرُوا في الأَرْضِ فَيَنْظُرُوا كَيْفَ كَانَ عَاقِبَةُ الَّذِينَ كَانُوا مِنْ قَبْلِهِمْ ، كَانُوا هُمْ أَشَدَّ مِنْهُمْ قُوَّةً وَآثَاراً في الأَرْضِ ، فَأَخَذَهُمُ اللهُ بِذُنُوبِهِمْ ، وَمَا كَانَ لَهُمْ مِنَ اللهِ مِنْ وَاقٍ(٢)). وقال تعالى : (تِلْكَ الـــدَّارُ الآخِرَةُ نَجْعَلُهَا لِلَّذِيــنَ لاَ يُرِيـــدُونَ عُلُوًّا في الأَرْضِ وَلاَفَسَادًا وَالْعَاقِبَةُ لِلْمُتَّقِينَ(٣)) . فإن الناس أربعة أقسام :

قَوْمٌ يريدون العلو على الناس والفساد في الأرض ، وهو معصية الله ، وهؤلاء الملوك والرؤساء المفسدون كفرعون وحزبه ، وهؤلاء هم شــر الخلـق . قال تعالى : (إِنَّ فِرْعَوْنَ عَلاَ في الأَرْضِ وَجَعَلَ أَهْلَهَا شِيَعـاً يَسْتَضْعِفُ طَائِفَةً مِنْهُمْ يُذَبِّحُ أَبْنَاءَهُمْ وَيَسْتَحْيِي نِسَاءَهُمْ إِنَّهُ كَانَ مِنَ الْمُفْسِدِينَ(٤)).

....

والقِـسـم الثـاني : الذيـن يريدون الفـسـاد بـلا علو كـالسـرّاق والمجرمين وسِفْلَة الناس .

والثالث : يريد العلو بلا فساد ، كالذين عندهم دِين يريدون أن يعلوا به على غيرهم من الناس .

.....

والقسم الرابع : فهم أهل الجنة الذين لا يريدون علوّا في الأرض
ولا فسادا ، مع أنهم قد يكونون أعلى من غيرهم كما قال تعالى :
(وَلاَ تَهِنُوا وَلاَ تَحْزَنُوا وَأَنْتُمُ الأَعْلَوْنَ إِنْ كُنْتُمْ مُؤْمِنِينَ (⁵)) . وقال :
(فَلاَ تَهِنُوا وَتَدْعُوا إِلَى السَّلْمِ وَأَنْتُمُ الأَعْلَوْنَ ، وَاللهُ مَعَكُمْ وَلَنْ يَتِرَكُمْ
أَعْمَالَكُمْ (⁶)) . وقال : (وَللهِ الْعِزَّةُ وَلِرَسُولِهِ وَلِلْمُؤْمِنِينَ (⁷)) .

Notes

(١) الإغلال : الخيانة في كل شيء .
(٢) غافر : ٢١ .
(٣) القصص : ٨٣ .
(٤) القصص : ٤ .
(٥) محمد : ٣٥ .
(٦) آل عمران : ١٣٩ .
(٧) المنافقون : ٨ .

(b) Read the following text by ابن كثير (1300–73) from his Qur'an commentary
تفسير القرآن العظيم (Beirut: دار الفكر, 1988), vol. II, p. 107, then
translate it into idiomatic English. The text is a commentary on verse 53 of sura
5, سورة المائدة. The verse itself reads:

أَفَحُكْمَ الْجَاهِلِيَّةِ يَبْغُونَ وَمَنْ أَحْسَنُ مِنَ اللهِ حُكْماً لِقَوْمٍ يُوقِنُونَ
'Do they seek a judgement of the Time of Ignorance?
Who is better than God in judgement for a people who
are certain in their faith?'

ينكر تعالى على كل من خرج عن حكم الله المحكّم المشتمل على كل
خيــر، الناهي عن كل شــر وعَدَلَ إلى مــا سواه من الآراء والأهواء
والاصطلاحات التي وضعها الرجال بلا مستند من شريعة الله ، كما
كان أهل الجاهلية يحكمون به من الضلالات الجهالات مما يضعونها
بآرائهم وأهوائهم، وكما يحكم به التتار من السياسات الملكية
المأخوذة عن ملكهم جنكزخان[1] الذي وضع لهم الياسق[2]، وهو عبارة
عن كتاب مجموع من أحكام قد اقتبسها من شرائع شتّى : من
اليهودية والنصرانية والملة الإسلامية وغيرها ؛ وفيها كثير من

الأحكام أخذها من مجـرّد نطره وهـواه ؛ فـصـارت في بنيـه شـرعـاً
متبعاً يقدّمونه على الحكم بكتاب الله وسنّة رسول الله (صلى الله
عليه وسلم) .

Notes

1. Genghis Khan (?1162–1227). Mongol ruler, supported also by other groups such as Turkic Tatars. He established an empire which stretched from the Black Sea to the Pacific and included Iran amongst its vassals.
2. The *yasaq* or *yasa* was Genghis Khan's codification of Mongol traditional law, along with other popular laws and customs. Very little is known about the *yasaq* (although Ibn Kathir's description of its sources in Jewish, Christian and Muslim law is certainly inaccurate).

7. Grammar/stylistics

(a) *Word order: postposing and middling*

i *Postposing*

In chapter 13, we discussed clause–initial elements as emphatics. There is another sense in which clause–final elements can be regarded as emphatic. In Arabic, as in English, the most new or newsworthy information is generally placed at the end of the sentence. The typical order of a sentence is to start with information which is well known (perhaps because it links back to previous material in the passage) or is at least relatively less newsworthy, and to place the more newsworthy information at the end of the sentence.

The fact that the principles of word order and clause–final emphasis are similar in both English and Arabic is reflected in the tendency for the order of ideas in a translation to be similar to that in the original version in the other language. For instance, a sentence هل أعجبتك مصر would typically translate into English as 'Do/Did you like Egypt?'. The grammatical features of the English nouns and pronouns are completely different from those of the Arabic, to the extent of being their mirror image; the Arabic subject مصر is translated as the English object 'Egypt', while the Arabic object, the pronoun suffix ـك, is translated as the English subject 'you'. In terms of word order, however, the two sentences are much more similar to each other than their grammatical structures would suggest. Most importantly, both the Arabic and the English put what is arguably the most newsworthy piece of the sentence مصر/'Egypt' at the end of the sentence.

A similar phenomenon has already been discussed with respect to the passive in English in chapter 3 (ch. 3, 7aii). As pointed out there it is common to find an English passive with an agent corresponding to an Arabic clause with V–O–S (Verb–Object–Subject) or V–Pp–S (Verb–Prepositional phrase–Subject) word order. Examples given there were:

وعندما أَضاءت وجهَ أَبيك {سيارةٌ عابرةٌ} ...
'When your father's face was illuminated by a passing car.' (ch. 6, 5a)

يجيب على هذا السؤال {الدكتور نيقولا الزيادة}.
'This question is answered by Dr Nicola Ziadeh.' (ch. 3, 8)

The grammatical structures of the English and the Arabic are quite different in these examples; in both examples the Arabic has an active verb and the English a passive, and the Arabic subject corresponds to the English *by*–phrase; in the first example the Arabic object corresponds to the English subject, and in the second example the Arabic prepositional phrase – على هذا السؤال – corresponds to the English subject. The word order in the Arabic originals and the English translations is, however, strikingly similar. In all cases the same noun phrase appears in final position in the English translation as in the Arabic original; سيارة عابرة – 'a passing car' in the first example, and الدكتور نيقولا الزيادة – 'Dr Nicola Ziadeh' in the second example. In fact, the Arabic V–O–S structures and V–Pp–S structures have the same informational effect as the English passives; by placing the subject in the case of Arabic, or the *by*–phrase in the passive sentence (which is the equivalent of the active subject) in the case of English, they allow this noun phrase to receive final emphasis and to be treated as the most newsworthy element of the clause or sentence.

This newsworthy element will often be indefinite, i.e. it will be 'unknown' to the extent of not having previously been mentioned in the text. So, in the first example وجه أبيك is grammatically definite in the Arabic, and the person's father has in fact been previously mentioned in the same paragraph. Similarly 'Your father's face' suggests previous mention in the English. By contrast, سيارة عابرة is grammatically indefinite and has not been previously mentioned in the text. This is therefore the more newsworthy piece of information. The same considerations apply to the English 'a passing car'.

In the second example, which is taken from a question–and–answer programme on the BBC Arabic Service, the listener's question has already been given, and على هذا السؤال – 'This question' is not, therefore, particularly newsworthy information. The name of the person who will reply to the question has not, however, previously been mentioned. It is therefore newsworthy information, and comes at the end of the sentence. (In fact the text then goes on with Dr Nicola Ziadeh himself discussing the topic raised by the listener.)

The fact that Arabic allows Verb–Object/Prepositional phrase–Subject word order effectively eliminates the need for an equivalent to the English passive+*by*–phrase. However, in modern Arabic, one sometimes comes across passive verbs, passive participles and verbal nouns with من قبَل , where من قبَل is the equivalent of the English *by*–phrase. Examples in this book are:

.. ان الجيش «سيستجيب بعزم لاستدعائه {من قبل} رئيس
الحكومة لحفظ الامن العام».
'... that the army will respond with resolution to any call from/by the
Prime Minister to maintain public security.' (ch. 15, 5d)

وهذا الاصرار الذي يتجلى في التوجه الرسمي بحاجة اكيدة الى
تضافر ومؤازرة باصرار مقابل وبخاصة من قبل الاحزاب
والتنظيمات السياسية ..
'This insistence which is abolutely clear in the official position
undoubtedly needs to be supported and strengthened through a similar
insistence particularly by/on the part of the parties and political
organisations ...' (ch. 15, 11a)

Elsewhere, forms other the من قبل may sometimes be found in a similar function,
such as ل:

وذلك انطلاقا من نسبة الاسهم المملوكة للحكومة ..
'This is based on the fact that the proportion of shares owned by the
government ...' (ch. 18, 4a)

Such usages, whether with من قبل or with other forms are frowned upon by
linguistic purists in the Arab world, and are mainly found in newspapers, either
through the direct influence of English or another European language in a
translation from that language, or through the indirect influence of English (etc.).
Accordingly, من قبل is felt by some writers to be part of newspaper style.

  The importance of postposing newsworthy elements in Arabic goes beyond
simple correspondence with the English passive+*by*–phrase. Consider the
following:

وتقول مانويلا كورتيس إن البحث عن الموسيقى الأندلسية يتكون
من شقين: الشعر والموسيقى، الشعر لا يزال في المخطوطات
{محفوظًا}، بينما طريقة العزف والموسيقى تناقلها المطربون
والموسيقيون جيلاً عن جيل ..
'Manuela Cortes says that the search for Andalusian music consists of
two parts: the poetry and the music. The poetry is still to be found in
manuscripts, while the method of playing and the music was passed on
from generation to generation by the singers and musicians ...' (ch. 12,
11)

Here the word محفوظا is postposed (the more normal word order would have
been لا يزال محفوظا في المخطوطات), since the fact that the poetry is preserved
is being treated as more important than the fact that it is in manuscripts (note also

the contrastive postposing of الشعر in الشعر لا يزال في المخطوطات محفوظا, and طريقة العزف والموسيقى تناقلها المطربون in طريقة العزف والموسيقى (والموسيقيون جيلاً عن جيل ..).

Similarly, in the following case:

وكما اختار الله لمصر {هذا الرجلَ الفذَ} ليكون وسيلة الى نصرها
وحفظها ورفع شأنها ..

'Just as God chose for Egypt this extraordinary man to be the means of
its victory, preservation, and uplifting ..' (ch. 16, 4c)

Here the phrase هذا الرجل الفذ is placed after لمصر, partly because the central
theme of the text is Sadat's greatness, and author is trying throughout to stress his
importance, and partly because the phrase هذا الرجل الفذ links directly to the
next phrase ..يكون وسيلة الى نصرها وحفظها ورفع شأنها.

ii *Pronominal middling*

The postposing of newsworthy information is closely related to another
phenomenon, which might be termed pronominal middling. This is the tendency
for phrases involving pronoun suffixes – and particularly prepositions with
pronoun suffixes – to be placed towards the middle of the sentence. This reflects
the fact that forms involving pronoun suffixes are unlikely to be particularly
newsworthy; such suffixes almost invariably refer to something which is well
known generally or which has been previously mentioned a relatively short time
before in the text.

Sometimes such middling is dictated by the grammar. For example:

كان {له} قاصّ يقال له عمر بن ذرّ ..

'He had a story teller called Umar ibn Dhurr ...' (ch. 17, 4c)

Here it would be at the least very unusual to find له in any other position than
before the noun قاص.

Such middling is also standard in relative clauses. For example:

والشوارع امتلأت بالبيريهات الزرقاء يتحرك {تحتها} جنودٌ
وضباطٌ ..

'The streets were filled with blue berets, under which moved men and
officers [officers and men] ...' (ch. 13, 11b)

وثمة تجارة مشتركة يعمل {فيها} كل قادر ..

'There is a common trade in which everyone who is able to works ...'
(ch. 17, 5a)

Elsewhere the choice of word order is a matter of context rather than grammar. For example:

فان الناس لم يعرفوا {عنه} شيئا الا اسمه هذا

'People knew nothing about him except this name [of his]' (ch. 17, 4c)

iii *Adverbial middling*
There is also a tendency to middle adverbial phrases, generally in nominal sentences.

'Today he is a Sufi ...' (ch. 13, 11b)   وهو {اليوم} متصوف ..

والجانب الامني {رغم اهميته البالغة} ليس وحده الحل ..

'Despite its vital importance, the security aspect is not alone the solution ..' (ch. 14, 5a)

وايران {وهي تودع هذه الايام زعيمها} بحاجة الى وقفة مع النفس ..

'At this time when it is paying its last respects to its leader, Iran needs to take stock [lit: 'stop with itself'] ...' (ch. 16, 5c)

Standard Arabic does not normally allow the word order in a clause Adv–S–P (Adverbial–Subject–Predicate) (cf. ch. 13, 7a). Therefore in the case of a nominal clause (in which by definition the subject precedes the predicate), the adverbial must come either immediately after the subject, or later in the clause, typically at the end. When an adverbial is the most newsworthy element in the clause, it will come at the end. Otherwise it will typically occur immediately after the subject. It is noteworthy that all the examples given here are translated into English with preposed adverbial phrases.

There are also numerous examples of adverbial middling with verbal sentences. Sometimes this also occurs in Adv–Vc sentences, as in:

وفي القرن الثاني عشر احتكر الرهبانُ {في اوروبا} مهنةَ التداوي بالاعشاب وزراعتها ..

'In the twelfth century in Europe, monks [and nuns] had a monopoly of herbal medicine and the growing of herbs ...' (ch. 19, 4a)

Here there is already an adverbial at the start of the sentence في القرن الثاني عشر, and the second adverbial في أوروبا is placed in the middle of the sentence after the subject, i.e. the same position as in which the middled adverbial is placed in nominal sentences. It is also possible to have two adverbials at the start of a verbal clause; an example discussed in chapter 13 (ch. 13, 7a) was: و{في هذا المكان منذ سنتين} ظهرت فتاة يونانية .. 'In this very place, two years ago, a

Greek girl appeared ...' (ch. 13, 11b). Doubled preposed adverbials, however, are fairly rare.

It is also possible to find adverbial middling in verbal clauses which do not have a preposed adverbial. So:

تجددت {الاسبوع الماضي} حوادثُ الشـغب في بعض مـدن صـعيد مصر ..

'Riots broke out again last week in a number of cities in southern Egypt ...' (ch. 13, 4d)

Here there are two adverbials, of which one, في بعض مـدن صـعيد مصـر, is postposed, while the other, الاسبوع الماضي, is middled. Adverbial middling here involves the placing of the adverbial phrase before the subject حوادث الشـغب. This is allowed where the verb is intransitive.

A slightly different case is presented in a verbal clause where the verb is transitive. If there is no subject noun phrase, the word order with a middle adverbial is Verb–Adverbial–Object, as in:

بدأ {في طفولته} تَعَلُّمَ القراءة والكتابة وحفظ القرآن الكريم في كُتَّاب القرية ..

'During his childhood he began learning to read and write, and to memorise the Qur'an in the village Qur'an school ...' (ch. 17, 4b)

In cases where the verb is transitive, and where there is a subject noun phrase, the word order is Verb–Subject–Adverbial–Object. An adapted version of the previous example, with a subject added would therefore read:

بدأ هذا الرجلُ {في طفولته} تَعَلُّمَ القراءة والكتابة وحفظ القرآن الكريم في كُتَّاب القرية ..

'During his childhood this man began learning to read and write, and to memorise the Qur'an in the village Qur'an school ...' (ch. 17, 4b)

The major word order possibilities with middled adverbials are therefore as follows:

1. V–first clauses and clauses with preposed adverbials:

  a. Where there is no noun subject:
  (Adv)–V–Adv–Other
  b. Where there is a noun subject without an object or objective prepositional phrase (an objective prepositional phrase being a prepositional phrase which is dependent on a verb, just as an object

is; for example, the phrase عَلَيَّ in ضَحِكَ عَلَيَّ 'he laughed at me'):
(Adv)–V–Adv–S
c. Where there is a noun subject with an object or objective
prepositional phrase:
(Adv)–V–S–Adv–Other
In these cases, 'Other' might be an object, an objective prepositional
phrase, or a combination of these two.

2. Subject–Predicate clauses:
    S–Adv–P
    The predicate may be a verb phrase, a noun phrase, an adjectival
    phrase, or an adverbial (cf. ch. 13, 7a).

(b) Pronoun of separation
As noted in chapter 13 (section 7a) it is possible to have nominal sentences of the
structure S–(S–Pc), i.e Subject–Predicate sentences in which the predicate itself
consists of a Subject–Predicate clause. One fairly common structure of this kind in
Standard Arabic involves the use of a pronoun of separation, or what is known in
Arabic as ضَمِيرُ الفَصْل. A simple example of this kind of sentence is:

'This is the boy'   هذا هو الولد

Here the subject of the entire sentence, i.e. the main subject, is هذا 'This'. The
predicate of the entire sentence is the phrase, in fact also a clause, هو الولد. This
predicate clause can itself be divided up into a subject and predicate, the subject of
the predicate clause being هو and its predicate being الولد. The overall structure of
the sentence هذا هو الولد can therefore be represented as follows:

هذا–(هو–الولد)
(P   – S) – S

This might be paraphrased into English as:

This – he [is] the boy

This structure involving the pronoun of separation has two basic functions: i.
structural disambiguation or identification; and ii. emphasis.

i *Structural disambiguation or identification*
Consider again the sentence هذا هو الولد 'This is the boy', and compare it with
an apparent potential equivalent هذا الولد. In modern Standard Arabic هذا الولد
can only mean 'this boy', i.e. هذا الولد has to be interpreted as a noun phrase,
(although an interpretation 'This is the boy' is possible in Classical Arabic). The

function of the pronoun هو in هذا هو الولد is to separate هذا from الولد, such that the form هذا هو الولد is interpreted as a sentence (or clause), rather than as a noun phrase; and it is for this reason that هو in this context is known as pronoun of separation.

One typical position in which the pronoun of separation occurs is between two definite noun phrases or a definite noun phrase and a definite adjective phrase. An example of the use of the pronoun of separation between two definite noun phrases is the following:

والقلق الفردي والعائلي والاجتماعي والدولي {هي} البركات التي
تتلقى بها تلك الآلهة الكافرة عبادها المتحمسين !

'Personal, family, social, and global anxiety are the blessings which those false gods bestow on their enthusiastic slaves!' (ch. 14, 11ai)

Here the pronoun of separation serves to mark off البركات .. as the start of the 'predicate proper', and makes sure that the reader does not misinterpret it, for instance as a noun phrase in apposition (cf. ch. 11, 7a) with the preceding phrase القلق الفردي. Similarly:

وأول من اشتغل في الصناعات {هم} أهل وادي الرافدين ..

'The first people to engage in industry were the people of Mesopotamia ...' (ch. 20, 4a)

Other examples of the pronoun of separation before definite noun phrases, this time involving subjects preceded by إنَّ and أنَّ are the following:

إن الديمقراطية {هي} خيارنا الذي لن نحيد عنه او نتراجع عنه
ابدا ..

'Democracy is our choice, which we shall never deviate or retreat from ...' (ch. 15, 11a)

وأكبر الظن أن الذي أنشأ هذه القصة ونماها انما {هو} هذا المكان
الذي احتلته قبيلة كندة في الحياة الاسلامية منذ تمت للنبي
السيطرة على البلاد العربية الى أواخر القرن الأول للهجرة.

'Most probably, what created and developed this story was the position occupied by the Kinda tribe in Islamic times from the Prophet's conquest of the Arabian peninsula until the end of the first century after the *hijra*.' (ch. 17, 4c)

It is also common to find a pronoun of separation before a predicate beginning with أنْ or أنَّ. For example:

ولكن الشيء الذي لا شك فيه أيضاً {هو} أنَّ للوحدة (وهي ما تعبر
عن الصفة العربية الشاملة) تقدماً ورجحاناً معنوياً ..

'But the thing about which there is no doubt as well is that unity –
which is what expresses the notion of the Arab totality [lit: 'what
expresses the total Arab description'] – is imbued with [lit: 'has'] a
moral progressiveness and superiority ...' (ch. 13, 11a)

والاهم من ذلك {هو} ان يكون هناك حزب وطني يحكم لانه يحصل
على اغلبية حقيقية دون تزوير.

'More important than all of that is that there should be a national party
which rules because it achieves a genuine non–fraudulent majority.'
(ch. 14, 5a)

It is not, however, obligatory to have a pronoun of separation before either a
definite predicate or a predicate beginning with أَنْ or أَنَّ. The following are
examples with أَنْ and أَنَّ. The symbol {X} marks where the pronoun of separation
would occur.

وأخطر من ذلك كله {X} أن المقولات الفكرية والسياسية لكثير من
تلك الجماعات بدأت تأخذ سبيلها إلى المزيد من الدوائر الشبابية
..

'Even more seriously, the intellectual and political slogans of many of
these groups have begun to make increasing headway amongst the
young ..' (ch. 14, 5b)

إن مهمتنا {X} أن نتميز وأن نحمل الشعلة للضالين في شعاب
الارض وفي متاهات الصحراء .

'Our task is to be aware and to carry the torch to the lost in the mountain
paths of the earth and the trackless wastes of the desert.' (ch. 13, 11b)

It is also possible to find pronouns of separation before indefinite predicates. For
example:

لا شك أن أهداف « البعث العربي » التي لخصناها في « الحرية
والاشتراكية والوحدة » {هي} أهداف اساسية ..

'There is no doubt that the goals of the Arab Ba'th [Renaissance] Party
which we have summarised as 'Freedom, Socialism and Unity' are
fundamental goals ...' (ch. 13, 11a)

وهذا الفرق أيضاً بين الحرية والاشتراكية كما تُفهمان في حالة
التجزئة (وفي عقلية التجزئة) وبينهما في عقلية الوحدة، {هو}
فرق في النوع وليس في الكم.

'And this difference as well between freedom and socialism as they are
understood in a state of division (and the mentality of division) and as
they are understood in the mentality of unity, is a qualitative and not a
quantitative distinction.' (ch. 13, 11a)

The pronoun of separation often occurs after a long subject. Here structural
disambiguation is involved in a general sense. More specifically, the pronoun of
separation provides a structural clue, functioning like a resumptive particle (ch. 10,
7b, ch. 17, 7a). For example:

الاتفاق الذي تم التوصل اليه بين شطري اليمن لحل المسائل
الحدودية المعلقة والاستثمار للنفط بين البلدين {هو} خطوة هامة
في مسيرة اليمن بشطريه ..

'The agreement which was reached between the two parts of Yemen to
solve the undecided border issues and oil investment [questions]
between the two countries is an important step for the destiny of Yemen
in its two halves ...' (ch. 13, 5a)

ان الحرية التي يطلبها حزب مصري او لبناني، والاشتراكية التي
يعمل لها حزب عراقي او سوري، {هما} غير الحرية والاشتراكية
اللتين تحتاجهما وتقدر على تحقيقهما الأمة العربية كأمة واحدة
ذات تراث حضاري ..

'The freedom which is demanded by an Egyptian or Lebanese party,
and the socialism which is striven for by an Iraqi party or a Syrian party
are not the freedom and the socialism which is required and is
achievable by the Arab nation as a single nation with a [single] cultural
heritage ...' (ch. 13, 11a)

ii *Emphasis*

The second major purpose of the pronoun of separation is to emphasise the
preceding subject element. The pronoun of separation often occurs where the
subject has been introduced by إنّ, as in the example beginning إنّ الحرية التي
يطلبها حزب مصري, which is itself an emphatic particle. The pronoun of
separation can also occur after a long subject which has not been introduced by إنّ,
as in the example beginning الاتفاق الذي تم التوصل اليه بين شطري اليمن,
cited above. Both structures beginning with إنّ and nominal clauses are potentially
emphatic (cf. ch. 15, 7a for إنّ, and ch. 13, 7a for nominal clauses). The use of the
pronoun of separation in these contexts, therefore, can partly be regarded as

confirming the emphasis which is already potentially present in such sentences.

Another case in which the pronoun of separation has a strong connection with emphasis is where this pronoun precedes a relative clause beginning with الذي. This very often translates appropriately into English as the so–called cleft–sentence, i.e. an emphatic sentence of the type 'It was John that I saw', as opposed to the more basic sentence 'I saw John'. For example:

بالإضافة إلى أن الاحزاب هي التي تدعو إلى الفتنة.

'... in addition to the fact that it is the parties which are stirring up dissension ...' (ch. 14, 11b)

Elsewhere a cleft–sentence may not be so appropiate. For example:

إن الاتفاق على مبادئ الاصلاح السياسي وعلى صوغها في دستور جديد هو الذي يعيد الحيوية الى المجتمع ..

'Only agreement on the principles for political reform and their fashioning into a new constituation will restore vitality to society ...' (ch. 14, 4b)

rather than:

'It is the agreement on the principles for political reform and their fashioning into a new constitution which will restore vitality to society ...' (ch. 14, 4b)

8. Aural Arabic texts 1

Listen to the following recording of part of a خطبة by the well–known Egyptian fundamentalist preacher الشيخ كشك, then complete the gapped transcription which follows. In this extract the Sheikh is mocking two members of the People's Assembly (the Egyptian Parliament) who have been elected on an 'Islamic' ticket for their concern with trivial matters relating to religion, while they ignore serious social problems to which Islamic principles should be applied. (Note that the quality of the original recording is rather poor.)

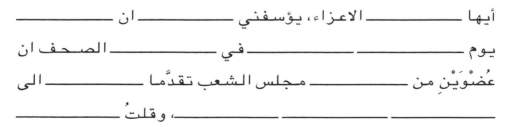

———— ، هل يسألانه « ———— ———— ———— تطبّقوا شرع

———— ———— سألاه « ————— » ؟

تُغلقوا شارع الهرم[1] ليفيض ———— ———— بالكرم؟ »

هل ———— ———— « ———— ———— تُغلقوا الخمّارات؟ »

———— ———— ———— « ———— تمنعون

———— الملاكي[2] التي تحمل ذئبا ونعجة[3] ————

يَزْنيان؟ ———— ———— تمنعوا موائد القمار في جبل

المقطّم[4] ———— ————؟ ———— يا

الاعلام لم تنظر ———— اولادنا بعين الرحمة فتحجب

———— الفاسدَ عن بيوتِنا؟ » ———— ———— على الابواب. لم

يبقَ ———— ———— إلا ———— أشهر ...

———— ———— ———— أفلامك؟ و ————؟

ومبارياتك؟ على أولادِنا ———— ———— هبط مستواهم ————

الدَرَك الاسفل ———— ———— ———— لماذا؟ ألأنك تملك

———— مدرِّساً يدرِّسُ لاولادك دروساً ———— وغالبية

الشعب لاتجد ———— ———— ولا ———— ولا الغطاء ولا الدواء؟

لماذا؟ ———— ———— اعلامك، ———— عن بيوتنا،

———— ، ———— مبارياتك،

هذا ———— الذي حطّم البيوت وحرّض ———— على

———— لكن ———— بالأسى وكأني ————

———— القائل « تمخّض ———— فوَلَدَ فأراً » . أتدرون

——————————— توجّب ..

توجّه .. به[5] اثنان من ——————————— الى ———————————

———————————؟ إنّ ——————————— سؤال ———————————

و———————————، ———————————— جدا. ——————————— سألاه عن مصير

——————————— ——————————— ——————————— الاقصى؟

——————————— ——————————— فلسطين؟

هؤلاء الذين يُضرَبون بالنابالم ويحاربون ——————————— الجراثيمية

——————————— افغانستان[6]؟ ——————————— انما سألاه و———————————

——————————— «لماذا ——————————— ——————————— على

الناصية[7]؟» يا خيبة الله غذّي السيرَ مسرعةً، ———————————

——————————— ——————————— اي ناصية؟ ناصية كاذبة خاطئة.

——————————— ———————————؟ ——————————— ناصية يا عضوي

——————————؟ يا مَن وضع الشعبُ أيديَه في يديكما

وعاهدتما ——————————— ——————————— على المطالبة بتطبيق ———————————

و——————————— ولكن فاقد الشيءِ لا يعطيه. أيقطعون يد السارق؟

اذا قطعوا ——————————— ——————————— فـمَن الذي يصفِّق. إنّ

——————————— بيد واحدة لا يقع ——————————— يكون. أيحرّمون

———————————؟ هل هم على ——————————— أن يفقدوا أمزجتهم؟ هل

——————————— أكل الحرام[8] وما مُلِئَت البطون إلا بالحرام؟

——————————— ——————————— كم خاب ظنّي فيكما

——————————— ——————————— ———————————، ولكنني

اشكوكمـا الى من يعلم خـائـنة الأعين ومـا تُخـفـي الصـدور . كـفـى

تهريجاً. ــــــــ ــــــــ ــــــــ ذقـون الشـعب.

ــــــــ وهل ، ــــــــ ــــــــ

ــــــــ سـيُطْعِم البطون الجوعى؟ ــــــــ

سـيـوجِد مـسكنـاً ــــــــ ــــــــ ــــــــ

ــــــــ شـابّ ــــــــ الـزواج؟ ــــــــ

سـيُكبِّرُ رغيف العيش ــــــــ ــــــــ

بـحـيث يُشـبع الطفل؟ ــــــــ ــــــــ خـيـبـة،

ما بعدها ــــــــ ــــــــ

Notes

1. The *Avenue of the Pyramids* is well known for its plush nightclubs. Muslim fundamentalists have demanded that these be closed down since the early days of the Muslim Brotherhood.

2. In Egyptian colloquial the word مَلاَّكِي does not inflect for number or gender. This pattern is followed here by the Sheikh.

3. Metaphorical to refer to the men preying sexually on innocent women.

4. Mokattam: chain of hills to east of Cairo.

5. توجِّب ; slip of the tongue, subsequently corrected to تـوجّـه بـه.

6. Islamicist volunteers went from Egypt, and other Middle Eastern countries, originally to fight the Soviet army which had gone into Afghanistan from 1979 onwards in order to shore up a Marxist regime there.

7. الناصية 'forelock'. ناصـيـة كاذبة خـاطئة is a quotation from sura 96 سورة العلق, verse 16 (cf. ch. 4, 8a). Note also the change from a more colloquial–influenced pronunciation, when the word is first used (roughly as نَصْيـة, in accordance with standard rules for reduction of vowel length, etc. in Egyptian Arabic) to the carefully enunciated classical form in the phrases أيّ ناصـيـة كاذبة خاطئة and the Qur'anic ناصية؟.

8. أكل الحرام. A general notion meaning to engage in anything which is forbidden in Islam, including corrupt financial dealings.

9. Aural Arabic texts 2
Listen to the following passage from حصاد الشهر, no. 7, side 1, item 4, هل
تستطيع الثقافة العربية أن تواكب العصر؟, then complete exercises i. and ii.
which follow.

i   Produce a complete transcription of the text. In your transcription you may find
     some of the following items of vocabulary of use.

نزعة	attitude; position
تبعية	dependency; subordination
غاز	invader; raiding
ارتقى (الى)	to rise to; advance
تأصل	deep–rootedness
انكماش	absorption; self–absorption

ii   In Arabic, discuss the speaker's view of modern Arab culture and Arab attitudes
     to modern Arab culture.

10. Written English texts
Using constructions and vocabulary encountered in the Arabic texts above as far as
possible, translate the following text from Dilip Hiro, *Islamic Fundamentalism*,
(London: Paladin, 1989), p. 274, into idiomatic Arabic.

Islamic fundamentalism

As economic development has accelerated in the Islamic countries in the
wake of political independence, cities have attracted vast numbers of
migrants from the villages. They feel lost and rootless in their new
environment. These alienated masses packed into the poor quarters of
urban centres provide a recruiting ground for radical and revolutionary
groups, secular and religious.

Muslim fundamentalists try to rally the alienated and underpriviliged
on the basis of Islam. They present it as a religion of justice and equity
and decry the current ruling elite as unjust, unIslamic and corrupt which
deserves to be overthrown, or at the very least replaced non–violently,
by true believers. The tactics used to achieve this objective vary: from
setting up secret cells to addressing large congregations inside a mosque
or outside, from bloody confrontations with the security forces to
peaceful participation in elections, from carrying out terroristic actions
to holding non–violent demonstrations, from subverting official
institutions through infiltration to total withdrawal from society, from
waging open warfare against an infidel state to conducting intelligent
debate with secular adversaries.

11. Précis

(a) The following texts (i) and (ii) are by the Egyptian writer and member of the Muslim Brotherhood سَيِّد قُطْب from نحو مجتمع إسلامي, pp. 7–9, and pp. 11–13. سَيِّد قُطْب was born in 1906 and was originally a member of the Wafd party. He went into *de facto* exile in the United States between 1948 and 1951, during which time he was shocked by what he perceived as the promsicuity and materialism of American society. He returned to Egypt in 1951 to become the leading thinker of the Islamic movement in Egypt. Read the following texts, then produce a précis of each in Arabic.

(i)

وكانت البشرية وقد انفلتت من قيود العقيدة الدينية قد انطلقت
إلى عبادات جديدة فأمريكا مـثـلاً قـد نبـذت كل المقدسات التي
عرفتها البشرية في تاريخها كله ، واتخذت لها آلهة ثلاثة جديدة :
الانتاج . والمال . واللذة . وروسيا على الضفة الأخرى كفرت بالله
الواحد واتخذت لها آلهة المادة ، والاقتصاد ، وكارل ماركس.

ولكن شيئاً فشيئاً اخذت البشرية تتبين أن هذه الآلهة وتلك إنما
تقود العالم كله إلى حروب طاحنة واستعمار بغيض . وحيوانية
تنتكس إلى مدارج البشرية الأولى ؛ وان العقد النفسية والأمراض
العصبية ؛ والقلق الفردي والعائلي والاجتماعي والدولي هي
البركات التي تتلقى بها تلك الآلهة الكافرة عبادها المتحمسين !

ولست أدري كيف يعيش الناس في روسيا السوفيتية وراء
الستار الحديدي ولو كانوا يعيشون - كما تدعي الابواق الشيوعية
- لما كان لهذا الستار الحديدي ضرورة ، ولرحبت الحكومة
السوفيتية بمن يطلبون زيارتها لرؤية ما فيها . ولتركت الشعب
الروسي يطلع على نظم العالم الأخرى وهي مطمئنة إلى أنه
سيؤثر نظامه ويتحمس له ، ويلعن النظم الاخرى.

ولكني أدري كيف يعيش الناس في أمريكا . بلد الانتاج الفخم
والثراء الفاحش واللذائذ المباحة .. لقد شهدتهم هنالك والقلق
العصبي يأكل حياتهم على الرغم من كل مظاهر الثراء والنعمة
ووسائل الراحة . إن متاعهم هياج عصبي ومرح حيواني وإنه

يخيل إليك أنهم هاربون دائماً من أشباح تطاردهم ، إنهم آلات تتحرك في جنون وسرعة وهياج لا يقر له قرار . وكثيراً ما كان يخيل إلي أن الناس هناك في طاحونة دائرة لا تني ليل نهار ، صباح مساء ، تطحن بهم ويطحنون ، لا يهدأون لحظة . ولا يطمئنون إلى أنفسهم ولا إلى الحياة من حولهم - إن كانوا يحسون ما حولهم - ليست هناك لحظة للتأمل ، ولا حتى للشعور بالحياة ذاتها وهي تدور حتى أوقات راحتهم ورياضهم في المنزهات والغابات وعلى شواطئ الانهار والبحيرات ... تراهم فيها فتحس انهم في « شغل ؛ » كأي شغل خلال العمل ؛ وكل ما هنالك من فارق أنهم في مكان غير المكان ، وفي عمل غير العمل . ولكن لا راحة ولا هدوء ولا تأمل ، ولا اطمئنان .

(ii)

والعقيدة في الله يجب في الوقت ذاته ألا تكون قيداً للعقل . ولا سجناً للفطرة ، ولا حائلاً دون الانتاج والنمو في الحياة . ومن ثم يبرز الاسلام وتتميز دعوة الاسلام ، وتتجلى حاجة البشرية كلها الينا في هذا الأوان .

حاجة الضمير الفردي إلى الاسترواح والثقة والاطمئنان .

وحاجة العقل البشري ألى الطلاقة والحرية والنشاط .

وحاجة الاسرة الخاصة إلى الحماية والرعاية والثبات .

وحاجة الاسرة البشرية إلى التعارف والتعاون والسلام .

وحاجة الفرد إلى الاعتراف بوجوده وخصائصه وفطرته .

وحاجة المجتمع إلى الحماية والتوازن والاستقرار .

إن شجرة الحضارة البشرية تهتز وتترنح اليوم كما كانت تهتز وتترنح قبيل مولد «الرجل الذي وحد العالم جميعه » فما أشد حاجة البشرية إلى رسالة هذا الرجل لتنفذها مرة أخرى.

إن البشرية كلها في حاجة إلينا : في حاجة إلى عقيدتنا ، وفي

حاجة إلى مبادئنا وفي حاجة الى شريعتنا، وفي حاجة الى نظامنا الاجتماعي ، الذي يكفل الكفاية لكل فرد ، ويكفل الكرامة لكل إنسان ويكفل سلام الضمير وسلام البيت وسلام المجتمع . كما يكفل السلام الدولي العام .

ومن هذه الحاجة الإنسانية – بعد عقيدتنا في الله – نحن نستمد قوتنا وثباتنا على الدعوة إلى عقيدة الإسلام وشريعته ونظامه الاجتماعي الخاص ، سنثبت بعون الله – ولو تخطفنا الشر والطغيان من كل مكان .

إن الذين يريدون لنا أن نذوب في حركة قومية ، أو في كتلة دولية أو في اتجاه عالمي – على فرض أن هناك اتجاهاً عالمياً – إنما يرتكبون جريمتهم في حق البشرية كلها ، قبل أن يرتكبوها في حق الإسلام أو الوطن الإسلامي ..

إن مهمتنا أن نتميز وأن نحمل الشعلة للضالين في شعاب الارض وفي متاهات الصحراء .

إن مهمتنا أن ننقذ البشرية من الحمأة الأسنة التي تتمرغ فيها اليوم ، لا أن نذوب معها في تلك الحمأة الأسنة والله معنا ، والبشرية كلها ستعرف يوماً ؛ أن نبوءة الله حق : « كذلك جعلناكم أمة واحدة لتكونوا شهداء على الناس » .

إن البشرية كلها في حاجة إلينا .. ومن ثم تبدو جسامة الجريمة التي يرتكبها من يحاولون ان نذوب في أية حركة أو أية منظمة أو أية اتجاه داخل الوطن الإسلامي أو خارجه على السواء .

(b) Read the following text by طارق اسماعيل المهدوي الاخوان from his book المسلمون على مذبح المناورة , pp. 19–20, then produce a précis in Arabic. How does Mahdawi's view of Islam contrast with that of Sayyid Qutb? What does text (b) reveal about Mahdawi's general ideological orientation? Consider in particular the use of terms such as: ليست الا تعبيرا, اغتراب ,جماهير نظرية متكاملة ,عقائدي ,سياسيا عن المحتوى الاقتصادي والاجتماعي. What other words and phrases used in the text are indicative of this orientation?

والتقط الإخوان المسلمون النفور التلقائي لدى الجماهير التي تعاني من الاغتراب عن التطورات الاقتصادية والاجتماعية والسياسية والفكرية وأعلنوا رفضهم المطلق لجمل هذه التطورات باعتبارها انهياراً شاملاً ناتجاً عن ابتعاد المسلمين عن دينهم الذي يحوي الشفاء لكل العلل في كل العصور، ورغم أن جماعة الإخوان المسلمين ذاتها ليست إلا تعبيراً سياسياً عن المحتوى الاقتصادي والاجتماعي للتطور فإنها لم تتوان في إعلان رفضها لكافة المؤسسات السياسية الأخرى كالدستور والبرلمان والأحزاب حيث لا دستور إلا القرآن كما أن البرلمان مخصص للصراع الحزبي وهو ما يعد فتنة والفتنة في النار بالإضافة إلى أن الاحزاب هي التي تدعو إلى الفتنة.

وانطلقت جماعة الإخوان المسلمين في دعوتها من التراث الديني المقدس الذي يصعب على الاتجاهات الفكرية الأخرى أن تنافسه كما اعتمدت في تحليلاتها للأحداث على رؤية بسيطة تتفق مع فطرة الغالبية العظمى من الجماهير والتي اعتمدت على تحليل كل ما يدور من صراعات في مختلف المجالات وعلى كافة الأصعدة المحلية والعالمية باعتبارها أشكالاً متعددة لرغبة أعداء الإسلام في تحطيم الإسلام والمسلمين الأمر الذي ساعد على توسيع عضوية جماعة الإخوان المسلمين بصورة لم يسبق لها مثيل بالنسبة لحزب عقائدي في مصر فقد بلغت خلال أقل من عشرين عاماً على ميلادها حوالى المليون من الإخوان المسلمين سواء هؤلاء الذين انتظموا كأعضاء عاملين في الجماعة أو اولئك الذين عملوا مع الجماعة كأعضاء منتسبين ويتقدم الجميع حوالى خمسة وسبعين ألف أخ مجاهد هم الكوادر المقاتلة للجماعة المنتظمة داخل صفوف الجهاز العسكري الخاص. هذا وقد حققت جماعة الإخوان المسلمين هذا النمو الصاروخي دون أي عناء في التنظير والتحليل أو في الدعاية والعمل الجماهيري أو في التجنيد

التنظيمي حيث كانت العضوية تبدأ بمجرد أن يتعاطف الفرد معها لكونها تهدف إلى إعادة مجد العصور السالفة التي كان المسلمون يسودون فيها العالم ويتحكمون في مقدراته وهو الأمر الذي لا يتطلب سوى تثقيف المسلمين بدينهم وتنظيمهم حوله لحمايته من أعدائه ، ولكن الوجه الآخر لهذه العملة كان الضعف الفكري والسياسي مما أفقد عضوية الجماعة الغفيرة القدرة على تقويم تنظيمهم عند انحرافه كما أفقدها القدرة على مواجهة الأفكار والقوى السياسية الأخرى بنظرية متكاملة بديلة فاضطروا إلى مواجهتها بالعنف !

هذا وقد أسهمت عدة عناصر أخرى في هذا النمو الصاروخي لجماعة الاخوان المسلمين كان في مقدمتها ذلك الغموض الذي اتسمت به في حركتها عندما راوغت الجميع بوجهيها حيث كانت تستمر في حركتها تحت ستار الدين عندما تصطدم بالسلطة السياسية وتنتقل الى الحركة السياسية بمجرد أن تتهادن مع السلطة كما كانت تمارس العمل السياسي باعتبارها حزباً وفي الوقت نفسه تهاجم الأحزاب والحزبية باعتبارها جمعية دينية ، هذا بالإضافة الى هروبها من تحديد مواقف واضحة تجاه قضايا الصراع الجذرية بدعوى انشغالها بأمور الدين مما جنبها خطر الانقسامات السياسية التي عانت منها كل القوى السياسية المصرية الأخرى ذلك أن كل أخ كان ينظر إلى المواقف المراوغة لقيادة الجماعة حسب نزوعه الشخصي إلا أن الوجه الآخر لهذه العملة كان غياب المعايير التي تهدي الجماعة في حركتها وتهدي العضوية في تقويم القيادة.

12. Oral

الأصولية الإسلامية
(a) One student to present a concise definition of الاصولية الدينية.
(b) A second student to present an account of الاصولية الاسلامية looking at its development, key figures and movements.
(c) A third student to present a speculative account of مستقبل الاصولية الاسلامية.
(d) Open lecturer–led discussion on الاصولية الاسلامية ومستقبلها.

13. Essay

Write an essay in Arabic of 200 words on the title الأصولية الإسلامية: الحل الوحيد لمشاكل الشرق الأوسط؟. In your writing address some of the following issues:

١ – ما هي الاصولية؟

٢ – ظهور الاصولية الاسلامية.

٣ – ما هي المشاكل الاساسية في الشرق الاوسط التي يجب حلها اليوم؟

٤ – كيف يقصد الاصوليون الاسلاميون حلَّ هذه المشاكل؟

٥ – الاصوليون الاسلاميون والديمقراطية: تجربة الانتخابات في الجزائر سنة ١٩٩٢ وفي دول عربية اخرى.

٦ – مستقبل الاصولية الاسلامية.

15
Democracy

1. Basic background material
Systems of government in the Arab world (as of 1997)

Algeria: Republic, with 'controlled' opposition. Former ruling party National Liberation Front (FLN), which had been in power since independence, agreed to liberalise the political system following civil unrest in October 1988. However, in the first round of democratic general elections in 1991 the Islamic fundamentalist party, the Islamic Salvation Front (FIS), won a decisive victory. In January 1992, the FLN–based Algerian government annulled the election results shortly before the second and final round. Since then there has been continual violence between the government and supporters of Islamic militant groups, most important of which is the GIA (Armed Islamic Group), amounting to virtual civil war, with 75,000 killed by 1997. Presidential elections called by the government in 1995 and local elections called in 1997 were boycotted by all the major opposition parties, which denounced them as a sham.

Bahrain: Emirate ruled by Emir Isa ibn Sulman al-Khalifa, who is a Sunni Muslim. During 1980s opposition to the regime came increasingly from pro–Iranian elements of the Shi'ite population, who form the majority in Bahrain. This was often severely repressed. In 1992 the government announced the formation of a Consultative Council, although this has little real power. Since then, there have been periodic demonstrations in favour of democracy.

Egypt: Republic under President Husni Mubarak and ruling National Democratic Party. Some opposition groups allowed to function, and take part in elections. Some opposition representation in parliament, mainly as independents.

Iraq: Republic under Saddam Hussein (since 1979) and ruling Ba'th party. All opposition subject to brutal repression, except for time in Kurdish north, where American–backed exclusion zone kept out Iraqi government and allowed holding of free elections in 1992. Subsequent collapse of Kurdish alliances.

Jordan: Monarchy ruled by King Hussein. Within these strictures, democratic local elections held in 1989. Relatively free multi–party general elections held in 1993 (although most citizens of Palestinian origin abstained from voting).

Kuwait: Emirate, with ultimate power held by Emir and royal Al-Sabah family. Elections for fifty–man National Assembly held in 1992 and in 1996, with some opposition representation.

Lebanon: Republic. In principle multi–party democracy with inbuilt constitutional guarantees for all major confessional groups (the President is to be a Maronite, the Prime Minister a Sunni Muslim, etc.). In practice democracy severely constrained by Syrian troops occupying part of country (as well as Israeli occupation of parts of southern Lebanon), giving Syria a veto over all aspects. Problems exacerbated by shift in confessional balance, such that the Shi'ites are apparently now the largest religious group, and Muslims more numerous than Christians (cf. ch. 2, 1).

Libya: State of the masses (جماهيرية) under Colonel Mu'ammar al-Qadhdhafi since military coup in September 1969. No political parties allowed to function.

Morocco: Monarchy ruled by King Hassan. Some opposition parties allowed to function, and take part in elections. Some opposition representation in parliament.

Oman: Sultanate under Sultan Qaboos since coup in July 1970. All members of the fifty–five–member national Consultative Assembly are nominated by the Sultan.

Palestine: Following PLO–Israel accord in September 1993 most observers predicted the gradual emergence of a Palestinian state in Gaza and the West Bank. However, subsequent Israeli colonisation of Palestinian lands in East Jerusalem, West Bank and Gaza plus lack of Israeli willingness to concede viable territory and power to nascent Palestinian entity (cf. ch. 6, 1). Doubts also raised about Yasser Arafat's leadership style, and willingness of himself and his Fatah organisation to abide by democratic process.

Qatar: Emirate under Sheikh Hamad, who deposed Sheikh Khalifa in a bloodless coup in 1995.

Saudi Arabia: Monarchy under King Fahd and ruling Al Saud family (5,000 members). Attempt in 1992 to establish Islamic–based forum for debate (Committee for the Defence of Legitimate Rights) repressed by government (cf. ch. 14, 1).

Sudan: Republic. Overthrow of Nimeiri dictatorship in 1985. Free elections in 1986, in which Sadiq al-Mahdi was elected President. Military coup in 1989 led to takeover by General Omar al-Bashir, with backing of Muslim Brotherhood. All opposition to regime repressed with extreme brutality. War against mainly non–Muslim southern Sudanese; since 1983 believed to have cost more than a million lives (mainly southerners). Persecution of southern Sudanese and other minority non–Arab groups (such as the Nuba) in northern Sudan (cf. ch. 14, 1).

Syria: Republic under Hafez al-Asad and ruling Ba'th party (since 1970). All opposition to regime banned.

Tunisia: Republic under Zine al-Abidine Ben Ali and ruling Democratic Constitutional Grouping (formerly the neo–Destour party). Most opposition organisations currently banned. Presidential and legislative elections held in March 1994. President Ben Ali re–elected for second term with 99.91% of vote.

United Arab Emirates Federation of emirates (Abu Dhabi, Dubai, Ras al-Khaimah, Sharjah, Ajman, Fujairah, Umm al-Qaiwain) ruled by a sometimes uneasy alliance of Sheikhs and their extended families.

Western Sahara: Occupied in part by Morocco in 1975 (in full 1979). Most Sahrawis claim the right for Western Sahara to be an independent state, a view rejected by the Moroccan government. Current UN–brokered plans for Western Sahara, to determine future status of territory.

Yemen: Republic, with free elections held in 1993, leading to a government consisting of a grand coalition of the three major parties: the Yemeni People's Congress – the former ruling party (and only legal party) in North Yemen, the Islamic–based Islah, and the Socialist Party – the former ruling party (and only legal party) in South Yemen. However, late 1993 saw increasing tension between the President and former ruler of North Yemen, Ali Abdullah Salih (head of the Yemeni People's Congress), and the Vice–President and former ruler of South Yemen, Ali al-Baidh (head of the Socialist Party), leading to war between the armies of the two former states in 1994, in which the northern army defeated the southern army. Following civil war de–facto coalition between YPC and Islah. The subsequent general elections in 1997 were boycotted by Socialist Party following the arrest of leading party members. In these elections, the Yemeni People's Congress gained a majority of seats in parliament, and subsequently formed the government, the major opposition being the Islah, which was the only other party to gain a significant number of seats.

2. Additional reading
(a) *The Times Guide to the Middle East*, relevant country sections.

3. Key vocabulary
Taking the texts in this chapter as a starting point, draw up lists of vocabulary in the following fields:
(a) Democracy, dictatorship, etc.
(b) Elections, votes, candidates, parties.

4. Written Arabic texts 1
(a) (i) Read the following definitions of ديموقراطيّة and دكتاتوريّة from المعجم العربي الأساسي, p. 474 and p. 457, then, without looking at the original text, paraphrase the definitions in Arabic.

ديموقراطيّة: ١ (في السياسة) إحدى صور الحكم
تكون السيادة فيها للشعب، ٢ (في الاجتماع) أسلوب
في الحياة يقوم على المساواة وحرية التفكير.

دكتاتوريّة: حكم الفرد المستبدّ الذي لا يلتزم
بموافقة المحكومين.

(ii) Read the following definition of شُورَى from المنجد العربي الأساسي, p. 708.

شُورَى: التشاور: (وأمرُهُمْ شُورَى بَيْنَهُمْ) (قرآن)،
«ترك عُمَرُ الخِلافَةَ شُورَى»، «الناسُ في ذلك
شُورَى»

(b) Read the following text from الشرق الأوسط, April, 17, 1993, which announces the official start of the Yemeni election campaign, then complete exercises i. and ii. which follow.

حملة الانتخابات اليمنية تبدأ رسمياً
4781 مرشحاً يتنافسون على 301 مقعد
والبيض ينافس الأحمر على رئاسة البرلمان
صنعاء: من حمود منصور
دخلت التحضيرات للانتخابات اليمنية مرحلة جديدة امس

بالاعلان رسميا عن بدء الحملة الانتخابية والسماح للمرشحين والاحزاب باستعمال وسائل الاعلام الرسمية حتى 26 ابريل (نيسان) الجاري اي قبل يوم واحد من الذهاب الى صناديق الاقتراع.

وكانت اللجنة المشرفة على العملية الانتخابية قد اقرت يوم اول من امس القوائم النهائية للمرشحين ، حيث تبين ان هناك 4781 مرشحاً يتنافسون على 301 مقعد بينهم 3429 مرشحاً مستقلاً و 1325 مرشحاً حزبياً ينتمون الى 19 حزباً وتنظيماً بينها حزب المؤتمر الشعبي العام الذي يتزعمه الرئيس علي عبد الله صالح وله 290 مرشحاً، والحزب الاشتراكي اليمني الذي يتزعمه نائب الرئيس علي سالم البيض وله 228 مرشحاً. وحزب تجمع الاصلاح الذي يتزعمه الشيخ عبد الله الاحمر وله 246 مرشحاً، وحزب البعث العربي الاشتراكي الموالي للعراق وله 160 مرشحاً، والتنظيم الوحدوي الشعبي الناصري وله 96 مرشحاً، وحزب رابطة أبناء اليمن وله 90 مرشحاً، ثم حزب الحق وله 62 مرشحاً.

وتشير خارطة توزيع المرشحين في الدوائر الانتخابية الى منافسة حقيقية بين الاحزاب السبعة للفوز باكبر عدد ممكن من مقاعد البرلمان، خاصة بين الاحزاب الثلاثة الرئيسية وهي المؤتمر الشعبي العام، والحزب الاشتراكي، وتجمع الاصلاح. ويمثل الوحدوي الناصري المنافس القوى للاحزاب الثلاثة في محافظة تعز، فيما يمثل حزب الحق اقوى منافس على الاطلاق في محافظة صعدة في اقصى الشمال اليمني، بينما يعد حزب الرابطة المنافس الاقوى في محافظتي شبوة وحضرموت اذ يواجه المؤتمر الشعبي، والاشتراكي، والاصلاح بنحو 20 مرشحاً، حيث يتمتع بنفوذ قوي. اما في ما يتعلق بحزب البعث فيشير المراقبون الى انه تعمد تقديم اكبر عدد ممكن من المرشحين، لكن فرص نجاحهم ضئيلة.

وفيما يجري اعلان اسماء المرشحين تباعا من قبل لجنة الانتخابات يجري الاعداد لبدء الحملة الانتخابية على مختلف

الاصعدة بما فيها من وسائل الاعلام الرسمية التي ستمنح جميع الاحزاب وقتا متساويا لعرض برامجها الانتخابية وتقديم مرشحيها للتنافس على مدى 9 ايام متوالية. الا ان هناك بعض الاحزاب التي تقدمت بمرشحين ولكنها لم تصل الى توفير العدد المطلوب الذي يسمح لها بممارسة الدعاية الانتخابية. وهذه الاحزاب هي التنظيم السبتمبري الديمقراطي، وهو حزب ممثل في اللجنة العليا للانتخابات وله 9 مرشحين، ثم التنظيم الشعبي لجبهة التحرير وله 8 مرشحين، والحزب القومي الاجتماعي وله 3 مرشحين ، والحزب الديمقراطي الثوري وله مرشحان، والتلاحم الوطني، والحركة الديمقراطية والجبهة الديمقراطية المتحدة ولكل منها مرشح واحد فقط.

الا ان ثمة 6 احزاب اخرى سيكون من حقها ممارسة الدعاية الانتخابية لبرامجها ومرشحيها عبر وسائل الاعلام الرسمية وفقاً لقانون الانتخابات، اذ تقدمت بأكثر من 15 مرشحا. وهي: تنظيم التصحيح الناصري وله 35 مرشحاً، والحزب الناصري الديمقراطي وله 26 مرشحاً، واتحاد القوى الشعبية وله 26 مرشحاً، والجبهة الوطنية الديمقراطية ولها 23 مرشحاً وحزب التجمع الوحدوي اليمني الذي يتزعمه عمر الجاوي وله 15 مرشحا.

وعلى الصعيد نفسه يلاحظ غياب الكثير من المسميات الحزبية في الترشيحات. وفي طليعة الاحزاب الغائبة حزب الاحرار الدستوري الذي قرر امينه العام عبد الرحمن احمد محمد نعمان خوض المعركة في الدائرة 63 بمحافظة تعز كمرشح مستقل، وينافسه في هذه الدائرة نحو 24 مرشحاً بينهم الدكتور محمد احمد الكباب، وزير الشباب والرياضة وهو مرشح المؤتمر الشعبي العام ويعد منافسا قويا. الا ان مصادر مقربة من النعمان تشير الى انه يحظى بدعم وتأييد من الحزب الاشتراكي اليمني. اما الشيخ محمد علي ابو لحوم، رئيس الحزب الجمهوري، فقد تقدم

بترشيح نفسه كمرشح مستقل في الدائرة 250 بمنطقة فهم –
محافظة صنعاء. كما ان الشيخ صادق عبد الله الاحمر نجل زعيم
«تجمع الاصلاح» ترشح نفسه هو الآخر في الدائرة رقم 225 كمرشح
مستقل بالرغم من انه كان يشغل منصب الامين العام للحزب
الجمهوري.

وعلى الرغم مما يتردد عن وجود تنسيق بين المؤتمر الشعبي
العام وحزب التجمع اليمني للإصلاح فإن هناك دوائر ستكون
المنافسة بينهما قوية، كما يتنافس «الاصلاح» مع الحزب
الاشتراكي في ما يزيد على 180 دائرة فضلاً عن المرشحين المستقلين
الذين دفعت بهم الاحزاب في عشرات الدوائر. ويستعد الشيخ عبد
الله بن حسين الاحمر لخوض معركة الانتخابات على امل الوصول
الى كرسي رئاسة البرلمان. وقد ترشح هو وولداه «صادق»،
و«حميد» في ثلاث دوائر مختلفة، فترشح الشيخ عبد الله في
الدائرة رقم 227 في منطقة خمر – محافظة صنعاء – فيما ترشح
صادق في الدائرة 225 وحميد في الدائرة 280 باسم تجمع الاصلاح
ايضا.

وتوقعت مصادر سياسية مطلعة ان تنحصر المنافسة علي
كرسي رئاسة البرلمان بين الشيخ عبد الله الاحمر ورئيس الحكومة
المهندس حيدر العطاس الذي تردد اخيرا انه سيتبادل المواقع مع
الدكتور ياسين سعيد نعمان.

وتجدر الاشارة الى ان المرأة سجلت حضورا مميزا في هذه
الانتخابات. وقد بلغ عدد المرشحات لخوض الانتخابات 49 مرشحة
منهن 13 مرشحة عن احزاب سياسية، والباقي من المستقلات.
واكبر عدد من المرشحات تم تسجيله في عدن (20 مرشحة)، ثم
امانة العاصمة صنعاء (17 مرشحة) وتوزعت باقي المرشحات بين
محافظات تعز، وإب، والحديدة، والبيضاء.

وتوقعت مصادر في لجنة الانتخابات انه اذا ما جرى التنسيق

او اقـامـة تحـالفـات حـقيـقيـة بـين الاحـزاب المشاركة في الانتخـابـات فانه سيـتم انسحـاب الكثيـر مـن المرشحـين في غضـون الايام المقبـلة.

i   Answer the following questions in English.

1. What two things were announced yesterday (the day before this report)?
2. What will happen on 27th April?
3. How many independent candidates are taking part in the elections?
4. How many political parties are taking part in the elections?
5. Which party is headed by President Ali Abdullah Salih?
6. Which party is supported by Iraq?
7. Which are the three main parties?
8. Which party has the strongest chance of election in Sa'dah?
9. Which party has the strongest chance of election in Shabwa and Hadramaut?
10. How does the report rate the chances of the Ba'th party?
11. Why is the National Socialist Party not permitted to put forward electoral propaganda?
12. Which other parties are in the same position?
13. Who is Abd al-Rahman Ahmad Muhammad Nu'man?
14. What has he decided to do?
15. Sources close to Nu'man say that he will gain the support of which party?
16. What does Sheikh Abdullah ibn Husayn al-Ahmar hope to do?
17. Where is خمر؟
18. Detail what the report says about women candidates.
19. What do sources expect will happen when coordination and alliances between parties takes place?

ii   Translate the first two paragraphs of the report into idiomatic English.

(c) Read the following newspaper extract from الاهرام May 2, 1993, which announces the results of the Yemeni elections, then answer the following questions in Arabic.

النتائج النهائية لانتخابات اليمن:
فـوز حـزب المؤتمر الشعبي بـ١٢١ مـقعدا والتـجمـع ٦٢
و٦٥ للاشتراكي

صنعاء: وكالات الانبـاء. اظهرت النتائج الرسمية لانتخابات مجلس النـواب اليـمني التي اعلنت أمس فـوز حـزب المؤتمر الشعبي العام

الذي يتزعمه الرئيس على عبد الله صالح باغلبية مقاعد المجلس الـ ٣٠١ غير انه فشل في الفوز بالاغلبية المطلقة. واوضحت اللجنة العليا للانتخابات في بيان لها ان المؤتمر الشعبي العام فاز بـ ١٢١ مقعدا بينما فاز حزب التجمع اليمني للاصلاح الذي يمثل التيار الاسلامي الاصولي بـ ٦٢ مقعدا في مجلس النواب. وأشار البيان الى ان الحزب الاشتراكي اليمني الشريك الثاني في السلطة مع المؤتمر الشعبي منذ اعلان الوحدة عام ١٩٩٠، حصل على ٥٦ مقعدا، وفاز حزب البعث الموالي للعراق بـ ٧ مقاعد، بينما فازت الاحزاب الناصرية الثلاثة بمقعد واحد لكل منها، وفاز حزب الحق بمقعدين، والمستقلون فازوا بـ ٤٧ مقعدا فى مجلس النواب. وكان المؤتمر الشعبي قد اعلن امس الاول ان ١٣ مرشحا من المستقلين الذين فازوا فى الانتخابات ينتمون لحزب المؤتمر. وذكرت اللجنة العليا للانتخابات فى بيانها أن النتائج النهائية لم تعلن بعد فى دائرتين وسوف تعلن في وقت لاحق بينما الغيت نتائج الانتخابات فى دائرة واحدة بسبب مخالفتها للقانون.

١ – من يترأس حزب المؤتمر الشعبي؟

٢ – كم عدد المقاعد التي يضمها مجلس النواب اليمني؟

٣ – ما هو اسم الحزب الذي يمثل التيار الاصولي في اليمن؟

٤ – اي حزب فاز بـ ٥٦ مقعدا؟

٥ – متى اعلنت الوحدة اليمنية؟

٦ – يعتبر حزب البعث اليمني قريبًا من أي دولة عربية؟

٧ – كم حزب ناصري يوجد في اليمن؟

٨ – ما هو عدد المستقلين غير المنتمين لحزب المؤتمر الذين فازوا في الانتخابات؟

٩ – في كم دائرة الغيت النتائج؟ لماذا؟

5. **Written Arabic texts 2**

(a) Read the following text from القبس الدولي May 23, 1990, then, without looking at the text, answer the comprehension questions which follow in Arabic.

بعض الجماعات الاسلامية تنتهك حرمة الرسالة

الرئيس الجزائري يتعهد بانتخابات نزيهة

الجزائر – رويتر – تعهد الرئيس الجزائري الشاذلي بن جديد في بداية الحملات الانتخابية لاول انتخابات حرة تجري في البلاد بأنها ستكون نزيهة وديمقراطية.

وقال الرئيس بن جديد ان الدولة ستحاول عن طريق استخدام جميع السلطات التي اعطاها لها الدستور ضمان ان اول انتخابات تؤدي الى الديمقراطية في الجزائر ستجري في جو من النزاهة والديمقراطية والوضوح.

وتخشى المعارضة ان يستخدم حزب جبهة التحرير الوطني الذي ظل يهيمن على السلطة في البلاد ٢٨ عاما رسوخ اقدامه في الحياة السياسية لمحاولة الاحتفاظ بالسلطة.

ووجه الرئيس الجزائري في كلمة القاها خلال اجتماع لمسؤولي القطاع العام في مدينة قسطنطينة في شرق البلاد انتقادات الى الجبهة الاسلامية للانقاذ المنافس الرئيسي لجبهة التحرير الوطني.

وبات في حكم المؤكد ان تظهر الجبهة الاسلامية للانقاذ بوصفها حزب المعارضة الرئيسي في الانتخابات التي تجري في البلاد في ١٢ يونيو المقبل لانتخاب المجالس البلدية والاقليمية. وكانت الحملات الانتخابية قد بدأت رسميا امس الاول.

ونقلت وكالة الانباء الجزائرية عن الرئيس بن جديد قوله ان بعض الجماعات الاسلامية تحاول بث بذور الفوضى والانقسام وسط المسلمين المتمسكين بالدين ممن لا يقبلون ان يلقي عليهم احد دروسا في هذا الشأن.

١ – كيف تمتاز هذه الانتخابات عن الانتخابات السابقة في الجزائر؟

٢ – كيف يصف رئيس الجزائر هذه الانتخابات؟

٣ – بأي وسيلة تحاول الدولة ضمان هذه الانتخابات؟

٤ – ما هي جبهة التحرير الوطني؟

٥ – ما الذي تخافه المعارضة؟

٦ – ما هو الاجتماع الذي حضره الرئيس الجزائري في قسطنطينة؟

٧ – لماذا انتقد الرئيس الجبهة الإسلامية ؟

٨ – هل الجبهة الإسلامية حزب قوي؟

٩ – متى بدأت الحملات الانتخابية؟

١٠ –حسب قول الرئيس بن جديد ماذا تحاول الجماعات الإسلامية أن تعمل؟

(b) Read the following extract from الاهرام Dec. 29, 1991, which announces the results of the first round of the Algerian elections, then complete exercises i. and ii. which follow.

جبهة الانقاذ تتوقع الفوز بـ٤٤ ٪ من مقاعد برلمان الجزائر
حشاني يعلن أن الجبهة ستطالب بانتخابات رئاسية مبكرة

الجزائر من هشام فهيم :

اعلن عبد القادر حشاني رئيس المكتب التنفيذي المؤقت للجبهة الاسلامية للانقاذ ان الجبهة قد حصلت على ١٨٩ مقعد من ٣٩٩ دائرة تم فرزها واعلان نتائجها حتى ساعة مبكرة من صباح امس بينما حصلت بقية الاحزاب الاخرى على ٤١ مقعد ، وبهذا تكون الجبهة قد حصلت على ٤٧ ٪ من الدوائر في انتخاب الدور الاول . وما زالت هناك ٣١ دائرة متبقية لم يتم فرزها حتى الآن فضلا عن ١٦٩ دائرة تجري فيها انتخابات الاعادة ، وهي المحدد لها يوم ١٦ يناير المقبل .

وقال حشاني ان الجبهة قد تحصل على ٤٤ ٪ من مجموع مقاعد البرلمان البالغ ٤٣٠ مقعدا مؤكدا ان الجبهة ستحصل على الاغلبية المطلقة في الدور الثاني مما سيمكنها من تشكيل الحكومة المقبلة واوضح ان احتمال عدم الفوز بالاغلبية غير وارد الان .

i   Answer the following questions in English

1. Who is the temporary head of the Executive Bureau of the Islamic Salvation Front (FIS)?
2. How many seats had the FIS won by the morning of 28th December?
3. How many seats had all the other parties won?
4. How many results were still to be declared?
5. When were the next round of elections to be held?
6. What did Hashani predict the FIS would obtain in the second round of elections?
7. What would this enable them to do?

ii   Answer the following questions in Arabic.

١ – على قول عبد القادر حشاني، ماذا سوف يحدث في الدور الثاني من الانتخابات؟

٢ – ماذا حدث فعلا بعد الدور الاول من الانتخابات؟

(c) Read the following text from الاهرام Dec. 30, 1991, which discusses reactions in Algeria to the results of the first round of the Algerian elections, then complete exercises i. – iii. which follow.

اتهامات متبادلة بين قادة احزاب الجزائر بعد الانتخابات
حمروش يلقي مسؤولية الهزيمة على عاتق حكومة غزالي
وآية احمد يتهم جبهة الانقاذ بارتكاب تجاوزات كبيرة

الجزائر – من هشام فهيم وعبد الحليم غزالي :

يعقد البرلمان الجزائري آخر جلسة له اليوم بصفته المجلس الذي كان يمثل الحزب الواحد في الجزائر ، وليبدأ الفصل التشريعي الرابع من خـلال مــجلس نيـابي جـديد يضم ممثلين لاول مــرة عن ٣ احــزاب بالاضافة الى عدد من النواب المستقلين وهو المجلس الذي ستتحدد خـريطته النهـائيـة بعـد اجراء الدور الثـاني من الانتخـابـات التشريعية والمحدد لها يوم ١٦ يناير المقبل .

وفضلا عن الانتقادات المريرة التي يبديها زعماء كافة الاحزاب تعليقا على ما احرزته جبهة الانقاذ الاسلامية من فوز ساحق في

الانتخابات فان رموز الحركة السياسية في الجزائر على مختلف اتجاهاتها لاتخفي مخاوفها العميقة من التوجهات الداخلية والخارجية للجزائر في الفترة المقبلة في ظل ما افرزته الانتخابات من نتائج كانت بمثابة المفاجأة الكاملة لحسابات جميع الاحزاب المشاركة.

فقد اتهم مولود حمروش رئيس الحكومة الجزائرية السابق واحد زعماء جبهة التحرير الوطنية حكومة سيد احمد غزالي ومعها الصحافة بانهما السبب في الهزيمة الثقيلة التي منيت بها الجبهة التي تحكم الجزائر منذ ٣٠ عاما .

واشار الى ان الحملات الصحفية درجت في الشهور الماضية على وصف زعماء الحزب الحاكم بالمافيا والمغتصبين مما اثر على الناخبين ، وقال ان انشقاق العديد من اعضاء الحزب الحاكم وترشيحهم كمستقلين كلف الحزب غاليا . واضاف ان الحكومة لم تبذل جهدا كافيا للتأكد على اهمية الانتخابات واجرائها في موعدها مما انعكس في عدم اشتراك نحو ٤٠ ٪ ممن لهم حق التصويت وكان يمكن ان يصوتوا لصالح جبهة التحرير بينما نجحت جبهة الانقاذ في حشد صفوفها وتجميع مؤيديها وانصارها في كل موقع .

ولم ينجح حمروش في اجتياز انتخابات الدور الاول في دائرته وسيخوض انتخابات الدور الثاني ضد مرشح جبهة الانقاذ . وفي الوقت ذاته اعلن عبد الحميد مهري الأمين العام لجبهة التحرير في حديث للتلفزيون الجزائري ان الدرس الذي يمكن استخلاصه من الانتخابات هو ان الاحزاب الجزائرية كانت تأمل في تحقيق نتائج اكبر لكن الشعب هو الذي اختار بحرية .

ومن ناحية اخرى اتهم حسين آية احمد وهو من زعماء جبهة التحرير الوطني والذي اختار صفوف المعارضة منذ عام ١٩٦٤ جبهة الانقاذ الاسلامية بارتكاب تجاوزات كبيرة للفوز

بالانتخابات مثل ملء البطاقات للأمين لصالح مرشحيها كما اتهم الحكومة في الوقت نفسه بتزوير الانتخابات والتآمر ضد جبهة القوى الاشتراكية لصالح الجبهة الاسلامية .

وقد فاز حزب جبهة القوى الاشتراكية الذي يتزعمه حسين اية احمد بالمركز الثاني في الانتخابات بعد جبهة الانقاذ الاسلامية حيث احرز ٢٦ مقعدا فقط . وقد أوضح حسين اية احمد في تصريحاته للأهرام أنه لاينبغي باي حال من الاحوال ان يكون الاسلام اداة في خدمة القوى السياسية فالاسلام منبع للفكر والاخلاق لايجب استحواز قوى سياسية متحزبة عليه ولايجب ان يستعمل لقمع المجتمع واقامة نظام سياسي متسلط ومنغلق على نفسه حتى لايصبح خطرا كبيرا على مستقبل المجتمع .

وحول رؤيته المستقبلية لحل المشكلات الاقتصادية في الجزائر قال حسين اية احمد : ان رهاننا كان ولايزال على ان الديمقراطية شرط من شروط التنمية واكد ان اهم ما أسفرت عنه الانتخابات هو بروز جبهة القوى الاشتراكية كقوة سياسية مهمة وذلك يقضي على تكريس ظاهرة القطبين جبهة الانقاذ وجبهة التحرير وهذا يعكس الواقع السياسي في الجزائر حيث تشكل جبهة القوى الاشتراكية قوة في ارضية الجزائر منذ زمن بعيد .

وشدد آية احمد من جديد على ان الانتخابات افتقرت للنزاهة والحرية والدليل على ذلك ان جبهة القوى الاشتراكية فازت في الانتخابات المحلية التي جرت في شهر يونيو من العام الماضي بـ٢٠٪ من المقاعد ولكن تقسيم الدوائر الجديد الذي تم تحت حكم غزالي رئيس الوزراء قلص من الدوائر في المناطق التي يهيمن فيها مؤيدو الجبهة وذلك دليل على ان النظام أخطأ في تحديد اعدائه فاتجه نحو المتطرفين على حساب القوى الاشتراكية التي لم يتوان عن تشويه سمعتها .

واضاف انه منذ زمن ليس ببعيد ونظام الحكم بما في ذلك جبهة

التـحـرير يسـتـعـمـل جـبـهة الانقـاذ الاسـلامـيـة كـوسـيـلة لمقـاومـة الديمقراطـية في البـلاد .

وفي الوقت نفـسـه نـدد حـزب الـطلـيـعـة الاشـتـراكي بنـتـائـج الانتـخـابـات ودعا الى الغائها فورا حيث انها تتعارض – حسب بيان اصدره الحزب – مع المصالح العليا للجزائر . بينما اكد حزب الوحدة الشعبـيـة على ضرورة احتـرام اختـيـار الشعب الجزائري مشيـرا الى ان هزيمة الحزب الحاكم ترجع الى غضب الاغلبية من النظام القائم.

i   Who are the following? Answer in English, giving as full details as possible about their official positions.

سيد احمد غزالي .1
عبد الحميد مهري .2
عبد الحليم غزالي and هشام فهيم .3
حسين آية احمد .4
مولود حمروش .5

ii   Who or what claimed the following? Answer in English, quoting the relevant section in the original Arabic.

1. The FIS succeeded ... in mobilising their supporters and activists throughout the country.
2. The FIS were guilty of serious electoral malpractice.
3. The regime failed to properly identify its enemies, and sought a rapprochement with the extremists.
4. The will of the people must be respected.
5. The defection of members of the ruling party, and their nomination as independents cost the party dear.
6. The election results should be annulled immediately, since they conflict with the supreme national interest.
7. The political parties had hoped to achieve better results, but the people had chosen freely.
8. The defeat of the ruling party is due to the anger felt by the majority towards the present regime.
9. Until recently the regime – and the government – had used the FIS as a means of opposing democracy in the country.
10. Islam should not be a tool in the hands of political forces.

iii Without looking again at the original text, answer the following questions in Arabic.

١ – من هما هشام فهيم وعبد الحليم غزالي؟

٢ – كم عدد الاحزاب التي ستتمثل في الجلسة الجديدة للمجلس؟

٣ – ما هو التاريخ المحدد للدور الثاني من الانتخابات؟

٤ – من هو مولود حمروش؟

٥ – من هو سيد احمد غزالي؟

٦ – منذ كم سنة تحكم جبهة التحرير الوطنية الجزائر؟

٧ – كم نسبة الذين لم يصوتوا في الانتخابات؟

٨ – من هو عبد الحميد مهري؟

٩ – من هو حسين آية احمد؟

١٠ – متى التحق بصفوف المعارضة؟

١١ – أي حزب فاز بالمركز الثاني في الانتخابات؟

١٢ – أي حزب فاز في الانتخابات المحلية في شهر يونيو الماضي؟

١٣ – إلى ماذا دعا حزب الطليعة الاشتراكي؟

١٤ – على ماذا أكد حزب الوحدة الشعبية؟

(d) Read the following text from الشرق الأوسط Jan. 13, 1992, then complete exercises i. and ii. which follow.

قيادة جماعية تحكم الجزائر
«الإنقاذ» تخرج عن صمتها
بلهجة تعكس حرج موقفها

الجزائر: من موفد «الشرق الاوسط» قصي صالح الدرويش

تسير الجزائر نحو صيغة جديدة للحكم قائمة على القيادة الجماعية عبر التفكير بالمجلس الاعلى للدولة الذي طرح بقوة في اليوم التالي لاستقالة الرئيس الشاذلي بن جديد ويفترض ان يضم هذا المجلس رئيس المجلس الدستوري «رئيس الجمهورية بالوكالة» ورئيس الحكومة ووزير الدفاع ووزير الداخلية ووزير العدل وربما وزير حقوق الانسان ايضا.

ومن مهام هذا المجلس ان يسد الفراغ السياسي الناتج عن

استقالة الرئيس بن جديد كما يفترض ان يسد الفراغ التشريعي الكبير الناتج عن غياب المجلس الشعبي الوطني الذي تم حله رسمياً قبيل الدور الاول من الانتخابات، وهذا يعني ان مجلس الدولة سيتولى صياغة القوانين واصدارها، كما انه قد يتولى مهمة تعيين كبار الموظفين مثل الولاة. والمشكلة التي طرحت تتعلق بالصيغة القانونية لمجلس الدولة. ذلك ان الدستور الجزائري لا ينص على وجود مثل هذه المؤسسة ولذلك فإن تشكيل مجلس الدولة او اي مجلس من هذا النوع تحت اسم آخر مرتبط باعلان الحالة الاستثنائية ومكمل لها. ذلك ان الحالة الاستثنائية التي ينص عليها الدستور تسمح بتعليق الدستور وتجميد نشاط جميع الاحزاب السياسية والجمعيات والهيئات النقابية.

واعلنت وزارة الدفاع الجزائري في بيان أذيع فجر امس ان الجيش «سيستجيب بعزم لاستدعائه من قبل رئيس الحكومة لحفظ الامن العام».

وتابع البيان ان «الجيش الوطني الشعبي يؤكد مجدداً ولاءه للدستور وثقته في المؤسسات الدستورية القائمة. وأكد الجيش انه سيدافع عن الامن. بينما توقعت مصادر عديدة إلغاء الانتخابات التشريعية.

وفي هذه الاثناء خرجت قيادة الجبهة الاسلامية للانقاذ من صمتها واصدرت بيانا يحذر الحكم من تعطيل المسار الديمقراطي. وقد جاء في بيان المكتب التنفيذي المؤقت للجبهة الاسلامية للانقاذ «بعدما عم جو الرحمة والبهجة الشعب الجزائري كله اثر اثبات وحدته وتوضيح ارادته وتأكيد عزمه على تثبيت مشروعه الاسلامي، ها هي جهات مشبوهة من النظام تثبت في مسرحية مفضوحة اصرارها المقيد على التسلط على رقاب الشعب الجزائري والسير به دون ارادته التي تجلت ناصعة يوم ٢٦ ديسمبر.

وأضاف البيان «أنه إثرَ هذه التطورات التي يهدف أصحابها

إلى إدخال البـلاد في دوامـة مـن التـوتر يمددون بهـا آخـر أنفـاس
تسلطهم فإن الجبهة الإسلامية للإنقاذ شعورا منها بمسؤوليتها أمام
الله ثم أمام الأمـة والتـاريخ تحـذر مـن أي إجراء يميع إرادة الشـعب
وتصر على إتمام المسار الإنتخابي » .

وحـمل نفس البيـان رئيس المجلس الدستوري ، بصفتـه مطلعـا
بمهـام رئيس الدولة، مسـؤوليـة حمـايـة المسـار الشـرعي الضـامن
الوحـيـد للاسـتقـرار وحمـايـة مصـالح البـلاد . وأكد البيـان على
ضرورة الإفراج عن المساجين السياسيين وعلى رأسهم قادة جبهة
الإنقـاذ . كمـا دعـا مـؤسسـة الجـيـش وأجـهـزة الأمـن إلى «تحـمـل
مسؤولياتها في الحفاظ على اختيار الشعب وعدم الاستجابة لأهواء
المغامـرين وشهـواتهم التـسلطيـة » الذين وصفهم البيـان بأنهم لا
يتـورعـون عن إدخـال البـلاد في دوامـة صـراع لا تخـدم سـوى أعداء
الإسلام والجزائر » مذكراً بـ«المسؤولية الفردية في إراقة الدماء » .

ولكن السـؤال المطروح هو مـدى قـدرة قـيـادة الإنقاذ عـلى ضبط
قواعدها وعلى ضبط التيار الراديكالي فيها الذي كان يعارض أصلاً
المشاركة في الانتخابات . وحتى هذه اللحظة لم تسجل تحركات أو
ردود فعل جماعية في مختلف أنحاء الجزائر .

i   Answer the following questions in English.

paragraph one
1. What happened the day before Algeria instituted a new type of government?
2. What form will this government take?
3. Who will definitely be in the Supreme State Council?
4. Who may be in the Supreme State Council?

paragraph two
5. What present gaps will this Council fill?
6. When was the National People's Council officially dissolved?
7. As a result of this dissolution, what will the State Council be in charge of?
8. Who will it be responsible for appointing?
9. What is there about the Algerian constitution which makes the formation of this council problematic?
10. Under what special circumstances could such a council be formed?

11. What would these special circumstances *then* allow?

paragraphs three and four

12. What two things did the Ministry of Defence announce yesterday at dawn?

13. What was expected to happen by a number of sources?

paragraph five

14. How did the Islamic Front (FIS) break its silence?

15. Who actually made the announcement?

16. What did the Islamic Front accuse 'dubious elements' of doing?

17. What can you infer happened on 26th December?

paragraph six

18. What does the Islamic Front's announcement accuse proponents of recent [political] developments of?

paragraph seven

19. In charging the President of the Constitutional Council with responsibility for protecting the legal process, the Islamic Front describes the legal process as the sole guarantor of what?

20. According to the announcement, what should happen to political prisoners?

21. Who do these political prisoners include?

22. What is asked to uphold the choice of the people and not give in to the whims of the reckless and their despotic desires?

23. Who is accused of not hesitating to plunge the country into a whirlpool of struggle?

24. Who is it said will benefit from this situation?

paragraph eight

25. About whom is it asked whether they can restrain their [political] bases and control the 'radical tendency'?

26. What did this 'radical tendency' initially oppose?

paragraph nine

27. Which party held a meeting yesterday?

28. Why was this meeting held?

ii Translate the first three paragraphs of the above text into idiomatic English.

6. Written Arabic texts 3 (classical)

(a) Read the following text by ابن تيمية from إصلاح السياسة الشرعية الراعي والرعية (Cairo: مكتبة دار الشعب), pp. 181–2, then translate the text into idiomatic English.

الشورى

لاغنى لولي الأمر عن المشاورة ، فإن الله تعالى أمر بها نبيَّه فقال :
(فَاعْفُ عَنْهُمْ وَاسْتَغْفِرْ لَهُمْ وَشَاوِرْهُمْ فِي الأَمْرِ [١]) . وقد روي عن

أبـي هـريـرة ، رضـي اللـه عنـه ، قـال : « لَمْ يَكُنْ أَحَدُ أَكْثَرَ مَشُورَةً مِنْ رَسُولِ اللهِ صَلَّى اللهُ عَلَيْهِ وَسَلَّمَ » . وقد قيل : إن الله أمر بها نبيَّه ليتألف قلوب أصحابه ، وليقتدي به من بعده ، وليستخرج مِنْهُم الرَّأي فيما لم ينزل به وحي من أمر الحروب والأمور الجزئية وغير ذلك ، فغيره صلى الله عليه وسلم أولى بالمشاورة ، وقد أثنى الله على المؤمنين بذلك في قوله : (وَمَا عِنْدَ الـلَّهِ خَيْرٌ وَأَبْقَى لِلَّذِيـنَ آمَنُوا وَعَلَى رَبِّهِمْ يَتَوَكَّلُونَ . وَالَّذيــــــــــــــــنَ يَجْتَنِبُونَ كَبَائِرَ الإِثْم والـــفَوَاحِشَ وَإِذَا مَاغَضِبُوا هُمْ يَغْفِرُونَ . وَالَّذيــنَ اسْتَجَابُوا لِربِّهمْ وَأَقَامُوا الصَّلَاةَ وَأَمْرُهُمْ شُورَى بَيْنَهُمْ وَمِمَّا رَزَقْنَاهُمْ يُنْفِقُونَ (٢)) .

.....

وأُولو الأمر صنفـان : الأُمراءُ والعلمـاءُ وهـم الذين إذا صلحـوا صلح الناس ، فعلى كل منهما أن يتحرَّى ما يقوله ويفعله طاعةَ الله ورسوله واتباع كتاب الله ، ومتى أمكن في الحوادث المشكلة معرفة مـادل عليــه الكتـاب والسنة ، كـان هو الواجب ، وإن لم يمكن ذلك لضيق الوقت أو عجز الطالب ، أو تكافؤ الأدلة عنده ، أو غيـر ذلك ، فله أن يقلد ما يرتضي علمه ودينه ، هذا أقوى الأقوال.

Notes

١ – آل عمران ١٥٩

٢ – الشورى ٣٦ ، ٣٧ ، ٣٨

(b) Read the following text by ابن قتيبة from كتاب السلطان, in الأخبار عيون,
p. 27 aloud, pronouncing all case and mood endings, then complete
exercises i. and ii. which follow.

المشاورة   والرأي

حدّثنا الزِّياديّ قال حدّثنا حمـاد بن زيد عن هشـام عن الحسـن قـال: «كان النبيّ صلى اللّه عليـه وسلم يستشيـر حتى المرأة فتشيرُ عليه بالشيء فيأخذُ به ».

وقرأت في التاج أن بعض ملوك العجم استشار وزراءه،

فقال أحدهم: « لا ينبغي للملك أن يستشير منا أحداً إلا خالياً به، فإنه أمْوَت للسر وأحرم للرأي وأجدر بالسلامة وأعفى لبعضنا من غائلة بعض، فإن إفشاء السر إلى رجل واحد أوثق من إفشائه إلى اثنين، وإفشائه إلى ثلاث كإفشائه إلى العامّة لأن الواحد رهن بما أُفشي إليه والثاني يطلق عنه ذلك الرهن والثالث علاوة فيه، وإذا كان سر الرجل عند واحد كان أحرى ألا يُظهر رهبةً منه ورغبة إليه، وإذا كان عند اثنين دخلت على الملك الشبهة واتسعت على الرجلين المَعاريض، فإن عاقبهما عاقب اثنين بذنب واحد، وإن اتهمهما اتهم بريئاً بجناية مجرم، وإن عفا عنهما كان العفو عن أحدهما ولا ذنب له وعن الآخر ولا حجة معه ».

وقرأت في كتاب للهند أن ملكاً استشار وزراء له، فقال أحدهم: « الملك الحازم يزداد برأي الوزراء الحَزَمة كما يزداد البحر بموادّه من الأنهار، وينال بالحزم والرأي ما لا يناله بالقوّة والجنود، وللأسرار منازل: منها ما يدخل الرهُط فيه، ومنها ما يستعان فيه بقوم، ومنها ما يستغني فيه بواحد. وفي تحصين السر الظفَرُ بالحاجة والسلامة من الخلل. والمستشير وإن كان أفضل رأياً من المشير، فإنه يزداد برأيه رأياً كما تزداد النار بالسليط ضوءاً. وإذا كان الملك محصّناً لسره بعيداً من أن يُعرَف ما في نفسه متخيّراً للوزراء مهيباً في أنفس العامة كافياً بحسن البلاء لا يخافه البريء ولا يأمنه المُريب مقدّراً لما يُفيد وينفق، كان خليقاً لبقاء ملكه. ولا يصلح لسرّنا هذا إلا لسانان وأربع آذان. ثم خلا به ».

i   Translate the text into idiomatic English.

ii   How do the views of Ibn Qutayba with regard to consultation differ from those of Ibn Taymiyya, as given in text 6. (a)?

7. Grammar/stylistics

(a) إِنَّ

The particle إِنَّ occurs immediately before a preposed subject in any of the
structures described in chapter 13 (ch. 13, 7a). Grammatically, إِنَّ causes the noun
phrase which follows it to be placed in the accusative, where the noun phrase is of
a type which takes case. Pronouns do not take case in Arabic, and إِنَّ is followed
by the same pronoun suffixes as follow nouns and prepositions. Thus: إِنَّها 'she',
إِنَّهُم 'they (m.pl.)'. The only forms which may cause problems are the alternatives
for the first persons: إِنِّي or إِنَّنِي 'I', and إِنَّا and إِنَّنا 'we'. Some other noun
phrases, i.e. nominal clauses, beginning with ما, for example, also do not take
case. Thus: إِنَّ ما قلتَه غيرُ صحيح 'What you (m.s.) said is not true'. Compare
the latter with إِنَّ قولَكَ غيرُ صحيح 'What you (m.s.) said is not true'.

إِنَّ is traditionally described as an emphatic particle. In modern Standard Arabic,
it is worth distinguishing two sorts of context where إِنَّ is used: i. cases where إِنَّ
is stylistically normal; and ii. cases where إِنَّ relays emphasis.

Where the predicate which follows إِنَّ starts with a noun phrase, this may be
introduced by لَ. For example:

وإِنَّه لَنبيُّ هذه الأمة ..

'He is indeed the prophet of this community ...' (ch. 4, 6)

The particle لَ is traditionally regarded as making the utterance more emphatic than
the particle إِنَّ on its own (see the discussion of stress, below).

i *Stylistically normal use of إِنَّ as a resumptive particle*
Particularly in long clauses with a preposed element (subject, adverbial; cf. ch. 13,
7av), the following element is sometimes introduced by إِنَّ with a following noun
phrase. This following element thus has a subject–predicate structure (the subject
being the noun phrase introduced by إِنَّ, and the predicate being what follows
this). إِنَّ in cases of this kind can be regarded as a resumptive particle, i.e. a
particle which is used to signal the start of the next major element in the clause or
sentence (ch. 10, 7b; ch. 17, 7a). Examples are:

والمستشير وإن كان أفضل رأياً من المشير، فـ{إِنَّ}ـه يزداد برأيه
رأياً كما تزداد النار بالسليط ضوءاً.

'The person who asks for advice, even if he has a better opinion than
the person whose advice he asks, has his opinion strengthened by
another opinion, just as the light of a fire is strengthened through oil.'
(ch. 15, 6b)

ويكتمل هذا التقدير لقيمة الديمقراطية الوعي بأنَّنا ومن خلال
نظامنا السياسي الديمقراطي بقدر ماحققناه من استجابة
حضارية لمطالب العقل السياسي أو الفكر السياسي العربي
فـ{إنَّ}نا نقدم البديل الذي طال انتظاره للخروج من واقع
الانقسام العربي ..

'This estimation of the value of democracy is made complete by the
awareness that we – through our democratic political system, and the
extent of our achievements in terms of a cultural response to the
demands of Arab political rationality and thought – are offering a
long–awaited alternative to escape from the facts of Arab division ...'
(ch. 15, 11)

In both these examples, the writer in effect interrupts his or her own train of
thought to introduce some parenthetical information. In the first example, this
information is وإن كان أفضل رأياً من المشير, while in the second example it is
ومن خلال نظامنا السياسي الديمقراطي بقدر ماحققناه من استجابة
حضارية لمطالب العقل السياسي أو الفكر السياسي العربي. In both examples
the sentences read oddly without the parenthetical information, indicating that the
use of إنَّ is a function of the inclusion of this information. Thus in the first
example: فـ{إنَّ}ه يزداد برأيه رأياً كما تزداد النار بالسليط ... والمستشير
ويكتمل هذا التقدير لقيمة الديمقراطية :and in the second example ;ضوءاً.
الوعي بأنَّنا ... فـ{إنَّ}نا نقدم البديل الذي طال انتظاره للخروج من واقع
الانقسام العربي .. In both these examples the pronoun following إنَّ refers to the
same thing as the same entity as was referred to by the noun/pronoun preceding the
parenthetical information. In the first example, this entity is المستشير–'the person
who asks for advice', and in the second example, this entity is نحن (cf. أنَّنا in
text)/'we'.

It is also common to find إنَّ as a resumptive particle in the main clause
(apodosis/جواب) of a conditional sentence, where this main clause does not have a
main verb. For example:

وايا كانت النتيجة فـ{إنَّ} الامر المؤكد ان سياسة تصدير الثورة ..
'Whatever the outcome, what is certain is that the policy of exporting
the revolution ...' (ch. 16, 5c)

For further examples in which فإنَّ is used resumptively see chapter 10 (ch. 10,
7b).

ii *Emphatic use of* إنّ

The most common function of إنّ is to give a sense of emphasis. It is possible to identify four emphatic uses of this particle: (i) stress, (ii) contrast, (iii) scene setting, (iv) linkage (cf. the list for emphatic uses of preposed adverbials and initial noun phrases without إنّ (ch. 14, 7a, etc.).

ii.i *Stress*

Preposing of adverbial phrases or subjects stresses the preposed element (ch. 13, 7a). The use of إنّ to mark stress, by contrast, may be regarded as either stressing the whole utterance or as stressing the predicate which occurs after the subject noun–phrase introduced by إنّ. That إنّ does not normally stress the noun phrase which immediately follows it is evident from the fact that إنّ is relatively often followed by a pronoun suffix. For example:

لقد تحطم التمثال وسقط فوق زورق صغير وانكفأ على وجهه
{إنَّه} غارق على سطح الماء ..

'The statue had been smashed and had fallen on top of a small boat, and tumbled over on its face. It was lying on the surface of the water ...' (ch. 13, 11b)

The most obvious cases of إنّ to mark stress for English speakers are those where an appropriate English translation involves an English stress–word, such as 'indeed' or 'certainly'. For example:

.. و{إنَّه} لَنبيُّ هذه الأمة ..

'He is indeed the prophet of this community ...' (ch. 4, 6)

Such examples are relatively rare.

Elsewhere the stress relayed by إنّ in the Arabic may have no correspondent in an English translation, although the situation in which إنّ is used in the Arabic is clearly one in which stress is involved. The easiest way to illustrate this is to consider what is sometimes called exhortatory material, i.e. material in which the writer is presenting opinions which he or she wants the audience to agree with. These opinions may or may not form part of an overall logical argument.

A good example of an exhortatory passage is the passage by سيد قطب from نحو مجتمع إسلامي in chapter 14 which begins وكانت البشرية (ch. 14, 11ai). In this the author is presenting Islam as the only alternative to what he regards as the failed ideologies of East European communism and Western capitalism. The following section concerns the behaviour of the people of the United States:

لقد شهدتهم هنالك والقلق العصبي يأكل حياتهم على الرغم من
كل مظاهر الثراء والنعمة ووسائل الراحة . {إن} متاعهم هياج
عصبي ومرح حيواني و{إن}ـه يخيل إليك أنهم هاربون دائماً من

أشباح تطاردهم ، {إنـ}ـهم آلات تتحرك في جنون وسرعة وهياج لا
يقر له قرار .

'I have seen them there, nervous anxiety eating up their lives despite all
the appearances of wealth and well–being, and the means for comfort.
Their pleasure is nervous excitement, and animal enjoyment. You
imagine that they are constantly fleeing from spectres which are
pursuing them. They are machines which move in madness, speed, and
excitement from which there is no respite.' (ch. 14, 11ai)

Here the use of إنّ is motivated by a desire to persuade the reader to agree with the
author's opinion of American society.

Consider also the second passage from نحـو مـجـتـمـع إسـلامـي in the same
chapter (ch. 14, 11aii). This consists of nine paragraphs, and also has as its central
theme the necessity for mankind to embrace Islam. The paragraphs begin as
follows:

paragraph one

والعقيدة في الله ...

Belief in God ...

paragraph two

ومن ثم يبرز الاسلام وتتميز دعوة الاسلام ...

Thus, Islam stands out, and its message is distinguished ...

paragraph three

إن شجرة الحضارة البشرية تهتز وتترنح اليوم ...

Today, the tree of human civilisation is shaking and tottering ...

paragraph four

إن البشرية كلها في حاجة إلينا ...

The whole of humanity is in need of us ...

paragraph five

ومن هذه الحاجة الإنسانية ...

From this human need ...

paragraph six

إن الذين يريدون لنا أن نذوب في حركة قومية ...

Those who want us to be absorbed into a nationalist movement ...

paragraph seven

إن مهمتنا أن نتميز وأن نحمل الشعلة للضالين ...

Our task is to be distinct and to carry the torch to those who are lost ...

paragraph eight

إن مهمتنا أن ننقذ ، البشرية من الحمأة الأسنة التي تتمرغ فيها اليوم ...

Our task is to save humanity from the stinking mire in which it is wallowing today

...

paragraph nine

إن البشرية كلها في حاجة إلينا ...

The whole of humanity needs us ...

Of the nine paragraphs here, six begin with إنَّ. These introduce an emotional element into the text; it is more than simply an attempt to convince the reader intellectually of the writer's position. It is a call to arms.

A similar emotional element can be seen in the use of إنَّ in the passage اتفاق اليمنين, which presents the agreement between the two Yemens as a great step forward for the Arab world generally (ch. 13, 5a). Here two of the five paragraphs of the text begin with إنَّ. These are:

paragraph one

ان نفط اليمن هو قوة للعرب.

Yemen's oil means [lit: 'is'] power for the Arabs.

paragraph three

ان يمناً فقيراً هو افضل الف مرة من وطن غني متقاتل ...

A poor Yemen is a thousand times better than a rich country which is a war with
itself ..

Both of these statements are intended to be emotionally powerful, and both include not only إنَّ as a marker of emphasis, but also the pronoun of separation هو (cf. ch. 14, 7bii). The use of إنَّ here can be contrasted with its non–use in what is otherwise an identical structure with a pronoun of separation in the first sentence of the same text. The essential relevant elements of this read:

الاتفاق الذي تم التوصل اليه بين شطري اليمن ... هو خطوة هامة
في مسيرة اليمن بشطريه ..

'The agreement which has been reached between the two halves of Yemen is an important step in the progress of Yemen in its two halves ...' (ch. 13, 5a)

Here the author is stating a basic thesis (i.e. a basic line of argumentation) for the text, or what is sometimes known as a topic–sentence or topic–clause. A topic–sentence, or topic–clause, is a sentence or clause at the start of a passage or paragraph, which introduces or states in general terms the topic of that passage or paragraph; i.e. it sets the scene for that passage or paragraph. One can also think of a topic–sentence or topic–clause as being marked out, or stressed (cf. ch. 13, 7ai.i, 7aii.i), in the way that underlining a sentence or clause (or putting it in bold or in capital letters) marks out, or stresses, that sentence or clause.

The reader is expected to be interested in this, and perhaps to agree, but it is not appropriate to introduce a strong emotive element. Accordingly, إنَّ is not used in this context.

It is also instructive to compare the clauses ان نفط اليمن هو قوة للعرب and ان يمناً فقيراً هو افضل الف مرة من وطن غني متقاتل with equivalent clauses in which إنَّ is replaced by the semantically light verb يُعتبَر (cf. ch. 1, 7d), other necessary changes also being made, i.e. يُعتبر نفط اليمن قوةً للعرب and يُعتبَر. The forms with يُعتبَر يمنٌ فقيرٌ افضلَ الف مرة من وطن غني متقاتل convey a much more detached attitude on the part of the writer.

While the emotive aspect of stress in the use of إنَّ is important, it is not the only aspect. In fact, any statement which is regarded as important – i.e. worth stressing – can be introduced by إنَّ. It is noticeable that statements by political leaders, for example, when quoted in newspapers, are often introduced by إنَّ. For example:

وحول رؤيته المستقبلية لحل المشكلات الاقتصادية في الجزائر قال حسين اية احمد : {إنَّ} رهاننا كان ولايزال على ان الديمقراطية شرط من شروط التنمية ..

'Regarding his vision for the future for solving the economic problems of Algeria, Hocine Aït-Ahmed said, "Our bet has been and remains that democracy is one of the conditions for development ..."' (ch. 15, 5c)

.. إذ لا يخلو خطاب او حديث من احاديثه من الاصرار على المضي في هذا التوجه بقوله : [{إنَّ} الديمقراطية هي خيارنا الذي لن نحيد عنه او نتراجع عنه ابدا] ..

'No speech or statement of his [President Ali Abdullah Salih's] omits an insistence on pursuing this orientation, as expressed in his words, "Democracy is our choice, [and one] which we will never deviate or retreat from ..."' (ch. 15, 11)

Another example in which the notion of the importance of the statement plays a role is the following, taken from Naguib Mahfouz's acceptance speech to the Nobel committee:

فاسمحوا لي أن أقدم لكم نفسي بالموضوعية التي تتيحها الطبيعة البشرية. {أنا} ابن حضارتين تزوجتا في عصر من عصور التاريخ، زواجا موفقا.

'Allow me to introduce myself to you with the objectivity which human nature allows. I am the son of two cultures which at a particular stage in human history entered into a successful marriage.' (ch. 17, 11)

Here the second sentence has as its subject أنا (placed in curly brackets above), rather than إني or إنّني. In this context, it would be inappropriate – since it would be immodest – of Nagúib Mahfouz to stress the importance of his own status. The use of أنا in this context rather than إني or إنّني expresses the intended message without introducing overtones of immodesty.

ii.ii *Contrast*

Sometimes إنّ is emphatic by virtue of providing a contrast with some previous element in the text. Sometimes this contrast is temporal, particularly where إنّ contrasts a subsequent state with previous actions. Examples are:

في بور سعيد قابلت كثيراً من الناس جاءوا من الشمال والجنوب
.. كلهم ليروا ماذا فعل العدوان بهذه المدينة الآمنة .. {إن} كل
شيء هادئ فيها ، الناس والحياة ..

'In Port Said I met many people who had come from both north and south, all of them to see what the attack had done to this secure city. Everything in it was calm, the people and life ...' (ch. 13, 11b)

لقد تحطم التمثال وسقط فوق زورق صغير وانكفأ على وجهه
{إنّ}ـه غارق على سطح الماء ..

'The statue had been smashed and had fallen on top of a small boat, and tumbled over on its face. It was lying on the surface of the water ...' (ch. 13, 11b)

Sometimes the contrast may be partially or totally non–temporal. The following is an example of a partially non–temporal contrast:

..فتاة يونانية كانت جميلة الصوت والشكل ، وكانت طيبة القلب
، وبهذه الطيبة خربت بيت أعز أصدقائي .. {إنّ}ني أستطيع أن
أروي قصته هنا وأنا آمن .. فهو غاضب مني ، وقد أقسم ألا يقرأ
شيئاً مما أكتب ..

'... a Greek girl who had a beautiful figure and a beautiful voice, and was good hearted. This good–heartedness it was which she used to destroy the household of my dearest friend. I am able to tell his story here in safety, because he is angry with me, and has sworn not to read anything which I write ...' (ch. 13, 11b)

In this example there is both a change of time, from past events (خربت بيت أعز أصدقائي, etc.) to present situation (أستطيع أن أروي قصته هنا, etc.), and a change of subject from the Greek girl (فتاة يونانية, etc.) to the writer.

ii.iii *Scene–setting*

إنَّ is sometimes used to introduce a topic–sentence or topic–clause (ch. 15, 7b). One can also think of a topic–sentence or topic–clause introduced by إنَّ as being marked out, or stressed (cf. ch. 13, 7ai.i, 7aii.i), in the way that underlining a sentence or clause (or putting it in bold or in capital letters) marks out, or stresses, that sentence or clause. A good example of such scene–setting is the following:

{ان} دول العالم الثالث قد قطعت منذ اوائل الخمسينات حتى الان شوطا في التصنيع ..

'Since the early fifties the countries of the third world have passed through a phase of industrialisation ...' (ch. 18, 5a)

Potentially at least, this clause can be contrasted with a similar topic–clause which begins with قد, of the type: قد قطعت دول العالم الثالث منذ اوائل الخمسينات حتى الان شوطا في التصنيع .. . If there is any difference between this latter sentence and the one which occurs in the text, beginning with إنَّ, it is that the sentence beginning with إنَّ presents دول العالم الثالث as the core of the topic of the paragraph, the information about industrialisation being only of secondary importance. The constructed sentence beginning with قد on the other hand could be said to present the entire clause as the topic of the paragraph (cf. ch. 15, 7b). Another example of إنَّ introducing a topic–clause is:

فـ{إنَّ} الناس أربعة أقسام : ..

'People are of four kinds: ...' (ch. 14, 6a)

The following paragraphs of this passage then go on to detail the four kinds of people. (This could also be regarded as a case where إنَّ involves linkage, since the argument also develops from points made in the previous paragraph; see the next section below for a discussion of the role of إنَّ in linkage.) A final example of إنَّ introducing a topic–clause is:

إن المراقبين يرون بشكل عام أن السياسة المصرية لن يطرأ عليها تغيير حتى شهر أبريل القادم أي حتى تتم المرحلة الأخيرة من الانسحاب الإسرائيلي من سيناء.

'In general, observers do not believe that there will be any change in Egyptian policy until next April, i.e. until the completion of the final stage of the Israeli withdrawal from Sinai.' (ch. 16, 4b)

Although this sentence constitutes an independent typographic paragraph, the next two paragraphs both contain information which is dependent on the scene established by the information in this paragraph. While this paragraph begins with إن المراقبين يرون, the next two paragraphs begin with ويقول المراقبون, i.e.

they start with non–emphatic initial verbs.

ii.iv *Linkage*

Sometimes إنَّ is used not to present a new topic, but to summarise, or draw a conclusion from, a previous argument. A good example is the following:

وقاطع الزوج أصدقاءه القدماء وصديقاته القديمات . . وهو
اليوم متصوف لا يقرأ إلا القرآن وإلا الأحاديث النبوية . . ويعيش
في أرضه التي يملكها بعيداً عن كل إنسان وكل زوجة وكل ميراندا .
{إن} هذا الصديق كأنه مات . .

'The husband cut himself off from his former male and female friends.
Today he is a Sufi, and reads only the Qur'an and the Prophetic
Hadiths. He lives on the land which he owns far from all people, all
wives, and all Mirandas.
      It is as if this friend has died' (ch. 13, 11b)

وهو لا يريد ان يعرف ان ما يحدث في تلك الاماكن لا علاقة له
بالدين من قريب او بعيد . {ان}ها حركات سياسية في احط
درجاتها . وهدفها الوحيد هو تمزيق اوصال مصر . ومن ثم ما
تبقى من الوطن العربي . وليس هذا اكتشافا . {إن}ها خطة معلنة
ومطبقة منذ اعوام وعلى رؤوس الاشهاد .

'It [the National Democratic Party] does not want to know that what is
happening in those places has no connection, whether close or distant,
with religion. These are political movements of the lowest orders. Their
only goal is to dismember Egypt, and consequently what remains of the
Arab nation. This is not a discovery. It is a plan which has been
announced and executed for years in the full view of witnesses.' (ch.
14, 5a)

In this example the two occurrences of إنَّ introduce a conclusion which is drawn
from the preceding statements.

إنَّ may also be used to introduce a justification, particularly an authoritative
justification, of a previous claim. For example:

يجب أن يُعْرَف أنَّ ولاية أمر الناس من أعظم واجبات الدين ، بل لا
قيامَ للدين إلاّ بها ، فـ{إن} بني آدم لا تَتِم مصلحتهم إلاّ بالاجتماع
لحاجة بعضهم إلى بعض ..

'It should be known that authority over the affairs of people is one of
the greatest duties of religion, indeed religion cannot exist without it.
For men can only achieve what is in their own best interest through
joint activity, due to the fact that they need one another ...' (ch. 14, 6a)

لاغِنَي لولي الأمر عن المشاورة ، فإن الله تعالى أمر بها نبيَّه فقال:

'It is essential for those in authority to consult other people, for God Almighty ordered the Prophet to consult: He said, ...' (ch. 15, 6a)

In the first of these examples, the authority of the statement introduced by إنَّ stems from its obvious and accepted truth. In the second example, the authority comes from the fact the statement following قال is a divine utterance from the Qur'an.

iii *Other uses of* إنَّ

The preceding discussion of إنَّ is not intended to be an authoritative or exhaustive statement of its uses. Nor are the categories of stress, contrast, scene–setting and linkage to be regarded as entirely distinct from one another. Rather, the intention is to provide a means of orientation regarding the ways in which إنَّ is used, particularly in modern Arabic. A good deal of variation will be found between different authors and different styles of writing. إنَّ is not used in colloquial dialects (although the related form إنْ is found in dialects of the Arabian peninsula); إنَّ may therefore be used as a marker of formality. Paradoxically, إنَّ seems particularly common in representations of colloquial dialogue, which are made in modern Standard Arabic – for instance in Arabic sub–titling of non–Arab films. In this case, the sub–titling seems to overcompensate for the typically informal style of film dialogue – as though the sub–titlers are concerned to assure their audience that the translation is in 'proper' Arabic.

Conversely, writers who use Standard Arabic for dialogue in short stories or novels, but who want to convey a colloquial flavour, may avoid the use of إنَّ because of its strong associations with the non–colloquial Modern Standard (and Classical) Arabic.

8. Aural Arabic texts 1

Listen to the following text from حصاد الشهر, no. 14, side 1, item 7, هل من خطر على البلاد العربية من الشيوعية؟, and produce a complete transcription of the text. You may find the following vocabulary items of use:

ارشيف	archives
الحبيب بورقيبة	Habib Bourguiba. Former President of Tunisia

9. Aural Arabic texts 2

(a) Listen to the following BBC Arabic Service news broadcast from Sept. 1995, then produce a complete transcription of the text. This extract reports the Arab League sending observers to the Algerian presidential elections.

(b) Listen to the following BBC Arabic Service news broadcast also from Sept. 1995, then produce a complete transcription of the text. This extract reports the release of prisoners arrested during pro–democracy demonstrations in Bahrain.

10. Written English texts

(a) Using constructions and vocabulary encountered in the Arabic texts above as far as possible, translate the following text from the *Guardian*, Jan. 1992, into idiomatic Arabic.

Rumblings from a distant outbreak of democracy

Yemen's new political freedom is worrying the neighbours.

When Yemenis go to the polls this year in the country's first multi–party elections they will do more than choose a new government. The election, which will mark the final stage of transforming Yemen into a fully democratic state, is likely to cause vibrations throughout the Arabian peninsula – a region where parliaments, if they exist at all, have limited power, where 'consultative councils' with appointed members are the preferred alternative, and where cabinet meetings tend to be family gatherings of brothers, uncles and cousins.

(b) Using constructions and vocabulary encountered in the Arabic texts above as far as possible, translate the following text from the *Guardian*, Jan. 13, 1992, into idiomatic Arabic.

Algeria cancels polls

Algeria's High Security Council last night cancelled general elections in what Islamic fundamentalists called an army–backed constitutional coup designed to rob them of victory.

In a statement, the council, meeting in emergency session after the resignation of President Chadli Benjedid on Saturday night, announced 'the impossibility of continuing the electoral process until necessary conditions were achieved for the normal functioning of institutions'.

Troops supported by tanks guarded the main government buildings and security forces manned roadblocks as the council, whose members include the acting head of state, Abdelmalek Benhabyles, who took over from Mr Chadli, top members of the army and security forces, the prime minister, and the defence, interior and justice ministers, met late into the night.

11. Précis

Read the following text from الثورة, June 8, 1991, then produce a précis in Arabic.

كلمة الثورة

الديمقراطية اختيار وطني للجمهورية اليمنية تبنى عليه اسسُ النظام السياسي الجديد القائم على التعددية السياسية المنتظمة في احزاب تتداول السلطة سلميا بالاحتكام الى قواعد واخلاقيات الديمقراطيةالحزبية..

وذلك الاختيار هو مايتكرر التأكيد عليه من خلال الخطاب السياسي الى الشعب والمواطن اليمني خارج وداخل الاحزاب والذي تتوجه به القيادة السياسية بزعامة الاخ الفريق علي عبد الله صالح رئيس مجلس الرئاسة ، إذ لا يخلو خطاب او حديث من احاديثه من الاصرار على المضي في هذا التوجه بقوله :

[إن الديمقراطية هي خيارنا الذي لن نحيد عنه او نتراجع عنه ابدا] .. وهذا الاصرار الذي يتجلى في التوجه الرسمي بحاجة اكيدة الى تضافر ومؤازرة باصرار مقابل، وبخاصة من قبل الاحزاب والتنظيمات السياسية على مستوى الممارسة العملية والواقعية وتمثلُّها للروح الديمقراطية ..

وتتأَكد هذه الضرورة كونها[1] مرتبطة ارتباطا وثيقا ليس فقط بالمهمة الوطنية لبناء دولة الجمهورية اليمنية وانما لانها تشكل جوهو عملية الحفاظ على دولة الوحدة وحمايتها، وهي المسؤولية الوطنية الحضارية والتاريخية الكبرى التي يشترك فيها الجميع نجاحا او ما لا نريد ان يكون وما ينبغي له ..[2]

وهذه المهمة تتطلب العقل السياسي اليمني الذي ينطلق من فهمه للعملية الديمقراطية الجارية والتفاعل في اطارها من الرؤية بأن هذه الديمقراطية التي اصبحنا ننعم بها لم تأت تلبيةً لرغبة أو احتياج تكتيكي، وانما هي تعبير عن ضرورة وطنية وبديل منطقي جديد وموضوعي لواقع سياسي تحكمت واستبدّت به اوهام

التشطير وتكرست في ظله كافة اشكال والوان المعاناة التي لحقت بابناء شعبنا في ظل التشطير .. واضعين دائما في الاعتبار مايعكسه ذلك ويجلبه من حقيقة الضريبة باهظة التكاليف[3] والتي سدّدت اليمن فواتيرها التي استنزفت سنوات من عمر بلادنا وامكانات شعبنا ودماء ابنائه ..

وخير سلوك[4] يبعث على الثقة والاطمئنان في النفوس الى عدم امكانية العودة او التراجع الى الماضي التشطيري هو السلوك الذي تبادر اليه دائما قيادتنا السياسية الوحدوية في ظل الجمهورية اليمنية كما كانت السباقة الى تحقيق الوحدة.

فبالعودة الى الزيارات الميدانية للقيادة السياسية الى العديد من المحافظات والمواقع العسكرية وبالذات زيارة الاخ الفريق علي عبد الله صالح للوحدات العسكرية باعتباره[5] رأس الدولة والقائد الأعلى للقوات المسلحة، تابعناه وهو يخاطب افراد جيشنا الوطني الباسل ويحدد مسؤولياتهم التاريخية في الحفاظ على الجمهورية اليمنية وحماية دولتها كدولة للنظام والقانون قائمة على التعددية الحزبية في ديمقراطيتها السياسية التي تقر بمبدأ التداول السلمي للسلطة .. وعلى ضوئه تتحدد واجبات رجال قواتنا المسلحة والامن البواسل بالابتعاد عن التحزب وتمسكها بعدم التدخل في الحياة المدنية التي تقررها الديمقراطية كجيش يمثل الوطن بكل فئاته واحزابه ويدافع عن حق شعبه في اختيار اسلوب حياته في ظل دولة ديمقراطية مستقلة ذات سيادة ..

والاخ الفريق علي عبد الله صالح وهو بما يفعله يقدّم أبهى معاني الوفاء والاخلاص وصدق التوجه الديمقراطي وحمايته وضمان مستقبله بإبعاد اخطر المخاطر التي تهدد الحياة الديمقراطية في العالم النامي، وتلك استجابة قيادية رائدة لمطالب هي في الاساس للمعارضة، وهو الذي يحمي في نفس الوقت قواتنا المسلحة من مخاطر استعداء الشعب عليها إنْ هي تحولت الى اداة

قمع لاختياره الديمقراطي.

وبذلك يتحقق التكاتف والالتحام الوطني الجماعي كأقوى ضمانات حماية دولة الوحدة من خلال الحرص والحفاظ على نظامها الديمقراطي الذي بيّنا مقدار ماتكبّده شعبنا وقدّمه من تضحيات لبلوغه.

ويُكْمل هذا التقديرَ لقيمة الديمقراطية الوعيُ باننا، ومن خلال نظامنا السياسي الديمقراطي بقدر ما حققناه من استجابة حضارية لمطالب العقل السياسي أو الفكر السياسي العربي، فإننا نقدّم البديل الذي طال انتظاره للخروج من واقع الانقسام العربي .. ونحن حرصنا على التذكير بهذا البعد القومي لمسألتنا حتى لايغيب عن ادراكنا حجم ماينتظرنا من مسؤوليات وما يتطلبه من وعي وحرص وطني ..

Notes

1. .. كَوْنَها = 'by [virtue of] the fact that it is ...'.
2. .. نجاحا او ما لا نريد ان يكون وما ينبغي له = 'with success or with what we do not want and what should not be'; i.e. 'successfully or in a way which we do not want and should not occur'.
3. باهظة التكاليف = 'extremely heavy [in expense]' – improper *idafa*. ضريبة 'tax' is being used metaphorically here.
4. .. خير سلوك = 'the best behaviour in order to ...', i.e. 'the best way of ...'.
5. باعتباره = 'as', 'in his capacity as'.

12. Oral

الديمقراطية في الوطن العربي

(a) One student to present a concise definition of الديمقراطية.
(b) Another student to present an account of فضائل الديمقراطية.
(c) Another student to present an account of مساوئ الديمقراطية.
(d) The presenters ask the other students questions relating to الديمقراطية. These questions should include some which require factual answers and some which require speculative, hypothetical, subjective and analytical answers. For example:

١ – ما هي مباديء الديمقراطية؟

٢ – هل الديمقراطية مفهوم غربي فقط؟

٣ – كيف تختلف الديمقراطية عن الدكتاتورية؟

٤ – ما هي فوائد الدكتاتورية؟

٥ – ما هي فوائد الديمقراطية؟

٦ – كيف تختلف الديمقراطية عن الشورى؟

٧ – هل للديمقراطية مستقبل في الشرق الاوسط؟

٨ – هل الديمقراطية القائمة في الدول الغربية مثل بريطانيا وفرنسا ديمقراطية في كل معنى الكلمة؟

(e) Open lecturer–led discussion on the advantages and disadvantages of الديمقراطية in comparison to other types of government.

13. Essay

Write an essay in Arabic of 200 words on the title مستقبل الديمقراطية في الوطن العربي. In writing your essay address some of the following questions and issues:

١ – ما معنى كلمة «الديمقراطية»، وما هو اصلها؟

٢ – ما هي مباديء الديمقراطية الرئيسية؟

٣ – ما هو تاريخ الديمقراطية في الوطن العربي؟

٤ – من يعارض الديمقراطية في الوطن العربي، وما سبب معارضته؟

٥ – ما هو موقف الدول الغربية من الديمقراطية في الشرق الاوسط نظريًا وعمليًا؟

16
Death and succession

1. Basic background material
The nature of authority

According to the German sociologist, Max Weber (1864–1920), there are three basic kinds of authority which may exist in a society: traditional authority, charismatic authority, and rational–legal authority. Traditional authority is authority based on a belief in the sanctity of the norms of everyday behaviour. The major example of traditional authority is patriarchalism, where authority is vested in the father, the husband, the senior man in the house, the feudal lord over his vassals, or the king over his subjects. In this form of authority, any infringement of traditional norms results in magical or religious evil.

Charismatic authority is based on the charisma of an individual, where charisma is defined as an extraordinary quality of a person (regardless of whether this quality is actual or imaginary), and typically (in pre–modern societies at least) involves that person having supernatural qualities, being regarded as a hero, and being the recipient of revelations. Charismatic authority implies rule over people, to which those who are ruled submit because of their belief in the particular qualities of the individual.

Legal–rational authority is based not on sacred tradition, nor on the charisma of the individual, but on an impersonal bond to the generally defined duty of office. This office is fixed by rationally established enactments, decrees and regulations. Rational–legal authority is the norm in modern democratic societies.

Max Weber believed that there was a general tendency to move from traditional and charismatic authority to rational–legal authority. Charismatic authority, in particular, he regarded as unstable, particularly with respect to succession following the death of the charismatic leader, because of the unique nature of the leader's claim to rule. For if the charismatic leader's gift of leadership is genuinely unique, there can be no true successor to him and, his movement must die with him.

If the movement is to continue, therefore, and assuming that the successor attempts to justify his claim to rule on charismatic grounds as well, it must be admitted that the charismatic leader's gift is shared by at least one other person. This, however, undermines the charismatic leader's claim to uniqueness. More importantly, the unlimited interpretive freedom which the charismatic leader enjoys tends to impede the formation of accepted criteria by which the claims of competing aspirants to the leader's role may be assessed. As a result, almost all charismatic movements experience a succession crisis following the death of the original leader, and before they have been traditionalised or transformed into a legal–rational structure (cf. Anthony T. Kronman, *Max Weber*, (London: Edward Arnold, 1983), p. 70).

In accordance with this analysis, the development of Sunni Islam with its emphasis on codes of law and the routinisation of the caliphate as an essentially political office lacking the power to interpret Islamic law independently of the codified tradition can be seen as a move towards a legal–rational authority (albeit within a traditional sacred framework). The development of Shi'ite Islam, by contrast, with its succession of divinely inspired caliphs, can be seen as a continuation of the charismatic authority of the Prophet (albeit that this charisma was somewhat rationalised). In democratic societies, political succession, in theory at least, takes place through rational–legal procedures, such as elections.

Some modern dictators may be regarded as charismatic (Nasser is a possible example in the Arab world). Other dictators present themselves as charismatic leaders, or at least allow their supporters to present them in this way. From a Weberian point of view, this might be regarded as an attempt to give such leaders an authority beyond the naked power which comes from control of the state apparatus. Democratic leaders, too, sometimes possess a degree of charisma, at least as far as their supporters are concerned (the Israeli Prime Minister Menachem Begin, 1913–92, is an example).

2. Additional reading
(a) Anthony T. Kronman, *Max Weber*, (London: Edward Arnold, 1983).
(b) Max Weber, translated, edited and with an introduction by H.H. Gerth and C. Wright Mills, *From Max Weber: essays in sociology*, (London and Boston: Routledge and Kegan Paul Ltd., 1948), pp. 295–301.

3. Key vocabulary
Taking the texts in this chapter as a starting point, draw up lists of vocabulary in the following fields:
(a) Death and succession.
(b) Assassination.

4. Written Arabic texts 1

(a) Read the following definitions of خلافة 'succession' from المعجم العربي الأساسي (Larousse dictionary), p. 418.

خلافة: ... ٢ إمـارة أو إمـامـة (ريـاسـة المسلمـين) «وَقـعت حروب الرِدّة في خلافة أبي بكر »، ٣ نيابةً عن الغيـر «خلّفتك على أهلي أثناء سفري فأحسن الخِلافَةَ ».

(b) Read the following text from an Arab newspaper, then, without looking at the original text, answer the questions which follow in English.

موت السادات المفاجيء يحدث فراغا سياسيا في مصر يصعب تقدير أبعاده

السّادات كان المحور المركزي لأمريكا في المنطقة واختفاؤه «كارثة كبرى لها!»

تساؤلات كبيرة حول الموقف الذي سيتخذه حُسني مبارك من الكيان الصهيوني

القاهرة وعواصم العالم – وكالات الأنباء

يتردد بشكل عام في القاهرة ومختلف العواصم الكبرى في العالم أن الاختفاء المفاجيء للرئيس المصري أنور السادات من ساحة السياسة الدولية سيترتب عليه انعكاسات ضخمة على صعيد السياسة الخارجية. ومن بين التساؤلات التي تتردد بإلحاح ذلك الذي يتعلق بالموقف الذي سيتخذه حسني مبارك المرشح الأوحد لخلافة السادات إزاء إسرائيل، إذ أنه لم يقم قط بزيارة للكيان الصهيوني.

وقد أكد مبارك فور إعلان نبأ وفاة الرئيس السادات أنه لن يطرأ أي تغيير على الخطوط العريضة للسياسة التي انتهجت حتى الآن وأن مصر سوف تحترم تحالفاتها.

ولكن هل يبدي مبارك نفس «التفاهم» الذي كان يظهره السادات إزاء «الدولة» اليهودية إذا عاودت القيام بعمليات مثل عملية قصف المفاعل العراقي وقصف بيروت؟!

إن المراقبين يرون بشكل عام أن السياسة المصرية لن يطرأ عليها تغيير حتى شهر أبريل القادم أي حتى تتم المرحلة الأخيرة من الانسحاب الإسرائيلي من سيناء.

ويقول المراقبون إن علامات استفهام كثيرة سوف تثار بعد ذلك ولكن هذا الموقف لم يكن ليختلف حتى لو لم يقتل الرئيس السادات وذلك بسبب الهوة الكبيرة جدا التي تفصل بين المصريين والإسرائيليين بشأن الحكم الذاتي الفلسطيني.

ويقول المراقبون إن موت السادات رجل كامب ديفيد والمحور المركزي للسياسة الأمريكية في الشرق الأوسط تنبيء بحدوث تغييرات جذرية عميقة ليس في المنطقة فحسب بل وحيال التوازن العالمي برمته. ذلك أن اختفاء السادات من المسرح السياسي يحدث فراغا سياسيا في مصر يصعب تقدير أبعاده.

ويضيف المراقبون أنه مهما كان الأمر فإن هذه الوفاة المباغتة تمثل بالنسبة للولايات المتحدة «كارثة ما بعدها كارثة»، إذ كان السادات بالنسبة لواشنطون الأساس الذي لا غنى عنه لأي محاولات تسوية أمريكية للنزاع العربي – الإسرائيلي.

1. How does the writer describe Sadat's death?
2. How does he describe Sadat's relationship with America?
3. Is it clear who will succeed Sadat?
4. What principal question is being asked about Sadat's successor?
5. Why is this question being asked in particular?
6. List the Arabic terms used to describe Sadat's death in this text (including terms used as metaphors for death).
7. How may the policy of Sadat's successor differ from that of Sadat vis–à–vis Israel?

8. In what type of circumstances does the writer believe Sadat's successor may behave differently from Sadat?
9. According to observers, what event may herald a change in Egyptian policy?
10. May this change still have taken place had Sadat not been killed?
11. Why?
12. How is Sadat described?
13. How does the writer sum up the effect Sadat's death will have on the Middle East and on the world as a whole?

(c) Taking no more than five minutes, read the following text from الأهرام, Oct. 7, 1981, which deals with the same event as text (b), then answer the questions which follow in English.

شــــهيد مصــــر

شاءت ارادة الله . ولا راد لقضائه . ان يمتحن مصر ببلاء عظيم، وحدث أليم جسيم ، دبره خصومه بليل ضمن سلسلة مؤامراتهم للايقاع بهذا البلد الكريم . شاءت ارادة الله ان يحرم مصر من قائد مسيرتها . ورب اسرتها ، وصانع نهضتها ، في وقت هي احوج ما تكون فيه لجهوده ، وبصيرته والهامه وزعامته .

لقد ذهب الرجل الحر الذي حقق لمصر حريتها ، الشجاع الذي علمها الشجاعة في ممارسة سياستها ، القوي الذي بث فيها القوة على مواجهة شدائد الاحداث الابي الذي علمها الاباء وكرامة الاداء ، في ظل ارادة مستقلة وكبرياء وطني لا يعرف الحدود .

لم يكن السادات هذا كله فحسب ، بل كان أصالة وقيمة ورمز ومعنى ، فيه تمثل عقل الشعب وروح الامة وعظمة الماضي ومجد الحاضر ورخاء المستقبل . كان حبا وحياة ونورا وسلاما . كان شعاعا قدريا والهاما من السماء لقيادة هذا الشعب الى مدارج الامن والامان لم يكن حاكما ولا رئيسا ولا قائدا الا لان شعبه أراده كذلك . بل كان أحب لقب ووضع يريده ويتمناه أن يكون رب العائلة الوفي ، يحرص على سلامة الامة

حرصه على حياته ، ويعامل جميع افرادها كانهم بعض أبنائه ،
يحمي بالحب والتآخي والوفاء والتضافر مسيرة شعب واحد
في السراء والضراء ، يريد ان يرفع أمته بالجهد والعرق والبذل
والارادة مكانا عليا بين الامم . وقد كان.

وكما اختار الله لمصر هذا الرجل الفذ ليكون وسيلة الى
نصرها وحفظها ورفع شأنها ، شاء ان يسترد وديعته بعد أن
تعلمت مصر على يديه كيف تحسن الاداء،

ان الرجل الذي حمل رأسه على كفه طول حياته لم يكن
ليهاب الموت في أي لحظة ، ولكم كان كل مصري يفخر بمصريته
التي حققها له السادات عن أصالة وانتماء ، يتمنى لو استطاع
أن يفتديه بروحه ودمه تحقيقا للشعار الذي طالما تغنى به
الشعب . بالروح والدم نفديك يا سادات .

ان مصر تعاهد روحك الطاهرة يا أعز وأغلى بنيها على أن
تكون وفية لذكراك بالوحدة والعمل والبناء . وسيظل كل
انجاز تحققه ، وكل مشروع تبنيه ، وكل عمل طيب تأتيه شاهدا
على ما نفخته من روحك العظيم .

وداعا ، ورحمة ، وسلاما ، من اخوتك وبنيك يا أوفى الاباء
وعهدا بمواصلة الطريق أسرة واحدة ، قوية ، شامخة ، على هدى
خطاك .

1. According to the writer, why was Sadat killed?
2. How is Sadat described in this text?
3. How does the tone of this text differ from the tone of text (b), موت السادات?
4. What does the writer say Sadat represented?
5. How does the writer describe Sadat's relationship with the Egyptian people?
6. Who is being addressed in the final paragraph?

(d) The following newspaper text from الوطن Nov. 1989, deals with the
assassination of the Lebanese President René Mouawad, shortly after the
signing of the Taif Accord (sponsored by the Saudis, and concluded in Taif in
Saudi Arabia). The Taif Accord was designed to put an end to the Lebanese civil
war by offering Muslims a somewhat greater say in the running of the country.

René Mouawad was succeeded by Elyas Hrawi, who was still President at the time of writing (1997). Read this text, then translate it into idiomatic English.

اغتيال معوض فاجعة عادية

لعل اهم درس يمكن استخلاصه من عملية اغتيال الرئيس اللبناني رينيه معوض هو ان الموقف السياسي الناتج عن اتفاق الطائف على درجة من الصلابة يصعب معها اختراقه الا من الباب الامني . واختراق الباب الامني من ثقب الاغتيال الغادر لا يعني سوى ان الحالة الامنية الناتجة عن وقف اطلاق النار الاخير لا تقل صلابة عن الموقف السياسي .

وفي هذه الحالة ليس من المبالغة القول ان اغتيال الرئيس اللبناني – بمعنى استمرار الكيان او انهياره ، واستمرار الموقف السياسي او تبديله – لا يختلف عن اغتيال اي رئيس او زعيم دولة مستقرة .

بعد اغتيال كيندي الديمقراطي خلفه نائبه جونسون واستمر الحزب الديمقواطي بقيادة البلاد .

ولدى اغتيال انديرا غاندي خلفها ابنها راجيف واستمر حزب المؤتمر بحكم البلاد .

وبعد اغتيال رينيه معوض يجب ان يخلفه « ابنه » السياسي او نائبه المفترض . أي ابنه او نائبه اللذان يمثلان نفس الموقف السياسي الذي حمل النواب اللبنانيين الى الطائف ثم قاعدة القليعات لبدء رحلة ترسيخ وثيقة الوفاق بسد الفراغات الدستورية .

بمعنى آخر اذا كانت النوايا العربية مستمرة باستخدام الدعم الدولي لجهود اللجنة الثلاثية وانجازاتها التي حققتها حتى الآن لا يشكل اغتيال الرئيس سوى فاجعة من النوع الذي يحدث في أي دولة وفي أي زمان.

5. Written Arabic texts 2

(a) Read the following newspaper text form العربي القدس, June 5, 1988 on the death of Khomeini, then complete exercises i. – iv. which follow.

ايران تودع الخميني

طهران – الوكالات – اعلن في طهران امس عن وفاة الزعيم الايراني الامام الخميني عن عمر يناهز السابعة والثمانين بعد حوالى اسبوعين من عملية جراحية لوقف نزيف دموي في قناته الهضمية. وقد اعلن عن عطلة عامة في ايران لمدة خمسة ايام وحداد وطني لمدة ٤٠ يوم، كما وضع الجيش في حالة تأهب قصوى ودعي مجلس الخبراء لاجتماع عاجل للاستماع لوصية الامام الراحل الذي يتلوها نجله احمد الخميني. وقالت وزارة الارشاد الاسلامي ان جثمان الخميني سيشيع اليوم ويسمح للصحفيين الاجانب بتغطيتها كما ينقلها التلفزيون والاذاعة على الهواء مباشرة. الجيش الايراني والحرس الثوري اصدرا بيانا اكدا فيه دعمهما لهاشمي رفسنجاني رئيس البرلمان والقائد العام بالوكالة للقوات المسلحة.

اما منتظري الذي نحي مؤخرا من منصبه كخليفة للزعيم الايراني الراحل فقد دعا الايرانيين الى الهدوء والحفاظ على الثورة. منظمة مجاهدي خلق هنأت الشعب الايراني وقالت ان وفاة الخميني نهاية محتومة لنظام دموي. وتوقع بعض زعماء المعارضة الايرانية اضطرابات في فترة ما بعد الخميني فيما اعرب ابو الحسن بني صدر الرئيس الايراني الاسبق عن امله في ان تفتح وفاة الخميني الباب للديمقراطية.

i   Identify the words or phrases in the Arabic text which correspond to the following in English.

1. bid farewell to
2. the death of the leader was announced
3. [it is/was] approximately
4. two weeks after an operation
5. state of top alert
6. emergency session
7. will, testament
8. late (/deceased)
9. son, offspring
10. his funeral will take place today
11. live [of a broadcast]
12. deputy commander in chief
13. he was removed from his post
14. predict
15. post–Khomeini era
16. while
17. former

ii   Answer the following questions in English.

1. How old was Khomeini at the time of his death?
2. What happened two weeks before his death?
3. Which two 'events' were announced in Iran following Khomeini's death?
4. To what purpose was the Council of Experts called into immediate session?
5. When will Khomeini's funeral take place?
6. How will the funeral be reported?
7. What did the Iranian army and the Revolutionary Guards declare in their statement?
8. Who was recently removed from his position as successor designate to the deceased Iranian leader?
9. What did he call on Iranians to do?
10. What did the Mojahideen-e Khalq organisation do?
11. What is predicted by Iranian opposition leaders?
12. Who is Aboulhasan Bani Sadr?
13. What is his expressed hope?

iii There are a number of word order cohesive features in this text which are atypical of written Standard Arabic. Why should this be? How would you rephrase the anomolous sentences, to make them conform more closely to the norms of Modern Standard Arabic?

iv Structure translations based on إيران تودع الخميني.

Translate the following English sentences into Arabic using relevant constructions found in the text at the points indicated.

1. The election of the new government will be announced shortly. (para. 1, line 1)
2. He died a month after the terrorist attack. (para. 1, line 3)
3. The students have a three–month summer vacation. (para. 1, line 5)
4. An immediate council session must be called. (para. 1, lines 6–7)
5. You're not allowed to smoke in this room. (para. 1, lines 9–10)
6. He was elected president of the Lebanese Republic. (para. 2, lines 1–2)
7. Radical changes are expected in the post–Gorbachev era in eastern Europe. (para. 2, line 6)
8. I hope they'll arrive soon. (para. 2, line 7)

(b) Read the following newspaper text from الحياة, June 5, 1989, then complete exercises i. and ii. which follow.

وفاة الخميني

لندن، طهران، واشنطن « الحياة »:

طويت امس الاحد صفحة في تاريخ ايران والمنطقة بوفاة الزعيم الايراني اية الله الخميني عن ٨٨ عاما. وبث التلفزيون الايراني ان مجلس الخبراء الذي يضم ٨٣ عضواً انتخب الرئيس علي خامنئي (٥٠ عاماً) باكثرية تفوق الثلثين، خليفة لـ«مرشد الثورة ».

لكن خبراء في الشؤون الايرانية قالوا ان «ترويكا» مؤلفة من نجل الخميني احمد ورئيس «مجلس الشورى» (البرلمان) علي اكبر هاشمي رفسنجاني وخامنئي نفسه تتولى السلطة عمليا في شكل موقت.

واوضح هؤلاء الخبراء ان نجل الخميني يستطيع السيطرة على الوضع الداخلي في البلاد بواسطة حليفيه وزير الداخلية محتشمي ووزير المخابرات ريشهري.

وقبل قطع خطوط الاتصالات بين ايران والخارج، افاد سكان طهران ان المئات من رجال «الحرس الثوري» نزلوا الى الشارع تحسبا لأي انقلاب، فيما وضع الجيش في حال تاهب. واذيع رسميا ان الخميني سيدفن اليوم. وكان ملفتا ان الاجنحة المتصارعة على السلطة حرصت على الظهور كانها موحدة بعد ان وضعت على راس

اولوياتها حماية النظام.

وتليت امس وصية الزعيم الايراني في جلسة عقدها مجلس النواب وهي تقع في ٢٩ صفحة اضافة الى ملحق من صفحة واحدة. وصرح نجله احمد ان الوصية ستذاع قريبا.

i   Translate the text orally into English.

ii Without looking at texts (a) and (b) above, translate the following English sentences into Arabic using the structures indicated in brackets.

1. The death of the president will be announced soon. (أعلن عن)
2. He died at the age of approximately eighty–three. (ناهز/يناهز)
3. The army arrived an hour after the attack. (بعد ... من)
4. There will be a three–day general strike.
5. Foreigners are not allowed to enter this area. (سمح ب ل)
6. Who's the deputy general commander of the armed forces? (بالوكالة)
7. He was elected president by a majority of over two thirds. (فاق/يفوق)
8. It was officially announced [broadcast] that the government had resigned. (أذاع/يذيع)
9. Hafiz al-Asad is anxious to appear democratic. (ظهر + كأن)
10. Yesterday the foreign minister began a visit to Egypt. (beginning of newspaper report)

(c) Translate the first two paragraphs of the following newspaper text from June 5, 1989 in written form into English.

ايران ما بعد الخميني

فتحت وفاة الامام الخميني فصلا جديدا من الصراع على الخلافة بين التيارات المتنازعة على السلطة في ايران. وعلى ضوء نتيجة هذا الصراع ستتبلور هوية ايران السياسية الجديدة وطبيعة علاقاتها مع جيرانها ودول العالم. وايا كانت النتيجة فإن الامر المؤكد ان سياسة تصدير الثورة التي ارتبطت بعهد وشخصية الامام الراحل اوقعت ايران في العديد من المشاكل والازمات، ابرزها الحرب مع العراق التي كلفت البلاد اكثر من مليوني قتيل ومئات الآلاف من الجرحى والمعاقين، وانهيارا اقتصاديا شاملا استنزف الثروات وتسبب في عجز مالي يفوق المئة مليار دولار حسب اكثر التقديرات حيادا.

وايران وهي تودع هذه الايام زعيمها بحاجة الى وقفة مع النفس ومراجعة دقيقة لكل حساباتها، وعلاقاتها وتراث السنوات العشر الماضية من تاريخها، فقد اثبتت الاحداث عدم جدوى توجهاتها السابقة لما الحقته بسمعة البلاد من ضرر وانهكتها داخليا، بصورة لم يسبق لها مثيل حتى في احلك عصورها.

وعندما نقول ان ايران بحاجة الى مراجعة، يحذونا الامل ان تتمثل هذه المراجعة بفتح صفحة جديدة من العلاقات العربية الايرانية، واحلال السلام الحقيقي بين الشعبين الشقيقين العربي والايراني، والتعاون سويا لمواجهة العدو المشترك، والقوى الخارجية التي تسانده وتعمل على بذر بذور الفرقة بين المسلمين. وايران ايضا بحاجة الى صفحة داخلية تعيد الوحدة والتماسك بين ابنائها بمختلف توجهاتهم وعقائدهم، حتى تقوم ديمقراطية حقيقية في البلاد تعيد اليها مكانتها السياسية والاقتصادية في العالم بأسره. فقد عانى الشعب الايراني كثيرا من المغامرات والصراعات والانقسامات وقد حان الوقت لوضع حد لهذه المعاناة، والالتفات الى اعادة تعمير البلاد، ووضع خطط تنمية طموحة، في مناخ من التسامح، لان هذا التسامح سواء كان داخليا، او خارجيا، هو الضمانة الاساسية لعودة الاستقرار والرخاء في البلاد.

باختصار ان ايران ما بعد الخميني يجب ان تكون ايران جديدة مختلفة عن ايران التي عرفناها طوال السنوات الماضية بما في ذلك ايران الشاه. وهذا يتطلب قيادة جديدة حكيمة عاقلة تتعامل مع الامور من منطلق المصالح المتبادلة. واحترام حق الجوار وتعميق الحريات الاساسية. والاستفادة من جميع الدروس السابقة، من حيث تطوير الايجابيات مثل وقف الحرب، ونبذ السلبيات بما في ذلك تشجيع خطف الرعايا الاجانب.

6. **Written Arabic texts 3 (classical)**

Read the following three texts, then translate (a) and (b) on the death of the Prophet, and (c) on the succession (خلافة) of the Prophet into idiomatic English.

(a) From سيرة الرسول by ابن هشام (sections 1009–10) .وفاة رسول الله

* (وفاة رسول الله صلعم) *

قال ابن اسحاق وقال الزُهْري حدثني أنَس بن مالك انه لما كان
يومُ الاثنين الذي قبض الله فيه رسوله صلعم خرج الى الناس
وهم يصلّون الصُبْحَ فرُفع السِتْرُ وفُتح الباب فخرج رسول الله
صلعم فقام على باب عائشةَ فكان المسلمون يفتتنون في
صلاتهم في رسول الله صلعم حين رأوه فرحًا به وتفرجوا
فأشار اليهم أن اثبتوا على صلاتكم قال فتبسّم رسول الله
صلعم سرورا لما رأى من هيئتهم في صلاتهم وما رايتُ رسول
الله صلعم احسنَ هيئةً منه تلك الساعة قال ثم رجع وانصرف
الناس وهم يُرَوْن ان رسول الله صلعم قد أفرق من وجعـه
فرجع ابو بكر الى اهله بالسنح ، قال ابن اسحاق وحدثني
محمد بن ابراهيم بن حارث عن القاسم ابن محمد ان رسول
الله صلعم قال حين سمع تكبير عمر في الصلاة اين ابو بكر
يأبَى اللهُ ذاك والمسلمون فلو لا مقالة قالها عمر عند وفاته لم
يشكّ المسلمون ان رسول الله صلعم قد استخلف ابا بكر ولكنه
قال عند وفاته إن أسْتخلفْ فقد استخلفَ من هو خير مني إن
أتركهم فقد تركهم من هو خير مني فعرف الناس ان رسول
الله صلعم لم يستخلف احدا وكان عمر غير متّهَم على ابي بكر .

(b) From تاريخ الطبري, vol. III, p. 202 (sections 1818–19) حدثنا زكرياء بن يحيى

حدثنا زكرياء بن يحيى الضرير، قال: حدثنا أبو عوانة، قال:
حدثنا داود بن عبد الأوديّ، عن حُميد بن عبد الرحمن الحميريّ،
قال: تُوُفّى رسولُ اللّه صلى اللّه عليــه وسلم وأبو بكر في

طائفة من المدينة، فجاء فكشف الثوبَ عن وجهه فقبّله، وقال:
فداك أبي وأمي! مـا أطيَبَك حيّا وميـتاً مـات مـحـمـد وربّ
الكعبة! قال: ثم انطلق إلى المنبر، فوجد عمر ابن الخطاب قائما
يُوعد الناس، ويقول: إنّ رسول اللّه صلى اللّه عليه وسلم حيّ
لم يمت، وإنه خارج إلى من أرجف به، وقاطع أيديهم، وضارب
أعناقهم وصالبهم. قال فتكلّم أبو بكر، وقال: أنصتْ. قال: فأبى
عمـر أن يُنصت، فتكلم أبو بكر، وقال: إن اللّه قال لنبيه صلى
اللّه عليه وسلم: «إنكَ مَيَّتٌ وَإِنَّهُمْ مَيِّتُون * ثُمَّ إنَّكُمْ يَوْمَ القيامَة
عنْدَ رَبِّكُمْ تَخْتَصِمُون» (١). «وَمَا مُحَمَّدٌ إلا رَسُولٌ قـد خَلَتْ منْ
قَبْله الرُّسُلُ أَفـإنْ مـاتَ أَوْ قُتلَ انْقَلَبْتُمْ عَلَى أَعْقَابِكُمْ ...» (٢) ،
حتى خَتم الآية، فمن كان يعبدُ محمدا فقد مات إلهه الذي كان
يعبده، ومن كان يعبد اللّه لا شريك له، فإن اللّه حيٌّ لا يموت.

قال : فحلف رجالٌ أدركناهم من أصحاب محمد صلى
اللّه عليه وسلم: ما علمنا أن هاتين الآيتين نَزَلتا حتى قرأهما
أبو بكر يومئذ.

(١) سورة الزمر ٣٠، ٣١.
(٢) سورة آل عمران ١٤٤.

(c) From تاريخ الطبري, vol. III, p. 203 (sections 1819–20) فتكلّم أبو بكر.

فتكلّم أبـو بكر، فلم يتـرك شـيـئـا نزل في الأنصـار، ولا ذكـره
رسـولُ اللّه صلى اللّه عليـه وسلم من شـأنهم إلا وذكـره. وقـال:
لقـد علمـتم أن رسـول اللّه قـال: لو سلك الناس واديا وسلكت
الأنصـار واديا سلكتُ وادي الأنصار، ولقـد علمتَ يا سـعـد أنّ
رسـول اللّه قال وأنت قـاعـد: قـريش ولاةُ هذا الأمر، فـبَرُّ الناس
تبع لبرّهم، وفاجرهم تبع لفاجرهم. قال: فقال سعد: صدقتَ،
فنحن الوزراء وأنتم الأمراء. قال: فقال عمر: ابسُطْ يدك يا أبا

بكر فـلأبـايعك. فـقـال أبـو بكـر: بـل أنت يـا عـمـر، فـأنتَ أقـوى لهـا
منِّي. قال: وكان عـمـر أشـدّ الرجـلين، قـال: وكان كلٌّ واحـد مـنهـما
يـريـد صـاحبـه يفـتح يـده يضـرب عليهـا، فـفـتح عـمـر يد أبـي بكر
وقـال: إن لك قـوّتي مـع قـوّتك. قـال: فـبـايع النـاس واستثبـتـوا
للبيـعة، وتخلّف عليٌّ والزبـير، واختـرط الزُّبـير سيفـه، وقـال: لا
أغـمـده حتى يُبـايع عليٌّ، فـبـلغ ذلك أبـا بكر وعـمـر، فـقـال عـمـر:
خُذُوا سيـف الزُّبـير، فـاضربـوا بـه الحجـر. قـال: فـانطلق إليهـما
عـمـر، فـجـاء بهـما تعبـا، وقـال: لتبـايعـان وأنتـما طـائعـان، أو
لتبـايعـان وأنتما كـارهـان! فبـايعـا.

7. Grammar/stylistics

قـد

The particle قـد can occur before either an imperfect verb or a perfect verb.

(a) قـد *with the imperfect*

The meaning of قـد with the imperfect is 'perhaps, possibly' 'maybe', 'may', etc. An example is:

وقـال حشـاني ان الجبـهة قـد تحصل على ٤٤ ٪ مـن مجـمـوع مـقـاعـد
البـرلمان ..

'Hashani said that the Front might obtain 44% of the total number of seats in the parliament ...' (ch. 15, 5b)

It is also possible to use قـد before an imperfect negated by لا. For example:

قـد لا تحصل الجبـهة على ٤٤ ٪ مـن مجـمـوع مـقـاعـد البـرلمان ..

'The Front might not obtain 44% of the total number of seats in the parliament.'

(b) قـد *with the perfect*

In contrast to its use with both positive and negative imperfect verbs, قـد is only ever used immediately before a positive perfect verb. The meaning of قـد with the perfect is more difficult to describe than its meaning with the imperfect. In modern Standard Arabic, it is worth distinguishing two sorts of contexts in which قـد with the perfect is used: i. where the use of قـد is either obligatory or at least stylistically expected; and ii. where the use of قـد conveys a specific meaning.

i *Obligatory or stylistically normal use of* قد *with the perfect*
There are a number of situations in which the use of قد is either obligatory or
stylistically normal.

i.i *In anterior* حال–*clauses*
قد is obligatory before an anterior حال–clause, that is to say, a حال–clause which
expresses previous time. Such a clause is constructed on the pattern وقد + *perfect*
verb. An example is:

وكـانـت الـبـشـريـة و{قـد} انفلتت مـن قـيـود الـعـقـيـدة الـديـنـيـة قـد
انطلقت إلى عبادات جديدة ..

'Having escaped from the bonds of religious doctrine, humanity has
taken up new forms of worship ...' (ch. 14, 11ai)

i.ii *In* كان + *perfect verb structures*
In the case of the so–called compound tenses involving the verb كان and a
subsequent perfect verb, the subsequent perfect verb is normally introduced by قد.
For example:

ولئن كـان {قـد} تسـمى بـالبـعث الـعـربـي، فـليـس ذلك لأنه أول حـزب
آمن بالوحدة العربية فكراً وعملا ..

'If it was called the Arab Ba'th Party, that was not because it was the
first party which believed in Arab unity in terms of both thought and
action ..' (ch. 13, 11a)

وكـان الـمؤتمر الشـعـبـي {قـد} اعلن امس الاول ان ١٣ مـرشـحـا من
المستقلين ..

'The popular conference announced the day before yesterday 13
independent candidates ...' (ch. 15, 4c)

وكـانـت الـحـمـلات الانتـخـابـيـة {قـد} بـدأت رسـمـيـا امـس الاول.

'The election campaign began officially the day before yesterday.' (ch.
15, 5c)

All the above examples involve the verb كان in the perfect. However, the verb كان
may also occur in the imperfect:

.. وبهـذا تكون الجبـهـة {قـد} حصلت على ٤٧ ٪ من الدوائر في
انتخاب الدور الاول .

'Accordingly, the Front will have gained 48% of the constituences in
the first round.' (ch. 15, 5b)

It is also possible, but relatively unusual, for the subsequent perfect verb in كان+ *perfect verb* structures not to be introduced by قد. The following – in which {X} marks the 'missing' قد – are examples:

.. وكان الاول {X} قُتل في اشتباك مساء الاثنين الماضي

'The first one was killed in a clash last Monday ...' (ch. 14, 4c)

.. و ليكتب لك اسم دواء كان {X} جرّبه هو او احد معارفه .

' ... or to write for you the name of a medicine he or one of his friends has tried' (ch. 19, 5c)

i.iii *As a resumptive particle*

In sentences with an emphatic word order and a main verb in the perfect, the verb is often marked by a preceding قد. This قد can be regarded as a type of resumptive particle, i.e. a particle which signals the beginning of the non–preposed part of the sentence (cf. ch. 10, 7b; ch. 17, 7a). The following sentence, for example, has the overall structure Subject–Predicate (the subject being تمثال الجندي المجهول and the predicate being قد انفصل حصاناه, while the predicate itself has the internal structure of a verbal clause (قد انفصل حصاناه) (ch. 13, 7a):

وتمثال الجندي المجهول {قد} انفصل حصاناه .

'The two horses of the statue of the unknown soldier had come away.' [Lit: 'The unknown soldier, his two horses had come away.'] (ch. 13, 11b)

Similarly following إنَّ:

تقول أوراق البردي إنَّ أحد الفراعنة {قد} نما إليه أن علاقة آثمة نشأت بين بعض نساء الحريم وبعض رجال الحاشية ..

'The papyrus sheets say that one of the pharaohs was told [lit: came to him that ...] that a sinful relationship had grown up between one of the ladies of the harem and one of the courtiers ...' (ch. 17, 11)

It is also possible to find قد used as a resumptive particle in other structures involving preposed elements. Thus, with a preposed subject, following أنَّ:

كذلك هنالك ما يثبت ان قدماء الهنود {قد} مارسوا، كقدماء المصريين هذه المهنة ايضا ..

'Similarly, there is evidence that the ancient Indians, like the ancient Egyptians, also practised this profession ...' (ch. 19, 4a)

Similarly with a preposed adverbial:

بدلاً من أن يؤدي هذا الضغط الأمني الذي تجاوز الحدود في بعض
البلاد العربية إلى اختفاء هذه الجماعات أو تغييرها لأساليبها أو
تنفير القواعد الجماهيرية والشعبية منها، فـ{قد} أدت الوسائل
الأمنية إلى نمو تيار من العنف المتبادل ..

'Instead of this security pressure ... leading ..., the security measures
have led to the growth of a current of mutual violence ...' (ch. 14, 5b)

قد is also typically used as a resumptive particle in an أما .. ف structure (ch. 17,
7a) following the ف:

اما الشيخ محمد علي ابو لحوم، رئيس الحزب الجمهوري، فـ{قد}
تقدم بترشيح نفسه كمرشح مستقل في الدائرة 250 بمنطقة فهم ..

'Meanwhile, Sheikh Muhammad Abu Luhum, the leader of the
Republican Party, put himself forward as an independent candidate in
Constituency 250, in the Fahm region ...' (ch. 15, 4b)

اما منتظري الذي نحي مؤخرا من منصبه كخليفة للزعيم الايراني
الراحل فـ{قد} دعا الايرانيين الى الهدوء والحفاظ على الثورة.

'Montazeri, meanwhile, who was recently dismissed from his post as
successor to the Iranian leader, has called on the Iranians to remain calm
and to preserve the revolution.' (ch. 16, 5a)

ii *Emphatic use of* قد *with the perfect*

The notion of emphasis was discussed in chapters 13 (ch. 13, 7a), 14 (ch. 14, 7a,
7b), and 15 (ch. 15, 7a). In most of the cases discussed in chapters 13, 14 and 15,
emphasis is used to emphasise a part of a clause. However, the particle قد with the
perfect tense is traditionally regarded as emphasising the whole of the clause in
which it occurs. Traditionally again the particle ل which can be prefixed to قد to
give the form لقد is felt to provide an even greater sense of emphasis (cf. the
discussion of ل with إنّ in ch. 15, 7aii.i). In modern Arabic لقد is sometimes used
as a slightly more formal alternative to قد.

It is possible to identify four emphatic uses of قد: (i) stress, (ii) contrast, (iii)
scene setting, (iv) linkage (cf. the list for emphatic uses of preposed adverbials (ch.
13, 7a) and initial noun phrases (ch. 13, 7aii–iii)).

ii.i *Stress*

Fairly commonly, قد can be regarded as relaying stress in Arabic. Much less
commonly, this stress can also reasonably relayed in an English translation by a
word or phrase expressing stress. For example:

وأي شيء أيسر من أن تأخذ ما {X} اتفقت عليه كثرة الرواة على
أنه حق لا شك فيه ؟ وكثرة الرواة {قد} اتفقت على أن اسمه حندج
ابن حجر ..

'And what is easier than accepting what the majority of reciters have
agreed is the indubitable truth? The majority of reciters have indeed
agreed that his name is Handaj ibn Hujr ...' (ch. 17, 4c)

Here the first اتفقت is not preceded by قد (this non-occurrence being marked in
the text by the symbol {X}), while the second is. A reasonable translation into
English might introduce the emphatic word 'indeed' into the translation.

Similarly:

يريد ان يرفع أمته بالجهد والعرق والبذل والارادة مكانا عليا بين
الامم . و{قد} كان

'He wanted to raise his people through effort, sweat, toil, and will to a
high status among the nations. And that was what in fact happened.'
(ch. 16, 4c)

..فمن لم يسعده الحظ بمشاهدة تلك الآثار فـ{قد} قرأ عنها وتأمل
صورها .

'Those who have not had the pleasure of seeing those monuments [in
person], will certainly have read about them and pondered pictures of
them.' (ch. 17, 11)

In these two examples, 'in fact' and 'certainly' in the English translation relay the
same kind of stress as is relay through the use of قد in the Arabic original.

ii.ii *Contrast*

A second identifiable use of قد is to express contrast with information which has
gone before in the text. This contrast may be of a simple temporal nature, such that
قد expresses a time reference either prior to the time being discussed in the
preceding section of text, or a time reference subsequent to the time being
discussed in the preceding section of text. قد may also express a specific time
reference in the past, as opposed to a general time in the past and/or present
expressed by the previous section of text.

On the basis of this general schema, the contrastive uses of قد be subdivided as
follows: prior time; subsequent time; specific time in contrast with general time:

– Prior time
The following is an example where قد expresses a time prior to the time being
discussed in the preceding section of text:

ويستعد الشيخ عبد الله بن حسين الاحمر لخوض معركة
الانتخابات على امل الوصول الى كرسي رئاسة البرلمان. و{قد}
ترشح هو وولداه «صادق»، و«حميد» في ثلاث دوائر مختلفة،
فترشح الشيخ عبد الله في الدائرة رقم 227 في منطقة خمر –
محافظة صنعاء – فيما ترشح صادق في الدائرة 225 وحميد في
الدائرة 280 باسم تجمع الاصلاح ايضا.

'Sheikh Abdullah ibn Husayn al-Ahmar is preparing to enter the
election campaign in the hope of becoming the Speaker of the
Parliament. He and his two sons Sadiq and Humayd have put
themselves forward as candidates in three different constituencies.
Sheikh Abdullah has put himself forward in Constituency 227 in the
Khumr region – in Sana'a Province, while Sadiq has put himself
forward in Constituency 225 and Humayd in Constituency 280 also in
the name of the Islah Grouping.' (ch. 15, 4a)

In this example it is particularly striking that the first use of ترشح is introduced by
قد, which establishes the new general time reference. The subsequent two further
uses of ترشح, however, merely maintain this new general time reference, and are
not therefore themselves independently introduced by قد.

Similarly:

في بور سعيد قابلت كثيراً من الناس ... والناس ينزلون من
القطار يبحثون عن تمثال دي لسبس .. {لقد} تحطم التمثال
وسقط فوق زورق صغير وانكفأ على وجهه ..

'In Port Said I met many people ... The people got off the train, looking
for the statue of De Lepsius. The statue had been smashed and had
fallen on top of a small boat, and tumbled over on its face ...' (ch. 13,
11b)

Here the phrase لقد تحطم describes a prior event to that of the people getting of
the train. Once this general prior time frame is established the following verb انكفأ
does not need to be similarly preceded by قد since the action of falling follows on
in a temporally predictable way from the action of being smashed.

The following are further examples of قد being used to express prior time:

والانقاض ترتفع من الشوارع ، ودخان البارود {قد} طغت عليه
رائحة البحر ، والناس ينزلون من القطار يبحثون عن تمثال دي
لسبس ..

'The ruins rise from the streets, the smoke of the gunpowder has been
overcome by the smell of the sea, the people get down from the train,
searching for the statue of De Lepsius ..' (ch. 13, 11b)

وكان الليل باردا في بور سعيد ، والبرودة تعلن حالة الطوارئ في
كل الشوارع حتى البوليس الدولي {قد} توارى في البارات . .

'The night was cold in Port Said, and the coldness announced the state
of emergency in all the streets; even the international police had
disappeared into the bars ...' (ch. 13, 11b)

As these last two examples illustrate, where قد is used to express prior time to an
event or state which is itself already in the past, the قد‑phrase is often translated by
an English past perfect (i.e. *had + past participle*).

– Subsequent time

قد is frequently used to express subsequent time, typically also with a change of
grammatical subject, and a change in the subject under discussion in a more general
sense, as in the following:

. . وكان أكثرهم عربًا أو تتلمذوا على يد العرب، و{قد} التقينا
الباحثة الاسبانية مانويلا كورتيس التي تحاضر في هذه المادة في
العديد من المؤتمرات التخصصية في الموسيقى بشكل عام
والاندلسية بشكل خاص . .

'.. Most of them [= these singers and musicians] were Arabs or studied
under Arabs. We met the Spanish researcher Manuela Cortes who has
lectured on this subject in a number of specialist music conferences in
general, and in conferences on Islamic Spanish music in particular ..'
(ch. 12, 11)

سيختفي التراب الذي أغمض العيون وسد النفوس . . تماماً كما
اختفى من المدن الألمانية . . {لقد} رأيت ميونيخ ودسلدورف ورأيت
هانوفر وهمبورج . .

'The dust which closed our [lit: 'the'] eyes and blocked our spirits will
disappear ... just as it disappeared from the German cities. I have seen
Munich and Düsseldorf; I have seen Hanover and Hamburg ...' (ch.
13, 11b)

As this last example illustrates, where قد is used to express subsequent past time to
an event or state which is further in the past, the قد‑phrase may be translated by an
English present perfect (i.e. *have/has + past participle*).

– Specific time, as opposed to general time

There are also cases where the change in time involves a shift from a general past to
a specific past. In the following example, for instance, the orders *were* clear and
had been made prior to the writer asking the officer, although they also remained in

force after the writer asked the officer:

والتعليمات صريحة بأن يلتزموا الأدب والوقار حتى إذا شربوا . .

إلا إذا ذهبوا إلى الصحراء فهم أحرار أن يفعلوا ما يريدون . .

و{قد} سألت ضابطاً دولياً رأيته يتطلع إلى السماء : كيف الحال ؟

'The orders were clear that they should maintain discipline and good behaviour even when they drank, except when they went to the desert, when they were free to do what they wanted. I asked an international officer whom I saw looking at the sky, "How are you?"' (ch. 13, 11b)

Similarly, in the following example, the type of life which Americans are described as living is to be regarded as having been lived both before and after the writer's witnessing of it:

ولكني أدري كيف يعيش الناس في أمريكا . بلد الانتاج الفخم

والثراء الفاحش واللذائذ المباحة . . {لقد} شهدتهم هنالك . .

'But I know how people live in America, the land of mass–production, fantastic wealth, and unbridled pleasures. I have seen them there ...' (ch. 14, 11ai)

Similarly, in the following example غاضب 'angry' expresses not only the fact that the friend got angry in the past (i.e. before he swore that he would never read anything which the writer wrote), but also the fact that the friend is still angry with the writer (i.e. after he swore that he would never read anything which the writer wrote). It can therefore be regarded as having something of a general time reference:

فهو غاضب مني ، و{قد} أقسم ألا يقرأ شيئاً مما أكتب . .

'He is angry with me, and has sworn never to read anything which I write ...' (ch. 13, 11b)

ii.iii *Scene–setting*

قد fairly frequently occurs at the start of a so–called topic–sentence, or topic–clause. As noted in chapter 15 (ch. 15, 7b), a topic–sentence, or topic–clause, is a sentence or clause at the start of a passage or paragraph, which introduces or states in general terms the topic of that passage or paragraph; i.e. it sets the scene for that passage or paragraph. One can also think of a topic–sentence or topic-clause introduced by قد as being marked out, or stressed (cf. ii.ii.i), in the way that underlining a sentence or clause (or putting it in bold or in capital letters) marks out, or stresses, that sentence or clause. The following is the 'skeleton' of a text from chapter 18 (ch. 18, 5b). The beginning of the two paragraphs of which the text consists are reproduced here in full. Other major verbs and a few relevant noun phrases and linking words which occur in the text are also listed.

paragraph one

لـ{قد} مر النشاط التجاري بين شبه القارة الهندية ومنطقة الخليج العربي بعدة مراحل من العصر الحديث ...

– شهدت ...

–كما شهدت ...

– وكانت العلاقات التجارية ...

paragraph two

لـ{قـد} تعـرض النشـاط التـجـاري بين الهند والخليج إلى صعود وهبوط، وامتداد وانحسار ...

– كما ان طبيعة العلاقات التجارية في المنطقة {قد} تغيرت ...

– حيث دخلت هذه الدول ...

paragraph one

'Commercial activity between the Indian sub-continent and the Gulf region has passed through several phases of the modern era ...

- they witnessed ...
- they also witnessed ...
- commercial relations were ...'

paragraph two

'Commercial activity between India and the Gulf has been subject to rises and falls, ebb and flow ...

- just as the nature of the commercial relations in the region changed ...
- such that these states entered ...' (ch. 18, 5b)

In this example, the first clause of paragraph one expresses the overall topic of the paragraph, and the text as a whole. This is introduced by لقد. None of the other verbs in the first paragraph are introduced by قد. The first clause of paragraph two is similarly introduced by لقد. This clause acts as a topic-clause to paragraph two. Of the other major clauses in paragaph two, one is not introduced by قد, while the other is; in this case, قد seems to signal temporal contrast, introducing a description of events subsequent to those previously described (cf. section ii.ii.ii, below).

Given the potentially emphatic nature of قد, one would expect paragraphs where an initial perfect verb does not express key information not to be introduced by قد. To some extent this seems to be the case. Consider the following from chapter 16 (ch. 16, 11). The symbol {X} marks the non–use of قد before a perfect verb.

paragraph one

و{قد} اصدر الرئيس محمد حسني مبارك اوامره بمشاركة طائرات القوات الجوية المصرية في البحث عن طائرة الرئيس الفلسطيني ياسر عرفات .

paragraph two

و{X}علمت وكالة انباء الشرق الأوسط ان اكثـر من خمس طائرات عسكرية مجهزة {قد} تحركت فى ساعة مبكرة من صباح امس من احدى القواعد العسكرية لتكون فوق منطقة البحث مع أول ضوء .

paragraph three

{X} جاء ذلك فور اعلان السلطات الليبية انقطاع الاتصال بالطائرة .

paragraph four

و{X}صرح متحدث رسمى بوزارة الدفاع المصرية بأن الرئيس محمد حسني مبارك القائد الاعلى للقوات المسلحة {قد} امر بمشاركة طائرات القوات الجوية المصرية فى عملية البحث عن طائرة عرفات ...

The following is a partial translation, with the use or non-use of قد noted before the English verb which translates the Arabic perfect (as above non–use of قد is indicated by {X}):

paragraph one
President Muhammad Husni قد issued his orders for the participation of Egyptian air-force planes ...
paragraph two
The Middle East news agency {X} has learnt that more than five equipped aircraft قد set off early ...
paragraph three
This {X} came/was revealed ...
paragraph four
An official spokesman in the Egyptian Ministry of Defence {X} announced that Predisent Muhammad Husni Mubarak, the supreme commander of the armed forces قد ordered ... (ch. 16, 11)

In this example, perfect verbs describing the relaying of messages, such as وعلمت جاء ذلك فور اعلان السلطات (paragraph two), وكالة انباء الشرق الأوسط وصرح متحدث رسمى الليبية انقطاع الاتصال بالطائرة (paragraph three), and بوزارة الدفاع المصرية (paragraph four) are not preceded by قد; the issue of who relayed the information, etc. is not particularly crucial. Perfect verbs giving more crucial information about orders given to actually do something, or physical events affecting the outcome of the incident, on the other hand, are introduced by قد. وقد} اصدر الرئيس محمد حسني مبارك اوامره بمشاركة طائرات Thus: اكثر من خمس طائرات عسكرية (paragraph one), القوات الجوية المصرية الرئيس محمد حسني مبارك القائد (paragraph two), مجهزة {قد} تحركت الاعلى للقوات المسلحة {قد} امر بمشاركة طائرات القوات الجوية المصرية فى عملية البحث (paragraph four).

The use of قد at the start of a text or a paragraph constitutes the most obvious cases of scene–setting. There are, however, also examples where قد functions as a scene-setter – or at least as a marker of a change of scene within a paragraph. For example:

> لاغنَى لولي الأمر عن المشاورة ، فإن الله تعالى أمر بها نبيَّه فقال : (فَاعْفُ عَنْهُمْ وَاسْتَغْفِرْ لَهُمْ وَشَاوِرْهُمْ فِي الأمْرِ). و{قــد} روي عن أبي هريرة ، رضي الله عنه، قال: ..

'It is essential for those in authority to consult other people, for God Almightly ordered the Prophet to consult: He said, "Forgive them and ask their pardon and seek their counsel." Abu Hurayra, may God be pleased with him, said ...' (ch. 15, 6a)

ii.iv *Linkage*

Sometimes قد is used as a linker, expressing a close relationship between the clause beginning with قد and what has gone before (a usage markedly in contrast with the use of قد to express temporal contrast or a new topic, discussed above). The use of قد as a linker is particularly common where قد is preceded by ف and the clause justifies or amplifies a previous statement. The following are examples:

> وكما يقول المؤرخ العربي الأندلسي ان وصول زرياب إلى الأندلس كان نقطة انطلاق في فنون الموسيقى والغناء، فـ{قد} جاء بآلات التخت الموسيقي الشرقي وأكثر من ألف أغنية شرقية كان يحفظها.

'As the historian of Arab Spain says, the arrival of Ziryab in Spain was a breakthrough point in the arts of music and singing. For he brought the instruments of the eastern orchestra and more than one thousand eastern songs which he had memorised.' (ch. 12, 11).

> .. الأمر الذي ساعد على توسيع عضوية جماعة الإخوان المسلمين بصورة لم يسبق لها مثيل بالنسبة لحزب عقائدي في مصر فـ{قد} بلغت خلال أقل من عشرين عاماً على ميلادها حوالى المليون من الإخوان المسلمين ..

'... something which helped to increase the membership of the Muslim Brotherhood in a way unprecedented for any other ideologically–based party in Egypt. In less than twenty years from its foundation, its membership reached around one million ...' (ch. 14, 11b)

Sometimes قد is found following و, but in a similar context to cases in which it follows ف, such that وقد provides further detail regarding the previous discussion:

وتجــدر الاشــارة الــى ان المرأة ســجلت حـضــورا مميــزا فــي هـذه
الانتـخـابـات. و{قـد} بلـغ عـدد المرشـحـات لخـوض الانتـخـابـات 49
مرشحة منهن 13 مرشحة عن احزاب سياسية ..

'It is worth noting that women have displayed an exceptional presence
in these elections. The number of women candidates for the elections
has reached 49, of whom 13 are candidates for political parties ...' (ch.
15, 4b)

وفي هذه الاثناء خرجت قيادة الجبهة الاسلامية للانقاذ من صمتها
واصدرت بيــانا يحـذر الحكم مـن تـعطيل المسار الديمقراطي. و{قـد}
جاء في بيان المكتب التنفيذي المؤقت للجبهة الاسلامية للانقاذ ..

'Meanwhile the leadership of the Islamic Salvation Front has emerged
from its silence and issued a proclamation in which it warns the
government against destroying the democratic process. The
proclamation of the provisional executive bureau of the Islamic
Salvation Front said ...' (ch. 15, 5d)

قـد is also commonly found following the linker هـذا و.., in which هـذا refers back
to (summarises) the information given in the preceding section of text, and و
indicates that the writer is going to talk further about this same topic. For example:

هذا و{قـد} حققت جمـاعة الإخوان المسلمين هذا النمـو الصـاروخي
دون أي عناء في التنظير والتحليل ..

'In addition, the Muslim Brothers achieved this phenomenal growth
without any concern for theorising or analysis ...' (ch. 14, 11b)

هذا و{قـد} أسـهـمت عـدة عناصـر أخرى في هذا النمـو الصـاروخي
لجماعة الاخوان المسلمين ..

'Several other elements played a part in this phenomenal growth of the
Muslim Brotherhood ...' (ch. 14, 11b)

ii.v *Other*
The above remarks on the use of قد are not intended to be exhaustive, and a good
deal of variation will be found between different authors and different styles of
writing. قد is not used in most colloquial dialects (although related forms are found
in dialects of the Arabian Peninsula). Like other Standard Arabic forms which are
not found in most dialects, such as إنّ (cf. 15, 7a), قد can therefore be used as a
marker of formality, drawing the reader's attention to the fact that what is being
written is 'proper' standard Arabic, rather than something which is relatively close
to the spoken language.

It is also possible to find places in texts where قد might be predicted to occur, but does not. For instance, it is perfectly possible to have a topic–clause with an initial perfect verb but without قد. For example:

نشأ الطب الاسلامي بعد بعثة النبي صلى اللّه عليه وسلم ..

'Islamic medicine grew up following the mission of the Prophet (God bless him and give him peace) ...' (ch. 19, 5b)

As a learner of Arabic, it is important to be aware of the various uses of قد, since this is an extremely common particle, and to be sensitive to the various ways in which قد can help to 'weight' the information in an Arabic text. It is also important to develop a facility for using قد in Arabic composition or translation in ways which are normal and acceptable to Arabs themselves.

8. Aural Arabic texts 1

Listen to the following text from حصاد الشهر no. 19, side 1, item 1, أضواء على الملك الراحل سعود, then summarise its contents orally in Arabic.

9. Aural Arabic texts 2

Listen to the following BBC Arabic Service news broadcast from Mar. 9, 1992, which deals with the death of the Israeli leader, Menachem Begin, then complete exercises i. and ii. below.

i   Answer the following comprehension questions in English.

1. Who is the newsreader?
2. When did Begin die?
3. How many people gathered in Jerusalem for his funeral?
4. Where was Begin buried and next to whom?
5. How old was he?
6. What prize was he awarded and with whom?
7. What did the Egyptian Foreign Minister say in tribute to Begin?
8. What did Jihan Sadat say about Begin?
9. What did the opposition Israeli Labour Party say about Begin?
10. Where was Begin born?
11. What happened to him at the beginning of World War II?
12. When did he go to Palestine?
13. What movement did he lead against the British mandate?
14. What did he do that lead to the killing of nearly 100 people?
15. What did his organisation do in 1948?

ii   Produce a complete transcription of the text in Arabic.

10. Written English texts
Making use of constructions encountered in the Arabic texts above, as far as possible, translate the following texts into idiomatic Arabic.

(a) Adapted from Maxime Rodinson, *Mohammed*, (Harmondsworth: Penguin Books, 1976), pp. 289–90.

The death of Mohammed
Umar refused to accept the stunning news. He stood squarely in the courtyard of the Prophet's house and harangued the crowds who came running from all directions, among them Usama's men. Mohammed, he declared, was not dead. He had gone to Allah for a while, like Moses on Mount Sinai. He would return and cut off the hands and feet of those who had spread the rumour of his death. Abu Bakr had been sent for and came hurriedly from Sunh. He went straight into Aisha's hut and, lifting the cloak which covered the corpse, kissed the dead face of his master and friend. Then he went out and tried in vain to calm Umar. After this he spoke authoritatively to the crowd. 'Men,' he said, 'those who have worshipped Mohammed must know that Mohammed is dead. But for those who worship Allah, Allah lives and will not die.' Then he quoted a verse from the Koran as proof: 'Mohammed is only a Messenger. The other Messengers have passed away before him. Yet, if he dies or is slain, will you turn back upon your heels?' (iii, 138) The odd thing – which might even look a little suspicious – was that no one had any recollection of this text; but they were impressed by it. There can be no further doubt. Umar collapsed. It was true. Mohammed was dead.

(b) Adapted from *Iran Yearbook 89–90*: (Bonn: MB Medien & Buecher Verlagsgesellschaft mbH).

Ayatollah Ruhollah Khomeini
Ayatollah Seyed Ruhollah Mostafavi, known as Mussavi Khomeini, the eighty–six–year–old founder and leader of the Islamic Republic of Iran died on June 3, 1989, twelve days after an operation.

Ayatollah Khomeini was the son of a cleric. He was born in 1903 in the small town of Khomein in Isfahan province. He completed his elementary education at fifteen and started his theological studies with Ayatollah Pasandideh, his ninety–seven–year–old brother who is still living in Qom. He left Qom for Arak in 1920 to continue his education and then moved to Qom in 1921 where he spent five years completing his advanced theological studies. He then began his career as an Islamic canonist and theology teacher.

In the early sixties Ayatollah Khomeini led the movement against the Shah of Iran's 'White Revolution'. As a result he was exiled in 1963, first to Turkey and then to the Islamic holy city of Najaf in Iraq. Following an agreement between Iraq and Iran he was expelled from Najaf and was forced to take up residence near Paris in the late seventies. On 2 February 1979, after a short stay in France, he returned to Tehran until after the Islamic revolution on 11 February 1979. He then moved to Qom, the religious capital of Iran, until heart problems forced him to return to Tehran where he lived in the northern suburbs for the rest of his life.

11. Précis

Read the following newspaper text from الأهرام, April 9, 1992, then complete exercises i. – iii. which follow.

التفاصيل الكاملة لأحداث الـ١٥ ساعة التي اختفت فيها طائرة عرفات

محطة سى. بى. إس الأمريكية : عرفات نجا من الموت بأعجوبة

طرابلس – تونس – وكالات الأنباء – وصل الرئيس الفلسطيني ياسر عرفات الى طرابلس بعد نجاته من محنة درامية مثيرة ، حبس العالم معها انفاسه لمدة ١٥ ساعة . وقد نجا الرئيس عرفات من الموت المحقق بأعجوبة عندما اجبرت عاصفة رملية شديدة الطائرة المقلة له على الهبوط على جسمها بدون عجلات فى الصحراء المفتوحة في منطقة «معاطن السرا» قرب الحدود الليبية مع تشاد والسودان وعلى بعد ١٤٠٠ كيلومتر الى الجنوب من طرابلس .

وطوال فترة اختفاء طائرة عرفات ، واحاطة مصيره بالغموض ، قامت مصر ، والولايات المتحدة ، وبريطانيا ، وفرنسا ، وايطاليا ، بالاضافة الى ليبيا بعملية مسح وانقاذ مكثفة لاستكشاف الصحراء الافريقية الكبرى لمحاولة رصد مكان طائرة عرفات.

طائرات مصرية تبحث عن عرفات

وقد اصدر الرئيس محمد حسني مبارك اوامره بمشاركة طائرات القوات الجوية المصرية في البحث عن طائرة الرئيس الفلسطيني ياسر عرفات .

وعلمت وكالة انباء الشرق الأوسط ان اكثر من خمس طائرات عسكرية مجهزة قد تحركت فى ساعة مبكرة من صباح امس من احدى القواعد العسكرية لتكون فوق منطقة البحث مع أول ضوء .

جاء ذلك فور اعلان السلطات الليبية انقطاع الاتصال بالطائرة .

وصرح متحدث رسمي بوزارة الدفاع المصرية بأن الرئيس محمد حسني مبارك القائد الاعلى للقوات المسلحة قد امر بمشاركة طائرات القوات الجوية المصرية فى عملية البحث عن طائرة عرفات وعلى اثر ذلك قامت وزارة الدفاع بتخصيص عدد من الطائرات المختلفة الأنواع لتنفيذ المهمة في ساعة مبكرة من صباح امس وذلك بعد التنسيق مع السلطات في الجماهيرية الليبية وجمهورية السودان وبعض الجهات الأخرى التي شاركت في عملية البحث من اجل المعاونة في العثور على الطائرة والاستعداد لتنفيذ اي اعمال انقاذ .

الاقمار الصناعية الامريكية

وفى واشنطن وافق الرئيس الأمريكي جورج بوش على طلب منظمة التحرير السماح للأقمار الصناعية الأمريكية بالبحث عن طائرة عرفات .

وقد رصد قمر صناعي امريكي عرفات ورفاقه بعد ان ظلوا مفقودين لمدة ١٥ ساعة وذلك على مسافة ٧٠ كيلومترا من منطقة «السرا» التي كانت الطائرة فى طريقها اليها قبل ان تصطدم بعاصفة ترابية قرب الحدود الليبية – التشادية المتنازع عليها .

إصابات عرفات

وقد اصيب عرفات في الحادث بسجحات واصابات طفيفة ،

ولكنه أعلن : « أنا بخير وأشكر كل من عاون وشارك فى عمليات الانقاذ » .

وقد أسفرت عملية الهبوط الاضطراري عن مقتل افراد طاقم الطائرة الثلاثة اذ ان الطائرة هبطت على جسمها بينما كانت عجلاتها غير مفرودة .

وكان برفقة عرفات على متن الطائرة ، تسعة من الحرس الشخصيين وافراد سكرتارية مكتبه بالاضافة الى طاقم الطائرة .

وقد وصفت محطة «سى. بى. إس » الأمريكية نجاة عرفات بأنها اعجوبة تصل الى حد المعجزة .

وقالت بعض محطات التليفزيون الأمريكية فى نشرات اخبارها ، التي تصدرها نبأ الحادث ، ان الرئيس عرفات له على ما يبدو « تسع أرواح » خاصة وان ملابسات الحادث كانت توحي باليأس التام في العثور على أي من ركاب الطائرة أحياء .

١٥ ساعة من القلق

وقد حبس العالم انفاسه طوال الـ١٥ ساعة التي ظلت طائرة عرفات مختفية خلالها بدون العثور على اثر لها .

وتقول الأنباء ان طائرة عرفات واجهتها عاصفة رملية شديدة ليلة امس الأول فقدت معها الاتصال بالمراقبة الجوية في طرابلس ثم اختفت من على شاشات الرادار .

وقالت مصادر فلسطينية ان قائد الطائرة قال في آخر اتصال له مع مركز الاتصالات بمقر منظمة التحرير في تونس انه يواجه ظروفا جوية صعبة فى الجزء الجنوبي الشرقي من ليبيا بالقرب من الحدود المصرية وان قائد الطائرة ابلغهم ايضا بأن وقوده على وشك النفاد ثم انقطع الاتصال به فى نحو الساعة ٩.٣٠ مساء امس الاول .

ويقول بسام أبو شريف مساعد عرفات ، ان طائرة الرئيس ، وهي من طراز «توبوليف » مجهزة للهبوط في الظروف الجوية

الصعبة وعلى الأراضي الوعرة .

وذكـرت وكـالـة رويتـر ، في تقريـر ساخـر لهـا ، ان الساحـر السياسي للشرق الأوسط ، تم انقاذه ، بمساعدة الأقمار الصناعية الأمريكية ، رغم ما لحق به من رضوض وكدمات » .

اتصالات   فلسطينية

وعلم مـراسل وكـالـة انبـاء الشـرق الأوسط فى تونس ، ان عـددا من المسؤولين الفلسطينيين اجروا صباح امس اتصالات مع عرفات شخصيا وانه قد وصل برفقة طاقم الطائرة الى معسكر «السرا» الفلسطيني فى ليبيا .

وأعلن بيان رسمى اصدرته منظمة التحرير الفلسطينية فى تونس ، امس ، ان عرفات ومن معه بخير .

وقالت مصادر فلسطينية انه سيجرى استقبـال رسمي للرئيس الفلسطينى لدى وصوله طرابلس كمـا يجرى استقبال جماهيرى له فى تونس لدى عودته إليها .

وأوضحت مصادر فلسطينية انه سيصدر بيان رسمي حول حادث اختفاء طائرة عرفات بسبب سوء الأحوال الجوية .

i   Produce a précis in Arabic of the contents of the above text.

ii This text is derived partly from English–language Agency reports. Pick out any features of the text which suggest original material in English.

12. Oral
الخلافة
(a) One student to present a definition/explanation of الخلافة.
(b) A second student to present an account of الخلافة في الاسلام.
(c) A third student to present an account of الخلافة في السياسة الحديثة.
(d) The presenters then ask the other students questions on الخلافة. The questions should include some which require factual answers and some which require speculative or hypothetical answers. For example:

١ – ما هي الخلافة؟
٢ – ماذا حدث بعد وفاة محمد رسول الله؟

٣ – من خلف الخميني؟

٤ – من خلف السادات؟

٥ – في نظرك، لو مات ياسر عرفات عند الهبوط الاضطراري لطائرته سنة ١٩٩١، فما كان الوضع بالنسبة للخلافة؟

٦ – ما هو الفرق بين الخلافة في الاسلام والخلافة في حكومة ديمقراطية؟

(e) Open lecturer–led discussion on الخلافة في المبدأ وفي الواقع.

13. Essay

Write an essay in Arabic of 200 words on the title الخلافة في المبدأ وفي الواقع.
In your writing address some of the following issues.

١ – ما معنى كلمة « الخلافة »؟

٢ – ماذا تعرف/ين عن مفهوم الخلافة في الاسرة العربية التقليدية؟

٣ – الخلافة في العهد الاسلامي الاول.

٤ – الخلافة في نظام اسلامي في القرن العشرين.

٥ – الخلافة في نظام ديمقراطي.

٦ – الخلافة في انظمة ديكتاتورية.

٧ – هل لمفهوم « الخلافة » مجال اليوم؟

17
Arabic literature

1. Basic background material
Chronology of Arabic literature

c. 500–633	Pre–Islamic poetry (المُعَلَّقات, etc.).
c. 610–632	Relevations to the Prophet Muhammad, subsequently collected as the Qur'an.
[622]	Date of the *hijra* (الهجرة), Muhammad's emigration from Mecca to Medina.
632–750	Period of the Rightly–Guided Caliphs (الخلفاء الراشدون) and the Umayyads.
750–1258	Abbasid period.
[750–1055]	So–called 'Golden Age' of classical Arabic literature.
c. 776–869	الجاحظ, leading writer of *adab* (الأدب) literature.
c. 814–856	أبو نواس, risqué poet who wrote on themes of drink and sex.
c. 915–965	المتنبي, court poet.
1258	Fall of Baghdad to the Mongols.
[1258–1798]	'Transitional period' of Arabic literature.
1332–1406	ابن خَلْدُون, author of المُقَدِّمة, the introduction to his History, which is considered by many to be the first work of sociology.
1798	Napoleon's invasion of France. Beginning of large–scale European influence on the Middle East.
c. 1850–c. 1914	Main period of النَهْضة (Arab cultural and literary revival).
1839–1904	محمود سامي البارودي, first neo–Classical poet.
c. 1914–1945	Flowering of 'Romanticism' in Arabic poetry.
1919	زينب by محمد حسين هيكل, first mature Egyptian novel.
1926–1927	First volume of الأيام by طه حسين.
1933	أهل الكهف by توفيق الحكيم.
1948	Palestine War; establishment of the state of Israel.
1952	Free Officers' Revolution in Egypt.
1947–	Free verse movement begins in Iraq.
1930–	أَدُونيس, leading modernist poet.

1952–	Period of 'committed' literature begins.
1953	عبد الرحمن الشرقاوي by الأرض.
1966	صنع الله إبراهيم by تلك الرائحة.
1911–	نجيب محفوظ Nobel Prize for Literature, 1988. Often combines descriptions of everyday life, with religious or metaphysical concerns expressed in allegorical form.
1927–1991	يوسف إدريس, Egyptian short story writer, whose themes reflect contemporary Egyptian society. Known for his inventive use of language, and frequent use of colloquial Arabic in dialogue.

2. Additional reading

(a) P.G. Starkey, and J. Meissner eds., *Encyclopedia of Arabic Literature*, (London: Routledge, 1998)

(b) M.M. Badawi, *A Short History of Modern Arabic Literature* (Oxford: Clarendon Press, 1993)

(c) H.A.R. Gibb, *Arabic Literature: An Introduction*, (Oxford University Press, 1962).

3. Key vocabulary

Taking the texts in this chapter as a starting point, draw up a list of literary terms, including: different types of literature – drama, prose, poetry, short story, novel, play; verse, line, chapter, section; plagiarism, innovation, extemporisation, راوٍ.

4. Written Arabic texts 1

(a) As a preparatory exercise for this chapter, read the following text from المعجم العربي الأساسي, p. 800, at home.

طه حـسـين (١٣.٧–١٣٩٣ هـ / ١٨٨٩–١٩٧٣ م): عـمـيـد الأدبـاء العرب، أديب كبير ومفكر حر وناقد كبير وسياسي محنك، ولد بصعيد مـصـر وكف بصـره وهو طفل. تعلم بالأزهر الشـريف وحـصـل على الدكتوراة من الجامـعة المصرية (١٩١٤) ومن الـسـوربـون (١٩١٨). ترقى في المناصب الأكاديمية إلى أن عين عمـيـدًا في كلية الآداب بالقاهرة ثم مـديـرًا لجامـعـة الإسكندرية ثم وزيـرًا للمـعـارف. نال جـائـزة الدولة التـقديرية (١٩٥٨)، وانتـخب رئيسًا لمجمـع اللغة العربية (١٩٦٣). كان غزير التـأليف متنـوعـه، له «ذكرى أبي الـعـلاء»، «قـادة الفكر»، «حديث الأربـعـاء»، «الأيام»، «في الأدب الجاهلي»، «علي وبنـوه»، «الشيـخـان»، «دعـاء الكروان»، «الحب الضـائـع»، وغـيـرها، وترجم عـدد من كتبـه إلى الكثير من لغات العالم. (من المعجم العربي الأساسي، لاروس ١٩٨٩).

(b) Read the following newspaper text from الشرق الأوسط Oct. 24, 1992, then answer the questions which follow in English.

في ذكرى قاهر الظلام

١٩ عاماً على رحيل عميد الأدب العربي طه حسين

القاهرة: «الشرق الاوسط»

تسعة عشر عاما مضت على رحيل عميد الادب العربي الدكتور طه حسين الذي ساهم في حركة التنوير والتغيير في الادب العربي مساهمة كبيرة. وكان ناقدا من اعظم النقاد فضلا عن دوره السياسي الذي مارسه بجانب كتاباته في الشعر والقصة والرواية ويعتبر احد ابرز رواد النهضة المصرية الحديثة.

ولد طه حسين علي سلامة في الرابع عشر من نوفمبر (تشرين الثاني) سنة ١٨٨٩ بقرية الكيلو في مركز مغاغة محافظة المنيا بصعيد مصر. بدأ في طفولته تعلم القراءة والكتابة وحفظ القرآن الكريم في كُتّاب القرية، وفقد بصره في طفولته نتيجة اصابته بالرمد، وكانت المحنة الاولى التي لازمته طوال مشواره الطويل. وبعد ان أتم حفظ القرآن الكريم التحق بالجامع الازهر في القاهرة ودرس علوم اللغة العربية والفقه الاسلامي وتاريخ الادب العربي ثم التحق بالجامعة المصرية القديمة وحصل على درجة الدكتوراة عام ١٩١٤ ليكون أول مكفوف توفده الدولة الى فرنسا لاستكمال دراسته. وفي عام ١٩١٨ حصل على درجة الدكتوراة في فلسفة ابن خلدون بالفرنسية من جامعة السوربون وعاد الى مصر عام ١٩١٩ ليعمل استاذا بالجامعة المصرية ثم عميدا لكلية الآداب عام ١٩٣٠ ثم وزيرا للمعارف «التربية والتعليم» عام ١٩٥٠. وفي عام ١٩٦٣ تولى رئاسة المجمع اللغوي خلفا لاحمد لطفي السيد وظل في هذا المنصب حتى وفاته.

وقد حصل الدكتور طه حسين على العديد من الاوسمة

والنياشين من جهات عربية واجنبية بجوار الاوسمة المصرية. منح العديد من شهادات الدكتوراة الفخرية من الجامعات الاوروبية.

قدم الدكتور طه حسين للمكتبة العربية اكثر من خمسين كتابا في القصة والنقد والأدب والشعر والتاريخ والفلسفة وترجمت كثير من مؤلفاته الى عدد من اللغات الأجنبية، ومن بين مؤلفاته «أديب» عام ١٩٣٥، «القصر المسحور» ١٩٣٦، «أحلام شهرزاد» ١٩٤٣، «المعـــــــذبون في الأرض»، «الأيام» ١٩٢٩، «على هامش السيرة» ١٩٣٣، «الوعد الحق» ١٩٤٩، «دعاء الكروان» ١٩٤١، «الحب الضائع» ١٩٣٧، «ما وراء النهر» ١٩٤٦، وكذلك «الشيخان» و«عثمان» و«علي وبنوه».

وصدر له كتابان بعد وفاته هما «شارع قولة» و«تجديد» ويضمان مقالاته التي نشرها في جريدة «كوكب الشرق» في منتصف الثلاثينات أثناء رئاسته لتحريرها، وقد كتب طه حسين في العديد من الصحف المصرية منها صحيفة «مصر الفتاة» و«الجريدة» و«العلم» و«الهداية» وتولى رئاسة تحرير جريدة «الجمهورية» في نهاية الخمسينات.

وقد ضرب د. طه حسين المثل الأعلى في تغلب الإرادة الإنسانية وانتصارها على العجز وتصديه للظروف القاسية التي عاشها بعد فقده بصره وهو طفل، ولم تقف أمامه أية معوقات ليحقق أعلى وأسمى ما يرنو إليه الإنسان. وقد أثرى المكتبة العربية بكتبه ومؤلفاته ومقالاته الأدبية والفكرية وساهم بجزء كبير في النهضة الثقافية المصرية الحديثة وكان له دوره في اللغة العربية وتعريب المصطلحات العلمية.

عاش د. طه حسين ٨٤ عاما منذ مولده في ١٤ نوفمبر ١٨٨٩ وحتى رحيله في ٢٨ أكتوبر (تشرين الأول) ١٩٧٣. صادف خلالها العديد من المحن والعقبات كان أولها فقدانه البصر وهو ما زال

طفلا ولكنـه لم ييأس أبدا إلى أن وصل الى أعلى الدرجات العلمية.

paragraph one

1. How is Taha Hussein rated as a literary critic?

paragraph two

2. Where did Taha Hussein memorise the Qur'an?
3. Why did he lose his sight?
4. Which two Egyptian universities did he study in?
5. What was the subject of his doctorate in France?
6. What was he appointed in 1963?

paragraph four

7. What types of work did Taha Hussein write?

paragraph five

8. What was the source of Taha Hussein's two books which were published posthumously?
9. What did he become editor of in the late fifties?

paragraph six

10. In what areas does the writer of this text suggest that Taha Hussein sets the highest example?
11. What was his contribution to the arabisation process?

paragraph seven

12. According to the writer of this text, what was the first obstacle Taha Hussein had to overcome?

(c) (i) As a preparatory exercise for the oral class (section 12), read and obtain a general understanding of the following text by طه حسين from في الأدب الجاهلي pp. 209–13. In order to help you with an understanding of the Arabic, an English translation has been included following the Arabic text. You may want to use this as a crib.

امرؤ القيس – عَبِيد – عَلْقَمة

لعل أقدم الشعراء الذين يروى لهم شعر كثير ويتحدث الرواة عنهم بأخبار كثيرة فيها تطويل وتفضيل هو امرؤ القيس.

ونحن نعلم أن الرواة يتحدثون بأسماء طائفة من الشعراء زعموا انهم عاشوا قبل امرئ القيس وقالوا شعرا ، ولكنهم لا يروون لهؤلاء الشعراء إلا البيت أو البيتين أو الأبيات . وهم لا يذكرون من أخبار هؤلاء الشعراء إلا الشىء القليل الذي لا يغنى . وهم يعللون قلة الأخبار والأشعار التي يمكن أن تضاف الى هؤلاء

الشعراء ببعد العهد وتقادم الزمن وقلة الحفّاظ . وقد رأيت في الكتاب الماضي أن قليلا من النقد لما يضاف الى هؤلاء الشعراء ينتهي بك الى جحود ما يضاف اليهم من خبر أو شعر . فلندع هؤلاء الشعراء ولنقف عند امرئ القيس وأصحابه الذين يظهر أن الرواة عرفوا عنهم ورووا لهم الشيء الكثير .

مَنْ امرؤ القيس ؟ أما الرواة فلا يختلفون في أنه رجل من كِنْدة . ولكن مَنْ كِنْدة ؟ لا يختلف الرواة في أنهم قبيلة من قحطان ، وهم يختلفون بعض الاختلاف في نسبها وتفسير اسمها وفي أخبار سادتها . ولكنهم على كل حال يتفقون على أنها قبيلة يمانية . وعلى أن امرأ القيس منها .

فأما اسم امرئ القيس واسم أبيه واسم أمه فأشياء ليس من اليسير الاتفاق عليها بين الرواة ، فقد كان اسمه امرأ القيس ، وقد كان اسمه حندجا . وقد كان اسمه قيسا . وقد كان اسم أبيه عمرا ، وقد كان اسم أبيه حُجْرا أيضا . وكان اسم أمه فاطمة بنت ربيعة أخت مُهَلْهِل وكُلَيْب ، وكان اسم أمه تَمْلِك . وكان امرؤ القيس يعرف بأبي وهب ، وكان يعرف بأبي الحارث . ولم يكن له ولد ذكر . وكان يئد بناته جميعًا . وكانت له ابنة يقال لها هند ، ولم تكن هند هذه ابنته وانما كانت بنت أبيه . وكان يعرف بالملك الضليل ، وكان يعرف بذي القروح .

وعليك انت ان تستخلص من هذا الخليط المضطرب ما تستطيع أن تسميه حقا أو شيئا يشبه الحق . وأي شيء أيسر من أن تأخذ ما اتفقت عليه كثرة الرواة على أنه حق لا شك فيه ؟ وكثرة الرواة قد اتفقت على أن اسمه حندج ابن حجر ، ولقبه امرؤ القيس ، وكنيته أبو وهب ، وأمه فاطمة بنت ربيعة . على هذا اتفقت كثرة الرواة واذا اتفقت الكثرة على شيء فيجب أن يكون صحيحا أو على أقل تقدير يجب أن يكون راجحا .

أما أنا فقد أطمئن الى آراء الكثرة ، أو قد أراني مكرهًا على

الاطمئنان لآراء الكثرة ، في المجالس النيابية وما يشبهها . ولكن الكثرة في العلم لا تعني شيئًا ، فقد كانت كثرة العلماء تنكر كروية الأرض وحركتها ، وظهر بعد ذلك أن الكثرة كانت مخطئة . وكانت كثرة العلماء ترى كل ما أثبت العلم الحديث أنه غير صحيح . فالكثرة في العلم لا تغني شيئًا .

وإذاً فليس من سبيل الى أن نقبل قول الكثرة في امرئ القيس، وانما السبيل أن نوازن بينه وبين ما تزعم القلة . وليس الى هذه الموازنة المنتجة من سبيل اذا لاحظت ما قدّمناه في الكتاب الماضي من هذه الأسباب التي كانت تحمل على الانتحال وتكلف القصص.

وإذاً فلسنا نستطيع أن نفصل بين الفريقين المختلفتين ، وإنما نحن مضطرون الى أن نقبل ما يقول أولئك وهؤلاء على أن الناس كانوا يتحدثون به دون أن نعرف وجه الحق فيه . ولعل هذا وأشباهه من الخلط في حياة امرئ القيس أوضح دليل على ما نذهب اليه من أن امرأ القيس إن يكن قد وجد حقًا – ونحن نرجح ذلك ونكاد نوقن به – فان الناس لم يعرفوا عنه شيئًا الا اسمه هذا، والا طائفة من الأساطير والأحاديث تتصل بهذا الاسم.

وهنا يحسن أن نلاحظ أن الكثرة من هذه الأساطير والأحاديث لم تشع بين الناس الا في عصر متأخر : في عصر الرواة المدوّنين والقصاصين . فأكبر الظن إذاً أنها نشأت في هذا العصر ولم تورث عن العصر الجاهلي حقا . وأكبر الظن أن الذي أنشأ هذه القصة ونماها انما هو هذا المكان الذي احتلته قبيلة كندة في الحياة الاسلامية منذ تمت للنبي السيطرة على البلاد العربية الى أواخر القرن الأول للهجرة . فنحن نعلم أن وفدا من كندة وفد على النبيّ وعلى رأسه الأشعث بن قيس . ونحن نعلم أن هذا الوفد طلب – فيما تقول السيرة – الى النبي أن يرسل معهم مفقّها يعلمهم الدين . نحن نعلم أن كندة ارتدّت بعد موت النبي ، وأن عامل أبي

بكر حاصرها في النجَير وأنزلهم على حكمه وقتل منها خلقًا
كثيرا وأوفد منها طائفة الى أبي بكر فيها الأشعث بن قيس الذي
تاب وأناب وأصهر الى أبي بكر فتزوّج أخته أم فروة ، وخرج –
فيما يزعم الرواة – الى سوق الابل في المدينة فاستل سيفه
ومضى في إبل السوق عقرا ونحرا حتى ظن الناس به الجنون ،
ولكنه دعا أهل المدينة الى الطعام وأدى الى أصحاب الابل أموالهم ،
وكانت هذه المجزرة الفاحشة وليمة عرسه . ونحن نعلم أن هذا
الرجل قد اشترك في فتح الشأم وشهد مواقع المسلمين في حرب
الفرس ، وحسن بلاؤه في هذا كله ، وتولى عملا لعثمان ، وظاهر
عليا على معاوية ، وأكره عليا على قبول التحكيم في صفّين .
ونحن نعلم أن ابنه محمد بن الأشعث كان سيدا من سادات الكوفة،
عليه وحده اعتمد زياد حين أعياه أخذ حجر بن عديّ الكندي ونحن
نعلم ان قصة حجر بن عدى هذا وقتل معاوية إياه في نفر من
أصحابه قد تركت في نفوس المسلمين عامة واليمنيين خاصة أثرا
قويا عميقًا مثّل هذا الرجل في صورة الشهيد . ثم نحن نعلم أن
حفيد الاشعث بن قيس وهو عبد الرحمن بن محمد بن الأشعث قد
ثار بالحَجّاج ، وخلع عبد الملك ، وعرّض آل مروان للزوال ، وكان
سببًا في إراقة دماء المسلمين من أهل العراق والشأم ، وكان الذين
قتلوا في حروبه يحصون فيبلغون عشرات الآلاف ، ثم انهزم فلجأ
الى ملك الترك ، ثم أعاد الكرة فتنقّل في مدن فارس ، ثم استيأس
فعاد الى ملك الترك ثم غدر به هذا الملك فأسلمه الى عامل الحجاج،
ثم قتل نفسه في طريقه الى العراق ، ثم احتُز رأسه وطوّف به في
العراق والشأم ومصر .

أفتظن أن أسرة كهذه الأسرة الكندية تنزل هذه المنزلة في
الحياة الاسلامية وتؤثر هذه الآثار في تاريخ المسلمين لا تصطنع
القصص ولا تأجر القصّاص لينشروا لها الدعوة ويذيعوا عنها كل ما
من شأنه أن يرفع ذكرها ويبعد صوتها ؟ بلى ! ويحدّثنا الرواة

أنفسهم أن عبد الرحمن بن الأشعث اتخذ القصّاص وأجرهم كما اتخذ الشعراء وأجزل صلتهم : كان له قاص يقال له عمر بن ذرّ ، وكان شاعره أعشى هَمْدان.

فما يروى من أخبار كندة في الجاهلية متأثر من غير شك بعمل هؤلاء القصاص الذين كانوا يعملون لآل الأشعث . وقصة امرئ القيس بنوع خاص تشبه من وجوه كثيرة حياة عبد الرحمن بن الأشعث . فهي تمثل لنا امرأ القيس مطالبًا بثأر أبيه . وهل ثار عبد الرحمن عند الذين يفقهون التاريخ إلا منتقمًا لحجر ابن عدىّ؟ وهي تمثل لنا امرأ القيس طامعًا في الملك . وقد كان عبد الرحمن بن الأشعث يرى أنه ليس اقل من بني أمية استئهالا للملك ، وكان يطالب به . وهي تمثل لنا امرأ القيس متنقلا في قبائل العرب . وقد كان عبد الرحمن بن الأشعث متنقلا في مدن فارس والعراق . وهي تمثل امرأ القيس لاجئا الى قيصر مستعينًا به . وقد كان عبد الرحمن بن الأشعث لاجئًا الى ملك الترك مستعينًا به . وهي تمثل لنا أخيرًا امرأ القيس وقد غدر به قيصر بعد أن كاد له أسديّ في القصر . وقد غدر ملك الترك بعبد الرحمن بعد أن كاد له رسل الحجاج . وهي تمثل لنا بعد هذا وذاك امرأ القيس وقد مات في طريقه عائدًا من بلاد الروم . وقد مات عبد الرحمن في طريقه عائدًا من بلاد الترك.

اليس من اليسير أن نفترض بل أن نرجح أن حياة امرئ القيس كما يتحدّث بها الرواة ليست إلا لونًا من التمثيل لحياة عبد الرحمن استحدثه القصاص إرضاء لهوى الشعوب اليمنية في العراق واستعاروا له اسم الملك الضّليل اتّقاء لعمال بني أمية من ناحية ، واستغلالا لطائفة يسيرة من الأخبار كانت تعرف عن هذا الملك الضليل من ناحية أخرى؟

(ii) English translation of text by طه حسين from في الأدب الجاهلي, pp. 209–13.

Perhaps the most ancient poet whose poetry is frequently recited and about whom tales are recounted at length and in detail by the reciters is Imru' al-Qays.

We know that the reciters mention the names of a group of poets claimed to have lived before Imru' al-Qays and to have recited poetry, but they can only recount one or two verses. They provide unsatisfactorily little information about these poets. They attribute the fact that there is so little information and lines of poetry ascribable to these poets to the length of time which has passed and to lack of documentation. In my last book, I claimed that even a rudimentary critique of [the works] which are ascribed to these poets brings you round to rejecting the information or poetry ascribed to them. So let us leave these poets and stop by Imru' al-Qays and his contemporaries who, it seems, the reciters knew well and described in detail.

Who was Imru' al-Qays? The reciters are all agreed that he was a member [lit: man] of the Kinda tribe, but who were the Kinda? The reciters are agreed that it is a tribe of Qahtan; they do not agree, however, over its lineage, the interpretation of its name, and the tales of its chiefs. But, in any case, they are agreed that it is a Yemeni tribe and that Imru' al-Qays was a member of it.

The name Imru' al-Qays, and the names of his father and mother, however, are things for which agreement is not easily found among the reciters. His name was Imru' al-Qays, his name was Handaj, and his name was Qays. His father's name was Umar, and his father's name was also Hujr. His mother's name was Fatima bint Rabi'a, sister of Mihalhil and Kulaib, and his mother's name was Tamlik. Imru' al-Qays was known as Abu Wahab and was known as Abu al-Hayth, but he had no male children. He buried all his daughters alive. He had a daughter called Hind; but this Hind was not his daughter, rather his father's daughter. He was known as the Errant King and was known as the One with Ulcers.

You have to sift through this confusion to extract what you can call true or half–true. And what is easier than accepting what the majority of reciters are agreed is the indubitable truth? The majority of reciters are agreed that his name is Handaj ibn Hujr, his nickname is Imru' al-Qays, his *kunya* is Abu Wahab, and his mother is Fatima bint Rabi'a. The majority of reciters are agreed about this, and if the majority are agreed about something then it must be true, or at the least it must be [highly] probable.

I sometimes rely on the views of the majority, or find myself forced to accept the views of the majority in parliamentary meetings and the like. In science, however, the [view of the] majority is meaningless: the majority of scientists denied the roundness of the Earth and its movement. After that it was apparent that the majority was mistaken. The majority of scientists thought that everything proven by modern science was incorrect. The [view of the] majority in science is worthless.

Therefore, we should not accept what the majority says about Imru' al-Qays.

The only way is to compare [what they say] with the claims of the minority. It is impossible to make this resulting comparison taking into account the reasons for plagiarism and fabrication of stories put forward in our last book.

Therefore, we are unable to distinguish the two different groups; we are simply forced to accept what is said by this [group] and that, since people used to talk about him without knowing the truth about him. Perhaps this and other forms of confusion about Imru' al-Qays' life are a clearer indication to what we are approaching than that Imru' al-Qays, if he really did exist – and we believe this to be probable and are almost convinced of it – all that was known about him was his name and a number of legends and stories connected with this name.

Here, it is appropriate to note that the majority of these legends and stories were not generally known to people until recent times: [namely,] the time of the reciters and story tellers. Therefore, they most probably came into existence at this time and were not really handed down from the Age of Ignorance. Most probably, what created and developed this story was the position occupied by the Kinda tribe in Islamic times from the Prophet's conquest of the Arabian peninsula until the end of the first century after the *hijra*. We know that a delegation from Kinda headed by al-Ash'ath ibn Qays visited the Prophet. According to the Sira, we know that this delegation asked the Prophet to send a religious man with them to teach them about the religion. We know that the Kinda apostacised after the death of the Prophet and that Abu Bakr's governor surrounded them in Nujayr, forced them to submit to his command, killed many of them, and sent a group of them to Abu Bakr including al-Ash'ath ibn Qays who [then] repented and became related to Abu Bakr by marrying his daughter Umm Farwa. According to the reciters, he went out into the camel market in Medina, unsheathed his sword and slaughtered his way through the camel market such that people thought him mad. However, he invited the inhabitants of Medina to eat and recompensed the camel owners. This dreadful butchery became his wedding banquet. We know that the man took part in the conquest of Syria, and witnessed the battles of the Muslims in the Persian war; he performed well in all of this, and undertook some work for Uthman; he supported Ali against Mu'awiya and forced Ali to accept arbitration at Siffin. We know that his son, Muhammad ibn al-Ash'ath, was a Kufan chief; Ziyad depended on him alone when he was unable to capture Hujr ibn Ada al-Kindi; we know that the story of Hujr ibn Ada and his killing by Mu'awiya in a party of his followers left such a strong impression in the minds of Muslims in general and Yemenis in particular that this man was portrayed as a martyr. Then we know that a grandson of al-Ash'ath ibn Qays – Abd al-Rahman ibn al-Ash'ath – rose up against al-Hajjaj, renounced Abd al-Malik, and exposed the family of Marwan to extinction; he was the reason behind the spilling of Iraqi and Syrian Muslim blood: those killed in his wars numbered tens of thousands. He was then defeated and sought refuge with the King of the Turks. He returned and wandered around the towns of Persia, then despaired and returned to the King of the Turks who betrayed him and handed him over to al-Hajjaj's governor. He killed himself on the way to Iraq. His head was severed and paraded in Iraq, Syria and Egypt.

Do you think that a family such as this Kindi family, occupying this position in Islamic life with such influence in the history of the Muslims would not fabricate stories or hire story tellers to spread their propaganda, praise them and further their influence? Of course they would! The reciters themselves tell us that Abd al-Rahman ibn al-Ash'ath made use of story tellers and paid them, just as he made use of poets and gave liberally to their relations. He had a story teller called Umar ibn Dharr, and his poet was A'sha Hamdan.

The tales of Kinda in the Age of Ignorance have doubtless been influenced by the work of story tellers who used to work for the al-Ash'ath family. In particular, the story of Imru' al-Qays is, in many aspects, similar to the life of Abd al-Rahman ibn al-Ash'ath. It depicts Imru' al-Qays seeking blood revenge for his father's death; according to those who understand history, did Abd al-Rahman rebel for any other reason than to avenge Hujr ibn Ada? The story depicts Imru' al-Qays craving sovereignty, and Abd al-Rahman ibn al-Ash'ath thought himself no less worthy of sovereignty than the Umayyads, and sought it. The story depicts Imru' al-Qays wandering among the Arab tribes, and Abd al-Rahman ibn al-Ash'ath wandered through the towns of Persia and Iraq. The story depicts Imru' al-Qays seeking refuge with Caesar and asking him for help, and Abd al-Rahman ibn al-Ash'ath sought refuge from the King of the Turks asking him for help. Finally, it depicts Imru' al-Qays having been betrayed by Caesar after prisoners in the castle conspired against him, and the King of the Turks betrayed Abd al-Rahman after al-Hajjaj's messengers conspired against him. Moreover, it tells us that Imru' al-Qays died on his way back from Rome, and Abd al-Rahman died on his way back from the lands of the Turks.

Is it not easy to suppose, and indeed consider likely, that the life of Imru' al-Qays as related by the reciters is no more than a colouring of the story of the life of Abd al-Rahman which the story tellers created in response to the wishes of the Yemeni people in Iraq? They gave him the pseudonym the Errant King to respect the Umayyad governors, on the one hand, and in order to exploit a small number of stories known about the Errant King, on the other.

5. Written Arabic texts 2

(a) Translate the following passage by نجيب محفوظ from the novel أولاد حارتنا pp. 115–16 (cf. ch. 14, 5c for background to this novel).

أقيمت بيوت الوقف في خطين متقابلين يصنعان حارتنا.
ويبدأ الخطان من خط يقع أمام البيت الكبير، ويمتدان طولاً في
اتجاه الجمالية. أما البيت الكبير فقد ترك خالياً من جميع
الجهات على رأس الحارة من ناحية الصحراء. وحارتنا، حارة

الجبلاوي، أطول حارة في المنطقة. أكثر بيوتها ربوع كما في حي آل حمدان، وتكثر الأكواخ من منتصفها حتى الجمالية. ولن تتم الصورة إلا بذكر بيت ناظر الوقف على رأس الصف الأيمن من المساكن، وبيت الفتوة على رأس الصف الأيسر قبالته.

كان البيت الكبير قد أغلق أبوابه على صاحبه وخدمه المقربين. ومات أبناء الجبلاوي مبكرين فلم يبق من سلالة الذين أقاموا وماتوا في البيت الكبير إلا الأفندي ناظر الوقف في ذلك الوقت. أما أهل الحارة عامة فمنهم البائع الجوال، ومنهم صاحب الدكان أو القهوة، وكثيرون يتسولون، وثمة تجارة مشتركة يعمل فيها كل قادر هي تجارة المخدرات وبخاصة الحشيش والأفيون والمدافع. وكان طابع حارتنا – كحالها اليوم – الزحام والضجيج. والأطفال الحفاة أشباه العرايا يلعبون في كل ركن، ويملأون الجو بصراخهم والأرض بقاذوراتهم. وتكتظ مداخل البيوت بالنساء، هذه تخرط الملوخية، وتلك تقشر البصل، وثالثة توقد النار، يتبادلن الأحاديث والنكات، وعند الضرورة الشتائم والسباب. والغناء والبكاء لا ينقطعان، ودقة الزار تستأثر باهتمام خاص. وعربات اليد في نشاط متواصل. ومعارك باللسان أو بالأيدي تنشب هنا وهناك. وقطط تموء وكلاب تهر وربما تشاجر النوعان حول أكوام الزبالة. والفئران تنطلق في الأفنية وعلى الجدران، وليس بالنادر أن يتجمع قوم لقتل ثعبان أو عقرب. أما الذباب فلا يضاهيه في الكثرة إلا القمل، فهو يشارك الآكلين في الأطباق والشاربين في الأكواز، يلهو في الأعين ويغني في الأفواه كأنه صديق الجميع.

(b) Read the following incomplete text from the short story شيء يجنن by يوسف
إدريس, from his collection آخر الدنيا, then translate the first two paragraphs
into idiomatic English (cf. also section 13 for completion exercise).

شيء يجنن!

لست في حل من ذكر اسم المدينة التي يوجد فيها ذلك السجن
العمومي ، فالقصة لم تصبح بعد حكاية ولا تزال في حكم الخبر الذي
يتناقله النزلاء وموظفو السجن وأقارب هؤلاء وأولئك . وعلى أية
حال فالسجون العمومية ليست كثيرة والحمد لله ، وبالكاد يوجد
منها سجن في عاصمة كل مديرية مخصص للمحكوم عليهم بالحبس
أو السجن من المديرية نفسها وما يحيط بها من مراكز أو
محافظات .

والبداية مثل فرنسي يقول فتش عن المرأة ، ولكننا لن نجد
امرأة واحدة في ذلك السجن العمومي فهو من النوع المخصص
للرجال ، والأنثى الوحيدة المسموح لها بالتجول في أنحاء السجن
ليست امرأة ولكنها كلبة ، أو على وجه التخصيص كلبة المأمور .
وللمأمور في أي سجن عمومي منزل مقام داخل السجن لاتستطيع
أن تفرقه عن بقية بناياته من الخارج ولكنه قطعا فاخر المنظر من
الداخل ، ويحتل في العادة مكانا قريبا من المدخل ، وله باب خاص
ولكنه محوط بالسور الرهيب الذي يحيط بالسجن من كل جانب .

وبالرغم أن «ريتا» (وهو اسم الكلبة) كانت تتمتع في السجن
بحرية تحسد عليها ، الا أنها ظلت سيئة الحظ لفترة طويلة ، لا لأنها
الحيوان الوحيد الذي يحيا في مكان كل ما فيها من البشر ولكن ...

6. Written Arabic texts 3 (classical)
Translate the following text by ابن الأنباري (المتوفى ٥٧٧هـ) into idiomatic
English. This text discusses the Abbasid poet أبو نواس (pp. 49–50).

أبو علي الحسن بن هانئ

وأما أبو علي الحسن بن هانئ المعروف بأبي نواس، فإنه ولد
بالأهواز ونشأ بالبصرة، وقيل كان مولى للجراح بن عبد الله

الحكمي والي خرسان، واختلف إلى أبي زيد الأنصاري، وكتب عنه الغريب وحفظ عن أبي عبيدة معمر بن المثنى أيام الناس ونظر في نحو سيبويه. قال عمرو ابن بحر الجاحظ: ما رأيت رجلاً أعلم باللغة من أبي نواس ولا أفصح لهجة مع حلاوة ومجانبة الاستكراه وقال الشعر وكان يستشهد بشعره. وقال أبو عبيدة معمر بن المثنى: كان أبو نواس للمحدثين كامرئ القيس للمتقدمين. وقال إسحق بن إسماعيل: قال أبو نواس: ما قلت الشعر حتى رويت لستين امرأة من العرب منهن الخنساء وليلى، فما ظنك بالرجال؟ وقال ميمون: سألت أبا يوسف يعقوب بن السكيت عما يختار لي روايته من الشعر فقال: إذا رويت من أشعار الجاهليين فلامرئ القيس والأعشى، ومن الإسلاميين فلجرير والفرزدق، ومن المحدثين فلأبي نواس فحسبك، فقال أبو العباس المبرد عن الجاحظ قال: سمعت إبراهيم النظام يقول، وقد أنشد شعر أبي نواس في الخمر، هذا الذي جمع له الكلام فاختار أحسنه وقال في حقه سفيان بن عيينة: هذا أشعر الناس. قال الجاحظ: لا أعرف من كلام الشعر أرفع من قول أبي نواس:

أية نار قدح القادح   [من السريع]

وأي جد بلغ المازح

وأنشد الأبيات قال الإمام محمد بن إدريس الشافعي رحمة اللّه عليه دخلت على أبي نواس وهو يجود بنفسه فقلت ما أعددت لهذا اليوم فقال:

تعاظمني ذنبي فلما قرنته   [من الطويل]

بعفوك ربي كان عفوك أعظما

7. Grammar/stylistics

(a) *More on* أما ... ف *clauses*

The أما ... ف structure has already been briefly discussed in chapter 2 (ch. 2, 7aii). In this structure أما introduces an emphatic preposed element (cf. ch. 13, 7a), while the resumptive ف introduces the rest of the sentence.

In most cases أما is not preceded by any other particle. It may, however, be preceded by و, ف or ثم (cf. ch. 20, 7ai). For example:

> فـ{ـأما} اسم امرئ القيس واسم أبيه واسم أمه فأشياء ليس من
> اليسير الاتفاق عليها بين الرواة ..

'The name Imru' al-Qays, and the names of his father and mother, however, are things for which agreement is not easily found among the reciters ...' (ch. 17, 4c)

> فأما عدنان فهو من وُلْد إسماعيل بالاتّفاق ... وأما قحطان فقيل
> من ولد إسماعيل ..

'Adnan are descended from Ishmael by common consent ... Qahtan are also said to be descended from Ishmael ...' (ch. 2, 6a)

Similarly, while a resumptive ف is found in the great majority of cases where the preposed element begins with أما, there are examples where no ف is used. A standard case is the stock phrase أما بعد, which is used to signal that a short introductory section of a text – usually praising God, the Prophet and his followers – is followed by the main section, in which the matter at hand is discussed. Since أما بعد serves merely to mark the end of an introductory section, it is not normally translated into English. The following, in which {X} has been added to mark the place of the 'missing' ف, is an example:

> {أما بعد، {X} إن القرآن الكريم هو معجزة الإسلام العظمى ..

'The Noble Qur'an is the supreme miracle of Islam ...' (ch. 4, 5a)

أما بعد is also typically used in letters following the initial greeting to the person to whom the letter is being sent, and before the main text of the letter.

It is also possible to find examples of أما without a resumptive ف in non–stock phrases, although such examples are rare. One example which occurs in this book, with {X} again marking the 'missing' ف, is the following:

> {اما} في شهر رمضان {X} ينخفض العمل الى ساعتين ونصف
> الساعة يوميا ..

'In Ramadan, work goes down to two–and–a–half hours per day ...' (ch. 9, 5b)

In أما ... ف structures the preposed element is typically a nominal. For example:

مَنْ امـرؤُ القيـس ؟ {أما} الـرواة {فـ}لا يـخـتلفـون في أنـه رجل من
كِنْدة .

'Who was Imru' al-Qays? The reciters are all agreed that he was a
member [lit: man] of the Kinda tribe ...' (ch. 17, 4c)

{أمـا} أنا {فـ}قد أطمـئـن الـى آراء الكثـرة ، أو قد أرانـي مـكرهًا علـى
الاطمئنـان لآراء الكثـرة ، في المجالـس النيابيـة ومـا يـشبـهها .

'I sometimes rely on the views of the majority, or find myself forced to
accept the views of the majority in parliamentary meetings and the like.'
(ch. 17, 4c)

The preposed element may also, however, be an adverbial. For example:

{أما} الآن فهو أمام السـيدة ..

'Now he is in front of the lady ...' (ch. 10, 11a)

{امـا} من جـانـب اسـرائيـل {فـ}إنهـا كـانت تعـرف انهـا تجلس مـع
منظمـة التحـريـر الفلسطينيـة عبـر طاولة المفاوضـات في مـؤتمر
مـدريـد ..

'As far as Israel was concerned, it knew that it was sitting down with
the PLO across the negotiating table at the Madrid conference ...' (ch.
6, 11)

{امـا} بالنسبـة للمناطق والاسـواق الحـرة، {فـ}قـد صـدر عـام ١٩٧٢
المرسـوم رقم ٨٤ لتنظيـم الاستثمار في هذه المناطق.

'Regarding free zones and markets, decree no. 84 was issued in 1972
in order to regulate investment in these zones.' (ch. 18, 11)

It is also possible for the element following أما to be a subordinate clause (a
subordinate clause is a kind of adverbial). This is particularly common where the
subordinate is the protasis (شرط) of a conditional clause. For example:

.. أمـا إذا قـدمت أنت خـدمـة لأحـد {فـ}يـجب أن تنسى هذا في
الحال!!

'... but if you do a service to anybody, you should forget this
immediately!' (ch. 11, 4bii)

{أمّا} إذا كان المقصود هو اشتراك شعب كامل في تقويض نظام
كامل للحكم، {فـ}إنَّني بالطبع أحد أبناء هذا الشعب.

'However, if what is meant is the involvement of the entire people in
bringing down an entire regime, then of course I am one of the people.'
(ch. 13, 5b)

Any of the major emphatic word orders outlined in chapter 13 (ch. 13, 7a) may
occur in أمّا .. فـ clauses. Specifically أمّا may be followed either by a noun or by
an adverbial (but not by a verb). It is worth noting particularly the use of إنَّ after
فـ as a kind of double resumptive particle (cf. also ch. 15, 7ai). For example:

و{أمّا} أبو علي الحسن بن هانئ المعروف بأبي نواس، {فـإنّه} ولد
بالأهواز ونشأ بالبصرة ..

'Abu Ali al-Hasan ibn Hani', who is known as Abu Nuwas, was born
in al-Ahwaz and grew up in Basra ...' (ch. 17, 6a)

Similarly, with a perfect verb قد is often used after فـ to produce a kind of double
resumptive particle (cf. also ch. 16, bi.iii). For example:

{أمّا} من العرب المسلمين {فقد} عوّل على الرازي حوالي 400 مرة ..

'Regarding the Muslim Arabs, he made use of al-Razi about 400 times
...' (ch. 19, 11)

Where the element after أمّا is a subject, and the predicate is not a verbal clause (cf.
ch. 13, 7a), the predicate may consist of a noun, adjective or adverbial plus
following element(s). For example:

{أمّا} جهاته الثلاث {فـ}خالية ..

'Three of its [the tomb's] sides are empty [open] ...' (ch. 11, 4a)

فـ{أمّا} اسم امرئ القيس واسم أبيه واسم أمه {فـ}أشياء ليس من
اليسير الاتفاق عليها بين الرواة ..

'The name Imru' al-Qays, and the names of his father and mother,
however, are things for which agreement is not easily found among the
reciters ...' (ch. 17, 4c)

Frequently, however, the predicate itself consists of a subject–predicate structure,
and the initial element after فـ is a pronoun which is coreferential with the nominal
following أمّا (i.e. it refers to the same thing as is referred to by the nominal
following أمّا). For example:

{أما} مشكلة ازالة الغابات {فـ}هي مشكلة متفاقمة ..
'The problem of deforestation is an increasingly serious problem ...'
(ch. 9, 4a)

{أما} الأسباب التي أدت إلى هذا الحب أو هذا الميل .. {فـ}هي أن الطبيب الكبير قد أصبح مشغولا عن زوجته ..
'The reason for this love or this inclination was that the great doctor became interested in other things than his wife ...' (ch. 10, 11b)

It is also possible to have أما .. فـ clauses in which there is a preposed nominal after the أما, and a coreferential pronoun in the element after the فـ, but where this coreferential pronoun is not a subject. For example:

{أما} أهل الحارة عامة {فـ}منهم البائع الجوال ..
'Among the people of the quarter generally were travelling sellers ...'
(ch. 17, 5a)

Here منهم is a preposed predicate (البائع الجوال is the subject of the clause following فـ). Similarly:

{أما} الذباب {فـ}لا يضاهيه في الكثرة إلا القمل ..
'The flies are only equalled in number by the lice ...' (ch. 17, 5a)

Here the pronoun ـه is coreferential with الذباب, and is the object of the verb يضاهي (to which it is suffixed).

i *Emphatic uses of the* أما .. فـ *structure*
A number of sub–types of emphasis can be identified in relation to the أما .. فـ structure. These are i. stress, ii. contrast and parallelism, iii. scene–setting, iv. linkage.

i.i *Stress*
Sometimes أما .. فـ corresponds to stressing (in an English translation, at least) of the element which occurs after the أما. For example:

مَنْ امرؤ القيس ؟ {أما} الرواة {فـ}لا يختلفون في أنه رجل من كِنْدة .
'Who was Imru' al-Qays? The reciters are all agreed that he was a member [lit: man] of the Kinda tribe.' (ch. 17, 4c)

In reading the English translation out loud, one might well stress the word 'reciters'.

i.ii *Contrast and parallelism*

Typically, أَمّا .. فـ involves some element of contrast. Sometimes this contrast may be very strong. For example:

ويعتبر العرب أصحاب الكيمياء العملية، {أما} اليونان {فـ}ـهم
أصحاب الكيمياء النظرية .

'The Arabs are considered the masters of practical chemistry, while the Greeks [on the other hand/by contrast] are the masters of theoretical chemistry.' (ch. 20, 5a)

إذا قدم أحدهم خدمة لك فيجب أن تتذكرها دائماً، {أما} إذا قدمت
أنت خدمة لأحد {فـ}ـيجب أن تنسى هذا في الحال!!

'If one of them does you a service, you should remember it for ever. But if you do a service to anybody, you should forget it immediately!' (ch. 11, 4bii)

Sometimes two pairs of أَمّا .. فـ phrases are used in close proximity, creating a kind of internal parallelism between them. For example:

{أما} الصيغة الشائعة في المشرق للاسم {فـ}ـهي قرطاجة و{أما}
الصيغة الأخرى الواردة في السؤال {فـ}ـهي قرطاجنة.

'The form of the name which is common in the eastern Arab world is *Qartaja*, while the other form which appears in the question is *Qartajanna*.' (ch. 3, 8)

فـ{ـأما} عدنان {فـ}ـهو من وُلْد إسماعيل بالاتّفاق ... و{أما} قحطان
{فـ}ـقيل من ولد إسماعيل ..

'Adnan are descended from Ishmael by common consent ... Qahtan are also said to be descended from Ishmael ...' (ch. 2, 6a)

In this last example, while there is parallelism, there is no real contrast.

i.iii *Scene-setting*

It is possible to use أَمّا .. فـ to establish a new topic. For example:

فـ{ـأما} اسم امرئ القيس واسم أبيه واسم أمه {فـ}ـأشياء ليس من
اليسير الاتفاق عليها بين الرواة ..

'The name Imru' al-Qays, and the names of his father and mother, however, are things for which agreement is not easily found among the reciters ...' (ch. 17, 4c)

Here there is some contrast with the previous paragraph, which dealt with the identity of Imru' al-Qays (rather than his name), as evidenced by the use of 'however' in the English translation. The أمـا .. ف structure in this example, however, also serves to introduce the topic of the current paragraph, which it occurs at the start of. The topic in this paragraph is the name of Imru' al-Qays and that of his father. Where أمـا .. ف is used to introduce a new topic, that topic covers only those elements which are included within the أمـا phrase, and before the resumptive ف.

Other examples of أمـا .. ف being used to introduce a new topic are the following:

{أمـا} المنهـج الذي اتبـعـه في تأليف كتـابه {فـ}لم يقتـصـر علی الاعتـمـاد علی المصـادر التي سبـقتـه بل علی البـحث الميـداني واستشارة اصحاب الخبرة والرأي.

'With regard to the methodology which he followed in composing his book, he didn't confine himself to reliance previous sources, but also carried out field work, and consulted experts and thinkers on the subject.' (ch. 19, 11)

This section of text is the start of a new paragraph, the previous paragraph having given a general assessment of the importance of Ibn al-Baytar's book. The phrase أمـا .. ف here introduces the topic of this paragraph, i.e. Ibn al-Baytar's methodology. Similarly:

{أما} أهم مؤلفاته التي وصلت الينا {فـ}هي:
1 – الجامع لمفردات الأدوية والاغذية.
2 – المغني في الادوية المفردة.

'His most important works which have come down to use are: (1) *The compendium of basic components of medicines and foodstuffs*, and (2) *The sufficient guide to the basic medicines.*'

Here the previous paragraph has discussed aspects of Ibn al-Baytar's life–story. The أمـا .. ف phrase introduces the new topic of Ibn al-Baytar's works.

i.iv *Linkage*
Contrast can be said to involve linkage in that the phrase following أمـا bears some relationship to what has gone before. In linkage proper, however, this relationship is closer than that of contrast or opposition.

Sometimes linkage involves reintroducing as the topic of the clause something which has been mentioned before, but was not the topic of the clause in which it was previously mentioned. For example:

ويبــدأ الخطان مـن خط يقـع أمـام البـيت الكبـيــر... {أمـا} البـيت
الكبـيـر {فـ}قد ترك خاليا ..

'The two lines began from a line in front of the big house. The big house [itself] had been left unsurrounded ...' (ch. 17, 5a)

Sometimes linkage involves further specification, from a general topic to a more specific one, or from one sub–topic to another sub–topic. This has already been seen in the example quoted above under scene–setting, where the previous paragraph had talked about the identity of Imru' al-Qays in general. The paragraph in question beginning with the ف .. أمـا clause then goes on: {فـأَمـا} اسـم امـرىء القـيـس واسـم أبـيـه واسـم أمـه {فـ}أشيـاء ليـس مـن اليـسيـر الاتفـاق عليهـا بـين الـرواة .., 'The name Imru' al-Qays, and the names of his father and mother, however, are things for which agreement is not easily found among the reciters.' (ch. 17, 4c)

Sometimes the link between what has gone before and the information following أمـا in the أمـا .. ف structure may be more vague. For example:

{أما} الذبـاب {فـ}لا يضاهيـه فـي الكثـرة إلا القمـل ..

'The flies are only equalled in number by the lice ...' (ch. 17, 5a)

Here the flies (and the lice) are mentioned after previous discussion of other kinds of vermin which infest the quarter – rats, snakes, scorpions. The use of أمـا .. ف here involves a recognition that flies are well–known features of poor quarters of traditional Egyptian cities. They can therefore be introduced as an emphatic topic following أمـا in this clause.

Finally, linkage may be a feature of listing of related elements. For example:

.. ولكن العلمـاء يسـتـبـعـدون أن يكون الملك قـد بنى للأولى أحـد
الهرمـين لأنها – كمـا حكى أحد وزرائه قد تآمرت عليه {أما} الثانية
والثالثة {فـ}كانتا ابنتـا أمير أبيدوس ونجع حمـادى وكان يـحبهمـا
الملك.

'... but scholars consider it unlikely that the king built one of the two pyramids for the first [wife of his] because, as one of his ministers recounts, she plotted against him. The second and third wives were daughters of the prince of Abydos and Nag Hammadi and the king loved them both.' (ch. 3, 5)

Here there is of course some element of contrast involved, although it is not as strong as in the examples listed under *contrast* above.

(b) *Resumptive particles: summary*

Resumptive particles have been discussed at a number of points in this book, particularly ch. 10, 7a; ch. 14, 7bi; ch. 15, 7a; ch. 16, 7bi.iii; and ch. 17, 7a.

There are four basic resumptive particles. These are i. ف, ii. أَنْ/إِلّا, iii. لِ, and iv. و. To these may be added the pronoun of separation (ch. 14, 7b), and also the emphatic particles إنَّ (ch. 15, 7ai) and قد (ch. 16, 7bi.iii) both of which typically occur in conjunction with ف. The uses of the four basic resumptive particles can be summarised in turn as follows.

i ف

As discussed in chapter 10 (ch. 10, 7b), ف as a resumptive particle is typically followed by إنَّ. Among the examples given in chapter 10 were:

وهكذا {فإنّ} المضيق أوسع بكثير مما يتصوره الناس

'Thus, the straits are much wider than people imagine.' (ch. 1, 5b)

وحسب إحصائيات اليونسكو {فإنّ} واحدا من بين كل أربعة من البالغين في العالم أمي.

'According to UNESCO statistics, one out of every four adults in the world is illiterate.' (ch. 10, 4c)

An example given in chapter 15 (ch. 15, 7ai) was:

والمستشير وإن كان أفضل رأياً من المشير، فـ{إنَّ}ه يزداد برأيه رأياً كما تزداد النار بالسليط ضوءاً.

'The person who asks for advice, even if he has a better opinion than the person whose advice he asks, has his opinion strengthened by another opinion, just as the light of a fire is strengthened through oil.' (ch. 15, 6b)

Here إنّ, along with the ف which precedes it, marks the resumption of the apodosis (جواب) following the intervening protasis (شرط) وإن كان أفضل رأياً من المشير.

In each of these cases there is a causal aspect to ف; the argument which develops after the ف builds on what has gone before. Causality – loosely defined – is a function of the meaning of ف whether it occurs as a resumptive particle or in another position, typically as a linker between two clauses.

It is also possible for ف to occur following a concessive phrase, e.g. one beginning with رغم 'despite'. Concessiveness can be regarded as a kind of causality in reverse, since it involves B happening despite A, i.e. where A would be specifically expected not to cause B, whereas causality involves B happening because of A, i.e. where A is specifically expected to cause B. For example:

ورغم أن جماعة الإخوان المسلمين ذاتها ليست إلا تعبيراً سياسياً عن المحتوى الاقتصادي والاجتماعي للتطور {ف}إنها لم تتوان في إعلان رفضها لكافة المؤسسات السياسية الأخرى ..

'Despite the fact that the Society of the Muslim Brothers itself is nothing but the political expression of the economic and social content of development, it lost no time in announcing its absolute rejection of all other political institutions ..' (ch. 14, 11b)

وعلى الرغم مما يتردد عن وجود تنسيق بين المؤتمر الشعبي العام وحزب التجمع اليمني للإصلاح {ف}إن هناك دوائر ستكون المنافسة بينهما قوية ..

'Despite numerous reports of an accord between the General Popular Congress and the Yemeni Grouping for Reform party, there are constituencies in which the rivalry between them will be fierce ..' (ch. 15, 4b)

While ف as a resumptive particle is typically followed by إنّ, it is also possible for it to be followed by قد (with the perfect verb). An example is:

بدلاً من أن يؤدي هذا الضغط الأمني الذي تجاوز الحدود في بعض البلاد العربية إلى اختفاء هذه الجماعات أو تغييرها لأساليبها أو تنفير القواعد الجماهيرية والشعبية منها، {فقد} أدت الوسائل الأمنية إلى نمو تيار من العنف المتبادل ..

'Instead of this security pressure ... leading ..., the security measures have led to the growth of a current of mutual violence ...' (ch. 14, 5b)

There are also cases where ف is used as a resumptive particle on its own, without قد or إنّ. For example:

وإذاً {ف}ليس من سبيل الى أن نقبل قول الكثرة في امرئ القيس ..

'Therefore, we should not accept what the majority says about Imru' al-Qays.' (ch. 17, 4c)

وعلى أية حال {ف}بالسجون العمومية ليست كثيرة والحمد لله.
'Whatever the case, public prisons are not common, thank God.' (ch. 17, 5b)

وقد كتب نجيب محفوظ هذه الكلمة بخط يده في ٨ ورقات فلوسكاب وقسمها إلى شقين، الشق الأول سياسي ويتعلق بالعالم

العـربي ومـشكلة الفلسطينيـين ... والشق الأدبي {ف}يـتــعـلـق
بإحساسه كأديب عن فوزه بنـوبـل ..

'Naguib Mahfouz wrote this speech in his own hand on eight foolscap
sheets, and divided it into two parts. The first part is political and deals
with the Arab world and the problem of the Palestinians ... and the
second part is literary, and deals with his feelings as a writer about his
winning the Nobel Prize ...' (ch. 17, 11)

وعن الحـضـارة الفـرعـونيـة لن أتحـدث عن الغـزوات وبناء
الإمبراطورية ... (start of paragraph)

...

وعن الحضارة الإسلامية {ف}لن أحدثكم عن دعوتها إلى إقامة وحدة
بشرية في رحاب الخالق تنهض على الحرية والمساواة والتسامح ...
(start of next paragraph)

'Regarding the Pharaonic civilisation, I will not talk about the invasions
and the building of the empire ...

...

'Regarding the Islamic civilisation, I will not tell you about its mission
to establish human unity in the vast realms of the Creator based on
freedom, equality and mutual tolerance ...' (ch. 17, 11)

These last two examples are similar to one another. In both there is parallelism
between two clauses, the first clause lacking a resumptive ف, and the second
having one. So in the former example, we find الشق الاول سـيـاسي [ويـتـعلق
followed by والشق الادبي {ف}يـتعلق باحساسه بالعالم العربي]. In the latter
example we find وعن الحضارة الفرعونية لن اتحدث followed by وعن الحضارة
الاسلامية {ف}لن احدثكم. The idea of causality is weak in these cases, but one
might think of the examples with ف as expressing a sense along the lines '[If you
ask me about ...] well then ...'.

The same is true of أمـا .. ف structures, discussed above (ch. 17, 7a). Here
there is a sense that the element following أما introduces a topic, almost as one
raises a notion to be questioned, and that the element following ف provides the
'answer' to the topic raised by the element following أما.

In this respect there is also a significant parallel with conditionals introduced by
إذا or إنْ. Here the main clause often follows the subordinate clause and in this case
is typically, but not necessarily, introduced by the resumptive particle ف. For
example:

واذا اتفقت الكثرة على شىء {ف}يـجب أن يكون صحيحا ..

' ...and if the majority are agreed about something then it must be true
...' (ch. 17, 4c)

إن أَسْتخْلفْ فقد استخْلفَ من هو خيـر مـني ..

'If he has appointed a successor, he has appointed someone who is better than me ...' (ch. 16, 6a)

In Arabic the protasis is termed the 'condition' شرط, while the main clause is termed the 'answer to the condition' جواب الشرط, just as it was suggested earlier that the element following ف in an أما .. ف clause provides an 'answer' to the topic raised by the element following أما.

ii إلا أنّ

While ف is causal, and includes both standard causal usages and concessive (i.e. reverse causal) usages, إلا أنّ is used only concessively. إلا أنّ was discussed in detail in chapter 10 (section, 7b), and will not be further discussed here. The following examples, given in chapter 10, are repeated here for convenience of reference:

ومع أنّ هذه المقولة شائعة {فإلا أنّها} ليست صحيحة إلى الحد الذي تلقاه من البعض ..

'Despite the fact that this view is widely held, it is not as true as some people would have you believe...' (ch. 2, 8)

ومع أنّها موزعة على مختلف بلاد العالم – النامية والصناعية – {إلا أنّ} معظمها يتركز في العالم الثالث

'Although it can be found in many countries throughout the world – developing and industrialised – it is concentrated in the third world.' (ch. 10, 4c)

iii لـ

One resumptive use of لـ has already been seen. This is where the predicate of an إنّ‑clause begins with a noun. An example given in chapter 15 (ch. 15, 7a, also 7aii.i) was:

.. وإنّه {لَ}نبيُّ هذه الأمة ..

'He is indeed the prophet of this community' (ch. 4, 6).

لـ in this context is traditionally said to give the predicate greater emphasis. This use of لـ can also be compared with the use of لـ in لَقَد which is also said to give greater emphasis than قد alone (cf. ch. 16, 7bii). In this respect it is interesting that in إنّ clauses what is emphasised is not the element following إنّ, but the element following the predicate of إنّ (cf. ch. 15, 7aii). It is not surprising therefore that the emphatic particle لـ should occur before the predicate, rather than before إنّ. In the case of قد, on the other hand, what is emphasised is the entire clause beginning with قد (cf. ch. 16, 7bii). The positioning of the emphatic particle لَ before قد in the form لقد is therefore also understandable.

لَ may also be used resumptively, in clauses involving the conditional particle لَو . Just as in the case of conditionals introduced by إذا or إنْ (see i. above), in conditionals with لَو, the main clause often follows the subordinate clause and in this case is typically, but not necessarily, introduced by the resumptive particle لَ. Examples are:

لو كان لنا دعوة مجابة {لـ}دعونا بها للسلطان ..

'If we had a prayer which was answered, we would use it to pray for the leader ...' (ch. 14, 6a)

ولو كانوا يعيشون – كما تدعي الابواق الشيوعية – {لـ}ما كان
لهذا الستار الحديدي ضرورة ..

'If they lived as the communist trumpets claim, this iron curtain would not be a necessity ...' (ch. 14, 11ai)

iv و

The final resumptive particle is و. This occurs only with the word منذ (also the rare, and more archaic, variant of this مذ) and even here relatively infrequently. The use of و here emphasis the simultaneity of the action described following the و and the time period described in the phrase beginning with منذ. Even more rarely منذ occurs with a resumptive فـ, where فـ emphasises that the action described in the phrase beginning with فـ is a consequence of an event described in the phrase beginning with منذ (cf. Cantarino vol. III, 1975: 79). One example of the use of منذ with a resumptive و in this book is:

واضاف انه منذ زمن ليس ببعيد {و}نظام الحكم بما في ذلك جبهة
التحرير يستعمل جبهة الانقاذ الاسلامية كوسيلة لمقاومة
الديمقراطية في البلاد .

'He added that recently [lit: since a period which is not far past] the ruling regime including the Liberation Front had been using the Islamic Salvation Front as a means of combatting democracy in the country.' (ch. 15, 5c)

While فـ is used as the resumptive particle where causal relations are involved, و, as a more general connector, is used with منذ, where a simple non–causal temporal relationship is involved.

8. Aural Arabic texts 1

Listen to the following text from the BBC Arabic Service news broadcast from Oct. 13, 1988, منحت جائزة نوبيل للآداب, then complete exercises i. and ii. below.

i Answer the following questions in Arabic.

١ – ما هو تاريخ ولادة نجيب محفوظ ؟

٢ – في رأي لجنة نوبيل على من تنطبق اعمال نجيب محفوظ ؟

٣ – منذ كم سنة يكتب نجيب محفوظ ؟

٤ – كم عدد الكتب التي كتبها نجيب محفوظ ؟

٥ – من هو بُلَند الحيدري؟

٦ – حسب قول بولند الحيدري ما هي المشاكل التي تعالجها كتب نجيب محفوظ ؟

٧ – ما هي كتب نجيب محفوظ التي يذكرها بولند الحيدري؟

٨ – بأي شكل صدر كتاب « أولاد حارتنا » أولاً؟

٩ – متى صدر في بيروت ؟

١٠ – حسب بولند الحيدري ماذا استهدف نجيب محفوظ في « أولاد حارتنا »؟

١١ – لماذا يفضل Denys Johnson Davies ترجمة نجيب محفوظ على ترجمة غيره من الكتاب العرب المعاصرين؟

ii Transcribe the first section of this passage from the beginning to المشاكله وآماله.

9. Aural Arabic texts 2

Listen to the following text from حصاد الشهر, no. 27, side 2, item 1, طه حسين يتحدث في حديث من إذاعة لندن, and produce a complete transcription of the text.

10. Written English texts

Making use of constructions encountered in the Arabic texts above, as far as possible, translate the following text from Hourani, *A History of the Arab Peoples*, p. 13, into idiomatic Arabic.

The language of poetry

Poems were composed to be recited in public, either by the poet himself or by a *rawi* or reciter. This had certain implications: the sense had to be conveyed in a line, a single unit of words of which the meaning could be grasped by listeners, and every performance was unique and different from others. The poet or *rawi* had scope for improvisation, within a framework of commonly accepted verbal forms and patterns, the use of certain words or combinations of them in order to express certain ideas or feelings. There may therefore have been no single authentic version of a poem. As they have come down to us, the versions were produced later by philologists or literary critics in the light of the linguistic or poetic norms of their own time. In the process of doing so, they may have introduced new elements into the poems, changing the language to suit ideas of what was correct and even forming *qasidas* by combining shorter pieces. In the 1920s two scholars, one British and one Egyptian, built upon these undoubted facts a theory that the poems were themselves the product of a later period, but most of those who have studied the subject would now agree that in substance the poems do come from the time to which they have traditionally been ascribed.

11. Précis
Read the following text, which is an extract from Naguib Mahfouz's acceptance speech for the Nobel Prize, then produce a précis in Arabic.

الوطن تنفرد بنشر خطاب
نجيب محفوظ للجنة نوبل

محمد سلماوي يلقي رسالة الأديب الكبير وكريمتاه
تتسلمان الجائزة من ملك السويد

استكتولم – أحمد كمال الدين

في الاحتفال المرتقب عالميا لاستلام أول كاتب عربي لجائزة نوبل، استمعت لجنة الأدب بالأكاديمية السويدية إلى خطاب عميد الرواية العربية الكاتب الكبير نجيب محفوظ بهذه المناسبة. وفي حضور ١٨ عضوا هم كل أعضاء اللجنة إلى جانب كريمتي الفائز فاطمة وأم كلثوم وفي حضور سفير مصر بالسويد عبد الرحمن مرعي وأعضاء السفارة والوفد الإعلامي المصري وكبار مثقفي السويد.

وأمس ألقى محمد سلماوي نيابة عن نجيب محفوظ الفائز بجائزة الشعب السويدي أو نوبل كما يطلقون عليها، وقد كتب

نجيب محفوظ هذه الكلمة بخط يده في ٨ ورقات فلوسكاب وقسمها إلى شقين، الشق الأول سياسي ويتعلق بالعالم العربي ومشكلة الفلسطينيين وما يعانيه الشعب الفلسطيني من اضطهاد داخل الأرض المحتلة ودور المجتمع الفلسطيني في هذا الخصوص من رفع الظلم عن هؤلاء البشر والشق الأدبي فيتعلق بإحساسه كأديب عن فوزه بنوبل وكيفية استقباله لها.. وهذا نص الكلمة التي ألقاها محمد سلماوي أمس أمام ٦٠٠ مواطن سويدي بالعربية والفرنسية والإنجليزية.

سيداتي، سادتي:

في البدء، أشكر الأكاديمية السويدية ولجنة نوبل التابعة لها على التفاتها الكريم لاجتهادي المثابر الطويل. وأرجو أن تتقبل بسعة صدر هديتي إليكم بلغة غير معروفة لدى الكثيرين منكم، ولكنها هي الفائز الحقيقي بالجائزة. فمن الواجب أن تسبح أنغامها في مراجعكم الحضارية لأول مرة. وإني كبير الأمل ألا تكون المرة الأخيرة، وأن يسعد الأدباء من قومي بالجلوس بكل جدارة بين أدبائكم العالميين، الذين نشروا أريج البهجة والحكمة في دنيانا المليئة بالشجن.

ساداتي:

أخبرني مندوب جريدة أجنبية في القاهرة بأن لحظة إعلان اسمي مقرونا بالجائزة ساد الصمت وتساءل كثيرون عمن أكون.. فاسمحوا لي أن أقدم لكم نفسي بالموضوعية التي تتيحها الطبيعة البشرية. أنا ابن حضارتين تزوجتا في عصر من عصور التاريخ، زواجا موفقا. أولاهما عمرها سبعة آلاف سنة وهي الحضارة الفرعونية، وثانيتهما عمرها ألف وأربعمائة سنة وهي الحضارة الإسلامية. ولعلي لست في حاجة إلى تعريف بأي من الحضارتين لأحد منكم وأنتم من أهل الصفوة والعلم، ولكن لا بأس من التذكير ونحن في مقام النجوى والتعارف.

وعن الحضارة الفرعونية لن أتحدث عن الغزوات وبناء الإمبراطورية فقد أصبح ذلك من المفاخر البالية التي لا ترتاح لذكرها الضمائر الحديثة والحمد لله. ولن أتحدث عن اهتدائها لأول مرة إلى الله سبحانه وتعالى وكشفها عن فجر الضمير البشري فلذلك مجال طويل فضلا عن أنه لا يوجد بينكم من لم يلمّ بسيرة الملك النبي أخناتون، بل لن أتحدث عن إنجازاتها في الفن والأدب ومعجزاتها الشهيرة الأهرام وأبو الهول والكرنك فمن لم يسعده الحظ بمشاهدة تلك الآثار فقد قرأ عنها وتأمل صورها. دعوني أقدمها – الحضارة الفرعونية – بما يشبه القصة طالما أن الظروف الخاصة بي قضت بأن أكون قصاصا، فتفضلوا بسماع هذه الواقعة التاريخية المسجلة. تقول أوراق البردي إن أحد الفراعنة قد نما إليه أن علاقة آثمة نشأت بين بعض نساء الحريم وبعض رجال الحاشية، وكان المتوقع أن يجهز على الجميع فلا يشذ في تصرفه عن مناخ زمانه، ولكنه دعا إلى حضرته نخبةً من رجال القانون، فطالبهم بالتحقيق فيما نما إلى علمه، وقال لهم إنه يريد الحقيقة ليحكم بالعدل. ذلك السلوك في رأيي أعظم من بناء إمبراطورية، وتشييد الأهرامات وأدلّ على تفوق الحضارة من أي أبّهة أو ثراء، وقد زالت الإمبراطورية وأمست خبرا من أخبار الماضي، وسوف يتلاشى الأهرام ذات يوم ولكن الحقيقة والعدل سيبقيان ما دام في البشرية عقل يتطلع أو ضمير ينبض.

وعن الحضارة الإسلامية فلن أحدثكم عن دعوتها إلى إقامة وحدة بشرية في رحاب الخالق تنهض على الحرية والمساواة والتسامح، ولا عن عظمة رسولها فمن مفكريكم من كرسه كأعظم رجل في تاريخ البشرية، ولا عن فتوحاتها التي غرست آلاف المآذن الداعية للعبادة والتقوى والخير على امتداد أرض مترامية ما بين مشارف الهند والصين وحدود فرنسا، ولا عن المآخاة التي تحققت في حضنها بين الأديان والعناصر في تسامح لم تعرفه

الإنسانية من قبل ولا من بعد، ولكني سأقدمها في موقف درامي مؤثر يلخص سمة من أبرز سماتها. ففي إحدى معاركها الظافرة مع الدولة البيزنطية ردت الأسرى في مقابل عدد من كتب الفلسفة والطب والرياضيات من التراث الإغريقي العتيد وهي شهادة قيمة للروح الإنساني في طموحه إلى العلم والمعرفة. رغم أن الطالب يعتنق دينا سماويا والمطلوب ثمرة حضارة وثنية.

قدر لي يا سادة أن أولد في حضن هاتين الحضارتين وأن أرضع لبانهما واتغذى على آدابهما وفنونهما، ثم ارتويت من رحيق ثقافتكم الثرية الفاتنة. ومن وحي ذلك كله – بالإضافة إلى شجوني الخاصة – ندت عني كلمات أسعدها الحظ باستحقاق تقدير أكاديميتكم الموقرة فتوجت اجتهادي بجائزة نوبل الكبرى، فالشكر أقدمه لها باسمي وباسم البناة العظام الراحلين من مؤسسي الحضارتين.

12. Oral

(a) In Arabic discuss the arguments put forward by طه حسين in the passage from في الادب الجاهلي (section 4).

(b) الادب العربي الحديث
i   One student to present an account of الشعر العربي الحديث.
ii A second student to present an account of القصة العربية الحديثة.
iii A third student to present an account of المسرحيات العربية.
iv The presenters then ask the other students questions about الادب العربي الحديث. These questions should include some which require factual answers, and some which require subjective, hypothetical or experiential answers. For example:

١ – ما هي انواع الادب العربي الجديدة في القرن العشرين؟

٢ – ما هي التأثيرات الرئيسة في هذه الانواع من الادب؟

٣ – كيف نشأت القصة العربية الحديثة؟

٤ – ما هو الفرق بين الشعر العربي الحديث والشعر الادبي القديم؟

٥ – كيف نشأت المسرحية العربية؟

٦ – ما هي الرموز السائدة في القصة العربية الحديثة؟

٧ – من هم اهم الادباء العرب اليوم؟

13. Essay

(a) Carrying on from ولكن at the end of p. 60, write your own alternative ending
to the short story شيء يجـن in section 5.

(b) Write an essay in Arabic of 200 words on the following title قصـة عربيـة
قرأتها. In your writing address the following issues:

١ – من كاتب القصة وما تعرف/ين عنه؟

٢ – متى كُتبت القصة؟

٣ – ما هي الشخصيات المهمة في القصة ؟

٤ – ما هي اهم الاحداث في القصة ؟

٥ – ما هي الشعور السائدة في القصة ؟

٦ – ما هي الرمـوز الرئيـسية في القصة ؟

٧ – ماذا تعرف/ين عن اللغة المستعملة في القصة؟

٨ – ما هي رسالة القصة؟

18
Economics

1. Basic background material

GNP, GNP per capita and average inflation in the Arab countries and Israel. Figures for Japan, Netherlands, United Kingdom and United States are given separately below for comparison.

	GNP (million US$) 1994	GNP per capita (US$) /annum 1993	1994	Average inflation (%) 1985–1994
Algeria	46,115	1,770	1,690	22.3
Bahrain	4,114	8,030	7,500	0.3
Egypt	40,950	660	710	16.4
Iraq	–	–	–	–
Israel	78,113	13,880	14,410	18.0
Kuwait	31,433	20,140	19,040	–
Lebanon	–	–	d	–
Libya	–	–	b	–
Morocco	30,330	1,020	1,150	5.1
Oman	10,779	5,320	5,200	0.1
Qatar	7,810	15,030	14,540	–
Saudi Arabia	126,597	7,570	7,240	2.7
Sudan	–	–	a	55.3
Syrian Arab Rep.	–	–	d	22.1
Tunisia	15,873	1,740	1,800	6.3
UAE	–	21,420	c	–
West Bank + Gaza	–	–	d	–
Yemen, Rep.	3,884	280	280	=
Japan	4,321,136	31,360	34,630	1.3
Netherlands	338,144	20,950	21,970	1.6
United Kingdom	1,069,457	18,050	18,410	5.4
United States	6,737,367	24,780	25,860	3.3

Notes: '–' means figures not available. **a.** Estimated to be low–income ($725 or less). **b.** Estimated to be upper–middle–income ($2,896 to $8,955). **c.** Estimated to be high–income ($8,956 or more). **d.** Estimated to be lower–middle–income ($726 to $2,895).

2. Additional reading
(a) Hourani, *A History of the Arab Peoples*, pp. 43–6; pp. 373–88; pp. 346–8.
(b) Maxime Rodinson, *Islam and Capitalism*, (Harmondsworth: Penguin Books, 1974).
(c) F. Nomani and A. Rahnema, *Islamic Economic Systems*, (London and New Jersey: Zed Books, 1994).

3. Key vocabulary
Taking the texts in the chapter as a starting point, draw up lists of vocabulary in the following fields:
(a) General economics.
(b) Finance.
(c) Industry – i. oil, ii. non–oil.
(d) Commerce (import–export, etc.)

4. Written Arabic texts 1
(a) Read the following newspaper text from الوطن, then complete exercises i. and ii. which follow.

البورصة

الاوساط المالية تحذر من الشائعات وتتوقع ارتفاع الاسعار مع شراء الشركات لأسهمها

قالت مصادر *الوطن* ان الانخفاض الذي حصل في اسعار الاسهم في البورصة امس كان نتيجة طبيعية للانهيار في البورصات العالمية وعلى وجه التحديد بورصة هونغ كونغ وذلك بعد ان تمت معالجة الانهيار فيها باساليب خاطئة اذا كان بالامكان ان تتم معالجة العامل النفسي باضافة اوقات الدوام في بورصة هونغ كونغ بدلا من اقفالها.

وتوقعت هذه المصادر ان تكون استجابة بورصة هونغ كونغ كبيرة لما سيحدث في بورصة نيويورك من تطورات ومستجدات ايجابية او سلبية مشيرة الى ان ردود الفعل في سوق الكويت للاوراق المالية ستكون اقل بكثير .

وذكرت اوساط مالية مطلعة ان عزم بعض الشركات المحلية على شراء ما نسبته ١٠٪ من اسهمها سينعكس بشكل ايجابي على معدلات

الاسعار وذلك انطلاقا من نسبة الاسهم المملوكة للحكومة في الشركات المدرجة في البورصة تقارب ٥٠٪ بالاضافة الى نسبة ٢٥٪ من اجمالي الاسهم المطروحة للتداول مرهونة او ان اصحابها لا يرغبون في بيعها ومتمسكون بها كمحافظ استثمارية ثابتة .

اذن لم يبق سوى ما نسبته ٢٥٪ من اجمالي الاسهم المطروحة للتداول لذا فان شراء الشركات ما نسبته ١٠٪ من اسهمها وهو ما يمثل ٤٠٪ من اجمالي الاسهم المعروضة سوف يدفع بالاسعار نحو الاعلى ويعزز من قيمة الاصول .

وتوقعت ان تتأثر حركة النشاط في البورصة باية تطورات سلبية حادة في اسواق الاسهم العالمية او اية تطورات سياسية على صعيد الوضع الاقليمي .

كما انها حذرت المتعاملين مع الاخذ بالاشاعات والتي كانت وراء موجة الخوف التي انتابت المستثمرين اثناء فترة التداول الصباحية .

i Identify the words or phrases in the Arabic text which correspond to the following in English (N.B. the English words and phrases are listed in the same order of occurrence as the corresponding Arabic words and phrases in the text).

1. financial circles
2. predict
3. according to sources ...
4. the fall in share prices
5. a natural consequence of
6. specifically/particularly
7. the fall ... was mishandled
8. trading hours
9. there would be a marked/dramatic response
10. future developments in the New York stock exchange
11. indicating that
12. informed ... sources
13. will have a positive effect
14. average prices
15. is approximately
16. [currently] traded shares
17. total shares
18. stable/fixed investment portfolios
19. will push up prices
20. those engaged in spreading rumours

ii Translate the text into idiomatic English.

(b) Read the following newspaper text from الوطن, then complete exercises i. and
ii. which follow.

المستثمرون السعوديون يعدون لمرحلة اكثر نشاطا

دب النشاط بالاسهم بعد ركود دام سنوات
التـحـسـن في اسـعـار النفط واعـلان الموازنة وراء زيادة
الاقبال على الاسهم

تدب الان حركة نشطة في اسعار الاسهم السعودية بالسوق الموازي
بعـد ركـود اسـتـمـر عـدة سنـوات، ومن المؤكـد ان الاجـراءات
التنظيمية الجديدة ستكون لها اثارها الواضحة في حركة السوق .
ومن العوامل الرئيسية التي ساهمت في حركة الاسعار الاعلان
عن الموازنة الحكومية لعام ١٩٩٠ والمؤجلة منذ ديسمبر الماضي،
بالاضافة الى التحسن الذي طرأ لاسعار النفط بالاسواق العالمية.
ومما لا جدال فيه ان الموازنة السعودية للعام الحالي خصصت
قدرا اكبر مما كان متوقعا للانفاق الحكومي خلال عام ١٩٨٩ مما
اعاد ثقة الاوساط التجارية التي ترى ان توسيع قنوات الانفاق
الحكومية بالاضافة الى انفاق الدول المنتجة والمصدرة للنفط
تعتبر من العوامل المشجعة للاقتصاد الوطني.
كل هذه العوامل ادت الى عودة الثقة الى القطاع التجاري مما
ادى الى زيادة الاقبال على الاسهم السعودية، فقد ارتفعت القيمة
المتوسطة للتداول الاسبوعي من قيمة تراوحت بين ثلاث واربع
ملايين ريال سعودي خلال نوفمبر الى ١١.٦ مليون خلال الاسبوع
المنتهي في ١٨ ديسمبر من العام الماضي. في حين بلغت قيمة
الاسهم المتداولة في الاسبوع التالي ١٧.٤ مليون ريال سعودي،
تراجعت بعدها الى ٥.٦ مليون ريال خلال الاسبوع المنتهي في ١
يناير ١٩٨٧، الا ان حركة التداول قد حققت قفزة كبيرة في
الاسبوع التالي المنتهي في ٨ يناير ١٩٨٧ وصلت معها قيمة
التداول الى ٣٧.٣ مليون من الريالات.

i Answer the following questions in English.

1. How is the current movement of share prices on the Saudi parallel market

described?
2. How long did the recession last?
3. How important was the Saudi budget in affecting the current state of share prices?
4. From when had the announcement of the budget been delayed?
5. What was the surprise element in the budget?
6. What has been the effect of this surprise element?
7. What two factors are mentioned as encouraging the national economy?

ii Translate the headlines and the first three paragraphs of the text into idiomatic English.

5. Written Arabic texts 2
(a) Read the following text from النفط والتنمية p. 72, then complete exercises i. and ii. which follow.

المنطق الثاني :

ضرورة تنمية السوق المحلية :

ان دول العالم الثالث قد قطعت ، منذ اوائل الخمسينات حتى الان ، شوطا في التصنيع لا تعود اهميته في نظرنا الى حجم النتائج المحققة وهي متواضعة ، بقدر ما تعود الى ضرورة الاستفادة من الدروس العلمية التي تمخضت عنها التجربة . وقد يبدو ذلك بديها ، لكن الواقع قد يشهد بأن غالبية الدول النامية ما زالت غير مستوعبة لهذه الدروس بالقدر الكاف . ذلك ان واقع التنمية الصناعية وما تقوم عليه من استراتيجيات وسياسات لم يشهد تغيرا حقيقيا واضحا يسمح معه بالقول بغير ذلك . ومن اهم الدروس العلمية المستفادة من تجربة التصنيع في العالم الثالث ، ما اسفرت عنه عملية الاختيار العشوائي أو الارتجالي للمشروعات الصناعية سواء في ظل سياسة الاحلال محل الواردات او الانتاج للتصدير من خلق مشروعات غير اقتصادية . الأمر الذي أدى الى زيادة نفقات الدولة لدعم هذه الصناعات وتوفير المناخ اللازم

لحمايتها من المنافسة الاجنبية محليا وعالميا بحجة انها
صناعات وليدة . والحقيقة التي لا مراء فيها ، ان الدولة
وجدت نفسها ملزمة باستمرار دعم هذه المشروعات رغم
ضخامة الاعباء ، لان هذه المشروعات صارت جزءا أو
واجهة للانظمة السياسية والاقتصادية التحررية في هذه
البلدان . وبذلك ظلت هذه الصناعات وليدة وقد شاب
شعرها.

i   Identify the words or phrases in the Arabic text which correspond to the following in English (N.B. the English words and phrases are listed in the same order of occurrence as the corresponding Arabic words and phrases in the text).

1. industrialisation
2. its importance lies in
3. not ... so much as
4. the experiment yielded these results
5. the reason for this is that ...
6. the strategies ... for handling industrial development
7. whether ... or
8. import substitution policy
9. uneconomic projects
10. state expenditure/government spending
11. supporting these industries
12. on the pretext that
13. the truth is that the state ...
14. forced to continue
15. thus
16. although/when

ii   Translate the text into idiomatic English.

(b) Read the following text, then complete exercises i. and ii. which follow.

ملخص

لقد مر النشاط التجاري بين شبه القارة الهندية ومنطقة
الخليج العربي بعدة مراحل من العصر الحديث، شهدت

نشأة ونشاط شركة الهند الشرقية الانجليزية ومنافستها للبرتغاليين والهولنديين في منطقتي الهند والخليج العربي، كما شهدت هيمنة بريطانية على تجارة المنطقتين ومواجهة منافسة غيرها من القوى الاخرى التقليدية والجديدة، وكانت العلاقات التجارية بين شبه القارة الهندية ومنطقة الخليج العربي نشطة في عمليات التصدير والاستيراد المتبادلة، ولكن في اطار ما سمحت به السياسة البريطانية المسيطرة على المنطقتين، وفي حدود مصالحها التجارية والسياسية وبخاصة بعد احتلال الهند وعدن.

لقد تعرض النشاط التجاري بين الهند والخليج الى صعود وهبوط، وامتداد وانحسار، نتيجة تطور الاحداث السياسية والعسكرية ولا سيما اثناء الحربين العالميتين، كما ان طبيعة العلاقات التجارية في المنطقة قد تغيرت نسبيا بعد استقلال دول شبه القارة الهندية عام ١٩٤٧، حيث دخلت هذه الدول مرحلة جديدة ولم تقطع جذورها بالماضي.

i In pairs produce your own vocabulary identification exercise structured in the same way as the vocabulary identification exercises given above, then exchange exercises for completion.

ii Translate the text into idiomatic English.

(c) Read the following text by عبد المغني سعيد from النظام الاقتصادي الاجتماعي الاسلامي وإنقاذ الاقتصاد العالمي (Cairo: مكتبة الانجلو–المصرية, 1985), pp. 76–7, then answer the questions which follow.

يمكن القول بما لا يفسح مجالا لجدل أو لشك ، ان المصارف الاسلامية، على الرغم من قصر المدة التي مرت على إنشائها قد اجتازت الآن ما يمكن أن يسمى بمرحلة التجربة والخطأ . وقد بلغ عددها نحو

الخمسين مصرفا وفرعا ، منتشرة في عدد كبير من الدول الاسلامية مثل مصر والسودان والامارات العربية وماليزيا وباكستان وبانجلاديش .. الخ . وهي جميعا تمارس عملها كمؤسسات اقتصادية حديثة لا تكاد تختلف في نظمها وأدواتها عن المصارف المعاصرة الا من حيث تجردها من استخدام الفائدة .

ولم يكن قيام مصارف لا تستخدم الفائدة الربوية بالأمر المتعذر علميا أو عمليا . فالفكر الاقتصادي الحديث لا يخلو من دعوات لاقامة مصارف لا تتعامل بالفائدة . ومصارف الادخار الشعبي والمصارف التعاونية على اختلاف أنواعها هي أقرب ما تكون الى المصارف الاسلامية بتركيزها على المشاركة والاستثمار ، دون الائتمنان التجاري البحت . وكما أشرنا في الفصل الأول سبق أن دعا الاشتراكيون التعاونيون وبعض رواد المدرسة الاشتراكية الفرنسية في أوائل القرن التاسع عشر ، الى إنشاء مصارف تعاونية أو مصارف استبدال تعمل بلا فوائد ...

وقد بدأت تجربة المصارف الاسلامية في السبعينات من هذا القرن كمظهر من مظاهر الصحوة الاسلامية ، وفي وقت كانت البنوك الرأسمالية الحديثة التي تتعامل بالفائدة الربوية منتشرة في سائر أنحاء الدول الاسلامية ، فكان من الطبيعي أن تأخذ المصارف الاسلامية بالكثير من نظم ووسائل هذه المصارف طالما هي لا تتعارض مع أحكام الاسلام في شيء . وما كانت ليعيب المصارف الاسلامية أنها تستخدم النظم المصرفية والآلات الحسابية والالكترونية الحديثة . فهي مجرد وسائل عصرية تسخر لخدمة الغرض . وفي بيت الله الحرام بمكة المشرفة تستخدم وسائل الانارة الحديثة ومكبرات الصوت والمكانس الكهربائية ، وعند توسيع دائرة المطاف منذ سنوات سمح بادخال سيارات اللوري لنقل مواد البناء الى أماكن العمل داخل الحرم .

1. What stage does the writer claim that Islamic banks have now passed?
2. How many Islamic banks and branches are there now?
3. To what extent do these differ from other modern banks?
4. According to the writer which western–style banks come closest to Islamic banks?
5. In what ways are they similar to Islamic banks?
6. Which western thinkers called for the establishment of cooperative banks in the nineteenth century?
7. What was the Islamic banking experiment in the 1970s one feature of according to the writer?
8. Why does the writer say that Islamic banks are not to be blamed for adopting modern techniques and machinery?
9. What comparison does he draw with the *haram* in Mecca?

6. Written Arabic texts 3 (classical)

(a) Read out loud the following two verses from the Qur'an on usury, then discuss the translation of the verses orally in class (سورة البقرة ii, 275–6).

٢٧٥ اَلَّذِينَ يَأْكُلُونَ الرِّبَوا لا يَقُومُونَ إلا كَمـــا يَقُومُ
الَذِي يَتَخَبَّطُهُ الشَيْطَنُ مِنَ المَسِّ ذَلِكَ بِأَنَّهُمْ قَالُوا إنَّمـا
الْبَيْعُ مِثْلُ الـرِّبَوا وأَحَلَّ اللّهُ الـبَيْعَ وحَرَّمَ الـرِّبَوا فَمَن
جَاءَهُ مَوْعِظَةٌ مِّن رَبِّهِ، فَانتَهَى فَلَهُ مَا سَلَفَ وأَمْرُهُ إلَى
اللّهِ ومَنْ عَادَ فَأُلَئِكَ أَصْحَبُ النّارِ هُمْ فِيهَا خَلِدُونَ
٢٧٦ يَمْحَقُ اللّهُ الـرِّبَوا ويُرْبِي الـصَّدَقَتِ واللّهُ لا يُحِبُّ
كُلَّ كَفَّارٍ أَثِيمٍ

(b) Translate the following text by ابن قتيبة from كتاب السؤدد in عيون الأخبار p. 250 into idiomatic English (there is no need to translate the footnote).

حدّثنا يزيد بن عمرو قال حدّثنا عَوْن بن عُمارة عن هشام بن
حسّان عن الحسن أَنّ عمـر بن الخطاب رضى اللّه عنه قال: من
تَاجَرَ في شيء ثلاث مـرات فلم يُصِبْ فيه فليـتـحـوّل مـنـه إلى
غيره. وقال: فرّقوا بـين المنايا، واجعلوا الرأسَ رأسَـين ولا تُلِثُّوا

بـدار مَعْجَزَة^(١). وقال: إذا اشتريتَ بعيراً فاشتره عظيمَ الخَلْق
فإن أخطأَك خيرُ لم يُخْطِئْكَ سوقُ. وقال: بع الحيوانَ أحسنَ ما
يكون في عـينك. وقـال الحَسن: الأسـواقُ مـوائدُ اللَّه في الأرض
فمن أتاها أصاب منها. ابن المبارك عن مَعْمَر عن الزُّبيري قال:
مـرّ رسـول اللَّه صلى اللَّه عليـه وسلم برجل يبيـع شيئـا، فقال
« عليك بالسَّوم أوَّلَ السـوق فـإن الرِّبَاح مع السـمـاح ». وكـان
يقال: اسْمَحْ يَسْمَحْ لك. وفي بعض الحديث المرفوـع: « أمـر رسول
اللَّه صلى اللَّه عليه وسلم الأغنياءَ باتخاذ الغنم والفقراءَ باتخاذ
الدَّجاج ». وقيل للزُّبَير: بمَ بلغتَ ما بلغت من اليسار؟ قال: لم
أرُدَّ ربحاً ولم أَسْتُرْ عيباً. دخل ناسُ على معـاوية فسـألهم عن
صنائعهم، فقالوا: بيعُ الرقيق. قال: بئس التِّجارةُ ضمانُ نفس
ومَؤنةُ ضِرْس.

Note

(١) رواه ابن الأثير في النهاية [أي ....] وابن منظور في اللسان [أي
« لسان العرب » وهو قاموس مشهور للغة العربية] « فرّقوا عن المنية
واجعلوا الرأس رأسين إلى أخ » وقالا في تفسـيره : إذا اشتريتم
الرقيق أو غير من الحيوان فلا تغالوا في الثمن واشتروا بثمن
الرأس الواحد رأسين فإن مات الواحد بقي الآخر فرقتم مالكم عن
المنية، « ولا تلثوا بدار مَعْجَزة » أي لا تقيموا بدار يعجزكم فيها طلب
الرزق وتحولوا عنها إلى غيرها.

7. Grammar/stylistics

Repetition: 1

An understanding of the use of repetition in Arabic is important for an understanding of what constitutes good Arabic style, and is also important for producing Arabic texts (whether translations from English, or composition in Arabic). In the grammar/stylistics section of this chapter and chapter 19, various forms of repetition in Arabic will be considered. Where useful, comparisons will be drawn with typical uses in English.

The following four major sections will consider (a) word repetition, (b) root repetition, (c) pattern repetition, (d) suffix repetition. Roots, patterns, and suffixes are three of the components of words in Arabic. The study of the components of words is traditionally known as morphology. These three forms of repetition, therefore, can be grouped together under the general category of morphological repetition. Section (e) finally will consider various forms of multiple morphological repetition.

(a) *Word repetition*
Word repetition is the repetition of the same word, or a dual or plural of that word, in close proximity. The use of word repetition in Arabic is striking for English speakers, because although words are repeated in English, the situations in which this is done and the frequency of repetition are strikingly different in the two languages.

Word repetition in Arabic is to some extent system–intrinsic. That is say it is grounded in the system of the Arabic language itself. Thus, a standard way of saying 'one day' in Arabic is في يوم من الأيام, and analogous forms can be produced for any other pluralisable noun. A similar example from this book is the following:

أنا ابن حضارتين تزوجتا في {عصر} من {عصور} التاريخ، زواجا موفقا.

'I am the son of two cultures which entered into a successful marriage at a certain stage of history.' (ch. 17, 11)

The use of word repetition in Arabic is, however, much wider than this, and is best studied by considering fairly large stretches of text. The following text is a press release for Brintons carpets, which was originally written in English and was subsequently translated into Arabic. The example is taken from Baker (1992: 208–9, 282–3), and the analysis is also based on that given by Baker. Some key words have been picked out in curly brackets with accompanying numbers. The number before the dot relates to the word used: 1 for 'Brintons'/برينتونز, 2 for 'company'/شركات/شركة, 3 for 'colours'/ألوان/لون). The number after the dot is the number of the occurrence of that particular word in the text in question. In the English text, for example, 3.1 means that this is the first occurrence of the word 'colours', 3.2 means that this is the second occurrence of the word 'colours', etc.

Original English text
{Brintons$^{1.1}$} have been manufacturing fine quality woven carpet for over 200 years. They are a privately owned {company^{2}} specialising in Axminster and Wilton carpets, using wool–rich blends. They have a totally integrated operation from the preparation of the yarn through to the weaving process. All their products are made on looms designed and built by their own engineers and recognised as the most technically superior weaving plant in the World. {Brintons$^{1.2}$} are one of the largest weavers with a production capacity in excess of 100,000 square

metres per week.

The recently introduced New Tradition Axminster range is already creating great interest and will be on display at the Exhibition. New Tradition offers a fascinating series of traditional patterns in miniature using rich jewel–like {colours$^{3.1}$} that glow against dark backgrounds, suitable for a wide variety of heavy wear locations from hotels, restaurants and leisure areas to high quality residential situations.

The successful Finesse and Palace Design qualities will also be displayed. Both carpets have geometrically styled designs suitable for both residential and contract use. Palace Design also incorporates a border and plain range in complementary {colours$^{3.2}$}.

Other {Brintons$^{1.3}$} products suitable for the commercial world, such as Bell Twist, Heather Berber, Broadloop, Bell Trinity and Trident Title will also be on display.

{Brintons$^{1.4}$} will be delighted to solve any carpeting problems as special designs and qualities can be produced for minimum quantities. Their standard range of {colours$^{3.3}$} offers 200 possibilities for the discerning designer to select from.

Arabic translation

تقوم {شركة$^{2.1}$} {برينتونز$^{1.1}$} بتصنيع أرقى أنواع السجاد المنسوج منذ أكثر من ٢٠٠ عام. وهي {شركة$^{2.2}$} خاصة، تتخصص في إنتاج سجاد الاكسمنستر والويلتون الذي تدخله نسبة عالية من الصوف. هذا وتقوم الـ{شركة$^{2.3}$} بتنفيذ جميع خطوات الانتاج بمصانعها، من إعداد الخيوط الى نسجها على أنوال من تصميم وصنع مهندسي الـ{شركة$^{2.4}$}، وتعتبر مصانع {برينتونز$^{1.2}$} أكثر مصانع النسيج تقدما من الناحية الفنية في العالم كله، كما تعتبر {شركة$^{2.5}$} {برينتونز$^{1.3}$} من اكبر شركات النسيج بطاقة انتاجية تزيد عن ١٠٠,٠٠٠ متر مربع في الاسبوع.

أثارت مجموعة «نيو تراديشين أكسمنستر» درجة عالية من الاهتمام منذ أن قامت الـ{شركة$^{2.6}$} بتقديمها حديثاً، وهي من ضمن أنواع السجاد التي سيتم عرضها بالمعرض. تقدم مجموعة «نيو تراديشين» عددا من التصميمات التقليدية الممتعة بحجم مصغر، في {ألوان$^{3.1}$} باهرة كـ{ألوان$^{3.2}$} الجواهر، تزيد الخلفية الداكنة من توهجها. وهي مناسبة للتركيب في العديد من المواقع التجارية ذات الاستعمال الكثيف، مثل الفنادق والمطاعم والاماكن الترفيهية وبعض المواقع السكنية ذات المستوى الرفيع.

كما يتضمن المعرض نماذج من سجاد «فينس» و«بالاس ديزاين» اللذين تم تسويقها بنجاح كبير. ويتسم هذان النوعان من

السجاد بتصميماتها الهندسية ويصلحا للاستخدام في كل من المواقع السكنية والتجارية. هذا وتشتمل مجموعة «بالاس ديزاين» على عدة {ألوان$^{3.3}$} سادة وتصميمات في شكل كنار تتماشى{ألوان}لها$^{3.4}$ مع باقي {ألوان$^{3.5}$} المجموعة.

هذا وسوف تقوم {شركة$^{2.7}$} {برينتونز$^{1.4}$} بعرض عدة أنواع اخرى من السجاد المناسب للاستعمال التجاري، مثل «بل تويست» و«هاذر بربر» و«برود لوب» و«بل ترينتي» و«ترايدنت تايل».

يسر {شركة$^{2.8}$} {برينتونز$^{1.5}$} مساعدتكم على حل اي مشاكل خاصة بالسجاد، حيث يمكنها انتاج تصميمات وانواع خاصة بكميات محدودة. كما ان مجموعة الـ{ألوان$^{3.6}$} المتوفرة لدى الـ{شركة$^{2.9}$} تزيد عن مائتي {لون$^{3.7}$} مما يتيح لاي مصمم فرصة كبيرة للاختيار.

The contrast between pattern and frequency of word repetition are quite different in the English original and the Arabic translation of this text. Taking only the words which appeared in curly brackets in English and their correspondents in Arabic, we get the following:

English original	Arabic translation
Brintons– 4 occurrences (1.1–1.4)	برينتونز – 5 occurrences (1.1–1.5)
	(شركة برينتونز 4 occurrences in combination)
company – 1 occurrence (2.1)	شركات/شركة – 9 occurrences (2.1–2.9)
	(شركة برينتونز 4 occurrences in combination)
colours – 3 occurrences (3.1–3.3)	ألوان / لون – 7 occurrences (3.1–3.7)

What is immediately striking is that the Arabic translation makes much more use of word repetition than does the English original. The word شركة/شركات in particular is used nine times in the Arabic translation, while the word 'company' is only used once in the English original. Some of the occurrences of شركة/شركات are explicable by its repeated occurrence in the phrase شركة برينتونز (four times). This use of 'classifiers' is typical of Arabic; cf. {مدينة} منفلوط 'the city of Manfalut' (ch. 14, 4b), {حي} عين شمس 'the quarter of Ayn Shams (ch. 14, 4c), {يوم} ١٩ يناير المقبل {الأمام} الخميني 'next 19th January' (ch. 15, 5c), 'Imam Khomeini' (ch. 16, 5a), منظمة مجاهدي خلق 'the Mojahed-i Khalq organisation' (ch. 16, 5a). Classifiers are sometimes used as a marker of formal style. An additional function which they have, however, is to identify a word as a proper noun (for which purpose English uses capital letters). For example Arabic readers might not know that the Mojahed-i Khalq is an Iranian political organisation opposed to the current regime, and might otherwise attempt to read the name as a common–noun phrase. Similarly, in the case of شركة برينتونز, the use of شركة alerts the reader to the fact that the foreignism برينتونز is the name of a company. This still leaves five other occurrences of شركات/شركة, however, only one of which corresponds to the English 'company'.

As this English text and its Arabic translation demonstrate, word repetition is a fairly typical feature of Arabic, whereas it is a much less typical feature of English. In Arabic, word repetition is, in some cases at least, an aesthetic feature of the text; the word is repeated because such repetition is felt to be attractive. More than this, however, in many cases Arabic word repetition contributes to the unity of the Arabic text, i.e. to the sense that what is being read is a coherent and well–constructed single entity, rather than simply a series of sentences which have some kind of theme in common.

In English, by contrast, multiple word repetition in close proximity is typically restricted to rather more obviously rhetorical purposes; for example, 'Victory at all costs, victory in spite of all terror, victory however long and hard the road may be; for without victory there is no survival.' (Winston Churchill). In English, in contrast with Arabic, text–building is typically achieved by semantic repetition, that is by repetition of synonyms or near–synonyms, rather than by word repetition.

The following examples illustrate word repetition in Arabic, not so much as a text–building device, but as something which is acceptable in many contexts where such repetition is not acceptable in English (specific comments are included after each example):

.. يمكن القول ان يوم 23 يوليو، وهو يوم ذكرى ثورة يوليو (تموز) يمر مثله مثل أي يوم عادي آخر في حياة المصريين، لكن يظل، بالطبع، يوم عطلة رسمية.

'It is reasonable [lit: 'possible'] to say that 23rd July, which is the anniversary of the July revolution, will pass like any normal day in the life of the average Egyptian [lit: 'the life of the Egyptians'], although it will of course remain an official holiday.' (ch. 13, 5c)

Here, the word يوم occurs four times in the original Arabic, while the word 'day' occurs only once in the English translation (or twice if the 'day' element in 'holiday' is included). Similarly the word مثل occurs twice in the Arabic, while the word 'like' occurs only once in the English translation.

ونحن نعلم أن الرواة يتحدثون بأسماء طائفة من الشعراء زعموا انهم عاشوا قبل امرئ القيس وقالوا شعرا ، ولكنهم لا يروون لهؤلاء الشعراء إلا البيت أو البيتين أو الأبيات .

'We know that the reciters mention the names of a group of poets whom they claim to have lived before Imru' al-Qays and to have recited poetry, but they can only recount one or two verses.' (ch. 17, 4c)

Here the Arabic repeats بيت/أبيات three times, while the English translation reduces this to a single mention 'verses'.

تعد ظاهرة التواجد بين اللغات في كتاب «الجامع» ظاهرة طبيعية

'The appeal to different languages in the *Compendium* is considered quite normal' (ch. 19, 11)

Here the Arabic repeats ظاهرة, but the English translation avoids a corresponding repetition.

(b) *Root repetition*

Just as word repetition involves repetition of a word in close proximity, so root repetition of a particular Arabic root in close proximity. A simple example of root repetition in Arabic is سأل سؤالاً 'He asked a question', where the root س أ ل occurs twice, once in the third person masculine singular of the first form perfect verb سأل, and once as the object noun سؤالاً.

i *System–intrinsic repetition*

Like word repetition, root repetition can to some extent be regarded as being linguistically intrinsic, i.e. built into the linguistic system of Arabic. In Arabic, it is normal to say سأل سؤالاً (although the more formal طرح سؤالاً is, for example, also available). In English, while forms such as 'live a good life' and 'die a horrible death' exist, they are not the norm. Much more common are non–repetitive forms such as 'ask a question' ('question a question' also exists, but has a specific, and relatively unusual meaning). Thus, Arabic has كتب كتاباً, but English has 'write a book', Arabic has أكل الأكل, but English has 'eat the food'.

Examples from this book where Arabic root repetition can be regarded as reflecting the linguistic system are the following:

.. والتعاون سويا لمواجهة العدو المشترك، والقوى الخارجية التي تسانده وتعمل على {بذر} {بذور} الفرقة بين المسلمين.

'... and cooperation to face the common enemy and the external forces which support it and work to sow the seeds of dissension among the Muslims.' (ch. 16, 5c)

لعل أقدم الشعراء الذين {يروى} لهم شعر كثير ويتحدث {الرواة} عنهم بأخبار كثيرة فيها تطويل وتفضيل هو امرؤ القيس.

'Perhaps the most ancient poet whose poetry is frequently recited and about whom tales are recounted at length and in detail by the reciters is Imru' al-Qays.' (ch. 17, 4c)

فنحن نعلم أن {وفدا} من كندة {وفد} على النبيّ وعلى رأسـه الأشعث بن قيس .

'We know that a delegation from Kinda headed by al-Ash'ath ibn Qays visited the Prophet.' (ch. 17, 4c)

ii *Absolute accusative*

One of the most common occurrences of root repetition is in the absolute accusative (in Arabic المفعول المُطْلَق). At its simplest, this involves using the verbal noun in the accusative following the verb of the same root. An example is ضَرَبَتـه ضَرْبًا, literally 'she hit him [a] hitting'. This simple form of the absolute accusative is relatively rare, and is used either for adornment or to give a sense that what was done was done with force, vigour, etc. So, in a given context ضَرَبَتـه ضَرْبًا might be translated as 'she hit him hard'.

Absolute accusatives most commonly occur in combination with an adjective. Examples are:

قـال جـابر رزق المتـحـدث الرسـمـي لجمـاعـة الاخـوان المسلمـين ان الاضطرابات التي شـملت مـدن الصـعـيـد الثـلاث {تدلّ دلالة} قـاطعـة على ان هناك أصـابـع خـفـيـة ومـشـبـوهة تريد اثارة الـفـتـنـة بـين عنصري الامة ، المسلمين والاقباط ..

'... Jabir Rizq, the official spokesman of the Society of the Muslim Brothers said that the disturbances which involved the three cities of Upper Egypt demonstrate with certainty that there are suspicious hidden hands [lit: 'hidden fingers'] which want to stir up dissension between the two elements of the nation, the Muslims and the Copts ...' (ch. 14, 4d)

ولقد {تطورت} ظاهرة التطرف الديني {تطوراً} سريعاً ..

'The phenomenon of religious extremism has developed quickly ...' (ch. 14, 5b)

.. وأن درجة التوتر العام في المجتمع قد {زادت زيادة} كبيرة ..

' ... and that the degree of tension in society has increased greatly ...' (ch. 14, 5b)

Grammatically the absolute accusative is adverbial. This is suggested in these cases by the English translations of تدلّ دلالة قـاطعـة 'demonstrate {with certainty}', زادت زيادة كبـيـرة .. 'has developed {quickly}', and .. تطورت ... تطوراً سـريعاً 'has increased {greatly}'. Here 'quickly' and 'greatly' are adverbs, while 'with certainty' could be replaced with an adverb such as 'indisputably'.

The commonness of the cognate accusative with adjective correlates with the fact that Arabic does not have many simple adverbs. It is possible to add the indefinite

accusative suffix to a number of adjectives to make adverbs; for example, سـريعا
'quickly', 'fast' from سـريـع 'quick', 'fast', كثيـراً 'often', 'frequently', 'much'
('muchly') from كثير 'much'. It is similarly possible to make adverbs by adding
the indefinite accusative suffix to adjectives having the *nisba*–suffix ـي, for
example, حكـومـيـاً 'governmentally' from حكـومـي 'governmental', عربيـاً 'on the
part of the Arabs' ('Arably') from عَـربي 'Arabic', 'Arab'.   There are also a
number of nouns from which adverbs are made directly by adding the indefinite
accusative ending; for example مَـثَلاً 'for example' from مَـثَل 'example', رأسـاً
'directly', 'immediate', from رأس 'head'.

It is also possible to make adverbials in Arabic from a preposition and a noun
(i.e. prepositional phrases are adverbials, as in English). For example بِسُرْعَـة
'quickly', 'fast' from سـرعـة 'speed', بِكَثْرة 'much' from كثرة 'abundance'.

The use of the absolute accusative constitutes a third, and fairly flexible, way in
which adverbials can be produced.

In adverbial accusatives, it is not necessary for the 'verbal form' which precedes
the verbal noun to be a verb. It may an active participle, a passive participle, or
itself a verbal noun, or some other form. In the following example the preceding
'verbal form' in question is itself a verbal noun (مـعـرفة) (and the example therefore
exhibits not only root repetition but also a particular instance of word repetition):

يقـوم الـوعي القـومـي أولاً علـى {مـعـرفـة} مـاضي الأمـة {مـعـرفـة}
صحيـحـة ..

'National consciousness is based on knowing the past of the nation
properly ...' (ch. 13, 4c)

The absolute accusative may itself appear in slightly different forms. In the
following the absolute noun الاخـتـلاف forms part of the absolute accusative element
of the sentence, but appears in the genitive after the accusative بـعض:

.. وهم {يخـتـلفـون} بـعضَ {الاخـتـلافِ} في نـسبـها وتفسيـر اسـمـها وفي
أخبار سـادتها .

' ... they do not agree, however, over its lineage, the interpretation of
its name, and the stories of its chiefs.' (ch. 17, 4c)

In the following example, the adverbial accusative حرص is followed by a pronoun
suffix:

..{يـحـرص} علـى سـلامـة الامـة {حرصَه} علـى حيـاته ..

'... having the same regard for the well–being of the nation as for his
own life ...' [Lit: 'aspiring for the well–being of the nation his
aspiring/aspiration for his life ...'] (ch. 16, 4c)

iii *Other types of root repetition*

While the absolute accusative is the most common use of root repetition in Arabic, it is by no means the only use. As the example كتب كتابا discussed above shows, it is possible to have accusatives other than absolute accusatives involved in root repetition. In the case of كتب كتابا of course كتابا is an object. It is also possible for other parts of speech to be involved in root repetition. The following is an example of subject–verb root repetition.

.. إنهم آلات تتحرك في جنون وسرعة وهياج لا {يقرّ} له {قرارٌ} .

'They are machines moving in madness, speed and turmoil, never experiencing repose.' (ch. 14, 11ai)

The following example involves verb–prepositional phrase repetition:

.. الذين نشأوا في ظل الإسلام و{ربوا} بـ{تربيتـ}ـه ..

'... who grew up in the shadow of Islam and were educated according to its teachings ...' (ch. 12, 5b)

The following are various other examples of root repetition involving a variety of parts of speech.

.. {طيلة} سنوات {طويلة} ..

'... throughout long years ...' (ch. 13, 5a)

.. بما {وقرَ} في نفوس الكافّة لهم من {الوقار} والتجلّة ..

'.. through the dignity and esteem with which they are standardly regarded by everyone.' (ch. 13, 6a)

وهو الفرق نفسه بين {الجامعة} العربية التي {تجمع} العجز الى العجز، والاستثمار والاحقاد والمصالح الخاصة بعضها الى بعض، وبين الوحدة العربية التي {تخلق} العرب {خلقاً} جديدا.

'This is exactly the difference between the League of Arab States, on the one hand, which joins impotence to impotence, and joins together investment, hatreds, and personal interests, and Arab unity which creates the Arabs anew.' (ch. 13, 11a)

.. بابعاد {اخطر المخاطر} التي تهدد الحياة الديمقراطية في العالم النامي ..

'... by banishing the gravest dangers which threaten democratic life in the developing world ..' (ch. 15, 11)

.. لقيادة هذا الشعب الى مدارج {الامن والامان} ..

'... to lead the people to the paths of security and safety ...' (ch. 16, 4c)

.. وكان جزءاً لا يتجزّاً منها ..

'... it was an inseparable part of it ...' (ch. 19, 5b)

Of these examples the last two at least – جزء لا يتجزأ and الأمن والأمان – can be regarded as stock phrases.

One major use of root repetition is for aesthetic effect. Such repetition makes the text sound attractive, and therefore enhances the message. There seems to be a greater tendency to use root repetition in texts which have a 'poetic' form. An obvious example is poetry itself, but also many types of prose writing fall within this category. Texts in which the author is trying to persuade also tend to make use of root repetition, the aesthetic power of the form being used to augment the logic of the argument itself. Root repetition is likely to be less prominent in texts where the precise detail of the message is important – for instance in scientific writing.

(c) *Pattern repetition*

Pattern repetition involves repetition of the grammatical pattern. A simple example is the following:

.. ولن يكون هناك {خَرَاب} ولا {دَمَار} ..

'... there will not be ruin or destruction ...' (ch. 13, 11b)

Here both خَرَاب and دَمَار are on the grammatical pattern فَعَال.

Since the pattern system of Arabic operates with regard to all the major grammatical categories – which can for current purposes be defined as noun, adjective and verb – it is possible to find pattern repetition for all these categories. Thus for nouns:

..وهو الذي يجنبنا {الانهيـارات} و{الانفـجـارات} العنيـفـة على النحو الذي اجتاح الدول الشيوعية الاوربية.

'... and it is this which allows us to avoid the collapses and explosions of the type which swept away the European communist states.' (ch. 14, 4b)

كافة {اشكال} و{الوان} المعاناة ..

'... all types and forms of suffering ...' (ch. 15, 11)

لقد تعرض النشاط التجاري بين الهند والخليج الى {صعود} و{هبوط}، و{امتداد} و{انحسار}..

'Commercial activity between India and the Gulf has been subject to rise and fall, ebb and flow ...' (ch. 18, 5b)

The following are examples of pattern repetition with adjectives:

'... tired and exhausted?' (ch. 19, 5c)   .. {متعب} و{مرهق}؟

                                            .. {كبار} إخوته و{صغارهم} ..
'... both his elder and his younger brothers and sisters ...' (ch. 19, 5d)

The following are examples of pattern repetition with verbs:

        .. من اجل بناء وطنهم الذي {قاسى} الكثير و{عانى} الامرين ..
'... in order to build their country which has suffered much and
endured terrible hardship [عانى الأمرين = 'to suffer terribly', 'endure
terrible hardship' (idiom)]' (ch. 13, 5a)

            .. وأشكر كل من {عاون} و{شارك} فى عمليات الانقاذ .
'... and I thank all those who helped and participated in the rescue
operation.' (ch. 16, 11)

As with root repetition, pattern repetition may be regarded as to some extent
grounded in the linguistic stystem of Arabic. Thus, to take the example {كبار} ..
إخوته و{صغار}هم .. discussed above, فعال is a standard plural pattern in Arabic
(particularly for nouns or adjectives having the singular patter فعيل). It is therefore
not surprising that in cases where a writer uses two plural adjectives together
(either for rhetorical purposes, or simply to express what he or she intends to say),
these two plural adjectives should sometimes display the same pattern.

As also with root repetition, pattern repetition is used partly for 'poetic' effect,
and can be expected to occur most frequently in texts of either an aesthetic or
persuasive intention.

Given the 'poetic' nature of pattern repetition and nature of the Arabic root
system, it is relatively common to find examples of pattern repetition which also
involve rhyme. For example:

            .. مسيرة شعب واحد في {السراء} و{الضراء} ..
'... the fate of the people in good times and bad ...' (ch. 16, 4c)

لعل أقدم الشعراء الذين يروى لهم شعر كثير ويتحدث الرواة
عنهم بأخبار كثيرة فيها {تطويل} و{تفضيل} هو امرؤ القيس.
'Perhaps the most ancient poet whose poetry is frequently recited and
about whom tales are recounted at length and in detail by the reciters is
Imru' al-Qays.' (ch. 17, 4c)

وانتشر الإسلام في ربوع هذا العالم الجديد، فكان الروح الهادية
لها كما كانت العربية سبيل {التفكير} و{التعبير} فيه وطريق
التعلم والتعليم.

'Islam spread in the lands of this new world, and was the guiding spirit of it, just as the Arabic language was the means of thinking and expressing in it and the means of teaching and learning.' (ch. 20, 4b)

Of these examples, the first السراء والضراء is a stock phrase. The final example is interesting not only because of the rhyming doublet involving pattern repetition التفكير والتعبير, but also because of the subsequent root repetition of التعلم والتعليم, yielding a second near–rhyme.

Examples of pattern repetition are easy to identify in Arabic because of the well–defined nature of what a pattern is in terms of the traditional grammar of Arabic. There are also, however, numerous cases which do not qualify as pattern repetition on formal grounds since the patterns in question are not the same, but which are intuitively similar to pattern repetition. Examples are:

وغاية مريد الرّياسة أن يكون كـ{فرعون} ، وجامع المال أن يكون
كـ{قارون} ..

'The goal of the man who desires leadership is to be like Pharaoh, and of the man who amasses wealth to be like Korah.' (ch. 14, 6a)

.. لو شكوت من الصداع امام {الاصدقاء} او {الزملاء} ، لسارع
بعضهم الى مد يده الى جيبه ..

'... if you complain of a headache in front of friends or colleagues, one of them will hurry to put his hand into his pocket ...' (ch. 19, 5c)

(d) *Suffix repetition*

It is worth recognising at least one more form of repetition within the word in Arabic – the repetition of suffixes. The following are examples of repetition involving pronoun suffixes:

شاءت ارادة الله ان يحرم مصر من قائد مسيرتـ{ها} . ورب
اسرتـ{ها}، وصانع نهضتـ{ها} ، في وقت هي احوج ما تكون فيه
لجهود{ه} ، وبصيرتـ{ه} والهامـ{ه} وزعامتـ{ه} .

'God chose to deprive Egypt of its leader, the head of its family, and the creator of its renaissance, at a time in which it was in the greatest need of his efforts, his insight, his inspiration, and his leadership.' (ch. 16, 4b)

ولكن مَنْ كندة ؟ لا يختلف الرواة في أنهم قبيلة من قحطان ، وهم
يختلفون بعض الاختلاف في نسبِ{ـها} وتفسير اسمِ{ـها} وفي
أخبار سادتِ{ـها} .

'But who were the Kinda? The reciters are agreed that it is a tribe of
Qahtan; they do not agree, however, over its lineage, the interpretation
of its name, and the tales of its chiefs.' (ch. 17, 4c)

.. وكثُر أنصارُ{هم} وإخوانُ{ـهم} ومعارفُ{ـهم} ..

'... They acquired many helpers, friends and acquaintances ...' (ch. 19,
6a)

In the last two examples here, suffix repetition is combined with some other form
of repetition. In the example نسبِ{ـها} وتفسير اسمِ{ـها} وفي أخبار سادتِ{ـها}
there is repetition of the letter س (alliteration), and in the final example أنصارُ{هم}
وإخوانُ{ـهم} ومعارفُ{ـهم} there is use of patterns, which although different,
sound similar to one another.

Other forms of suffix repetition are also fairly common. The following is an
example of repetition of the plural suffix اتَ (with additional repetition of sounds
in the main body of the words involved):

فقد عانى الشعب الايراني كثيرا من المغامر{ات} والصراعـ{ات}
والانقسامـ{ات} ..

'The Iranian people has suffered greatly from adventures, conflicts and
divisions ...' (ch. 16, 5c)

It would, of course, be possible to list other types of repetition of parts of words,
such as repetition of prefixes (initial elements of words) such as the م which occurs
at the start of مُحيط, مِفْتاح, مَكْتَب, مَدْرَسَة, etc. These do not, however, seem to
play such an important role in Arabic as root repetition, pattern repetition and suffix
repetition.

As with the other forms of morphological repetition discussed above – root
repetition and pattern repetition – suffix repetition typical has a 'poetic' function,
and can be expected to occur particularly not only in poetry and poetic prose, but
also in persuasive texts.

(e) *Multiple morphological repetition: pattern repetition plus suffix repetition*
By far the most common and important form of multiple morphological repetition is
the combination of pattern repetition with suffix repetition. Two examples (the first
of which was discussed earlier under pattern repetition) are the following:

..وهو الذي يجنبنا {الانهيارات} و{الانفجارات} العنيفة على النحو الذي اجتاح الدول الشيوعية الاوربية.

'... and it is this which allows us to avoid the collapses and explosions of the type which swept away the European communist states.' (ch. 14, 4b)

فقد كان واسعًا دون حدود يُسمَح للمرء أن يتنقل فيه {سائحاً} أو {تاجرًا} أو {عالًما} أو {حاجًّا}.

'It [This society] was widespread, having no borders, and allowing people to move about in it as travellers, traders, scholars or pilgrims.' (ch. 20, 4b)

8. Aural Arabic texts 1

Listen to the following text from حصاد الشهر, no. 30, side 1, item 1, البنوك الإسلامية وكيف تعمل, then complete exercises i. – iii. below.

i Answer the following questions in English.

1. What is meant by usury?
2. What does the Qur'an forbid?
3. How does interest differ from usury?
4. What are we told about Sheikh Ibrahim al-Tayyib al-Rayyih?
5. What does he say about the purpose of an Islamic Bank in Europe?

ii Transcribe the text in Arabic from the beginning until على وفق دينهم وشريعتهم.

iii Listen to the remainder of this text, and answer the questions below in Arabic. The questions relate to the remainder of this text from الفرق بين البنوك الإسلامية والبنوك التقليدية.

١ – حسب قول المذيعة ما هو الفرق بين البنوك الإسلامية والبنوك التقليدية؟

٢ – حسب قول الشيخ بماذا تعمل البنوك الغربية؟

٣ – هل الفائدة ربح أم ربا؟

٤ – هل تقدم البنوك الإسلامية الخدمات المصرفية العادية؟

٥ – هل الخدمات التي تقدمها البنوك الغربية محرّمة؟

٦ – لا يأخذ البنك الإسلامي الفائدة. فماذا يأخذ بدلها؟

٧ – في حالة الشراكة أو المشاركة يُعتبر المال والعمل شركة بين من ومن؟

٨ – في المشاركة هل تتعلق الأرباح على رأس المال أم لا؟

٩ – في المشاركة متى يتمّ الاتفاق بين الطرفين على تقسيم الربح؟

١٠ –كيف يربح البنك في حالة المشاركة؟

١١ –على ماذا يقوم النوع الثاني من المشاركة؟

١٢ –في هذه الحالة من يشتري الماكينة في البداية؟

١٣ –يُقسم ثلث الربح للبنك وثلثه للعميل. فماذا يحصل بثلث الثالث؟

١٤ –ماذا يحصل بعد أن يدفع العميل مبلغ الماكينة؟

١٥ –ما رأي المذيعة بالقرض من أجل شراء بيت؟

١٦ –ما هو البديل الإسلامي للاقتراض من شراء بيت؟

١٧ –بين من يُقسم إيجار البيت في هذه الحالة؟

١٨ –هل نصيب العميل عادة أكثر من نصيب البنك أم لا؟

١٩ –في النظام الغربي ما هو ضمان البنك في حالة شراء بيت؟

9. Aural Arabic texts 2

Listen to the following text from الشهر حصاد no. 23, side 2, item 1, هي ما
الكويت؟ في المناخ سوق ازمة ذيول اسباب, then complete exercises i. and ii.
below.

i   Produce a complete transcription of the text. In your transcription write dates in
figures, not words.

ii   Paraphrase the following terms in Arabic in the same sense they have in the
text. Some terms will require more explanation than others. The terms are given
here in their order of occurrence in the text:

١ – سوق المناخ

٢ – المعروض

٣ – انتعش

٤ – اندلاع الحرب

٥ – مستثمرون

٦ – صوب

٧ – ولم تخضع هذه السوق

٨ – شيكات آجلة

٩ – اصبح جليا

١٠ –موعد الاستحقاق

١١ -بغض النظر عن

١٢ -تعويض

١٣ -ممتلكات سائلة

10. Written English texts

(a) Using constructions and vocabulary encountered in the Arabic texts above, translate the following text from the *OAPEC Monthly Bulletin*, Feb. 1990, p. 14, into idiomatic Arabic.

Natural gas reserves

The petroleum map of Egypt shows that most of the present wells are concentrated in the Gulf of Suez basin, work on which dates back more than a hundred years. No discoveries were made in other areas until the mid–sixties when the first oil field in Egypt's Western Desert was discovered (the Alamein field, 1966). This was followed by discoveries in other areas, such as the Abu Madi field in the Great Nile Delta and, later, the offshore Abu Qir field in the Mediterranean Sea. As exploration work continued, a number of new oil fields were added, but the State did not attach sufficient importance to the gas released, and most of the associated gas was flared. The many reasons for this policy included the availability of other, relatively cheap energy sources that met the needs of industry.

(b) Using constructions and vocabulary encountered in the Arabic texts above, translate the following text from *Islam and Economic Development*, p. 124, into idiomatic Arabic.

One objection to interest is simply that it is a reward gained without productive effort. Western economists regard it as a reward for waiting, or postponing consumption. Goods consumed in the future are worth less today, and their value has to be discounted. This process of discounting introduces the interest element. For Muslims, as time is not money these western concepts cannot apply. Interest, however, is also viewed as objectionable because of its adverse redistributive effects. It makes the more productive indebted to the less productive, and can also result in the poor being indebted to the rich. Where a debtor gets into difficulty with repayments, the Qur'an urges leniency with debt rescheduling: 'If your debtor be in straights, grant him a delay until he can discharge his debt; but if you can waive the sum as alms it will be better for you if you but knew it.'[1]

Notes

1. وَإِنْ كَانَ ذُو عُسْرَةٍ فَنَظِرَةٌ إِلَـــى مَيْسَرَةٍ وَأَنْ تَصَدَّقُوا خَيْرٌ لَكُمْ إِنْ كُنْتُمْ تَعْلَمُون

سورة البقرة, v. 280.

11. Précis

Read the following text from ضمان الاستثمار vol. II, no. 5, Feb. 1983, then produce a précis in Arabic.

مناخ الاستثمار في الجمهورية العربية السورية

مقدمة:

تقع الجمهورية العربية السورية على الساحل الشرقي للبحر الابيض المتوسط، حيث يحدها من الشمال تركيا، ومن الشرق العراق، ومن الجنوب الاردن وفلسطين، ومن الغرب لبنان والبحر المتوسط. ويشكل هذا الموقع اهمية من الوجهة الاقتصادية فسوريا تربط الوطن العربي – اقطار الجزيرة العربية وما وراء سوريا كالاردن والعراق – باوربا عبر تركيا كما تربطها بالاضافة لايران بالبحر الابيض المتوسط والاقطار المطلة عليه.

ويكسب هذا الموقع البلاد اهمية كمركز مواصلات جوية وبرية هامة. وكمعبر لتجارة الترانزيت، ويتمتع الساحل السوري الغربي المطل على البحر الابيض المتوسط بامكانات سياحية هائلة وتعتبر امتدادا للساحل والجبال اللبنانية بالاضافة الى توفر الاثار والمدن التاريخية القديمة كمدينة اوغاريت قرب اللاذقية وفي الداخل تدمر ومدينتي ماري وايبلا. تبلغ المساحة العامة لاراضي البلاد ٩٧١ ، ٥١٧ ، ١٨ هكتارا منها حوالي ٨ مليون هكتار اراضي زراعية تبلغ نسبة المستغل منها ٦٣ ، ٣٪، وتغطي الجبال والصحاري بقية المساحة. اما السكان، فقد بلغ عددهم عام ١٩٨١ نحو ٩ ، ٣ مليون نسمة، ويبلغ معدل نموهم السنوي حوالي ٦ ، ٣٪.

يتميز الاقتصاد السوري بتعدد مصادره المولدة للدخل بعد ان كان اقتصادا زراعيا في بداية الخمسينات وكانت الصادرات الزراعية تشكل العنصر الاساسي في جملة الصادرات السورية. الا

ان السياسة الاقتصادية ركزت ومنذ بداية الاتجاه نحو التخطيط الشامل في بداية الستينات، على الاهتمام بالتصنيع واحلال الواردات واحداث تنمية صناعية في سوريا. وقد ادت هذه السياسة الى بروز قطاع الصناعة وتفوقه على القطاعات الاقتصادية الاخرى من حيث مساهمته في الناتج القومي الاجمالي، ساعد على ذلك الاستكشافات النفطية وتصديرها بكميات تجارية تبلغ في المتوسط حوالي ٩ مليون طن سنويا وزيادة كميات الفوسفات المستخرج وتطور قطاع الصناعات التحويلية.

الاطار القانوني للاستثمار:

لقد اصبح معلوما، انه بالاضافة الى المصادر الذاتية التي تشكل العنصر الرئيسي، فان عملية التنمية الاقتصادية والاجتماعية تستند الى حد كبير على تدفق الاستثمارات واستيعابها في المجالات الانتاجية المولدة للقيمة المضافة والمؤدية الى تزايد نمو الناتج القومي. وقد ادركت الحكومة السورية اهمية الدور الذي يمكن للاستثمارات الوافدة القيام به، واعطت اولوية لاستثمارات المغتربين السوريين ورعايا الدول العربية، ومنحت هذه الاستثمارات التسهيلات والمزايا والضمانات.

- ويأتي المرسوم التشريعي رقم ٣٤٨ لعام ١٩٦٩ في مقدمة التشريعات المنظمة لاستثمار رؤوس اموال السوريين المغتربين والعرب. وينص المرسوم على السماح باعادة تحويل صافي قيمة الاستثمار بانقضاء خمس سنوات على ابتداء تنفيذه، اضافة الى تحويل ٥٠٪ من ربح الاستثمار الصافي.

- وفي مجال الصناعة، فقد صدر المرسوم التشريعي رقم ١٠٣ لعام ١٩٥٢ ليمنح المؤسسات الصناعية بعض الامتيازات والاعفاءات، والقانون رقم ٢١ لعام ١٩٥٨ بشأن تنظيم

الصناعـة وتشجيعهـا، كمـا صدرت بتـاريـخ ٥/١١/١٩٧٦ تعليمـات وزارة الصناعـة المتعلقـة بتسهيل الترخيص الصناعي.

– وفي مجال الزراعة، صدر قرار وزير الزراعة رقم ٥٢/ت لعام ١٩٧٩ والقرار رقم ٤٥/ت لعـام ١٩٨٢ المتعلقين بمنح تراخيص اقامة مزارع الابقار والدواجن على التوالي.

– وفي مجال السياحة، صدر في عام ١٩٦١ المرسوم التشريعي رقم ١٩٨ بخصوص المؤسسات الفندقية والمحلات العامة.

– امـا بالنسبـة للمناطق والاسواق الحرة، فقد صدر عـام ١٩٧٢ المرسوم رقم ٨٤ لتنظيم الاستثمار في هذه المناطق.

حوافز الاستثمار:

١– الاعفاء من ضريبة الدخل:

١–١ في مـجال الصناعـة – الاعفـاء من ضريبـة الدخل مع ارباح المؤسسات الصناعيـة لمدة ثلاث سنوات اعتبارا من تاريخ البدء بالاستثمار. امـا المبالغ الاحتياطيـة للتوسع بما لا يتجاوز ١٠٪ من الارباح السنوية فتعفى من الضريبة.

٢–١ في مجال الزراعة – الاعفاء من ضريبة الدخل على ارباح الاستثمارات الزراعية والحيوانية.

٣–١ في المجال المصرفي – اعفاء شهادات الاستثمار وفوائدها من جميع الضرائب والرسوم، واعفاء الودائع المصرفية من رسوم الطوابع.

٤–١ وفي مجال السياحة – الانهاء من الضرائب والرسوم لمدة سبع سنوات للاستثمار السياحيـة من المستوى الدولي، ولمدة خمس سنوات للمشاريع السياحـة من الدرجتين الممتازة والاولى واي مشروع يعطي الصفة السياحية.

٢– الاعفاء من الرسوم الجمركية:

١–٢ في مجال الصناعـة – تعفى من الرسوم الجمركية كافة

الالات والادوات والاجهزة ومواد البناء المستوردة لحاجة المشاريع الصناعية، وتحدد برسوم الصناعات والمستوردات ومقدارها التي تستفيد من هذا الاعفاء. اما بالنسبة للصناعة غير المشمولة باحكام قانون تشجيع الاستثمار، فان الضريبة تخفض الى معدل ١٪.

٢-٢ في مجال الزراعة – تعفى الحيوانات الحية وتخفض الرسوم مع التجهيزات الزراعية والمبيدات الحشرية.

٢-٣ وفي مجال السياحة – تعفى المؤسسات السياحية المشتركة (عام – خاص) من جميع الرسوم الجمركية على السيارات السياحية المستوردة. اما المؤسسات الخاصة فتعفى من نصف الرسوم.

٣- التسهيلات النقدية والتسهيلات الاخرى:

٣-١ اضافة الى التسهيلات التي يمنحها المرسوم التشريعي ٣٤٨ المذكورة آنفا، فقد نص المرسوم التشريعي رقم ٧٧٩ لعام ١٩٧٩ على السماح للمصارف باداء فائدة عن الودائع بالعملات الاجنبية، كما ينص القرار رقم ١٧٢ الصادر عن وزارة الاقتصاد على السماح للمقيمين في القطر بادخال العملات الاجنبية واخراجها دون اية قيود.

٣-٢ السماح للمواطنين العرب باكتساب حقوق عينية وتملك العقارات.

٣-٣ ضمان حرية التنقل والاقامة لموظفي المشاريع الممولة باستثمارات خارجية.

٣-٤ توحيد جهات اتصال المستثمرين بمكتب شؤون الاستثمار العربي والاجنبي في هيئة تخطيط الدولة الذي يصدر الموافقة على طلبات الاستثمار، يقدم بعدها المستثمر طلب الترخيص للوزارة المعنية.

12. Oral

اقتصاد الوطن العربي

(a) One or two students to present an account of الاقتصاد والبنوك في الشرق الاوسط.

(b) The presenter(s) then ask(s) the other students questions about الاقتصاد والبنوك في الشرق الاوسط. These questions should include some which require factual answers and others which require subjective or speculative answers. For example:

١ – ما هي المفاهيم المهمة في الاقتصاد؟

٢ – ماذا تعرف/ين عن انظمة الاقتصاد في الشرق الاوسط؟

٣ – كيف تختلف انظمة الاقتصاد في الشرق الاوسط عن نظيرتها في الغرب؟

٤ – ماذا تعني كلمة «الربح»؟

٥ – ماذا تعني كلمة «الربا»؟

٦ – هل زرت بنكا في الشرق الاوسط؟

٧ – ماذا فعلت في هذا البنك؟

٨ – هل رأيت فرقا بين هذا البنك والبنك في بلادك؟

13. Essay

Write an essay in Arabic of 200 words on the title الإسلام والاقتصاد. In your writing address some of the following issues.

١ – ماذا يحدث في البنوك الغربية غير الاسلامية ؟

٢ – ماذا حرّم الاسلام ولماذا حرّمه ؟

٣ – ما هو الفرق بين الربح والربا؟

٤ – ماذا تعني كلمة «المشاركة» وكيف تجري المشاركة في البنوك الاسلامية اليوم؟

٥ – كيف يقترض المسلم من البنك الاسلامي مثلا إذا اراد شراء بيتا للايجار؟

19
Medicine

1. Basic background material

(a) *Three types of medicine*

It is possible to distinguish two major types of medicine in the pre–modern Islamic world. The first of these is folk–medicine. This existed not only amongst pre–Islamic Arabs, but also amongst the people they conquered. Folk–medicine involved not only the use of herbs and other natural products to treat disease, but also magical cures rooted in local folklore, or in aspects of popular Islam.

In addition to folk–medicine, there was also a tradition of 'scholarly' medicine, which grew up in the Islamic world. This was based originally on traditions of previous civilisations particularly the Greek tradition, although it also included Indian, Syrian and Persian elements. From c. 830 AD onwards under the patronage of the Abbasid Caliphs, Greek medical works were translated into Arabic often via intermediate Syriac translations.

Within a hundred years of the first translations, there was large–scale teaching and learning of 'scientific' medicine in the Islamic world. Centres of medical teaching developed in Iraq, which benefited from the relative proximity of the Greek–based Sassanian medical school of Jundishapur

It is also worth mentioning a third form – or source – of medicine in the Islamic world. This is what is known as 'Prophetic Medicine' الطب النبـوي, which derives from a body of Prophetic Hadith, to be found in various places, including the authoritative Hadith collection of al-Bukhari, where it occupies two chapters. These sayings of the Prophet cover various topics to do with illness, such as visiting the sick and giving consolation to the sick, the evil eye, talismans, amulets, and protective prayers. A small number of the Hadith deal directly with medicine and surgery, and the principal methods of treatment are listed as honey, cupping and cauterisation (the latter to be used sparingly).

(b) *Medicine in the modern Middle East*

In the modern Middle East the 'scholarly' medicine of the Middle Ages has been entirely supplanted by modern 'western' medicine – which is in any case a development of medieval 'scholarly' medicine. Modern medical treatment varies from the ultra–modern, particularly in the wealthy oil–states of the Peninsula, to the basic, and in some cases unreliable, in the poorer countries of the region.

Particularly for poor people in the poorer Arab countries, even basic modern health care is expensive, and because of this and a mistrust in the efficacy of what are sometimes poorly–delivered modern remedies, many people still resort to traditional cures and traditional curers. Ailments which in the west would typically be analysed as psychological are often regarded by more traditional people as spiritual in origin; and cures will often by sought from 'spiritual' figures, whether these figures are officially recognised in Islam, or have a more dubious status vis-à -vis religious orthodoxy.

2. Additional reading
(a) E.G. Browne, *Arabian Medicine*, (Cambridge University Press, 1921).
(b) M.J.L. Young, J.D. Latham and R.B. Serjeant (eds.), *The Cambridge History of Arabic Literature*, vol. III, *Religion, Learning and Science in the Abbasid Period*, (Cambridge University Press, 1990), pp. 342–63.
(c) M.S. Khan, *Islamic Medicine*, (London: Routledge and Kegan Paul, 1986).

3. Key vocabulary
Taking the texts in this chapter as a starting point, draw up lists of vocabulary in the following fields:
(a) Herbs, plants, etc.
(b) Islamic medical terms.
(c) Modern medical terms.

4. Written Arabic texts 1
(a) Read the following text by التداوي بالأعشاب from أمين رويحة (Beirut: دار القلم, 1983), pp. 15–16, then complete exercises i. and ii. which follow.

تاريخ التطبيب بالاعشاب قديم جدا يرجع الى العصور الاولى من التاريخ. وبعض المحفوظات من اوراق البردي وقبور الفراعنة، دلّت على ان الكهنة في ذلك الوقت، كان عندهم معلومات كثيرة بأسرار الاعشاب والتداوي بها، حتى ان البعض من هذه الاعشاب الشافية وُجد بين ما احتوته قبور الفراعنة من تحف وآثار.

كذلك هنالك ما يثبت ان قدماء الهنود قد مارسوا، كقدماء المصريين هذه المهنة ايضا، وحذقوا بها، ومنهم «سرسروتا Susrata».
ثم جاء بعد ذلك قدماء حكماء اليونان ووضعوا المؤلفات عن التداوي

بالاعشاب في القرنين الرابع والخامس قبل الميلاد، واشهرهم في هذا المضمار «هيبوقراط»[1] و«تيوفراستوس»[2] و«ديسكوريدس»[3] و«كالينوس»[4].

وظلت مؤلفات هؤلاء عن التداوي بالاعشاب المصدر الاساسي لهذا العلم، حتى جاء بعدها من الاطباء العرب من اخذ العلم عنهم، وزاد عليه وتوسع فيه بتجارب جديدة وفي مقدمتهم «ابن سينا»[5] والرازي»[6].

وفي القرن الثاني عشر احتكر الرهبان في اوروبا مهنة التداوي بالاعشاب وزراعتها واشهرهم الراهبة «القديسة هيلديكارد»، ومؤلفها الذي سمته «الفيزياء Physika» كتاب مشهور.

Notes
1. Hippocrates (?460–?377 BC), commonly regarded as the father of medicine.
2. Theophrastus (?372–?287 BC); Greek philosopher.
3. Discorides (first century AD); Greek physician.
4. Galen (?130–?200 AD); Greek physician, anatomist, and physiologist. Codified existing medical knowledge. Authoritative writer throughout Middle Ages.
5. Known as Avicenna in medieval Europe.
6. Known as Rhases in medieval Europe.

i   Identify the words or phrases in the Arabic text which correspond to the following in English (N.B. the English words and phrases are listed in the same order of occurrence as the corresponding Arabic words and phrases in the original text). Also add any synonyms for any of the listed words, phrases or parts of phrases which you are able to think of.

paragraph one   *Synonym(s)*
1. herbal medicine
2. earliest historical times
3. papyrus leaves
4. priests
5. medicinal herbs
6. the contents of the graves of the pharoahs
paragraph two
7. there is [conclusive] evidence that
8. ancient Indians
9. they were skilled/experts in it

10. in this area
paragraph three
11. they were followed by
12. who inherited the science from them
13. foremost amongst whom was
paragraph four
14. monopolised
15. monks

ii Answer the following questions in Arabic.

paragraph one

١ – إلى متى يرجع تاريخ التداوي بالأعشاب؟

٢ – من كان عندهم علم في التداوي بالأعشاب في ذلك الوقت؟

٣ – كيف نعرف هذا؟

٤ – ماذا وُجد بين التحف والآثار الموجودة في قبور الفراعنة؟

paragraph two

٥ – من هم الذين مارسوا مهنة التطبيب بالأعشاب غير المصريين القدماء؟

٦ – من هو «سرسروتا»؟

٧ – ماذا عمل اليونان في القرنين الرابع والخامس قبل الميلاد؟

paragraph three

٨ – ممّن أخذ العرب علمهم في مجال التداوي بالأعشاب؟

٩ – بأي طريقة وسّع العرب هذا العلم؟

١٠ – من هما أشهر الأطباء العرب؟

paragraph four

١١ – ماذا عمل الرهبان في القرن الثاني عشر في أوروبا؟

١٢ – من هي «القدّيسة هيلديكارد»؟

١٣ – ماذا كتبت؟

(b) Read the following passage from مجلة الشرق الأوسط Mar. 25–31, 1992, then answer the questions which follow.

لكل عشب فائدة

* البابونج: البابونج دواء للصداع والحميات شربا. يقوي الكبد ويفتت الحصى، وينقي الصدر من الربو، ويذهب الاعياء ونزلات البرد، ودهنه يزيل الشقوق في الثدي والفم وهو دواء لاوجاع

المفاصل والنقرس، وهو مهدئ للاعصاب خافض للحرارة ينفع لسوء الهضم. يقوي الشعب وينفع لعلاج السل الرئوي.

* الرواند: ينفع لبرد الكبد والمعدة والاستسقاء واليرقان، يقطع الحميات وفساد الاغذية، مفيد للسعال المزمن والربو اذا مزج بالصبر انقذ الدماغ من نوبات الصداع ويتم تناوله هنا شربا او شما. واذا تم تناوله مع اليانسون اوقف النزف المعوي ونوبات المغص الحاد. واذا تم تناوله مع السكنجبين ساعد على تفتيت الحصى واسهم في تخفيف اضطرابات المثابة.

* عشب الشيخ:[1] نبات صحراوي شديد المرارة ينفع لتخفيض مستوى السكر في الدم لدى مرضى داء البول السكري.

* القطب: عشب يفيد في علاج الحصى وامراض المثابة الاخرى.

* الدارسين: يفيد شاي الدارسين لعلاج تشنجات الامعاء وفي علاج الاسهال.

* الهندباء: نبات يثير نشاط الجهاز الهضمي، ينفع لاضطرابات الطحال والمرارة. وينفع لازالة الامساك وعلاج الديدان.

* قشر الرمان: دواء للاسهال والديدان الشريطية، وينفع لتقوية بصيلات الشعر.

* الحنظل: ينفع للفالج والصداع وعرق النسا والمفاصل واوجاع الظهر، طبيخه مع الزيت ينفع لعلاج الجذام واوجاع الاذن والصم، فيه صلاح للاسنان واللثة.

* الكزبرة: تفيد لاطفاء جذوة العطش وتوصف للحكة والجرب والقروح عن طريق الاكل. كما تستعمل على هيئة طلاء وينفع ماؤها المحلي لفتح الشهية. وفيها فائدة للقلب وهي دواء للخفقان، واذا اكلت مع الزعتر تنفع للزحار، وهي دواء مضاد لديدان البطن اذا تم تناولها مع اليانسون.

* الكمون: شاي الكمون طارد للريح مضاد لسموم البدن وسوء الهضم وتخمر المعدة، فيه تسكين لضيق النفس والمغص الحاد، يسكن

وجع الاسنان اذا عمل على هيئة غرغرة مع الزعتر، دهن الكمون يمنع اقتراب القمل والحشرات من جلد الصغار، وهو مدرّ للحليب كما انه مسكن لآلام الحيض.

Note

1. عشب الشيخ = sarsaparilla

Which herbs are used to treat the following ailments?

1. headache
2. diabetes
3. indigestion
4. diarrheoa
5. persistent coughs
6. ulcers
7. constipation
8. stomach cramps
9. bladder disturbances
10. earache

(c) Translate the following text into idiomatic English.

أول كتاب صيدلة في العالم

لم يكن القانون هو الحقل الوحيد الذي برع فيه السومريون قبل سواهم من البشر، فقد توصلت التنقيبات الى اكتشاف وثيقة تحمل أول دستور للصيدلة في العالم. إن هذه الوثيقة تتحدث عن طب وعلاج لا أثر فيهما للسحر والتعاويذ والرقي، وإنما هما طب وعلاج على مستوى علمي. وقد كان مثل هذا الطب متداولا في سومر خلال الألف الثالث قبل الميلاد.

لقد وجدت الوثيقة المذكورة أعلاه مكتوبة بالخط المسماري على لوح من الصلصال، وتحمل ما يزيد على اثنى عشر نوعا من العلاج، ويعتبر هذا اللوح أول كتاب صيدلة عرفه الانسان. وقد عثر على هذا اللوح في التحريات التي أجريت في نفر، وهو موجود الآن في متحف جامعة فيلادلفيا. وتشير المعلومات الواردة في هذا اللوح

الى أن الطبيب السومري الذي كتب الوثيقة كان يلجأ، كزميله في
وقتنا الحاضر، إلى النبات والحيوان وكذلك الى المعادن كمصادر
أولية لاستخراج الأدوية.

5. Written Arabic texts 2

(a) As a preparatory exercise for this section, read the following text at home.

اعتاد بعض المؤرخين الذين كتبوا عن الطب العربي أن
ينزعوا عنه صفة الاصالة ويدعوا أنه مستقى من المدنيات
السابقة ولا سيما مدنية اليونان والفرس والهنود. وكان
المؤرخون الغربيون أقلّ اهتماماً من هذه الناحية بالعرب
ولم يخصصوا في كتبهم إلا صفحات قليلة للعرب وللمدنية
العربية إجحافاً بحقهم وحقها، وجعلوا ما حققه العرب
والمسلمون في هذا الميدان لا يزيد عن النقل والترجمة من
كتب الأقدمين. ومنهم من قال إن الأساس النظري لكثير من
نواحي الطب العربي لم يكن في أصل عربي المنبع بل كان
غير عربي.

(b) Translate the following text by أحمد طه from الطب الإسلامي, p. 8, into idiomatic English.

بسم الله الرحمن الرحيم
الحمد للّه الذي هدانا لهذا وما كنا لنهتدى لو لا أن هدانا اللّه
والصلاة والسلام على صفوة رسله وخاتم أنبيائه سيدنا محمد
وعلى آله وصحبه وسلم ...

تمهيد
نشأ الطب الاسلامي بعد بعثة النبي صلى اللّه عليه وسلم وظل
طيلة قرون الحضارة الاسلامية. ويُطلق البعض على هذا الطب اسم
« الطب العربي » غير ان هذه التسمية ليست دقيقة. فهذا الطب
نشأ في ظل الحضارة الاسلامية وكان جزءا لا يتجزأ منها واضمحل
عندما غربت شمس تلك الحضارة عن العالم، والعرب قبل الاسلام لم

يكن لهم طب مميز فقد كانوا في جاهلية شملت معظم انشطة الحياة وحتى العلوم الطبية التي كانت لديهم لم تتبلور الا بعد الاسلام، ثم إن معظم الاطباء الذين اشتهروا وكانوا روادا للطب الاسلامي، كالرازي وابن سينا وعلى بن عباس، لم يكونوا عربا بل كانوا اعاجم عربهم الاسلام الذي جعل العربية لسانا، لا عصبية ولا جنسا، فكتبوا بلغة القرآن. اضف الى ذلك ان عددا غير قليل من اطباء الطب الاسلامي لم يكونوا مسلمين وانما عاشوا تحت ظل الدولة الاسلامية ذميّين وساهموا بنصيب وافر في الترجمة والتأليف الطبي. ولم يكن ذلك ممكنا اذا لم يعيشوا في ظل الحضارة الاسلامية التي كفلت لهم من الحقوق ما كفلته للمسلم.

(c) Read the following text from الحوادث Feb. 27, 1987, then complete exercises
   i. and ii. which follow.

الاوروبيون يستهلكون الأدوية اكثر مما يستهلكون الفواكه
الفقر لا يعطي المحتاج حق ممارسة دور الطبيب!

بسبب الاهمال او عدم الاكتراث ببعض الامراض البسيطة، واحيانا بسبب الثقة بالنفس انتشر في السنوات الاخيرة ما يمكن تسميته بـ«التطبيب الشخصي» او العلاج الذاتي .

صداع ، انفلونزا خفيفة ، سعال ، رشوحات في الانف ارق طارئ ، هذه امراض يعتبرها عدد كبير من الناس بسيطة لا تستحق مراجعة الطبيب . ويعمد هؤلاء الى الاستعانة بالصيدلي الذي انتفخت خزائنه بأصناف وانواع من الادوية الخفيفة المضادة لهذه الامراض ، والتي تتسابق شركات الادوية في تصنيع العلاجات لها ، لأنها من جهة اولى اكثر ربحاً من ادوية الامراض قليلة الانتشار ، ولان الناس ، من جهة ثانية ، يشترونها ويتناولونها كما يشترون الخضار او الحلويات والشوكولا . والاعلانات المتلفزة والمذاعة تضع في متناول المستهلك مئات الاصناف من هذه الادوية ، التي لا تحتاج في معظم بلدان العالم الى وصفة طبية من طبيب .

الم في المعدة ؟ عليك بالكبسولة «الفلانية» . الم في الرأس ؟

تناول « علانة » من الحبوب . متعب ومرهق ؟ الحل في تناول هذا الدواء الذي يحتوي على كمية كبيرة من الحديد . نقص في الحيوية والنشاط ؟ هناك لائحة من الفيتامينات المقوية . هذه الادوية ذات الاستهلاك العالي ، اصبحت اليوم مثل «العلكة» ، يتناولها الناس دون اهتمام بحقيقة مضارها وفوائدها. اصبحت عادة يومية . وتفاقمت هذه العادة الى درجة انك لو شكوت من الصداع امام الاصدقاء او الزملاء ، لسارع بعضهم الى مد يده الى جيبه ، ليقدم اليك حبة دواء اعتاد على استعماله ، او ليكتب لك اسم دواء كان جربه هو او احد معارفه .

i   In Arabic explain the following words which occur in the text using synonyms or phrases.

١ – استهلك

٢ – اكترث بـ

٣ – سعال

٤ – رشوحات

٥ – أرق

٦ – عمد على

٧ – استعان بـ

٨ – انتفخ

٩ – خزينة ج خزائن

١٠. –وصفة طبية

١١ –لائحة

١٢ –علكة

١٣ –مضرّة ج مضارّ

١٤ –تفاقم

١٥ –اعتاد

١٦ –معارف

ii Structure translations based on الفقر لا يعطي حق ممارسة دور الطبيب. Translate the following English sentences into Arabic using relevant constructions found in the text at the points indicated.

1. We eat more bread than cheese. (title, line 1)
2. It's possible to call this 'self–treatment'. (para. 1, line 3)

3. They consider sciences easy, [and] unworthy of deep thought. (para. 2, line 2)
4. Which are the widespread problems which you mentioned? (para. 2, line 6)
5. You should take a short holiday. (para. 3, line 1)
6. She suffers from a lack of self–confidence. (para. 3, line 3)
7. These are highly productive industries. (para. 3, lines 4–5)
8. The matter has reached the point where we cannot turn back. (para. 3, lines 6–7)
9. She rushed to open the door. (para. 3, lines 7–8)
10. This letter was written by him or one of his friends. (para 3, line 9)

(d) As a preparatory exercise for the essay class (section 13), read the following text by طه حسين from الأيّام, p. 128.

أَقبل الشابُّ آخر هذا اليوم كعادته باسماً ، فلاطف أُمَّه وداعبها
وهدّأ من رَوْعها وقال: لم تُصَبِ المدينةُ اليومَ بأكثر من عشرين
إصابةً ، وقد أخذتْ وطأة الوباء تَخفّ ، ولكنه مع ذلك شكا من
بعض الغَثَيان ، وخرض إلى أبيه فجلس إليه وحدّثه كعادته ، ثم
ذهب إلى أصحابه فرافقهم إلى حيث كان يذهب معهم في كلّ
يوم عند شاطئ الإبراهيمية . فلما كان أوّلُ الليل عاد وقضى
ساعةً في ضحك وعبث مع إخوته . وفي هذه الليلة زعم لأهل
البيت جميعاً أنَّ في أكل الثّوم وقايةً من الكوليرا ، وأَكَلَ الثّومَ
وأخذ كبارَ إخوته وصغارَهم بالأكل منـه ، وحاول أن يُقْنِعَ أبويه
بذلك فلم يُوَفَّق .

6. Written Arabic texts 3 (classical)

The following text is an extract from الرسالة الثالثة, one of the epistles of the إخوان الصفاء , رسائل إخوان الصفاء, pp. 14–15. The إخوان الصفاء, 'The Brethren of Purity', was a fellowship of men in Basra (and possibly also Baghdad) in the late tenth century, who espoused the myth of the microcosmic return; i.e. that 'the world in all its complexity emanated for the Ultimate One [i.e. God], which was expressed in cosmic reason; and that all this complexity was resumed in human beings as microcosms; who by purifying their individual reasoning powers could reascend in intellectual contemplation to the original One' (Hodgson 1974, vol. II: 170). Although the Brethren seem to have been independent of any particular Islamic sect, their views were influenced by those of Ismailism. The following text can be read as an allegory for the spreading of spiritual enlightenment. Translate the text into idiomatic English.

اعلم أيها الأخ ، أيّدك اللّه وإيانا بروح منه ، أنّا قد فرغنا من بيان ماهيّة الطريق إلى اللّه تعالى ، وكيفيّة الوصول إلى معرفته وهي الغاية القصوى ، فنريد الآن أن نذكر في هذه الرسالة بيان اعتقاد إخوان الصفاء ومذهب الربّانيين ، وبيان أن النفس تبقى بعد مفارقتها الجسد التي عُبّر عنها بالموت الطبيعي بطريق مقنع لا بطريق البرهان فنقول :

اعلم أنه في الزمان السالف ذكروا أنه كان رجل من الحكماء رفيقاً بالطب ، دخل إلى مدينة من المدن ، فرأى عامة أهلها بهم مرض خفي لا يشعرون بعلتهم ، ولا يُحسّون بدائهم الذي بهم ، ففكر ذلك الحكيم في أمرهم كيف يداويهم ليبرئهم من دائهم ويشفيهم من علتهم التي استمرت بهم ، وعلم أنه إن أخبرهم بما هم فيه لا يستمعون قوله ولا يقبلون نصيحته ، بل ربما ناصبوه بالعداوة ، واستعجزوا رأيه ، واستنقصوا آدابه ، واسترذلوا علمه . فاحتال عليهم في ذلك لشدة شفقته على أبناء جنسه ، ورحمته لهم وتحننه عليهم ، وحرصه على مداواتهم طلباً لمَرضاة اللّه ، عز وجل ، بأن طلب من أهل تلك المدينة رجلاً من فضلائهم الذين كان بهم ذلك المرض ، فأعطاه شربة من شربات كانت معه قد أعدها لمداواتهم ، وسعطَه بدُخْنة كانت معه لمعالجتهم ، فعطس ذلك الرجل من ساعته ، ووجد خِفّة في بدنه ، وراحة في حواسّه ، وصحة في جسمه ، وقوة في نفسه . فشكر له جزاه خيراً وقال له : هل لك من حاجة أقضيها لك مكافأةً لما اصطنعت إلي من الإجسام في مداواتك لي ؟ فقال : نعم ، تُعينني على مداواة أخ من إخوانك . قال : سمعاً وطاعة لك . فتوافقا على ذلك ، ودخلا على رجل آخر ممن رأيا أنه أقرب إلى الصلاح ، فخَلَوَا به من رفقائه وداوياه بذلك الدواء ، فبرأَ من ساعته . فلما أفاق من دائه جزاهما خيراً وبارك فيهما وقال لهما : هل لكما حاجة أقضيها لكما مكافأةً لما صنعتما إلي من الإحسان

والمعروف ؟ فقالا : تعيننا على مداواة أخ من إخوانك . فقال : سمعاً
وطاعة لكما . فتوافقوا على ذلك ، ولقوا رجلاً آخر ، فعالجوه وداووه
بمثل الأول فبرئ وقال لهم مثل قول الأوّلين ، وقالوا له مثل ما قال
الأول .

ثم تفرقوا في المدينة يداوون الناس واحداً بعد آخر في السر ،
حتى أبرؤوا أناساً كثيراً ، وكثُر أنصارهم وإخوانهم ومعارفهم ، ثم
ظهروا للناس وكاشفوهم بالمعالجة ، وكابروهم بالمداواة قهراً ،
وكانوا يَلقَون واحداً واحداً من الناس ، فيأخذ منهم جماعة بيديه
وجماعة برجليه ، ويَسعطه الآخرون كَرهاً ، ويسقونه جَبراً حتى
أبرؤوا أهل المدينة كلهم .

7. Grammar/stylistics
Repetition: 2
(a) *Semantic repetition*
While word repetition involves repetition of form and meaning, and morphological
repetition (root repetition, pattern repetition and suffix repetition) involves
repetition of form only (i.e. part of the form of two or more words), semantic
repetition involves repetition, not of form, but of meaning.

Semantic repetition is a rather imprecise notion, but for practical purposes two
basic sub–categories can be established: i. synonymy or near–synonymy; and ii.
antonymy or near–antonymy.

i *Synonymy or near–synonymy*
Synonyms are words, or by extension phrases, which mean the same thing.
Near–synonyms are therefore words or phrases which mean nearly the same thing.
Beeston (1970: 112) points out that Arabic (unlike English) frequently makes of
hendiadis, that is the use two words which are partially synonyms (i.e. they have at
least one sense in common) in order to specify the sense which the two words have
in common.

Beeston gives the following example of three partially synonymous words:

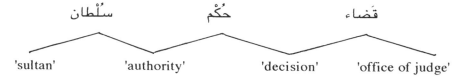

| سُلْطان | حُكْم | قَضاء |
| 'sultan' | 'authority' | 'decision' | 'office of judge' |

In this example, سُلْطان has the two meanings 'sultan' and 'authority', حُكْم has the two meanings 'authority' and 'decision', and ﻗَﻀﺎﺀ has the two meanings 'decision' and 'office of judge'. Accordingly, ﺳﻠﻄﺎﻥ and ﺣﻜﻢ are partial synonyms with respect to one another; they have the shared sense of 'authority'. However, they are not total synonyms; they have at least one meaning which is not shared, 'sultan' in the case of ﺳﻠﻄﺎﻥ and 'decision' in the case of ﺣﻜﻢ. For corresponding reasons ﺣﻜﻢ and ﻗﻀﺎﺀ are also partial but not total synonyms.

Beeston says that in order to express the concept 'authority', an Arabic writer will often use ﺍﻟﺤﻜﻢ ﻭﺍﻟﺴﻠﻄﺎﻥ, while in order to express the concept 'decision' he or she will useﺍﻟﺤﻜﻢ ﻭﺍﻟﻘﻀﺎﺀ. Expressions of this kind are not tautological, as they might appear to be if they were translated with two English words; they represent a single concept and should translated accordingly into English.

The following is an example of the kind of hendiadis in Arabic which Beeston talks about:

ﻭﻟﻴﺲ ﻣﺎ ﻳﻤﻨﻊ ﺍﺗﺤﺎﺩ ﺍﻭ ﺍﻧﺼﻬﺎﺭ ﺍﻷﺣﺰﺍﺏ ﺍﻟﻘﻄﺮﻳﺔ ﺫﺍﺕ ﺍﻻﻫﺪﺍﻑ ﺍﻟﻮﺍﺣﺪﺓ {ﺍﻟﺤﻮﺍﺟﺰ} ﻭ{ﺍﻟﻌﺮﺍﻗﻴﻞ} ﺍﻟﺘﻲ ﺗﻀﻌﻬﺎ ﺍﻟﺤﻜﻮﻣﺎﺕ ﺃﻭ ﺿﻌﻒ ﺍﻟﻮﺳﺎﺋﻞ ﻓﻲ ﺳﺒﻴﻞ ﺫﻟﻚ ..

'What prevents the merging or unification of regional parties with single goals is not [so much] the obstacles which are placed by governments or the weakness of the means of achieving this [that] end ...' (ch. 13, 11a)

Here ﺣﺎﺟﺰ (pl. ﺣَﻮﺍﺟﺰ) means in a concrete sense 'partition', 'fence', 'gate', and in an abstract sense 'obstacle', 'barrier', 'impediment'. ﻋَﺮْﻗَﻠﺔ (pl. ﻋﺮﺍﻗﻴﻞ) means 'obstacle', 'encumbrance', 'impediment', 'difficulty'. The use of the two words together rules out a concrete meaning (since ﻋﺮﺍﻗﻴﻞ only has an abstract meaning). Therefore ﺍﻟﺤﻮﺍﺟﺰ ﻭﺍﻟﻌﺮﺍﻗﻴﻞ in this context is to be taken to mean 'obstacles', or similar.

Another example of the same kind is:

ﻭﺑﺬﻟﻚ ﻳﺘﺤﻘﻖ {ﺍﻟﺘﻜﺎﺗﻒ} ﻭ{ﺍﻻﻟﺘﺤﺎﻡ} ﺍﻟﻮﻃﻨﻲ ﺍﻟﺠﻤﺎﻋﻲ ﻛﺄﻗﻮﻯ ﺿﻤﺎﻧﺎﺕ ﺣﻤﺎﻳﺔ ﺩﻭﻟﺔ ﺍﻟﻮﺣﺪﺓ ..

'In this way collective national solidarity is achieved, as the strongest [surest] guarantor for protecting the unitary state ...' (ch. 15, 11)

ﺗﻜﺎﺗﻒ means in a concrete sense 'standing shoulder to shoulder' and in an abstract sense 'supporting one another', while ﺍﻟﺘﺤﺎﻡ means in a concrete sense 'sticking to', 'being in immediate contact with' and in an abstract sense 'being united'. When the two words are put together the differing concrete senses are ruled out, and the shared abstract sense – along the lines of something like 'solidarity' – emerges as the only contextually acceptable meaning.

There are two other aspects of repetition of synonyms which are important. The first is that such repetition is a traditional feature of Arabic writing, particularly in 'poetic' or persuasive material, and is regarded as elegant in Arabic. The second aspect, and one which is closely connected to the first, is that such repetition often gives a sense of emphasis in Arabic. For example:

هل لكما حاجة أقضيها لكما مكافأة لما صنعتما إلي من {الإحسان} و{المعروف} ؟

'Is there anything I can do to recompense you for the good deed you have done to me?' (ch. 19, 6)

Here semantic specification is involved in the use of the two words الإحسان and المعروف. إحسان has the more general verbal sense of 'acting well' in addition to the specific sense it has here of '[performance of] good deed[s]'. معروف has a basic sense of 'known' in addition to the sense it has here of 'favour rendered'. However, either of these two words on their own would almost certainly be correctly interpreted in this context (and the same is true of either member of the pairs الإحسان التحام-تكاتف and عراقيل-حواجز discussed above). The use of والمعروف together provides an emphasis which would be lacking were only one of the words used on its own.

Semantic synonyms are most commonly joined by و, as in the above examples. They can, however, also occur with أو. For example:

وليس ما يمنع {اتحاد} او {انصهار} الأحزاب القطرية ..

'What prevents the merging or unification of regional parties is not ...' (ch. 13, 11a)

The translation here maintains the two elements 'merging' or 'unification' – and it might be that there is some technical difference between the two notions. Idiomatically, however, it would probably be more normal in English to opt for one of the two terms, rather than both, e.g. 'merging' or 'merger'.

In the case of adjectives, it is possible to have two or more adjectives which are connected asyndetically, i.e. without و or any other joining word. This has been discussed in chapter 2 (ch. 2, 7b). As noted there, adjectives are coordinated asyndetically – that is to say, they are linked with no conjunction such as و – when they refer to inseparable aspects of the noun. This notion of inseparability, although different from the notion of hendiadis of nouns in Arabic, bears some similarity to it; and it is fairly normal for adjectives which are coordinated asyndetically to be translatable by a single adjective in English:

وكان فهمه للحرية وفعلها {الخطير} {الاساسي} في بعث الأمة العربية فهما لم تسبقه اليه حركة أخرى من حيث العمق والنضج والوضوح ..

'Its understanding of freedom and its profound/dramatic and
fundamental effect in reviving the Arab nation was an understanding
which had not been previously achieved by any other movement in
terms of its depth, maturity and clarity.' (ch. 13, 11b)

Here, instead of the doublet 'profound/dramatic' and 'fundamental', an English
translator might opt for just one word, for example 'fundamental'. Bearing in mind
that one aspect of repetition of synonyms in Arabic of this kind is emphasis, an
alternative in English would be to combine an adjective such as 'fundamental' with
an emphatic adverb such as 'absolutely', resulting in an English translation
'absolutely fundamental effect' of the Arabic الخطير الاساسي وفعلها. Similarly:

ويقول المراقبون إن موت السادات رجل كامب ديفيد والمحور
المركزي للسياسة الأمريكية في الشرق الأوسط تنبيء بحدوث
تغييرات {جذرية} {عميقة} ليس في المنطقة فحسب بل وحيال
التوازن العالمي برمته.

'Observers say that the death of Sadat, the man of Camp David and the
central pillar [axis] of American policy in the Middle East, presages
radical and profound changes not only in the region but also in relation
to the balance of power throughout the world.' (ch. 13, 11a)

Here again, an idiomatic English translation might drop either 'radical' or
'profound'. (In this case a translation along the lines 'absolutely radical' or 'utterly
profound' seems ruled out by the fact that the words 'radical' and 'profound' do
not readily admit of further definition in terms of degree in English.)

Just as Arabic makes use of lexical synonymy, i.e. two words which mean
roughly the same, so it also makes use of phrasal synonymy, i.e. two phrases
which mean roughly the same. For example:

فلم يعد إذن عمل الأحزاب القطرية مرحلة توصل الى الوحدة، بل
{اتجاهاً جديداً} و{طريقاً مختلفاً} يبعد عنها ويضعف امكانياتها ..

'So the work of the regional parties is not to be considered as a stage
leading to unity, but rather as a new direction and a different path which
leads away from it and weakens its chances of success ...' (ch. 13,
11a)

Here the phrases جديداً اتجاهاً and مختلفاً طريقاً are near–synonyms; and in an
English translation one might render them by a single phrase, such as 'a new path',
or if the sense of emphasis is felt to be important, by a phrase along the lines 'a
completely new path'.

Similarly:

فـرأى عـامـة أهلهـا بهـم مـرض خـفـي {لا يشـعُرون بعلتـهم} ، و{لا
يَحسّون بدائهم الذي بـهم} ..

'He saw that the mass of its people were afflicted by a hidden illness
whose ill effects they could not feel.' (ch. 19, 6)

Here the translation reduces the Arabic double phrase to a single English phrase, in
order to avoid a repetition which would seem unnecessary in English.

ii *Antonymy or near–antonymy*
Repetition of antonyms or near–antonyms is less problematic from an English point
of view than repetition of synonyms or near–synonyms, since English also makes
use of this form of repetition quite regularly. An example of repetition of lexical
(i.e. single–word) antonyms is the following (already discussed under pattern
repetition above):

.. {كبار} إخوته و{صغارهم} ..

'... both his elder and his younger brothers and sisters ...' (ch. 19, 5d)

Note that English often signals antonymic contrast more strongly than Arabic.
Here, for example, the English translation introduces 'both' and repeats 'his',
which occurs before both 'elder' and 'younger'.
    The following is an example of phrasal antonyms:

الأمر بالمعروف والنهي عن المنكر.

'... to order what is known [i.e. the good], and to prohibited what is
unknown [i.e. the bad]'. (ch. 14, 6a)

This well–known Islamic saying involves two phrases, الأمر بالمعروف and النهي
عن المنكر which are not only global antonyms, but whose elements are
individually antonymic. Thus أمر 'ordering' is the opposite of نهي 'forbidding' ب
in this context can be regarded as the opposite of عن (cf. رغب بشيء 'to desire'
vs. رغب عن شيء 'to dislike', 'to detest'), and المعروف 'the known', 'the good'
is the opposite of المنكر 'the unknown', 'evil', both in the basic senses 'known'
vs. 'unknown', and in the secondary senses 'good'/'bad'.
    An example of phrasal near–antonyms is the following:

..وفي ما تكوّن من هذا الامتـزاج مـن أمـة {مـختـلطة الدم والجنس}،
{مـوحّدة في ما هو أهم من هذا كثيـرًا} ..

'... regarding the development from this mixture of nation which is of
mixed blood and ethnicity, but is united in that which is much more
important than this ...' (ch. 13, 4c)

Here the two phrases مـختـلطة الدم والجنس and مـوحّدة فـي مـا هـو أهـم مـن هذا

كثيرا begin with the near–antonyms مختلطة and موحدة. The two phrases are also contrastive taken as a whole, a fact which is reflected in the use of 'but' in the English translation.

(b) *Semantic repetition plus morphological repetition*

It is fairly common for semantic repetition to be combined with morphological repetition (ch. 18, 7b), i.e. with partial repetition of form. Given that morphological repetition and semantic repetition both have an aesthetic effect, it should be expected that a combination of the two forms of repetition would have a stronger effect than that of either form of repetition on its own. In general, this seems to be the case. Complex repetition of this kind is a normal feature of Arabic.

i *Semantic repetition plus root repetition*

Words in Arabic are grouped into roots principally on the grounds of sharing the same root letter. Another feature of roots, however, is the sharing of some basic area or areas of meaning among all the words having a single root. Thus, as is well known, words sharing the root ك ت ب tend to share some notion of writing – e.g. كَتَبَ 'to write', كاتِب 'writer', 'scribe', مَكْتُوب 'written', 'letter', مَكْتَب 'office', مَكْتَبَة 'library', 'bookshop', etc. Given this, it is virtually inevitable that root repetition will go hand in hand with semantic repetition, and there is therefore no need to comment on this combination in more detail.

ii *Semantic repetition plus pattern repetition*

More interesting than the combination of root repetition with semantic repetition is the combination of pattern repetition with semantic repetition. This turns out also to be extremely common, and can be considered under the following heads: ii.i. synonymy or near–synonymy plus pattern repetition, ii.ii. antonymy or near–antonymy plus pattern repetition.

ii.i *Synonymy or near–synonymy plus pattern repetition*

The following, all of which were previously discussed under pattern repetition, are examples of pattern repetition in combination with synonymy or near–synonymy:

.. ولن يكون هناك {خَرَاب} ولا {دَمَار} ..
'... there will not be ruin or destruction ...' (ch. 13, 11b)

كافة {اشكال} و{الوان} المعاناة ..
'... all types and forms of suffering ...' (ch. 15, 11)

.. {متعب} و{مرهق}؟
'... tired and exhausted?' (ch. 19, 5c)

.. من اجل بناء وطنهم الذي {قاسى} الكثير و{عانى} الامرين ..

'... in order to build their country which has suffered much and endured terrible hardship ...' (ch. 13, 5a)

As noted in the discussion of semantic repetition, there is a tendency in idiomatic English translation to reduce Arabic synonyms to single terms in English or to a complex such as an adjective plus a noun, or an adverb plus an adjective. So, a more idiomatic translation of كافة اشكال والوان المعاناة might be 'all types of suffering', or 'all the various types of suffering'.

ii.ii *Antonymy or near–antonymy plus pattern repetition*
The following are examples of pattern repetition in combination with antonymy or near–antonymy:

.. مسيرة شعب واحد في {السراء} و{الضراء} ..

'... the fate of the people in good times and bad ...' (ch. 16, 4c)

.. {كبار} إخوته و{صغار}هم ..

'... both his elder and his younger brothers and sisters ...' (ch. 19, 5d)

This example has been already discussed under both pattern repetition and semantic repetition.

iii *Semantic repetition plus suffix repetition*
A number of examples can be found in which suffix repetition combines with semantic repetition. These are dealt with under the following heads: iii.i. synonymy or near–synonymy plus semantic repetition, iii.ii. antonymy or near–antonymy plus semantic repetition.

iii.i *Synonymy or near–synonymy plus suffix repetition*
The following are examples of suffix repetition in combination with synonymy or near–synonymy:

.. كارثة وطني{ة} وقومي{ة} ..

'... a national disaster ...' (ch. 13, 5a)

.. على مستوى الممارسة العملي{ة} والواقعي{ة} ..

'... on the level of actual practical activity ...' (ch. 15, 11)

.. لم يكن {حاكم}{اً} ولا {رئيس}{اً} ولا {قائد}{أً} الا لان شعبه أراده كذلك .

'... he was only a ruler, head, or leader head because his people wanted him to be thus [i.e. these things].' (ch. 16, 4b)

iii.ii *Antonymy or near–antonymy plus suffix repetition*
An example of suffix repetition in combination with antonymy is the following:

.. دون اهتمام بحقيقة {مضار}{ها} و{فوائد}{ها} .

'... without any concern for the benefit or harm which they can do.'
(ch. 19, 5c)

(c) *Complex cases, and* سجع

It is possible to combine the various forms of repetition discussed in the preceding sections into patterns of great complexity. A fairly prosaic example involving root repetition, suffix repetition, and a degree of semantic repetition, as well as word repetition (ch. 18, 7a) is the following:

أفتظن أن أسرة كهذه الأسرة الكندية تنزل هذه المنزلة في الحياة الاسلامية وتؤثر هذه الآثار في تاريخ المسلمين لا تصطنع القصص ولا تأجر القصّاص لينشروا لها الدعوة ويذيعوا عنها كل ما من شأنه أن يرفع ذكرها ويبعد صوتها ؟

'Do you think that a family such as this Kindi family, occupying this position in Islamic life with such influence in the history of the Muslims would not fabricate stories or hire story tellers to spread their propaganda, praise them and further their influence?' (ch. 17, 4c)

The following example makes use of semantic repetition, pattern repetition and suffix repetition:

..بل ربما ناصبوه بالعداوة ، واستعجزوا رأيه ، واستنقصوا آدابه، واسترذلوا علمه.

' ... indeed they may be openly hostile to him, reject his point of view, and dismiss his learning, and disdain his knowledge.' (ch. 19, 6)

The use of complex repetition in combination with rhyme is termed in Arabic سَجْع and although سَجْع in its pure form is now scarcely used (cf. Beeston 1970: 113), it is still possible to find examples of this kind in modern Arabic, particularly when the writer wishes to achieve an classical, formal or solemn effect. Thus, in the obituary to Sadat from الأهرام in chapter 16:

شاءت ارادة الله . ولا راد لقضائه . ان يمتحن مصر ببلاء عظيم ، وحدث أليم جسيم ، دبره خصومه بليل ضمن سلسلة مؤامراتهم للايقاع بهذا البلد الكريم.

'God has willed, and there is no recourse in the face of what He decrees, to test Egypt with a terrible affliction, and a painful and momentous event, which was plotted by his enemies at night amidst their series of conspiracies to bring down this noble nation.' (ch. 16, 4c)

لقـد ذهـب الرجل الحـر الذي حـقق لمصـر حـريتـها ، الشـجـاع الذي علمـها الشجـاعة في ممارسة سيـاستها ، القوي الذي بث فيها القوة على مـواجهة شـدائـد الاحداث الابي الذي علمـها الابـاء وكرامـة الاداء
..

'The free man has passed away who achieved Egypt's freedom, the courageous man who taught it courage in the practising of its politics, the powerful man who gave it the power to face the worst of events, the proud man who taught it pride and the honour of achievement ...' (ch. 16, 4c)

(d) *Apparent semantic anomoly*
As discussed under semantic repetition, it is sometimes necessary to translate two Arabic synonyms or near–synonyms as a single word in English, or as a single word (e.g. a noun), plus another word (e.g. an emphasising adjective). If such phrases were translated literally into English the result would be semantically anomolous.

There are also a number of cases of apparent semantic anomoly in Arabic which can be traced back to forms of semantic repetition. The most basic examples of this type is where elements of meaning are repeated in two different parts of speech. Consider the following example:

{يرجع} {السبب} في ذلك الى قلة الاهتمام بالأمور الاقتصادية.
'The reason for this goes back to a lack of interest in economic matters'.

In the Arabic, the word يرجع is used metaphorically to express a sense of causality, while the word سبب also expresses causality. While this is a possible translation in English would be 'The reason for this goes back to a lack of interest in economic matters', this might be felt to be tautological. A more appropriate translation might therefore be 'The reason for this is a lack of interest in economic affairs' or 'This goes back to a lack of interest in economic affairs'.

A similar example from this book is:
{شاءت} {ارادة} الله.
Literally: 'God's will has willed.' (ch. 16, 4b)

Here the noun ارادة 'wish', 'will' repeats the notion of 'willing' already expressed in the verb شاءت. In this context, this repetition is used in the Arabic as a rhetorical device, and is designed to heighten the drama of the statement. (It is significant that this is the opening sentence of the text, which is an 'official' obituary of Sadat from الأهرام).

Another form of apparent semantic anomoly occurs where two words, particularly nouns, are co–ordinated by و, and stand in a superordinate–hyponym relationship to one another – a superordinate being a word whose meaning fully encompasses the meaning of another word, this other word being described as a hyponym of the first word. Thus, 'animal' is a superordinate with respect to 'horse'. Everything which could be correctly called a horse could also be correctly called an animal. Conversely, 'horse' is a hyponym with respect to 'animal'; not everything which could be correctly called an animal could also be correctly called a horse. (Cows, pigs, goats, etc. could be correctly called animals, but they could not correctly be called horses.)

Typically in Arabic, apparent semantic anomolies involve a superordinate followed by its hyponym.

وهم لا يتحدثون إلى أحد من الناس . . ولكنهم يداعبون {الباعة} و{المتجولين}.

Literal translation: 'They don't talk to anyone, but they joke with the sellers and the barrow–men.' (ch. 13, 11b)

Here, الباعة 'the sellers', is a superordinate of المتجولين 'barrow–men' (literally 'travelling [people]'), but normally used to describe people who sell goods from a barrow or handcart); all barrow–men are sellers but not all sellers are barrow–men.

In cases such as this, the meaning of the first word in the particular context has to be taken as excluding that of the second word. In this context, therefore, باعة has to be interpreted as meaning not sellers in general, but that group of sellers who are not المتجولين 'the barrow–men'. Accordingly, باعة here means the 'non–barrow–men sellers', and could be translated idiomatically as something like 'shopkeepers', giving an overall idiomatic translation along the lines, 'They don't talk to anyone, but they joke with the shopkeepers and the barrow–men.'

The following are examples are also to be understood along the same lines (individual comments are given after each example):

.. أن سياسة تصدير الثورة ... اوقعت ايران في العديد من {المشاكل} و{الازمات} ..

'... that the policy of exporting the revolution ... led Iran into a series of problems and crises ...' (ch. 16, 5c)

Here المشاكل is a superordinate (or virtual superordinate) of الازمات. It is not possible (or hardly so) to have a crisis which is not a problem, but it is possible to have a problem which is not a crisis. (All crises are problems, but not all problems are crises.) Here the best solution from a translation point of view might be to go for the more dramatic 'crises', and to abandon the notion المشاكل. Alternatively, given that semantic repetition in Arabic is often used for emphasis (ch. 19, 7ai), one might use an emphatic adjective such as 'grave', or 'serious' in combination with 'crises', giving an idiomatic translation along the lines, '... that the policy of exporting the revolution ... led Iran into a series of grave crises ...'

.. الحرب مع العراق التي كلفت البلاد اكثر من مليوني قتيل
ومئات الآلاف من {الجرحى} و{المعاقين} ..
Literal translation: '... the war with Iraq, which cost more than two million dead and hundreds of thousands of wounded and disabled ...'
(ch. 16, 5c)

Here الجرحى 'wounded' is a virtual superordinate of المعاقين 'disabled' (although it is in fact possible for someone to be disabled from birth, the disabled people referred to here are those who have become disabled by virtue of wounds which they received in the war with Iraq). A more idiomatic translation might take this into account by rearranging the information, perhaps along the lines '... the war with Iraq, which cost more than two million dead and hundreds of thousands of disabled and other wounded ...'. Alternatively, if it were felt that the major intention of the writer was to stress the seriousness of the wounds by this use of a form of semantic repetition, one might, in an English translation, sacrifice a certain amount of accuracy for a greater degree of idiomaticness and go for a translation along the lines, '... the war with Iraq, which cost more than two million dead and hundreds of thousands of seriously wounded ...'.

The previous examples of superordinate–hyponym pairs have been cases in which the superordinate occurs first. It is, however, possible to find cases in which the hyponym comes first, as in the following:

.. هوية ايران السياسية الجديدة وطبيعة علاقاتها مع {جيرانها}
و{دول العالم}.
'... the identity of Iran and the nature of its relations with its neighbours and the states of the world.' (ch. 16, 5c)

In this context, جيران is effectively a hyponym and دول العالم a superordinate. That is to say, what is meant by جيران 'neighbours' in this context is the neighbouring states; and since all neighbouring states are states of the world (but not vice versa), this looks like a hyponym–superordinate relationship. In fact, دول العالم should be interpreted here as referring to the other non–neighbouring states only, and an adequate idiomatic translation can be achieved by adding the word 'other', resulting in an idiomatic translation along the lines, '... the identity of Iran and the nature of its relations with its neighbours and other states of the world'. An alternative might be to eliminate the word 'states' altogether, on the basis that it is clear from the context that what are being talked about are states, giving an idiomatic translation along the lines, '... the identity of Iran and the nature of its relations with its neighbours and the rest of the world'.

In considering cases of apparent semantic anomoly in Arabic, it is also worthwhile being alert to the possibility of polysemy, that is one word having two (or more) meanings, and sometimes two very closely related meanings. The following two examples – with detailed comments below for each – are cases in point:

والشوارع امتلأت بالبيريهات الزرقاء يتحرك تحتها {جنود}
و{ضباط} . .

'The streets filled up with blue berets under which moved officers and men ...' (ch. 13, 11b)

Here it looks as though جنود 'soldiers' is a superordinate of ضباط 'officers' (all officers are soldiers, etc.). In fact, as well as meaning 'soldiers' generally, جنود has the more specific sense of 'privates' (i.e. non–officers). The notion of officers and non–officers, which is what is intended here, is idiomatically expressed in English by the phrase 'officers and men'.

Similarly:

فالقصة لم تصبح بعد حكاية . .

'The story has not yet become common gossip [or: common knowledge] ...' (ch. 17, 5b)

According to the dictionary (Hans Wehr), قصة means 'narrative', 'story', 'tale', while حكاية means 'story', 'tale', 'narrative', 'account'. Clearly, however, the context requires that a proper differentiation is made between the two forms; and context suggests one along the lines of the proposed translation above.

Finally, some cases of apparent semantic anomoly may be to do with other ways in which the conventions of Arabic differ from those of English. For example:

.. ليسوا صغار السن كالدنماركيين والسويديين، بل معظمهم على
أعتاب {الأربعين} و{الخمسين} . .

'... they are not young like the Danes and the Swedes; in fact most of them are nearing forty or fifty ...' (ch. 13, 11b)

Here the Arabic uses و, between the two numbers الأربعين and الخمسين, while the English uses 'or' between 'forty' or 'fifty'. There is no semantic anomoly, whether in the English or the Arabic; it is simply that they use different forms of expression to relay the same idea. (One might 'justify' the Arabic form by saying that some soldiers are approaching forty *and* others are approaching fifty.)

As a general strategy in dealing with the kind of problems dealt with in this section, it should be assumed that the original Arabic text does make sense. The task of the reader is to work out what this sense is – something which is typically fairly apparent from the context, while the task of a translator is to work out how this sense can be fairly accurately, but also idiomatically, conveyed into English.

8. Aural Arabic texts 1

(a) Listen to the following Arabic text from حصاد الشهر, no. 35, side 2, item 5, starting from ونقل الدكتور الصيدلة والعقاقير عند العرب في القديم بجانب كتاباتهم في مواضيع أخرى until محمد زهير, then answer the following questions in English.

1. What is the work of Dr Muhammad Zuhayr?
2. What did the Prophet Muhammad say about the relationship between disease and treatment?
3. Which three areas did the Prophet divide treatment into?
4. What did Edward Browne intend by presenting the information in this way?
5. What demonstrates the falsity of Browne's claim? (Do not bother to list specific names.)
6. Why does Ibn Khaldoun say that medicine is essential in cities, but not amongst the Bedouins?
7. What are the three traditional divisions of medicine?
8. What was the most important branch of medicine in the Middle Ages?
9. What kind of medicinal drugs are there?
10. What two aspects of medicine are the Arabs said to have invented?
11. How did the Arabs supplement their knowledge of medicinal drugs which they gained from the Greeks and others?

(b) Listen to the following Arabic text from حصاد الشهر, no. 33, side 1, item 5, ما هو الفضل الذي أداه العرب للطب؟, and produce a complete transcription of the text.

9. Aural Arabic texts 2

Listen to the following Arabic text from حصاد الشهر, no. 13, side 2, item 3, starting from حينما دخل تلك البلاد هل يا ترى الطب الحديث until, then answer the following questions in Arabic.

١ – ما هو سؤال المذيعة الأوّل؟

٢ – ما هي إجابة الدكتور؟

٣ – هل يجب أن يهمل باقي التراث الطبي العربي؟

٤ – لماذا؟

٥ – ما هو سؤال المذيعة الثاني؟

٦ – كيف يجاوب الدكتور على هذا السؤال؟

٧ – كيف يوضّح هذه الإجابة؟

٨ – حسب قول الدكتور على ماذا تعتمد المدن الصغيرة؟

٩ – ماذا يقول عن التداوي بالوخز بالإبر؟

10. Written English texts

Using constructions and vocabulary encountered in the Arabic texts above, translate the following text by Sami K. Hamarneh, 'The life sciences', in John R. Hayes (ed.), *The Life Sciences in The Genius of Arab Civilisation: Source of Renaissance*, (New York University Press, 1975), p.178, into idiomatic Arabic.

Hospitals and Medical Education

The early Arab concept of the hospital became the prototype for the development of the modern hospital – an institution operated by private owners or by government and devoted to the promotion of health, the cure of diseases, and the teaching and expanding of medical knowledge. Within the Islamic domain, from the beginning of the ninth century onward, hospitals were generously endowed from the state treasury and operated under lay administration and management. They served both men and women, in separate wards. In the tenth century, during the reign of al-Muqtadir (908–32), Sinan bin Thabit bin Qurrah extended hospital services to meet the needs of neighbouring rural areas, prisons and the 'inner city' – a program that has only recently been adopted in the West.

Sinan's contemporary ar-Razi considered hospitals of primary importance in providing practical training in the health professions and in disseminating health information. Late in the tenth century, the fame of 'Adudi hospital in Baghdad had spread far and wide. This remarkable institution had twenty–four doctors on its staff and was equipped with lecture halls and a generously supported library.

11. Précis

Read the following text from الشرق الأوسط Aug. 14, 1993, then produce a précis in Arabic.

«الجامع لمفردات الأدوية والأغذية» لابن البيطار

موسوعة من الصيدلة والنبات لا تزال تنتظر جهود الباحثين

باريس: من جليل العطية

قدم المسلمون الكثير للحضارة الانسانية. وقد شمل عطاؤهم

مختلف العلوم والآداب والفنون وبينها علم النبات.

ويقف «ابن البيطار» في طليعة العلماء الذين تركوا بصماتهم في علم النبات والأعشاب، ومن أسف ان اكتشافهم له جاء متأخرا وبالتحديد القرن التاسع عشر للميلاد فترجم كتابه «الجامع لمفردات الأدوية والأغذية» - موسوعته الكبيرة في الصيدلة وعلم النبات - الى اللاتينية 1833 ثم ظهر في ترجمة المانية 1840.

غير ان افضل ترجمة لهذا الكتاب المهم تمت على يد لوسيان لكلرك ونشرت في باريس بين سنتي 1877 و 1883.

والغريب ان العرب لم يهتموا بابن البيطار، إذ ان كتاب «الجامع» لم يصدر إلا سنة 1291 هـ - 1874 م في طبعة سقيمة بمطبعة بولاق - القاهرة، ولا يزال هذا الكتاب الخطير ينتظر جهود المحققين لاخراج طبعة علمية منه تأخذ مكانها اللائق في مكتبة التراث الاسلامي.

سيرة ابن البيطار

هو ضياء الدين ابو محمد عبد الله بن احمد المعروف بالعشاب والنباتي والمشهور باسم: ابن البيطار.

ولد في مالقة في الاندلس نحو سنة 1194م واهتم بالنباتات منذ صباه ثم انصرف الى الدراسة مع اساتذته وبينهم أبو العباس النباتي وعبد الله بن صالح وابن الحجاج الاشبيلي وكان اكثرهم فائدة «النباتي» الذي انصرف الى التعشيب معه في اشبيلية وضواحيها.

وفي سنة 617 هـ - 1219 م غادر ابن البيطار الاندلس في رحلة طويلة الى المشرق لم يعد بعدها، وقد زار اقطار المغرب العربي، حيث أمضى فيها فترة من الزمن ثم زار المشرق وواصل رحلته حتى آسيا الصغرى، واقصى بلاد الروم، ويبدو ان رحلته كانت علمية تطبيقية حيث كان ينصرف في كل بلد يزوره الى دراسة اعشابه ونباتاته، وبعد رحلة طويلة استقر في مصر حيث انصرف

الى خدمــة سلطانه الايوبي الملك الكامل 635 هـ الذي عينـه رئيسا على سائر الصيادلة والعشابين في مصر. وكان اثناء اقامتـه في مصر يقوم برحلات علمية عديدة انتهى في احداها الى الاستقرار في دمشق، حيث واصل نشاطه العلمي حتى وفاته سنة 646 هـ – 1248 م.

أما أهم مؤلفاته التي وصلت الينا فهي:

1 – الجامع لمفردات الأدوية والاغذية.

2 – المغني في الادوية المفردة.

4 آلاف مصطلح فني

يعد «الجامع لمفردات الادوية والاغذية» من المؤلفات الاسلامية في علم النبات، وهو يشتمل على 2324 فقرة فيها 4 آلاف مصطلح فني، ويقول الباحث ابراهيم بن مراد (من تونس) ان نصيب ابن البيطار كان عظيمــا في الفقرات التي احتواها كتابه، إذ نجد مائتي دواء جديد – من النباتات خصوصا – ادخلها ابن البيطار لأول مرة في تاريخ الطب والصيدلة.

أما المنهج الذي اتبعه في تأليف كتابه فلم يقتصر على الاعتماد على المصادر التي سبقته بل على البحث الميداني واستشارة اصحاب الخبرة والرأي. اعتمد ابن البيطار على آراء نحو مائة وخمسين مؤلفاً وعالماً ابرزهم: ديوسقريديس وجالينوس وأرسطو وأبقراط وأريباسيس ورونس وبولس وكلهم من اليونان.

وكذلك اعتمد على علماء من الفرس والهند والسريان والكلدان، أما من العرب المسلمين فقد عوّل على الرازي حوالي 400 مرة، وابن ماسويه 160 مــرة، وابن مـاسـة وابي حنيفــة الدينوري 130 مـرة، والمسيح بن الحكم 100 مـرة، ويلاحظ ان ابن البيطار لم يعتمد على اصحاب الاختصاص بل تجاوز ذلك الى الادباء والنحويين وعلماء اللغة مثل:

الخليل بن احمد الاصمعي، الفراء، الجاحظ، المسعودي وغيرهم.

تجارب ميدانية

اتبع ابن البيطار الطريقة العلمية في تأليف كتابه وذلك عندما أفاد من تجاربه الشخصية وعلمه، وفي ما يلي أمثلة على بحوثه الميدانية.

– اكثار

شاهدت نباته في ارض الشام بموضع يعرف بعلمين العلما بين نبات الذرة. ورأيته بموضع آخر يعرف بقصر عقراء في قرية بالقرب من نوى.

– أبو فايس

هو الفاسوب الرومي، شاهدت نباته – والنبات الذي يذكر من بعده – في بلاد انطاليا ورأيت أهل تلك البلاد يغسلون بأصولهما الثياب، كما يفعل أهل الشام باصول العرطنيتا.

– حدق

هو ايضا كثير في أرض القاهرة من الديار المصرية. رأيته في المطرية في البستان الذي فيه المبلسان في عين شمس.

– صفيرا

شجرته لا تسمو من الأرض كثيرا وورقها يشبه ورق الخرنوب الشامي سواء، إلا انه أمتن من ورق الخرنوب وفيه نقط سود وحمر. على أغصانه قشر يميل الى السواد. هكذا رأيته في بلاد أنطاكيا.

– أوقيموا يداس

هو النبات المعروف عند الشجاريين في افريقيا، وخاصة في مدينة تونس في اللسيعة، وكثيراً ما ينبت عندهم في جبل ماكوص، ومن هناك جمعته أيام كنت هناك.

– هذيلية

اسم لنبات يعرفه شجارو الاندلس خاصة، ولم أره في أرض الشام وانما اكثر ما رأيته في الأندلس في مدينة غرناطة على النهر الذي يشق مدينة مسيلة.

هذه نماذج من طريقة البحث الميداني التي مكنت ابن البيطار من استيعاب معلومات واسعة عن النباتات، وهذا ما جعل كتابه «الجامع» مصدراً أساسياً لدراسة علم النبات عند المسلمين.

ومن الأمور التي تزيد في أهمية (جامع ابن البيطار) أنه لم يكن مجرد ناقل، بل أنه ينقد ويوازن، ولنأخذ مثلا في كتابه:

– أقحوان

هو عند العرب البابونج المعروف في مصر، وهو الكركاش وهو أنواع، فبعض شجاري الاندلس جعل الاقحوان نوعاً صغيراً من انواع الكركاش. وزعم قوم أن المراد به ما تحت هذه الترجمة، وليس الأمر كما زعم – لأن الدواء المذكور تحت هذه الترجمة – وهو المسمى باليونانية فرتانيون – ليس من أنواع الكركاش وانما هو في الحقيقة النبتة المعروفة في الأندلس اليوم وما قبله بشجرة مريم، وتعرف في افريقيا واعمالها بالكافورية. ومنها في مدينة الموصل شيء كثير مزدرع وتعرف في الموصل بشجرة الكافور، وهي نوعان: جبلية تنبت في الحال الباردة جداً، ومزدرعة في البساتين وفي البيوت وفي المراكز.

......

كان ابن البيطار يجيد عدة لغات بينها اليونانية والبربرية واللاتينية والفارسية، اضافة الى العربية. وقد دفعته معرفته الواسعة هذه الى الاهتمام بمختلف التسميات النباتية والحيوانية والمعدنية للأدوية والمستحضرات الصيدلية التي اشتمل عليها كتابه.

تعد ظاهرة التواجد بين اللغات في كتاب «الجامع» ظاهرة طبيعية، فقد ذكر فيها: العرض السادس من اسماء الأدوية بسائر اللغات المتباينة في السمات، مع اني لم أذكر فيه ترجمة دواء إلا وفيه منفعة مذكورة او تجربة مشهورة.

وذكرتُ كثيراً منها بما يعرف به في الأماكن التي تنسب اليها

الأدوية المسطورة كالالفاظ البربرية واللاتينية، وهي عجمية إذ
كانت مشهورة عندنا وجارية في كتبنا. وطريقته في ذكر أسماء
الأدوية (بما تُعرف به في الأمكان التي تنسب اليها) أي بالعربية
والبربرية واللاتينية – تضاف الى طريقة اخرى مهمة أيضا
تجسدت في ذكر مختلف الأسماء لمختلف الأدوية، كما توجد في
المصادر القديمة التي استقرأها المؤلف وخاصة المصادر اليونانية
منها.

12. Oral

الطب التقليدي والطب الحديث

(a) One student to present an account of الطب التقليدي في الوطن العربي.

(b) A second student to present an account of الطب الحديث في الوطن العربي.

(c) The presenters then ask the other students questions about الطب التقليدي
والطب الحديث. These should include questions which require factual answers
and others which require speculative, hypothetical or subjective answers. For
example:

١ – ماذا أُستعمل في الطب التقليدي في الوطن العربي؟

٢ – كيف يختلف الطب الحديث عن الطب التقليدي؟

٣ – ما هي فوائد الطب التقليدي؟

٤ – ما هي فوائد الطب الحديث؟

٥ – هل من الممكن ان نستفيد من الطب التقليدي؟

٦ – هل هناك مظاهر غير مفيدة في الطب الحديث، ما هي؟

(d) Open lecturer–led discussion on الطب التقليدي والطب الحديث.

13. Essay

(a) Carrying on from where the text in section 5 (c) leaves off, write your own
ending to the story told in الأيام.

(b) Write an essay in Arabic of 200 words on the title الطب العربي. In your
writing address some of the following issues.

١ – الطب التقليدي في الوطن العربي – استعمال الاعشاب.

٢ – الشخصيات المهمة في الطب العربي.

٣ – نشوء المستشفيات في الوطن العربي.

٤ – الطب الحديث في الوطن العربي.

٥ – الفروق الرئيسة بين الطب الحديث والطب التقليدي.

٦ – تأثير الطب التقليدي في الطب الحديث.

٧ – مساوئ الطب الحديث في الوطن العربي.

٨ – ما هو مستقبل الطب العربي؟

20
Islamic heritage

1. Basic background material

(a) *Islam in a unitary world*

European colonialism (including the colonisation of the Arab world from the end of the eighteenth century onwards), and the development of a world economy with mass production, mass movement of goods and people, multinational corporations, and instant communication can be said to have destroyed an autonomous Islamic civilisation, just as it has destroyed an autonomous Japanese or Chinese civilisation. The world is in a more profound sense one than at any previous time in history.

However, the terms on which this unity has been achieved have been largely dictated by the West: in the nineteenth century by the European powers, and in the twentieth century increasingly by the United States. Formerly, the communism of eastern Europe offered some alternative to Western capitalism, at least on an ideological plane. However, even for those who are socially discontented, the fall of east European communism in the early 1990s and the return of these states to capitalism, along with the increasingly capitalist orientation of China, have largely deprived this potential alternative of its remaining credibility. Forms of socialism, or more generally 'statism', which were attempted elsewhere (in the Arab world, under Nasser in Egypt, for example) have similarly been largely abandoned, and are now widely regarded as having led to inefficient industries, parasitic bureaucracies and economic corruption.

It is possible that in the twenty–first century China will emerge – perhaps along with Japan and other major states of east Asia such as Indonesia – as a major centre of world power, perhaps the centre of world power. If this happens, there may be some de–Westernisation (de–Europeanisation) of culture throughout the world. Alternatively, the United States may remain the dominant power in the world, probably continuing to pursue policies of international free trade and deregulation of markets, including labour markets. Or moves towards a united Europe (at least on the economic plane) might lead to a resurgence of social–market structures, characterised by markedly redistributive tax systems (reducing income inequality), universal social welfare, and employee participation in what are otherwise capitalist enterprises. Currently, however, with the continuing relative lack of competitiveness of Europe, this last possibility seems somewhat unlikely.

The possibility of the development of an Islamic bloc as the centre of world economic and social power appears even more unlikely, with the relative failure to industrialise of most Islamic states (Indonesia and Malaysia are major exceptions), and the continuing reliance of the oil–rich states of the Arab world on both oil and Western support, as seen in the 1991 Gulf war (cf. ch. 7, 1).

Running counter to this relative economic weakness of the Islamic world, however, is an extraordinary religious vitality. This is particularly striking in comparison with Japan, where only a small proportion of the population professes any religious belief. It is also fairly striking in comparison with Western Europe where religious belief in a general sense has more or less maintained itself over the past fifty years, but where mainstream Christianity has steadily lost adherents. In more traditional societies, such as India, religion has not declined as it has in Western Europe, and even in the United States the decline has been less pronounced.

In contrast with the relative decline of organised religion elswhere, religious sentiment in the Islamic world has become much more pronounced over the past few decades. In the Middle East, this sometimes manifests itself by adherence to Islamic organisations which are radical to varying degrees, and often explicitly anti–Western. Even among those not attracted by 'Islamic politics', however, there is an increase in Islamic observance – of the five daily prayers, and the Ramadan fast, for example.

Outside the Middle East, Islam is advancing rapidly in Africa, making as many as 1,000,000 converts a year. Missionary efforts are well funded (by the oil–rich Arab states, among others), and converts are attracted by the simplicity of the Islamic message, and its general compatibility with existing African ways of life, as well perhaps with its lack of association with the colonialism of the West.

More evident from a western point of view is the growth of Islam in the West. This is partly because of Muslim immigration (from India and Pakistan into Britain, from North Africa into France, from various Arab states into North America). There is now, however, also a significant process of conversion to Islam amongst groups which previously had no Islamic affiliations, most strikingly among Black Americans. There are now estimated to be two million Black Muslims in the United States (out of a total American Muslim population of almost six million), some belonging to mainstream Islamic sects, while others are affiliated to non–orthodox groups, such as the Nation of Islam, led by Louis Farrakhan. The current rate of conversion to Islam among Black Americans has been claimed to be as high as 250,000 a year. A similar conversion movement also seems to be underway among black (Afro–Caribbean) people in Britain, though it is probably too early to say whether this will maintain itself.

(b) *The Islamic heritage in high and popular culture*
Regardless of the future of Islam in the world, the Islamic civilisation of the pre–modern era has made a significant contribution to world civilisation in general, and Western civilisation in particular, in the areas of both high culture and popular culture.

In the area of high culture, the Islamic contribution ranges from philosophy, to medicine, to music, to poetry (the poetry of the troubadours, who flourished in Provence and northern Italy between the eleventh and thirteenth centuries owes much to Andalusian poetry), to geography, chemistry, and mathematics. The Arabic numerals now used in the West – including, crucially, the zero, which had eluded the Greeks and Romans – are derived from an Andalusian and North African variant of the numbers used generally in the Middle East (which themselves originate in India, as indicated by their Arabic designation, أرقام هندية). And without Arabic translations, much of the Greek heritage of antiquity would never have come down to the West.

Perhaps the most obvious feature of Arabic popular culture which has come down to the West is astrology. Astrology has ancient roots in Greece, the Middle East, Iran and India, but it is at least in part through the forms developed by the Arab astrologers, relayed by medieval translations of Arabic astrological works into Western languages, that astrology is now typically practised in the West.

2. Additional reading
(a) Lewis, *The Arabs in History*, pp. 131–43.
(b) Hourani, *A History of the Arab Peoples*, pp. 434–58.
(c) Young, Latham and Serjeant (eds.), *The Cambridge History of Arabic Literature*, vol. III, *Religion, Learning and Science in the Abbasid Period*, pp. 290–300.
(d) G. Kepel, *Allah in the West*, (Cambridge: Polity Press, 1997).
(e) Hodgson, *The Venture of Islam*, vol. III, pp. 411–41.

3. Key vocabulary
On the basis of your reading of the texts in this chapter, draw up lists of vocabulary in the following fields:
(a) Islamic scientific vocabulary
(b) Astrological terminology

4. Written Arabic texts 1
(a) As a preparatory exercise for this chapter, read the following text at home.

كان العرب في مجال العلوم ورثة للبابليين والمصريين
القدامى والهنود واليونان والرومان بحكم الاحدار البيئي
والاجتماعي والتاريخي. وأول من اشتغل في الصناعات هم

أهل وادي الرافدين وبعدهم طور أهل مصر التعدين وأبدعوا
فيه وعلى الأخص تعدين المعادن الثمينة، وفي مقدمتها الذهب.
ثم كانت الصباغة وصناعة الزجاج وتحضير الأدوية وما يتصّل
بها من مواد التحنيت والعطور فتطورت على أيديهم.

(b) Read the following text from عبقرية, حصاد الشهر, no. 32, side 1, item 3,
الحضارة العربية, then in pairs produce and exchange your own
comprehension questions; produce questions firstly in Arabic, then in English.

عبقرية الحضارة العربية

بُعيد وفاة الرسول صلى الله عليه وسلم بدأ العرب فتوحهم التي
وضعت تحت تصرفهم خلال قرن واحد جميع المنطقة الشاسعة
الممتدة من أواسط آسيا وحوض السند شرقًا إلى شمال إسبانيا
غربًا. وبذلك أقاموا دولة الخلافة التي انتقلت عاصمتها من المدينة
المنورة أولاً إلى كوفة ثم إلى دمشق أيام الأمويين وأخيرًا إلى بغداد
لما قامت الدولة العباسية في أواسط القرن الثاني للهجرة والقرن
الثامن للميلاد وبنى المنصور مدينة السلام. وقد ترتّب على قيام
هذه الدولة نشوء مجتمع جديد فريد في نوعه لم يعرف له التاريخ
مثيلاً من قبل. فقد كان واسعًا دون حدود يُسمَح للمرء أن يتنقل
فيه سائحًا أو تاجرًا أو عالمًا أو حاجًا. وتلا الفتح العسكري فتح
لغوي إذ انتشرت العربية في أنحائه لغة الإدارة والعلوم الإسلامية
والمنقولة عن الحضارات الأخرى. وانتشر الإسلام في ربوع هذا
العالم الجديد، فكان الروح الهادية لها كما كانت العربية سبيل
التفكير والتعبير فيه وطريق التعلم والتعليم. وفي هذا المجتمع
الجديد تعرّف العرب إلى التراث الحضاري المتنوع للشعوب المختلفة
التي خضعت له والتي احتكّوا بها مباشرةً.

فنقلوا ما كان أولاً عند السريان من ترجمات للطب والفلسفة
والمنطق منقولة عن اليونانية.. ذلك بأن الكنيسة المسيحية
الشرقية على تنوع اتجاهاتها كانت قد نقلت هذه الأمور عن

اليونانية وذلك لاستخدام الفلسفة والجدل في المناقشات والخلافات الدينية بين الفرق المسيحية. لكن هذا الدور الأول لم يَطُل إذ أخذ العرب يترجمون عن اليونانية إلى العربية رأسًا. وقد وجد العرب في البلاد التي فتحوها مدارس كبيرة كانت مراكز البحث والتعليم وأهمّها بقية مدرسة الإسكندرية القديمة ومدرسة غزة ومدرسة أنطاكيا ومدرسة روها – أو إيديسا – ومدرسة جنديسابور في جنوب غرب إيران. وهذه بالذات كانت فيها مدرسة مهمة للطب كما كان فيها بيمارستان كبير، أي مستشفى. وترجم العرب أدبًا فارسيا مثل «كليلة ودمنة» واتصلوا بالتراث العلمي خارج الدولة نفسها إذ حُملت مخطوطات يونانية إلى بغداد لنقلها إلى العربية كما كان أول كتاب فلكي نقل إلى العربية هنديًا وهو المعروف باسم «السد هند». وقد ترك القدامى في أرض الرافدين وبلاد الشام ووادِيَ النيل آثارًا مختلفة بعضها ظاهر كالآثار الفنية وبعضها توارَثه القوم علمًا ممزوجًا بالأسطورة مثل التنجيم. هذه جميعها انتقلت إلى الحضارة العربية بالواسطة، أي عبر التوارث الاجتماعي.

وفي أواخر القرن الثاني عشر بدأ التراث العربي يجد طريقه إلى أوربا على يد المترجمين الذين اجتهدوا في نقل كتب العلوم والطب والفلسفة إلى اللغة اللاتينية كما قام من جاء قبلهم بنقل التراث اليوناني إلى العرب في القرنين الثامن والتاسع. ومن الجدير بالذكر أن الكثير من الفكر الإغريقي لم يصل إلى علماء الأوربيين قبيل عصر النهضة سوى عن طريق دراسات العلماء العرب له – كابن سيناء وابن رشد وغيرهما. وظلت التراجم اللاتينية لتلك الدراسات المرجع الأول للبحاثة في الغرب إلى ما بعد القرن السادس عشر.

وفي تصنيف العلوم في عهد الدولة الإسلامية سعى كثير من المؤرخين العلماء في عصرنا هذا بمفهومهم الحديث وتعريفهم

المتخصص الدقيق، فقسموها إلى علوم نظرية وعلوم تطبيقية، أو علوم طبيعية وعلوم حية. والواقع أن العلوم في ذلك الزمن لم تأبه بالحدود أو الاختصاصات. فكان العالم الرياضي الفيلسوف طبيبًا عالمًا بالعقاقير والأعشاب وربما بالموسيقى أيضًا. وقد يدرّس الفلكي الرياضيات والكيمياء ويؤلف في علم الحيوان وربما الشعر.

(c) Read the following text from حصاد الشهر, no. 8, side 2, item 3, المسلمون هم الأوائل في تأسيس أقدم جامعة في العالم, and predict and fill in the words and phrases missing from the text. Discuss orally in class in Arabic why you have chosen these particular words.

الجامعات العربية الإسلامية العريقة نذكر ـــــــــ كثيرة

ـــــــــ الأزهر ـــــــــ الزيتونة و ـــــــــ جامعة القرويين و

المستنصرية والنظامية ونيسابور ـــــــــ و قرطبة و ـــــــــ

أقدم الجامعات أن ـــــــــ بغداد، ويكاد الإجماع ينعقد ـــــــــ

ـــــــــ طُرًّا العالم ـــــــــ الجامعات ـــــــــ العربية الإسلامية بل

تأسست ـــــــــ فاس بالمغرب ـــــــــ جامعة القرويين

ثماني مائة وثمان – ـــــــــ وخمسين وخمس مائتين ـــــــــ

أحد ـــــــــ أكثر ـــــــــ ـــــــــ وستين ميلادية. فقد مضى

علمي إشعاع منارة خلالها ظلت القرن، ونصف ـــــــــ عشر

و ـــــــــ إلى جانب شقيقتيها جامعة الزيتونة وجامعة الأزهر.

مساجد تأسيسها عند كانت العريقة ـــــــــ هذه ـــــــــ يُذكر

ـــــــــ أساسًا الدينية العلوم لتدريس حلقات فيها تُعقد للعبادة

التعليمية مناهجها وتطورت ـــــــــ التدريس نطاق اتسع

ـــــــــ بالمعنى جامعات أصبحت ـــــــــ وتشعّبت وانتظمت

واثنتين مائة ـــــــــ المغربية فاس مدينة تأسست ـــــــــ

وتسعين هجرية كان في عداد الذين هاجروا إليها ———— ———— تونس

محمد بن عبد الله الفِهري القيرواني ———— ———— توفي بُعيد وصوله

———— فاس تاركا ثروة طائلة لكريمتيه فاطمة ومريم. ————

منتصف ———— ———— الثالث الهجري بنت فاطمة أم البنين

القيروانية ———— القرويين بعدوة القرويين في ————

الغربي ———— نهر فاس. وسرعان ما أصبحت ———— فاس

قبلة أنظار العلماء والأدباء فقد جعلت منها جامعتُها الجديدة

عاصمة ثقافية يحج إليها الطلاب لا ———— شمال إفريقيا

———— بل ومن أطراف أوربا ———— ومن جملة من وفد عليها

البابا سلفستر الثاني ———— ———— درس في القرويين الأرقام

———— ، ثم أدخلها ———— أوربا ———— ارتقائه سلطة

البابوية.

ويلي القرويين ———— العراقة ———— الأزهر في ————

التي ———— ———— تسع مائة واثنتين وسبعين ميلادية،

فيكون ———— مضى ———— تأسيسها أكثر ———— ألف

———— ، وبعدها جامعة الزيتونة ———— تونس بنت جامعها

عطف أرملة المستنصر الحصي ———— ألف ومائتين وثلاث

وثمانين ميلادية، ونذكر في هذا ———— أنّ ———— ————

في أوربا ———— جامعة أكسفرد التي ———— ———— ألف

ومائة وسبع وستين ميلادية، أي بعد جامعة القرويين بـ ————

ثلاثة ———— ، وتلتها جامعة كيمبريج ———— ———— بعد

أكــســفــرد ———— مـن قـرن ———— الـزمـان ———— ألـف
ومـائـتـين وأربـع وثمـانـين ميـلاديـة.

5. Written Arabic texts 2

(a) Translate the following text into idiomatic English.

الكيمياء

الكيمياء من العلوم التي لها علاقة بالطب ، وقد بلغ فيها العرب
شأوا بعيدا حتى ان علماء أوروبا يضعون العرب في المقام الأعلى
عند بحثهم في تاريخ الكيمياء . وأول من أدخل الكيمياء خالد بن
يزيد الأول المتوفى ٨٥ هـ حين استخدم بعض العلماء من مدرسة
الاسكندرية . ومن الأسباب التي دعت العرب الى العناية بالكيمياء
(١) الرغبة الشديدة في تحويل المعادن الرخيصة الى ذهب (٢)
محاولتهم اكتشاف الالكسير الأعلى أو ما يسمى بحجر الفلاسفة
لاعادة الشباب واطالة العمر . وجابر بن حيان أول من حضر
حامض الكبريتيك المعروف بزيت الزاج ، واكتشف حامض
النيتريك وهيدروكسيد الصوديوم . وأوجد العرب التقطير ،
والترشيح ، والتبخير ، والتذويب ، والتبلور . واكتشفوا القلويات
، ونترات الفضة . وقد ظلت تعاليمهم في الكيمياء معمولا بها حتى
القرن الثامن عشر . ويعتبر العرب أصحاب الكيمياء العملية ، أما
اليونان فهم أصحاب الكيمياء النظرية .

(b) Read the star signs in the following horoscope, then complete exercises i. – iii.
which follow.

اليوم   برجك

* برج الجدي ٢١ ديسمبر الى ٢٠ يناير
علاقة عاطفية قديمة مطلوب منك ان تنهيها
قريبا.

* برج الدلو ٢١ يناير الى ٢٠ فبراير

احترس من رسالة هامة تصلك من شخص لا
يضمر لك الحب او المودة.

* برج الحوت من ٢١ فبراير الى ٢٠ مارس
دعوة توجه اليك لحضور حفل لا بد من تقديم
هدية خلاله.

* برج الحمل من ٢١ مارس الى ٢٠ ابريل
الحكمة تقول ما استحق ان يولد من عاش لنفسه
فقط.

* برج الثور من ٢١ ابريل الى ٢٠ مايو
تركيزك على الاشياء الهامة يجعلك تفقد بعض
الاشياء الصغيرة المفيدة.

* برج الجوزاء من ٢١ مايو الى ٢٠ يونيو
اليوم تحصل على بعض اللمحات المفيدة ممن
تحب قد تجعلك تغير من رأيك.

* برج السرطان من ٢١ يونيو الى ٢٠ يوليو
لا تكن انانيا وحاول مساعدة الاخرين قدر
استطاعتك وعندها ستشعر بالسعادة.

* برج الاسد من ٢١ يوليو الى ٢٠ اغسطس
مشروعاتك الشخصية وخاصة المالية منها في
توسع مستمر فاحترس لنفسك.

* برج العذراء من ٢١ اغسطس الى ٢٠
سبتمبر
يوم مزدحم بالاعمال لن تجد خلاله وقت لالتقاط
الانفاس.

* برج الميزان من ٢١ سبتمبر الى ٢٠
اكتوبر
موقف مفاجئ تتعرض له سيكشف لك عن

اصدقائك المخلصين من حولك.

* بـرج العـــقـــرب مـن ٢١ اكـتـــوبـر الى ٢٠
نـوفـمـبـر

الاهتـمـام والجـدية في العـمل يجعلك مـحـط انظار
واهتمام الرؤساء.

* بـرج القـــوس مـن ٢١ نـوفـــمــبـــر الى ٢٠
ديسمبر

انت في حاجـة الى سـلوك طـريـق السـلامـة والامـان
ولا داعي للمغـامـرات الفاشلة.

i   Find your own star sign and paraphrase its predictions or message orally in
Arabic.
ii Ask other students for their birthdates and let them paraphrase the predictions or
message of their sign orally in Arabic.
iii Using the same kind of abbreviated 'sentences' as those given in the horoscope
above write three or four of your own star signs in Arabic.

6. Written Arabic texts 3 (classical)

Translate the following text by ابن صلت from الطب الفلكي into idiomatic
English.

الباب الثاني

فيما يحتاج اليه المتطبّب من علم طبائع البروج

اعلم أنّ البـروج الاثنا عـشــر تـدلّ على الأسْطُقُسّـات الأربعـة دلالةً
عـامـيّـةً أعـنـى النار والهـواء والماء والأرض ، فـالحـمل والأسد والقـوس
مثلّثـة ناريّـة حـارّة يابسـة تدلّ على الصفراء والأشياء المرّة الناشفة
والحرارات والنيران ، والثور والسُنْبُلـة والجـدى مثلّثـة أرضيّة باردة
يابسـة تدلّ على السـوداء والأشـيـاء الكريهـة الجـافّـة والبـردات
الأرضيّـات ، والجَوْزاء والميزان والدلو مثلّثـة هوائيّة حارّة رطبة تدلّ
على الدم والأشـيـاء الحُلوة المعـتـدلة والحـرارات والهـوائـيـات ،
والسـرطان والعـقـرب والحـوت مـثلّثـة مـائيّة باردة رطبة تدلّ على

البلغم والأشياء العذبة السيالة والرطوبات والمائيّات ،
واعلم أنّ الحمل والسرطان والميزان والجدى منقلبة تدلّ على تقلّب
الأحوال وتغيّرها في سرعة ، والثور والأسد والدلو والعقرب ثابتة
تدلّ على البطء وعسر الانتقال والتغيّر من حال الى حال ، والجوزاء
والسنبلة والقوس والحوت ذوات جسدين تدلّ على التوسّط في
تنقّل الأحوال والأمور .

7. Grammar/stylistics

(a) *The basic connectors:* ثمّ *and* ف ، و
Arabic has three basic connectors و ، ف and ثمّ. In Classical Arabic these are said to
be properly used as follows (cf. Bohas, Guillaume, Kouloughli 1990: 134):

ف involves either temporal or logical sequence or both. That is to say what
comes after ف is either logically dependent on what comes before, or occurs after
what comes before, or both.

ثمّ also involves temporal or logical sequence or both. But in addition it also
involves non–immediacy; that is to say, the event described after ثمّ does not occur
immediately after the event described before, and it is not an immediate logical
consequence of the event described before.

و by contrast, simply involves association. That is to say, it simply implies there
is some link between what is described before the و and what is described after it.

It is also possible for there to be no connectors between adjacent sentences. This is
said to occur, either (i) where there is no link whatever between the adjacent
sentences, or (ii) where the two sentences completely agree in formal structure and
meaning, such that the second simply echoes and reinforces the first, or (iii) where
the second sentences follows on quite predictably from the first, as in a
question–answer sequence, such as the following line of poetry قال لي كيف أنت
قلت عليل سهر دائما وحزن طويل 'He asked me, "How are you?". I said, "Bad.
Endless insomnia and chronically sad".' (cf. Bohas, Guillaume, Koughouli 1990:
133). Here there is no connector between the question كيف أنت and the reply
قلت عليل, since the question makes some kind of reply predictable.

In practice, the use of basic connectors in modern Arabic is not as
straightforward as the above description might suggest. ثمّ presents relatively few
problems, and in its basic temporal usage corresponds closely to English 'then'.
Three things are, however, worth remembering about ثمّ. The first is that ثمّ cannot
be preceded by و or ف (just as ف cannot be preceded by و or ثمّ, and و cannot be
preceded by ف or ثمّ). This means that *وثمّ* is not an acceptable translation of
'and then'. Secondly, ثمّ can be used in a logical rather than temporal sense to mark
the forward movement of an argument from one point to another. For example:

هي دينية من حيث أنها تُلْغي الغيبيات التي ترتكز عليها الدين
{ثم} أيضا تأخذ مكان الدين في تعيين الأخلاق والقيم الإنسانية {ثم}
هي فلسفية ...

'It is religious, because it does away with the supernatural elements on
which religion is based, and because it takes the place of religion in
determining morals and values. It is also philosophical ...' (from أدب
للشعب by سلامة موسى 1961: 107; quoted in Cantarino 1975, vol.
III: 38).

Finally, when ثم joins two clauses, it must normally be followed by a verb (or a
particle, such as لم, لن, سوف plus a verb). It is not standardly followed directly
by a noun or adverbial. In this respect ثم contrasts with و and ف which can be
followed by either a verb, or a noun, or an adverbial (cf. ch. 13, 7ai, 7aii, 7aiii).

The major problems for an English speaker with respect to the basic connectors
are the difference in usage between و and ف, and the tendency in modern Arabic to
use no connector in circumstances where و might be expected.

With respect to the difference in usage between و and ف, consider the
following:

اسم عُرف به جنوب اسبانيا بعد أن احتلها القاندال {فـ}أَخذ عنهم
اسمه: واندالوسيا.

'[Andalusia] A name by which southern Spain was known following its
occupation by the Vandals, whose name it took [lit: 'and it took its
name from them']: *Vandalusia*.' (ch. 12, 4ai)

تلاشت الإمارة {فـ}عقبها دويلات حكمها ملوك الطوائف ..

'The Emirate collapsed and was followed by mini–states ruled by the
Party Kings ...' (ch. 12, 4ai)

قدمه ابن طفيل لأبي يعقوب يوسف خليفة الموحدين ١١٨٢،
{فـ}عيّنه طبيباً ثم قاضياً في قرطبة.

'He [Ibn Rushd] was presented to Abu Ya'qub Yusuf, the Mohavid
Caliph in 1182, and he appointed him physician and later judge in
Cordova.' (ch. 12, 4avi)

ثم جاء عبد الرحمن الثاني {فـ}رفع من قيمة الطرب والموسيقى ..

'Then came Abd al-Rahman the Second who [lit: 'and he'] increased the
prestige of singing and music ...' (ch. 12, 11)

Each of the above sentences makes use of ف as a connector in situations where an

English speaker might expect و. In each case there is some kind of 'causal' relationship. In the first example, the adoption of the name *Vandalusia* is an outcome of the fact that the Vandals had settled in Spain; if they hadn't the country would never have come to be named after them. In the second example, the emergence of the Party Kings was a result of the breakup of the Emirate. In the third example, the appointment of Ibn Rushd as physician (and later as judge) stemmed from his prior presentation at court; and in the final example Abd al-Rahman the Second's increasing of the prestige of singing and music was dependent on his prior accession to the throne.

The problem from an English speaker's point of view in each of these cases is that the 'causal' relationship is rather weak. In none of the examples given above is there a question of strict causality. It was not a necessary consequence of the occupation of Spain by the Vandals that the country subsequently became known as *Vandalusia*. Nor is it even a question of relative predictability or expectedness. It is not particularly expected that the occupation of a country by a certain ethnic group will lead to that country being renamed after that ethnic group (the invasion of England by the Normans did not lead to England being renamed 'Normanland', for example). Rather these examples involve a weaker sort of 'causality' such that the second event follows on from the first, but it is neither the only event which might have followed on from the first, nor even necessarily the expected outcome of the first event. It would be odd in all the examples given above to replace 'and' (etc.) with 'so' as the translation of ف. The first two examples (with additional changes where necessary) are sufficient to illustrate this:

اسم عُرف به جنوب اسبانيا بعد أن احتلها الڤاندال {فـ}أَخذ عنهم
اسمه: واندالوسيا.

'[Andalusia] A name by which southern Spain was known following its occupation by the Vandals, {so} it took its name from them: *Vandalusia*.' (ch. 12, 4ai)

تلاشت الإمارة {فـ}عقبها دويلات حكمها ملوك الطوائف ..

'The Emirate collapsed {and so} it was followed by mini–states ruled by the Party Kings ...' (ch. 12, 4ai)

The reason for the oddness of 'so' in these cases is that 'so' implies either strict causality or at least that the second event is an expected outcome of the first. It is therefore important for an English speaker in writing Arabic or translating into Arabic, to consider not only whether 'so' would be a possible connector in the context in question, but more generally whether the situation involves a 'logical' or 'causal' relationship in a looser or more general sense. If it does, ف may be used rather than و.

Because و is a general connector, implying only some link between one event and another, it may be used in a variety of contexts. Particularly striking for an

English speaker are cases in which و is most naturally translated as English 'but', 'although', 'however', etc. and can accordingly be said to have an adversative sense in Arabic. For example:

.. حـيـث دخلت هذه الدول مــرحلة جــديدة {و}لم تقطع جــذورها بالماضي.

'... when these states entered a new era, although their roots in the past remained intact.' (ch. 18, 5b).

.. فقسموها إلى علوم نظرية وعلوم تطبيقية، أو علوم طبيعية وعلوم حية. {و}الواقع أن العلوم في ذلك الزمن لم تأبه بالحدود أو الإختصاصات.

'... they have divided them into theoretical sciences and applied sciences, or natural sciences and life–sciences. The truth, however, is that sciences at that time were not concerned with boundaries or specialisms.' (ch. 20, 4b)

Less commonly, ف may also be translatable as 'but', etc. For example:

وحاول أن يُقْنِعَ أبويه بذلك {فـ}لم يُوَفَّق.

'He tried to convince his parents of this, but did not succeed.' (ch. 19, 5d)

In some styles of modern Standard Arabic, و is not used in a variety of contexts in which the rules of Classical Arabic would dictate that it should be used. This is particularly the case where what is intended is a concise and unemotional factual statement of something. The following example is an encyclopedia entry for ابن زيدون from the dictionary and encyclopedia المنجد في اللغة والأعلام. {X} marks a point at which و might be expected in a more standard text:

ولد في قرطبة وتوفي في إشبيلية. {X} وزير من شعراء الأندلس. {X} اشتــهر شعره بولّادة بنت المستكفي. {X} أخبــاره مـعها ومع منافسه فيها الوزير عبد عبدوس كثيرة. {X} كان له بـين الأمـراء منزلة عـاليـة لمواهبـه الأدبيـة ومـعرفتـه بأحـوال المسلمـين في الأندلس. له «ديوان».

(In the case of the sentence which reads وزير من شعراء الأندلس, one would also expect in a more standard text an additional initial verb with وزيرًا in the accusative.)

This kind of 'staccato' style is also reminiscent of compound newspaper headlines (of the type favoured in الأهرام for example), where there is no link between the individual statements making up the compound headline. For example:

موت السادات المفاجيء يحدث فراغا سياسيا في مصر يصعب تقدير أبعاده السّادات كان المحور المركزي لأمريكا في المنطقة واختفاؤه «كارثة كبرى لها!» تساؤلات كبيرة حول الموقف الذي سيتخذه حُسني مبارك من الكيان الصهيوني

(ch. 16, 4c).

This kind of style owes something to the style of newspaper and dictionary writing in English and other western languages (for discussion of word order and tense in newspaper Arabic, see ch. 6, 7b and 7c).

In newspaper writing more generally, there is some variation but most writers adhere roughly to the Classical Arabic norms for using و. In modern fiction, there is a tendency amongst some writers to adopt a style in which و, and other connectors, are used more sparingly than might be expected. This may be partly due to the influence of European styles of writing. It can also reflect an attempt to write a form of Arabic which adheres to the grammatical rules of Standard Arabic, but has something of the feel of colloquial speech. Colloquial Arabic, if anything, uses fewer connectors than English, and is therefore quite different in this respect from Standard Arabic. The following is an excerpt from the beginning of موسم الهجرة الى الشمال by the Sudanese author الطيب صالح. Points at which و or another connector might have been expected to occur but does not are marked by {X}.

عدت الى اهلي يا سادتي بعد غيبة طويلة، سبعة أعوام على وجه التحديد ، {X} كنت خلالها أتعلم في أوربا. {X} تعلمت الكثير وغاب عني الكثير ، لكن تلك قصة أخرى . {X} المهم أنني عدت وبي شوق عظيم الى أهلي في تلك القرية الصغيرة عند منحنى النيل . {X}؟ سبعة اعوام وأنا أحن اليهم وأحلم بهم ، ولما جئتهم كانت لحظة عجيبة أن وجدتني حقيقة قائماً بينهم ، {X} فرحوا بي وضجوا حولي ولم يمض وقت طويل حتى أحسست كأن ثلجا يذوب في دخيلتي ، فكأنني مقرور طلعت عليه الشمس . {X} ذاك دفء الحياة في العشيرة ، فقدته زماناً في بلاد « تموت من البرد حيتانها » . {X} تعودت أذناي أصبواتهم وألفت عيناي أشكالهم من كثرة ما فكرت فيهم في الغيبة ، {X} قام بيني وبينهم شيء مثل الضباب أول ما رأيتهم . لكن الضباب راح واستيقظت ثاني يوم وصولي ، في فراشي الذي اعرفه في الغرفة التي تشهد جدرانها على ترهات حياتي في طفولتها ومطلع شبابها وأرخيت أذني للريح .

Here the quasi–spoken nature of the passage is underlined by the inclusion of يا
سادتي in the first line, as though the author is telling his story to a group of friends
or acquaintances. Other forms reminiscent of spoken language are also included in
the text, such as المهم (line 3). It is also noteworthy that the form لكن occurs twice
in this passage, while the form ولكن does not occur at all. Again, this use of لكن
rather than ولكن is reminiscent of colloquial usage.

(b) لكنْ and لكنَّ

Given that و in Arabic may have an adversative sense, and may therefore be
translatable into English by 'but', etc. (cf. above), it is reasonable that و may be
combined with the adversative particles لكنْ and لكنَّ to give the compound forms
ولكنْ and ولكنَّ. In fact the compound forms ولكنْ and ولكنَّ are the more
commonly used forms, although the forms لكنْ and لكنَّ without و are also fairly
frequently encountered.

i لكنْ

The forms لكنْ and ولكنْ are typically used in the following circumstances: where
there is no noun or pronoun suffix available to be used after لكن; where the use of
a noun or pronoun suffix after لكن would render the phrase less concise and
effective; or where there is a fronted adverbial. Examples where there is no noun or
pronoun suffix include the use of لكن before imperatives and before question
words, as in the following:

.. {ولكن} اذهب إليها الآن وأرني أثراً واحداً لقنبلة أو طوربيد ..
'... but go there now and show me a single sign of a bomb or a torpedo
...' (ch. 13, 11b)

{ولكن} هل يبدي مبارك نفس «التفاهم» الذي كان يظهره السادات
إزاء «الدولة» اليهودية ..
'But will Mubarak show the same "understanding" which was shown
by Sadat towards the Jewish "state" ...' (ch. 16, 4b).

'But who were Kinda?' (ch. 17, 4c)   {ولكن} مَنْ كندة ؟

Another situation where no noun or pronoun suffix is available to follow لكن is
after the لا of absolute negation (لا followed by the accusative without تنوين
meaning 'there is not [at all]', etc.). Examples which occur in this book are:

{ولكن} لا راحةَ ولا هدوءَ ولا تأملَ ، ولا اطمئنانَ.
'But there is no rest, no calm, no contemplation, and no peace of
mind.' (ch. 14, 11ai)

ولعلي لست في حاجة إلى تعريف بأي من الحضارتين لأحد منكم وأنتم من أهل الصفوة والعلم، {ولكن} لا بأس من التذكير ونحن في مقام النجوى والتعارف.

'I probably do not need to tell any of you about either of these two civilisations, since you are members of the educated elite. However, there is no harm in reminding you, since we are in a situation where we can exchange confidences and get to know one another.' (ch. 17, 11)

Examples where ولكنْ is used rather than ولكنَّ with a following pronoun suffix on the grounds of concision or effectiveness are the following:

.. فأنا لست أبرئ نفسي مما وقع، ولكن على نحو آخر ومختلف عن التفسير البوليسي « للمؤامرة » كما دعوها.

'I do not absolve myself of guilt for what happened, but [I am guilty] in a completely different way [lit: 'in another and different way'; cf. ch. 19, 7ai)] from the police explanation of the "conspiracy" as they called it.' (ch. 13, 4b)

.. وكانت العلاقات التجارية ... نشطة ...، ولكن في اطار ما سمحت به السياسة البريطانية ..

'Commercial relations ... were ... active, but [they were active] within the framework allowed by British policy ...' (ch. 18, 5b)

The following two cases are examples of fronted adverbials triggering the use of (و)لكنْ, rather than (و)لكنَّ:

لكن بعد سقوط غرناطة، هجر الموسيقيون الأندلس إلى المغرب والجزائر وتونس ..

'But following the fall of Granada, the Spanish musicians emigrated to Morocco, Algeria and Tunisia ...' (ch. 12, 11)

ولكن شيئاً فشيئاً أخذت البشرية تتبين أن هذه الآلهة وتلك إنما تقود العالم كله إلى حروب طاحنة واستعمار بغيض .

'But slowly humanity began to realise that these different gods [lit: 'these gods and those'] were leading the entire world into ruinous wars and odious colonialism.' (ch. 14, 11ai)

In both these above examples, a subject noun phrase is available – الموسيقيون الأندلس in the first example and البشرية in the second – which could otherwise have been placed after لكنْ. However, the fronting of the adverbial occasions a subsequent word order in which the subject follows the verb (cf. ch. 13, 7a).

Accordingly, the form for 'but' which is used is لكنْ and not لكنَّ.

Finally, there are occasional cases where لكنْ is used, but where لكنَّ with a following pronoun suffix could equally have been used. An example from this book is the following:

.. يمكن القـول ان يـوم 23 يوليـو، وهـو يوم ذكـرى ثورة يوليـو (تموز) يمر مـثـله مثل أي يـوم عـادي آخـر في حيـاة المصريـين، {لكنْ} يـظل، بـالطبـع، يـوم عطلة رسمية.

'... it is possible to say that 23rd July, which is the anniversary of the July revolution passes just like any ordinary day in the life of the Egyptians, although it remains, of course, an official holiday.' (ch. 13, 5c)

Here, it would have been perfectly possible for the writer to have written لكنّه يظل without any significant change in meaning or emphasis.

ii لكنَّ

The form لكنَّ followed by a pronoun suffix is standardly used when a noun has been previously mentioned, such that the pronoun suffix can be coreferential with this previously mentioned noun. Typically the pronoun suffix following لكنَّ precedes a verb of which it is the subject. This gives the potentially emphatic word order لكنَّ+subject–verb (where the subject is the pronoun suffix) (cf. ch. 13, 7aii). In most cases, this word order does not carry any sense of emphasis, reflecting the fact that it is the most normal word order with لكن. The following are examples of this structure:

وتشيـر البـاحثـة إلى أنه ربما كـانت التـأثيـرات في موسيـقى الفـلامـنكو أكـثـر وضـوحًا ...، {لكنهـا} تقول إن مـا بقي من المورسكيين بعد سقوط غرناطة هربوا إلى الداخل ..

'The researcher points to the possibility that the influences on flamenco music were clearer, but she says that those who remained of the *Moriscos* following the fall of Granada fled into the interior ...' (ch. 13, 11b)

ولست أدري كيف يعيش الناس في روسيا السوفيـتـية وراء الستار الحديدي ..

...

{ولكني} أدري كيف يعيش الناس في أمريكا .

'I do not know how people live in Soviet Russia behind the Iron Curtain ...

...

But I do know how people live in America.' (ch. 14, 11ai)

وقد اصيب عرفات في الحادث بسجحات واصابات طفيفة ، {ولكنه}
أعلن : « أنا بخير .. »

'Arafat suffered bruises and slight injuries in the accident, but he announced, "I am well ...".' (ch. 16, 11)

It is also possible for no noun to have been previously mentioned but for the reference of the pronoun (particularly a first person pronoun) to be clear from the context:

{ولكننا} لن نجد امرأة واحدة في ذلك السجن العمومي ..

'But we will not find one woman in that public prison ...' (ch. 17, 5b)

In this example, there has been no previous mention of نحن (etc.), but the context is sufficient to determine that what is being referred to here is a generalised 'we' (= 'one', 'people', etc.).

Occasionally, this kind of structure might be somewhat emphatic, as in the following:

وهم لا يتحدثون إلى أحد من الناس .. {ولكنهم} يداعبون الباعة
والمتجولين.

'They don't talk to any of the people, but they [do] tease the shopkeepers and the travelling barrowmen.' (ch. 13, 11b)

Here the word order *pronoun subject–verb* following ولكنهم mirrors the previous clause which also has the word order *pronoun subject–verb*, and the لكن–clause might be regarded as having the same kind of emphasis as occurs in the first clause وهم لا يتحدثون ..

It is also possible to have other kinds of structures involving لكنَّ and a pronoun suffix. Most numerous are cases where the predicate following لكنَّ+*pronoun suffix* is not a verb but an adjective or noun. For example:

وقد امتلأ بالبوليس وعيونهم تتجه إلى من يدخل من المدنيين
{ولكنهم} حريصون على أن يضيقوا اتصالهم بالناس إلى الحد
الأدنى ..

'It [The cabaret] had filled up with policemen, their eyes turning towards any civilian who entered, although they were keen to keep their contacts with people to the absolute minimum ...' (ch. 13, 11b)

والأنثى الوحيدة ... ليست امرأة {ولكنها} كلبة ..

'The sole female ... isn't a woman, but a dog ...' (ch. 17, 5b).

More complex structures following لكنَّ also occur, involving, for example, a

580 Islamic heritage

pronoun of separation (ch. 14, 7b). For example:

وأرجو أن تتقبل بسعة صدر هديتي إليكم بلغة غير معروفة لدى
الكثيرين منكم، {ولكنها} هي الفائز الحقيقي بالجائزة.

'I hope that you will generously accept my present to you in a language
which is not known to many of you, but it is the real winner of the
prize.' [or: '... but it is this language which is the real winner of the
prize.'] (ch. 17, 11)

Occasionally لكنّ occurs with a following pronoun suffix plus a fronted adverbial
(cf. ch. 20, 7aiï.i.), as in the following:

ولكن مَنْ كندة ؟ لا يختلف الرواة في أنهم قبيلة من قحطان ، وهم
يختلفون بعض الاختلاف في نسبها وتفسير اسمها وفي أخبار
سادتها . {ولكنهم} {على كل حال} يتفقون على أنها قبيلة يمانية .

'The reciters are agreed that it is a tribe of Qahtan; they do not agree,
however, over its lineage, the interpretation of its name, and the tales of
its chiefs. But, in any case, they are agreed that it is a Yemeni tribe ...'
(ch. 17, 4c)

.. {ولكنه} قطعا فاخر المنظر من الداخل ..

'... but it [the prison governor's residence] is undoubtedly magnificent
looking inside ...' (ch. 17, 5b)

Examples in which لكنّ is followed by a noun in general show a greater tendency
towards emphaticness than examples in which لكنّ is followed by a pronoun
suffix. Emphaticness is not, however, an automatic result of the combination لكنّ
+noun. The following are cases in which the subject noun following لَكنّ is
followed by an adjective predicate:

{ولكن} الشعرة رفيعة جداً بين « الجريمة » و« الثورة ».

'But there is a very thin line [lit: 'But the hair is very thin'] between
"crime" and "revolution".' (ch. 13, 4b)

اما في ما يتعلق بحزب البعث فيشير المراقبون الى انه تعمد
تقديم اكبر عدد ممكن من المرشحين، {لكن} فرص نجاحهم ضئيلة.

'As far as the Ba'th Party is concerned, observers point to the fact that it
intends to field the largest possible number of candidates, although their
chances of success are slim.' (ch. 15, 4b)

In neither of these two examples does there seem to be much sense of emphasis in

the structure following لكنَّ, and the use of the *noun phrase + adjective phrase*
following لكنَّ seems to be motivated purely by the fact that this is the simplest way
of expressing what the writer has to say.

More interesting are cases in which لكنَّ is followed by a nominal clause
consisting of a noun phrase followed by a verb phrase. Some examples of this kind
do not seem to be emphatic. For example:

وشـدد أية احمـد مـن جـديد علـى ان الانتـخـابات افـتـقـرت للنـزاهة
والحرية والـدليل علـى ذلك ان جبـهة القـوى الاشـتـراكيـة فـازت فـي
الانتـخـابـات المحليـة التـي جـرت فـي شـهـر يـونيـو مـن الـعـام الماضي
بـ ٢٠ ٪ مـن المقـاعـد {ولكن} تقسيـم الدوائـر الجـديد الـذي تم تحت حكم
غـزالـي رئـيس الـوزراء قلـص مـن الـدوائـر فـي المناطـق التـي يـهيـمـن
فيـها مؤيـدو الجبـهة ..

'Aït-Ahmed reiterated the point that the elections were insufficiently fair
[lit: 'clean'] and free, the proof of this being that the Socialist Forces
Front gained 20% of the seats in the local elections which were held last
year, but the new division of constituencies which had taken place
under the Prime Ministership of Ghazali reduced the number of
constituencies in regions dominated by supporters of the Front ...' (ch.
15, 5c)

In other cases involving لكنَّ plus a following *subject+verb*, however, there is a
sense of emphasis. Typically, this takes the form either of contrast with what has
gone before, or scene–setting, or linkage with what has gone before. An example
of contrast is the following:

{ولكن} {الوجه الآخر لهذه العملة} كان الضـعف الفكري والسيـاسي
مما أفقد عضوية الجماعة الغفيرة القدرة على تقويم تنظيمـهم عند
انـحرافـه ..

'But the other side of this coin was an [lit: 'the'] intellectual and political
weakness, which deprived the widespread membership of the Muslim
Brotherhood of the ability to rectify its organisation when it deviated
...' (ch. 14, 11b)

Here, the phrase الوجه الآخر لهذه العملة 'the other side of this coin' provides a
contrast with a previous description of the dramatic growth of the Muslim
Brotherhood, due to openness to anyone who sympathised with its general aims.

Similarly:

.. وقد زالت الإمبراطورية وأمست خبرا من أخبار الماضي، وسوف
يتلاشى الأهرام ذات يوم {ولكن} {الحقيقة والعدل} سيبقيان ما دام
في البشرية عقل يتطلع أو ضمير ينبض.

'... the empire has disappeared and become one of the stories of the
past, and the pyramids too will disappear one day; but truth and justice
will remain, as long as mankind continues to possess an intelligence
which strives, and a conscience which beats.' (ch. 17, 11)

As can be seen, the contrast here is between the physical glories (empire, the
pyramids) of ancient Egypt, and the abstract virtues which نجيب محفوظ is
claiming are ultimately of greater permanance (there is also linkage here, since
الحقيقة والعدل has been mentioned earlier in this text).

The following can be regarded as an example of scene–setting involving لكنّ
plus a following *subject+verb*:

{لكن} {خبراء في الشؤون الايرانية} قالوا ان «ترويكا» مؤلفة من
نجل الخميني احمد ورئيس «مجلس الشورى» (البرلمان) علي اكبر
هاشمي رفسنجاني وخامنئي نفسه تتولى السلطة عمليا في شكل
موقت.

'But experts in Iranian affairs said that a troika consisting of
Khomeini's son Ahmad, the Head of the Consultative Council (the
parliament) Ali Akbar Hashimi Rafsanjani, and Khamanei himself are in
de facto control of power for the time being.' (ch. 16, 5b)

This sentence occurs at the beginning of a new paragraph. Here the phrase لكن
خبراء في الشؤون الايرانية قالوا involves some contrast with the description in
the previous paragraph of the official position regarding power in the country (that
the Council of Experts had elected Khamanei as successor to Khomeini).
It also sets the scene for the information about the real power situation which is to
be given in this paragraph.

Examples of linkage involving لكنّ plus a following *subject+verb* include the
following:

ويقول المراقبون إن علامات استفهام كثيرة سوف تثار بعد ذلك
{ولكن} {هذا الموقف} لم يكن ليختلف حتى لو لم يقتل الرئيس
السادات ..

'Observers say that a number question marks will subsequently be
apparent, but that this situation would not have been different even if
President Sadat had not been killed ...' (ch. 16, 4b)

Here the phrase هذا الموقف links back to the idea expressed by علامات استفهام

كثيرة سوف تثار بعد ذلك, with which it is coreferential. Similarly:

> أمـا أنا فـقـد أطمـئن الى آراء الكثرة ، أو قـد أراني مكرهًا عـلى الاطمئنان لآراء الكثرة ، في المجالس النيابية وما يشبهها . {ولكن} {الكثرة في العلم} لا تعنى شيئًا ..

'I sometimes rely on the views of the majority, or find myself forced to accept the views of the majority in parliamentary meetings and the like. In science, however, the [view of the] majority is meaningless ...' (ch. 17, 4c)

Here the phrase الكثرة after لكنَّ provides linkage with its previous mention (twice) in the phrase آراء الكثرة. There is also a contrastive aspect, in that when it is used after لكنَّ the word الكثرة is followed by في العمل, i.e. in contrast with other areas of human life. This is reflected in the English translation in which 'In science' is placed at the start of the sentence. Finally:

> {لكن} {هذا الدور الأول} لم يطُل إذ أخـذ العـرب يتـرجـمـون عن اليـونانيـة إلى العـربيـة رأسًا.

'But this first phase did not last long, since the Arabs began to translate directly from Greek into Arabic.' (ch. 20, 4b)

Here the phrase هذا الدور الأول links back to a previous description of the first phase of translation in the Islamic era, when translations of Greek works into Arabic were made not directly but from existing Syriac translations of these works.

Fairly commonly, لكنَّ is followed by a structure involving a pronoun of separation (ch. 14, 7b). Typically, such cases involve emphasis (cf. ch. 14, 7bii), which may be contrastive. For example:

> ..اعلن عبد الحميد مهري ... ان الدرس الذي يمكن استخلاصه من الانتخابات هو ان الاحزاب الجزائرية كانت تأمل في تحقيق نتائج اكبر {لكن} {الشعب هو الذي اختار بحرية} .

'... Abd al-Hamid Mahri announced that the lesson which could be drawn from the elections was that the Algerian parties had hoped to achieve better results, but that it was the people who had chosen freely.' (ch. 15, 5c)

Here the contrast is between the political parties (and their aspirations) and the people (and their choice).

Sometimes, the structure with the pronoun of separation after لكنَّ has a scene–setting aspect to it. For example:

ولكن} {السؤال المطروح هو مدى قدرة قيادة الإنقاذ على ضبط قواعدها وعلى ضبط التيار الراديكالي فيها الذي كان يعارض أصلاً المشاركة في الانتخابات} .

'But the question which is being posed is the extent to which the leadership of the Front is capable of controlling its grass–roots and of disciplining the radical tendency within it, which was fundamentally opposed to participation in the elections.' (ch. 15, 5d)

This example occurs at the start of a paragraph. The previous paragraph has dealt with various demands made by the Islamic Salvation Front, including the release of political prisoners. The phrase السؤال المطروح shifts the topic away from the demands made by the Islamic Salvation Front which were described in the previous paragraph towards the next topic, the ability of the Front to control its own supporters.

Finally, the structure with the pronoun of separation after لكن may function to provide linkage in a more general sense. For example:

لا شك أن أهداف « البعث العربي » التي لخصناها في « الحرية والاشتراكية والوحدة » هي أهداف أساسية متساوية في الاهمية لا يجوز فصل او تأجيل بعضها عن البعض الآخر. {ولكن} {الشيء الذي لا شك فيه أيضاً هو ان للوحدة ... تقدماً ورجحاناً معنويا} ..

'There is no doubt that the goals of the Arab Ba'th Party, which we have summarised in [the slogan] "Freedom, Socialism and Unity" are goals which are of equal importance, and none of which can be divorced or detained from the others. But the thing about which there is also no doubt is that unity ... has priority and moral precedence.' (ch. 13, 11a)

Here the phrase ولكن الشيء الذي لا شك فيه أيضاً echoes the phrase at the beginning of the quoted section (and in fact the beginning of the text) لا شك أن and أهداف « البعث العربي » and thus provides a form of linkage with what has gone before.

8. Aural Arabic texts 1

Listen to the following text from حصاد الشهر, no. 3, side 1, item 5, من أول من وضع كتابا في الحساب؟, then complete exercises i. and ii. below.

i   Produce a transcription of the text in Arabic. You may find the following list of words and phrases useful. The words and phrases are listed in their order of occurrence.

يسرّنا	it pleases us
نبذة	snippet, bit
عبد الحليم منتصر	[name]
احتجب عن	to be concealed from
الخوارزمي	[name]
خوارزم	[place name]
الرياضيات	mathematics
الفلك	astronomy
الجبر	algebra
مدين ل	indebted (to)
تبويب	classification
زيج ج أزياج	astronomical almanac
معادلات	equations

ii Answer the following questions in English.

1. Where did Khawarizmi live?
2. According to the speaker, he was the first person to do what?
3. What value does his book have?
4. Who translated his book into Latin?
5. When was the book published in London?
6. Which numbers are used in the Arab East?
7. Which numbers are used in the Arab West?
8. Where else are these latter used?
9. What was السند هند الصغير؟
10. What continues to be used until the present day?
11. How does the speaker support his claim for Khawarizmi's fame among the Europeans?
12. Which counting system was used before the number system?

9. Aural Arabic texts 2

Listen to the following text from ما رأي, حصاد الشهر, no. 26, side 1, item 4, العلم بما يسمى بقراءة الطالع والأبراج؟, then complete exercises i. and ii. below.

i Answer the following questions in Arabic.

١ – ماذا يشغل أفكار أكثر الناس؟

٢ – من يهتم بالمستقبل اهتماماً خاصاً؟

٣ – ما هي أغرب ظاهرة تتعلق بالمستقبل؟

٤ – أين نجد هذه الظاهرة؟

٥ – على رأي المؤمنين بالتنجيم ماذا يؤثر على مزاجنا؟

٦ – ماذا يحدد ميول الشخص وملامحه؟

٧ – ما هو موضوع بحث ميشال وفرنسوا غديلا؟

٨ – هل دراسات الزوجين علمية أو غير علمية؟

٩ – ما هو هدف البحث؟

١٠ – متى نُشر البحث؟

١١ – أين نُشر؟

١٢ – ما هي نتائج البحث؟

ii Translate the text into idiomatic English. You may find the following words and phrases useful. They are listed in the same order as they occur in the text itself.

خَلا من	to be free of, lack (often used in negative to mean 'be concerned with' etc.)
طالِع	rising star, ascendant (believed to indicate good fortune)
هاوٍ pl. هُواة	devotee, fan
لا يهدأ لهم بالٍ	they don't feel content
مُنجِّم	astrologer
بَالَى ب	to be concerned about, worry about
مزاج	temperament
انبرى على	to undertake, embark on
ركاب	stirrup
مستفيض	detailed, extensive, exhaustive
أوْحى	to inspire, suggest, create the impression
رَصين	calm, composed (here in the sense of being scientifically 'respectable')

10. Written English texts
Using constructions and vocabulary encountered in the Arabic texts in this chapter, as far as possible, translate the following text from Lewis, *The Arabs in History*, p. 142, into idiomatic Arabic.

During the period of greatness of the Arab and Islamic Empires in the Near and Middle East a flourishing civilisation grew up that is usually known as Arabic. It was not brought ready–made by the Arab invaders from the desert, but was created after the conquests by the collaboration of many peoples, Arabs, Persians, Egyptians and others. Nor was it even purely Muslim, for many Christians,

Jews and Zoroastrians were among its creators. But its chief
medium of expression was Arabic, and it was dominated by Islam
and its outlook on life. It was these two things, their language and
their faith, which were the great contributions of the Arab invaders
to the new and original civilisation which developed under their
aegis.

11. Précis

(a) Re–read the text عبقرية الحضارة العربية used in section 4. (a), then produce
a précis in Arabic.

(b) Read the following text by جمال الطيب احمد entitled العرب في غرب
افريقيا which is cited in مختارات من الادب السوداني edited by علي المك,
pp. 64–6, then produce a précis in Arabic. This passage follows a description
of the role of the Arabs in East and Central Africa and is part of an introduction
to the Arabic translation of a book by Basil Davidson entitled افريقيا تحت
أضواء جديدة.

العرب في غرب افريقيا

هذا عن شرق القارة ووسطها البعيد ولكن الرباط العربي بغربها
في القديم لا يقل قوة عن هذا الذي رأينا بعضه في الشرق والوسط ،
اتصلت هذه وتلك بجنوب الجزيرة العربية منذ فتح التاريخ عينيه
ينظر ، واتصل الغرب بالشمال الافريقي وشماله الشرقي منذ
احقاب ممعنة في القدم ، وكانت الصحراء هنا كالبحر هنا ، تتناثر
على حوافيه في الشمال والجنوب المدن كالموانئ ، تخرج القوافل
من فاس ومراكش وقسطنطينية والقيروان ، تحمل الملح ، وكانت
سلعة عزيزة في الجنوب والغرب ، لغانا ومالي وجن وجاوا وتمبكتو
وكانو ، وتعود قوافلها تحمل الذهب والرقيق . عرف الجانبان من
الصحراء ، طرقا ثلاثة للقوافل ، أولها غربية تقلع من مراكش
متجهة للمنحنى الشمالي من النيجر ، والى الاقليم الشاسع غربه
صوب المحيط وثانيها طريق وسط يبدأ عند تونس ويتجه للاقليم
الكبير الواقع بين بحيرة شاد ونهر النيجر ، وطريق ثالث من
الشرق لدى طرابلس ومصر ، يسير للاقليم الواقع حول شاد كله ،
طرق كلها تدلك على ما كان من صلات قديمة قريبة بين الشمال

الافريقي ، والاقليم العريض الذي عرف من بعد بالسودان ، حين جاءه الرحالة العرب ، ويقص عليك كتابنا هذا الذي بين يديك كثيرا من مفاخرهم في هذه المسالك الوعرة . ظلت هذه الصلة تجارية صرفا حتى كان أول العهد المسيحي ، حين دفعت التقلبات السياسية في الشمال ، شعوبا عدة وقبائل مختلفة للنزوح عبر الصحارى للجنوب ، هربا من الحروب . توالت هذه الافواج حتى القرن الثالث عشر ، ونشأت معها منازل من المهاجرين العرب والبربر المتهودين ، تعيش آمنة وسط أرض الزنج ، يتراحمون ويتقاسمون العيش ، ويتبادلون ما عندهم من ثقافات ، كما فعل اهل جنوب الجزيرة العربية في شرق القارة ، وابتلع بحر الزنج هذه القطرات الوافدة ، فلم يعد ما يميز قادما من مقيم ، وظلت حياتهم هكذا آمنة لا يروعها شيء ، حتى وجدت أروبا طريقها اليهم ، تتاجر في الرقيق ، بادئ الامر وتتوالى شئونها شيئا فشيئا منذ القرن الخامس عشر ، تمهد لاستعمارها في النهاية .

وللعرب في هذه القصة دور مركزي ، فقد اندفعوا بعد الاسلام للشمال الافريقي على النحو الذي يعرفه القارئ العربي ، وكانوا قبلهم جماعات لا خطر لها ولا شأن من المخاطرين ، فتح الطريق لهم سهلا معبدا بعد فتح مصر (٦٣٩-٦٤٢) ، فاستولوا على الشمال بعد غزوات موفقة معروفة ، يقدر المؤرخون ان ربع مليون من العرب استقرت بعدها في الاقليم واختلطت بأهله البربر ، فاتخذوا الدين الجديد عقيدة ، واللغة الغالبة لسانا وترعرع سلطانهم وامتد بين القرنين الحادي عشر والثاني عشر ، على يد بنى هلال وبنى حسن ، وغيرهما من قبائل العرب ، وهي القرون التي شهدت بدايات الامبراطوريات الاسلامية التي يتحدث عنها كاتبنا هذا في اختصار لا يخل . كانت هجرات الشمال الافريقي والشمال الشرقي في السودان القديم الممتد بين النيل والنيجر - متقطعة ، قبل ان يستقر العرب استقرارا في الشمال ، ولكنها اتصلت اتصالا واسعا

بعد هذا العهد ، فاتسع نطاق التجارة والهجرة والاستيطان فبعد اثر العرب في حياة الزنج وعمق . ما كان مجيئهم للاغارة كما فعل البربر قبلهم ، ولا للاقامة الهاربة من الاضطهاد كما فعل اليهود والبربر المتهودون ، حين شق عليهم العيش مع الروم . كان التجار والمهاجرون العرب يحملون رسالة ويتحدثون لغة مرموقة وكانوا بعد هذا يبحثون عن مجال للعيش والتجارة أوسع ، واتخذت آثارهم هذه سمتها القوية التي بقيت لليوم في سحنة الكثيرين ، ودين الاكثرية ، ولغة الاقلية ، خضع المزيج الذي تكون في الأقليم من بربر وزنج لسلطان العرب الفتى فاستأثروا بالتجارة والثقافة والحكم لا يشركهم فيها احد ، وترى آثار هذا في التكوين الجسدي للشعوب التي تعيش شمال الغرب جنوب الصحارى ، فالدم الغالب شمال السنغال والنيجر هو الدم الخليط من الزنج والبربر والعرب ، والدين الغالب هو الاسلام ، واللغة العربية ليست عربية على الاكثرية ، ثم يغلب الدم الزنجي جنوب هذين النهرين وان كنت ترى حتى يومنا هذا الاثر الذي تركته تجارة القادمين ودينهم وعاداتهم ، رغم القرون التي مضت الآن على تلك الصلة .

12. Oral

(a) One or two students to present an account of التراث العربي الاسلامي.

(b) The presenter(s) then ask(s) the other students questions about التراث العربي الاسلامي. These questions should include some which require factual answers and others which require subjective, speculative or analytical answers. For example:

١ – ماذا يشمل التراث العربي الاسلامي؟

٢ – لمن كان العرب وراث في مجال العلوم؟

٣ – كيف استخدم العرب الفلسفة والجدل؟

٤ – ما هي اهم المدارس في الوطن العربي؟

٥ – ما هو دور المترجمين في الوطن العربي؟

٦ – ما هو دين الغرب للعرب في مجال الكيمياء؟

٧ – ما رأيك بقراءة الطالع والابراج؟

13. Essay

Write an essay in Arabic of 200 words on the title تأثــيــر الحـضــارة العـربيـة-الاسـلامـيـة على اوربا. In your writing address some of the following issues.

١ – دين الغرب للعرب في مجال الطب.

٢ – من هم اشهر العلماء العرب؟

٣ – ما ترجم العرب من كتب فلسفة وعلم اغريقية؟

٤ – ماذا عمل العرب في مجال الحساب؟

٥ – ماذا اوجد العرب في مجال الكيمياء؟

٦ – من من العرب قد ادخل الكيمياء؟

٧ – ما هي اشهر المدارس التي اسّسها العرب؟

Bibliography

Abboud, Peter F. and Ernest N. McCarus (eds.), *Elementary Modern Standard Arabic*, vols. I–II, Cambridge University Press, 1986.

Al-Nassir, A.A., *Sibawayh the Phonologist*, London and New York: Kegan Paul International, 1993.

Al-Sa'dawi, Nawal, *The Hidden Face of Eve: Women in the Arab World*, London: Zed Books, 1980.

Ashtiany, Julia, *Media Arabic*, Edinburgh University Press, 1993.

Badawi, M.M. *A Short History of Modern Arabic Literature*, Oxford: Clarendon Press, 1993.

Baker, Mona, *In Other Words*, London: Routledge, 1992.

Beeston, A.F.L., *The Arabic Language Today*, London: Hutchinson, 1970.

Bernal, Martin, *Black Athena: The Afroasiatic Roots of Classical Civilization*, London: Free Association Books, 1987.

Bohas, G., Guillaume and Kouloughli, *The Arabic Linguistic Tradition*, Brill, 1990.

Browne, E.G., *Arabian Medicine*, Cambridge University Press, 1921.

Bushnaq, Inea (trans.), *Arab Folktales*, Harmondsworth: Penguin Books, 1986.

Cantarino, Vicente, vols. I–III, *A Syntax of Modern Arabic Prose*, Bloomington and London: Indiana University Press, 1975.

Crystal, David, *Dictionary of Linguistics and Phonetics*, 2nd edition, Oxford: Blackwell, 1985.

Gabrielli, F. "Asabiyya' in *Encyclopaedia of Islam*, vol. I, p. 681.

Gibb, H.A.R., *Arabic Literature: An Introduction*, Oxford University Press, 1962.

Hinds, M. and El-S. Badawi, *A Dictionary of Egyptian Arabic*, Beirut: Librairie du Liban, 1986.

Hodgson, Marshall G.S., *The Venture of Islam*, vols. I–III, Chicago and London: University of Chicago Press, 1974.

Holes, Clive, *Modern Arabic: Structures, Functions and Varieties*, London: Longman, 1995.

Hourani, Albert, *A History of the Arab Peoples*, London: Faber & Faber, 1991.

Kepel, Gilles, *Muslim Extremism in Egypt: The Prophet and Pharoah*, University of California Press, 1993.

Allah in the West, Cambridge: Polity Press, 1997.

Koning, Hans, *Columbus: his Enterprise*, London: Latin America Bureau, 1991.

Kronman, Anthony T., *Max Weber*, London: Edward Arnold, 1983.

Lewis, Bernard, *The Arabs in History*, Oxford University Press, 1993.

Mernissi, Fatima, *Beyond the Veil*, London: Al-Saqi Books, 1985.

Nomani, F. and A. Rahnema, *Islamic Economic Systems*, London and New Jersey: Zed Books, 1994.

Penguin Atlas of World History, vols. I–II, Middlesex and New York: Penguin Books, 1974.

Rodinson, Maxime, *Islam and Capitalism*, Harmondsworth: Penguin Books, 1974.

Israel and the Arabs, New York: Penguin Books, 1982.

Ruthven, Malise, *Islam in the World*, Middlesex and New York: Penguin Books, 1984.

Starkey, Paul and J. Meissner (eds.), *Encyclopaedia of Arabic Literature*, London: Routledge, 1998.

Sluglett, Peter and Marion Farouk–Sluglett, *The Times Guide to the Middle East: The Arab World and its Neighbours*, London: Times Books, 1993.

Watson, J.C.E., *A Syntax of San'ani Arabic*, Wiesbaden: Harrassowitz, 1993.

Weber, Max, translated, edited and with an introduction by H.H. Gerth and C. Wright Mills, *From Max Weber: Essays in Sociology*, London and Boston: Routledge and Kegan Paul, 1948.

Wehr, Hans, *A Dictionary of Modern Written Arabic*, Wiesbaden: Harrassowitz, 1974.

Wikan, Unni (translated by Ann Henning), *Life Among the Poor in Cairo*, London and New York: Tavistock Publications, 1980.

Wright, W., *A Grammar of the Arabic Language*, Cambridge University Press, 1859 (1971).

Young, M.J.L., J.D. Latham and R.B. Serjeant (eds.), *The Cambridge History of Arabic Literature*, vol. III, *Religion, Learning and Science in the Abbasid Period*, Cambridge University Press, 1990.